NATIONAL SERMONS.

SERMONS,

SPEECHES AND LETTERS

ON

SLAVERY AND ITS WAR:

FROM THE

PASSAGE OF THE FUGITIVE SLAVE BILL TO THE ELECTION OF PRESIDENT GRANT.

BY

GILBERT HAVEN.

BOSTON:
LEE AND SHEPARD.
1869.

Electrotyped at the Boston Stereotype Foundry,
No. 19 Spring Lane.

Presswork by John Wilson and Son.

TO

The Reverend Fathers and Brethren

OF

THE NEW ENGLAND CONFERENCE OF THE METHODIST EPISCOPAL CHURCH,

The first organized body in America that accepted and proclaimed the duty of the immediate and unconditional abolition of slavery, after its announcement by William Lloyd Garrison; and that adhered faithfully to this cause, through evil report and good report, until God gave it the victory:

This Volume,

Devoted to the consideration of this reform, in its past, present, and future relations to the Church, the Nation, and Mankind,

Is Cordially Inscribed,

In gratitude for their fatherly guidance, in memory of their fraternal coöperation, and in hope of the early obliteration of the unchristian prejudice, growing out of the abolished iniquity, that still afflicts the American people, and for whose extirpation this Conference has so long and so ardently labored and prayed.

"These things came to pass
From small beginnings because God is just."

INTRODUCTORY.

THE New England ministry, like the Jewish, from its origin, has been faithful in setting forth the relations of the Gospel to the laws and customs of man. From the times of John Cotton until now, twice every year, and oftener if events demanded, have their words proclaimed the alarm or the exultation, as national sin or national virtue gave the occasion.

So great was the clerical influence in these matters, that in the earliest days it was well nigh a clerical supremacy; and the election sermon was not unfrequently a more important document than the Governor's message.

In the exercise of this prerogative occurred the natural division of the human mind on every topic submitted to its consideration, and radical and conservative were developed, at the start, with a violence never surpassed in later controversies. The history of the Province of Massachusetts Bay, even in the days of Governor Winthrop, discloses this furious pulpit war upon questions of civil and social import.

But witl this natural divergence, its main drift was ever toward political righteousness. It fostered the spirit of independence in the colonies, long before the people gained strength to assert it. It was the supporter of Congress and the army through all that war, so long, so wasting, so often seemingly lost.

Rev. Jonas Clark, of Lexington, was the chief cause why the untrained militia of that hamlet dared to confront the armed and disciplined troops of their own government. A sermon of Rev. Jonathan Mayhew of the West Church, Boston, on the Higher Law, by the confession of John Adams, was the opening gun of the Revolution. President Langdon, of Harvard College, blessed, on that June night, the troops that marched from College Green to Bunker Hill. President Styles, of Yale, was a most ardent advocate of the national cause, as was his eminent successor, President Dwight, who had also served as a chaplain in the Revolutionary army.

The later and greater struggle through which America has passed, was equally honored and upheld by the pulpit of New England. It found its earliest martyrs among this class. Torrey and Lovejoy, the first two witnesses who laid down their lives for the abolition of slavery, were New England ministers. Channing sprang to this conflict in the maturity of his powers and his fame. The New England Methodist clergy very early identified themselves with this cause. June 4, 1835, the New England Conference, sitting in Lynn, organized an anti-slavery society on the basis of the immediate and unconditional abolition of slavery, and invited George Thompson to address them. He preached a very powerful sermon from Ezekiel xxviii. 14–16. "Thou art the anointed cherub that covereth; and I have set thee so; thou walkest upon the holy mountain of God; thou hast walked up and down in the midst of the stones of fire. By the multitude of thy merchandise they have filled the midst of thee with violence, and thou hast sinned; therefore I will cast thee as profane out of the mountain of God: and I will destroy thee, O covering cherub, from the midst of the stones of fire." North Bennett Street Methodist Episcopal Church, in Boston, was opened to him that year, on Fast Day, for a sermon, and received these words of commendation for their courage from the pen of Mr. Garrison: —

> In these days of slavish servility and malignant prejudices, we are presented, occasionally, with some beautiful specimens of Christian obedience and courage. One of these is seen in the opening of the North Bennett Street Methodist Meeting-House, in Boston, to the advocates for the honor of God, the salvation of our country, and the freedom of enslaved millions in our midst.

He, however, declares that every other church was closed to him at that time, in this strong, possibly too strong, assertion: —

> As the pen of the historian, in after years, shall trace the rise, progress, and glorious triumph of the abolition cause, he will delight to record, and posterity will delight to read, the fact that when all other pulpits were dumb, all other churches closed, on the subject of slavery, in Boston, the boasted "CRADLE OF LIBERTY," there was one pulpit that would speak out, one church that would throw open its doors in behalf of the down-trodden victims of American tyranny, and that was the pulpit and the church above alluded to. The primitive spirit of Methodism is beginning to revive, with all its holy zeal and courage, and it will not falter until the Methodist churches are purged from the pollution of slavery, and the last slave in the land stands forth a redeemed and regenerated being.

When Mr. Thompson, persecuted for this righteousness' sake, was compelled to hide himself from his enemies, he took shelter with Rev. S. W. Wilson, at Andover, a member of the same Conference, from whose house he went to the ship that bore him from the country. Rev. Orange Scott, also of this Conference, commenced writing against slavery in "Zion's Herald," in 1834, and during the same year sent "The Liberator" free, for six months, to all the ministers of his Conference.* This faithful culture brought forth early fruit, and the very next year, when the society was formed, delegates were elected to the General Conference, who had the honor of initiating this conflict at Cincinnati, and of arousing a large church to the controversy, before their associates had widely extended their growing influence. Two of the members from New Hampshire were censured for attending an anti-slavery prayer meeting, — a censure which remained a blot upon the church until 1868, when, on petition of members from Maryland, it was expunged, and the church relieved from the blame which she had for so many years fastened upon herself in their condemnation.

Equally zealous were other New England ministers: A. A. Phelps, Joshua Leavitt, Dr. Osgood of Springfield, James Porter, Dr. Ide of Medway, George Storrs, John Pierpont, Nathaniel Colver, Samuel J. May, J. D. Bridge, Daniel Wise, Phineas Crandall — everywhere began to spring up this good seed in this good soil. True, the churches and clergy were not all, or instantly converted, and many severe and just scourgings both received from those who devoted themselves exclusively to the great reform. Yet they made

* For these facts we are indebted to Rev. R. W. Allen, of Newton, one of the original members of this New England Conference Anti-Slavery Society.

greater progress than was sometimes conceded, and before twenty years had elapsed, so universal had become their adhesion to this cause, that in the conflict over the repeal of the Missouri Compromise, more than three thousand ministers of New England protested, "in the name of Almighty God, and in His presence," against that measure, and Charles Sumner, then fresh in the seat he has so long and so highly honored, gave them this just and noble tribute: —

> From the first settlement of these shores, from those early days of struggle and privation, through the trials of the Revolution, the clergy have been associated, not only with the piety and the learning, but with the liberties of the country. For a long time New England was governed by their prayers more than by any acts of the legislature; and, at a later day, their voices aided even the Declaration of Independence. The clergy of our time may speak, then, not only from their own virtues, but from the echoes which yet live in the pulpits of their fathers.
>
> For myself, I desire to thank them for their generous interposition. They have already done much good in moving the country. They will not be idle. In the days of the Revolution, John Adams, yearning for independence, said, "Let the pulpits thunder against oppression!" and the pulpits thundered. The time has come for them to thunder again.

These discourses have, therefore, a natural origin. They are of the root of the fathers, alike of the oldest and the youngest of the churches of New England. They were delivered on the days appointed by the State or National government, for the consideration of State and National duties, except in a very few instances, when the occurrence of remarkable events demanded the solemn consideration of the will of God in respect to a sinning nation. They are upon nearly all the salient events in the controversy, from the hour when the nation, through her government, avowed herself the propagandist of slavery, to that when she declared that the last vestige of the iniquity should be swept from the land.

The passage of the Fugitive Slave Bill was the beginning of her active coöperation with slavery, after the revival of the reform. Before this, she had only sought to stay the progress of that movement. In this act she cast herself earnestly into the support and extension of slavery. With rapid steps she plunged downward, till all the departments of State, executive, judicial, and legislative, were leagued together in its baleful service. She descended to the utmost possible degree of degradation. Another step would have been annihilation, and even that, her executive and supreme judiciary essayed to take. Only the mighty uprising of the people, under the inspiration of God, saved her from being blotted out from among the nations. From the hour of that return, her steps have been equally rapid in the right direction. Eighteen hundred and sixty beheld her President and Chief Justice prostrate at the feet of the power that had seized half the land, and proclaimed its independence of the United States. Eighteen hundred and sixty-eight saw that power destroyed, its foundation abolished, its rulers fugitives, its slaves rulers, and one, at the hour of her downfall, unknown of men, put by the popular voice at the head of the government, while all the world acknowledged him the first general of his age. Great and mighty are Thy works, Lord God Almighty!

These religious orations, as they should properly be called, cover this field of the long controversy. They rise and fall with the tide of national feeling, and thus the more faithfully photograph their times. Being delivered at different places, and upon one general theme, they may contain some repetitions, though such passages have been omitted as far as possible consistent with the symmetry of the discourse.

The range of topics is not confined to narrow, local, or momentary limits, but embraces nearly every field into which the controversy legitimately entered. Objection may not be improperly offered, in this colder period of quiet and victory, to occasional expressions. But the rifle and the cannon grow hot in the battle, and the cool words of careful rhetoric are unsuited to the fearful crises when everlasting ruin or renown wait on the decree of the moment. If faithful to the hour of their utterance, they should still burn, like lava, long ejected from the blazing volcano.

More than half the contents of the volume have been published in other forms, — in pamphlet and book, in the daily and weekly newspaper, in the monthly and quarterly. They are printed in the order of the national events. A few speeches and letters, that have a unity of substance with the discourses, are inserted in their appropriate place. The work thus presents what may be a novelty in printed, yet is far from being one in spoken literature, — a series of speeches that shows the sympathy and oneness of the pulpit with the events, political and military, of the mightiest movements of God in this generation.

But it would be unjust to the main purpose of this volume to declare that it was chiefly a recollection. It looks before as well as after; before more than after. Its object is not to gather up memorials of the past, but to enforce the duties of the future. History, that simply describes vanished events, is as purposeless and profitless as a moralless tale. All history, like the Bible, should describe the past only to sanctify the present and perfect the future. This would fail of its object if it left the reader indifferent to the evil that still possesses too largely the American heart. Despite the mighty panorama of divine events that has passed before this people, their hearts are hardened toward those for whom God has wrought such great deliverance. We are still cursed with a curse, even this whole nation. Chattel slavery is dead. Political slavery is nearly at an end. Social slavery still prevails. Trade yet shuts its gates against the aspiring and competent youth of this complexion. Pulpits yet bar their doors to the accredited and popular ministers of Jesus Christ as their regular pastors. Society too generally abhors their companionship. Aversion thus defiles the whole national heart.

The victims of our contempt feel the yoke of bondage with which we still burden their souls. The liberties they have won only make these chains the more galling. Not until every such fetter is broken will God's controversy with America come to an end. To their removal these pages are consecrated. The past is past; the future beckons us. The words that urged to duties done, call to the discharge of duties that must be done. May this crown be won and worn by the American people. They only need to conquer this prejudice, to become the model and the inspiration of all the nations of the earth. May Church, State, and Society, in all their life, speedily reveal the perfect cleansing of the American heart from the unbrotherly distinction of man from man. May the Father and Brother of all men, who has created them in His image, and seeks their unification in His grace and nature, hasten the accomplishment of this most desired of His earthly consummations.

CONTENTS.

I. THE HIGHER LAW.

"*Render unto Cæsar the things that are Cæsars's; and unto God the things that are God's.*" — Matthew xxi. 12.

ARGUMENT. — The need of examination of the principles of action, especially when these principles are in controversy. The divided duty before every citizen of the Free States; loyalty to country or to conscience. On what rests the obligation to obey the State. I. Man the subject of law. 1. Distinction in the kind and authority of law. Law of body and of spirit; of sensibilities, mind, and moral being. The lower authoritative only, when not hostile to the higher. If man were holy, all his nature would work symmetrically. Sin the disturber of this harmony. 2. The civil government a creature of the social nature of man. It must therefore by virtue of its origin be in subjection to conscience, or the higher nature, if any conflict arises. II. How shall we know the relations of the human laws to the law of God? By Conscience, by Providence, by the Scriptures. How act if such a decree is thus decided to be wrong? Refuse to coöperate in its enforcement. Refuse to desist from duties it forbids. Cast all our influence against it. III. Application to the Fugitive Slave Bill. It comes from the State. Slavery, its nature; condemned by instincts, conscience, Providence, and the Bible. Our duty, to refuse obedience; to befriend these whom it outlaws, and to oppose it by voice and vote. IV. The plea of constitutional protection. The Constitution a creature of civil government, and therefore of the social nature. It is consequently subject like that nature to the moral sentiments. Its words allow liberty not slavery. Our trust in Christ not the Constitution. Encouragements in the conflict. No slave hunters in our borders.

ARGUMENT. — The right and duty of ministerial utterance on national questions proved from Bible history and orders. Especial obligations in view of the enormity of the national transgression. I. What has triumphed? 1. Not the Democratic party. 2. Slavery. Study this victor; trace its power in a human being from birth to death. Robbed of name, of parents, of education, of property, of religion. What shall the end be if the victors retain their strength? Enslavement of Kansas; because of their purpose, their necessity, and the fact that this is the center of the conflict. This won, all is. 2. Extension of slavery to Oregon. 3. Annexation of Cuba and Central America as slave States. 4. Reopening of the Foreign Slave Trade. 5. Suppression of freedom of speech, everywhere. 6. Adjudging slaves as property everywhere. Slavery must make these attempts. It must advance or die. III. What has caused the defeat? 1. No real national sympathy with the slave. 2. No earnest prayers for the victory of Freedom. 3. More anxious to conquer a party than to abolish slavery. IV. Encouragements. None in the ruling party. 1. First organized success of political anti-slavery in a single State. 2. A stimulant to friends of liberty in the slave States to organize against slavery. 3. The growth of the religious sentiment.

"*We are verily guilty concerning our brother.*" — Genesis xlii. 21.

ARGUMENT. — Foundation for American Slavery. I. Not in man as man, but in his color or origin. Scripture stolen to array an idol. This color is declared to be a mark of degradation, and separation. II. This feeling, 1. General. 2. Deep-rooted. 3. Unnatural. Because, (1.) Not towards any other class of men. (2). They have the gifts of music, manners, the culinary art, aptness of imitation, wit and humor, patience, and sunniness of temper. (3.) No repugnance to this color, as seen everywhere else than in America. (4.) No disunity in spiritual nature. (5). Caused by social condition. (6.) Contrary to the Scriptures. 4. The feeling is the chief bulwark of American slavery. South could not resist the North were she free from this prejudice. III. How shall it be cured? 1. Cease to dwell on the distinction of color. 2. Welcome those of this hue to your society. 3. Encourage them to enter all branches of trade. IV. Result, intermarriage; its right and fitness. True marriage. Shakespeare's foresight and courage. Othello and Desdemona.

VI. THE BEGINNING OF THE END.

"*Surely oppression maketh a wise man mad.*" — Eccl. vii. 7.

"*I am not mad, most noble Festus.*" — Acts xxvi. 25.

"*So I returned, and considered all the oppressions that are done under the sun: and behold, the tears of such as were oppressed, and they had no comforter; and on the side of their oppressors there was power, but they had no comforter. Wherefore I praised the dead which are already dead, more than the living which are yet alive.*" — Eccl. iv. 1, 2.

ARGUMENT. — Opening of a new act. Its influence. Its purport and effect. The beginning of the end. It has taught the slaveholder his weakness. It has strengthened the heart of the slave. His right to liberty, even through blood. It will tend to unite us to our enslaved brethren; stimulate all peaceful modes of assault on slavery; abate the haughty assumptions of the slave power. The benefit of his death, if he dies. Honors the American scaffold, as Vane, Russell, and Sidney did England's. His future fame.

VII. THE MARTYR.

ARGUMENT. — A new date in American Annals. A national day in character and interest. The righteousness of his deed. His right to interfere to save his fellow-men. Its wisdom. He wins the fight in his dying. The slayer slain.

VIII. TE DEUM LAUDAMUS.

"*I will sing unto the Lord, for he hath triumphed gloriously. The horse and his rider hath He thrown into the sea.*" — Exodus xv. 1.

"*But promotion cometh neither from the east, nor from the west, nor from the south. But God is judge: He putteth down one, and setteth up another.*" — Ps. lxxv. 6, 7.

"*Jesus saith unto them, Did ye never read in the Scriptures, the Stone which the builders rejected, the same is become the head of the corner; This is the Lord's doing, and it is marvelous in our eyes.* — Matt. xxi. 42.

THE HIGHER LAW.*

"Render therefore unto Cæsar the things that are Cæsar's, and unto God the things that are God's." — *Matt.* xxii. 21.

IT is well frequently to lay bare the springs of our being, to examine their nature, and see if their present movement is in accordance with their original design.

This is especially necessary when conflicting sentiments obtain respecting a course of action which we are required to pursue. When we cannot remain idle spectators of a contest which is raging around us, but from the orders of leaders in the battle are compelled to take definite positions, then it is our solemn duty to examine the nature of these commands, that we may see whether we must obey or resist them.

Such is the condition in which every person is placed throughout the Free States. The government of the country has arrayed its mighty strength upon the side of Slavery, and issues its mandate to all the people, to lend

* A sermon preached at Amenia, New York, November, 1850, on the occasion of the passage of the Fugitive Slave Bill. See Note I.

their aid in its defense. The conflict between the eternal foes of freedom and slavery has by this act changed us from unconcerned spectators, if we had chosen to assume that position, into actors, and requires every one to take his place under one of the hostile banners. If, therefore, there were no previous claims upon our feelings of brotherhood, we cannot avoid considering our duties under this assertion of the will of the State.

In such circumstances it is our highest duty to examine the Nature and Extent of the Authority of Human Government, and to see if the late decrees of our nation are in agreement or hostility with its delegated rights.

Man is created subject to law. Enactments originating in the wisdom of God control every faculty of body and soul. In whatever direction he seeks activity, he finds laws inducing the desire and limiting its gratification. Around him as well as within him ever operates the same infinite energy under the guidance of the same infinite wisdom, coöperating through all the lower orders of being with his highest faculties, or by the same obedient officers modifying or suppressing their unhealthy activity. The world without us is our servant or our scourge, according as we are the servants or enemies of God within us.

But while there is no portion of our nature free from the authority of law, there is an evident distinction in the degree of this authority. As a being intended for different states of existence, and for different duties in each state, the Divine Lawgiver must assign to each faculty authority proportionate to its original design. Each is allowed full powers within its own borders, with restrictions against any intrusion upon the rights of adjacent faculties, and unhesitating submission to the Conscience, the governor of the whole realm, and through that to the Creator and Proprietor of All.

The laws that regulate our body are felt to be inferior to

those which control the soul. Though constructed with measureless skill, and acting under impulses of divine origin, the body is only a servant of the soul. Its mechanism, its vitality, its appetites, its instincts are all acknowledged to be subordinate to other powers which inherit it for a season, and which can mar its structure or even suppress the instincts necessary to its self-preservation with the approval of the Divine Author of both natures.

Among the faculties of the soul there exists no less distinction of rank and authority. There are powers which seem especially designed for the present life, whose action is essential to its earthly preservation, happiness, and progress. There are others that are evidently of a higher grade and sublimer destiny, which, for the most part, are kept in abeyance here, and allowed only in rare instances to assume the supremacy and to reveal the latent powers of their being. There are yet others that oversweep all these inferior energies, and claim their obedience on penalty of leaving them to the fatal anarchy of the lowest passions.

These faculties are called generically the propensities or sensibilities, the intellect and the moral nature. Most of the propensities, though capable of coöperating with the higher powers of the soul, in by far the greater portion of their activity and the greater part of mankind, act independently of all moral guidance. They are confined too, largely, to this state of existence. Self-love is generally considered as the basis solely of earthly pleasure; esteem regards earthly favor; desire for existence includes mainly a passion for earthly life; curiosity is limited to earthly inquisition; and sociality to the divers forms of affections arising from, and centering in, earthly relations.

In our devotion to this portion of our nature, the demands of the intellect are often neglected. Passion rules the hour, rules every hour, and Thought toils as its bond slave. The mind is chiefly studious to obtain means for gratifying the propensities. It seeks gain, frames plans, pursues studies chiefly that vanity, pride, or lower lusts may have the larger indulgence. Only in occasional moments does it tower before mankind, when the over-sated passion reveals its own inferiority, or when some Leibnitz or Newton has mounted above the narrow skies that bound their vision, and transmitted some of their discoveries to these slaves of mere desire.

Above the intellect rises the moral nature, and claims the service of both these classes of faculties. It asserts its authority over them by allowing them, if rebellious, to run into ruinous excess of riot and of skepticism, and by enabling them, if obedient to its dictates, to grow harmoniously and happily, after their original design.

It was not intended that this diversity of constitution should lead to discord and mutual injury. The law of the body had no original hostility to that of the soul. Our selfish and our social nature were made to act in unison. The duties pertaining to earthly life had no essential opposition, but rather an essential oneness with those that lead out to another existence. The mind, and heart, and conscience were designed to be as harmonious as the nature of God himself, in whose image they are created. These complex duties and interests, so marvelously interwoven, have no constitutional defects or variances. There was no entangling of threads, no jarring of chord with chord, as they came from the hand divine. It was a microcosm combining in outward form and inward action the same multiplicity in unity, and complexity in simplicity, that is exhibited by that infinite macrocosm, the universe itself. Under their united action every institution of man, domestic, social, or civil, every outgrowth of his nature, could have been established and matured without possibility of imperfection or collision. The family would have been an harmonious unit, full of life and love. The State would have respected every right, and aided while it embraced all minor movements in its rounded fullness. The Church would have been identical with the State, though superior to it, informing it with the more subtile life of the soul, hanging its humbler dome in the heaven of heavens. Art, commerce, handicraft, every form and force of activity, would have each moved righteously and efficiently in its own sphere, while they aided, rather than impeded, the congenital vocations. Earth and Man would have been one with Heaven and God.

But a hostile element invades the soul, and anarchy prevails. Satan mars the machinery of God. Excess of indulgence or of abstinence becomes the mode of human action, and ignorance of the true law, or inability to pursue it steadily, prevents their perfect harmony and growth. This disorder possesses every man, and is revealed in all the organizations into which his wants and nature are expanded.

"The trail of the serpent is over them all."

Under such conditions, it becomes us to study carefully our duty in every relation we sustain, whether to ourselves, our fellow, or our God, remembering that all these relations meet and melt into Him who is their only Source and everlasting Life.

Among these qualities are those feelings and ties that compose the organism called the State, or civil government. The last has the narrower significance. Civil government means, primarily, the authority of a city. It shows that a condensed population gathered around competent leaders, subdued and then ruled the scattered peoples beyond their walls. But the State — that which stands — has the calm look of permanence, the solid shape of eternity. It expresses the confidence and the restfulness of man. "Here I have peace. Here I have room for the quiet growth of all my being. These arms of power are around me to shield and to support. By it my weakness is made strong, my littleness enlarged, my single-hand made myriad-handed, my poverty is changed to unmeasured affluence, and my paltry personality becomes majestic and mighty as the oneness of the sea."

Well may we be careful how we assail or undermine this hope of the Race. Well may enmity to its will be branded by the word second only to murder, if second to that, in the abhorrence of man — treason. For what is he who destroys individual life, compared with him who slays the State?

But if the State has such a root in the instincts of mankind, it, too, must beware lest it pervert its office from the protector to the destroyer of its people. For as high as it is exalted in love and power by its willing subjects, when it is an instrument of justice, so low will it plunge in the execrations of its people, in weakness within and abroad, if it make itself the instrument of injustice. Exalted to heaven, it shall be cast down to hell.

In this hour, then, when the people are perplexed by the action of the State, it is our solemn duty to examine the ground of its origin, and the relations it sustains to the higher law of our nature,—the voice of God in the soul of man,—before we consider how its late enactments comport with that law, and what are our individual duties under the circumstances it has forced upon us.

Civil government exists by the will of God. The social element in man in its development into its natural forms reveals itself in that of the State. This is its last expression. Under it this propensity has the fullest range and action. Solitary man becomes the family, the community, the nation.

But since the idea of nationality springs from this propensity, its government must be under the supervision of the faculties which govern its source; that is, the Judgment and Conscience. If not, then the gregarious habits and laws of beasts are civil government, for their instinct is identical with this propensity in its original action.

If this desire for social organization originates with our Creator, and is placed under the control of our intelligent and moral nature, then must it be developed only in accordance with the will of the Creator, and under the direction of His law written in our hearts and in His Word. It cannot grow to its due and destined height without coming into connection, and perhaps into collision, with other faculties and duties. Only the appointed ruler of the soul can decide between conflicting passions, or lead them each to their proper fullness, and so make the whole an harmonious unit.

Since, then, the process of forming a civil government must be guided by our moral nature, the duties we owe it, in its right or wrong procedure, are all referred to the same tribunal. Before the judgment seat of the Conscience must it stand. If that condemns it, then must it plead guilty; if that forbids obedience to its wrong behests, they must be disobeyed; if that demands that it should repeal its laws and make them conformable to the law of God, it must hasten to obey on pain of the righteous displeasure and sure judgments of God, who will sustain the authority of the Conscience, His vicegerent, against all combinations and all adversaries.

Two questions here arise: —

1st. How shall we know when the decrees of the State are inconsistent with the Will of God?

2d. How shall we act when we are satisfied that such an inconsistency exists?

I. How shall we know when the decrees of the State are inconsistent with the Will of God?

We should include the institutions with the acts of government, for the error of its customs usually precedes and produces errors in its acts. The leprosy lies deep within in most cases of spiritual disease. Society is wicked inwardly before it is formally. It is the corrupt tree that bringeth forth corrupt fruit.

This should be the more carefully noticed, since transgressors are always inclined to shelter their conduct under the prevailing power of the evil that produces it. Intemperance exists, — therefore it must be legally protected. Idolatry is universal, — therefore it is wrong to resist it. Kings reign, — therefore they rule by right divine, and disobedience to any of their behests is treason against God.

This plea has been the strongest weapon of offense and defense in our great controversy. Slavery exists in society, and is recognized in the Constitution; therefore edicts for its protection are right. And all hostility to it, or them, is contrary to the preservation of the State and the Will of God.

Are there any means of learning our duty, other than what the laws and customs of society itself afford? Has God transferred all His authority over the human soul to the State? Has He made that the solitary receptacle of His wisdom, and declared that obedience to its mandates is the sole ground of acceptance with Him? Has He delegated to it power over the future destiny of the immortal beings intrusted to its care, saying to its governors, "Whatsoever thou shalt bind on earth shall be bound in heaven, and whatsoever thou shalt loose on earth shall be loosed in heaven"? If this is not the case, but if, on the contrary, civil government derives its strength and stability from laws originating *out of* and *above* it, then is it binding upon us to seek to know what these means of moral illumination are, and where they are to be found.

As God is one, His moral law must be one and the same, in whatever way it may be revealed to us. He has chosen three ways of revelation—through Conscience, Providence, and His Word. Whatever these clearly agree in must be of the highest authenticity and authority.

Our moral being, though rendered imperfect and obtuse by reason of sin, is still, in some respects, true to its original character. The needle may be drawn by wrong attractions, for the moment, from its true direction; but still within it dwells the force that is ever pressing it against all temptations to point to its pole. Conscience, however perverted, ever possesses this instinct. In respect to some of its duties, no amount of influence can destroy its attraction towards the true and the excellent. No state of barbarism has sunk so low as to make disobedience to parents, ingratitude, or maternal hatred of offspring appear right. No matter what brutality of degradation may have obscured these sentiments, — they still and ever live. They cannot be destroyed. They spring up spontaneously, and no edict of the State, no seduction of priestcraft, no brutality of condition, has been able to suppress them. Maternal love will yearn over its helpless babe. Gratitude will gush forth from the most hardened subject of unmerited kindness. Reverence for parents will arise in the heart of every child. Every effort of the State to destroy them only proves its own weakness and folly. They are above and in advance of human power, and to them must it bow if it seek extension or permanence.

These instinctive actions of our moral nature are confirmed by its cooler, if not clearer, utterances. The Conscience sits sovereign. However much beguiled from its steadfastness by the force of education, custom, fear, or flattery, it cannot be wholly perverted. It is still employed by our Creator as His representative in the soul. It is still one of His appointed guides to us in all perplexed and devious ways. Though often drawn into a seeming support of sin, in its depths it has remained faithful to the truth. It has favored persecution, because it thought it was thus doing service both to God and its victim. It has never approved of incest, adultery, blasphemy, murder, any vice which could not steal some garment of virtue in which to hide its hatefulness. This faculty, therefore, is a chief ally in the detection of the will of God. If enlightened and assisted by its Creator, it may become to us, as it is to the sinless of Heaven, the oracle of God, —

"A light to guide, a rod
To check the erring, and reprove."

Its slightest suggestion demands our most solemn attention. Its positive decisions cannot be opposed or evaded without bringing us into condemnation with God, and subjecting us, if unrepentant, to the full measure of His just indignation.

Another mode of discovering the will of God is by His Providence. As He rules over all kingdoms and ages, a faithful seeker of His will can draw many safe conclusions from the rise and fall of customs and opinions. He will discern two great laws. Nothing enacted by God for the race of man has ever died out of society. Temporary institutions of His planting, like the Jewish government, may disappear; but then only to reappear in a fuller and finer form. No influences, however strong, or united, or persistent, have been able to extirpate or to permanently retard these divine germs. On the other hand, no principle nor practice in opposition to the law of God has been able to gain and retain enduring sway. Though upheld by every interest and fortified by every power which the god of this world could summon to his aid, though fed by the passions, the prejudice, the timidity, the ambition of man, they have shrunk before the breath of the Almighty, and have either faded slowly away before the gradual diffusion of His truth, or have been suddenly consumed by the brightness of His coming. Idolatry, atheism, absolutism, infanticide, witchcraft, what evils that have ruled mankind with a rod of iron, has He not broken in pieces as a potter's vessel? In these great laws written along the ages, the will of God and the duty of man can be most vividly discerned.

The last mode He has adopted to make known His wishes, which are to be our law, is in His writings. In them we have eternal truth. They are a lamp unto our feet, and a light unto our path. Not that every difficulty we meet on that path is especially noted in this chart of our voyage; but the general principles that fit these particular cases are scattered over all its pages, run, a stream divine, through its entire limits. If wild and wicked fantasies have sought refuge under its panoply, if single passages have been wrested from their connected and evident meaning to the support of criminal opinions and the destruction of their advocates, still these perversions of men of corrupt minds do not disturb its marvelous unity and consistency. They may teach us not to seek to shelter our depraved propensities under its sacred shadow. They do teach us to seek prayerfully its real and consistent meaning. They do not deprive us of its counsel and support in matters of honest inquiry and conscientious desire to know and do the will of our Father which is in heaven. And if we find any local word in seeming hostility to the sense of right, we must seek to adapt that expression to its declarations of universal application rather than to sacrifice these truths at the shrine of permitted but condemned infirmities.

If, when thus examined, we find the whole drift of its teachings, whether of precept or example, coincident with the course of Providence, the declarations of Conscience, and the instincts of Humanity, we have the strongest possible ground for assurance.

Hence we conclude that any act which violates the instincts of our nature, clashes with the decisions of Conscience, deviates from the path of Providence, and disagrees with the Word of God, is clearly contrary to His will, and must be treated as an enemy of mankind.

But, if it is possible for us to come to any positive conclusions upon the moral quality of any decree of State, and if these divinely appointed arbiters upon the case have decided that it is wrong, then the question arises : —

II. How shall we act in reference to the immoral decree?

1. We should refuse to coöperate in enforcing it. It has been not unfrequently asserted in the present strife of opinion, that we are bound actively to support a law, however bad, so long as it remains on the statute books. It is a law of the land. Obedience to its behests is the first duty of a virtuous citizen. But, as we have already proved, civil government is an institution founded on an inferior element of our nature, and hence has no power to bend the higher faculties to its will, unless it first conforms to their requirements.

We know that in our private action we are compelled to refuse compliance to any habit which opposes the decrees of Conscience. No evil desire, however strong, however habitual, however essential, seemingly, to our comfort, and even to our existence, can rightfully command the coöperation of the will. One's vicious habits may have become so powerful that their indulgence is absolutely necessary to the preservation of his life. Yet if he obeys them, he saves his life and loses his soul. "If thine eye offend thee, pluck it out and cast it from thee. For it is profitable for thee that one of thy members should perish, and not that thy whole body should be cast into hell."

In the family, the earliest form in which this social nature reveals itself, the same law obtains. Though the obligations of its members to its general laws have the clearest approval of the Creator, yet it has often been true that a man must forsake his father and mother, wife and child, if he would be Christ's disciple. Will a Christian not say that circumstances may arise which will make it supremely necessary for the child to refuse compliance with his parents' commands? that he cannot obey his Father in heaven without disobeying his father on earth? And shall our personal habits and family ties both be sundered in obedience to the will of God, and we still be compelled to assist in enforcing a statute of society, which is far more at enmity with the law of God, and injurious to His cause, than any private practice can possibly be? If we must refuse to obey ourselves or our parents when ordered into sin, much more must we refuse obedience to the more sinful and more dangerous demands of government.

2. But there is an additional duty imposed upon us. We must not only refuse to assist in the execution of an unrighteous law, — we are required of God to refuse to desist from those duties whose performance this law has forbidden.

Many may have moral courage enough to refuse to do a wicked act, and not have sufficient to nerve them to do a righteous one in opposition to the ungodly decree. Many a follower of Christ has shrunk from a defense of His cause, when they would have equally shrunk from a denial of Him. Yet there are claims which our Maker has upon us, compliance with which is essential to our growth in grace, and even to the possession of His favor. "He that is not for Me is against Me, and he that gathereth not with Me scattereth abroad." Were it not so, the principles of the Gospel never could spread through the world. Sin has gained possession of the hearts and the heads of men. It has organized governments, and established itself in the high places of influence and authority. It would be careless respecting passive resistance to its demands, save when prompted by its instinctive hatred of goodness to pour upon the servant of God the fury of its malice. It is only by doing what is impiously forbidden that the soul gains the approval of God and extends His dominions.

The history of Christianity affords innumerable examples of this obligation. From the career of Christ to that of His latest disciple who has thus followed his Master, come to us lessons of instruction and encouragement. Those who passed through great tribulation, who fought the good fight, who opposed the world, the flesh, and the devil, and are now surrounding the throne of God, esteem it their chief honor that they trod the path of Duty, though human customs, opinion, edicts, and power combined to keep them motionless, or to force them upon the broad and crowded road of popular, legal, governmental sin.

3. There is still another duty, coextensive with the law which it opposes.

We are required to cast our influence against it, and to endeavor to create a public sentiment which shall nullify its action and obtain its repeal.

There may be some unholy edicts which the majority of the subjects of government can oppose only in this way. But even this many shrink from doing. Feeling but little their responsibility for immoral laws, they allow them to be enacted and executed without their opposition, in deed or word. In this they act contrary to the practice and commands of Christ. He was bold to reprove all wrong institutions and edicts. He faithfully shed the light which He brought into the world upon all the habitations of cruelty. If we would receive His approval, we must pour the light of truth upon the nefarious laws and practices that yet curse mankind. In this way all can serve their God and create a moral power that shall sweep all these solidified and imperious iniquities from the world. These fires kindled in solitary breasts, spreading through their nearer circles of family, church, and community, shall meet and enkindle other like fires in other hearts, and other localities, until the mighty flame shall blaze over all the land, and consume the evil that had long enjoyed supreme possession.

When, then, we are convinced of the immorality of a law, if we would render to God the things that are God's, we are oath-bound of conscience to refuse compliance with its demands for coöperation, to disobey its commands to desist from the right which it opposes, and to throw our influence against it, so as to destroy its energy and compel its repeal.

III. Let us apply these fundamental principles to the subject which is so fearfully agitating the nation.

The law for the rendition of fugitives comes to us clothed in the majesty of that authority which we all feel bound to respect, and, if possible, to obey. Yet its form and features, despite this stateliness, are repugnant to our feelings and judgment. Cæsar, though in set array and claiming sovereign honors, is demanding clearly not the things which are his own, but the things which are God's. The question of obligation is therefore brought home to our hearts. It is no theory merely that we have been discussing, no scholastic bout of words, but a present and pressing duty. We may feel at a loss how to proceed. We may fancy our sympathy for the slave is an impulse of benevolence which cooler decisions of the reason should restrain, while the duty of sustaining the authority of law is confirmed by every consideration of benevolence and justice, human and divine.

Amid this contest of principles, when the pulpit and press are urging the decree of State as of superior claim to the decree of Conscience, when we are told obedience to Cæsar fulminating his edicts against God is a greater duty than obedience to God Himself, uttering his decrees in every heart against this law of Cæsar, in such a moment of wide-spread and increasing conflict, we must reëxamine the charts divinely granted us, to see if we can track the course marked out by the King of kings, the Cæsar of Cæsars, which alone will lead us to the desired haven.

The ground of our opposition to all laws that protect

slavery is the feeling against slavery itself. We may profess to give political or other reasons for this feeling, but we fail to see, or to acknowledge, the true reason by any such pretenses. It is an abhorrence to the claim of Property in Man that is the inspiration and the vitality of the passion that now belts the North with a burning zone. Is this conviction based on immutable foundations in the moral nature? or is it a transient emotion, the offspring of a perverted fancy? or is it a fanatical indulgence of a rightful emotion which we should curb within its appropriate limits? There are many who advocate the last opinion, whose influence greatly retards the progress of the truth. How deep this cause is seated may be learned from considering the nature of the crime which it is opposing.

Slavery is the most extreme and terrible violation of human rights. Appeal to your moral instincts. Do they not revolt from a state of servitude? Would you yield up your liberty of thought, of speech, of act, and become the possession, body and soul, of another? History shows the supreme vitality and energy of this feeling. All other passions and purposes of men are weak in comparison with this innermost nature. It is read in the insurrections which disturb the serenity of tyrants, in the revolutions that have wrought such mighty changes in society, in the haughty bearing of the savage, in the elastic step of the freeman. It impels every colony to proclaim its independence from its parent State when its strength is sufficient to sustain its desires. It is the soul of eloquence, of poetry, of art, of patriotism. It feeds the sacred fires of religion. Right over myself, a right given by God, and only to be annulled by Him, or for reasons which He approves, — this is the first law of our individual being.

But it is cruelly said, these emotions are not common to the enslaved people of America. They are beneath this universal sentiment of humanity, because they are beneath the grade of man. See how those who have known nothing of freedom save by the undying promptings of their nature are making efforts to obtain it, by as great courage and sufferings as have made illustrious the annals of the world.

"Their pulses beat with floods of living fire."

They hide themselves in the perilous holds of tiny coasters; they put on disguises and thread fearfully the paths of travel. A lady, soft and delicate, wears, like Imogen, the garb of men, and employs as a servant her darker-favored husband, both slaves now, both unspeakably despised because slaves and of African blood, but both to be held in honor abroad and at home, and to become noted persons in the history of their times.* One has himself nailed in a box, and in this coffin-like carriage is rudely tossed hither and thither, as freight, after the rough mode of public carriers, who, had they dreamed they were handling a living man, and he a black slave, would have torn off the cover, not to relieve, deliver, and hail such unexampled endurance, but to reject him with loathing, as of a race that neither deserves nor desires its liberty, and to hurl him hotly back into the hell from which they were unwittingly bearing him.

Thus does the nature of man break through every crust, however thick, of oppression and degradation, and assert its supreme prerogative. Thus does its immutable decree declare the wrongfulness of that iniquity which most positively prevents its rightful exercise.

Not only do our instincts thus condemn slavery, but our conscience approves their decision. Whatever palliatives may be thrown around it, whatever texts of Scripture may be wrested most wickedly to its support, whatever glamour Church and Society may seek to throw around its horrid nature, it can never seduce the Conscience to its service.

* William and Ellen Crafts. He has been employed in the Foreign Service of the British Government.

That tears away all these masks, pierces all these pretensions, strips off the sacerdotal and social robes, and shows the devil of devils in this livery of the court of heaven. The Conscience of the North, sometimes against the treachery, frequently despite the timidity, of its professed exemplars and teachers, has exposed it to the execration of the world, and made all true souls shrink from its awful presence.

The Providence of God vividly supports the same truth. Slavery was almost the first born of sin, and has settled in midnight blackness on every nation. No scruples existed as to the color or nationality of the victim. If he was the weaker, he became the property of the stronger. Black stole white, and white black. The children of Ham sold and scourged the children of Japhet, and those of Japhet unrighteously fulfilled prophecy by dwelling thus cruelly in the tents of Shem.

What has caused, in the slow march of the world, its steady disappearance? Why have the most advanced peoples of mankind outgrown this barbarism? It is the Providence of God declaring its sinfulness, by the evils He inflicts on its disciples, — evils in the state of anarchy, of corruption, of poverty, of weakness, of dissolution; evils in the individual transgressor of ignorance and brutality. He demanded its extinction as the first step in civilization. He led the advancing races further and further from its black abyss, until now, the mere idea of property in man is as abhorrent to the Christian world as the eating of man, its twin abomination in birth and dominion.

The Word of God confirms these witnesses to this truth. If it does not, then must this mode of revelation be in disagreement with the other which its Author has adopted, which would be equivalent to saying that God approved in the Bible that which he condemns in the conscience, and in His Providence, and that He is not, therefore, ever and everywhere, One and the Same. No such fear need possess our souls. The written law of God is identical with that inscribed on the tables of every heart, on the annals of every people, on the pages of every age. Every sentiment of general application, every decree of eternal obligation, is inspired with the idea of liberty. The commands of Sinai are penned on every Conscience. Had they said, "Worship other gods and all gods beside or with Me, disobey your parents, kill, commit adultery, steal, covet, bear false witness against your neighbor," we should universally declare the Bible the worst of books, and its Author the worst of beings.

Far otherwise is the truth. Its every precept is instinct with human liberty. Every line burns against human bondage. "Thou shalt love thy neighbor as thyself." "If a man love not his brother, whom he hath seen, how can he love God, whom he hath not seen?" "Love worketh no ill to his neighbor." "Ye are called unto liberty." "Whom the Son maketh free is free indeed." "Do unto others as ye would that they should do to you." Every command, and reflection, and incident of general import is a silent or vocal protest against slavery. Whatever words may there be found seemingly recognizing this evil, were designed to mitigate a system that could not yet be extirpated. While the State with its every arm protected the sin, and raged against its victim, it was almost impossible to escape from its toils. Its meshes covered the earth, and wherever fugitives fled, they would be caught in the snare of a vigilant tyranny. Their duty was, therefore, ordinarily, to abide in their oppressed condition, enjoying spiritual liberty, and looking forward to the hour when death should break the chain and admit them to the rights and joys of the eternally free. But while the apostle to slaves — himself boasting, so as to get nearer their estate and thus their hearts, that he, too, was a slave, but of Jesus Christ, who also, he declared, had taken upon Himself the form of a slave, — carefully advised their patient endurance of the ills they suffered, he constantly showed how wicked was the state they were compelled to endure, how glorious was liberty in its highest and proportionally in its lowest forms, how proper it was for them to escape, if possible, from their doom, how obligatory it was upon Christian masters to give their slaves that which was just and equal, which could be nothing less than their emancipation, and how masters, if Christian, must receive their own slaves no longer as slaves, but above slaves, even as brethren beloved in the flesh and the Lord.

The early history of the Church proves the true character and influence of the Bible. Christians were bound to emancipate their slaves, and the plate was often sold from the altar to deliver their brethren from this dreadful yoke. Within a few centuries of her beginning, and almost in the first of her political domination, she had cast out the evil not only from the Church, but from the State, that ruled over all the civilized earth, and had fostered this iniquity till Christianity assailed it, as the most precious jewel of the realm.

Such is the Word, such the work, of the Bible against slavery. It is designed to enforce the law written in our hearts by the light of nature, with the clearer utterances of revealed will. It cannot clash with the central impulse of that earlier law. It is intended for the guidance of man in every stage of his human, perhaps of his heavenly career, in the full glory of the millennial age, as well as the full darkness of the pagan era; and it can never approve a practice which the Providence of God is clearly removing to make way for the full triumph of the Gospel of Christ.

A Book of such vastness of aim and expression, bound indissolubly to every attribute of God, can never be perverted to the service of Satan. Its frequent declarations in the polity of Moses; its pathetic descriptions of the enslavement of Joseph, of the Hebrew people, and of the kingdoms of Judea and Israel; the odes of its prophets, bewailing the bondage, or exulting in the salvation of their people; the sublime teachings of the Savior; the sympathizing advice of the apostle, — all show that the Word of God, from its every page, in one steady, changeless beam of light divine, portrays and consumes this crime of crimes.

Tested, therefore, by all the means given us for discerning moral quality, slavery is condemned. At every tribunal to which it has successively appealed, it is adjudged guilty. Finding no protection at any court of divine decree, it has fled to the civil power, and is now striving to find under its shadow safety from the ministers of divine justice, and liberty to pursue unmolested its nefarious career. Here it defies our assault, and profanely presumes to execute vengeance, spiritual no less than civil, on all who dare oppose its hellish sway.

What is our duty in respect to it?

If it did not directly put itself athwart our path, if it laid no commands on us to assist in its extension or perpetuity, if it ruled in a distant realm, and our land was happily free from its baleful presence, we should still be morally bound to raise our voices against it, to strive to enlighten its supporters, to relieve its victims, and to seek in every right way its extirpation. We acknowledge this duty binding in respect to every other vice. Our Missionary and Bible Societies attest its depth and fervor. Our sympathies for Greece, France, Hungary, and Italy, expressed not only by the general press and voice, but in some cases by the solemn resolves of the National Legislature, show how vain and wicked it is to suppress the feelings of brotherhood, and the actions by which they demand expression.

If this be right concerning religious and political errors separately, shall it be declared wrong if indulged toward an institution which is evil of every kind, which annihilates all civil rights, corrupts all moral sentiments, and dethrones God from His sovereignty in the soul? If it is, then, our unquestionable right and most imperative duty to exert our influence for its abolition, if it prevailed in another country, does this duty diminish as the evil approaches our shores, and disappear as it lands upon them? Have the ignorant perpetrators of this crime no claim on our superior light, and their intelligent supporters on our indignation? Have its victims no demand on our tears and prayers?

But if this duty be ours when the iniquity is united with us by national jurisdiction, though not directly influencing the society in which we live, it becomes, if possible, more imperative when the unholy institution has seized the power of the government, and is using it for its basest purposes; when it intrudes its hateful presence into the seats which, till now, were free from its sway, and seeks to make us abject slaves of its satanic will. Then are we compelled by every consideration of the present and future, of national honor, of our own life even, to labor for its removal. Not with the corrupt means which itself gladly uses for its diffusion, not with its own favorite weapons, the stake, the knife, the bloodhound, but with the more fatal though less speedy weapons of speech, and prayer, and vote—powers given us by the God of nations and of men for the overthrow of every stronghold which sin erects in the institutions of society.

A government, therefore, which indorses slavery, which orders the recovery of those who have escaped from its dreadful dungeon, ought to be met with one general burst of execration, one united prayer and effort for the repeal of its wicked enactment, and the deliverance of those so unrighteously bound.

If this duty is not embraced by all, it is none the less binding upon us. Our individual action should have this tendency. Our prayer, our voice, our oath, our effort, should be devoted to the destruction of this engine of oppression, and the driving back of its director and inspirer to his native hell.

More than this we may not be able to do. The foot of the fugitive and his pursuer may not pass our door. But if occasion should occur which should bring us into immediate contact with it, by present or future laws, (for we know not what edicts may yet issue from this perverted seat of power,) other duties will arise, severe, authoritative, unavoidable. What do they demand?

We have shown that when any human law is opposed to the evident decisions of divine law, those edicts are to be disobeyed both in what they command us to do, and in what they command us to refrain from doing. To give us a right to act in this manner, the law must be clearly immoral. Laws requiring obedience to any peculiar system of government are not of this class, as no form of government, as such, can be proved to be hostile to the divine will. But an act designed to defend a system abhorrent to every virtuous faculty of our nature, stamped with infamy by the hand of God in the ruin of the countries and nations which cherish it, opposed by the Conscience of every man, and the Spirit of God, — such a system finds no defense for its demands in any laws it may impudently set up. With God as our Guide and Inspirer, we should not hesitate to advance in the way that He marks out against such a stronghold of Satan.

Should we be called upon to assist in the execution of this law, we must refuse. Ready as we should be to aid the executors of laws which we have no sound reasons to consider morally wrong, we should refuse any assistance in the execution of those clearly criminal. We must suffer, if need be, the penalty of disobedience, rejoicing that we are counted worthy to endure such contradiction of sinners, and that Christ gives us strength sufficient for the high resolve.

If the minions of government should not attempt to execute upon us its penalties, it will not be from want of willingness on their part to engage in such work, nor from the benevolence of the State which approves such decrees. Those who are ready to execute a cruel law on an unoffending woman — as the slave-catchers of the North are, and will be — will delight to wreak their vengeance upon those who dare to decline coöperation. Malice always burns the fiercest against those who, like the Hebrew captives, refuse to follow their fellows into known sin at the orders of popular power. This is already seen in the diabolic hate with which disgrace and suffering are heaped upon those who have allowed their philanthropic feelings to cause them to assist in the escape of fugitives. Some of these disciples of Christ have died under their cruel mockings, bonds, and imprisonment; others have, till lately, pined away in solitude and misery, within the walls of the national jail; and still others are to-day toiling under the lash in a Kentucky prison-house. A like fate would befall us even in this section, boastful of its liberty of speech, were we few and weak. But, by the grace of God, the fangs of this serpent have here been drawn. It has lost much of its deadly venom, and slight is the liability of injury from obeying this command of our Conscience.

Yet it may be inflicted. We may be in those sections where the opposing influence reigns, and where any resistance, even so mild as declining to coöperate in the bloody work of reënslaving a free man, may meet with instant vengeance. There and then should we commit our ways unto the Lord, and meet our appointed fate in Christian heroism, in Christian hope. Never should our hands be stained by more than the blood of the oppressed — the freedom of which that grasp may deprive him. Never should our ear feel the everlasting burning of that cry of despair which bursts from the captured fugitive as our clutch fastens upon his body and his soul. Never should our hearts be rived with the consciousness that we have been accessory to the reburial alive of one who had raised himself, with the invisible help of the Divine Rescuer, from that grave of living death. Far better that the arm wither, and the ear cease forever to catch any sound of thought or joy, than that such memories should curse our future hours.

But we have another duty forced upon us by the State, which compels us to defy the State. We are forbidden to harbor the fugitive, or to assist him in his endeavors to escape his pursuer. This command conflicts with the positive decree of God none the less than those which demand our aid in catching and binding the unhappy victim. It must be disregarded. If the man seeks our assistance whom the government is seeking to reduce to the awful bondage, from which, against great odds and amid great perils, he has effected his escape, even though it forbids us to oppose its vile attempt, as servants of Christ we should unhesitatingly disobey it, and obey Him. We must receive him to our fireside as cordially as we would receive our Lord, had He sought the shelter of our roof from the wicked rage of His persecutors. We must conceal him from his pursuers. We must aid him to escape from his native land, that is thus refusing the protection to its native-born citizens under its own flag, and on its own soil, which it claims for those who but partially adopt it as their own, and are under the flag beneath which they were born, sacrificing these primal and dearest rights of its people to the lusts of godless traffickers in human flesh.

This duty may be attended with greater peril to our

property and liberty than the refusal to assist in his recapture; but whatever sacrifices attend such a course, we should willingly make them, feeling that the release of our brethren from perpetual slavery is far more than a temporary loss of our own liberty, or the sacrifice of all our property. It is a duty we owe to him as our brother, of our own flesh and blood, made in the same image as ourselves, by the same God, endowed with the same nature and rights, responsible to the same justice, and heir of the same immortality.

We cannot shun this command of God and be guiltless concerning our brother. We cannot obey the law of the land and have a conscience void of offense toward God and toward man. We have let the sufferer be stretched again upon the rack, from which, torn and weary, he has broken away. We have permitted him who had escaped from this most horrible pit, to be again plunged into its abyss of despair. We have shut our eyes to his outstretched arms and imploring appeal. We have withheld our hand from the guidance and support he entreated. How, then, can we meet His eye, His voice, His frown, when He shall say, "Forasmuch as ye did it *not* unto one of the least of these My brethren, ye did it not unto *Me*. Depart from Me, ye that work iniquity." Not doing our duty when it is thus made a proof of our love for Christ, is doing iniquity. Beware how this sin lieth at your door.

Thus clearly does the will and Word of God mark out our path in the solemn trials of the hour.

IV. But a plea is set up by some teachers, political and religious, with much vociferation and pertinacity, that attracts attention, bewilders the judgment, and therefore merits consideration.

It is said, that although, under some circumstances, the course here laid down may be our duty, yet, as we are situated, under a Constitution that, it is declared, recognizes this system, as a national institution, we are morally bound to obey the laws based on this recognition, even if they clash with the laws of our Creator.

We have shown that civil government is based on the social faculty, an inferior propensity of our nature, which cannot rightly control the faculties acknowledged to be superior. If this be so, any peculiarities in the institutions of that government, whether in its Constitution, or laws, or their operation, are inferior in their very nature to the duties arising from our higher being, and can rightfully secure the weight of its approval, only by conforming to its character and claims.

The Constitution is a peculiarity of our national government, designed to effect the union of many independent governments under one head for certain specific and limited purposes. It is not generally considered as minute in its authority as an ordinary government, since it only exercises its power within specified limits. If it is thus limited, the obligations to obey its claims can only be coextensive with its written powers to make these claims. Where is the written authority for this demand? Where does the Constitution say, "Congress has power to compel the restoration of a runaway slave, even to the infliction of penalties upon those who aid in his escape, or refuse to aid in his return?" Is it so nominated in the bond? Ere we give up the pound of flesh, cut from the centre of the heart, bleeding with the dying life of a murdered Conscience, we demand the letter of the sinful law. According to the favorite argument of the slaveholder, on his most petted theory of State rights, he is powerless to enact or execute this great crime against humanity and God. No step can he go beyond the expressed permissions of the Constitution. He is hoisted with his own petard.

But if it be allowed, with other statesmen, that the Constitution is of equal authority with the States, or even supreme in its claims, it cannot trample on the rights which itself guarantees, nor can it justly command the violation of that higher law under which its own existence alone endures. If the clause on which the law is based can, or ought to be construed to support slavery, then that clause conflicts with the preamble of the Constitution, and hence can only be of superior weight on condition that it more closely conforms to the law of God. If we must choose between them, we must choose that which agrees best with the law written on our hearts. The preamble *decrees* liberty, the parenthesis of an article only *suggests* slavery. Under which king? God and man actually come together in one part of the Constitution, man and the devil are, perhaps, united in another. Who is to be worshiped?

Many other legal objections are made to the binding efficiency of this clause. It contains no power to execute itself, says one, and therefore must be left to the moral sense of the States themselves. It was not designed, says another, and no less an authority than Daniel Webster, to support slavery, but only the system of apprenticeship, then very popular. Thus diversity of opinion among leading and legal minds teaches us to be cautious about placing the instrument, and the laws which may be said to be founded upon it, above the intuitions of our moral nature, and the teachings of the Word of God. We should ever remember that there is a Law above the Constitution, a Lawgiver more exalted than Congress, obedience to whose will alone can make a people virtuous, prosperous, and happy.

It has become too much the fashion of late to center all moral excellence and natural prosperity in the Constitution. We acknowledge with gratitude the debt we owe our fathers, and the value of the bond which unites our great country. We believe that through these ties the Maker and Redeemer of the race will display His attributes more clearly to mankind than has yet been seen. We believe that here the religion of Christ is to have full course and be glorified. But while such are our opinions and desires, we believe that this result can be consummated only by bringing the souls of men into subjection to Christ through their vital regeneration in the principles of the gospel. Shut up the Bible House, the Tract Depository, the Church; break the presses, whose frequent issues, like sacred doves, fly over all the land; put out the light of Christianity in its renewing power upon some, its restraining power over all; and this land would soon present a spectacle to the eyes of men and of angels more hideous than any that glares upon us from the worst epochs of human history, — full of activity, of enterprise, of intelligence, of ambition, of culture, but without God, without restraint of law or love, a vast menagerie of untamed, cruel, and insatiable lusts, without bar, or bolt, or keeper, — a tropical luxuriance of civilization, full of more than tropical beasts of passion and destruction. The Constitution would be trampled under foot by all, as it now is in those States whose devotion to slavery brings them into collision with its claims, and a greater than antediluvian corruption would cry mightily to God for a greater than antediluvian ruin.

In Christ, not in the Constitution, must we put our trust. On His law should we meditate, not on that which again nails Him, scourged and bleeding, to the fatal cross. His Name should be our badge of honor, our stamp of manhood. Then, and then only, shall we truly render not only unto Cæsar the things that are Cæsar's, but unto God, also, the things that are God's.

I have endeavored to explain the grounds of our relation to civil government, the extent of the obligation it imposes, the modes of determining its usurpation of rights not belonging to it, and our duty when it assumes these unbestowed prerogatives for unrighteous ends.

I entreat you, as you love the Lord your God, as you love your neighbor, as you desire the approval of a good

Conscience now, and the approving welcome of Christ the Judge in that day, I entreat you, declare your hostility to any system or edict that retards the progress of the Gospel, violates the teachings of the Conscience, defrauds your neighbor of rights as truly his as they are yours, and as far above all price for himself, his wife, his children, as they are to you and yours, and that crowns its height of iniquity by blasphemously rejecting the laws most expressive of infinite love and holiness, the foundations of the universe and of God Himself.

Let these expiring struggles of one of the most fell destroyers of human happiness meet with no sympathy from you. Let not the eye melt with pity over its narrative of injuries inflicted by a just God and people. Let not the hand of charity relieve its most deserved distress. It assumes these postures of petition from the weakness that precedes dissolution. There would be no need of a Fugitive Slave Act, had not the conscience of the North given these poor victims a home at every Christian hearth-stone, were not the hideous crime of slavery staggering in its strongholds under the light and strength which Christ and the hour are sending forth upon it mightily.

Be not deceived by its new assumption of national forms and phrases, the robes of Congressional decree and presidential signature. How will that signature yet glare upon its signer, as Faust's in the legend. It will stain his memory to all generations. Give it no support in any form. It is the same fiend that crucified the Master. It is ready to feast its ravenous appetite upon the bodies and souls of your brethren. If by your silence or connivance it regains its strength, it will only use it for the transformation of the whole country into one vast grave of liberty and law. It has been driven from the firesides, the capitols, the churches of the North. It has thrown off the cloak of hypocritical philanthropy and piety, of Biblical approval, of pecuniary profit, of social advantage, in which, till most recently, it strove to make itself divine. It has fled for shelter to the Constitution, hoping to find under its folds protection and opportunity to regain its lost dominion.

Be not deceived. If allowed to coil itself around that symbol of national unity, it will not relax its hold until it has pressed all vitality not only from the American Constitution, but from the American people. If permitted to cling to that altar of our national faith, it will defile the whole temple of our liberties with its pestiferous breath. Like Laocoon's will be our condition, like Laocoon's our fate.

There is no permanent union between liberty and slavery. God and Satan can have no compact nor compromise. One or the other must be triumphant. If you wish for the cause of God to prevail, you must enroll yourself among the active opponents of every institution and effort designed to support or extend the cause of sin, and labor earnestly and persistently for the righteous victory.

Let your tears flow for the oppressed rather than for the oppressor, for those by this wicked decree made unjustly lawless, rather than for those impiously lawful. Think upon the long, long hours which the poor slave spends in pining for freedom; think of the perils and sufferings he undergoes in making his escape from the house of bondage. Remember his outcast and despised condition even among the free, and, in some respects, Christian States to which he has fled. Dwell upon the struggles, fears, toils, sufferings, loathings which he has endured, and then say, if you be a Christian, if you be a man, if a human soul beats in your bosom, can you place the manacles again upon those bleeding hands? Can you allow him, through your vigilance in assisting in his arrest, or your negligence in affording him the means of escape, to be dragged back in chains to the lash, the block, the more than death, from which God and his strong will have rescued him? Can you refuse to contribute your voice and vote, your purse and prayers, every means in your possession, or your influence, to remove this curse from the Church and the land? Lift your hearts above the thick air of cowardice and crime that to-day invests this whole nation, into the serene, eternal day of the truth of God. Say to every one who solicits your aid in this work of immeasurable crime, in the mighty words of Freedom's Laureate: —

"*We* hunt your bondmen, flying from Slavery's hateful hell?
Our voices at *your* bidding take up the bloodhounds' yell?
We gather at your summons above our fathers' grave,
From Freedom's holy altar-horns to tear the wretched slave?

"Thank God, not yet so vilely can Christian freemen bow;
The spirit of our early times is with us even now.
Think not because our Pilgrim blood flows slow, and calm, and cool,
We thus can stoop our chainless neck, our brother's slave and tool.

"All that a brother should do, all that a free man may,
Heart, hand, and purse we offer as in that early day;
But that one dark, loathsome burden ye must stagger with alone,
And reap the bitter harvest which ye yourselves have sown.

"Hold while ye may your struggling slaves, and burden God's free air
With woman's shriek beneath the lash, and manhood's stern despair.
Cling closer to the cleaving curse that writes upon your plains
The burden of the Almighty's wrath against a land of chains.

"We wage no war, we lift no arm, we fling no torch within
The fire-damps of the quaking mine beneath your soil of sin;
We leave you with your bondmen to wrestle, while ye can,
With the strong upward tendencies and godlike soul of man.

"But for us and for our children, the vow which we have given
For freedom and humanity is registered in heaven;
No slave hunt in our borders, no pirates on our strand,
No fetters for our brethren, no slave upon our land."

THE DEATH OF FREEDOM.*

"THE BEAUTY OF ISRAEL IS SLAIN UPON THY HIGH PLACES." — 2 *Samuel* i. 19.

"AND SAUL WAS CONSENTING UNTO HIS DEATH." — *Acts* viii. 1.

"THERE WAS DARKNESS OVER ALL THE LAND." — *Matt.* xxviii. 45.

E gather to-day around the corpse of Freedom. Our nation has given up the ghost. Her deadly sickness has met with but feeble resistance to its progress; and to-day it waves its black banner in acknowledged triumph over her prostrate, corrupting form. The beauty of Israel is slain upon her high-places. As we bend over this fallen glory and strength, I shall try to speak of that vanished strength and glory, of the means and the foe that murdered it: —

> "Show you sweet" Freedom's "wounds, poor, poor, dumb mouths!
> And bid them speak for me."

I ask you to consider your duty as Christians in this dreadful hour, and to see with the eye of prophecy either her resurrection in a greatness never before displayed, like that of her Divine Author on His reappearance from

* A sermon preached at Wilbraham, Mass., May 28, 1854, on the occasion of the passage of the Nebraska Bill, by the Senate of the United States, on the midnight of Thursday, May 25, 1854.

the grave — a resurrection that shall send despair and ruin through the ranks of her murderers, or, if we are permanently stupefied by the dragon that has triumphed over us, behold with the same clear vision the still more fearful spectacle of a contending, ruined, obliterated nation.

> "A curse shall light upon the limbs of men,
> Domestic fury and fierce civil strife
> Will cumber all the parts of this fair land."

You may say "This is a sick man's dream." "Is not this a free land? Has it not been consecrated by the prayers and sacred sufferings of the Pilgrims, honored by the patriotic valor of the revolutionary fathers, made illustrious by the wisdom of Washington and Jefferson, of Hamilton and Adams? Is it not a land whose institutions are based on the broadest principles of liberty — a land of wealth and enterprise, comfort and culture, churches and piety? And can this land be wrapped in its grave clothes, and be even now an offense and a loathing among the nations of the earth? Impossible! Does not trade rush through its crowded channels? Does not the earth bring forth abundantly, laughing ever with its munificent harvests? Does not labor 'strike with its hundred hands at the golden gates of the morning'? Does not steam toil in our factories, and whirl its products over all the land? Do not sweet bells call to church? Are we not the greatest, freest, happiest of nations?" Alas! "Gray hairs were on him, and he knew it not." "When ye say peace and safety, then sudden destruction cometh upon him, and he cannot escape." Material life flows on after the spiritual has gone. Chemical laws keep the atoms of a dead body for a while as compact as when it tented a soul.

There is no national life. What exists, exists in obstruction, weakness, obscurity. Last Thursday we surrendered all our glorious heritage. We gave up the Declaration of

Independence, the revolutionary speeches, and battles of fire and blood, the Constitution of our country, the names of our Pilgrim and Puritan ancestry, our hopes and prospects, our morals and religion. We have laid them all at the feet of Slavery. We confess ourselves her slaves. We open our gates for her triumphal march to unquestioned, universal power.

I ask no pardon for bringing this subject before you on this sacred day. I have waited till the strife raging at the seat of government should end, feeling that I had no need to stimulate you to your duty to pray for those there and then engaged in the contest, and that this word should be spoken when that battle was decided. I had hoped against hope that the right would triumph, and that I could have congratulated you on the first national step that liberty had taken towards a final victory. But that day is not yet, if ever. A far different task awaits me, and by God's grace I hope to discharge it. Let us, with sackcloth and ashes upon our souls, sit around this corpse of American Freedom; deliver its funeral sermon, and gather, if we can, some reasons for its resurrection, and of our part and lot in bringing about the glory of that distant hour. Let us try to answer the question, How can these things be?

Five years ago, or fifty, — any previous year since we became a nation, — such a deed could not have happened. Southerner and Northerner would have responded in burning indignation to a charge of his devotion to such a crime, "Is thy servant a dog, that he should do this thing? Does not my belief that slavery is an evil, my sensitiveness to the honor of the country through its pledge faithfully made in the compromise agreement of 1820, show the injustice of your imputations?" And yet this act is a necessary result of all previous acts. It is the perfect fruit of germs long since planted, and constantly nurtured. It is a link in an iron chain of our whole national history. In the first concession made to the slave power, this monster was born.

Though the letter of the Constitution does not use the word "slave," yet in its representative basis, if not in its fugitive clause, there is a recognition of its existence, a bowing to its behests. Two small States, by their firmness and vehemence, brought the other eleven to their feet, made them surrender their convictions, and obey the soft voice, but mailed arm, of Belial. What though Franklin and Jay organize abolition societies, and Washington and Jefferson favor emancipation, and Madison gets the word "slavery" excluded from the Constitution? What though every eminent man of the age is hostile to the iniquity? Still they let it find entrance into their Constitution. It is there, intrenched in the national fortress; it mocks at all objections and objectors, and commences its march to universal dominion.

When the sons of God came together for their sublime deliberations, Satan came also; and though, as in the days of Job, he gained not every point, yet, more than with him, he gained the chief, and, with the gleefulness of perdition, he snatched at his success, and plotted and waited, waited and plotted, year and year, for larger prizes. He won them.

A law to execute more perfectly the Fugitive Slave clause followed within six years. A law which never could have passed the First Congress passed the Third. A law which would have been pronounced unconstitutional by the founders of the Constitution triumphed under the very eyes of those founders. And the hand of Washington signed his name as president to an edict which five years before he would have abhorred himself for approving.

New territory is sought. Louisiana is purchased. She seeks erection into States. The strife commences afresh. Again the slave power gains all it wants by asking for more; and Missouri, Louisiana, Arkansas wheel into line under its pirate flag, while the desert lands, which will not be needed for a generation, are professedly abandoned to freedom, then, as of old, driven into the wilderness; thence, also as of old, to be driven out when its enemy would make this desert his dwelling-place. In that controversy slavery triumphed. Many then saw that when those remoter regions became the seat of population, it would claim them as its own, would make them its own. But then it could not have been done. The spirit of the fathers was not yet utterly lost. One half only of the fair acres was given up to this ravenous beast. One half alone of its pure soil was to be wet with the blood of God's persecuted saints. One half of its air was to be filled with shrieks under the scourge, with moans over sold and stolen children, with the unutterable agony of that prison-house of humanity. The anaconda rested content with its gorged appetite, which two hundred thousand square miles had momentarily satisfied, assured that those who had granted him so much would bestow the balance when his appetite returned. His assurance was well grounded.

But before that hour came, the old religious and philanthropic anti-slavery sentiment, which had glowed in the souls that burned with the revolutionary fires, was kindled afresh. A little, despised sect, their name a stench in the nostrils of the country and the Church, cast out of men as evil, lifted up their voice like a trumpet, and told the house of Israel its transgressions, and the house of Judah its sins. They started from the only Christian, the only true basis — sympathy with the slave as a son of man and a son of God, an heir of heaven, a joint heir with Jesus Christ. This was new doctrine to our degenerate fears — a doctrine no Church in this land had ever fully and faithfully preached. We mocked at and reviled them. We drove them from our churches, halls, and homes. We haled them before our judgment-seats. We issued edicts against them from State and National Congresses, and executive speeches from the chairs of governors and presidents. What the Madisons and Jeffersons, the Hancocks and Storys, would have approved was denounced and proscribed by the Van Burens and Everetts of this generation.

Still they fought for the right. It may be with lack of discretion, yet how shall you and I in our idleness dare to take up a railing accusation against them? How dare you say that William Lloyd Garrison, George Thompson, Orange Scott, and their compeers were not the wisest of their generation in action, as they certainly were in their fears, their prophecies, and their entreaties? Their errors will yet be lost in the splendor of their daring, sincerity, and zeal. If ever freedom becomes the possession, as it is the birthright, of every man in this land, he who will be honored with the loftiest monument — a monument built by every hand that has been raised against him — will be that yet hated and proscribed, that somewhat error-led, but far more truth-led, man, William Lloyd Garrison.

This stone, cut out of the mountain without hands, rolled by few but tireless arms, grew, and grew, until, when the slave power set up its claim to national domain, a new voice mingled in the tumults of the hour, and made its triumphs Bunker Hill victories, that betokened an ultimate destruction.

Again the anaconda stirs. It demands Texas — Texas with a war; and it wins. It claims that the new regions acquired by war should be his, and they are given it. Maddened with lust and success, it says, "Return to me my fugitives hiding in your own Free States; give me that nurse and playmate of your children; that industrious citizen whose family looks up to him for protection; the minister from the altar. They are mine." And all the people hasten to give them up. No, not all. Among the faithless, faithful stood a few. Seven thousand were found who bent not the knee to this Baal of America.

May they soon become seventy times seven, and deliver the land from this idolatry and the Jezreel abominations which so fiercely flourish under its dominion.

Even then the proposition that has just been successfully carried would have been rejected with abhorrence. Great and little politicians declared that these concessions were made only because the Constitution demanded it. Their sacrifice was Jephtha's, but so was their necessity, and their lamentation. But any attempt to remove an ancient landmark, any disturbance of ancient settlements, will never be allowed. No concessions to slavery. O, no! Only a painful fulfillment of agreements which our fathers made, only a declining to exasperate our brethren of the South by a useless proviso; and so, by soft words and a flattering tongue, by a heart that deceived itself, the government became the bloodhound of the slaveholder, to track and catch his God-like property. So our vast possessions, acquired by our blood and treasure, became an Aceldama, a field of blood unto this day. And great men and good men shouted loud hosannas over these peaceful measures, and declared that He who holdeth the winds in His fists would bind these contending breezes, and that there should be a great calm.

Ah! the anaconda was only resting from his bloody feasts. Now and then he opes his ponderous jaws, and swallows down, as a sweet morsel, the body and the soul of a Long, or a Sims, some poor Christian free man or free woman. But its fell hunger does not yet gnaw within. And we only said, "It is the price of the Union, this precious Union. It is the condition of our country's existence. Throw the slave Daniel into the Southern den of lions. Our farms, our stores, our schools, must flourish even if a few negroes suffer slightly. They are half brutes. They cannot feel the chains, the whip, the auction-block, the breaking of heart-strings, the fiery stake of death. What are they compared with our great and glorious Union? 'Off with their heads!'" And on we marched, and boasted, and declared ourselves the standard-bearers of the race, and called on Europe to witness our glory, to fall at our feet, and follow our illustrious leadership to universal democracy. But that great serpent awoke; nay, rather, he never slept. He bided his time; and when our boasts were loudest, and political calm the deepest, he said, "Give up that useless Missouri Compromise. It aggravates the South. It does you no good. It will make no difference in the end. Slavery can never flourish in those territories. Don't wound our feelings by adhering to its punctilios. You very generously abandoned the Wilmot Proviso, because of our sensitiveness. Do the generous thing once more."

We were struck aghast. "'Give up the Compromise'? Open the gates of the Eden of the continent to this river of death, that has burned and blackened so many fair fields? Never! The Thirteen States fought eight years rather than submit to foreign tyranny. We will fight as long rather than surrender a domain twice as large as the Colonies embraced to a domestic tyranny immeasurably worse." Loud rose the cry: "It is ours. It shall remain ours." And behold, while we cry, our representatives hold it out to the greedy clutch of the slaveholder. It is grasped. It is swallowed, and to-day the arch tempter is the sole ruler in that Paradise. Freedom, intelligence, and enterprise, art, civilization, and Christianity, every grace and strength of humanity, have fled, as the angels that frequented the holy Eden, and Satan, sin, and death revel in its desecrated forests and prairies, their unquestioned possession.

Thus these things are. Not by one step, nor two, have we reached this goal, but by a practical imbruting of the conscience, by yielding to the demands of this awful iniquity, by violently opposing and abusing its earnest enemies. Had not these members of Congress fought against the anti-slavery movement with furious passion, they would not be found to-day enacting this bill. The light that was in them is darkness; and how great is that darkness! What an awful depth upon depth of darkness! Great men in the pulpit and the forum set the bad example of mocking at the higher law, and now their bayers on deride the very law which they so idolatrously worship. So comes Pandemonium, no law, but Chaos and old Night.

> "Nor public flame, nor private, dares to shine;
> Nor human spark is left, nor glimpse divine!
> Lo, thy dread empire, Chaos, is restored;
> Light dies before thy uncreating word:
> Thy hand, great Anarch, lets the curtain fall,
> And universal darkness buries all."

Verily as we have sown, so do we reap this day. Saul is consenting to the martyr of this first-born of Christianity. Saul, the Pharisee of Pharisees, we, who tithe mint and anise and cummin, and neglect the weightier matters of the law, judgment and mercy and truth, we stand by while the murderous rocks are being hurled at its head; we share in the robber's spoils — its sacred lands, with all their hidden but real wealth of happiness and prosperity. You and I, my brethren, have too much to do with this dire act. Have you not said, "Party first, liberty afterward"? Have you not cried, "Union, Union, Union, now and forever," carefully omitting the word "Liberty," which alone makes that Union an honor or a blessing? Have you not filled your ears with the shouts, "Our Nation, however bounded, and however ruled," so that you could not and would not hear the wail of your oppressed fellow-citizens, that heart-broken entreaty from the depths of that vast dungeon, covering a half million of square miles — "Am I not a man and a brother?" Have you not said, "The slave belongs to his master; how can I interfere?" Have you not acknowledged the right of man to say to his brother, his sister, "Thou art my property, to be worked, whipped, starved, sold, ravished, killed, as I will?" Have you not forgotten often in your daily prayers to pray for those in bonds as bound with them? In insolence of heart have you not despised "God's image cut in ebony;" ay, cut in ivory too, if that seems to you the more precious? for the blue-eyed, yellow-haired Saxon, no less than his swarthier brother, groans to-day in that prison-house. Have you not joined in jeers and slanders against the abolitionists, and given ground for the remark of a senator from Georgia, Mr. Toombs, but last Thursday, that "the government has but little to fear from the abolitionists. Their greatest achievements have been to raise mobs of fugitives and free negroes, and to incite them to murder and other crimes, and their exploits generally end in subornation of perjury, to escape the criminal courts. The whole concern is not worth an ounce of powder."

Have you not apologized for, defended, and even applauded the system of slavery, commending the graces of the masters, the submission, contentment, and even happiness of the slave? Have you not cherished a pride of caste, declared complexion a Heaven-appointed barrier of separation between the children of Adam, a great gulf, across which no white and wealthy Dives could pass to mingle in perfect unity of feeling and life with a black or tawny Lazarus, barbarous, beggarly, and sore-smitten, as you saw and said, albeit he was even then lying in Abraham's bosom, the best beloved of all his children? Have you not thus declared the diversity of the human race, and given your sinful aversion the authority of a divine decree?

Let him that is without sin among us cast the first stone at those lofty in position and power, who but give the logical and inevitable conclusion to these feelings; who say, "The negro has no identity of rights with the white," as you say he has none of blood; "the abolitionist is a madman, scattering firebrands, arrows, and death. Money is everything. Make money. Extend slavery. Crush out abolitionism!" And it is done. In their grand if gloomy palace of hell sit these slave masters of the people, all of whom are their slaves, and most of whom, if of white faces, hug their chains and kiss their conquerors' feet. They exult, as did the Pandemonium chiefs over their magnificent structure. They exclaim with the Babylonian monarch, "Is not this great Babylon that I have builded?" "Surely all the principalities and powers, all the offices and honor of the American continent, shall be ours, and ours forever." They heed not the footstep of the descending God; they hear not that avenging voice whispering in their heart of hearts, "Thou fool, this night thy soul shall be required of thee;" then what becomes of thy stores of power, pomp, and pride?

"An answer sweeps through the troubled night
With a shout for the slave and a shout for the right.
Hear ye not, hear ye not, through your marble arch,
The iron tramp of the millions march?
The earthquake awakes in a giant start,
And breaks the chain which has bound his heart."

By such slow and steady approaches the citadel of liberty has been enclosed, undermined, taken. America is no longer a free nation. No longer can she boast that in her borders the rights of man are inviolable. Here may the oppressed find liberty, and the heavy laden rest. Not in obedience to constitutional scruples, not by a sudden surprise, temptation, or fall, has this destruction come upon her. This act is against all constitutional statements or suggestions. She gives her hand, if not her heart, to the vote. So far from being the first triumph of the Tempter, it is the autumnal fruit of seeds sown by our fathers' hands, and nurtured and enriched by the assiduous culture of three generations. From the ordinance of 1787, which admitted slavery to all our country south of the Ohio, by forbidding it north of that line, and which built up the enormous power of this crime in four of the largest and most influential of our Slave States,—Kentucky, Tennessee, Alabama, and Mississippi,—we have descended to the ordinance of 1854, which prohibits freedom in all the territory that had been pledged sacredly to liberty, which practically and intentionally forbids any restrictions on the march of this demon over any part of the national domain.

There is no national life in us. Before the world, before God, we stand to-day in a blacker infamy than rests upon any other power. We have become the basest of kingdoms. The lowest of the nations of the earth look down upon us. France has liberated its slaves in Algiers and the West Indies. Russia has emancipated its serfs, Mexico its citizens. Brazil discourages slavery and encourages its extirpation. Turkey represses this accursed trade. We alone, of all Christian, of all heathen lands, avow the divine origin of slavery, and accord it unlimited life. We alone tear down the wall of separation our fathers had built, and say to the sea of unspeakable crime and agony, "No longer shall it be said to thee, by man or God, 'Here shall thy proud waves be stayed;' but dash, roar, roll onward and onward, engulfing all those vast and blessed regions with an arkless deluge of death."

If Jefferson could say, in his day, "I tremble for my country when I remember that God is just," what must we say, who have seen that country descend from one point of baseness to another, until now African cruelty, Egyptian degradation, or Roman corruption, in the heights of their excesses, were hardly more vile, were far less guilty? There should be no more Fourth of July, — its celebration is a mockery; no more reading of the Declaration of Independence, — we are independent no longer: the slave's collar and manacles burden our neck and arms; no more boast of our Christianity as a nation, when our President and Congress exceed Nero and his senate in pagan edicts and crimes; no more vaunts of our greatness among the nations of the earth. They have heard of our shame, they have seen it, and they rejoice in it. We, raised to heaven by free institutions and all the culture that has ever yet been given to man, have voluntarily cast ourselves down to hell.

Before God and all the world, America stands to-day the propagandist of slavery, the advocate and practicer of the dogma that man can, and should, and shall own his fellow-man; that we are endowed by the Creator, not with inalienable rights of life, liberty, and the pursuit of happiness, but of murder, bondage, and the destruction of happiness; that there is no sacredness in the marriage tie, no duty to believe in or regard the affections of father or mother, husband or wife, brother or sister; that the "peculiar" and very domestic "institution" of home life and love is confined exclusively to those who have not a drop of African blood in their veins; that the human auction-block, the whipping-post, the branding-iron, the bloodhound, the gallows-tree, and the stake — in a word, every barbarism — are the true elements of a nation's growth and glory. These are the doctrines enacted by the present Congress of the United States, approved by our present President, and published to the world as the consummate flower of Christian civilization in this land of the Puritan, Huguenot, and Quaker, in the year of our Lord and Savior Jesus Christ, the eighteen hundred and fifty-fourth. The pen that put the figures of that date of our redemption upon this satanic bill must have shrunk from the profanity, if the heart and hand that it served were so depraved as to be unconscious of the horrible sin.

The deepest depth is reached. There may be a table-land of darkness upon which future legislators and executives shall erect other trophies of their wickedness, — the abolition of all laws which now prevent the bringing or keeping and trading of slaves in the Free States; the reinstatement of the African slave trade — a trade far less cruel than that which is regularly carried on under the protection of our government between Baltimore and New Orleans; the enslaving of white laborers as well as those of the darker hue, who now pine in chains; the acquisition of Cuba by robbery or by open war with Spain, as we fought with Mexico, to win a new region for this crime; and, at last, and not improbably, a war with Great Britain, to prevent Canada's harboring the fugitives from our oppression. Then cometh the end — a return to violence, ignorance, idleness, and bestiality surpassed only by those in that "outer darkness," the "dogs, sorcerers, whoremongers, murderers, idolaters, and whosoever loveth and maketh a lie."

Is this our future? Must our star be hurled from the heavens up whose steeps it was marching with such a rapid, vigorous, and lustrous step? Shall our fine gold become dim, our name, long the terror of tyrants, become their byword, our strength for the oppressed of all lands change to a rotten reed which pierceth the hand that leans upon it, and snaps while it stings? *This* we *are!* It is no *shall* be. The eclipse is *on* the sun. Darkness is now over all the land. The glow is faded from the heavens, and all isles and continents, even to distantmost Asia and Africa, gaze with awe and sadness at the pale, cold light which we shed upon their dreary realms. But yesterday the nation

> "Stood against the world; now lies she here,
> And none so poor to do her reverence."

But is the eclipse total? Is there not a ring — a faint and little ring — of light around the blackened orb, that will yet re-cover all its face with glory? Will not this darkness pass away, and the true light again shine? Step by step has this obscuration moved on, a small segment in 1789, the whole face in 1854. The shadowy edge of brightness gives token of a brighter day to-morrow. The administration triumphed, but its forces were divided; and had not its foes come to the rescue it would have failed in its attempt. Its own party threw a larger Northern vote against it than for it. A hundred Democrats were found to resist the crime — a hundred in a body of whom almost every one was elected on a pro-slavery platform. This is a star in the midnight, a ray of morning lying athwart the denseness of gloom.

But not upon this hundred do we rely for deliverance. Behind them is a mass of millions, whose eyes are freed from the scales of party obligations, whose souls thrill with novel sympathies for their brother in chains, whose indignant voices have gone up to God in petition after petition against this outrage, who have seen the slave struggling for freedom before their own eyes, branded and bleeding, but still defying his robbers; who have read tales, real or fictitious, — the latter far less than the reality, — that burned through their hearts like fire, filled them with an agony of sensibility and sympathy, and nerved them with an abhorrence of slavery and a resolution to destroy it. This mighty mass are recognizing their rights as members of the great Republic. Their numbers grow rapidly; their spirit, and resolve, and consciousness of power outrun in increase the additions to their adherents. They are almost stupefied at this awful horror. They feel that it is beyond the scope of dreams. But they are not unnerved by the spectacle. They are preparing to confront it boldly, legally, effectively.

Behind the Congressional hundred, behind these masses, rocking with prophetic throes, stands the Church of Christ, too often, alas! dumb and paralyzed before great and general sins, whose robes much blood of the innocents stains, who in this long conflict has too frequently forgotten that she was the Church of Christ, and has once and again become the synagogue of Satan, and who is even now far from representing perfectly her Author and Founder, and only Life. For this crime has polluted the sanctuary, and set up the abomination that maketh desolate in the most holy place. Yet still, with all her faults and failures, she is by far the best organization among men for the extirpation of national no less than individual sins. The Church of Christ abolished idolatry, gladiatorial shows, Roman and European slavery. She is beating down with her gigantic arm the strongholds of modern idolatry. She is moving into the van, and marshaling the hosts against this evil.

Slowly but surely she is emerging from those waters of pollution into which she was led by a criminal love of the world, or a delusive dream that, by conforming to the lusts of the flesh, she could deliver souls from those lusts. We have all gone down into Egypt, holy Jacob and Joseph as well as worldly-minded Simeon, cruel Levi, changeable Reuben, and carnal-hearted Judah. From Egypt we are returning. Here comes an individual church and pastor, there a conference, or association, or synod of churches and pastors, until this act has shot, like a crystallizing force, through Church and ministry, transforming multitudes averse to agitation and abolitionism into the warmest friends of both.

It has opened the eyes of the apologists of the system, and those opposed to any attempt to extirpate it, to the truth long since seen by the clear-eyed friends of Freedom, that Slavery cannot remain at ease, eating its bread in quietness and singleness of heart. It must work. Like its father, the devil, it ever goeth about seeking whom it may devour. It encroaches on the sacred territory of the Church. It ascends from her obscure layman and preacher to her pillars in pew and pulpit. It climbs into the high seats of the bishopric, paling the fires and blackening the brightness of the holy breastplate of the highest of the priests of God. It has entered her organizations, and disciplined her discipline. Thus it stood in the Church, as it now does in the State, unquestioned, uncontrolled, supreme in authority and power. From this seat it has measurably fallen, from that of the State may it fall speedily and forever.

This act will give an impetus to the work of Church purification such as a smaller evil might not have done. May God hasten the day when every Christian Church shall say to her slaveholding member, "Repent, and forsake that sin. Let your oppressed go free, or release my hand from the grasp of Christian fellowship. Leave the holy inclosure of those who would fain live unspotted from the world. Stand without until you can come in as one who shows that he loves God by loving his neighbor as himself." This national shame, like the act of the Church forbidding colored testimony, will convert thousands of the timid into the brave, and incite every communion to the work of purging itself and its country of the fearful sin.

In front of the sacramental hosts of God's elect appears the Captain of our salvation. He has said the wickedness of the wicked shall come to an end. He has declared He will give deliverance to the captive, and open the prison door to the bound. He stands with the gathering multitude, bringing their hearts into closest sympathy with His purposes, and inspiring them with a zeal and energy that, through their communication, descend on less lofty and holy masses like a mighty rushing wind that fills every heart, however ignoble in its general tendency, however unbelieving concerning its own salvation, with these most Christly principles and resolves.

4

Are these sufficient grounds for hope? We see the close-knitted squadrons of error. Their faces are flushed with victory. Their passion for conquest is growing with wonderful rapidity by its late successes. They do not stand still. Far from it. Does a victorious army, in an enemy's country, halt and surrender on its field of victory? They march on. Ere the coming month is over, your ear, if watchful, will catch the pass-word from lip to lip in the presidential mansion, the Senate Chamber, the Hall of Representatives, "Forcible occupation of St. Domingo, that Hayti may be returned to its chains; war with Spain, that Cuba may be ours; yet another slice of Mexico for our slaves." Before this Congress rises, if the black cloud of war does not again shut down upon the land by the decree of President and Senate, all this may be done. The future is full of portents dire. The wicked rule; the righteous are hidden.

But the growth of the anti-slavery sentiment has been more rapid and strong than that of pro-slavery dominion. So far as opinion is concerned — and that is very far — the North is disinthralled. Opinion will soon ripen into conviction of duty, and conviction work itself into action. We shall see, I hope, men of every political and religious faith bound together by one feeling, one vow, one act, never to rest from battle till our government is emancipated from this sin. Not only may we see this feeling in the North, but the Spirit of God and the Conscience of man are bound by no sectional limits. Over that vast region the light is breaking. May it prove the light of the morning. A free press, full of denunciations against slavery, lives and even flourishes in Virginia. The people of Kentucky thrust a slaveholding murderer from their borders.* He is preserved from a felon's fate solely in consequence of his

* Matt. Ward, of Louisville, Kentucky, who killed Professor Butler for chastising Ward's brother, who was one of his pupils.

wealth and rank, even as every such murderer is throughout that whole region. But he alone of them all has fled before the indignation of the people. If he is not the last who murders school teachers as they would vermin, he is not the last, we trust, who will find a popular verdict that shall override the unjust wrestings of the courts, and vindicate, if roughly, the majesty of law, and the rights of the humblest citizen.

Frequent cases of manumission, the increased dissemination through the South of anti-slavery books and papers, their more intimate connection with a North becoming purer and purer with every year and every trial, — these blessed signs betoken the coming of the resurrection morn to that benighted region, to our now benighted land. Mighty as stands this iniquity to-day, like Nebuchadnezzar's image, its feet are clay. Speedily shall its power vanish away. Speedily, but not this month, nor year. Perhaps the war may be one of many years; it has already been; but it shall vanish away. Not in an unexpected or unseen manner; not by some miraculous act in which man meddles not, but by one effort, prolonged, intense, gradually successful. It has grown by progressive acts. So it may die.

A few reflections will conclude our sad service.

First. This dark hour should fill us with humiliation. Perhaps you have been very valiant for the truth, now prostrate under insulting feet, and you may presume on that faithfulness to reproach your neighbor for his idleness and recreancy. But it is not the false so much as the faithful that in such hours cast themselves penitently and with self-reproaches before God. When Jerusalem lay a desolation, upon which the curse of God had been executed, it was the elders of the daughter of Zion, not the blasphemers and idlers, who cast dust upon their heads, and bowed before the Lord. It was not some worldly and timid Jew, captive to his fears and lust more than to his Babylonish master, but the holy Daniel, that said, "I set my face unto the Lord God to seek by prayer and supplication, with fasting, and sackcloth, and ashes; and I prayed unto the Lord my God, and said, 'O Lord, the great and dreadful God, we have sinned, and have committed iniquity, and have done wickedly, and have rebelled even by departing from thy precepts and from thy judgments. O Lord, to us belongeth confusion of face, to our kings, to our princes, and to our fathers, because we have sinned against thee.'" Such were the tears and confessions of this man of God; not Pharisaic in exclusiveness, but deeply conscious of his own sins. So the zealous Nehemiah, when his people had gone backward, says, "I sat down and wept, and mourned certain days, and fasted and prayed before the God of heaven; and said, 'I pray before thee now, day and night, for the children of Israel, thy servants, and confess the sins which we have sinned against thee; but I and my father's house have sinned.'"

Even so must we, my brethren, fall before our God, and confess that we have sinned. Have we done our whole duty always? Have we wrestled with God as fervently as we have with men? Have we sought his aid as much as that of our brother? Have we not sometimes forgotten the slave in our contest for local and temporary political triumphs? The judgment of Heaven is upon us. Let us imitate the elders of Jerusalem, the godly Daniel, and Nehemiah, and pour out tears and prayers before their God and ours, who alone casts down, who alone can build up.

Second. What works shall be added to these penitential words? The crown has fallen from the head of our country. She sits in the dust. The heathen have come into the inheritance of our Christian fathers, and all our pleasant places lie waste. The fetter is riveted the more firmly on the neck of your poor brother and sister, and shouts of hellish exultation over this victory go up this sacred day around the slave-pens of Richmond, Alexandria, Baltimore, and the great multitude of similar prison-houses of death. The saintly victim within hears their notes of blasphemous glee, and, learning the cause, his faint hopes fall, and despair

"Closes around, above him as a shroud."

Christian, what is your duty? — to contend about tariff or free trade? to hold back, in Pharisaic pride, from association with publicans and sinners, as you call those of the party opposite your own? to strive about words to no profit but to the subverting — the utter and eternal subverting — of their hearers and speakers? Is it to say, "That party which represents freedom is bigoted, fanatical, of one idea?" Better have one idea than none. Do you declare, "I have ridiculed and fought it. I cannot now join myself to it. I have friends and kindred involved in this crime. I cannot openly oppose their course or wound their feelings"? "Whosoever loveth father or mother, husband or wife, brother or sister, more than Me, cannot be My disciple." Is not the slave, too, your father and mother, your brother and sister? Does not this very tie of blood bind you to the oppressed as closely as to the oppressor? In Adam, in Noah, you are of one blood; in Christ, of one redemption.

Will you see this gigantic cruelty marching northward, invading your threshold, subduing your State, possessing confessedly, triumphantly, our whole land and our whole life? Christian man, Christian woman, ask for the straightest path of duty, and follow it, whatever sacrifices it may require of pride, of former opinions, of friendship, of kindred, of reputation, of life itself. Let not the platform of action be made narrow by intolerance. If it be of one plank, and that not an inch in breadth, leap upon it, labor on it, seek to widen it, never desert it until all the land stands erect upon its broad base. Toil until the mustard seed becomes a mighty tree, the stone by rolling enlarges and fills the whole earth. The stone which the builders so disdainfully reject shall yet become the head of the corner, the capstone of universal liberty and joy. Fear not the names that are flung at you, as if of themselves abominable. They are good words, and will yet be the most choice and honored titles of this hour. The brave Senator Wade, of Ohio, said, in that fight in the night and with the night, that until this warfare was ended by the triumph of the right, "I am an Abolitionist* at heart while in the slave-cursed atmosphere of this capital, whatever I may be at home. But here pride and self-respect compel a man either to be a doughface, flunky, or an abolitionist, and I choose the latter. I feel that my hatred to slavery justly entitles me to wear it — a name which I never yet denied, and which present, passing events are fast rendering glorious." Be an abolitionist at Washington, at home, everywhere. It is the highest title to-day of honor from God, and will be to-morrow of like honor from men.

Finally, forget not prayer. This kind cometh not forth but by prayer and fasting.† If it has fascinated the nation by its wealth, its strength, its culture, and its statesmanship, if it has gained possession of our greatest men, it can be expelled. They can again become clothed and in their right mind — the mind which one‡ had at Chicago, when he declared himself "opposed to the extension of slavery;" of another§ at New Boston, when he said, "The Fugitive Slave Law is a great evil;" of another|| at Newburyport, when he wrote letters

* This word was afterward printed in the Congressional Globe in Italics, as if it was, as it was, an extraordinary expression of boldness. It is possible that this was the first adoption of this title by a member of Congress in his seat.

† Frequent national proclamations of prayer and fasting were made during the war, beginning with that of President Buchanan, in the winter before his administration terminated.

‡ Stephen A. Douglas. § Edward Everett. || Caleb Cushing.

full of the warmest, noblest sentiments of freedom. Who knows but that this mind may return?

Perhaps the final act by which this iniquity is consummated may yet be stayed. Perhaps compunction may paralyze the hand that would subscribe the death-warrant of the nation. Pilate's wife may perhaps successfully warn her husband to have nothing to do against this most just cause — to sign no decree which shall consign millions of sons and daughters of the Lord Almighty, whom Christ has declared to be his brothers, and sisters, and mothers, to shames, and agonies, and welcome deaths.

If the national governor's wife should fail in duty, or in success; if Herod, and Caiaphas, and Pilate — the Senate, the House, and the President — unite in this crucifixion of Freedom; if it lies in its sepulcher, pierced and lifeless, before a mocking South, a tearful, timid North, an amazed world, still let us pray. Death cannot bind it forever. God will not suffer this holy one to see corruption. It will rise again. It will come forth in greater glory than it ever wore before. With powers then vailed, but now disclosed, it shall sit in the seat of judgment. It shall be itself Congress and President. It shall fill its votaries with praise and might, and its enemies with shame and everlasting contempt. Its foes shall be its footstool. With our great Senator, at that midnight hour of its passage, may we say, "Sorrowfully I bend before the wrong you are about to perpetrate. Joyfully I welcome all the promises of the future." *

Roll away the stone from the door of the sepulcher! Be vigilant. Be tearless. Be prayerful. Be believing. We shall triumph, not through disunion, not with perpetual feuds, but through the help and Spirit of God. Some Washington or Jefferson will yet arise, who will lead North and South to the battle and the triumph of true freedom and

* Charles Sumner.

true democracy. The South will not forever keep back, and our Jerusalem, the seat of this death, shall be the seat of its revival in perfect power and glory.

While, therefore, we weep over this death and burial of national righteousness, as David, when the government fell into the power of apostate sons and priests, went weeping up Olivet, and looked back on the sacred city left desolate, let us also weep with a purpose and hope of regaining the lost sovereignty. Labor in the closet, at the family altar, in the community, at the polls, with prayer, and speech, and purse, and vote. Labor with a largeness of soul that seeks not only this grand and spacious land for freedom, but freemen everywhere in a free land. Labor till every yoke is broken and every family unbroken, until the feet of tender women no more sow blood along the paths their taskmasters drive them, until their hearts no more sow richer drops of sacred blood over sundered families and desolate households, — soon to be reaped in what terrible judgments upon our nation, ourselves, our posterity, God only knows, and the future alone can tell.

We may go into deeper blackness, but we shall come forth into brighter light. May every soul be a worker together with God in this the hour and power of darkness, that he may rightfully be a partaker in the glory that shall follow.

THE STATE STRUCK DOWN.*

"But those husbandmen said among themselves, This is the heir; come, let us kill him, and the inheritance shall be ours." — *Mark* xii. 7.

LAST Sabbath many of us — would it had been all — ate the body and drank the blood of the great Martyr of Humanity, of Deity. In grateful, solemn, humble devotion, we commemorated that event which at the time seemed, and was, the victory of hell. A band of men, eminent in station, armed with swords and staves, came upon that Martyr, in the dusk of a Thursday evening, in the retirement of a garden. They beat Him with deadly blows, they thrust in His head the cutting thorns, they mock Him, spit upon Him, murder Him! All for what? Professedly for blasphemy. False hypocrites! Great zeal theirs for their National Religion, for the Constitution of their fathers, for the quiet and harmony of their nation. This was the reason: "Then gathered the chief priests and the Pharisees" (President and Senators), "a council, and said, What do we? for this man doeth many miracles. If we let Him thus alone, all

* A sermon preached at Westfield, Mass., June 11, 1856, on the occasion of the assault on Hon. Charles Sumner. See Note II.

men will believe on Him." It was because He was an eloquent orator, whom the common people heard gladly; because He was a bold and sarcastic denouncer of these same official criminals; because He strove to restore the principles and practices of the fathers to their true seat of authority and power; because He pleaded for the primitive Constitution of their Washington in its true meaning; because He was a real democrat, who loved the people and sought their good, who was not ashamed to talk and abide familiarly with the Samaritans, whom his countrymen hated and despised, as we do the black race among us,— it was for these reasons that they hated, beat, and murdered Him. Not on account of His blasphemy or unconstitutionality; not because He surpassed the bounds of propriety in His speech, though no sharper nor severer personalities are found in all oratory than those He uttered. Far deeper, more malignant, more powerful, were the motives which impelled them. They were the central fears of a wicked oligarchy, who saw their power giving way under the mighty words of this Master of the Hearts, soon to have been Master of the Acts of the people. They were the central passions of their viperous souls, which felt that if He was stricken down, all the powers of virtue, conscience, ancient name, divine religion, would fall into the same grave, and their tyranny be perfect and perpetual. Therefore "those husbandmen said among themselves, This is the Heir; come, let us kill Him, and the inheritance shall be ours."

Let it not be thought, in the suggestions of this analogy, that we would limit the experience of our adorable Savior, in that hour of grief and pain extreme, to that of any follower of His, however exalted. It was not Christ as God, but as man, that the Jews intended to slay. For if it had been as God, then they must have been fiends, not men, and He could not pray for them as we must for all — "Father, forgive them, for they know not what they do." They meant to kill Him as a man; He laid down His life as our divine Redeemer.

The feelings and actions of His persecutors come afresh before us in the tragedy of to-day — persecutors, then, as now, blind to the divinity of the principles and powers they seek in the person of their advocates to utterly destroy.

Every sufferer for the truth is an associate of that Infinite Sufferer in His sorrows, His joys, His renown. They who fell in the obscurity of ancient martyrdoms, of Italian dungeons, of Hungarian gallows, of Southern swamps and cells; those who molder or are hardly yet cold under the grassy plains of Kansas; and he whose blood stains, and will forever stain, the floor of the hall of our highest legislation, who now lies pale and weak, with that brain full of great thought and high resolve, a festering pulp of dead matter struggling for the mastery, and almost sure of carrying its victory to a fatal perfection, and of laying the noble temple of that sovereign soul in ruins; all these, known and unknown by men, are in the eye of God, and stand at the right hand of Christ, in the work and reward of human redemption.

Eminent among these, when we consider the powers which he represents, and which are combined against him, is he who closes our catalogue. There has been no such martyr, in the position and purposes of his assailants, in the variety, wealth, and importance of the established and prosperous Ideas thus assailed. It is not because of personal feeling at the keenness of his sarcasm, nor because he broaches unconstitutional heresies, or disturbs the harmony of the nation, that he is smitten with the tongue of Senatorial vituperation, and the bludgeon of Representative bloodthirstiness. It is because he is the plainest, strongest, most eloquent, most single-eyed, most unscheming, ministerial, and prophetical of all the defenders of Liberty on the floor of Congress. It is because his great powers of wisdom, learning, rhetoric, and oratory, have been sanctified and set apart for the Master's use. It is because his appropriation of these eminent gifts to the before degraded cause of Abolition has raised that from the dust, and made the hooted, dreaded name of Abolitionist like the very glory of God, in the light which his protecting and illuminating genius has cast upon it. It is because in him thus dwelt personally and officially the desires and purposes of freedom, that these, its enemies, have singled him out for years as the central mark of their venomous hate. "It is *the cause*, it is *the cause*," my friends. Therefore it was that in that hall of dignity and authority, on that Thursday afternoon, but a few days after the anniversary, and a few hours before the time that the Divine Orator and Reformer was assailed, a band of men, eminent in station, armed with swords and staves (how significant the analogy! — bowie knives and loaded canes, the modern substitutes and striking likenesses of the Roman glaive and club), instigated and supported by their still more eminent leaders, set upon this unarmed disciple of the mighty and hated Nazarene, and left him senseless in his blood.

Many murders of the advocates of the truth are in the pages of humanity. Yet no one embodies so many perfected fruits of evil on the one hand, and of goodness on the other, as this.

Others were smitten down while bearing and sowing the seed of life yet ungrown. So fell the first martyr, Abel. So fell all the forerunners of Christ. So fell the disciples in those early persecutions. So Luther freed the long-imprisoned truths, and flashed them out in all their purity upon the conscience of the world, and it rushed upon him with swords and bludgeons. So the Puritans suffered as seed-bearers, the Wesleys and their associates, Kossuth and his people, Mazzini and his, Washington and his. I know not an instance in which the principles of Civil and Religious Freedom, in the very summit of their lofty power, have been so murderously assailed. Roman purity and honor had already fled when Cæsar clove down the statue of Liberty; when the Goths replaced her effeminacy with their wild, rude vigor. France had no national piety nor morality when Napoleon grasped her sceptre. These were Jehus, appointed to smite down anarchy, voluptuousness, and intolerable vice.

But here, in the Senate House of this Christian Republic, on the person of this simple man of God's desires, there fell the blows of Arch-Iniquity. It was anarchy assaulting order; the deepest ignorance, the highest learning; savage habits, the finest culture. It was idleness murdering industry; piracy, honorable trade; disunion, the federation of Free and Equal States; barbarism, civilization; grossest impiety, holiest Christianity. It was progressive debasement in every wish and want of man, cleaving down progressive enlightenment in every walk of the soul. It was, in fine, every vice throttling every virtue; Satan attacking Christ.

Sumner is not, like the fathers of the Revolution, a rebel without any authority save that which God had inwardly given. He is not like Clarkson, and Wilberforce, and Garrison, at the beginning of their career, eloquent revealers of the yet generally unseen. He embodies the awful sovereignty of a Nation,—for every State is a Nation in its rights and dignities. He embodies the whole civil, social, and personal character of that State. He represents its wealth, its enterprise, its education, its philanthropy, its religion, its perfect life.

As it was not a mere man, but the liberties and humanities of a great State and Nation that were thus felled, so the aggressor was something more than a man. Brooks, much less than a man as he is, would not have dared to strike Massachusetts. It was a confederacy of the abandoned men who wield the sceptre of our government, whose strong hand hurled Brooks at the defenceless head of this State. It was a systematic, mighty, ruling Sin, the sum and essence of all villainies, that swayed that league, as the will the arm, and hurled its cowardly implement at the sum and essence of all virtues in the person of your Representative. Hence the inspiration and the judgment which made them say among themselves, "This is the heir; come, let us kill him, and the inheritance shall be ours."

Sympathy with the sufferer is, therefore, the least of your duties in connection with this crime; would be the least agreeable to him in his perils and pains, and the least satisfactory to Him whose he is and whom he serves. We bleed in him; liberty, humanity, the future of our race in time, the future of unnumbered members of it in eternity, religion, Christ, — all are faint, and bleeding, and ready to die in the feeble body and suffering soul of this representative man.

Standing amid the smitten and shaking pillars of all national, of all human perfection, let us ask ourselves — First, Are we guilty in this matter? Second, If so, what works meet for repentance shall we bring forth?

I. Are we partakers of the sin and guilt of this Cain? We sharers of his sin? you will say; we, so vehement in our denunciations, so valiant in our boasting, so bloody in our revenge? we, accessories before the fact to the murder of the whole past and future of human attainment? It cannot be. "Out of thine own mouth will I judge thee, thou slothful servant." As this thing was not done in a corner, so it was not done in a moment. A long series of assaults and martyrdoms of principles and their advocates, patiently endured, often as violently applauded by us as this deed by the South, have been the necessary preamble to the civil war in Kansas and the brutality in Washington. Sumner's fall, the murder of Barbour, the butchery of John Brown's son, the sack of Lawrence, the ravages of a guerrilla war, legislative and executive falsehood and violence, — these are but the central scenes in the national tragedy, whose future acts threaten to be so bloody, but whose first scenes were performed before a nation of spectators wavering between indifference and applause of the wrong doer and his deeds. See where the great principles of the Declaration were stricken down and slain along the path of our national legislation.

In the Constitution, framed thirteen years after that sublime assertion of the political equality of all men, there creeps in, in the intention of its framers, though in such phrase as permits us otherwise to understand it, the recognition of Slavery as a power in the land — a coheir with Liberty, of the great inheritance just won from Britain. Six years later, that Slavery gets embodied in a statute, the ancestor of our present accursed Fugitive Slave Bill — a puny father of a monstrous son, yet still the father. Twenty years later, the son of this first born of Slavery was born into legislation, and we still submitted our necks to the yoke. Then came the Missouri Compromise, by which three States — Louisiana, Arkansas, and Missouri — were admitted into the Union under its baleful protection, while the more distant lands, being without inhabitants, were graciously surrendered to liberty. And instead of demanding its instant repeal, and keeping up that cry till it drowned all contending voices, we said, "It is done; it can't be helped; it is well to make the best of a bad bargain. So, 'Hurrah for the Compromise, healing, uniting, enduring!'" Then came the gagging of the free speech of the people in the refusal to receive petitions for freedom — a gag formally revoked, yet as really the law of the Senate to-day, and of the House till this session, as when its author won for himself a hapless immortality in securing its pssage. Then came the orders to open the mail, and rifle it of all free words, where free speech was incendiary — and it was done. Then comes the Texas annexation; then the Mexican War; then the refusal to protect the new territories from the invasion of this evil; then the new atrocity of a Fugitive Slave Bill, by far the most wicked thing ever done by our nation; then the repeal of that protection which had been so laboriously constructed; then and now the full power of the government to deprive these unprotected lands of any of the rights of freedom, and to compel their submission to the foul embrace of slavery; then and now the gagging of free speech and act in Congress and Kansas, not by vote, as the people suffered themselves to be, but by the red hand of war.

We are indignant to-day, and indignant, I hope, not too late: but our cowardice and lack of moral principle have brought all this upon us. Think you, if the South had lost the Missouri Compromise, they would have been so ready to declare the thing settled, and in conventions and resolutions heartily, and with hurrahs, shouted over their defeat? We did, and do. Think you the slave power would have let their numerous petitions on their favorite subject be treated with the contempt which petitions for freedom receive? Would they be content with the barren form of a speechless reception? Would they not storm Congress and the country till their demands triumphed, if triumph were possible? Would we have allowed requests for legislation on far inferior subjects to suffer such sovereign disdain? Yet this all-involving interest has been spurned from their doors, and we have been quiet. We have gone into active political association with those who thus choked both our liberties, and those of our enslaved brethren in the South, in one effectual clutch of death.

Thus has "that great serpent, which is the Devil and Satan," in the guise of slavery, swallowed our territories, our constitutional principles, our judicial decisions, our national legislation, our religious organizations, our whole peculiar and honorable character. "The beauty of Israel has been slain on her high places," and we have not even kept silence. We hastened after the godless conqueror. We applauded his victories. We carried the feeble representative and tool of this power by an almost unanimous vote into the office he now desecrates.* We cast the words of righteousness so far behind us that for half a generation Freedom lay a breathless corpse in the midst of our land. Thus fell the great moral and legal principles of true government along the path of our baleful progress.

But these lie not alone. As, upon some field where Right fell under the death-strokes of Might, the faithful standard-bearer lies dead beside his torn and trampled flag, so these principles have not been without those human souls who lifted them up before the people, and who fell with them into the grave of the martyr; ascended the rather with them, like Astrea, into the glory which is with the God and Father of all truth and its worshipers.

A little more than twenty years ago the spirit of God breathed the breath of life into a few men and women, and sent them out into this great wilderness, crying, "Repent ye." But so far from acknowledging them as anointed of God for this work, and obeying their commands, we cried, "Away with them! Away with them! Crucify them! Crucify them!" The whole North is blazing with rage to-day on account of the murders in Kansas, and the assaults and threats in Washington. But there have been other attacks upon other abolitionists which we have openly approved, or easily and silently allowed.

* There were only four States that did not cast their votes for Franklin Pierce, of New Hampshire.

A few Christian women and an earnest exhorter for the slave were mobbed by a crowd of gentlemen of property and standing in the streets of Boston, within sight of Faneuil Hall, but a score of years ago. How many Northern villages and cities, how many persons, rebuked the deed? Their number could be easily counted. Lovejoy fell a martyr to free speech on the shores of the Mississippi. Did indignation meetings take place in all hearts and homes? Alas! he entered an unhonored grave. Torrey sickened and died in a Baltimore prison for the noblest philanthropy which the present age has witnessed.* Did you weep over his death? Did pulpits and presses everywhere lift up one cry of horror to Heaven at the deed? Drayton and Searle languished in the National Jail at Washington for offering their vessel to a band of oppressed Christians who had heard and believed in the Declaration of Independence. Dr. Bailey's press was thrown into the Ohio; Dr. Cox's church sacked in New York; Pennsylvania Hall burned in Philadelphia; Prudence Crandall mobbed in Connecticut for teaching little children to read and write. Almost every State has its stool of infamy on which it has placed itself, not with shame and sorrow of heart, but with boastful pride. Gallio-like, we cared for none of these things, and drove the new apostles of Jesus Christ everywhere from our judgment-seats.

Ay, more than this. As a people we have upheld and executed the enormity of the Fugitive Slave Bill. The orders of our taskmasters have been faithfully obeyed. We have cast the poor slave to Moloch. We have cried to all the beasts of the South, "Come and devour." Like Athens of old, we sent our sons and daughters to this man-eating Minotaur of the South; but no Theseus went with them to slay the monster, and lead them back to freedom.

* The same in which Mr. Garrison had been previously confined for publishing an anti-slavery newspaper.

No black sails and funeral dirges are on our Acorns and Revenue Cutters,

> "Built in the eclipse, and rigged with curses dark,"

but with extraordinary governmental promptness and pleasure, with military pomp, "following the flag, and keeping step to the music of the Union," they marched into the crushing teeth of the dreadful monster. Did your arm rise for their rescue? Did your hearts bleed for their agony? Alas! no tear enriched our eyes. But a momentary sigh responded in our hearts to their faintings even unto death. "They are only black folks," we cried, as we recovered our breath after the short spasm of conscience. "'What do they know about feelings?' 'Is it not so nominated in the bond?' 'The Constitution, it must be preserved.' 'Our dear white brethren shall have their rights.' 'So back to your rice swamps, your mud huts, your coffles, your bloodhounds, your unwilling pollution, your torn hearts, your slaves' graves.'" Great statesmen said, "Conquer your prejudices." Great ministers preached, "The powers that be are ordained of God, and therefore, whatever they ordain (though they frame iniquity by a law) is God's decree." Great merchants and manufacturers cried, "Our craft is in danger. So,

> 'Hence, home! you slavish creatures, get you home!
> Ye blocks, ye stones, ye worse than senseless things!'"

and all the people, through the ballot-box, with a cruel unanimity, said, "Amen."

Beneath this lowest deep there is a lower deep, out of which this prince of darkness has arisen to sit in power and great glory in the midst of our land.

The fearful consummations of this hour have their primal root in our infixed repugnance to those who suffer this wrong. The least touch of their blood is as leprosy to our self-important Caucasianism. Have you not, do you cherish not, this pride of caste? Do you not declare complexion a Heaven-appointed barrier between the children of Adam? Is there not in your feelings (I will not say judgment, for the reason has nothing to do originally or secondarily in this matter) a loathing of your brethren? Have you not proclaimed the disunity of the race, and given to your unnatural prejudices the authority of the divine will? Let him that is without sin cast the first stone at those who, standing on the godless sentiment, have laid the yoke of bodily chattelism, with all its horrible consequences, on these our brethren, and the yoke of political chattelism, with its past and present shames and sorrows, upon us who sympathize, but will not fraternize with these sufferers.

Hence come the present motions of the nation. Up from this deep and long enslavement of our judgment, our sympathies, our conscience, attended by the obedient and conspiring forms of the National Legislation, Judiciary, Executive, and Religion, like "archangels ruined," this evil Power rises to its present infamous hight of oath and covenant breaking; the invasion of sovereignties; the robbery of our dearest rights, and the murder of our national life. Judges like Loring, Kane, and Lecompte utter their execrable decisions as the solemn declaration of supreme law. The president uses the cunning of his brain, the strength of his mailed hand, to carry into execution these judicial lies, and to destroy the beautiful house which our fathers builded of truth, freedom, and happiness.

Up along the bloody path of the cruelties of our enslaved brethren, of the cruelties and murders of Northern freemen, it has marched to the fatal victories of this hour. How vividly the parable which climaxes in our text portrays our national history! When God planted this vineyard with the seeds of a holy religion and civil liberty, and left it to our fathers to keep and dress it, they, with great grief of heart, and, alas, with as great feebleness of will, let the enemy sow his seed of sin, so that when His earliest servants came seeking the fruit of a perfect freedom, they were beaten and sent away empty. And again He sent other servants, commanding in yet louder tones to let the oppressed go free, and to break every yoke; and at them we "cast stones, and wounded them in the head, and sent them away shamefully handled." Remember you how that aged and eminent representative of the majesty of this State was driven from the chief city of a sister State, whither he went to ask the fruit of righteousness for the Master of us all? and did we make that a ceaseless issue with our government till we righted that wrong, and those which he went to remove? If we had but put our heel on that serpent then, it would not a second time have thrust its venomous fangs into the sacred head of Massachusetts, and hissed in triumph over our servility. "And again He sent another, and him they killed; and many others, beating some and killing some." Growing bold by victories tamely endured, or only vociferously and spasmodically resisted, when the Compromise appears, converted from its original blackness into an angel of light, and asks the erection of its lands into free territories and free states,—when the free speech of an awakening North rings through the halls of legislation in weighty argument, cutting sarcasm, pathetic entreaties, bleeding at every vein in agony for the enslaved,—these robbers of God, and murderers of His children and His principles, "said among themselves, This is the heir; come, let us kill him, and the inheritance shall be ours."

"Strike down the Compromise," they say, "and these consecrated lands are open to our defiling foot. All lands, organized though they be into States, will yield to the same assault! Freedom flees the heritage, and all the grapes of God are ours. Strike down Sumner, chief among his peers, who, robed in the majestic sovereignty of their several States, wield their delegated power with the might of Samson, the wisdom of Solomon, the eloquence of Isaiah, smite to the earth this beloved son of liberty, and all mouths are dumb. Quiet reigns in Warsaw. We will call the roll of our slaves on Bunker Hill with no opposing voices. We will give slavery the right of passage through the Free States, the right of abode there, the right of way across the ocean, the right of traffic through all the land; and you ranting abolitionists shall 'roar as gently as a sucking dove,' if your most sweet voices do not chime with ours."

As one of the most eminent and conservative of the lawyers of New York city, speaking of the Sumner outrage, says, "If the Senate be destroyed, the Union is destroyed, because the union of the States exists in the Senate. There the States are equal. There Rhode Island measures Ohio, Texas and Florida out-double New York. A blow, therefore, aimed at the Senate is aimed most effectually at the very heart of the Union. The refusal of this body to defend itself against such aggressions of its rights has pulled down to its foundations the only model ever existing of a free government. It has struck a blow not only at our own country, but at the existence of all government among men."

Our masters reason rightly. There is no more that they can do to conquer the Constitution and the Declaration. Every vine of this vineyard of God, every grape of every vine in which was His blessing, is trodden down by this wild boar of slavery. The Border Ruffian policy triumphs to-day as completely in Washington as in Kansas. Calhoun's official proclamation, as the first minister of state, to all foreign powers, that slavery is the corner-stone of this Republic, is unquestioned law in two of the great branches of government, — the Judicial and Executive, — and triumphant in the third. If these things are borne, if they are not speedily and effectually resisted, farewell, a long farewell, to all our greatness! The land must be given over to the Sodomites who now possess it, and its iniquity will be speedily full.

"What will the Lord of the vineyard do? He will miserably destroy those wicked husbandmen, and let out his vineyard unto other husbandmen, which shall render him the fruits in their season." Do we say, as did those affrighted hearers, seeing themselves included in the vengeance coming on their land and nation, "God forbid"? Then may we rightly consider the second part of our duty.

II. What works meet for repentance shall we bring forth?

We have been consenting to this death. Perhaps, like Pilate, we have washed our hands in the presence of those whose arm and vote struck the blow. Perhaps, like Paul, we now preach the faith we once destroyed. Yet, as a people, as a State, I hope not; but I fear too many of us, as individuals, have washed our hands in vain. We were indifferent to the perils and defeats of freedom. We eagerly snatched and swallowed the few beggarly slops of office and enactments which our shrewd Southern masters tossed us. We selfishly let Christ be scourged and crucified in many of these His dear children in chains; in many priceless principles, the equally dear and vital offspring of His. We may cry, "Thou canst not say I did it." But God says, "Inasmuch as ye did it not unto one of the least of these my" children, "ye did it not to Me." Look on your hands. Blood! Cry, "Out, damnéd spot! out, I say!" It flees not; it blears our eyes; it stains our souls; it smells to heaven. Not all the perfumes of Arabia can sweeten this Northern hand.

> "Nor bleeding bird, nor bleeding beast,
> Nor hyssop branch, nor sprinkling priest,
> Nor running brook, nor flood, nor sea,
> Can wash the dismal stain away."

What can?

1st. Penitential abasement before a just and holy and good God, whose justice, goodness, and holiness we have nationally rejected. The North must bend the knee in godly sorrow before His arm brings salvation. We must bewail our manifest sins toward our oppressed brethren, toward an oppressed Gospel, oppressed in its preaching, in its discipline, in its literature, in its whole character and claim. We must have God on our side if we would dispossess the giants that are in the land of their baleful power. And He will not be with us heartily, unless, like that other defender of truth who was once a persecutor and injurious, we beg forgiveness for the past and strength for the future.

2d. We must entertain brotherly feelings toward the slave.

You are not going to deliver yourself without delivering him. This revolution has far greater objects, and will have, if successful, results far greater than that of 1776. That was chiefly for the political salvation of the European race. It answered the question, "Is the highest of the families of men capable of self-government?" This is for the political and social salvation of all men. Extremes here providentially meet. The lowliest of your kindred has hold of your hearts. Their welfare is inextricably inwrought in your own. They are around your necks. You cannot shake them off. You are, you must be, if a defender of your own rights, a defender of theirs. "Abolitionist," "Negro-worshiper," "Black Republican," whatever name is attached, honorably or contemptuously, to the upholders of the great sentiment of perfect human equality and brotherhood, must be your title.

If this be not the basis of our present indignation, what is? Why this furor against the slaveholder, if the colored race is not one with our own? He has no objection to *our* holding slaves and carrying them to Kansas or elsewhere. "Because free labor dies beside slave labor"? Wherefore? It does not die where horses and oxen abound; it does not where the dark free man works. Why should it where his slave brother toils? Simply because in our heart of hearts we see our oneness. Take away this conviction, and we can trade in them as easily as in cattle or grain. The argument is simple and unanswerable. If essentially different and inferior, then they are, and of right ought to be, servants, slaves, merchandise. There is but ONE race of men, and God has put all things under its feet. If the negro is a man, then he is the unquestioned equal in every right of every other man. If not an equal, not a man. If not a man, a merchantable thing.

All this prejudice of ours is peculiarly superficial. The seat of the disease is in the skin, not in the vitals, much less in the spirit within. Social and civil rights hang on the fibers of the flesh, dwell in cellular tissues and animal pigments. Driven from one fortress after another by the spirit of human equality, caste has made its last refuge in the surface of the body.

Divine right of Kings has become a mockery. Blood no longer flows an impassable gulf between men. Wealth lords it not over worth with universal consent. Might is not Right. The theories, if not the practices, of men recognize the equality and fraternity of all men, save the colored. They are outcasts. Chisel a man's features a little apart from the European standard; shade his skin a trifle darker than our hue; ay, let his features and his complexion be after our most perfect models; yet let the fact be known, that in his veins flows one drop of Afric's blood, and he dwells not as an equal in the presence of his brethren. No church opens her pulpit to receive his regular ministrations. No school employs his talents and education as its teacher. No store gives him the knowledge of business life. No workshop allows him to handle its tools and acquire its knowledge. Exceptions may be found to the rule, but they are most rare and startling. All this must be changed.

We must recognize our kindred. We must acknowledge that every man, of every complexion, has in his genealogical chart, as Christ had in His, "which was the son of Adam, which was the son of God." It is their wrongs, and not ours, that are shaking this land. The prostrate orator closed his first great speech for Freedom with a quotation that has since been more fearfully verified, and unless heeded will yet rive our souls with untold agonies. "Beware," said he, "beware of the groans of wounded souls. Oppress not to the utmost a single heart; for a solitary sigh has power to overset a whole world." We shall be distracted by a thousand side issues, betrayed by a thousand false lights, unless this great truth is our inspiration and our aim.

"While the truckling jurist sitting, as the slave-whip o'er him swings,
From the tortured truths of Freedom the lie of Slavery wrings,
And the solemn priest to Moloch on each God-deserted shrine
Breaks his bondmen's heart for bread, pours his bondmen's blood for wine, —

"While the multitude in blindness to a far-off Savior kneels,
And spurns, the while, the temple where the *living* Savior dwells, —
Thou must see HIM in the task-field, in the prison shadows dim,
And thy mercy to the bondman, it is mercy unto Him."

3d. If we thus have a conscience void of offense in the sight of God and man, the future is clear before us. We know not the exact course wisdom may dictate in every exigency, but we know its general bearings and its inevitable goal. As the traveler sees the desired summit in the light that overflows both it and the interjacent vales, though he knows not what forests, gorges, and ravenous beasts are between him and it, so the glorious hight of a Universal Freedom rises before the eye thus divinely illumined, and the path built by Divine Providence for our advancing steps, however perilous and bloody, will lead there.

Two duties are laid upon the Emancipationist to-day — duties as imperative and as valuable as those which will be given to those who shall in some future, I hope not distant, day, complete the long and painful work, and break the last yoke from the neck of the last slave.

The duties of the lover of Liberty now are, —

1st. Resumption, if necessary, by force, of the millions of acres stolen from us by the slave power, and defense of those who, as the agents of the Free States, are struggling to retain it in their possession against legalized thieves and murderers.

2d. The instantaneous and complete conversion of the government from Slavery to Freedom in all its ideas and acts, in every branch and office of its power.

1. How shall these be done? The first by the stout hearts and strong arms of freemen, equipped as our fathers were against the less cowardly and less brutal assassin of the forest, and the array of foreign tyranny. Do you cry, "What! a servant of the Prince of Peace, in His house, on His day, recommend the weapons of war!" "By what authority do you these things, and who gave you this authority?" "I will also ask you one question, and if you will answer me, I will tell you by what authority I do these things."

Suppose the city of Springfield and the adjacent towns on the other side of the river, on account of their earnest advocacy of the Maine Law, are invaded by armed bands of rumsellers from Connecticut and remoter States. They sack the city, burn and blow up its chief buildings, imprison its mayor in the center of their bloody camp, murder some of its unarmed and unoffending citizens, and overrun the neighboring territory, robbing and killing at will. They strike down not only the offending law, but all protections against anarchy. They declare the soil their own, and will, if unopposed, inevitably turn their pestilent march upon us, who are associated with the helpless sufferers in the same reform, and in the malice of its enemies. What would you do about it? What should the minister of Jesus Christ do about it? As brethren, as men, whither would your eyes, your feet, turn? "And this know, that if the good man of the house had known what hour the thief would come, he would have watched, and not have suffered his house to be broken up." How could he have prevented it? By soft speeches? By referring it to the ballot-box as to whether it belonged to the thief or the owner, knowing that the bands of the robber would outdo in violence, if not in power, his own allies? And if Christ commands, in effect, the good man of the house not to suffer its invasion, does He not demand him to expel the invaders, especially if that house has in it all the treasures of wisdom, and knowledge, and happiness gathered by the Providence of God for the sustenance of his earthly children?

The shapes hot from Tartarus, that ravage those plains, are unfortunately encased in bodies, and wield weapons of death, and are able and willing to drive every free soul from its body unless they can scare them, body and soul, from their inheritance. Men, and women, and children are now suffering in Kansas the pains and evils of civil war. Its clouds overhang that fair land. Satan and his hosts have entered that Eden, and finding that they could not seduce the new Adam and Eve that God had placed there, they are employing all their forces to expel them. All the officers of the government join in the dreadful work. It must be resisted. *We must not suffer the house to be broken up.* Not so great an hour passed over those who lived in '75. Not so great a work was committed to a Tell, a Kossuth, a Washington, as is given to this hour and people. "To-day is a king in disguise," says one of our finest brains. To-day will be the emperor of the past and future days of this Republic. Shall it be the Lucifer leading it from the heaven to which God has exalted it, or the Messiah raising it to a yet loftier heaven of grace and glory?

Kansas is the theater where the conflict between the rebellious and the faithful angels is renewed. "Of form and gesture proudly eminent," he stands who was the second officer of this nation, and the head of the (officially) most grave and reverend council in the globe. Beside him are Governors, Senators, Representatives, Judges, Cabinet officers, and he who is the head of this Republic, —

> "Thrones and imperial powers, offspring of Heaven,
> Ethereal virtues; who, these titles now
> Justly removed, are called Princes of Hell."

Shall they triumph? Shall that land be drenched with the blood of the slave? Shall its sweet airs reek with the foul breathings of the master's lust, echo and moan with the groans of the poor bondmen under the tortures of their tyrants, often bone of their bone and flesh of their flesh, "always of Christ's body, of his flesh and of his bones." Shall the abomination which maketh desolate there be set up — the abomination which includes, as its lesser evils, idleness, beggary, ignorance, licentiousness, murder, every form and fruit of sin? Or shall liberty, righteousness, temperance, education, love, peace, holiness, every virtue, honor, and joy, flourish and abound there?

If the latter, those who are seeking their establishment must be sustained; ten thousand armed settlers ought to march there before these summer months close. Do you say, "Let them hold it for a season, till we play with them the great game of the Presidency?" If so, what will you do if you lose? What can you do if they win? Remember that possession is nine points in law. What will you do with those who defend your rights in the presence of these marauders? The voice of our brother's blood cries to us from that ground. Has he not been hacked to death by more than savage mobs? Has he not been shot, "the only son of his mother, and she a widow," after having given up his weapons, and while going peaceably to his home? Has not the voice of Rachel gone up to the ear of the All-pitying, "weeping for her children, and would not be comforted because they were not"? Is not the gray-haired Jacob, going down to his grave in sorrow for his beloved son, torn to pieces by those fierce beasts in the shape now, as then, of men and brethren?

> "Alas! that country sinks beneath the yoke;
> It weeps, it bleeds, and each new day
> A gash is added to its wounds. Each morn
> New widows howl, new orphans cry, new sorrows
> Strike Heaven on the face, that it resounds
> As if it felt with Kansas, and yelled out
> Like syllable of dolor."

Shall we let these demons rage there, while we merely get up processions and mass meetings to carry the next election? "These things ought ye to do, and not leave the other undone." The land is ours: it has been solemnly deeded to us by the voice of the country, and the deed is recorded in the nation's registry. It is ours, for ourselves and our children, for God and His Christ. And shall we basely abandon it? If patriots, fearless and firm, will but go thither, and peaceably assume their rights under the Compromise and the Constitution, the murderous villains will flee as the thief at the approach of the sheriff; their duped followers will become our ally, and peace shall be in all her borders.

If this is not done, we can do nothing in the great political contest at the polls and at Washington, nothing in the great moral war in the South for speedy, peaceful emancipation.

2. Doing this courageously, and in the fear of God, we should, secondly, put the whole force of the government instantly and thoroughly on the side of freedom.

Let not party names or men becloud your judgment, bewray your steps. There are but two parties in this land, the Slave and the Free. All the buffets of compromising machinery that have heretofore prevented these from coming face to face, have been crushed to death in the violence of the collision. Other names may float on other banners in the field: only two combatants are there. Every issue is set aside, *must* be set aside, but this. We have thrust Liberty into the outer darkness as long as we can. It is put directly before us by our Creator, the Creator of all progress in national and spiritual life. Will we again spurn it? Will we again let a name and a party lead us astray from the truth? If the present power, though under other leaders, retains its dominion, Sumner's reeling swoon, speechlessness, and possible death, are the type and forerunner of the dumbness and death of all the liberties of this people. Free speech can no more be heard in Washington than in Charleston. The North, with its wealth of noble principles and practices, is trodden down of the Gentiles. The last ounce is thrown upon the back of Issachar. The lion of the tribe of Judah bends his neck to the yoke. Lucifer, the light-bearer of the Nations, falls from heaven.

If the kidnapping of the wandering fugitive from under the shadow of Faneuil Hall and Bunker Hill, — if the dragging back to death and despair of that more than Virginius, who with her motherly arm struck the life out of her own child to prevent prospective, not impending shames and woes, — if these, repeated again and again in increasingly aggravated forms, cannot rouse our sympathies sufficiently to demand, with a voice as the roar of many waters, the instant repeal of the nefarious statute, what can bring philanthropy from dream-land into actual life? If the robbery of our land, the robbery of our franchise and our legislation, the imprisonment and murder of their defenders, the extinction in blood of freedom of debate and of State Equality, — if these cannot bring us to unite against the mighty foe, what can? Will the mere abrogation of a commercial restriction, whereby our ships cannot bring slaves from Africa, set the country into convulsions, if these produce only momentary spasms? Will the declaration that internal slave trade is as lawful as the internal flour trade, and that no State can restrict it, bring us to action? These are all that are left, and these are but merchantable things. They cannot thrill the heart, as the dreadful scenes have through which we have passed for the last few years, and are still passing. They will no more restore us to life than the last faint struggles of the dying will throw off that conqueror whom the fearful agonies of preceding hours had wrestled with in vain.

Say not so, aged, eminent, conservative a man as he who is put at the head of these hosts, will never lead us whither we have been moving. As the President has just said in reference to this very nomination, "Men are but instruments." Pierce has done no more than Fillmore, Fillmore than Polk, Polk than Tyler, Tyler than Van Buren. Each did all that the Slave Power asked of them. Each did worse than his predecessor, simply because he was the successor. If the present Chief Magistrate had occupied his seat four years before, he would have said, had you charged him with his present deeds, "Is thy servant a dog, that he should do this thing?" He would only have signed the Fugitive Slave Bill, and defeated the Proviso. Four years earlier he would but have carried on the war with Mexico. Four years earlier merely annexed Texas. Four years earlier simply purged the mails of free speech, and opposed the purging of the District of Columbia of Slavery. "Men are but instruments."

Who secured the nomination of this venerable man by the withdrawal of his potent name from the canvass? Who dictated the platform on which this Image is set up? Who will be the chief instrument in his election, if he obtains it?

— which may God in His mercy prevent. Who will be his right hand supporter in his administration? The boldest and wickedest of all the bold and wicked men that blacken our history, beside whom Arnold and Burr are models of decency and religion. They sought to strangle in his cradle the Hercules of our political being, when as yet his divinity could be seen only by the eye of faith. He assails him in the height of his strength, when he stands among mankind the only cleanser of its Augean stables of royal corruption, the only annihilator of its hydra oppressions, the only one able to conquer the guards of the pit, and bring out of its long death the beautiful form of Civil and Religious Freedom.

He it is that by a previous assault, unparalleled for its coarseness and threats of violence, instigated those blows, whose remotest as well as immediate effects he foresaw and intended. He it is, that, having been urged to the rescue of his fellow-senator, sat calmly through the beginning of the attack, and climbed, as he himself says, on a high back seat at its close, that he might catch a glimpse of the bleeding victim as he was borne away; as a little fraudulent leader of bad men in an ancient time climbed to a high seat that he might see Him who was to be the great Sacrifice for Eternal Freedom, though unlike Zaccheus, no penitence smote his conscience, no submission and conversion followed the sight. He did more than begin and enjoy an assault on a peaceful Senator; he led those troops of Sin against and over the prostrated landmarks of Freedom, prostrated Territorial and State sovereignty, prostrated law, and right, and peace, and honor, and chastity, and life. This is the head and fang of that huge serpent which "in many a scaly fold, voluminous and vast," coils itself around the pillar of our confederacy, and from its capital "hangs hissing at the nobler men below." He is the power greater than the President, present or to be, who, with the crowd of violent men behind him, will seek to carry the Evil, whose they are and whom they serve, to a permanent, universal dominion.

Then cometh the end. One of two things follows. Unquestioned prostration of the whole country under the hoof of the slave power. As the unslaveholding South to-day is dumb before the shearers of its power and prosperity, so shall the whole land be. We shall be thrust into a seat of infamy lower than any living or dead nationality can occupy, beside which Roman anarchy, Greek cowardice, and Jewish impiety are highest excellence. A nation of Slaves! One hundred thousand ignorant and brutal men the monarchs of twenty-five millions! driving us into the Atlantic, if they so list, as they now declare they can, with a lady's riding whip,* — filling our land with poverty, vice, and murder, and making the very dust of our patriot sires beg the winds of heaven to bear them from the dishonored soil!

What a spectacle to the world! That great nation, stretching over more territory than ever saw the wing of the Roman eagle, whose songs have all been set to the tune of Liberty, whose Constitution and laws beat, with but few discordant notes, the same inspiring measure, whose name has been a terror to tyrants and a watchword to patriots, that people whose God has been the Lord, under the feet of the pirate of perdition! The star-spangled banner torn down, and the blood-red flag with which South Carolina marches through fallen Lawrence, the black flag the slave ship carries across the free ocean, — these shall wave

> " O'er the land of the free and the home of the brave!"

Your meadows and mountains shall be covered with slaves, not necessarily black in the face, certainly white in the blood, the very images of us their fathers and mothers; — poorest of whites, ruled over by the desperadoes of the

* A remark made in Congress by Alexander H. Stephens.

South, and their satanic allies of the North! O disastrous eclipse! O shadow worse than death! The light gone from earth, the hopes of man blotted out, the howl of tyrants exultant and universal! "The glory of kingdoms, the beauty of the Chaldees' excellency, shall be as when God overthrew Sodom and Gomorrah. Wild beasts of the desert shall lie there; their houses shall be full of doleful creatures; owls shall dwell there, and satyrs shall dance there. And the wild beasts of the islands shall cry in their desolate houses, and dragons in their pleasant palaces; and her time is near to come, and her days shall not be prolonged." May God through our present faithfulness prevent this fast-speeding doom.

The second alternative, if we postpone our political reformation to the presidential contest of 1860, will be civil war. If the North has courage enough to fight, though not enough to vote for Liberty, before that not distant period arrives the struggle may have been begun. This power, if again triumphant, will triumph as never before. Not smuggled and disguised, but openly will it start on its new career. And if its insolence is so great now, if its demands are so unendurable, what will they be when it puts on the crown of authority that the People will offer it? If resisted, it must be under the smoke of battle. The barbarities of Kansas and Washington will be repeated in aggravated forms along the whole border — over the whole land. Those extremes will be joined by a river of fire and blood, and this great Republic expire in the ashes of fraternal flames.

"A curse will light upon the limbs of men,
Domestic fury and fierce civil strife
Will cumber all the parts of this fair land.
Blood and destruction shall be so in use,
And dreadful objects so familiar,
That mothers shall but smile when they behold
Their infants quartered with the hands of war.

All pity choked with custom of fell deeds,
And Freedom's spirit ranging for revenge,
With Fury by her side, come hot from hell,
Shall in these confines with a monarch's voice
Cry 'Havoc,' and let slip the dogs of war,
That these foul deeds shall smell above the earth
With carrion men, groaning for burial."

It is for the Christian and Patriot of this day to say whether or no one of these dreadful fates shall not be ours. It is for us to say if Sumner's seat, the site of Kansas' Lexingtons, the graves of Barbour, Dow, Brown, Stewart, and other martyrs, whose sod is for the first time green above them, shall be visited by a victorious, free people, reverently gazing on that blood shed for the first time in our history in defense of freedom of national debate, and those ruins and graves, attesting the zeal, discretion, and courage of the first banded defenders of our principles in the field of fraternal strife, or if they shall be disregarded, as the Greek of to-day knows not, and cares not to know, the spot where the three hundred saved Greece and the world their liberties, or where the great orator patriot, Demosthenes, banished, fell by a sacred and privileged altar, anticipating but for a moment the tortures intended for him by his persecutors — the tyrants of Athens, and the destroyers of her name and power unto this day?

Read the great speech which excited such rage, and well nigh won for its author the crown of a martyr. For before he uttered a word he knew its probable effect; he measured the danger before he struck the blow. But three or four in all history are its equals in beauty and strength of thought and language. Demosthenes against the Philipizing Douglas of Athens, the keen, ready, insolent tool of her tyrants; Cicero against the Atchison Catiline of the Roman republic; Burke against Hastings, the wholesale enslaver of India; Webster against the South Carolinian traducer of freedom and its fruits, — with these four, this stands, and will always stand, equal to the highest in all the literary qualities of an oration, higher than the highest in the sweep of his theme — the preservation of the liberty, culture, and religion of a great Christian nation. Let every man, and woman, and child frequently read it. Read it in a spirit of humiliation and prayer. Read it for our guidance in this crisis as we do the Bible for our guidance in this and all.

Let us repent and forsake our slothfulness, our prejudices, our cowardice. Let us surrender all minor duties to this preëminent human duty, second only to the salvation of souls, and even involving their eternal weal or woe in its measureless results. Let us engage in the great civil and moral warfare before us with a oneness of heart and will that insures the victory. The sun that shall roll over this earth for the next few months will look down on as important a conflict as has ever been waged upon it. The sons of God who shouted together over its creation never more anxiously watched the movements of men, never more heartily identified themselves with the friends of freedom, than they watch over and work with us to-day. The lovers of our race, wasting in exile, or rotting in European dungeons will be our heartiest allies. The poor slave will pray in many a cabin that the North may win.

If we conquer, the long nightmare of our country is gone, the overflowing scourge is stayed. Wisely, lovingly, steadily, we shall move up out of the ghastly gloom into the light of our earlier day. Shouts of joy will echo in the cells of European liberty, pallor and trembling seize on European tyrants. Let us once stand forth in the full glory of constitutional freedom, and the millennium morn breaks full-orbed upon our land. Unspeakable gladness will overwhelm the hearts of four millions of our kindred, grinding in these prison-houses of the South. Unspeakable fears and smitings of the knees will shake their fierce devourers.

But if we should fail, — if the cunning and vehemence of our enemies, the heartlessness and blindness of the masses, continue the power with its present blood-stained possessors, the victory, though in another path less peaceful, will surely come. Though they kill the Freedom of the State, the heir of all the treasures of the nation, though they exult in the inheritance which they will then say is incontestably theirs, the heir shall rise again with twenty, ay, with twenty thousand mortal murders on his crown to push them from their stools. The principles of His government and attributes of His nature that have been given to man shall not be blotted from the earth. Through the tearing asunder of the national ties perhaps, through the flames of awful war, through blood up to the horses' bridles, we may have to wade to the peaceful glories of a Republic of universal freedom. May He preserve us from this calamity, yet give us grace to meet it if it come upon us. If it shall come, and after it is passed, from the Atlantic to the Pacific, from Labrador to Virginia, shall stretch a vast confederacy of free and prosperous States, even if over those Southern valleys of the plain a dead sea of tribulation shall continue to roll.

"Our bleak hills shall bud and blow,
Vines our rocks shall overgrow,
Plenty in our valleys flow;
And when vengeance lights their skies,
Hither shall they turn their eyes,
As the damned on Paradise.
We but ask our rocky strand,
Freedom's true and brother band,
Freedom's brown and honest hand,
Valleys by the slave untrod,
And the Pilgrims' rugged sod,
Blessèd of our Father, God."

THE NATIONAL MIDNIGHT.*

"AND WHEN I LOOKED, BEHOLD, A HAND WAS SENT UNTO ME; AND LO, A ROLL OF A BOOK WAS THEREIN; AND HE SPREAD IT BEFORE ME; AND IT WAS WRITTEN WITHIN AND WITHOUT; AND THERE WAS WRITTEN THEREIN LAMENTATIONS, AND MOURNING, AND WOE."
— *Ezekiel* ii. 9, 10.

HE great battle is over, and the Slave Power, as of old, as in all our national conflicts, when its dominion has been contested, remains master of the field. We come, my brethren, under its permission, to consider the results of the battle — a permission granted us for the present, and because we are in this remote New England; a permission forbidden our brothers under the hoof of this Satan, forbidden even our own national representatives, who are soon to assemble at the foot of its throne; a privilege soon to be forbidden us in this distant locality, and soon to be resigned by us, unless God, in His infinite grace and providence, shall interpose for our national salvation.

Before we unroll the book which the hand of experience

* A sermon preached at Westfield, Mass., November 16, 1856, on the occasion of the election of James Buchanan to the Presidency of the United States. See Note III.

and truth has sent out to us, the roll of our fast-coming history, — we will seek to remove two obstacles that some think should seal our lips with dumbness. They are, that we are attacking an ancient and honorable political party, and that we are intruding in priestly vestments upon forbidden ground.

Both of these objections are answered by an examination of the battle-cries of the campaign. What were the shouts that went up from every corner of the vast field? that rung out over all the land and all the world? Not tariff and free trade, not banks and sub-treasury, not retrenchment in the public expenditures, not foreign aggressions or sailors' rights — a cry that shook the land in the days of Madison.

Three war-cries freight the air — Disunion, Romanism, Slavery. These three fears assailed the hearts of the people. Every one of them is a moral, a religious, a Christian question. Every one of them demands the earnest attention of the minister of Christ. If he cannot discuss these evils; if he cannot present to your consciences that among them which is the most threatening and deadly, when it excels all others, and thrusts its poisoned dagger into the vitals of the national honor, and even life; if he cannot descry and declare the form and the coming of Antichrist, and rally the allies of the Lord Jesus to his overthrow, — when can he speak?

These censures come chiefly from those who have no experimental knowledge of Christian faith and duties; who are rejecters of Christ, and especial haters of His ambassadors. They are hardly competent to teach the preachers of the Gospel the message He commissions them to bear. It will be well for these self-appointed, and somewhat too self-important, overseers of the ministry, to remember that not one word of instruction, as recorded in this Book, forbids the discussion of every question that affects humanity. Their mission is to preach a full salvation, salvation from all sin, personal, social, national. It is to rebuke all iniquity in high places or low, whether centering in the palace or rioting in the multitudinous madness of the whole nation. So far from being forbidden to intermeddle in national and political matters, they are, by the especial orders of God Himself, given to many of their predecessors, and by His general orders, issued alike to all, especially commanded to interfere in the affairs of men. While to all other dignitaries it is said, "Touch not mine anointed, and do my prophets no harm;" to them He commands to preach before all offenders the preaching He gives unto them. While David, the general and the politician, for only eating the bread of the priests, endangered his life; while he was forbidden to touch the ark, priest and prophet were commanded to meddle with his private as well as official affairs, and to pierce his soul in the very hour of his pride and vain-glory.

While King Uzziah was smitten with leprosy for his interference with the duties of the minister, the ministers Elijah and Elisha, confronted, by God's order, the ungodly king of Israel, when he was seeking, for personal ends, the ruin of the nation. Paul reasoned with Governor Felix on his official no less than his personal sins. Everywhere God puts this peculiar honor on His servant, giving him authority to rebuke kings and nations, and forbidding them to rebuke him.

It is one of the devices of Satan by which he seeks to harden your hearts against the truth, and make you deaf to your duty against the greatest sin of this or of any age, that the servant of Christ must not expose it, because, forsooth, it has compelled a political party to become its most active slave. What is this "consecrated politics" that is beyond the reach of the Word of God, and too sacred to be condemned by Him? Ah, my friends, it is not the sacredness, nor the political relations, of the theme that causes this denunciation of God's ministers, but because it is so thoroughly interwoven with the ambition, wealth, trade, and fashion of the land. Therefore they seek to screen it from the wrath of God, and defame His servants, who dare denounce it, as traveling beyond their province in human affairs over which God has set them.

They cry out, as did Mr. Douglas to the thousands of God's ministers, "Let State affairs alone." "Attend to your concerns, while we are allowed to plunder and murder at our will all the interests of freedom and religion." Far more properly may the highwayman, while he is knocking down and plundering his victims, command them to desist from preaching against theft, and confine their discourse to the abstract nature of God, or sin, or holiness.

Ministers are tarred and feathered, are scourged and shot by the nefarious power of slavery, and that, too, because they are ministers. Aged and eminent members of the church have been killed in attempting to save the lives of their ministerial brethren. Clergymen are treated with foul slanders, by the chiefs of the Republic, for a respectful and solemn petition. But when all these persistent and organized acts of hostility are waged against them and their cause, they must not open their lips in defense, not of themselves, but even of Christ and His children, bought and sold by wicked men, because it is interfering with politics.

Away with all such blasphemous folly. We ask no pardon for entering this arena. The greatest crimes that ever broke away from hell, and emerged on this fair earth, are being defiantly committed by the rulers of this nation — crimes against every virtue, every grace, every joy; crimes of which robbery of purse and murder of the body are its least expressions. Robbery of the man himself, not his pennies, murder of his soul, not his body merely, are its daily, its hourly deeds. God forbid that I should keep silence. "Son of man," says the same Voice to the same listener, whose words are the motto for our discourse, says the same Voice to every one of His ambassadors in every age, "Son of man, get thee unto the house of Israel, and speak My words unto them. For thou art not sent to a people of a strange speech and of a hard language, but to the house of Israel, son of man."

But not from these rebellious hearts do we expect a favorable ear. There are, however, a few who, though knowing the power of Christ and the obligation of Christians, have fallen into this error. Not because they doubt the right and duty of the minister of Christ to denounce national sins, but because they deny that these sins have become the life and power of the party they support. Prove this to them, and they will be among the most earnest supporters of their brethren in these declarations. It is to these and all other followers of Christ, and well-wishers of His cause, that I appeal to-night. I ask your serious and prayerful investigation of the subject before us. I come in no partisan spirit. The Spirit of the Lord God, I humbly trust, is upon me. I come not to secure the triumph of any political organization as such, but to present the truth as it exhibits itself in the roll of recent history, and is rapidly unfolding its fearful future — lamentations, mourning, and woe.

I must speak plain words. I shall not hesitate, as have not my forerunners in this sacred office, to mention by name the individuals and organizations that have wrought our fall, and are preparing to lead us onward and downward to yet more horrible crimes, even to the spoiling of the whole people of all the treasures of freedom and religion which their fathers left them. I may speak to incredulous ears. So did Jeremiah and Josiah, and John the Baptist, and Christ. How vividly the authority that commissioned Ezekiel sounds in our ears, both its orders and the reception of them and of those who proclaim them by those to whom the word is sent! —"Son of man, I send thee unto the children of Israel, to a rebellious nation, that have rebelled against me; they and their fathers have transgressed against me even to this day. For they are impudent children and stiff-hearted. I do send thee unto them, and thou shalt say unto them, 'Thus saith the Lord.' And thou shalt speak My words unto them, whether they will hear or whether they will forbear: for they are most rebellious. But thou, son of man, hear what I say unto thee. Be not thou rebellious, like that rebellious house. Open thy mouth, and eat that I give unto thee. And when I looked, behold, a hand was sent unto me, and lo, a roll of a book was therein. And He spread it before me. And it was written within and without. And there was written therein lamentations, mourning, and woe."

By God's grace, I will obey His equally painful command to-night, and speak His words to a house that I hope and pray will not treat them as Israel did those uttered by His servant of old, but who will be earnestly sorry, and will heartily repent of all their misdoings, and who will proceed so far as in them lies to renew the land again in repentance and salvation.

We shall consider, —

1. What it is that has triumphed.

2. What are its present and imminent claims and prospects.

3. Why Freedom is defeated.

4. What are our encouragements and obligations in this hour of our failure.

I. What is it that has triumphed?

Not the Democratic party. Not any mere political organization working for political ends. I know the name it takes. As Satan entered that creature that was above all its fellows in beauty and intelligence, in order that he might overthrow a still higher creature who was made in the image of God, and whose destruction would be, in his judgment, as the conquest of God himself, so has Satan entered this creature of human wisdom and attraction, this chiefest of the instruments of our political excellence, in order to ruin that very life which makes us a people, the peculiar people of God. It is not, therefore, any mere form in which this Evil is embodied that must be called the victor. The serpent did not claim nor receive the honor of inducing Adam to sin. This party in American politics, as that form of the animal kingdom, unless it is penitent and abandons speedily the evil that possesses it, will be cursed above all the other instrumentalities that have been the favored servants of the nation, and be doomed to the basest fate. Upon its belly shall it go, and dust shall it eat, till it returns to dust and nothingness.

But while the Democratic party may lose its high position, as it has lost its high character, the Evil that has ruined it, that has already corrupted, and afterward destroyed, two other great parties will still confront us. The Slave Power, not any political party, exults in this victory, and rejoices in hope of everlasting dominion.

To prove this, it is only necessary to revert to the scenes and sounds that have filled the land in the last few months. Look on the banners that have brightened or gloomed the air. Hardly a topic has had any prominence in the canvass that did not concern slavery. Shall Kansas be free or slave? Shall the Ostend Manifesto prevail, which declares we will steal Cuba for slavery, if its government will not sell her for that purpose? Shall all the territories be thrown open to the foul foot of this monster under the wicked lie of popular sovereignty? Shall Nicaragua bring her gift of trampled freedom, and lay herself at its grateful feet? These have been the warnings of the friends of liberty and their country. How have they been met? By cries of reform, free trade, specie currency, and equal rights — any of the ancient watchwords of that party, by which it has so often, and so rightfully, swept the field? Not a syllable of these. How glad would they have been to have used those famous battle-cries? Their transparencies and banners, their papers and speeches, have rung no change on these their favorite themes. Disunion, sectionalism, popular sovereignty, have been their declaration of principles; the first two as bulwarks against the destructive artillery of their foes; the last, the specious form in which this demon now arrays himself to tempt and slay the nation. Therefore, by the forced confession of its unwilling confederates, as well as by the earnest assertion of its passionate devotees, Slavery is the actual victor. It shouts defiance over prostrate liberty. Read the Southern journals; read the speeches of those who made the platform and appointed its Executive attorney, and you will see that Slavery alone is the crowned monarch of America for the coming reign. Said Judge Johnson, of Georgia, under the shadow of Independence Hall, "The question of this campaign is whether we can buy and sell labor as we buy and sell cattle."

And now, my friends, let us pause and gaze a moment at the monster we have set over us. We are so familiar with the word "slavery" that its real scope and character do not smite the eye with a true horror. If this nation stood to-day perfectly free from this iniquity, and could behold it approaching its shores, and demanding the sovereignty, we should rise up as one man against the hellish foe. Our fright at the coming of the Pope, and his enthronement among us, at our possible subjection to Czar or Sultan, would be a courage and a joy to that which would palsy our soul when this prince of darkness rose up before us. We talk about it as flippantly and thoughtlessly as we do about the weather. We shudder at Mormon polygamy, at Mexican anarchies, at British domination on the North, at the surrender of a fraction of the Pacific Coast to her hands. All these are angels of light in comparison with that which excites but the feeblest fear. We call it patriarchal, scriptural, domestic, respectable, Christian. We declare that it has the right to enter and abide in any State or Territory, if a majority of its white men, who care enough about the matter to vote upon it, shall choose to allow it. Many pleasant things are said concerning it, and, though it has some bad features, as an eminent New York divine has said, "they are only such as are incident to every other human relation."

What is it that is so nice and honorable, and pious and Biblical? It is the taking of a human being, and selling him like a beast. It is the working of him without recompense; refusing his mind the light it seeks; refusing his soul the grace it needs; refusing his heart the affections it craves; making his conjugal, parental, and filial ties depend upon his master's pleasure. This is Slavery, American Slavery, the only Ruler in the Republic of the United States.

Consider the abominations it sets up, not casual, incidental, perishable offshoots, but its essential and inevitable life; its blood and being.

Begin at its beginning. In the cot of poor parents a child is born. Not in Africa, but in America, under the Capitol itself, that stands so proudly in the very heart of the land. Their breasts thrill with joy unspeakable, as yours, parents, when God sends such an angel to your arms. They feel and accept the sacred responsibility. The father lays plans for his future, in all of which this babe holds a prominent place. "He shall bear my name," he says to himself, "to coming generations. 'Through him I will build up my family in the earth." The parents talk over the name by which he shall be called, his education, his profession, his whole future life. They grow happy in his growth, famous in his fame. In the midst of their blissful dreams, a man enters, perhaps a member of the church, a minister even of Jesus Christ, and, paying no attention to the outflow of the parental nature, not even regarding its first wish, — that of a name of their choice, — says, "Don't trouble yourself about that. Call him Tom, or Cæsar, or January," or whatever odd or fancy name comes into his mind. "Don't worry about his future. Though his father, you have nothing to do with that." He follows the condition of his mother. She is a slave. All the freedom enjoyed by his father, if he happens to have a little nominal liberty, avails him nought. She is, perhaps, allowed to care for him, for a few moments a day, taken from her toil in the field. But this privilege may be taken away at any moment. The master's whim or necessity may sell the babe from his mother's breast. Hastening to her hut to feed him, she may find him gone. Put upon the block with him, the purchaser may decline the incumbrance, and the child is tossed aside as a worthless bit of baggage, and his mother driven away in an agony that God only knows or can avenge. These cases occur by the thousands. This it is to be born a slave. Thus is this wonderful gift of Heaven, this soul fashioned in the similitude of God, this beautiful house of clay, tented with his loving and artistic hand, debased by the wickedness of man. It is snatched from its father's arms, and, after being left perhaps for a day or two upon its mother's breast, is set up in the market-place, knocked down to the chance bidder, and sent on the doleful path of a horrible future.

Who gave this crime power to thus legally tear the child from its father, and declare its mother was its sole representative? Whence comes that law? Is the woman the appointed head of the family? Is she its exclusive head? Does the son never represent the father? Is the law of primogeniture so popular in all ages, and so frequently suggested in the Scriptures, contradictory to all human experience? Is there any such law among even the lower animals, with whom their "owner" rates them? Nay, it is simply the arbitrary will of the robber who has stolen this child from his parents, as he has stolen the parents from themselves; who robbed him of his freedom before he was born, and now steals him from his father, to whom he is born, and will soon steal him from his mother, from whom he is born. It claims to be from Rome. It is from the Devil.

But the crime does not stop here. If the babe was actually given to its mother, though its father were excluded, it might yet be well. She would act her own and her husband's part, and lavish on the bereaved and beloved one a double portion of her heart. But it is not hers. It follows her condition, not her. She is property. So are her babes. She is not her own property. They are not hers. She is subject to her master's fortune. They must follow her fate. Her daughter — what horrors arise in her soul as she looks upon that lovely infant — her daughter! What a fate awaits her! What a life of toil, of infamy, of ignorance, of suffering! the more beautiful, the more awful. Naturally may she be tempted to deliver, by the stroke of death, that beautiful body, and more beautiful soul, from its unutterable future.

Both parents are thus robbed of this darling gift of God, not by the gipsy snatch, rare and lawless, not by a whirl of maddening passion, but by sober and written *Law*, whereof ministers and members of the professed Church of Christ, statesmen of the highest rank, judges of most rigid legal righteousness, and even philanthropists of tender hearts, are the enactors, advocates, and supporters. How horrible our sin! How more horrible will be our punishment!

If left with its parents for a season, it is as the calf is left with its dam, awaiting the owner's need or wish. Nay, it has less privileges than that creature, for the animal's mother may train it after her nature, to the utmost of her capacity. These sons and daughters of the Lord Almighty are not suffered to be developed by their affectionate parents according to the nature He has given them. Though permitted to remain in their arms, they are forbidden to receive any real education. They must not be taught to read or even pray. They grow up, a youth manly and self-reliant, a maiden modest and comely. Are these blessings? To your sons and daughters they are. Not so with this piece of marketable flesh. Their heaviest curse is their intelligence, their manliness, their modesty, their beauty. For their fate violates and crushes these noble instincts. They enter the holy estate of matrimony. It is a cheat and a lie. They are coupled like cattle subject to their owner's will. He takes that wife from her husband at any impulse of passion, the husband from his wife under any purpose of self-interest. They are parted or united as indifferently as you would separate a yoke of oxen.

And this is Biblical, patriarchal, Christian. This is what Abraham practiced and Paul commanded. God forbid! It is a vile slander on the Word and the children of God. The servitude of Abraham and of the Hebrew bondmen was as the servitude of factory hands to their employer, or feudal retainers to their master. They were his property only as you are the property of the man who employs you. Abraham's servants could have left him at any time. One he sent away with her child free, by the orders of his wife — a generosity no Southern Abraham is equal to. Our jealous Sarahs sell their Hagars and Ishmaels; they never emancipate them. They were retainers, armed and independent. One of his slaves was the head of his house. Paul's advice was to you, whether in shop or store, "Servants, obey your masters." God in this word sets before us the law of employer and employed — the great rule for the management of free industry; a rule that is fitted for every estate on earth, for every relation, duty, and hour of eternity.

This sin of sins against God and man has no small and obscure being. It rules over four millions of immortal souls. It covers with its death-shade one half of the Republic. It has held the reins of power under other drivers these many years, and now, in its own person, it openly ascends the

chariot-seat. A weak old man, and a debauched party, profess to be charioteers, but this demoniac power sits on their necks. He is the avowed, he the sole, owner and lessee of America — her imperator and tyrannus, her single sovereign and lord.

Before the eyes of the world, beneath the eyes of Heaven and of Christ, thus stands the American Republic to-day. It has seen its threescore years and ten, and if, by reason of the immense strength of the principles received from its fathers, it has reached fourscore years, yet is its strength labor and sorrow. It will be soon cut off and fly away, unless it hastens to repent and forsake utterly this unspeakable iniquity. Its glory is gone. "Ichabod," "Ichabod," is on all its walls. Freedom, humanity, religion, are excluded from the national policy, and national idea. The Declaration of Independence, which inspired Jefferson, and Adams, and Lafayette, and Washington, which sustained the hearts of the people with its breath of life divine, amid the terrible pressure of years of conflict, which received political form and substance in our Constitution, — that Declaration, as avowed by one of the ablest advocates of this triumphant power, and as adopted by all its leaders, is but glittering generalities, unworthy the regard of sober men, although these glittering generalities are those very principles without which Christianity is a lie and civilization a dream.

Thus we stand. Clouds and darkness are round about us. The air is pierced with lightning, and shaken by mutterings of avenging thunder.

II. What shall the end be?

Some suppose that the party retaining the power, the party, rather, ascending to power, will be very gentle, encroaching on no one's rights, and doing nothing to advance its own ends. We read in some journals great professions of this character. They have thus influenced many votes, and doubtless decided the contest. Are they well grounded?

I have no desire to be an alarmist. I shall strive to state only what is probable, and what is logically certain to be attempted. I know there are thrills of terror at the immense vote for freedom, and that these emotions may restrain its progress along the course which its position and existence compel it to march. I do not say the slave power will attempt to carry out *all* its designs; but it will and *must* push forward the most advanced of them to completion, and encourage the less developed in their growth. Such necessity is laid upon it. It is consistent with every human, with every inhuman, principle that actuates its disciples.

Read the dreadful programme which the nation by last Tuesday's action has declared shall be hers for the next quadrennian. Note that in all the list there is not one sentiment of true Democracy, humanity, or Christianity.

First and foremost, the administration will put forth all its power to make Kansas a Slave State. Hear the reasons for this opinion: —

1. They have set their heart upon it — carried all the preliminaries up to the last act but one; carried them with a rush, a violence, a madness, which has not hesitated at fraud, robbery, arson, and murder. They will not abandon the lands they have stolen from the Free States, and which they have many times ravaged by bloody hordes; where they have committed such brutal murders as to give them a name below every name in the annals of man; where they now "sit, shapes hot from hell," in all the form and pomp of sovereignty that obtains in Pandemonium itself. They never will resign that power at the call of an administration of their own right hand's making. These bull-dogs will not let go their grip upon the throat of Kansas by any cry from Washington, if one should be made. But it will not be made. They know too well that *they* are Washington. These janizaries have made the Sultan, these cardinals the Pope; and they are too wise to have made one greater than themselves.

2. But not only will they have Kansas because they have steeped themselves in such iniquity to get it, they must have it of political necessity. They want no Free State cordon around Missouri. They will have none if their fierce and tireless zeal can prevent it. It will be impossible to keep this Slave State in their hands, shot through as it is with free sentiments, if Kansas becomes free. And if Missouri falls, the whole demoniac arch totters to its base, and tumbles to the nethermost hell. Kansas or nothing, is their clear discernment and purpose. For slavery in Kansas they will fight, because they are thus battling for slavery in Virginia and South Carolina.*

3. They will wage this conflict to its issue, because success here is triumph everywhere. Kansas theirs, all the Territories will be. They wish for no more compromises. They want no barter with Freedom, whereby Slavery and Liberty shall divide the Senate between them. They mean to have slavery national, and freedom not even sectional. Kansas theirs, and this triumph is sure. The law of the nation will then decree that a slaveholder can take his "property" with him into any of the Territories, and that no local organization can emancipate them!

Every other Territory thus subdued, all the new States will wheel into the Union under this flag, and its triumph at the capital is assured forever. Utah is at our doors with her twin institution, in its professed patriarchal and less abominable nature. She unites lovingly with slavery in the edict of her ruler to all the "saints" to vote for him, who declares he is the platform upon which these barbarisms are

* The hero of Kansas became the martyr of Virginia. In the name and strength of his Master, John Brown struck at the head of the serpent after he had, in Kansas, effectually bruised its tail. That blow revealed and confirmed the instincts of both contestants on this then distant field. Kansas included the whole in its every part.

to dwell together under their own territorial vine and fig tree, with none to molest nor make them afraid.

Oregon has slaves on her soil, and is in the hands of men who have kept off a State organization for several years, because they saw that the country was not ripe to receive her as a Slave State, and they were determined she should be nothing else. Washington Territory is in their hands. So are New Mexico and Nebraska. Every spot of our national domain but Minnesota. And she, in the insolence of this triumph, may be refused admission, unless she will put this broth of abominable things in her sacred constitutional vessel.

Outside of our present boundaries, where sweeps not her eye, greedy and devouring? Central America is under her feet. Cuba is hotly lusted after. The three-headed dog of war across the seas, England, France, and Spain, guards the Hesperides, and alone preserves these golden apples from her clutch.

The African slave trade will be reopened practically, if not by legislative act. This does not need Congressional enactment or presidential signature. Let Charleston, New Orleans, and Mobile offer to receive these Africans, and they will be introduced, as enslaved Americans now go to these ports from Baltimore and Richmond, under the protection of our national flag and cannon.

Silence will be imposed on Congressional lips. Sumner's still bleeding head and wasting frame will be ever before the representatives of the Free States, as an index of their fate, if they dare to assail this execrable shape. Not gutta percha canes, but knife and pistol, will speedily end the controversy at the Capitol. Moving northward, silence will be laid upon the press, which is the mouth of the people. No journal will be allowed to condemn the national institution. The fiery "Independent," the vehement "Tribune," the solid white heat of the "Liberator," the long uplifted trumpet of "Zion's Herald," the first of all journals of the Christian Church in this warfare, and not the least in energy and influence, the "National Era," grand oracle of grand men, the growing multitude, local, urban, and rural, that have joined their voices to the swelling volume of indignation, — upon them the administration will lay its hand, and stifle their speech or their life. With them will sink into dumbness every minister of Christ and Liberty, every speaker who urges this great reform from any stage, every book that paints the horrors of the hell of bondage, and fires the hearts of the people with a burning detestation of it and of its defenders; all these will this power essay to repress, for its tyranny will be everywhere, and will everywhere be in peril if this liberty is allowed. Napoleon's treatment of the press will be as the little finger to the thick loins of this American despot.

Finally, slaves will be adjudged property anywhere, while in transitu, and the transit may be months in occurring. Slave-pens will, therefore, be a necessity of New York and Boston, and the slaves, instead of being sent thither for shipment alone, will be sold as openly in their market-places, as in those of Richmond. Then comes the universal reign of the demon. The nation everywhere submits her neck to the yoke.

You turn away with loathing from this cup of horrors, and denounce it as the offspring of a disordered brain. My friends, every one of these claims is openly made in the leading administration journals of the South, and avowed by its political representatives, while their Northern allies make no objection, but keep a close silence upon these preparations, and expend their strength of argument and invective in assailing the defenders of Jefferson and Washington, of the Declaration and the Constitution, of humanity and Christ.

Say not, "Prophesy smooth things, pleasant things, hopeful things." When a servant of the Most Holy God was requested to preach a political sermon before his king, that should conform to the general current of expression and flatter the pride and prospects of his sovereign, he said, "As the Lord liveth, what my God saith, that will I speak." So must I say, so far as I, anxiously seeking for the light, am able to discern it. This contest is very different from all this nation has previously waged. If it had not been, ministers would not have engaged so earnestly in the canvass. I suppose more men have addressed audiences on the issue of this campaign from the pulpit than from the platform. The three thousand ministers that sent up from New England alone that solemn denunciation, in the name of Almighty God, against the Nebraska sin, have probably, in nearly every case, uttered their warning to their hearers in the last few months, while thousands in other parts of the land have lifted up their voices in the general appeal.

These "political," "gunpowder priests," as they are called, have no desire to interfere in mere political matters. They are servants of no names except the Name that is above every name, whose orders they dare not and desire not to disobey. I warned and entreated you before the leader of the hosts of freedom was selected, indifferent as to who he should be, far from confident that one of a more decided anti-slavery character would not have been a better captain. I have no devotion to men. It is the cause that has brought these ministers from their sacred studies, wherein they delight, from the beds of the dying and the side of the penitent inquirer after Jesus, into the tumult of the market-place, the dust and whirl and thunder of battle. It is Christ for whom they are preaching and praying and voting, in these works as much as in the more regular duties of their calling.

The fact that Antichrist has secured this victory proves that it will not, cannot be tamely abandoned. The Slave Power is no Hannibal, to waste its victorious forces in luxury, while Rome is not yet completely captured. Therefore will the administration be forced to serve its baleful ends.

Two other reasons confirm this view. 1. The slave power must advance or die. It is a bankrupt swindler, who will have to abandon his show of wealth, unless he can extend his villainies. The late articles in the "Charleston Standard," on the opening of the foreign slave trade, — articles of great power, which should be pondered by every thoughtful man, — prove conclusively that they will die unless they move forward. Talk about resting in quiet on their plantations, undisturbed by the North. Impossible. Their plantations would soon be deserts, their homes poorhouses, and not even almshouses, for no gifts would relieve their poverty. They must grow. Land, land, they must have, to be rifled of its virgin sweets, and then abandoned. Slaves, slaves, cheap and numerous, to till these lands and multiply their wealth. Thus they are driven deeper and deeper into this gulf by the highest pressure on man, his necessity to live. They are on the steed of destiny. They cannot escape this progress in evil except by emancipation, and emancipation will not immediately relieve them. They must leap into the chasm before they can fill it.

2. But they are driven on in this inevitable path by what will be to them a yet higher motive — the total loss of all their present possessions. Two of their chief men have said that the election of a Free State President would have killed slavery in twenty years. They see by the mighty uprising in the North, that a Free State President will soon be elected, and under the inspiration of despair they will work with startling vigor during this brief space of power for their future safety.* Fifty thousand men, representing three thousand millions of property, who have the national power

* How vigorously they did work, history shows. They transported all our fleet into distant parts, and all our arms into Southern arsenals. They appropriated our treasury, navy and war departments to their ends, and left this administration, at its close, without spirit or means for defense, much less for aggression.

in their hands, know that it is surely passing over to those who will make this vast property valueless.* Will they not fight as no men have ever fought in this nation to preserve their power and possessions? Suppose that a system of measures were already commenced, or soon to be inaugurated, which would make every bank and factory and farm, in a few years all the property of the State, but beggars' rags, would not our citizens do all in their power to avert the catastrophe? † Would not fifty thousand robbers defend three thousand millions of gold which they had stolen, against all the bands of justice, and provide in every possible way for its preservation. These thousands of robbers, from whom I exclude all conscientious or indifferent slaveholders, are the assumed protectors of three thousand millions of stolen property — God's property, made, bought, and redeemed by Him, to be His treasure and joy forever. They have the government. Are they going to be easy and indulgent, and give you, their enemies, all the victories which you would have had, if you had defeated them? I speak as unto wise men. Judge ye what I say.

III. What has caused this defeat? Why did not truth and right prevail? Why were not the horse and his rider cast into the sea? For reasons such as are seen in all the struggles of liberty and Christianity for the subjugation of the world to God. Huss and his people must die before Luther could slay their murderer. Bunker Hill must be lost before Yorktown could be gained. Why did we not win?

* The slave property was valued from $2,000,000,000 to $4,000,000,000, the slaveholders of every class about 250,000. This includes minors, women, and aged men. Its controllers were far less than 50,000.

† A striking illustration of the absorption of all industry into the business of slavery is shown by the statistics of Virginia for this very year. She exported over $7.000,000 of her property in slaves; more in value than her tobacco, wheat, or corn. Slaves rose in that State from $62 apiece in 1789, to $500 in 1856. Abolitionism financially ruined her, and she knew that it would.

1. Because there was no deep repentance of the real cause of these shames and crimes, and no true sympathy with their chief victims. The cause is slavery; the real victim is the slave. For the crime we have sorrowed, but not after a godly sort. We have not bemoaned our sins of omission and commission connected with it. The nation has been the abettor and supporter of the President and his iniquity. Who has cried, as he saw his own coöperation in this sin of sins, "God be merciful to me a sinner"?

We have had no tears for the slave. His fate has not been the battle-cry of any party. "Free Labor is in peril!" "*White* Labor, *our* labor!" This has been our watchword: not the rights of our brethren, but our own purses. How much better are you than those white and black brethren that groan in that prison-house of death? Millions on millions are scattered over more than half our organized territory, suffering the unspeakable horrors of the worst tyranny outside of the pit. Bomba of Naples—before whose crimes all Europe, even bloody Napoleon and the Nero of Austria, stand aghast, and cry aloud—inflicts no such punishment on his victims as our own Southland does on hers. He never tears asunder those whom God has joined together, so that each never knows through all their bitter life where the other lives, or if they live. He never snatches the babe from its mother's arms, and sells it into distant lands. He does not employ the fair and pious maidens of his realm, as the other domestic animals, for the raising of stock for the market, or strip them of every protection of the law, and cast them helpless into the lustful clutch of every vagabond of the palace and the street. He does not hunt his laboring people through the thick tangled ravines of his lands with trained bloodhounds, nor flog them to death at whipping-posts on every farm and in every market-place, nor burn them at the stake, nor pour burning-fluid over their head and neck, and set fire to it in order that he may enjoy the sport, as two of our noblemen did not long since in Kentucky; and no press, nor pulpit, nor public voice in all their land spoke a syllable against them. This king does not put his subjects into such agonies that mothers slay their children rather than expose them to his cruelty. He does not refuse them the offices of religion, and try to shut upon them the door of the kingdom of heaven as well as the kingdom of earthly knowledge and happiness. We do! Close beside us, but a few hundred miles from our doors, begins this valley of the shadow of death, this valley of real death, not its shadow. There abound these tears, and groans, and agonies. Families are being torn asunder this hour. "They ravish the women in Zion, the maids in the city of Judah." They are on auction-blocks knocked down to vile merchantmen; in slave-pens, awaiting the hour of their march to their Southern grave; in coffles, handcuffed and fettered, walking wearily over those dreary paths to unknown horrors. They are wading in rice swamps, sweating in sugar houses, stooping in cotton fields, screaming under their father's lash, falling before their brother's bullet. How many a mother, crouching in her desolated cabin, is wailing and moaning with groanings that cannot be uttered, as she thinks to-night of her tender and beautiful daughter, your sister and mine, crucified on the awful cross of slavery!

"Gone, gone! sold and gone
To the rice swamps dank and lone,
Where the slave-whip ceaseless swings,
Where the noisome insect stings,
Where the fever-demon strews
Poison with the fallen dews,
Where the sickly sunbeams glare
Through the hot and misty air.
There no mother's eye is near them,
There no mother's ear can hear them;
Never when the torturing lash
Seams their backs with many a gash,

Shall a mother's kindness bless them,
Or a mother's arms caress them.
Toiling through the weary day,
And at night the spoiler's prey.
O that they had early died,
Sleeping calmly side by side,
Where the tyrant's power is o'er,
And the fetter galls no more.
Gone, gone! sold and gone
To the rice swamps dank and lone,
From Virginia's hills and waters:
Woe is me, my stolen daughters!"

Poets have essayed to paint the mouth of hell. Homer, Virgil, Dante, and Milton have imagined its horrors. Yet the chief of them — the artistic Roman, the painfully minute Tuscan — fail to convey, in their imaginations of the lost, a true picture of the living fate of millions of Americans, born under our flag and on our soil, heirs with us to every right and privilege of an American citizen. Howlings and writhings, and fiery streams, and caves of ice, and blackness of darkness were the pigments on their palette. But the power that mingled them was Sin. Here virtue lies distressed; here innocence writhes in flames; here piety is encased in thick-ribbed walls of everlasting ice; here chastity is embruted by human beasts; here Christ is crucified afresh. And we, what have we done as a nation, or as a political party striving to gain the reins of government? We dared not raise a cry for them, for fear of being called "abolitionists." For that word is so unpopular, no party assuming it can rise to power. We shouted, and planned, and fought for suffering Kansas. Her woes filled our eyes and lungs. Great as they are, they are nothing to those suffered by other Americans in the larger part of the land. And these we feared even to mention.

We did not deserve the victory. We shall not win it till this sympathy possesses the heart and bursts from the lips of the people. An American citizen attempted to leave

Richmond lately. He was nailed in a box, and the box put on board of a vessel so carelessly, that he stood upon his head, and in that condition he went reeling along the billowy ocean to New York. When he reached that harbor, half dead, — thrice dead we might rather say, — he made himself known to the captain; and that Northern wretch, a New England wretch probably, kindly sent him back to Richmond. He had suffered Peter's fate for weeks, crucified head downward, and yet he was treated with less leniency. For had not death released the apostle, his persecutors might have had pity on such courageous endurance of so long and so horrible a martyrdom. They certainly would not have remanded him to severer tortures. Did we make the skies ring with our indignation? How many wept because of him? We talk of our Congressional and Kansas heroes. Have they suffered like this man for freedom? And yet he was honored by hardly a half dozen lines in the journals. Not a burst of rage at the poltroon captain, not a cry of pity for the redeemed brave, hurled back into the burning pit from which he had by such immensity of endurance well nigh escaped. Indignation meetings should have been held over the atrocity of that Northern captain, and against the system that compels such heroism to escape from its tortures.

2. We have failed because we were not, as a people, earnest in prayer for the triumph of Freedom. "I will be inquired of," saith God, "by the house of Israel to do this thing for them." Politicians despise election prayer-meetings, and too many Christians did not see their necessity. Though frequently appointed in this place, they were poorly attended. Men were busy at the caucus, but not at this true caucus — the coming together with and before the Lord. Women would talk politics over their tables, but declined to come up to the temple and pray it on their knees. Voters thought this to be just like other contests,

and supposed mere party-talk and machinery would give them the victory. Unless the Lord go up with us, we go in vain; we go to defeat, not triumph. He will be sought unto for this great salvation. We should all have done as was done in some places. Christians of all sects should have met together on the morning of election, and marched from the prayer-meeting to the ballot-box. If this duty had been done for the preceding months, we should have received the desired blessing. Christ is more deeply interested in this work than we can be. He is King of kings and President of presidents. To Him the earth is given for an inheritance. He requires His children to call for His aid. His arm alone can bring us salvation. Had the whole land been one atmosphere of prayerful incense, — had the Church alone been earnest, and instant, and universal, in this cry, — many a doubting heart would have turned rightward instead of wrongward; many a hand lifted against Him would have been raised for Him; many a vote that said "No" to this call of God and man, would have said "Yes."

Pennsylvania is not the keystone of this nation. It is prayer. When we pray for the slave as one with him, we shall speak for him, vote for him, and win for him and ourselves individual, national, universal liberty. "I will be inquired of by the house of Israel to do this thing for them."

3. We have failed because we were, as a whole, more anxious to beat a party than to destroy a gigantic sin. We have opposed the President and his supporters as politicians, not as sinners against a just and angry God. We have sought their overthrow for personal and party aggrandizement, and not for the sake of God and man. We have been unwilling to see that that unfortunate Pilate in the history of liberty, enshrined forever in the execrations of mankind, was, in reality, no greater offender than those who went before him. Pierce was no worse, though a weaker instrument of this sin, than his predecessors, Fillmore, and Webster,

and Clay. Those who voted for him were no worse than the most of those who voted for his rival. All avowed their joy that agitation on this subject had ceased, shutting the hatchway on our miserable brethren and sisters in the hold of our Ship of State, and stifling their shrieks and moans, while she sails over sunny waters of credit and renown.

We are all partakers of our Pilate's crime. The innocent blood he has shed is on us and our children. It will be demanded of us, drop for drop, by the God of justice.* We must look behind that poor man to the Judases and Caiaphases who, for money and power, have set on this weak-willed governor to his dreadful deeds and fame. We must go behind even these traitors and enemies of our liberties and our God, to the arch Sin which possesses them like the Legion, the wanderer in the tombs, the greatest of modern, nay, greater than any ancient crime—American Slavery.

It is a system the smoke of whose torment blackens all our sky. No such organized iniquity exists elsewhere on the earth. If it prevailed in China precisely as it does in Virginia, we should vent our loudest thunders against it. If it possessed a European foothold, it would be expelled by the united cannon of all nations. Ezekiel's denunciations of the Judean infamy, in all its minute and horrible fullness, does not express the full deserts of this abomination. See all the present population of New England in the condition of our kinsfolk of the South; their number is about our number. Go from city to city, from village to village, and behold only the worst of huts, the most meager fare, the raggedest dress. Note their condition. Not one allowed to read; not one permitted to go from his allotted place; no Westfield man visiting Springfield, nor Springfield man, Boston. No one riding on the railroads, except in the cattle cars, and in chains; sold on your and every village green; driven through every street as beasts for the

* See Note IV.

slaughter, only that cattle go freely in their droves; these go lashed together, the sound of the whip ever falling on their quivering flesh; the sound of agony ever rising on the weary air; and below, beyond all this, crimes against God and nature, which defiled Sodom, and buried it in wrath and fire, everywhere occurring. Traverse all these Puritan States, and gaze on this universal horror, with not a single exception, and say, Is there any sin like ours? That is the sight which spreads over our land for a thousand miles. Is it not strange that God's thunders still sleep in His arm? that the earth does not gape, and the heavens break forth in fire?

We should demand that these horrors shall cease, or that we should throw off the body of this death that makes the United States a stench in the nostrils of the world, a byword and hissing among the nations.

A dislike of this evil, joined with unwillingness to extirpate it, is a characteristic of no especial party. The Democratic party, now in power, is as much opposed to slavery, so far as most of its Northern elements are concerned, as the party that opposes it. The foreign and native elements of its Northern wing have no desire to see slavery established in Kansas, extended into our Territories, or spread over our whole land. The President elect, and ruling, are undoubtedly, in their private sentiments, opposed to its extension. The fault is not in their private, abstract feelings; it is in their attachment to a party, because they see in it the road to political success. Unprincipled men, trading politicians, are the Northern leaders of this party, whose conscience and heart, if they have any, never interfere with their plans or deeds. Their followers are believers in its original creed, who fought its battles in the days when it defended the cause of the people, when the greatest good of the greatest number was its motto and endeavor, and who cannot yet believe that it is in the hands of the most haughty and wicked aristocracy on the face of the earth. They still think its enemies are their ancient foes, whom they esteemed the enemies of the people and of the rights of man.

The leaders know for whom they are working. The slave-traders, who have stolen this Democratic livery of a popular name and popular rights, to serve the devil in, have put the mercenaries of the North into office in order that they may keep the masses on their side, and thus retain the national power. We have not, as a party, sought so much to convince these Democratic voters as to subdue them. This party management of ours has retained them in the hands of the enemy. In Pennsylvania alone multitudes were thus kept from our ranks. It is not natural to submit to the man that smites you. We may christianly turn the other cheek, — we are not christianly required to make him our companion and guide. Not until we rise above the passion for party success or the vindictive assaults on men for mere partisanship, shall we win this great victory for God.

These are the chief reasons for our failure: bitterness of party feeling and ambition for party triumph, lack of sympathy, deep and all-pervading, for the slave, dread of the reproach of Christ and of abolitionism, and neglect of prayer to God, that His right arm might give us the victory.

IV. Is there any bow upon these clouds? Have we any ground for hope in the ultimate triumph of Freedom, in the restoration of the Declaration and the Constitution to their true seat of power? Is the roll filled only with lamentations, mourning, and woe. Written it is within and without with these doleful exclamations. The hosts of Pharaoh have not yet sunk like lead in the mighty waters of a popular uprising. The chain yet clanks about the neck of the nation. Our bondage is to be yet more grievous. But will it come to an end? I can prophesy good concerning Israel. There is ground for hope. "I shall see Him, but not now. I shall behold Him, but not nigh." It is the hour and the triumph of darkness. Satan conquers in Eden and on Calvary. Yet Christ hath bruised his head, and will lead him captive even in the hour of his victory. Not without great toil and suffering and defeat and death will this deliverance come.

Two questions address us. Will the programme already prepared be carried out? Will the defeated principles be inthroned by the next quadrennial in the seat of national power? 1. We answer, In the prevention of the execution of the dreadful catalogue of aggressions on the nation's liberty and life, we have no hope from the managers of the dominant party. Undoubtedly its Northern leaders are terrified at the mighty expression of Free State sentiment; but they are not the leaders of the party; they are but the tools of the slave-drivers, whose slaves, sooner than these men, will rebel against them. We have nothing to hope from a President who has been for thirty years the foremost worshiper at this Baal; who has advocated all their measures with a readiness of zeal that surpassed even John C. Calhoun himself; who alone, of all Northern senators, urged the enactment of a law, making the postmaster responsible, under heavy fines, for the passage through his office of any document condemning slavery; who alone, of all Northern men, advocated the annexation of Texas, on the ground that the South ought to have more slave territory; who wrote in favor of extending the Missouri line to the Pacific, when this tyranny demanded it, in order to secure to themselvés, without fail, New Mexico, Arizona, and all Southern California; who dared to do what Mr. Pierce, with all his subservience, and Mr. Douglas, with all his boldness, would have shrunk from, and in the center of Europe, and under the eyes of all Christian powers, draughted and published with his name first, and two slave-drivers after him, a plan for America to steal a province from a nation with whom we are at peace, unless she will consent to its sale, in order that the area of this crime may be extended, and its power made more secure.

What should we say if Great Britain should threaten to take Massachusetts unless the Republic sold it to her; stolen with all its wealth, its history, its patriotism, its every material and spiritual bond of union, stolen to make it a bond-slave of her own, that her favorite iniquity might be the more firmly planted and widely extended. But this did James Buchanan on the continent of Europe, when he asserted the purpose of the Slave Power to seize Cuba, unless Spain surrendered it. Such is his past career. Can any change for the better be augured therefrom? Is there any hope for the amelioration of this evil drawn from his character or history? Alas, none! While as a minister of Christ I shall pray for our new President, while I shall not shut the door against his penitence and return, in the fear of God, before whom princes are but men, and who commands His servants not to fear or favor the face of unrighteous rulers, I solemnly declare that we have no right to hope for any act favorable to liberty from Mr. Buchanan. The dying dynasty will be forgotten, I fear, in the subtle, cruel, tireless criminality of the coming administration. The last woe is nearly past; the next cometh quickly, and cometh sure. The bow, if it is one, is of the clouds, is not on them. The Judicial Bench is the servile oracle of this Power. The Senate will be no less vindictive than it has been against freedom, and no less supple to slavery. It cannot be more so. The House may stand against the waves of this gulf of death. It may. God grant that it will. Here is our only hope, so far as our national action is concerned, for the success of freedom, or rather for the prevention of further successes of slavery. You know how feeble it is. Men who turned a deaf ear to the wail of Kansas, who have joined loudest in insults upon the advocates of liberty, who have worked zealously for what they knew was the cause of sin, will not be apt to stand up against their leaders. Their backs are stiffened to the stooping posture in which they have so long been bent. They have no power to walk erect. Such men as John P. Hale and Hannibal Hamlin have not taken seats in the House as they have in the Senate; nor can we hope, unless the people shall change their mind, and then their representatives, that its immediate future will differ from its past. A body which voted not to arraign the murderer of Keating, because its Southern masters forbade it; which voted not to expel the murderer in intent, and probably yet in fact, of Charles Sumner; which voted that the Border Ruffian sitting among them, by votes which he and they confessed were fraudulent, should still hold his seat; which voted against any search into the Kansas troubles, and after it had received the report, and knew of its truthfulness, voted not to believe it; which fought for weeks to give the President the forces he is now employing to rob and murder peaceable citizens of their own districts in their new home,— these are not the men to go backward, and confess and forsake their sins, and do works meet for repentance. They will grow more desperate against the light and summons of the hour, and strive yet more fiercely to strangle the babe divine in its growing grace and greatness.

We turn away with hopeless heart from the national government. As well expect to find Judas returned to the apostleship, and outstripping Paul and Peter in his devotion to Christ, as well dream that Arnold would again become the companion of Washington, that Francis of Austria will make Kossuth his prime minister, as that the slave party shall act with the disciples of Christ, the followers of Washington, and of Kossuth in abolishing this wrong.*

As we turn sadly away, we rejoice to see two governmental barriers to this baleful progress, foreign and domestic. The powers of Europe will forbid the annexation of Cuba

* The House was better than these fears. The next year, on the one hundred and thirty-third ballot, by a plurality of three, but four less than a majority, Mr. Banks was chosen Speaker. The "American" vote and a year's discussion contributed this victory.

and Central America, the powers of the Free States the annexation of Kansas to the South. All these States, with one exception, have governments favorable to freedom, and by ways sagacity, prudence, and firmness will devise and execute, will, we trust, keep Kansas unsubdued. By grants of money to those citizens settling there, and by other equally legal and potent methods, they will, we believe, maintain our rights and her liberty, though all the powers of the national army, purse, and judicial subtlety, shall be employed for her destruction.

The fear of foreign invasion, which shall set their captives free, may keep these Southern pirates peaceable on the high seas, and confine their slave trade to our own afflicted citizens and our own degraded coast. The united front of Northern administrations may stay its progress on the land, and compel it to confine its ravages to the lines that already inclose it, and over which, like fires girdled by bounds which they seek to pass, it shoots its tongues of flame, and leaps, in mad desire and endeavor, to lay waste the whole national heritage, and whelm State and Territory, old and new, east and west, north and south, in one common ruin. Only these powers can prevent the accomplishment of its designs. We shall soon see whether even they are able to resist its progress.

2. Looking away from the material relief which we so much need and desire, but which is so little to be expected, let us see if there are any good hopes of the overthrow of this Power after the coming calamities shall have overpassed. Here we have glimpses of light. Thanks be unto God who giveth us the victory through our Lord Jesus Christ. The morning cometh, though also, and previously, the night.

Our hopes are based on these foundations: —

(1.) This is the first time in our national history that the cause of Anti-Slavery has prevailed, openly and avowedly, in a single State. Other issues have been foremost, and this put at the end of the resolutions and the party. An Anti-slavery political organization has long been formed, and is the real seed of the present harvest. But never till this election did it carry a single State. Now the last is made first. Though its demands are the least of the claims and duties of Abolitionists, — the sharp edge of the wedge, — yet it is an edge. More than a million of the citizens of this nation have declared their hostility to this sin, and their determination to resist its progress. They cannot stop here. While faithfully abiding by their doctrine of the independence of the States in their own jurisdiction, they must say an evil which cannot go over the continent cannot abide under the national flag. Washington must be free. The national piracy on the high seas from Virginia and Charleston to the Mississippi and the Gulf, must be stopped, and the government be put openly and entirely on the side of Freedom. This party, being in its beginning right, will in the end be successful.

(2.) Again, this vote for freedom will stimulate those who dwell in the midst of slavery to shake off the terrors that have kept them dumb. Said Governor Wise, one of the leaders of this host of fallen spirits, "What we have most to fear is an insurrection of our white citizens." The vote for Mr. Fillmore is almost entirely a vote against the extension of slavery. They dared not put their desires in its true form; but by voting against the candidate of the secessionists and slavocrats, they voted for the cause of Freedom. This large party at the South has carried one State, and perhaps more, and has prevented all the rest from going by large majorities for slavery propagandism. It will dare to speak more freely under the countenance of such a Northern vote for liberty. Had we been successful, every Southern State, with perhaps one exception, would have wheeled into line within four years. As it is, their day of deliverance, though delayed, draweth nigh. What they have wanted was the erection of a free spirit here, — sober, guarded, conservative, but earnest and mighty. Having these, we shall see in those regions light springing up. Western Virginia, Kentucky, Missouri, — who has sent one Representative to Congress, — Maryland, — who has one there now,* — Louisiana, North Carolina, Tennessee, — in all these the tree of Liberty will again put forth its leaves, and be pouring, we trust, its ripened fruit into the successful harvest of Freedom in 1861.†

(3.) Lastly and chiefly, we hope for success because of the religious sentiment that has been developed. Never has a great party, since the dawning of the revolution, had so much of the life and power of religion flowing through its veins. A hearty sympathy with our suffering kindred in Kansas, a patriotic devotion to our ancient and imperiled liberties, an earnest calling upon God that He would come and save us, — these have been the great elements of its being. Never has the conscience of this nation been so aroused; never its dependence upon God so tested. That feeling is not sufficiently deep yet. The horrors of the coming years, whose gloomy clouds cover all the land, and drop their rain of misery and death upon its political and geographical centers, Washington and Kansas, — these sufferings and sins will make our cry go up yet more earnestly unto God, and He will hear and answer.

It is this character in these issues that has brought the Church and the ministry so actively into the canvass. They have not gone out of their way. The political march of events and duties has come upon their way. For years

* Henry Winter Davis, one of the truest friends of Freedom the country ever possessed.

† Though the Southern allies failed to rally, except in Western Virginia, as soon as is here suggested, they were the loyal element, that did us good service in many parts of the South, and are now the associates of their emancipated brethren in securing that land to righteousness.

have they striven with this sin in their churches, often too feebly, always too unsuccessfully. They have not engaged in it in order to make the Church, as such, the head or controller of the State. Not till the millennial dawn, when the Church and the State shall both be perfect, and become one, will that position be assigned to her. They have not marshaled their forces as the Papist bishops have theirs, and ordered them to vote so that their church organization shall be recognized as one of the ruling powers, and shall be represented, as such, in the offices of the nation, — which act, united with the marshaling of white serfs, gave the Slave Power the victory. Papal priest and slaveholding tyrant have entered into power as one force. It only needs, what it has in heart and voice, and, as far as possible, in vote, the Mormon abomination, to complete its organization.

"Devil with devil damned firm concord holds."

The true Church of Jesus Christ has engaged in this duty as Christians. They have voted as they prayed, and prayed as they voted — for Christ and Cæsar; not for Cæsar only; for eternal as well as for temporal good; for man rather than for his transient accidents. The entire North, though not all, and actually but a small part Christian, has been moved by the Spirit of God.

This is our surest confidence that darkness and chaos will soon disappear, and light and liberty, in the beautiful order of heaven, be our heritage forever.

Thus stands our cause. The bow glitters in the heavens. Though the waters yet cover the earth, — though the waves roar with the swelling thereof, — though winds howl, and clouds press close and heavy, and thunders crash, and lightnings slay, — still there gleams the bow. Before us rises the pillar of fire. We must follow it. We may die in the wilderness, die without the sight of the promised land; yet that fiery guide will lead this enslaved nation, with those in her deepest dungeons of bondage, — all of us, black and white, North and South, — into the land of holy liberty.

> "Oppression shall not always reign:
> There comes a brighter day,
> When Freedom, burst from every chain,
> Shall have triumphant sway."

Let us not grow weary in our toils and prayers. Scoff as the wicked may, the effectual, fervent prayer of the righteous in this great war has availed much. It will, if continued, in God's good time, — and that seems not far off, — give us the glorious victory. Let us refresh our sympathies with the agonies of our brethren and sisters in slave hut and prairie cabin. May God quicken the consciences of our rulers, so that they may fear Him and work righteousness. May He distract the counsels of the wicked, and break their bows asunder. May you all seek the power of a Christian faith and a godly life, that you may join your prayers to those that are going up to the throne of God for the salvation of this nation. Without this, your labors are but half perfect; with it, they will have the symmetry and strength of angelic works. For Christ labor; to Christ pray; and He will prosper His servants, and spread His millennial glory over all this land. The cruel and deceitful men that now govern us shall be driven into obscurity; the weak and fearful shall be made strong; the slave arise to his true estate of civil and social manhood; the lover of liberty abroad gather new inspiration from our victories; and the whole world be filled with our praises and our power.

> "Down shall the shrines of Moloch sink,
> And leave no traces where they stood;
> No longer shall its idol drink
> His daily cup of human blood;
> Another altar standeth there,
> To truth and love, and mercy given;
> And Freedom's gift and Freedom's prayer
> Shall call all blessings down from heaven."

CASTE THE CORNER-STONE.*

"We are verily guilty concerning our brother."

Genesis xlii. 21.

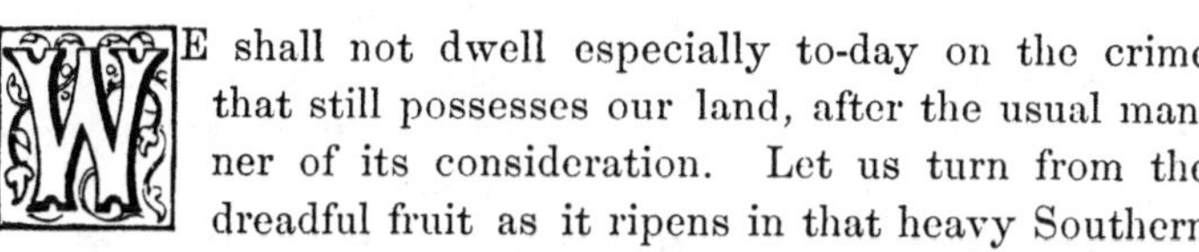

WE shall not dwell especially to-day on the crime that still possesses our land, after the usual manner of its consideration. Let us turn from the dreadful fruit as it ripens in that heavy Southern air, and examine its seed-grain that is growing profusely in every heart. The corner-stone of this system is prejudice against color. Upon this almost universal feeling the slaveholder builds an impregnable fortress. Slavery will never be abolished until it gives way. As one that must render an account to God for what I say, I shall speak. As those that must give like account before the same God, I beseech you, take heed how you hear. Though I assail a deep-rooted but God-forbidden sentiment, as you would obey the command of Christ, "Thou shalt love thy neighbor as thyself," I

* A sermon preached on the occasion of the State Fast, at Wilbraham, Mass., in 1854, and at Roxbury, Mass., in 1858. It was also delivered at the Forsyth Street Methodist Episcopal Church, New York.

entreat you to give the subject your candid and Christian attention.

I. Upon what is slavery grounded? Is it upon the right to hold in slavery the black man, or the man who has any blood relation, however remote, with that portion of the sons of men? The most arrogant defender of slavery in this country has never dared to advocate the enslavement of *any* race of colored men, for all men are colored. The lighter, though sometimes very dusky, shades of the Caucasian, the yellow Chinese, the tawny Malay, the copper-hued Indian, are all painted by the hand of their Creator another color than white. No doctor of diabolic divinity has ever picked from the sacred page any text for the enslavement of Indian, Mexican, Englishman, or Greek, though every argument which they wrest from the writings of Paul (as did those of old for their own destruction and the destruction of the brethren of Christ) must, on their principle, be applied chiefly to white persons, as these were almost the only slaves of Rome in the days of Paul. One text alone, in the whole Bible, can they bring to the support of African slavery. Every other reference to it is human, not specific — the slavery of Man, not Ham. And even that text supports no such theory. It was a prophecy announced and completed four thousand years ago, when Joshua made the Gideonites his servants, and David ruled over the whole land of Canaan.* A broader view of the history of these three families only confirms this position. The sons of Canaan ruled in Nineveh, and were the first conquerors of the world. They became subject to the posterity of Shem, under Cyrus, and Shem had to allow Japhet, under Alexander, to abide in his tents. To-day, Shem, in the person of the Turk, holds Canaan in bondage in Syria and Egypt, and Japhet, in that of Russia and England, dwells in many of the tents of Shem.

Scripture is stolen to deck a false idol. It is a new argu-

* See Note V.

ment for an old sin, an argument without any antitype in history, or any authority in the Word of God. Abraham, they say, was a slaveholder; but the sons of Shem were his slaves. Egyptians and Babylonians enslaved Hebrews, Hebrews enslaved the Canaanites, not for reasons of race, but for the sole reason of power. The Persian owned the Greek; the Greek, the Roman; the Roman, the Norman; the Norman, the Saxon. No one of them regarded color, but condition only. The last of these slaves, the Saxon, having gained his liberty, and following the devil's maxim, "Do to others as you do not wish should be done to you," goes out and binds his fellow-servants. He is an adventurer, and when he conquers, enslaves. He steals men and women from Africa, and sells them in America. Here he enslaves every new-born child of the daughters of these captives in every following generation. For two hundred years he pursues this traffic, and when the conscience of the world begins to rise up against his iniquity, behold, he clothes himself with these fig leaves of prophecy, which he gets professed ministers of Christ to sew together, and hopes to perpetuate his sin and shame with a pretension that blasphemes God and empties His Word of its sovereign power. For if that Word could be proved to indorse this crime, its sanctity and authority flee instantly and forever.

No other modern race but the Saxon makes this pretension. Spanish, French, Russ, Turk, all but the English, claim no Scripture text for their protection. Nor can all the last people be charged with this folly. It is the child of the American Saxon, not of the British. It was born on our soil, of our lusts, of which it is the meanest offspring.

Away with all such mockery of God and his Gospel. Stand forth, transgressor, in thy own vileness. "Lie down in thy shame, and let thy sins cover thee." Pretend not to shelter thyself in the Word of God. It burns with intolerable flame against all such hypocrisy. No one ever before made such a cowardly excuse for his indulgence in avarice, power, and lust. No sinner in all the Bible ever arrayed his wicked passions in such a cloak of holiness. It was left for preachers and professors of the Gospel in this free and Christian America, in this nineteenth century after the coming of Christ, to weave such a garment of sanctity for the body of their death. How will He whom they thus mock, put them to open shame for this profanity of His name and claims. Better defy Him in word, as they do in act, than to thus proclaim that in their most godless deeds they are especially observing His most godly law.

Thus was it left for Satan, in his last resort, to transform himself into an angel of light, and enter this Paradise, which the Bible and Christian institutions were making the garden of the Lord, and by the deft handling of the Word of God, seduce His Church to her ruin. As he showed his skill in selecting apt texts of Scripture with which to assail our Lord and Savior, so has he tempted His disciples — alas! in their case, with a too baleful success.

II. But another root this iniquity puts forth. It is claimed that this mark of color is a badge of separation and of degradation; that, because they are black, they are without equal rights, and cannot mingle indissolubly with the rest of mankind. Their white neighbors shrink from them with horror. A leper is not so offensive.

This sin of caste prevails here as much as where it has borne its legitimate fruit — the transforming of this separated, darker, and inferior class into the property of the lighter and superior.

To its consideration we of the North are especially called. It is a sin at our own doors, in our own hearts. It makes us naked before our enemies. It ties our tongues before their taunts. It must be extirpated ere God gives us perfect and perpetual peace. It is the most general, deep-rooted, unnatural, and destructive of all the sins of the nation.

1. Its universality none can doubt. The familiarity of the South, the philanthropy of the North, have not yet weakened this feeling. Now and then a Richard M. Johnson publicly avows his tinged companion to be his wife. Here and there, in the North, equally fervent loves are legally consummated. But these are solitary stars in the midnight clouds of this superstition. "Darkness is over all the land."

2. It is the most deep-rooted. I could not have mentioned a subject that would have excited such instant and profound loathing as this. I rejoice that you have so patiently listened to its uncongenial truths. I believe that it is because reason commands you, though your feelings yet refuse obedience. Let reason have her perfect work, and see if she cannot subdue this feeling to herself, and convert it to the perfect truth.

The presence of a drop of this blood excludes its possessor from all white society, North or South. But a few years since, a wealthy man in New Orleans, in a heated conversation, was charged with having a colored ancestor, a free black, some four or five generations before. The blood of his antagonist was not sufficient recompense for the injury he suffered. He prosecuted him, and laid his damages at twenty thousand dollars. Though the defendant could not prove his charge, he proved enough to throw a stain of doubt on his opponent, which is said to have excluded him from the society where he had moved. It would have excluded him from any circle in the North. A gentleman in a New England town brought an elegant and wealthy bride from the West Indies, who was slightly tinged with this hue. Her wealth, culture, and beauty could not secure for her admittance into a society below that in which she had moved at home, and she remained in seclusion till death admitted her to the equal company of heaven. These instances could be reproduced everywhere. It is not the amount, it is the *fact*, of African blood that puts its inheritor without the pale of those who boast that they are of Caucasian origin.

A Virginia court has lately refused freedom to some persons, three fourths white, saying such a precedent would free one tenth of the slaves in the State. We grant no real freedom to those who are nine hundred and ninety-nine thousandths white, if the other thousandth be of African blood. A young lady, at a Northern seminary, the slave daughter of a Southern slaveholder, was the acknowledged belle of the school, and so remained for many terms. On the discovery of her being slightly affected with Afric blood, she fell from her high estate, and only her affiance with an honorable gentleman, whom she afterwards married, prevented her becoming an outcast. If this prejudice works so powerfully in these extreme cases, how must it rage in the general feeling toward the great masses of our brethren, whose skin is touched with a browner hue than that which bleaches upon our bones?

3. But you will say a sentiment so deep and all-pervading is not prejudice; it is nature. Is it so? If so, our opposition ceases. We shall not ask you to violate the laws of Nature. On the contrary, we affirm that it is unnatural. We use this word not in a moral sense, but physical. It is unnatural physically; it is inhuman morally. It is so, because,—

(1.) We have no such feelings toward any other class of men. We may dislike the Indian, but some of the greatest men of this nation boast of their Indian blood. Patrick Henry and John Randolph were honored the more from this circumstance. This blood is no bar to any society, employment, or dignity. No man has been refused a pastorate or any office on its account.

Yet eminent physiologists affirm that the blacks are superior to the Indians. A grander nature, more original, more divine, has God conferred on them. I heard a distinguished naturalist of Baltimore say that this despised people was far superior to the Indians in all manly qualities. Every observer of the two must acknowledge it. The "poor Indian," with all his oppressions, has been comparatively a petted protegé of the nation.* He has been the ally of warring whites for two hundred years. Missionaries have been sent him from every church. No legal bars have been raised against him. Yet where is he to-day? Running before the white man, or abiding among us, scarcely changed in dress, habits, or disposition from his barbaric ancestors. Negroes were brought here as slaves; were kept as slaves everywhere for one hundred and fifty years. Most of them are kept in that condition until this day. Every curse and sneer that our souls could conceive, or tongues pronounce, have been thrust upon them. Yet to-day they have some of the most attractive orators in the country. Through both South and North are found negro preachers, without learning or culture, of such natural wit, pathos, and sublimity, as make the mass of their white brethren in the ministry, before their brightness, pale their ineffectual fires.

They have given the nation a style of music which has become more diffused and more popular than any other in the world. Tasso's songs are said to be sung by Venetian boatmen. A few ballads live by the genius of Burns in the glens of Scotland. Such national strains are found elsewhere, confined to the lands where they were born. But the songs of our enslaved brethren have taken captive the whole world. Bayard Taylor says that Arabian minstrels on the Nile sing them to their tamborines, instead of their old humdrum discords. The singers of Hindostan relieve the audi-

* This statement has been confirmed by the appointment by General Grant of a half breed, Colonel Parker, as the chief of his military staff, who also, since the war, has married a white lady of high position. Not a paper, nor tongue, however hostile, has spoken a word against either of these events. Why should they if he should make Frederick Douglass, another half breed, of far higher abilities, the chief of his presidential staff — his Secretary of State?

tors of ennui and money by the merry or plaintive strains of our favorite airs. Borne by their masters on the wings of commerce, these plaints and consolations are carried to all the world, and all the world repeats their strains.

They are in highest honor here. Every street corner attests their popularity. Every city has its band of minstrels, who blacken their faces, and reproduce plantation melodies and manners, for the greedy delight of every class in society. One of the wealthiest gentlemen of New York, of the highest social rank, said to me, "I very much prefer to visit the negro minstrels than the opera." The unabated success of these companies — a success beyond that of any other class of amusements — shows its deep and extensive popularity. It has made those rich who can catch these wild wails of our national captives, and fashion them into songs. If these composers invent melodies, and give them this dialect, they still keep close to the character they assume, and make both words and tones sound forth the depths of breaking hearts. Few more pathetic pieces are in all musical literature than "Lucy Neal," "Uncle Ned," "Old Folks at Home," or "Carry Me back to Old Virginny." How wonderfully does this experience of our slaves agree with that of their Hebrew brethren by the side of the rivers of Babylon! "They that wasted us required of us a song." God grant that, like these their ancient brethren, their wailings may soon become rejoicings over their own liberty, in their own homes, free and happy forever.

Not in music alone do they attain national eminence, and even preëminence. In courtesy of manners they have no equals among our whiter populations. They are our truest gentlemen, in that quiet good breeding that knows what perfect courtesy requires. Not the crouching servility that the slave-master requires and receives, but the unconscious adaptation to the requisites of the street, or the parlor, which forms the law of good society, this they instinctively exhibit. Compare the manners of our African and Indian brethren. The latter are stiff, ungainly, feeling ill at ease, in house or city. The former slide instinctively into the best postures, looks, and actions, putting every one at ease in their own unconscious propriety.

In the culinary art they have no rivals. The French alone equal them in both these graces. No Anglo-Saxon touches by hard study that deft handling of the mysteries of the kitchen which his negro servant and slave attains by a sort of instinct. They will frequently introduce new dishes — a thing as rare in an ordinary housewife as the creation of a new world; and when asked where they learned these felicitous combinations, they reply, "Out of my own head." No cook-book helps them; for they cannot read. They make new dishes, as a Lowell or Browning makes new rhymes, or Mozart new melodies, by sheer instinct of genius.*

In other gifts they excel. In aptness of imitation, in wit and humor, in patience and sunniness of temper,† in fidelity and integrity, they are of the highest rank. Duplicity they have been trained in by the conduct of their oppressors; and this sin hangs to too large a degree around those who are relieved from its immediate temptation. In their ready reception of the Gospel in all its simple truth and heartiness, they are without an equal.

Such are the gifts and graces of those millions of our brethren whose oneness with us we declare to be most unnatural. Compare their character with those of other trans-Atlantic races, and then compare our feeling toward each.

* "Cooking is an indigenous talent of the African race."

"Now, there's Dinah gets you a capital dinner, — soup, ragout, roast fowl, dessert, ice-creams, and all, — and she creates it all out of chaos and old night." — *Uncle Tom's Cabin.*

† I never saw a negro angry, nor heard a word of profanity from his lips. Undoubtedly they fall into these sins. But their indulgence in them is most rare in comparison with that of their whiter brethren.

We profess no such aversion to the Asiatic tribes, or the Polynesian, or the various branches of the European family. A cultivated member of any of these families of men might move with perfect freedom in any of our circles.* Why should we so vehemently declare a prejudice to be founded in nature which puts a class far superior to many of these without the pale of humanity?

What is there, then, we solemnly ask, in view of these facts, in this portion of the human family, that justifies the idea so powerful in this and every American community, that they are, by divine decree, set forever apart and below the rest of mankind? Are they the children of Cain, bearing his mark on their foreheads? Much rather are their haughty oppressors his offspring. Theirs is the faith and fate of Abel.

(2.) On what do we base our dogma of necessary segregation? On color? What degree of color is requisite to enslave or liberate a man? Where is the Mason and Dixon's line among pigments,—on one side of which a man is changed from a brother to a beast, and crossing which,—if he can cross it, as many do,—transforms a beast into a brother? Where run the boundaries that put a son of Adam, of Noah, of God, among another order of beings than the rest of his brethren? Will not this border line, in its course, enter the families of proud-blooded Caucasians, and set husband against wife, father against daughter, brother against sister? Does it not to-day, in many a household in this land, make one half of the family the property of the other? † Will not this law go yet further, and give the lightest complexioned race dominion over their darker kindred? Cannot

* This was confirmed by the visit to America of the Queen of the Sandwich Islands, in 1864, as well as that of Japanese and Chinese embassadors. All of these were received freely into our best society, and all of them were far less attractive in contour of face, or even complexion, as well as in manners, than the better class of Afric-Americans.

† See Note VI.

England quote this plea as the conclusive argument for its subjugation of Ireland, the yellow-haired Saxon being the natural superior of the dark-skined Celt? How like an unsubstantial shadow, as it is, does this fantasy fade into nothingness before the clear and sober light of reason!

But say you, "Other physical features—the contour of face, or head, or foot, some real or fancied divergence from the Caucasian model—are proofs that God never designed we should live as one family on the closest and most sacred terms of intimacy." How do you know they are proofs? Is there a suggestion in the Word of God, is there an impulse in the universal heart, is there an instinctive abhorrence, mutual and potent, as it must be, if it is an instinct, in regions where both classes abound. We all know that these questions cannot be answered in the affirmative. The Bible teaches no such doctrine. The conscience utters no such decree. The world has recognized no such law. Ethiopia swayed the world from Memphis. Ham ruled all mankind from Nineveh and Phœnicia and Carthage.* The loves of the Shemite Æneas and the Hamite Dido (for the Phœnicians were of Ham's family) were celebrated by the daintiest scholar of imperial Rome, the Japhethite Virgil. Black Ethiopians held generalships in Roman armies, professorships in Greek schools, and bishoprics in Christian churches. Men with all their physical peculiarities founded empires, and the blood of Europe's nobility and royalty, your own blood, if traced far enough, may be found to possess this direful drop of tainted color.

(3.) If no physical reason can be given for this deep-rooted prejudice, the argument in its favor is still more fallacious, when we look at the real nature of humanity. The soul's dress is the body—dress like that the body itself wears, of all shades, from black to white, and all shades alike

* See article in the Methodist Quarterly, for January, 1869, entitled "The Negro in History;" written by Professor Blyden, of Liberia College, a gentleman of pure African origin.

agreeable and comely. It is a dress in which God, and not our own vanity, has arrayed our spirits, and therefore, so far from being a ground of repulsion, it ought not to offer any barrier to the perfect communion of those it clothes. Are there natural, vital, eternal distinctions in the spiritual being of man? All confess there are none. When we meet these outcasts at the table of the Lord, when we hear their experiences of Christ in all these highest exercises of the mind and heart, there is no knowledge of black or white. All are one in Christ Jesus.

(4.) But again you will say, "If this is not unnatural, why does it so powerfully possess the national heart?" I answer, Because of their social condition. Two things chiefly create this prejudice among nations — religion and social condition. Religion may breed caste. You do not abhor the black to-day any more than the Christian of the middle ages abhorred the Jew, or than the Jew in earlier ages abhorred the Christian. Neither would have treated the other, when he was in the supremacy, with any more respect than a Southern white man now treats his colored brother. Each would have felt the heaviest curse resting upon him, had he admitted his religious antagonist to his table or his bed. Thus, too, the Mohammedan, in the days of his power, and where he still holds undisputed sway, treats his Christian brother. "Dog" and "infidel" are his best compliments, death his best hospitality. Thus, in India, religion builds its mighty walls between the same blood. Men whom you cannot distinguish apart in complexion, or any feature, are separated by a gulf which it is death, and worse, to attempt to span.

Social condition breeds the same feeling. The English Norman would have felt unutterable disgust had his Saxon neighbor claimed social equality and intimacy. To this day the English noble, or even gentleman, would profess that he had a "natural" aversion to the serf, though of one parentage a few generations back. So a rich, especially if an old, family among us feels toward its poor neighbor, though equally old and as truly honorable. The members of it may meet in the same party, and attend the same church, but for the rich man to invite his poorer brother to his table, for his family to associate with his neighbors on perfect equality, is a grace far above their attainment.

Their social status has wrought this prejudice in us. It is the lowest any class can occupy toward their fellows. They are slaves. And as the Egyptians loathed the Jews, their whiter neighbors, because they were their slaves, as Greeks and Romans shrunk from fraternal communion with their slaves, though of their own blood, so we have allowed this condition to work in us its baleful power. They are slaves, bought and sold. We are free. The separation is immeasurable.

Of course, if those who are in slavery have a difference of appearance added to their condition, we should very readily defend ourselves on the plea that this appearance was the *cause* of slavery, and that thus we were separated, not by condition only, but by *nature*. And from this we should easily conclude that they were by race necessarily removed from us, and there could be no community of interest, or friendship, or life.

Hence arises American caste. The slave is black. The free are white. If the slave is black, then the black man is, and of right ought to be, a slave. If the black man ought to be a slave, and the white man free, then there is a vital, natural and eternal distinction between them — a great gulf fixed by God.

Thus the diabolic argument is framed, and our consciences seared as with a hot iron. Slavery alone has caused this creed; its abolition, as all history attests, will cause its destruction.

(5.) Another proof that this aversion is unnatural is, that

it is largely confined to countries where the black man is a slave. No strong prejudice exists in Europe. Queen Victoria, at the marriage of her eldest daughter, placed in a prominent position among her retinue a black lady, a princess from Africa. A black man sits in the legislative chamber of France. Students of this color are in the English universities, and in the society of Propaganda at Rome. Dumas, the most popular of French writers, is the grandson of a negro, and possesses marked African features. Fugitives from our shores melt into the current of European society as easily as their whiter brethren.*

If it is a natural sentiment, it must be universal. It must exist outside of the region that is cursed with a system which, in its living presence, or in its almost equally powerful memories, has wrought within us these convictions. As it has no such existence, it is contrary to nature.

(6.) Finally, we declare this prejudice unnatural because it is contrary to the Scriptures. The Scriptures never speak disrespectfully of the black race. "I am black, but comely," says Christ of Himself, in the Canticles. It says, "Can the Ethiopian change his skin?" — not because it is desirable, but because it is impossible. If you claim that a change is desired here, then it is also in the parallel passage, "or the leopard his spots." But as the skin of the leopard is the handsomest that clothes any animal, it may be intended to affirm that the skin of the Ethiopian is the handsomest of all human cuticles. The parallelism of the Hebrew writers would approve that conclusion.

* Later events multiply these instances. The most celebrated dragoman I met in Alexandria was as black a Nubian as was ever sold in Richmond, and far blacker than most of that property. Yet all rivals gave way to him as being far more accomplished, as well as more capable. Rev. Dr. Bellows commends, in his late Travels in the East, the beauty of the blacks of Cairo. Colored gentlemen's daughters, in Paris, are sued by white lovers as flatteringly and as earnestly as other ladies of wealth and position.

It finds no place in all Bible history. Solomon treated the Queen of Sheba, a negress of Abyssinia, with the utmost respect and cordiality; Philip ran reverently by the side of the chariot of a negro, the chief minister of the court of her successor; Moses married an Ethiopian; a negro was called of God and his brethren to be one of "the prophets and teachers of the church at Antioch," with Barnabas and the foster-brother of Herod, and was also called by the Holy Ghost to lay his hands, in company with those of his brethren, upon the heads of Paul and Barnabas—the first Christian ordination that is upon record, and one that our ministers would do well speedily to imitate.

More than this: the Bible constantly proclaims the absolute oneness of the race of man, in Adam, Noah, and Christ. Against this divine rock every wave of infidelity beats today, and beats in vain. Let the church, let every Christian, beware how they aid this assault of false science by a more false humanity. Cling to the central doctrine of the Word of God—one man, one Savior, one God. Whatever opposes or rejects this truth, reject and oppose it. Pluck out your right eye, if it sees, or professes to see, any separation among the children of men. Cut off your right hand, if it strikes down your brother because the same blood, and of the same color as your own, puts on a darker hue, but not unlovelier as it appears upon his countenance, than upon your own.

Thus falls the plea that this sin is according to nature. It was never heard of till within less than two hundred years, and then only within our territorial limits. It will never be heard of two hundred years hence; and in far less time than that, if the iniquity out of which it flourishes shall disappear. When slavery dies, this its child and parent, whose foul breast preserves its fouler life, shall fast follow it to its unholy grave. May God hasten to deliver the land from both abominations. Already is the mingling of the diverse complexions going forward. In the West Indies, so general is amalgamation that men and women of a culture and beauty, of a wealth and lineage, that the proudest Bostonian or Virginian would envy, boast of their mixed blood. The Chief Justice of Jamaica is of this origin. No reflection on color is allowed in any fashionable circle in that island. It would be a taunt at many of the gentlemen and ladies in the assembly.

In Brazil, so utterly extinct is this prejudice, — if it ever existed, — that the black and mixed bloods are in the highest national offices. When Governor Wise, of Virginia, was sent as minister to Brazil, his wife was compelled to accept the service of a colored physician to escort her to the shore, whom she would have flogged at home for assuming such a profession, or if he had not bowed his head, and spoken in the most cringing manner, with the enforced dialect of his brethren.

4. The great objection to this feeling is, that it is almost the sole bulwark of slavery. Other systems of slavery are based on other pretensions. The slaves of India are held in that estate by the combined strength of wars and creeds: the ruling class having subdued the aboriginal peoples in war, and then bound them in the fetters of caste. Slavery in Russia is simply that of noble and serf. Our slavery can have no such basis. Slaves are not captives of war waged by present masters. They are not separated in their religious life by form, or ceremony, or creed, although many attempts are made to create such distinctions. The glorious Gospel of the blessed God, much as it has been perverted and suppressed, there and here, in its teachings and inspirations as to the oneness of man, and especially of all believers, has often broken through this wall of prejudice, and both theoretically and practically compelled the white to recognize his slave as his brother. Colored churches, pews, galleries, and all the other high walls and huge that

the enemy has erected in the house of God, sometimes disappear like walls of black cloud before the powerful beams of the Sun of Righteousness and of love.

The only basis of this system is the divinely ordained separation of the colored man from his whiter brother. Were they white, they could not be kept in slavery a year. But the South says, "They are so distinct a people that it is impossible for us to ever mingle together." How the complexion of their slaves gives the lie to this pretense! "If they are so distinct a people, they cannot become one with us by any process. If inferior, we must be their natural protectors; if protectors, possessors. If they were not created equal, they are perpetual servants, and involuntary servitude is thus entailed upon them and their children forever. We will make this paternal, patriarchal, considerate as possible, but we cannot change fate." Thus, from our cruelty of soul toward our brother's face springs forth the horrid form of chattel slavery. We may abhor the conclusion. We consent to its basis. Only by denying the premise, earnestly, practically, constantly, shall we escape the fatal snare that makes us dumb and powerless before these enemies of the human race and its Divine Father.

The South could not long withstand the influence of the Free North, were we not thus partakers in this sin — its feeders and nurturers. When they observe, with all our abolitionism, no recognition of the unity of man; when they see these, our brethren, set apart in churches and schools, or, if allowed to enter our churches, driven into the lowest seats; when they behold every avenue of honorable effort shut against them, — that no clerk of this complexion is endured in our stores, no apprentice in our workshops, no teacher in our schools, no physician at our sick-beds, no minister in our pulpits, — how can we reproach them for their sins, or urge them to repentance? Where is there a colored family dwelling in perfect intimacy with its neighbors? Where is there a friendly party in which they appear as welcome and equal guests? Where is the neighborhood, we might almost ask, the person, who communes with this brother, heart in heart, neither noticing nor thinking of the difference of complexion? How deep, how wide-spreading, how exceeding bitter, are these roots of bitterness!

Till this iniquity is done away, we are verily guilty concerning our brother. We are speechless before Southern effrontery and sophistry. We are approving and acting upon the very ideas they faithfully carry out in their laws, their customs, their "domestic institution." When our churches are not based on the practical disunity of the race, when our workshops, our stores, our juries, our halls of legislation, our family relations, give no evidence of the existence of this iniquity in our hearts or lives, then we can say to our Southern brethren, "Go thou and do likewise." When Frederic Douglass stands in Congress, with other members, and above them, as he will stand when he arrives there; when Charles Remond can move in the circle to which his wealth and culture give him the passport; when Dr. Pennington is settled over a congregation of faithful worshipers of every hue and one heart; when we see our colored brethren moving around our conference appointments with no more thought of their color than there is of those who now occupy them; when these things are witnessed among us, we shall no longer need to entertain this topic as a subject of humiliation, fasting, and prayer. Till then, we must humble ourselves, and pray earnestly for our deliverance from the chains of a bondage so inhuman and ungodly.

But you may say, "My prejudice has nothing to do with this iniquity. Can there not be equality without fraternity?" Certainly, but not without capacity for fraternity, if the necessary conditions are fulfilled. For instance: A rich democrat may grant that his poor political brother is his essential equal, and yet not fraternize with him. But if he says that brother's hair, or eyes, or contour, or complexion, is such, that if every other disability were removed, — poverty, ignorance, and rudeness, — he could not, nor could his family, for a thousand generations, be his real companion and brother, — such a democrat could never believe in the real equality of his poorer kinsman with himself. So, if we say the colored man is our equal, but we will never fraternize with him; never invite him to our houses and tables; never give him a seat in our pulpits or pews; never have him as our teacher or pupil, as our apprentice or master-workman, — all our talk about equality, without fraternity, is a mockery and a lie.

Hence it is that the great majority of those who go South, not having wrought into them this sense of his perfect equality with us in all the essentials of manhood, but looking on him as of an outcast race, are powerless before the sophistries of the slavocrat, and soon concede that the system is necessary in order to their existence, while it is necessary solely because of this wicked feeling that pervades the whole land.

Thus, my friends, we have carefully and honestly examined this feeling of aversion to our colored brethren, as of one blood and destiny with ourselves, in the light of history, of reason, of the general sentiment of mankind, of the Scriptures, and of the strength which it gives to the system of Slavery. All of them condemn it. Notwithstanding its depth and universality with us, it is unnatural and inhuman. It is the great author and sustainer of slavery, its chief corner-stone, and the cement of its walls. It must die before this great crime fully ends.

In the divine condemnation, are we not ourselves included? We, so active in political strife for Northern supremacy, so furious against Southern aggression — "We are verily guilty concerning our brother." We refuse to call him our brother in our heart and in our life.

We treat him far worse than the children of Jacob did their brother, and must yet, for this conduct, meet, as did they, the judgments of a just and angry God.

III. What is the cure of Slavery? Not Kansas; not presidential triumphs; not reversals of the infamous decisions of a packed and slavish court; not the removal of wicked judges from the seat they have stained with their shameful edicts; not the complete triumph of Anti-slavery in all the National Councils, so that Freedom shall be national, as it now is sectional. None of these things will completely extinguish this horror of sin. Four millions of persons will yet be held in profitable, in unspeakable, bondage. The wealth, and fashion, and refinement of the slaveholder will control the whole land as it does to-day; for Charleston and Richmond give tone to the fashion of the nation. Fifth Avenue and Beacon Street submit to their sway as easily as the rich manufacturers and merchants of England follow the style set by their nobility; as easily as our new rich men imitate, as far as possible, the style of those who have grown up amid the refinements of wealth and luxury. We shall still hate and despise those who have any drops of African blood in their veins. We must do these first duties in politics, and in the Church, but we must not leave the great duty undone. We must extirpate this prejudice from our hearts. We must set the reason, the conscience, against this sentiment, and work all their power till it is completely obliterated.

But you may ask, How shall I begin the cure?

1. By resolving to think no more of the color of the skin than you do of the eyes, and to like its color, as you do that of the eyes. Look at the heart, at the divine likeness there, and let your feelings be excited only by sympathy with its virtues.

2. You must be willing to welcome them to your house and table, if they are worthy of such a welcome. You must give them this hospitality, if they have been prevented

by the prejudices of society from attaining that style of manners which you see they are capable of reaching under proper encouragement. I do not say that every one possessing this blood should be thus treated. Our tastes differ in our friendships as in our food. Only those whose native traits resemble yours, or such as are agreeable to you, are you under obligation to admit to this intimacy. But you must not let your unnatural aversion keep you from doing this social duty. You must admit them, if otherwise agreeable, to all these rights and privileges. You will find them among the most charming of all the guests of your family. They will prove the shining lights of your table.

But last Sabbath, I had the pleasure of introducing a brother minister — a fugitive slave — to the table where I was a guest; and, though many others surrounded that table, none surpassed or equaled him in giving animation to the hour. Among the many who honor my house and table with their presence, none have more refinement, originality of thought and language, rich and playful natures, and none give more elevation to the society, in piety or in talents, than some of these despised men and women You lose some of the best opportunities to enliven and improve your social life by refusing these kindred spirits an equal place at your board. If you could have the humor of an Irving, the wit of a Holmes, or the refinement of an Everett, to adorn your table, you would feel that you were exalted by their presence. I know of some of these so-called repulsive men and women whose wit is as brilliant as Mrs. Stowe's, whose manners are as refined as Everett's, whose conversation is a perfect mine of genial sportfulness and clear-headed wisdom.*

3. You must go further than this. They have a right, and ought to be encouraged, to enter the various paths of indus-

* Among these visitors was one since famous in all the land — Sojourner Truth. She is an admirable guest, full of genius and of grace.

try and enterprise. Where is the colored clerk, the colored apprentice, the colored foreman, or physician, or preacher, that practices his vocation among his whiter brethren? True, these men are found, but only among and for those of their own color. You can find them in Brattle Street, and behind the West End aristocracy of Boston, like the kitchen behind and below the parlor; but that is no better, nor as good, a position as their free brothers hold in the South. You must give them a chance to develop their talents. The ablest salesman in a large wholesale house, in a city where I once resided, was a colored man; but he was only allowed the name and salary of a porter, notwithstanding his acknowledged capacity. We should put the smart and intelligent colored boy or girl into just as good stations, and open before them just as good opportunities, as their white playmates have. In one of the outer schools of Northampton I saw a very handsome colored lad. He surpassed all his schoolmates in every attraction, and, had he had equal chances, would have surpassed them in the struggles of manhood. But his superiority ended there. They could go to the town, to Boston, to New York, and, by force of character and favorable circumstances, could rise to wealth and social power. The majority of the present rulers of this region were poor back country children. Had their dusky playmates had equal chances, they would hold now equal, if not superior, positions. We have a poor shoemaker leading our State at Washington; a poor mill-boy and machinist leading it at home. If these men had had the least drop of Afric's blood, with all their present abilities, — yea, with vastly greater abilities, — they would never have been allowed to be even a poor shoemaker or mill-boy. These offices are too high for the colored man.

We curse them with a bitterer curse than any proud empire of Europe lays on its lowest population. England's nobles, in not a few instances, are children of the lowest class. Sir Robert Peel's grandfather was a poor hireling; Napoleon's counselors and generals, and Austria's greatest chieftain, — Radetzky, — were from the lowest class. Slaves born, and still held as slaves, are among the first officers of Russia; men who pay twenty thousand dollars a year to their owners as a rent for themselves, and grow rich with that deduction from their income. But with us, if a colored man becomes rich, it is in a low or contraband way, and his riches give him no ingress to society, which his talents and accomplishments merit and demand.

The South is superior to us in this matter of prejudice, for the same reason that the Tories of England are more liberal in their treatment of their ignoble associates than their rivals, because, though they make a Jew their parliamentary leader, there is yet a great gulf betwixt him and the nobility. So the slaveholder, despising all labor, can make his slave his overseer or master workman. The Northern workman, living by labor, is foolishly sensitive lest the South should make him one with the black, if he admitted the black to be one with him. These things ought not so to be. Let them enter not above, but according to their ability; let the simple take the simple's place, the able, the able's.

IV. But you will say this social, business, and political equality may lead to another, the very thought of which is insufferable. My friends, all I have said is, I am aware, very unpalatable to you. It would be insufferable if spoken two hundred miles south of us. It could not have been spoken below Washington, nor there save by one protected by the State whom he represents. We must not fear to declare the whole counsel of God in this matter. The question that has been uppermost in your hearts in all this discourse, that will leap from your lips as soon as their enforced silence is broken, let us briefly and calmly consider. When Governor Banks, by whose authority we meet to-day,* was asked

* At Roxbury, 1856.

by the Southern catechist, when he was a candidate for the Speaker's chair, in order to cover him with infamy, whether he believed in amalgamation, with a promptness, independence, and courage, that but few ministers of the Gospel, and fewer of any other class, would have exhibited, he answered, that "the more powerful race would absorb the weaker, and it was an undecided question of physiology yet, which was the stronger." So, when you ask us if we believe in the intermarriage of the races, we answer, True marriage is a divine institution. Such hearts are knit together by the hand that originally wove them in separate but half-finished webs. God makes this unity. If He does not, then it is a conventional, human thing, subject to the whims of human society. As it respects such marriage, all I need to say is, "It is none of our business. It is the business of the two souls that are thus made one by the goodness and greatness of their Creator." Parents have advisory power to a certain extent. If it is not of God, but only of transient passion, of pride, of ambition, of desire for wealth, then parents may have complete, or nearly complete, control until their children have attained a legal age. But if heart is one with heart, then with Shakspeare must you say,—

> "Let me not to the marriage of true souls
> Admit impediment."

That greatest of poets and thinkers carries this principle to its full expression in the marriage of the most womanly of his women and the most manly of his men. He sets the loves of Desdemona and Othello far above the range of groveling criticism. The whole story of that event seems to have been made for our land and hour. It is a protest against this curse such as no subsequent poet in all literature has ever attained. Read it and see the feelings of the American heart painted and denounced by this master of human nature.

Desdemona's father, a rich and proud Venetian, full of the spirit of caste, like many such a father in this nation to-day, when he learned of his daughter's secret marriage, cries out thus against her distinguished and noble husband: —

"O thou foul thief, where hast thou stowed my daughter?
Damned as thou art, thou hast enchanted her;
For I'll refer me to all things of sense,
If she in chains of magic were not bound,
Whether a maid so tender, fair, and happy,
So opposite to marriage, that she shunned
The wealthy curléd darlings of her nation,
Would ever have to incur the general mock,
Run from her guardage to the sooty bosom
Of such a thing as thou!"

In his unrestrained rage he again bursts out: —

"That she, in spite of nature,
Of years, of country, credit, everything,
To fall in love with what she feared to look on!
It is a judgment maimed and most imperfect
That will confess perfection so could err
Against all rules of nature, and must be driven
To find out practices of cunning hell
Why this should be."

To this storming American, Othello before the Duke makes reply — a reply so dignified, so manly, so majestic in rhythm and in feeling, that it seems as if Shakspeare felt that he was pleading for God and humanity against the contemptible prejudices of this age and nation. The great Duke, at the close of Othello's speech, says truly, as you and every one unprejudiced would have said, —

"I think this tale would win my daughter too."

Even Brabantio, her father, softens in his prejudices, and declares, —

If she confess that she was half the wooer,
Destruction on my head, if my bad blame
Light on the man."

And after Desdemona's frank acknowledgment of her love, he generously gives her to him "with all his heart" — an example many a now wrathful father among us will yet faithfully follow.

In all cases of true affection, this higher law than man's must have sway. If God makes such marriages between the white and the colored, who art thou that refusest to bless His bands? Such marriages, Heaven-made and blessed, have occurred. In Jamaica, in Brazil, in Mexico, happy souls, whose outward hue is varied, whose inward blood arises from remote fountains, are made one in a perfect marriage. In our own land it is already no uncommon thing.

The necessities of the heart demand it. The loveliest maidens of the South are often of mixed blood. A pure and noble man will seek a pure and noble mate, and he is more apt to find her in that class than any other, for the pride and bitterness of the white and slaveholding women do not defile her soul. Society lays its heavy hand on his affections and crushes them. It lays its hellish laws on her, and despoils her of her virtue, so far as she can lose it, against every remonstrance of her whole nature. Here and there a rich man rises superior to society, and abides honorably to his love and vows, though no minister will consecrate them. Said a clergyman to Mrs. Johnson, the God-given wife of Vice-President Richard M. Johnson, "You cannot join the Church, because you have not been married." She told her husband what had been said to her. He replied, "Tell your minister, my dear, that I am ready, and always have been, to be publicly married, and ask him to come and marry us this very night." The clergyman dared not do his duty, even at the request of one so high in station. Thus he kept a Christian woman from the Church for a sin which he and his Church fastened upon her. No wonder that her husband, in his official career, hurled indignant epithets at the Church, and died without its pale. Many a man, were this curse removed, would follow his honorable instincts, and rejoice in the wife of his love and youth, proud of the very charms her tropical blood has given her. When slavery dies, this prejudice will die. There will be no more objection to this blood, if its possessor is attractive, than the long bigoted New Englander or Englishman objects to his heart's love, though every drop of her blood flows from foreign fountains. The grand ladies of the South will yet be the mixed bloods of that region, and many a white, fastidious, and wealthy Solomon will solicit the duskier, yet none the less loving and lovely daughter of Pharaoh, to give his house her perpetual blessing.

I have spoken, my friends, with great plainness of speech, my honest, and earnest, and long-held convictions on this subject. I believe that caste is the great sin of this nation, and that it is the great duty of every one to extirpate it first from himself, and then from every heart which he can influence. The reform must begin here. I rejoice that it has begun. We have abolished from the statute books laws forbidding intermarriage, creating separate schools, and depriving them of the right of suffrage and office. In the eye of the law they are equal; but the Gospel must effect "what the law cannot do, in that it is weak through the flesh." It must work its perfect work. We must feel the brotherhood of man. We must sympathize with the most oppressed of the human family.

The African has been despised and rejected of men, for the same reason that woman has been. Not because of lack of talent, but excess of a submissive, peaceful, religious spirit. Had he been as bloodthirsty as the Indian, he would have been as free. His elements are needed to make the perfect man. He is the John of the Apostles, milder than the rest, yet superior to all of them in many of the highest traits of soul.

We may justly lament the aggressions of the slave power.

We may be surprised at their open robbery from the North of its acquired and conceded territories. We may be horror-struck at the sight of president, cabinet, and grave senators, hastening to break obligations as solemn and reverend as oaths at the marriage altar, or on the bed of death. We may lift our voice against these crimes. We may struggle manfully to repel this invading abomination. But we cannot expect, we shall never see, the complete removal of this curse from our land until we stand boldly and heartily upon the divine foundation — the perfect unity of the human race.*

In dragging up our brother from this horrible pit of mire and clay, — this bottomless pit of death and despair, — into which we have cast him, we shall find ourselves compelled to move higher and higher in our apprehension and adoption of the principle and obligations of human brotherhood. We cannot, by a cord coiled around our feet, raise him up so that he shall stand where we stand, and no higher; but we must take him in our arms, and bear him with us, on and up into all the light and liberty with which God shall crown our path. Till then shall the nations hear of our shame. Till then our cry shall fill all lands. Till then shall, as now, the mighty man stumble against the mighty, and both fall together.

Let us not turn from this truth with loathing. Let us look our cruelties in the face. Let us look our duties in the face. Let us look stern facts in the face. Over four millions of this people are here. What are you going to do with them? Send them to Africa? If they should agree to go, and great ocean steamers carried them all there, it would take eight thousand such steamers, or that number of voyages, to

* The whole course of the war, and of reconstruction since, is the comment on this declaration. Only as we advanced to these truths did our cause prosper, and only when we "boldly and heartily" embraced them did we triumph. The completion of this work and success yet await the Church and society.

transport them. They will never leave us nor forsake us. A handful may go, as a few of us go to California; but the millions will stay. Even if colonization could be carried out, it would not cure the evil. It would intensify it. If every son and daughter of Africa, however far removed by Anglo-Saxon intermixture from their original blood, were removed to those shores, it would only make the feeling more bitter. The unnatural doctrine of natural distinctions would be sustained, and Christianity would have no perfect sway in the earth. They must abide with us till we acknowledge by word and act that they are one with us. And when we confess and embrace them as brothers, we shall never listen to their expatriation. The idea will be as abhorrent as the expulsion of your own children from your arms, or your wife from your bosom. God will keep them with us till He has cured us of our sins. Then shall we rejoice to abide with them always, and to build up a grand nationality of one humanity, of one language, having one Redeemer, and one future on earth, and, if in Christ, forever.

Do you still ask, What shall we do? You can do but one thing — your duty —as Christians, as men. Be honest, be honorable, feel yourselves one with these children of your earthly and heavenly Father. Follow Christ, and He will guide and bless you.

Thus shall you cure the sin of sins that so fearfully possesses our nation. Thus will love subdue hate, and the slaveholder, beholding your conquest over your prejudices, will approve your course, and vie with you in giving his slave that which is just and equal. Then shall we stand forth before the world, a nation where civil and social equality and fraternity, where the humanity of man, is the passport to every station.

Purge yourself of this old leaven, as Paul had to purge himself of his prejudice against the Gentiles, as the Athenians had to purge themselves of their disgust at his proclamation that God made of one blood all nations of men, — Greek and Barbarian, Scythian and Jew, — a proposition offensive beyond conception to those cultivated and contracted spirits. Let us each see that we are without sin concerning our brother. Labor to make others equally free from prejudice, and equally ready to build up on the solid foundations of the Oneness of Man such a power as shall strengthen every part of the army of freedom, and shall melt the hearts of those who hold our brethren in bondage. Then shall the cloud, surcharged with thunder and fire, that is settling down over those Southern plains, be lifted, and peaceful Emancipation shall be proclaimed, with its growing train of unspeakable blessings, throughout all the land, to all the inhabitants thereof.

Such is our duty. It is enough for us to know it. As said the Iron Duke to his clerical inquirer, who asked if he ought to go as a missionary to India, "How read your orders?" So should every soul say, What is duty? If heart and flesh revolt, if the world sneers, and frowns; if we are doomed to tread a solitary path with mocking sons of Belial assailing us, God give us grace to move onward and upward in the only way which will relieve our land of its curse, and make all nations see and acknowledge its glory.

Thus acting, of you, and to you, a Voice from out the golden cloud of the Divine nature will sound sweet and deep through your humble, happy soul, —

"Servant of God, well done! Well hast thou fought
The better fight, who singly hast maintained
Against revolted multitudes the cause
Of truth, in word mightier than they in arms,
And for the testimony of the truth hast borne
Universal reproach, far worse to bear
Than violence; for this was all thy care, —
To stand approved in sight of God, though worlds
Judged thee perverse."

THE BEGINNING OF THE END.*

"Surely oppression maketh a wise man mad." — *Eccl.* vii. 7.

"I am not mad, most noble Festus." — *Acts* xxvi. 25.

"So I returned, and considered all the oppressions that are done under the sun: and behold, the tears of such as were oppressed, and they had no comforter; and on the side of their oppressors there was power, but they had no comforter. Wherefore I praised the dead which are already dead, more than the living which are yet alive." — *Eccl.* iv. 1, 2.

NEW act opens in the great drama of the rights and destiny of humanity, which is now being performed by this nation, in the presence of an astonished world. It opens with a sound of war, a cry for blood. Is it the last act of the tragedy, when deaths are frequent; where the innocent first fall, the wicked follow; or is it but a slight interruption to the former movement, and without effect on that which shall come after? Let us consider it in the sacred light that falls upon us from Heaven. Let us dwell upon it in no frivolous spirit, but in deep solemnity.

* A sermon preached at Harvard Street Methodist Episcopal Church, Cambridge, November 6, 1859, on the occasion of the capture at Harper's Ferry of Captain John Brown and his associates. See Note VII.

"Things now,
That bear a weighty and a serious brow,
Sad, high, and working, full of state and woe,
Such noble scenes as draw the eye to flow,
We now present."

Let us keep before us the great fact — the violent enslavement of forty hundreds of thousands of our kindred in the flesh and in the Lord, in Adam and in Christ. Let us not forget what this system is and does; how it thrusts its miscreated front athwart the path of all national and religious progress, breaks churches to pieces, rules and ruins great Christian charities; and above, beyond all this, sets its satanic foot on man, created in the image of God, crushes out his freedom, his culture, his piety, his every God-given right and privilege. Connect with this defiant, triumphant on-marching institution of perdition this little act of a score of men, and see if, and how, such a small stone can indeed sink into the forehead of the mighty Goliath and smite him to the dust. And may God help us to speak and hear in all sincerity and godly fear.

You all know the published history of the transaction. About twenty men, led by one before famous, now immortal, seized a few slaveholders, and a United States arsenal, delivered a few score of slaves, were taken, most of the number instantly killed, a few captured, their leader tried, condemned, and sentenced to be hanged. That is all. How can this, you may say, be the beginning of the end of American Slavery? A glance at the excitement it has created may guide you to a perception of this great fact.

Not less than three orations upon it were published in the papers of last week; every journal has abounded with editorials upon it; every political speech has been burdened with attempts to fasten it upon their opponents and ward it off from themselves. Within a month, ten thousand thanksgiving sermons will dwell upon its lessons. Every car and tongue, from Galveston to Eastport, is on fire for every item pertaining to it. Never has any single event in our annals so enthralled the whole nation. The court of justice instantly takes up the wondrous tale. With an astounding speed it connects itself with the moans of the wounded and bereaved, drags its bleeding prisoners to its bar, refuses all demands for needed and brief delay, heeds no claim of judicial impartiality, driving its deadly business at this fearful rate, and only breathing freely when it has pronounced over the doomed gray head the sentence of death. Nay, it does not breathe freely yet. He is in prison, and the centurion and his band keep watch day and night over him, lest his friends come and steal him away, and the last error be worse than the first. Whether released or hung, his influence has but just begun. If dead, he will speak as no dead have spoken in this land, since Warren fell asleep in his bloody shroud. If alive and in prison, to no walls will such a multitude of earnest eyes be aimed as to those that shut him in. If at liberty, his steps will be followed by myriads of sympathizing friends or curious foes.

What does all this mean? What does it portend? Is it simply the excitement of politics, which periodically ebbs and flows? Politicians may seek to use and abuse it; but the feeling that produced it, and that it has produced, is vastly greater than any they can create or control. Theirs is but the tiny vessel, — Great Eastern though it be, — this is of the mighty upheaval of the ocean underneath. The vessel may reach its desired haven, or go down among the billows it has sought to ride; the waves sweep on, under the laws of their Creator, to the goal He has set for them. Is it the ordinary excitement over a murderous riot? Other riots are constantly occurring. One has transpired since this event, by which several men were killed and wounded, and a great city surrendered to a lawless mob; and yet a brief telegram satisfies the general hunger for the bloody feast.

Why this difference? Because the one is exceptional, transient, easily and palpably curable; the other connects itself with the great iniquity that covers half, and darkens all the land. It is the first blow that gigantic power ever felt. It is a blow from which it cannot recover. How is this the case? How can this brief, and apparently unsuccessful, act be considered as the beginning of that long-prayed for — we can hardly say, long looked-for hour, the death of Slavery? For two reasons: —

I. 1. It has taught the slaveholders their weakness. Never has such trembling shaken their knees before. Never has such a thrill of horror made so many great States to quake. Over fifteen States, over a million of square miles, there has run one feeling, one fear, one Belshazzar sense of awful guilt, and awful weakness, and awful punishment. That handwriting on the wall of the great Southern palace of pleasure needed no slave prophet, like Daniel, to interpret it. They understood its meaning; they feared its instant accomplishment. Their action, or want of action, in this conflict, has placed them before the world as totally incapable of defending themselves against any moderately well-devised and well-executed rising of the slaves. Had John Brown been half as successful as he anticipated, had but five hundred slaves joined him there, he could have marched to New Orleans, freeing all the slaves on his way, for all the slaveholders could have done to stop him. His folly appears to be, not in counting on the weakness of the South, but in neglecting to count on the strength of the Federal arm.

Well may they tremble. They are but men — men most guilty, and therefore most weak. We who are so free with our gibes, would be palsied with equal horror and faintness, if we stood on the same rocking and cleaving soil, over the same mine which we had wickedly filled with deadly explosives, as we saw the torch approaching it.

"Thus conscience doth make cowards of us all."

Suppose you had stolen a man's wages from his youth, had trampled out his manhood, beat him often and cruelly, robbed him of his wife and children and sold them from his arms, — how would you feel if you saw, or dreamed you saw, that man stand before you, rifle in hand, demanding his freedom? This is their condition. They slept but little before, they will sleep less now. The planters in the vicinity of the outbreak dare not spend the night on their plantations. They flee when no man pursueth. Let us not revile them. Let us with larger, and so tenderer, heart lament their state, while we call them, by these fears, to repentance. They may thus be led thither. The terrors of the Lord have persuaded multitudes of men to be holy. God surrounds all His laws with great punishments, so that those who will not be led by love may be driven by fear. May we not hope that this sense of helplessness, and dread of the just vengeance of their oppressed brethren, will persuade them to give them that which is just and equal?

Had Pharaoh hearkened to his fears, he would have emancipated his bondmen before the great wrath of God fell so awfully upon him. So, if these Pharaohs, who have so long combined against the Lord and against His children, will but heed these feelings of danger and powerlessness that their loving Creator has given them, as warnings and incentives to duty, they will instantly inaugurate the work of emancipation.

Mr. Thackeray has said that Great Britain, in the Revolution, never overcame the influence of Bunker's Hill. Much less will the slaveholders overcome Harper's Ferry. Whether bloodier outbreaks follow, or more peaceful counsels prevail, be assured that the lessons of this hour will not be lost on them. They may, for a season, wear the bold face they have borne so long. They may still utter great swelling words of vanity, and defy the armies and the truths of the living God, but their hearts are moved out of their place;

there is no strength in them. The march of the cause of emancipation is far from being stayed by this affair. Crazy, and broken with age and grief, as everybody seems so anxious to paint the leader of this band, that they may defend themselves from all complicity in his plans, he has taught the haughty South what she cannot, dare not forget. His apparition will undoubtedly incite them to the work God will yet perform through them, or over them.

2. The second reason for considering this the beginning of the end of this accursed crime against God and man, is the confidence it will breathe into the slave. If England never forgot Bunker's Hill, much more America never did. The sight of the falling or fleeing forms of their arrayed oppressors, on that memorable day, never lost its tremendous power over their hearts. So the millions of the enslaved will never forget the dismay, which turned the hearts of their masters to water, at the first gleaming of the rifle, the first stern demand for Freedom. Harper's Ferry is the turning-point in their history. Though they responded but feebly, though they have maintained a most wonderful silence since, though they seem to be the only cool men in the whole country, excepting their would-be deliverer, still they are not feelingless, they are not thoughtless. We sneer at them because they did not avail themselves of this opportunity, at the same time that we brand Captain Brown with insanity for offering it to them. Wiser thoughts will find less fault with both parties. The slaves are men. As one born to that fate said, centuries ago, amid the applause of a vast theater of slaveholders, "I am a man; nothing human is foreign from me."* They are *but* men, and, therefore, like all the white races, however much they may say they prefer liberty to death, they will want some well-grounded hope of obtaining that liberty before they imperil their lives. See Hungary to-day, rest-

* Terence was a slave in Rome.

less yet warless, in the talons of Austria; Rome, under the cloven hoof of the pope; France, in the clutch of Napoleon. Our slave brethren are of like passions with ourselves. They have acted wisely; they bide their time; it will come.

This great deed, as it must and ought to appear in their eyes, will be talked of in every cabin. The underground telegraph will carry the tidings where no underground railroad yet runs its blessed trains of liberty. The two chief features of the event — the interposition of Northern white men for their deliverance, the ghastly fright and feebleness of their masters — will leave an indelible impress on their hearts. Their consciousness of their rights as men will grow mightily under the influence of the fact that those of the same race as their oppressors are willing to die, if need be, for their redemption. The consciousness of their strength will grow with equal rapidity, when they see thousands of these armed masters trembling before a dozen wounded and imprisoned men, and compelled, by their fears, to let a handful of troops, mostly foreigners, win their battles.

You may say, Is not all this wrong? Has the slave any right to demand his freedom? We are not now defending theories, we are only stating facts. We are showing the grounds for our belief that this movement is to hasten the glad day of universal emancipation. Yet we do not shrink from answering the question. The slave *has* a right to demand his freedom. They have a right to unite in this demand. They have a right to fight for it if it is refused them. It is not their uprising that is to be condemned — it is the resistance to that uprising. It is the master, throttling the slave, and thrusting him into a bloody grave, if he dare say, "I will be free!" that is the great criminal before God and man; not the slave, claiming to exercise his inherent and inalienable rights, and resisting all who oppose him.

Can you find fault with this, you, whose government is based on that great sentence wrought out in the fires of a fierce rebellion, "*All* men are created free and equal"? You, whose highest boast is, that you descend from *revolutionary* fathers, whose greatest holiday is that whereon they proclaimed their independence from an ancient but unjust power, whose whole creed, of whatever party — Democratic, American, or Republican — is, "All government must be based on the consent of the governed"? "Who is blind, like my servant, or deaf, as the messenger I have sent?" You do not shrink from applying your formula to Italy, to France, to Ireland, everywhere, save to your own countrymen, whose fathers were as valiant as ours, in that insurrection against Britain.

But we dare not say that wicked thing, and sin against God. We dare not affirm that any child of Adam, any child of God, has not the same right to himself that we have; and if he can secure it without bloodshed, has a right to take it. If he can obtain it only by bloodshed, it is not for us, with our ceaseless praises of Kossuth, and Garibaldi, and Washington, to say him nay.* God help him to his rights without the shedding of a drop of human blood! God help him to his rights, even if, like Israel, He shall see fit to have him thrust into freedom by the terror-stricken, sorrow-stricken masters; made so now, as then, by the Angel Jehovah, the Lord Jesus Christ himself.

There will be no such redemption, for the slave has no thirst for revenge. Vast and numerous as are the temptations to it, no such cry has ever leaped in his soul, much less from his tongue. Some there may be, of the many Legrees, that may have commended to their lips the chalice of agony they have so foully forced upon their brethren. But these revenges will be rare. No such design moves the hearts of their sympathizers. He who has gone furthest

* Are not our eulogies, and statues, and monuments of Washington, — the peculiar fashion of our time, — designed by Providence to prepare us to welcome that greater than Washington, who may yet arise to lead the oppressed race to Freedom?

in this work of neighborly love and duty, expressly and repeatedly denies the intention of creating or allowing a bloody insurrection. "I never did intend," he says, "murder or treason, or the destruction of property, or to excite or incite the slaves to rebellion, or to make insurrection. I never encouraged any man to do so; but always discouraged any idea of that kind." Let us refrain from charging these dead and dying men, who have sacrificed their lives for the freedom of a despised people, with any such imputation. Let us rejoice that other human agents are in this work beside Pharaoh and his bondmen, and that their external sympathies and energies will peacefully melt the iron from these necks.

We have only said that, in the dread alternative of freedom through blood or perpetual slavery, we have no right, as men or as Christians, to decide for the latter. For consider, that one quarter of a million hold four millions of innocent people in chains. By our American arithmetic the majority rules. Apply the rule here, and let it peaceably work itself out. If violence attend its working, ask yourself which is the better — the short but fierce conflict of sixteen men, with their one pretended owner, or the violent subjugation to the master of those sixteen, and their posterity. On the one hand, some masters slain, some matrons dishonored, some falsely rich made poor, and then liberty, equality, fraternity in all generations; no chains, no whips, no pollution, no unconsecrated marriages of lovers, no separation of families, no robbery of a man's labor and its rewards, of all chances of elevation, socially and mentally, of all the rights which all men respect and strive after. On the other hand, generations upon generations of these millions suffering unspeakable loss, and shames, and agonies. There may be no war nor bloodshed, thanks to the great Northern, the great Christian sentiment; but if there shall be, God has often blessed it, and will again.

II. This event will lead to a more general recognition of our oneness of blood and destiny with the despised race. The past movements of this reform have made astonishing changes in the Northern feeling. The colored race to-day are treated with a thousand-fold more respect and fraternal familiarity than they were twenty years ago. Yet there remains much to be done. Our walls of prejudice still rise high between us and them. We must tear them down. We must cease separating them from us in our churches — perpetuating, under another form, the negro-pew abomination of our fathers. We must open the doors of our schools and colleges to them, not only as scholars, but as teachers, if they show themselves capable. We must let them enter our shops as apprentices, our stores as clerks, our firms as partners. We must open the doors of all our varied departments of human enterprise, and say to them, "Show yourselves capable, we will show ourselves liberal." How high the walls that now hem them in! how narrow and poor the soil they are permitted to cultivate! The lightest quadroon, no less than his darkest kindred, is confined within the range of one or two modes of industry, and they the least intelligent and remunerative. I heard a worthy lady say, not long since, she might allow one of this class to work in her kitchen; she would revolt from letting her sew for her. However light in hue, however neat and nimble in this most womanly of accomplishments, she could not avail herself of it to get a living in that family. Could she in yours? We must crucify this lust of pride and caste, if we would be the friends of Christ, if we would deal truly and justly with the slave and his master.

No one act in the whole movement, thus far, can contribute to this end what the deeds done and suffered by John Brown and his associates will do. That sublime speech, on receiving his sentence, so manly, so womanly, so full of generosity and frankness, full of modesty and courage, has a few sentences that, with the deeds that accompany them, will be living forces for the cleansing of this nation from the base prejudices that now infect it. Hear him, and let his words work their perfect work in all your hearts: "Had I interfered in the manner which I admit, and which I admit has been fairly proved, — for I admire the truthfulness and candor of the greater portion of the witnesses who have testified in this case, — had I so interfered in behalf of the rich, the powerful, the intelligent, the so-called great, or in behalf of any of their friends, either father, mother, brother, sister, wife, or children, or any of that class, and suffered and sacrificed what I have in this interference, it would have been all right, and every man in this court would have deemed it an act worthy of reward, rather than punishment. This court acknowledges, too, as I suppose, the validity of the law of God. I see a book kissed, which I suppose to be the Bible, or at least the New Testament, which teaches me that all things whatsoever I would that men should do to me, I should do even so to them. It teaches me further to remember them that are in bonds as bound with them. I endeavored to act up to that instruction. I say I am yet too young to understand that God is any respecter of persons. I believe that to have interfered as I have done, — as I have always freely admitted I have done, — I have done in behalf of his despised poor no wrong, but right."

III. Another benefit is the new life it will give to the varied modes which have long been at work against this wrong. Had it not been for their previous activity, it would have been utterly powerless for good or evil. Twenty-five years ago such an act would have created no general uproar. The slave power was too strong, the anti-slave power too weak. It is far different now. The speeches, and sermons, and editorials, and votes, and prayers of a quarter of a century have not been without their effect. The quickening of the moral sense of the nation, the increase of sympathy and fraternity with the oppressed, the collisions of churches and parties, the very fierceness of the wrath of the slaveholder, have all been as fuel preparing for this spark. The quenching of this spark will not cause the work to cease. It will go on as never before. Not arraying the North against the South, but the whole nation, North and South, against this sin. The end is at hand. Let us not be weary in well doing until that end is reached. However hostile to this work this enterprise first appeared, new light is breaking upon the general mind. The party journals that fancied their party aims were ruined are gaining their better reason. Let every right way of assailing the trembling fortress not cease because of this diversion. They will not. The fires of Freedom will burn the brighter, for that which seemed to quench the flame is but fuel. The peaceful triumph must be hastened by the very failure of any scheme which seems to be infected with war.

IV. This will not be the least beneficial in stilling the haughty and horrible assumptions of the leaders and managers of the Slavocracy. They have preached doctrines from the stump, the hall of legislation, the pulpit, the bench, during the last ten years, more blasphemous, more satanic than any that have been uttered in the civilized world since Christianity overthrew Paganism. No bull of the Vatican in the midnight point of the dark ages, no Torquemada defense of the Inquisition, ever made half so ungodly apologies, or announced half so demoniacal decrees, as the Southern press and pulpit have done in the last decade; and they were waxing worse and worse. A slave code for the territories, slave trade for their harbors, slave transportation over the whole country, — this is their avowed programme. Their strides have been rapid and vast; their steps are raised for mightier paces. This infernal march — I speak soberly and solemnly — this tramp of men, possessed by him whose name is Legion, over all human and divine law and life, has suddenly been made to halt. They have seen the Angel of the Lord; they are pale and piteous; they cry for quarter, though His sword has not left His thigh. Where, now, is your senatorial imperiousness? Where your judicial perversions of law and history? Where your executive hauteur? Their demands, decisions, decrees, suddenly cease. They will revive them again, but with bated breath. Outwardly they may be more vociferous and abominable, but inwardly they fear, and whisper, "See there! that strange, awful sight; how it burns our eyeballs! Northern whites as mad for Freedom as we are for Slavery. Made so by us, they are adopting our tactics and our weapons. As we have murdered men for Slavery in Kansas, as we have struck down great and high defenders of Freedom and the Constitution in the Senate House, so they are murdering us in the cause of Liberty; they are arming our slaves for their freedom. We shall lose our lives, perhaps; we shall certainly lose our property and our power." They see in this more than votes, more than the triumph of any political party; they see the death of Slavery. They see themselves the murderers; the favorite offspring of their lust of pride, and power, and wealth dies by their own hands. Well may we say to them, as our prophet bard of Freedom did to their great leader, Calhoun, years ago, when a less fright congealed his soul, —

"Are these your tones, whose treble notes of fear
Wail in the wind? And do ye shake to hear,
Actæon-like, the bay of your own hounds,
Spurning the leash and leaping o'er their bounds?
Sore baffled statesmen, when your eager hand,
With game afoot, unslipped the hungry pack,
To hunt down Freedom in her chosen land,
Had ye no fears that, ere long, doubling back,
These dogs of yours might snuff on Slavery's track?"

Let their proud knees quake. They ought to fall before their slaves with cries of forgiveness for their inhuman conduct towards them; before their country, asking her pardon for the dishonor with which they have stained her fair fame before the world; and, above all, before their God, imploring His mercy for their false and cruel treatment of His truth and children. This little event will be magnified by them a thousand-fold; yet, perhaps, not too highly. May it lead them to instant penitence, and its all-important work.

If I speak aught that offends your present judgment, weigh it carefully before you reject it. I declare only what I have thought, and prayed, and spoken for years. I believe no such sin is laid at the door of any nation as is laid upon us. I believe no such sufferings are seen by the all-loving Omniscience in the wide earth, as He sees in the breasts of multitudes of powerless victims in the Southern shambles. I speak in the interest of no party. Politics are tossed on this wild and mighty sea that sweeps over the whole land, as fishing boats off Newfoundland, —

> "When descends on the Atlantic
> The gigantic
> Storm wind of the equinox."

So are rocking all other great interests. The Church fears her dissolution; free labor, in its grand and lesser divisions, fears her destruction; the throes of this great birth of freedom and fraternity to the least among the races of men, make all classes and callings to writhe. Yet there shall be no death of any vital force. Government, Religion, the Church, the Gospel, free and varied industry, all shall live, and live a higher life for the struggles through which they are now passing. I speak with no hardness to the slaveholder. Some of these that I know, I esteem. All God has loved, and has given His only-beloved Son, that they, believing on Him, might not perish. May they receive the grace of God in its fullness, and let it lead them to give that which is just and equal to the slave, lest "the great and terrible day of the Lord come." Would to God they would treat their fellow-citizens in bondage as our fathers treated theirs — declare Slavery incompatible with their Constitutions, and that it ceases henceforth to exist in their midst. So easy, so peaceful is the way of duty in this matter.

I speak in no love or expectation of a murderous uprising, or of armed intervention to aid them in rising. Their rights I have defended. Their duty it is not for me to decide. I have striven to remember them as bound with them. I see them as they are to-day, sitting under vines and fig trees not their own, with everything to molest and make them afraid. I see them, as they are plodding in coffles, or crowded in holds, on their dreadful march to their unknown fate. With bleeding feet, and backs, and hearts, they are scourged from the miserable hut of their childhood, to the miserable grave of their early prime, from the dungeon of ice to the dungeon of fire. "They have no rights," says the solemn and supreme tribunal of the land, "no rights which white men are bound to respect." The husband has no right to his wife, which you are bound to respect; the maiden no right to her honor; the mother no right to her babe, the babe no right to its mother; the mind no right to culture; the soul no right to its Savior; no rights which *white* men are bound to respect! My God, what a decree! Let us obey God rather than man, and hold in higher respect their natural and divine rights, for the very contempt and loss they suffer at the hands of those now so powerful and so cruel.

Let us not be discouraged. This deluge of hell has heard a voice it will obey, saying, "Hitherto shalt thou come, but no further, and here shall thy proud waves be stayed." The very dilemma of the captors of these men is itself propitious. They dare not hang them; they dare not release them. If they pardon John Brown, it is saying to all the world, "We are verily guilty. Any man may come among us, invite our slaves to assume their freedom, give them arms to defend that freedom, and even slay those who seem to oppose it, and yet we dare not hang him. Why? Because we know he is right, and we are wrong." They can never defend their system again if John Brown is allowed to live.

If he dies, if he mounts the scaffold for Freedom, which may Heaven prevent, he will slay the monster which seems thus to slay him. He will make the scaffold in this land as sacred and potent as it became in England when Vane, and Sidney, and Russell mounted it. Such a thrill of indignation and remorse will freeze the soul of every man, North and South, slaveholder and abolitionist, as never struck through the heart of a great Christian nation before. Let John Brown's great words be fulfilled: "Now, if it is deemed necessary that I should forfeit my life for the furtherance of the ends of justice, and mingle my blood further with the blood of my children, and with the blood of millions in this slave country whose rights are disregarded by wicked, cruel, and unjust enactments, I say, let it be done."

Out of that death life will leap: life for those miserable millions now worse than dead. To his memory honors will be paid; statues will bear his stern, mild features to posterity; and when Virginia is free,—as free she will be,—one of her first acts will be to erect a monument to his memory, on the very spot where disgrace, defeat, and death now overwhelm him — as one of the first acts of this Commonwealth, after she had achieved her liberty, was to raise the lofty memorial to the "monomaniac" Warren, and his slain and defeated comrades, rebels, like these, against a legal but tyrannical power.

May God help us all to give ourselves to Him, in the consecration of a holy heart and life, and then to the great moral warfare with every vice, chiefest of which, in the cry of the down-trodden, and the crime of the down-treader, is American Slavery.

THE MARTYR.*

NOTHER date has been added to our national history — to the history of the world. Next to July 4, 1776, is to stand in the world's chronology, against the name of America, December 2, 1859. None between them can be placed beside them. These will stand with the two dates immediately preceding the former, — April 19 and June 17, 1775, — and with two preceding that — October 10, 1492, and December 22, 1620 — the Discovery of the Continent and the Landing of the Pilgrims, as the chief days of her history unto this hour. The striking of the clock of Humanity only happens when events of mighty influence on the destiny of nations and races occur. Solferino, as the moment when Italy came out of its grave of centuries, may have such honor. Waterloo, because it had no moral nor national significance, will descend from its high place, and rank only with Philippi, Actium, Cannæ, New Orleans, when dynasties are affected, not races.

* An address prepared for a public meeting arranged to be holden at Malden, Mass., on the evening of the execution of John Brown. The meeting was not held, and the address was published in "Zion's Herald," December 8, 1859.

This day is not only in its events, but in in its physical character, a national day. It is a Virginia winter's day, so warm and sunny in this region that we have sat without fires and with open windows; a halcyon day, when the bird of freedom broods in its nest; a day, probably, almost identical in character from New Brunswick to Mexico. It would seem as though Providence had made the universal feeling, calm, warm, unusual, infect the day.

Everybody gathered about that gallows; everybody saw that gallant man march serenely to his grave; everybody felt to say, "Let us also go, that we may die with him." We knew, South and North, slave and slaveholder, we knew in our inmost hearts that he was being crowned by the Divine Lover of all men, the Divine Sufferer for all men, with glory, honor, immortality, eternal life.

Why this interest? Why this conviction? Some say he was mad; some say he was bloody-minded. He took the sword; it is right that he should perish with the sword. Was he insane? Was he a monomaniac? Did he labor under a mental hallucination? So some of his many friends represent; but if so, why this mighty, instinctive, irrepressible approval? Why do our hearts belie our lips? Why do we have to put our nature under the hatchways when we condemn him? Let us look at him as our children will a half a century hence — ay, as we shall ere a decade of years passes over us. We have read the affidavits which were said to prove his insanity, and though we condemn the Virginia court that slew him for many of its rulings, we think it showed good sense in excluding that testimony. His madness, according to that record, consisted in feeling that he was called upon to oppose slavery. He only lived to kill that murderer. If that is insanity, we shall find no madhouse large enough to contain a tithe of his companions. He was not mad. However erroneous his judgment, as to his resources or his expectations, he was a cool, shrewd, sane man; and they who now, from terror or ignorance, brand him with insanity, will, ere many years have flown, acknowledge the greatness of his wisdom.

But whether his undertaking was wise or foolish in a politic, worldly sense, was it right? We as Christians can defend no act which does not stand on this foundation. The question is more important; is it more difficult? It seems to be, by the utterances which have gone forth concerning it. "It is destiny," says one. "It is divine sovereignty," says another. "It is an inscrutable Providence," says a third. They see the handwriting, but cannot interpret it any more than the terrified Belshazzar. But it ought not to be a hard thing to understand John Brown. It is not hard to see through every other deed of that transparent life, whether those by which he saved Kansas from the clutch of slavery, when he from the robber rent that prey, or those by which he has won all hearts since his capture. His words are so plain that he that runs may read them. Why is not this central act apprehensible? Simply because we have not yet *dared* to study it. We have been as afraid of it as they of him. He was too ripe for us, but not for the cause. The instinct of every heart declares the latter; the perplexities of every head the former.

Now, this country has not gone crazy over a madman; it has not forgotten its Christianity in the fascinations of a great murderer. The men and women that love and praise him are pious, humble, God-fearing, man-loving, war-hating men and women. Why do they praise and love him? Because he did simply this: He gave the slaves their freedom, and means to defend that freedom; that is all. Not a pike nor pistol was for aggression, for murder or rapine, but for defense against their otherwise murderous masters. This was the only new thing about this enterprise. Hundreds have been run off without arms of defense. Torrey has preceded Brown to martyrdom for doing, in this way, as he would be done by. Brown merely added weapons of defense. His own assertion, repeated over and over again, establishes this. He was not like Warren, to whom he has been compared, in all respects, though he was in many. Warren armed himself and his men with the intention of fighting. Brown armed himself and his slaves with the intent to prevent bloodshed. Was this wrong? Our Master says, "He that hath no sword, let him sell his coat and buy one." Not that His disciples should engage in aggressive or vindictive war, but that they should defend themselves, their families, and their liberties, against the enslaving armies of their enemies. The church has never adopted the doctrine of non-resistance: it never will. As long as man feels that he has a right to raise his hand to protect his head against the murderer's blow, he will feel that he has a right to mail that hand, to arm that hand, for this sole purpose. For this alone he gave his slave brethren weapons. Can we say he had no right to give them?

But it may be said "all such interference is unjustifiable." Then we are verily guilty if we aid a fugitive to escape; for the law holds him in slavery here. If we say armed intervention on the soil puts a very different aspect on the case, let us ask ourselves what we have said of Louis Napoleon's armed intervention in Italy. Not like John Brown's, — a war of defense alone, — but purely and intentionally from the beginning a war of offense. How pæans went up to him as long as he was faithful to that cause! How he was honored with the title of the Liberator of Italy! And did Italy call Napoleon with half the imploring voice that Virginia called Captain Brown? Were the Italians suffering what our brethren in that country are suffering? Did the Austrian sell the Venetians into hopeless bondage far into Southern Italy? Did he steal the Milanese peasant from his wife? Did he seize their dark-eyed daughter, and sell her to his light-haired German neighbor for purposes too horrid to think of? Were the Italians fettered and lashed, driven from Venice to Rome, or carried in slave ships from Genoa to Naples, as they are to-day from Richmond to Memphis, from Baltimore to Mobile? Before we judge John Brown we must judge every attempted liberator of his own or another people from tyrannical servitude. Let us cast the beam out of our own eye, and then shall we see clearly to take the mote out of our brother's eye. We shall cast it out. We shall see clearly. We shall unitedly say ere many days that this man, whom all call a Christian, has violated no Christian obligation in this remarkable undertaking.

If it was the work of a sane and pious man, was it that of a wise one? This seems to demand two answers. Wisdom is sometimes gauged by success, sometimes not. Kossuth has always been called a wise man, though he failed; so Warren; so Socrates. Did Brown fail? The day of his death was the day of his greatest victory. Two things were in his heart. God gave them to him: Inspiration of the slave with such a desire for freedom as will make him ready to die to obtain it; and inspiration of the pretended owner, with such a conviction of his sin, and such fear to continue in it, as will make him haste to escape from it. The first will appear. All who know the slaves, and dare to speak, know how this deed has inspired them. The last is already his. Every eye sees it; every slaveholder's heart feels it. Conviction of duty, and the terrible danger of neglecting it, have gone through that whole Southern land like an earthquake. They may appear very confident; they may shout over his gallows, "Abolitionism is dead; long live Slavery!" But the terrible Nemesis, shod with wool, suddenly stands behind them, and whispers in their affrighted ears, —

"If the red slayer thinks he slays,
Or if the slain think he is slain,
They know not well the subtle ways
I keep, and pass, and come again."

The slain knew he was not slain. No man ever went to a martyr's death with such assurance of success; no man ever had better grounds. And that red slayer, the slave power, that has driven Governor Wise to wash his unwilling hands in this saintly blood, already beholds the dread Avenger come again. They are not eating their festal feasts of victory without seeing the terrible spectre, and they cry, with chattering teeth, —

> "Hence, horrible shadow!
> Unreal mockery, hence! The times have been
> That when the brains were out the man would die,
> And so an end. But now they rise again
> With twenty mortal murthers in their crowns
> *To push us from our stools.*"

They surround the gallows with an army. Also propitious; for thus they bring the first citizens of Virginia from every section of the Commonwealth to escort their captive to his crown. And those clear-eyed, strong-minded soldiers could not have witnessed that wonderful death without feeling that he and his cause were right, and would triumph. They must have said, hundreds of them, in their hearts, like Balaam before Israel, "May I die the death of that righteous man, and may my last end be like his!"

Then, too, the fact that this institution could only be upheld by the bayonet, shows it is near its end. No cause in this land can long stand which requires such support. That very display, which was not for us, not to keep their prisoners in their toils, but to inspire terror in the slave, shows that the cause that asks its aid is dying. We hail the omens; the sacrifice is slain on the altar of Slavery; the auguries foretell the speedy destruction of that abomination.

Let us not murmur at this deed, or its doer. So murmured some of our fathers at the mad enterprise of Prescott, and Putnam, and Warren. "Foolhardy men," they doubtless said, "to throw themselves against a force so far above them in numbers, equipment, and training! What property destroyed! What lives lost! And he, our Commander-in-Chief, has flung himself most foolishly away." Not so murmurs the sea of applause that beats around that great deed to-day from the vast ocean of humanity, even as the waves of every clime murmur at the base of its immortal hill. The Charlestown of Virginia shall stand forever beside, and yet above, the Charlestown of Massachusetts.

Let Slavery then proceed to the bloody end of her unnatural revenge. Let her crunch her remaining captives, as she has their great leader, in her dripping jaws, grin horribly a ghastly smile, settle down upon the burning marl, and gloat over the miserable victims that daily feed her hellish maw. Let her use their survivor to decoy the anti-slavery leaders to her den, so that they, too, served up by Judge Lynch, may tickle the delicate palate of this eater of men. Will the haughty slavocracy cease the less to fear her slaves? Cowards fear the dead more than the living. She fears both. She is fast rushing to her grave. Great signs in the religious, the political, the social heavens, betoken her overthrow. All forces are uniting against her, — Church and State, society and civilization, — and like every tyrant, she loses everything, and loses it instantly, if she loses her Waterloo. Ere long she will lose Waterloo. Within this first century of our national life she will disappear. Then will all men unite in praising this Samson who first tore down the pillars of this soul-devouring Dagon. Then will Virginia set aside the judgment of her courts against these brave and true men who loved her better than her rulers, better than she loved herself, and will place beside her Washington, him whom she has just hung, and whose dead body she has spewed out of her land.

Let every one measure this whole character and career by the true Christian standard, and let them so far obey the voice of duty and of God in their hearts as he did in his.

We shall be compelled by our conscience to utter the whole truth to the master; to withhold no word of sympathy and rightful succor from the slave. We shall be required by the Father of all, the Sacrifice for all, the Illuminator of all, to feel our oneness with this race. Almost John Brown's last act was one whose fitness none can question, whose large lesson all must learn. As he left the jail, he saw a slave woman and her babe near its door, and, as she, with a smiling countenance, addressed him, he, stooping over, kissed her babe. Who of that crowd could have done that? Who of the readers of the story? He, face to face with his coffin, face to face with his God, recognizes the cause for which he was to die, and teaches us the lesson this nation is set to learn, and to teach all other nations — the union and fraternity of Man.

Let the bells toll, then, on the return of this great day. Soon will their knell be changed to merry peals of gladness over the glorious consummation of Universal Emancipation, for which he laid down his heroic life, and received his eternal crown.

TE DEUM LAUDAMUS.*

"I WILL SING UNTO THE LORD, FOR HE HATH TRIUMPHED GLORIOUSLY. THE HORSE AND HIS RIDER HATH HE THROWN INTO THE SEA." — *Exodus* xv. 1.

"BUT PROMOTION COMETH NEITHER FROM THE EAST, NOR FROM THE WEST, NOR FROM THE SOUTH. BUT GOD IS JUDGE: HE PUTTETH DOWN ONE, AND SETTETH UP ANOTHER." — *Ps.* lxxv. 6, 7.

"JESUS SAITH UNTO THEM, DID YE NEVER READ IN THE SCRIPTURES, THE STONE WHICH THE BUILDERS REJECTED, THE SAME IS BECOME THE HEAD OF THE CORNER; THIS IS THE LORD'S DOING, AND IT IS MARVELOUS IN OUR EYES." — *Matt.* xxi. 42.

NE year ago last Sabbath evening, we assembled in this house to meditate on the beginning of the end of American slavery. A fortnight before, a score of men had made a descent on a national arsenal, freed some slaves, been captured by the soldiers of the Federal Government, their leader tried, condemned, and sentenced to be hung. You well remember the month that

* A Thanksgiving sermon delivered in the Harvard Street Methodist Episcopal Church, Cambridge, Sunday evening, November 11, 1860, on the occasion of the first election of Abraham Lincoln to the Presidency of the United States.

The following dedication was appended to the sermon when published: —

"To the HONORABLE CHARLES SUMNER,

Who has spoken the bravest words for Liberty in the most perilous places; who has suffered in behalf of the Slave only less than those who followed — far more exciting than the one through which we have just passed. For thirty days, from Calais to Galveston, only one name was on every lip, only one feeling in every heart. You all remember the day of his death: —

> "Sweet day, so cool, so calm, so bright,
> The bridal of the earth and sky."

You remember, far more clearly, the death itself, — more sweet, more cool, more calm, more bright, his soul's great bridal of earth and heaven. No death of greater beauty adorns the pages of secular history — no one sublimer is in the annals of Christian martyrdom. Socrates, with the hemlock at his lips, was not more charming and child-like. Latimer, in the fire, was not more cheerful. Paul, among the lions, was not more triumphant. It was by far the greatest death-scene in American history, and will shine forth purer and nobler with every passing year, and passing age.

We come to-night not to sorrow over Liberty enslaved afresh — Liberty, tried by the jury of the country, and without cause, without consideration, found guilty — Liberty under sentence of death, and on her way to the scaffold. No, thanks be to God, the beginning of the end of slavery gives us gladder scenes in the opening of this act of its fast accomplishing drama.

The defeat at Bunker's Hill and the death of Warren — a lost day and a lost leader — cast an immeasurable gloom, for a season, in spite of some redeeming features, over the

wear the martyr's crown; who has come forth from that suffering with the profoundest, because experimental, sympathy with the Oppressed, with a more intense hatred of the Oppression, yet without any bitterness of heart against the Oppressor; who will stand forth in the future times as the clearest-eyed, boldest-tongued, and purest-hearted Statesman of the age, — these few words of Thanksgiving and Praise for the manifestation of the Presence and Power of the Almighty Redeemer in this greatest work of our time, are most respectfully dedicated."

American heart. But the second great act, executed, like this, in but little less than a year from the first, executed, like this, under the leadership of the chosen captain of their hosts, by which a proud and mighty enemy, flushed with long success, and backed by the gigantic strength of a powerful nation, without the firing of a gun, evacuated their most important post in the whole country, left it, never to return, — the great deed by which Washington purged Boston of its insolent and murderous foe, — thrilled the whole nation with unmitigated joy. So this peaceful evacuation by the arrogant, wealthy, and long-ruling Slave Power of the most important post it ever held or can hold, never to return, has caused such a flood of ecstasy as never before filled the hearts of this people since the bells rang out the first declaration, and the bewildered multitudes awoke to the realization of their existence as a united and free nation. The perplexing and saddening features of the event of last year do not mar this victory. No gallows tree stretches its black arms athwart the golden sky; no dying groans, no stiffened forms, attend the triumphal shout and march. Shall we not, then, come before His presence with thanksgivings whose right hand and holy arm hath gotten Him the victory? For promotion cometh neither from the east, nor from the west, nor from the south. But God is judge: He putteth down one and setteth up another.

Not in the interest of the great party through whom He has done this work do I appear, but in the interest of that cause which swells far, far beyond the power of that or any party to embrace — the redemption of millions upon millions of my fellow-men. In their behalf I raise the song of praise. That redemption draweth nigh. Power is passing away from the side of the oppressor. Power which belongeth unto God is being employed by Him to break this infamous yoke. Shall we not laud and magnify his Name, in whose hand are the hearts of the children of men, that he has turned them as the rivers of water are turned, and made them sweep upon, soon, we trust, to sweep away, this rooted and massy iniquity in their overflowing, swift-rushing flood?

You may ask, Is it not a profanation of the sanctuary to employ it for rejoicings over mere political strifes? This is very far from an ordinary victory, and for its celebration we have the unanimous voice of all ages and all religions.

Abraham praised God, in a temple not made with hands, for the defeat of his enemies, and Melchizedek, the priest of the Most High God, the type of Christ, poured upon his head the divine benedictions. The victories of the Hebrew kings were celebrated in the temple, and some of the grandest psalms were written in praise of national deliverances. The heathen have followed this natural sentiment, and in all ages and nations have hung the trophies of their triumphs in their temples; have made their praises to their gods rise above their shouts over their fallen foe. So the Philistines rejoiced before Dagon, when they had captured Samson; and, in a later day, when they gained possession of the Ark of God. The history of Delphi and other templed spots is but a catalogue of such thanksgivings. The Christian world has, from the first, obeyed the ancestral, human law. "*Te Deum laudamus*," "We praise thee, O God," has rung through the lofty arches of great cathedrals, and against the dome of heaven, for more than a thousand years, when the Lord had given their country deliverance in the day of battle.

We have, therefore, abundant precedent in the universal practice of our race for entering these courts, to-night, with thanksgivings, and these walls with praise. Have we abundant reason? It may be said that these religious national rejoicings were because of victories won on bloody fields, won over a foreign foe, and at the expense of human life. Is a mere periodical strife, peaceful and bloodless, between brethren of the same family, for the honors of civil life, — is this to be placed beside the overthrow of the Egyptians, the destruction of the Assyrians, the redemption of Europe at Waterloo, of Italy at Solferino? Is it not straining a point to thus elevate the mad whirl of quadrennial politics into a great national, a great world battle, which marks an epoch in the history of the race?

These questions are very proper. For if it be but the ordinary strife of ordinary politics, although the Church has the guardianship of these as she has of every other matter pertaining to human duty, yet she might safely leave them to the general course of her counsel and authority, without making their ephemeral victories subject of especial exultation.

Let us then ask, as a needful preliminary to our songs of gladness and of hope, What was the subject of controversy in the late conflict?

The only subject set before the people was Slavery; its extension and nationalization, or its relegation to the regions now blackened with it, there to

> "writhe in pain,
> And die amid its worshipers."

Four parties were professedly in the field, but only two combatants, — only one question. In different parts of the land, the two intermediate parties took different positions, according to the sentiment ruling there. In the South they contended against the domineering passion for the national supremacy of Slavery. In the North they fought with equal zeal against its ruling passion, the national supremacy of Liberty. Their bands flew across the field, now striking at the haughty Slave Power, and now at the iron legions of Freedom.

Behind them advanced steadily the main hosts with their banners flying, each glowing with its one word. On the one "Slavery;" on the other, "Liberty." Marching beneath them, each party instinctively, immeasurably felt, that the issue involved the most vital questions ever submitted to this nation; and that the result was sure to be disastrous to freedom, if defeated, fatal to slavery, if it should go down in the battle.

No other question was debated by the leading advocates of all parties. One of the candidates for the Presidency,* and one of the ablest men in the country, traversed its length and breadth, making many addresses; and the burden of every one was Slavery. He endeavored to exclude it from the canvass, but he could not exclude it from his own speeches. It rounded every sentence, pointed every line. And it was not a little remarkable that so sagacious a statesman should not have perceived, that what had filled all his public life, good and evil, for a decade of years, was not to be banished from the general mind, nor settled in the national councils, except by a fair fight on the appointed field.

The other party, though attempting to banish it from its platform, showed the impossibility of the attempt in its very phraseology. For its two chief words, "Constitution and Union," proved that it felt or fancied these to be endangered by the struggle with slavery. Its worthy appendix, "the enforcement of the laws," was aimed solely at the execution of the most unchristian and inhuman act that ever issued from a Christian legislature.

From the unwilling but universal confession of neutrals, therefore, no less than from the declarations of real opponents, do we see clearly the field of conflict. The real weapons of the real fighters were all drawn from one armory, all waged in one battle. The only speaker that advocated the Southern party in this region made the strongest defense of human slavery ever made in Massachusetts. There was an honest boldness that was refreshing to wit-

* Stephen A. Douglas.

ness, in inviting Mr. Yancey to give a pro-slavery speech in Faneuil Hall — a boldness no party would have been equal to in any previous campaign. The invitation was not accepted by a timid man. No abler, no more courageous speech was ever made in Boston than Mr. Yancey's, viewed as a eulogy on a system abhorrent in the utmost degree to almost every one of his audience. As he was here, so were his associates everywhere on slave soil. As he was here, so would the advocates of freedom have been, had they been allowed to speak in Richmond, Charleston, Mobile, or New Orleans. So were they on their native heather, the broad, free soil of the North.

Not a syllable was breathed against the candidate of Slavery, except his devotion to that system; not a syllable against the victorious leader of the hosts of Freedom, except his opposition to it. "It is the cause," then, "it is the cause, my friends," that has organized, inspired, waged and won this national battle. It is the cause, too, that commands me to speak to-night, to speak in my official capacity, as an ambassador of Jesus Christ, upon one of the especial objects of His mission — the freedom, equality, and fraternity of the human race.

Some may yet complain that we drag the holy vestments of the altar in this mire of social strife. Do you remember how Phinehas, the priest of the Most High God, possibly while arrayed in most sacred robes, and in his hand the sacrificial knife consecrated exclusively to the service of the altar, rushed in among the sinning Israelites and their idolatrous associates, slaying heathen and Hebrew in the midst of their profane abominations? And do you remember how that Most High God said to Moses, "Phinehas, the son of Eleazer, the son of Aaron, the priest, hath turned my wrath away from the children of Israel, while he was zealous for my sake among them, that I consumed not the children of Israel in my jealousy? Wherefore say, 'Behold,

I give unto him my covenant of peace: and he shall have it, and his seed after him, even the covenant of an everlasting priesthood: because he was zealous for his God, and made an atonement for the children of Israel.'" Was it a greater deed for this minister to stay the plague of voluntary passion, than for us to seek to stay that plague which makes pure and pious men and women the victims of every conceivable lust that power, avarice, or passion breeds?

If Christ showed that the zeal of the house of the Lord had eaten him up, by scourging from the temple, the seat of civil as well as religious authority, those that sold doves, shall we say His servants are not His followers when they seek to scourge from our temple of civil and religious liberty those that sell MEN? The temple of our national life has become defiled. Woe to that priest who is dumb before the defilers! In Christ's day some of them shared in the business that profaned his house. In our day some of them share in the honors and profits of this far greater profanation. Let us obey the example He has set us, — not the decrees of timid, time-serving, wicked men.

But this defense is unnecessary before this congregation. The contest as to the rights and duties of the ministry to engage in this work has long been settled in this region. Here and there, the rare exceptions requisite to prove a rule rise before us, denying the privileges of humanity to those who are set to apply to the hearts of men all the laws of the Divine Author of humanity. Not so with the multitudes. Slavery is to them an object not only of civil, but of religious detestation. Its defeat, on any field, is a cause of religious thanksgiving. Its defeat on the field where it has just fallen, — the field it has ruled the longest and the ablest, where its chief seat is by choice, and by necessity if it retain any seat in the land, its overthrow and its expulsion from the throne of the national government, its flight to its native lair, and the soon coming fight there for bare existence, — these are subjects of the most devout, the most rapturous praise. "Not unto us, O Lord, not unto us, but unto Thy name give glory, for Thy mercy and Thy truth's sake."

Let us, then, gratefully meditate on the late victory, considering its cause and its consequence.

I. *Its Cause.* Why has Freedom triumphed?

For two chief reasons among a multitude of lesser ones: First, the growth of conscience as to the nature and effects of slavery; and, Second, the growth of fear as to its political power and prospects.

1. The first and profoundest cause is the awakening of the conscience of the nation as to the dreadful character and workings of slavery.

There must always be two periods, at least, of attack upon any organized iniquity before the tide of moral sentiment deluges and drowns it forever. The first awakening is moderately efficient, but the mighty sin is too strong for complete overthrow. The besieging hosts get weary and slumber on their arms. The enemy sallies forth and triumphs over them. They dwell in captivity to the evil which they rose up against. Again the conscience grows, again the vice is attacked, and in the new assault is left weaker than before, perhaps completely destroyed; if not, the victorious right yields anew to the slumber of sloth and sin; is chained and ruled afresh, again bursts its bands and sweeps on irresistibly to victory. Thus, by tidal waves of flux and reflux, the huge mountain of sin is finally buried beneath the deep, abounding ocean of truth.

So the Jews moved forward, from Joshua to David, in the subjugation of Canaan. So Christianity has marched, is marching forward in the subjugation of the world. So Grecian idolatry, in a hand-to-hand fight with early Christianity, fell and rose, fell and rose, weaker at each resurrection, till, three hundred years after its first defeat, that form, eminent and potent for more than a thousand years, fell, never to rise again. So Roman slavery staggered and tumbled before the sharp blows of the same Apostolic Christianity, — sprang to its feet with the ferocity and strength of a wounded lion, and rent its enemies in pieces; again felt the shafts, again reeled and fell, again rose and raged, till, after half a millennium, the golden rule of the Savior and the golden command of His apostle to Christian masters to give their servants that which was just and equal, were finally obeyed, and throughout Christian Europe, property in man passed into the execrable list, abjured and abominated by every person.

The black race, in consequence of its seclusion and degradation, was separated almost entirely from this influence. True, Africa had been honored with the earliest, and, in many respects, the ablest of Christian schools. Her sons had worn the consecrated mitre, and sat in equal authority with the Bishops of Rome and Jerusalem in Episcopal Councils. But the ravages of the Vandals nipped this budding civilization, and Mussulman fanaticism perpetuated the work northern Paganism had achieved.

Christian Europe, hemmed in by Mohammedanism on the south and south-east, and by the wildest heathenism on the north and north-east, without extensive commerce and without mechanic arts, itself the child of northern idolatry, baptized with the childish Christianity of Rome, grew, by slow and unequal steps, to a true manhood in Christ. So far had she retrograded from her earliest faith in the last two centuries, that traffic in human flesh was again found among her lawful commerce. And though she never fell back so far as to acknowledge the right of property in the white and Christian man, she did finally recognize the idea of ownership in the African race.

It was reserved for this land to inaugurate the work of universal emancipation. That work began with the beginning of our history, and has risen and fallen, with mingled success and failure, to the victory of this hour. Massachusetts first refused to receive a cargo of slaves at the same time that Virginia first welcomed them. The principles involved in those two deeds have been in conflict, violent or latent, throughout our whole history.

The fundamental law, on which universal personal freedom must stand, the law of perfect equality before God, has long been settled here, has never yet been acknowledged elsewhere in the world. America was settled by the flower of Protestantism before it had fallen into the sear and yellow leaf of formalism, or the thrice dead infidelity which covered all Europe, Protestant and Papal, in the last century, with thorns and briers fit only for cursing, and doomed to be burned.

Our fathers, the Pilgrims and Puritans of Massachusetts, the Baptists of Rhode Island, the Quakers and Lutherans of Pennsylvania, the Episcopalians of Virginia, the Romanists of Maryland, and the Huguenots of Carolina, were all refugees from religious persecution. Every State was settled or largely populated by sufferers for conscience' sake. And after a few ineffectual struggles to employ the same cramps and fetters upon others that had been visited upon themselves, they arose, one after another, to the true apprehension of the rights of conscience, and Puritan and Episcopalian, Baptist and Pedobaptist, Quaker and Lutheran, Huguenot and Romanist, came to that broad table-land of universal freedom for the religious sentiment which is still the most wonderful characteristic of this nation.

So thoroughly had this doctrine filled the air of common life, long before the formation of our confederacy, that only the briefest and most incidental reference to the whole subject is found in our Constitution. I have heard a scholarly Englishman complain of it for this very defect — a defect like that found in the Bible, where proofs of the existence of God and the obligations of Religion are never given, its every line assuming these as accredited, universal truths.

So did our fathers settle the other great question — the greatest that affects our human relations — the absolute right of every man to himself. Advancing, not ascending, on the lofty table-land of the equality of every man before God, they stood upon that first of human truths — the equality of every man before his fellows. While Europe bowed down to certain families and individuals as royal and sovereign by right divine, and, as a natural consequence, esteemed the other extreme of society, whether peasants or slaves, as void of all rights which the crouchers were bound to respect, the American people, coming together, through their representatives, themselves the nominal holders of slaves, unanimously, unhesitatingly, enthusiastically declared that "all men are created equal." Such a declaration by the founders of a nation the world had never heard before.

Their first struggle was to establish their own equality before King, and Nobles, and Parliament, and a haughty people. They must prove the fallacy of the divine right of kings on the battle-field. Only one great inspiration can possess at a time a man or a people. This broad platform must rest on the head of king and slaveholder, but it must be planted on that of the king first, as the most imminent and dangerous foe. Hence the revolutionary struggle and victory.

When they had emerged from that conflict — when George the Third saluted George Washington, and, through him, the American people, as his perfect equal, then came a second duty — to preserve this equality among themselves. How perilous was their state you can faintly conceive, by seeing how all classes have just been swept into the current of an unnatural reverence for the youthful heir of that throne.

These patriots were born royalists. A vast proportion of the people were, in feeling and theory, royalists. Every city was full of wealth and fashion thus devoted. If England's royalty and nobility were expelled, might not America substitute one of her own? Italy has just proved the passion of a people for a king. Mazzini and Garibaldi had to yield to Victor Emanuel, republicanism to royalty. So might it have been here. Our fathers saved us by self-denial. It was a greater work to deliver themselves from themselves than from England. "Greater is he that ruleth his spirit than he that taketh a city."

Every member of that Constitutional Convention could have had an American title of nobility. Lands for the support of the title were far more abundant than William's barons found them in England in the eleventh century. The leaders of the people, Washington, Hamilton, Adams, and Jefferson, would have been of the blood royal, or next the throne. They saw the peril. They must meet it. They did. They especially guarded against inequality of rank, forbade the receipt of titles from foreign courts, and steered clear of the currents that might sweep them into that channel — a senate without pay or for life, an executive for life or for a long term of years. And they consummated their precautions by one of their earliest acts of legislation — forbidding the increase of the Society of the Cincinnati, or even its continuance among the sons of the original members, as this society, being composed of the officers of the Revolution, might, through the fascination of the military spirit, endanger their primal and most vital idea — equality, liberty.

As we have said, only one fever can rage at a time, only one great duty be done at once. Therefore, while their sympathies went out for the slave population, while their conscience told them they should be equally faithful and honest to these as to themselves, their exhausting labors were in another direction. They rested from their labors, fondly hoping their children would take up and apply their great principles to this oppressed people.

Of the chief revolutionary patriots, Franklin alone was an avowed abolitionist. Jefferson wrote against slavery, or rather wrote reflections upon it, but never worked vigorously for its extinction. Franklin cast his influence on that side, probably more because he dwelt among the liberty-loving Quakers than from an inherent passion of his own. Washington disliked it, but when urged by Lafayette to make the experiment of emancipating and hiring his negroes, he declines on account of the embarrassed state of his property; and yet he died shortly after, leaving an estate estimated at half a million of dollars, which is more than a million at the present valuation of money.

The fact must be stated, that, while faithful to one half of their theory, they were practically indifferent to the other. While abolishing all titular distinctions and equalizing all the white inhabitants, they failed to abolish the title of slaveholder, and to give their colored brethren that which was just and equal.

The battle on this field exhausted all their energies. To keep this liberty from licentiousness, this equality from familiarity, to preserve an aristocracy, to sustain democracy against aristocracy, to secure state rights, to maintain the federal unity and strength,—on these important fields the war raged, and the servant of servants was unnoticed in his servitude among the great questions of social and political equality that so violently agitated the governing classes.

This work was perhaps as much as one age could do. It was certainly more than any one age had previously done. The men who achieved it were more than thirty years in accomplishing it. Thomas Jefferson wrought wondrously for the rights of man, from 1776 to 1809—thirty-three years of most remarkable service in a most remarkable cause. He was then past sixty — an old man, weary with the cares of State — not fit in vigor or vehemence for the great work of emancipation. Failing to keep progressive, he slid backward, and dishonored his gray hairs by apologizing for slavery and defending the Missouri Compromise.

The generation that succeeded them, as great men's sons are apt to be, were very poor imitators of their illustrious fathers. Most trees bear only biennially. Most generations are under a similar law. A great calm follows a great storm. The children of these revolutionary parents were feeble in principle, low in moral tone. They were tired of great ideas and great deeds. The overstrained nature sprang back to the narrower range which men naturally prefer. The leading men of that age, men who have just left us, were far below their fathers in greatness of nature, and will be incalculably beneath them in greatness of fame. Clay, Calhoun, Adams, Webster, and Jackson, its five representative men, present to the historian no such lofty traits of character or service as shine in the names of five representatives of the preceding era — Washington, Samuel Adams, Jefferson, Hamilton, and Franklin.

John Quincy Adams alone of his peers held forth the light that glowed in his youth. But not he till he had descended from the presidential throne into the vale of age and comparative political obscurity. Hardly a word of his can be quoted before his seventieth year, that has the ringing sound of liberty. How different from the young John Adams in the mass meetings of Boston, the provincial Congress, and Independence Hall. Fortunate was he that those last few years and that congressional opportunity were given him.

It was an era of the deadening of the conscience, on the subject of freedom. Church and State alike fell into the slumber. Political and religious compromises became the order of the day. The *sentiment* of the fathers was against slavery. But sentiment can do nothing against sin. And so the sons came to endure, to pity, to embrace the unclean thing, and, from Calhoun to Webster, fell down and worshiped the abominable idol their pious fathers had neglected to destroy.

"New times demand new measures and new men."

The new times had arrived. New men and their new measures were not wanting. The third generation appears on the stage of action. The grandsires find their likeness in their grandchildren, not their children. Thirty years passed from the triumph of Jefferson to that of Jackson, the representatives of the ideas of their generations. Thirty years have passed from the triumph of Jackson to that of the Anti-slavery sentiment, not in the person of its recognized exponent, but still in the strength of its mighty feeling and purpose. These last thirty years cover the era of this agitation, cover the adult life of the agitators. You will find on "The Liberator" of this year, "Volume XXX.:" and this sheet has the honor of initiating the movement in this nation.

The conscience was aroused very slowly. The deadly slumber was pleasant. Churches, societies, parties, every body disliked to be disturbed. But the young men sympathized with young Mr. Garrison and his young idea. Young Mr. Seward, then emerging into public life, felt the throbbings of the new inspiration. Young Mr. Phillips and Mr. Sumner, then students at Harvard or on their way thither; the youthful Tappan, and Leavitt, and Lovejoy, and Giddings, and Gerritt Smith, caught the flame in their fresh and sympathetic hearts, and commenced kindling it in the breasts of others. Dr. Channing and John Quincy Adams were almost the only men of accomplished fame that indorsed the enterprise, and they did not publicly coöperate with its youthful managers.

Soon bitter conflicts sprang up in the breasts of these young philanthropists. The fresh-armed men began to bite and devour one another, and were well nigh consumed one of another. Yet still the great inspiration moved on, through them, in spite of them. New measures were required by the progress of the sentiment. It demanded a chance to express itself at the ballot-box, and began to feebly, but faithfully, reveal its power on this field where it stands to-day victorious.

Thus steadily have advanced the conscience and the cause. The vast majority of the men of to-day have grown up under its power; for the mass of men are under forty-five years of age. The impressible youth of fifteen, who drank of this new wine when it was first pressed from the grapes of a fresh experience, is to-day the governor elect of your commonwealth. The poor youth of twenty, toiling in the solitude of western rivers and forests, learning to abhor slavery because of its contempt for honorable industry, is to-day the civil leader of the cause and country.

Thus has the principle which moved our grandsires to the great work of personal liberation moved us toward the completion of their work, in the liberation of more persons than their valor saved, from a bondage infinitely worse than that which pressed them down.

2. But fears created by the rapid march of the slave power have aided in this work. The growth of this power has been a necessary complement of the corresponding growth of the abolition sentiment. The Gospel is a savor of life unto life and of death unto death. Conscience is one and the same in every man. But conscience trampled upon is sure to revenge itself by allowing the passions that expel it from its seat to assume a diabolic sovereignty. The Southern mind felt as keenly as the Northern that slavery was a sin. There was but one testimony from the whole land in our early history, and even as late as the

beginning of this agitation. But when the spirit within began to be heard, saying, clearly, "Extirpate this evil. Let my oppressed go free, and break every yoke,"—self-interest said, "Nay; I shall impoverish myself by so doing. My money is invested in slaves. My habits and tastes are educated in slavery. My heart inclines to it." So they resisted the Spirit of God. They trampled under foot the national life-principle. They counted the revolutionary blood shed for them an unholy thing. They turned and rent those who cast these pearls at their feet, and who called upon them to adorn themselves with their luster.

They began to defend the system through the press, in the forum, on the bench, from the pulpit. They sought to extend it. They sought to open the accursed trade which should populate their wildernesses with the barbaric merchandise. They enthroned themselves in the national legislature, in the presidential chair, in the supreme court. They trod out freedom of the press, freedom of speech, almost freedom of thought, in all the Slave States. They were on the point of nationalizing slavery in the Territories, in every free State. Their children, fifty years hence, will not believe their fathers zealously advocated practices so abhorrent to human nature.

There was no real change in the Southern conscience. That still told them, "You are verily guilty concerning your brother." "Slavery *is* the sum of all villainies." I never saw a slaveholder who did not, when he spoke his real sentiments, make this confession.

A gentleman who long lived in Alabama told me he had often heard slaveholders, worth a million dollars in this property, say, "The slaves have just as much right to their freedom as I to mine." It was this conscience that made the whole South shake with undisguisable terror, when they heard that hero-martyr saying to their bondmen, "You are as free as I or your master. Here is a weapon to defend yourself, if they attempt to enslave you. Here is one who will aid you in using that weapon, if they dare to attack you." Their audacious course consummated its malignity in the murder of that man, who, every one of them knew, was in the right and doing right. For *they* saw, however blind we might be, that he was of the blood royal of mankind, most of whom rule the race from the scaffold. They felt that he was proving in this deed his lineal descent from the patriotic but defeated Gracchi, and Demosthenes, and Wallace, and Hampden, and Vane, and Russell, and Warren.* But time would fail me to mention the grand list of martyrs for liberty into whose front ranks they beheld him enter, who all died in the faith, not inheriting the promises.

This God-defying march of the hosts of Satan upon the sacred institutions, the more sacred inspirations of the land, helped to stimulate the already quickening conscience of the North. The heaviest eyes began to open — the dullest natures to stir. Every one whose heart throbbed with any of the life of their fathers, of their fathers' God, felt that the evil must be rebuked, must be repressed, must be extirpated, so far as any constitutional or moral power could do it. So the Church and the State have moved together, — here slowly and cautiously, there boldly and manfully, everywhere motion, everywhere life, until the mighty work is wrought which puts our government, openly and entirely, on the side of Freedom.

This, then, is the cause, this alone — the Spirit of God moving on the hearts of the children of men. "This is the Lord's doing, and it is marvelous in our eyes." "Not unto us, O Lord, not unto us, but unto Thy name give glory." The Lord hath triumphed gloriously. "The horse and his rider," the Northern political slave and his Southern political master, "hath He cast into the sea."

* See Note VIII.

II. *Consider the consequences of this victory, which is one in fact, though threefold in form.*

1. It will suppress all efforts to extend slavery. The battle was waged at this point. Here, too, was it won. For the first time in all this long conflict the hostile parties agreed as to the object in dispute. Every previous Democratic Convention shut off the real issue from the people. The Whig and American parties, when alive, were equally careful. Tariff, banks, the Roman Catholic question, retrenchment and reform, — all these have turned away the gaze of the masses from their real danger and duty. Mr. Douglas supposed that what had been would still be, and therefore attempted to get up a war-cry that should mean nothing, while under its delusion the people should again put in power their haughty tyrant. But the honesty of the slave power swept away this subterfuge. They boldly placed at the head of their columns the universal supremacy of slavery. The free sentiment hailed the conflict. The deadly embrace is passed, and slavery lies prone upon the field. A tyrant once slain is slain forever. Error can never survive its Waterloo. Freedom had often fallen, but it rose ever the more beautiful and strong from its momentary defeat. Slavery has fallen, never to rise again defiant, successful. It will rule in New York and Boston before it ever rules again at Washington. It ruled there first only by our consent. We must rehabilitate it at home before we allow it to return thither.

This absolute and unquestioned gain — the point, the center of the fight — is almost incalculable. Some speak slightingly of it, and say nothing is done. The Fugitive Slave Act is recognized by President Lincoln as constitutional. He will favor the admission of Slave States if they come constitutionally to the door of the nation. These are not agreeable sights. Yet, consider how unlikely they are to occur. What Slave State will seek admission to an Anti-

Slavery confederacy? As for the fugitive from slavery, unless vital modifications are made in the present law, the people will take care that he is not returned. Can one here be seized, and sentenced to bondage again, as Anthony Burns was, passing down State Street in broad daylight, fettered by a squad of foreign mercenaries, when more than a hundred thousand of the citizens of Massachusetts have put the most eloquent defender of the Personal Liberty Bill in the chair of State?

The accursed oceanic slave trade will forever cease. New York will be relieved from the miserable honor of sending out these vessels, — Savannah and Charleston, the more miserable honor of receiving their cargoes. Africa and Cuba will be girdled with a moving wall of fire through which but few of the dreadful craft can pass. If nothing more were done than is assuredly done, it is wonderful, it is worthy of unbounded thanksgivings.

2. But, secondly, we have done still more. We have set ourselves right before the world. We shall cast our influence, as a great nation, on the side of universal liberty. For years we have been a by-word and a hissing among the nations. Not a word for freedom could escape the lips of our representatives abroad, for they were bound, hand and foot, mouth and tongue, with the grave-clothes of the body of this death. Our influence has been against liberty everywhere, in every man. The conscience of the slaveholder, the conscience of the tyrants of France and Austria and Rome, were stifled in the deadly air which our government exhaled. All this is changed. America will stand forth in the glory of her earlier, better days; in a glory greater than that, for we now appear as the upholder of the rights of every man, of every hue and condition. Italians contend for the rights of Italians, Hungarians for Hungarians, Englishmen for Englishmen; we, alone, for the black race, the weakest and least favored of the children of

Adam. Napoleon boasted that he went to war for an idea. We fought for vastly more, — the foundation principle of humanity, — the oneness of man in blood and destiny.

This influence is worth everything. It is irrepressible, it is unavoidable. The acts and words of the Administration will be most careful and moderate, but this power it cannot repress. It is an Anti-slavery Government. It was created because it was anti-slavery. This word assures us that a new life is breathed into the soul of the nation. It will thrill with its enthusiasm every section of the land, every corner of the globe. Distracted Mexico will now turn entreating eyes upon us, certain to see no wolfish leer in our gaze, hungering to reduce her citizens to slaves. The South American Republics will sit at our feet, and follow our footsteps in the upward march to perfect freedom. Hayti will stand at our Capitol among the great nations, its representative sitting with those of England and France, in the seats of ambassadorial dignity and equality.* Italy, and France, and England, will, as never before, admire and imitate the mistress of nations, sitting in the glory of universal liberty on the highest seat of earthly authority.

What is better than all, the sweet, summer morning air of freedom will once more steal over the hot and arid plains of Southern despotism. Blowing from the whole North, through Washington, through the Executive mansion, it will nerve with vigor many a soul now paralyzed with fear. The minister of Christ, who has there, for these many years, denied his Master, will weep bitterly, and speak earnestly against the fearful crime that has so long cursed the Church and his own soul. Literature will feel it. Southern Whittiers will arise, who shall make her hills and glades echo with their trumpet blasts of denunciation, their trumpet calls to the conflict and the victory. Mrs. Stowes will

* The representative of Hayti was admitted in the first year of President Lincoln's administration.

spring from their own soil, who will portray the evils and wrongs of their cherished "institution," the duty and blessedness of universal emancipation, in colors that shall outshine their marvelous prototype, because they will be drawn from personal experiences, and filled with the enthusiasm that only such experiences can inspire. The whole people will be made alive with the mighty wind, blowing from the hills of God over their fields of dry bones, and they shall stand upon their feet, an exceeding great army, for freedom.

What is already seen on the northern border of the black abyss will be seen everywhere. St. Louis gives almost ten thousand votes for liberty, as many as Boston, and, better than Boston, with these votes sends a bold and earnest abolitionist to the national councils. Baltimore gives over a thousand votes for freedom, — as many as the whole State of Massachusetts gave twenty years ago. That thousand has become a hundred thousand here in a score of years. It will become that there ere half that time has passed. In every Southern city, even Charleston, the worst, will be found representatives of an anti-slavery government. In every State, papers will be advocating its principles; in every heart, the Spirit of God, which is liberty, will assert its claims, be acknowledged and obeyed. Soon that Serpent shall be bound, shall be hurled into the bottomless pit, shall disappear from this first and best of lands, and, with it, from the earth, forever.

3. For this glorious victory assures the speedy abolition of slavery. I say speedy, not with a few months, or a Presidential term, in view, but with only a few years, in comparison with its long life and wide dominion.

The knell of slavery was struck last year in the heroic deed, and more heroic death, of John Brown. He first shook the tottering Bastile to its foundations. It had been riddled, it had been undermined, but it had not rocked on its base till he put his hand upon it. It reeled to and fro like a slave ship in a storm, and well nigh foundered, then. I have frequently mentioned this event with words of approval such as but few, probably, in this audience will reëcho. It is proper, therefore, that I should pause, and give a brief reason for my opinions. Our witty neighbor says the millennium is near at hand, —

"When preachers tell us all they think."

I have not shunned to declare to you the whole counsel of God on the highest of our duties. I shall not play the hypocrite now. Allowing the largest liberty of opinion to others, I claim equal liberty for myself. I know how the tide of misconception and condemnation still sets against Captain Brown. I know that the "Tribune" and "Independent," — anti-slavery journals of deserved influence, — still speak of his attempt as a "raid" — a term of disparagement, if not of reproach. I know Mr. Seward said he was "justly hanged." I know that many cry out with horror at the bare idea of putting weapons in the hands of the slaves, to maintain their freedom, and say that he that apologizes for such an act defiles his sacerdotal garments, and is become a companion with murderers.

But, on the other hand, I see how Victor Hugo and the other great and pure patriots of Europe can find no words to express their admiration of the deed and its doer.* Struggling in chains of despotism at home, they know how to appreciate the intense humanity of one who strove not to save himself, but others, from a far worse tyranny than crushes them down. I see Hayti, the only really independent and enterprising African State, hailing the man with a spontaneous reverence and admiration, and out of

* In the winter of the execution, Victor Hugo etched and published with his autograph a print of John Brown on the gallows, hanging in thick darkness, with only a slight gray light falling on the head. It had a great sale in Paris.

her poverty sending to his family thousands of dollars as a token of her gratitude. I see the strong arm of Massachusetts wielding a sword, while she pronounces the sentence first uttered by the slaughtered patriot, Algernon Sydney, which might have been properly emblazoned on John Brown's banners, "*Ense petit placidam sub libertate quietem*"—"She seeks, with the sword, serene quiet under liberty." Virginia's motto should also shine there. That stately maiden, with her foot on a prostrate and fiendish foe, with "*Sic semper tyrannis*"—"Thus always may it be to tyrants,"—encircling her victorious brow,—how happily it answers to his creed and career! Surely what Massachusetts and Virginia have put upon their seals may be put into action against the worst tyrant that ever desecrated American soil or trampled on American hearts. The maiden, called Liberty and Humanity, is under the hoof of the fiend. God will bless him who rescues her, and puts his heel on the head of the destroyer.

There is nothing in human nature, human history, or the Word of God, that rebukes this sentiment. The gospel of Peace does not always require of its disciples non-resistance to every form of revolting oppression, but sometimes demands of them a stern resistance even "unto blood, striving against sin."

The Savior himself, among his last injunctions, commands those of His disciples who had no sword, to sell their tunic, or chief garment, and buy one; thereby clearly teaching us that the clothing needful for the protection of our bodies is not to be esteemed above the means of *defending* our liberties and our lives. This enterprise, as we understand it, sought to put the sword in the hands of the slave, *only* that he might *defend* his God-given freedom against his enslavers. So deep and universal is the conviction of this right, that had the people whom he strove to deliver been of our own race, or even of any race but the African, that we hold in such inhuman contempt, there would have been no more question as to the *rightfulness* of the enterprise than there was to the many unsuccessful attempts of our fathers to release their brethren from the far less terrible slavery in which they were held by the corsairs of Algiers.

In the light of these facts and principles, I find no condemnation for this man or his deed. In the light of its influence on the hideous wrong it assailed, I see much in it to approve. I cannot but conclude, therefore, that the words of censure so rife at present are the offspring of long-indulged prejudice, or when uttered by some of our wise leaders, have been prompted either by an unwise desire to commend the anti-slavery chalice to the lips of slaveholders, by removing some of the bitter but essential ingredients that strengthen the potion, or else by the temptations of ambition, —

> "That last infirmity of noble minds."

In either case they will yet be regretted more than any other of their utterances.

If this be called fanaticism, I am content to bear the imputation. I am not alone in this State, however it may be elsewhere, if the late election truly expresses the sentiment of the people. The election to the governorship, by the largest vote any candidate ever received, of the man who, more than all others, labored to save him from that "just" death, who publicly indorsed his character, if not the abstract rightfulness of the attempt, — such an elevation of his best friend to our best office is a strong evidence that our common sense and common humanity are getting the better of our fears and prejudices. The hated Mordecai already descends here, from the gallows of public condemnation on which the Haman of a subtle pro-slaveryism had hung him, and rides through our streets in the royal apparel of executive sovereignty, as the man whom the people delighteth to honor. As if to show that this remarkable act of the people of Massachusetts was not the blind following of blind political leaders, but a silent yet real voice of approval, her favorite lyric poet comes forth and places a garland of exquisite beauty and perfume on the grave of the hero. Under the influence of his religious training, the Quaker Whittier cast upon his coffin a hastily gathered wreath of bitter herbs. But true also to the fundamental principles of his faith, through the influences of the events and reflections of the past year, he has discovered the "Inner Light" of superior truth, and with characteristic frankness, has published the revelations of that Light. A late poem, written on the liberation of Italy, by its own confession, covers the whole ground of the present controversy. The laurel which he places on Garibaldi's brow, he hangs alike on John Brown's tomb. Hear the sentiment of almost every Christian in these true and tender and solemn words: —

'I dreamed of Freedom slowly gained
By Martyr meekness, patience, faith,
And lo, an athlete grimly stained,
With corded muscles battle-strained,
Shouting it from the field of death!

* * * * *

I know the pent fire heaves the crust;
That sultry skies the bolt will form
To smite them clear; that nature *must*
The balance of her powers adjust,
Though with the earthquake and the storm.

And who am I, whose prayers would stay
The solemn recompense of time,
And lengthen Slavery's evil day
That outraged Justice may not lay
Its hand upon the sword of crime!

God reigns, and let the earth rejoice!
I bow before His sterner plan.
Dumb are the organs of my choice;
He speaks in battle's stormy voice,
His praise is in the wrath of man!"

If the violent act of one man thus paralyzed this iniquity, much more will the peaceful act of two millions tend to its annihilation. Our righteous and gentle course will not be instantly answered in a similar spirit. It may at first, it undoubtedly will, intensify the rage that already burns in the Southern breast, seven-fold hotter than it did aforetime. In this rage they will gnash upon us with their teeth, will seek to frighten us, by financial crises and threats of secession, into submission. Let us not be alarmed. Let but Wall Street look on and hold on, calm and cool, as Menelaus did when Proteus sought to elude him by assuming terrific shapes and making beastly noises, and the monster now, as then, will become tame and humble. Our greatest danger is in the cowardice of the moneyed power. The Church is getting ready to do her part. Politics is doing hers, and now the third of our social forces must do hers. If she fails, if she whines and grows pallid, and begs her dear slave-holding brethren to desist, and promises Northern repentance and its meet works, she will only encourage them in their course. She can *never* change the course of the Republic. Freedom is more than trade, liberty than wealth. Our fathers have said so twice. We shall not fail to repeat the word, if it must be spoken.

The poor slave will also burn in the hot breath of this fiery furnace. The master fears his slave more than he hates the North. He will feel the scourge of that fear. It is one of the necessities of tyrants that they can preserve their power, and even their life, only by the frequent deaths of their enslaved subjects. In Sicilian prisons, Neapolitan dungeons, Roman inquisitions, every-where, every-when, has triumphant sin taught us that this necessity is laid upon it. So it is now where this worst of sins holds completest sway. No dungeon of Venice or Rome or Naples ever vied with Carolina prisons or Alabama plantations in the excruciating cruelty which the helpless victims of their fear and hate receive at their hands. When the secrets of this prison-house shall be revealed, you will cease to wonder at the tortures of Messina and Palermo. No woman suffered there, only a few score of men. Here tenderest women suffer such cruelty daily, as hard-hearted heathen Rome, the most cruel of the ancient nations, would have shrunk from inflicting. Read Olmstead's late "Tour through the Back Country," and you will find incidents of these tortures, inflicted so coolly and carelessly, as show them to be a common matter of daily and indifferent outrage. But he never saw the slave roasting at the stake. He never saw the fierce blood-hounds tearing in pieces the tender flesh of fainting women. He never saw, as a friend of mine did, himself once a slave-holder, a frantic mother torn from a nursing babe, less than a year old, and dragged shrieking down the public street of a Missouri village, by men who bore Christian names and a white skin, and were, not unlikely, born in Puritan New England, of pious parents.

"On horror's head horrors accumulate,"

We emerge from the dungeon so full of

"Horrid shapes and shrieks and sights unholy,"

and breathe the upper air of liberty, with the feeling of an angel who had escaped from Pandemonium revelry and out-rage into the pure society of the blessed. Alas! unlike the angel, we do not leave only sinners and damnéd spirits be-hind us, rioting in their willing wickedness, but pure and lovely souls, pure as the spirits of the just made perfect, lovely as their angels, who do always behold the face of their Father which is in heaven: these we leave behind, suffering such shame, such sorrow, such anguish of body and of soul, as only God can relieve, only He can avenge.

Thank God, that worse than hell shall be swept from the earth. The Administration may not, will not, directly, aid it. The party in power is forbidden to do it — rightfully, constitutionally forbidden. It can only be done peacefully and properly by themselves. It will be so done. The warm air of freedom gliding over all that icy region will relax, will dissolve these chains. The great example of eighteen States of the Union, voluntarily emancipating their slaves, or voluntarily indorsing the act by which the nation rescued their domain from its polluting presence, will not be lost upon them. They have lost the post of master. They will soon be willing to take that of a pupil. They will begin to see as they are seen. They have pompously proclaimed to the despised North, "I am rich and increased with goods, and have need of nothing." They will now see that they are "wretched, and miserable, and poor, and blind, and naked." They will then come to that state of humility which will incline them to buy of us "gold tried in the fire," the gold of universal emancipation, "that they may be rich, and white raiment," the wedding robes of liberty and holiness, "that they may be clothed, and that the shame of their nakedness do not appear." "They will anoint their eyes with the eye-salve" of Northern prosperity, "and will see." Thus learning, thus seeing, the generous spirits that now pant speechless in that prison of silence and death will give their heart a tongue. The free, white, ruling South will speak everywhere, and speak one voice. Tokens of such coming utterance are already given. North Carolina has spoken through the lips of Mr. Helper and Professor Hedrick; South Carolina hailed this reform, at its inauguration, in the persons of her Grimkés and Brisbane; and in this very canvass, Professor Lieber, late of her University, has boldly denounced her treason and its cause, and cast his vote for freedom. Kentucky and Virginia already pour forth consenting voices, like the volume and the sound of many waters, while Missouri is upon the verge of planting the standard of emancipation on the summit of its Capitol.

This revival of Jeffersonian, of Washingtonian abolitionism, with more than the fervor and with more than the practical purpose of those reformers, on their own soil and among their own posterity, will sweep through the masses, and one fire blaze in all breasts — the celestial fire of universal liberty. The struggles of the enslaved, their sufferings, their deaths for personal freedom, not infrequent and not powerless even now, will increase, and increase the zeal of their generous advocates; and ere the hundredth anniversary of our nation's birth is reached, —the Fourth of July, 1876, — we shall have completed the work undertaken at our beginning. The bell that rang out the first birthday in the ears of all the nations, will ring out its first centennial with the prophetic words inscribed upon it, "*Proclaim Liberty throughout all the land to* ALL *the inhabitants thereof*" — no longer prophecy to be accomplished by a long and perilous and bloody path, but blessed, unchanging history.

We have given it a long lease of power, brief as it may appear to you, in allowing four presidential terms to pass before it disappears. But we know that three thousand millions of property are not to be destroyed in an instant, except by a bloody uprising. We hope and pray that there may be no such reprisals. It may go down by a bloodless revolution. Garibaldi has shown how nearly bloodless an insurrection may be in this age of the world. Had there been no standing armies in Sicily and Naples, they would have achieved their liberty without the sacrifice of a single life. There are no standing armies in the Slave States. A Garibaldi from the enslaved race may secure their liberation without the shedding of a drop of blood. God grant that it may be so.*

* The statement of Mr. Buchanan, in his late Message, that the slaves are becoming "uneasy," is a most remarkable confession of a most important witness. This uneasiness exists more in the Gulf States than on the border. For the latter gets rid of its dangerous element through

But we look more to the liberal action of the white race than to any violent action of the black. We shall see the sentiment of the States gradually changing. Then their policy will change. Law after law, the worst first, will be repealed; until, under one grand impulse of conscience, they will pull down the whole fabric, and the slave shall stand beside his master, his free and acknowledged equal.

All this will not take place without such commotion as we have not yet seen nor dreamed of. Threats of disunion, and probably a brief indulgence in that suicidal remedy, will be made by the more insane of the maniacs. We have seen some agitation at the North, in the last thirty years; some mobs and murders have desecrated the Free States in their endeavors to relieve themselves from the *influence* alone of slavery. What will not that bloody power do in a life-and-death struggle which is now to arise in its own dominions, where it has held unquestioned and unlimited sway for two hundred years? The war has passed from the North to the South, and the thirty thousand votes just cast there for liberty show that the war will not cease, come what may, fall who may, till that twelve millions are delivered from their few hundred thousand masters, and freedom of every kind, for every man, shall be the glad possession of the whole people.

This must be the work of time. Yet the change is rapid from daybreak to dawn; more rapid and brief from dawn to sunrise. And when the sun rises, darkness flees to its caves,

the two outlets of Southern trade and the underground railroad. These Northern slaves, that have been sold South because they were unmanageable, are united with the superior native slaves of that section, who, if on the border, would escape to Canada. These violent and restless men, kept from liberty by a wall five hundred miles thick, will, in time, in the very nature of things, rise upon their masters. These masters, by their madness, are tempting the insurrection. There is the fire, there the powder. If an explosion comes, it will come there first. God grant the masters may escape the terrible danger by immediate preparation for ultimate, if not instant, emancipation.

though a few shadows may linger among the rays till the midday brightness burns them up. So will it be with this cause. The day is breaking. A gray light streaks across the darkened heavens. The next presidential election will bring the rosy dawn that will send its warm flush athwart the whole horizon. The third will be the perfect sunrise. The fourth the noontide glory, that shall consume every ray of slavery blackness that has lain so thick and heavy across the nation's sky.

Let us rejoice. Let us shout for joy. Oppression shall not always reign. Oppression has ceased to reign in its highest, strongest seat. It will soon abandon its lower thrones of State sovereignty, cast down headlong by the people whom it has so long deluded and betrayed. It will then flee from those private, domestic seats of tyranny, upon the multitude of which the fifteen seats of State authority have been erected, upon which fifteen, faithfully knit together, the throne of their national power has been elevated. An aroused people will extirpate it from these obscure, but central seats, and the gigantic sin that swells vast to heaven, will flee from the earth to its native, nethermost hell.

Let us pray for this hour; let us labor for it in all righteous and loving ways. Our real work is just begun. We have only broken down a barrier that opposed our march. That march must yet be made. We have only compelled the haughty transgressors to listen. Our entreaties, our warnings, our encouragements are yet to be poured into the opened ear. We have only attained the outmost edge of the broad table-land of free discussion. The high land must yet be traveled. Remember that this deed is nothing unless it bring forth fruit better than itself. The object upon which we must fix our eye, the prize that must be won, the goal that must be reached, is the *abolition of slavery*, THE LIBERATION OF EVERY SLAVE.

Let us discuss, in a spirit of prudence and liberality, every measure that seeks this end. Let us bring every reason that worldly success, humane sentiment, or religious obligation can suggest to bear upon the hearts of their masters. Let us aid those who are anxious to be released from this relation out of the abundant wealth of the North, that they may not be kept from this duty by the gaunt form of poverty staring them in the face, and certain to be their portion, if they strip themselves of all their inherited, though unrighteous possessions. Let us, at least, assist them, if they need, or will receive, no remuneration for the discharge of their duty, by providing for these emancipated brethren a home on free soil, which they cannot enjoy on the slave. We must bring our money to bear upon this sin, if we would see it peacefully die. Let us do it wisely, generously, speedily.

Let us especially feel for the slave. The lot, the loss of the master is nothing to his. His is a hapless, horrible fate. Never forget him. In your morning prayers remember him upon whom the morning breaks only to light him to his rewardless tasks. When gathering round the family altar and the family table, pity those who have no such comforts. At your evening devotions pray for those who go to cheerless couches, bowed down with dreadful memories and more dreadful fears. Remember that the Lord had these sufferers before Him, no less than His chosen people, when He said, "This is a people robbed and peeled; they are all of them snared in holes, and they are hid in prison-houses; they are for a prey, and none delivereth; for a spoil, and none saith, *Restore!*" Never, never forget them. They are your brothers and sisters. They shall stand in equal liberty with you, delivered by the right arm of Him who saved your fathers, and who has just cast down their leagued oppressors from their lofty seats.

What a day that day of deliverance will be, — the great and acceptable day of the Lord, — a day sure to come; a day, I believe, soon to come! Behold that vast and beautiful region, from the peaceful Ohio to the sunny Gulf, from the swift Mississippi to the raging Atlantic, as it now rests under the gloom of this awful sin. All the refinements, all the enterprises of civilized life, pause at its borders, or creep feebly through it, like solitary star-rays through midnight clouds. The magnificent landscape is rarely cheered with the flying train, rarely adorned with the lovely hamlet, the prosperous village, the mighty city. The church lifts but seldom its defiled hand to heaven, and lifts that hand only to point to the judgment of God on its fearful sin in compelling the bride of Christ to commit adultery with Belial. No school-house appears, full of the neighborhood's children, no farms trodden by their humble, but independent, owners; no culture, prosperity, piety. The sight most frequent is the miserable slave toiling with barbaric implements in the rudest forms of menial service; or the more miserable white man, degraded beneath the slave he despises, idle, intemperate, ignorant, and brutal.

Thus stands that vast land to-day. Let the hour come for which we are praying and laboring, to which the great deed of the past week has made the grandest stride that the century has seen; let but that hour come, when every man shall be free, and how changed the spectacle. The wilderness, that blossoms like the rose in wild fertility, shall be transformed into the smiling abode of free, industrious, intelligent man. Railroads shall rush through every valley, bearing the famishing of all nations to the rich treasures nature has there in store for them. Beautiful roads will wind beside every stream, scale every mountain, pierce every forest. Rich embowered cottages, such as no Northern sun nor soil can give, will line every pathway, will cluster in frequent centers, will multiply, at brief intervals, into great communities, with the gigantic factories, and warehouses, and spacious stores, and crowded streets of growing cities. The school-house, modest or majestic, as it stands in village or city, will be filled with the young of all families, white and black, as with us, unconscious of difference or prejudice ; alike growing in knowledge and affection. No slave-whip whistles through the resisting air, rushing down upon the shrinking flesh of saintly woman. No agonizing husbands and wives, mothers and babes, are dragged to the market-place, and there torn, husband from wife, mother from child, never to meet again till they appear together as witnesses on the stand at the bar of God against these murderers of their liberty, their love, their life. No gangs of men and women, silent and sad, move monotonously over the broad acres, to the ceaseless look and lash of the cruel overseer. No wretched hovel, with its earthen floor and heap of straw, filled for a few short hours with the half-starved slaves, blotches the lovely landscape. All these are gone, and gone forever.

The white fields shall blossom under the free and active industry of every class. Comfort shall gladden every home. Willing labor shall garner the soil. The free and happy, busy and populous, wealthy and cultivated North, shall cover the whole land, and equal freedom and happiness, energy and prosperity, culture and piety, will be the possession of every man. Above all, the Church of Christ, the Divine Liberator, will point its sacred finger to the Infinite Lover and Redeemer of all men, to the everlasting freedom of heaven. In its walls, without distinction of color or condition, without negro pews, or negro galleries, or negro corners, all souls shall bow in the loving unity of "one Lord, one faith, one baptism," before "the one God and Father of all, who is above all, and through all, and in all" that love Him, equally and eternally.

No dim and distant prophecy of millennial glory is this. The day is nigh at hand. It has already dawned. It shall speedily arise. "Surely I come *quickly*. Amen! Even so, come, Lord Jesus!"

LETTERS FROM CAMP.*

I. TO ARMS.

FIRST GATHERING OF THE STATES.

STEAMER ARIEL, OFF ANNAPOLIS,
Wednesday, 9 A. M., April 23, 1861.

NE always wishes to know the condition of his correspondent. Let me give you a crayon sketch of this one. On the after deck of a California steamer, sitting on a camp-stool, with his sheet of note-paper on a pocket account-book, and the book resting on his knees, with a military cap on his head, a military beard on his face, and a military weapon peeping out of his breast pocket, putting its possessor in far greater peril than any real or imaginary foe, — thus sitteth the sketcher. His immediate surroundings are admirably adapted to habits of reflection and composition. Crowding around him are soldiers of many uniforms, and many religions and irreligions, having two bonds of unity — fury against the

* The three following sections contain extracts from letters written from the army at Washington, the Relay House, and Baltimore, during the first three months of the war, and published in "Zion's Herald," "Christian Advocate," and "Harper's Magazine."

rebels, and noisy welcomes to neighboring troops. Some eight or ten vessels lie near us, with troops from Rhode Island, New York, Philadelphia, and Boston, vociferating their hurrahs and "tigers" across to each other in a most enthusiastic manner. Outside of this trampling and talking, singing and shouting, screaming of steam pipes and rattling of muskets, lie the quiet Chesapeake and its more quiet banks. The sun is preparing to give us a warm reception, whatever the citizens may give. He pours his sheets of flame on the bay, and it glitters in his radiance with charming beauty. It is a beautiful field of silver, about a mile wide here, but opening into an area three or four miles wide a little way below. The banks are low, yet very pleasant. The grass is green, and the trees are clothed in that "mist of greenness," as Tennyson so happily describes the intermediate state between leaflessness and leafage.

A War Night in Faneuil Hall.

I have seen old Faneuil Hall under many excitements since my first memory of it, which, by the way, was beholding General Jackson shake hands with Boston dignitaries. I was chiefly anxious, I recollect, then to see the famous Major Jack Downing, and eagerly inquired of my Mentor which of the attendants on the General was the great Major. Since that childish faith was then and there broken to pieces, I have had my faith broken or confirmed many times by the sights and sounds within its walls. But Faneuil

> "saw another sight,
> When the drums beat at dead of night."

My experience of many delectable Methodist camps had trained me for the enjoyment of the scene. So I lay on a straw mattress under the rostrum, from whence I had heard Webster, Choate, Parker, Sumner, Burlingame, and a host of others thunder, and saw the sights in which their speeches were culminating — the bodying forth of their airy nothings. Troops marching and countermarching, up stairs and down stairs, bands playing, men whistling or singing, packing and nailing boxes, shouting orders, going through drills, — every conceivable noise; melting into one mighty patriotic symphony. The grand old eagle seemed to enjoy the scene, —

"The fierce gray bird with a bending beak,
With an angry eye and a startling shriek,
Which nurses his brood where the cliff flowers blow."

How he exulted in the daring of his Northern associates! On his breast glowed the stars and stripes, and round his talons waved the *E Pluribus Unum*, not to be changed to *Ex Uno Plura* by the combined fraud and force of any or all the leagued oppressors on our Southern shores. Below the symbols of the United States stood the haughty memorials of Massachusetts sovereignty, — her Indian and his weapons, — and her motto, looking far from "Algerine," in this hour of her quick response to the call of her country.

Opposite these, the patriotic faces of Samuel Adams, Washington, Hancock, and Warren, glowed with animated enthusiasm; while, by a sort of prophetic inspiration, Calhoun had been placed on the walls, but covered with a cloud, evidently nursing his wrath with difficulty, as he saw the formidable array to suppress his treasonable desires and efforts, and to give the final blow to his favorite Power as a ruler in the nation.

Among the tunes were often heard, just as I hear them here and now, the familiar songs of the camp-meeting and prayer-meeting. "I am going home to die no more," "There'll be no more sorrow there," "We're bound for the kingdom, Will you go to glory with me?" mingled with *America* and *Yankee Doodle*, showing how great was the power of these melodies over the masses.

First War Sunday.

That Sabbath day's journey ought to be chronicled. We marched through saintly Boston in the gray twilight to the tune of Yankee Doodle. All along the route, cannons and bells, bands and flags, and waving handkerchiefs, soldiers and crowds upon crowds, gave us a hearty hail and farewell. At Springfield the crowd was immense and enthusiastic. At Hartford we were told the women were all at home driving their sewing machines, and the men busy making cartridges for their troops. Not a few, however, filled the depot and the track to salute us. But Meriden gave us the heartiest welcome. All the town left their churches, and gathered round the depot, where they had had preaching and singing while waiting for us. They had also provided refreshments enough for five thousand persons, and plied us with sweetmeats and benedictions.

New Haven and Bridgeport were equally alive and multitudinous in their enthusiasm. At the last place an incident occurred which strikingly, not to say grotesquely and harshly, showed the fierce fire that glowed in every breast. A man had been killed the day before while firing a salute to a company going to Washington. They had his body wrapped in American flags, in a hearse trimmed with flags, and drawn by four white, dancing horses, also trimmed with flags. The force of the fever could go no farther. It did not seem to me that it ought to have gone so far. Yet the great crowds, the bands, cannons, bells, soldiers, and shouts, showed that the people did not seem to feel this novel expression to be exceptional.

Opening the Way to the Capitol.

Washington, April 23, 1861.

The Massachusetts Eighth Regiment first reached Annapolis, and would have first opened the way, solitary and alone, to Washington, had not an accident prevented their landing. One of their officers informed me that when they reached Philadelphia they heard of the Baltimore riot, and the murder of their comrades. They left that city expecting to follow their predecessors on the same route. They prepared a corps of sappers and miners, selecting some forty of their most brave and dashing men for this service. These were to head the troops, and, upon attack, spring into the houses, set them on fire, and otherwise open, if possible, a path through the city. "As they marched down the streets of Philadelphia," said he, "the lowest weight of any soldier was one ton," so full of weighty matter and solid courage were they. They found, after a while, that they were going to Perryville, hoping to get possession of the steamer there that is connected with the railroad. They heard that the Baltimore secessionists held it, and had no doubt that they would have to fight to recover it. So, as they drew near the place, their guns were loaded, and their names called, to see if all were present. As the roll was called, one of the soldiers said, "When it is called again we shall not all be here to answer." Tears rolled down many cheeks at this remark, and at the thoughts which it revived of home and friends left perhaps forever, of the first real battle in which they were about to engage, of all the sudden, strange, and terrible experiences of war. But they did not faint nor falter. They were children of their fathers, and they went forward cheerfully to the expected conflict.

Leaving their cars about a quarter of a mile from the depot, they formed a line, with orders to rush upon the enemy, and force their passage into the boat at the point of the bayonet. They found they were as those that beat the air. The terrible enemy was not. They quietly took possession of the steamer, and ran down to Annapolis, which they reached about two o'clock on Sunday morning, and anchored off the Naval Academy.

Here occurred one of those puzzles which diplomacy often meets with. The commandant of the Naval School had heard that a secession steamer was coming from Baltimore to take possession of that spot. He had not heard of the movements of this regiment, and supposed, of course, that this steamer was the one promised and dreaded. On the other hand, General Butler had heard that the secessionists were already in possession of the Naval School, as well as of the city. A lieutenant came to the steamer to find out who they were. But as he did not like to reveal his position to parties of whom he was in doubt, and as General Butler did not choose to reveal his name and purpose, their conversation was brief and cipherish. Soon the lieutenant said he must go, as a signal had been made for his return. They learned afterward that this signal was to be given, after a certain time had elapsed, so that he might escape to the shore, as they should then consider them secessionists, and open the guns of the fort upon them. The commandant, Captain Blake, however, finding that his lieutenant knew nothing, came off himself, and he and the general talked back and forth in the dark for some time, till gradually they began to find out that they could trust each other.

He then asked for help to get the Constitution into the bay, as it was exposed where it lay to guns from the shore. So the church-going, and many of them church-loving, citizens of Lynn, Marblehead, and their vicinage, worked all day to cut out the famous Old Ironsides. Their steamer ran aground in the effort, and stuck there till Tuesday morning. They could get no help, and had no food nor water, and some of them, in the fury of their thirst, drank the salt water of the bay. The midshipmen, on learning of their condition, brought water in boats to their relief. They lay here in great peril, for there were no means of getting ashore. The people of Annapolis knew of their presence, and it was currently stated that a war steamer was coming from Baltimore to sink them — a thing that could easily have been done.

An accident happened here that was a strong confession of the value of religion to a man. There was only one boat on the steamer, and the general was afraid that one of the crew, or some traitor who might have smuggled himself on board at Perryville, would take it, and give information to the enemy. So he commanded two men to be put in charge of the boat, with orders, if any one touched it, to warn him off; if he did not leave instantly, to shoot him dead. "And," said he, "if you have any praying men in your company, appoint them, for they will conscientiously obey their orders."

On Monday morning the Boston arrived from Philadelphia with the Seventh Regiment, and worked nearly all day to get their steamer afloat, so that the Eighth Regiment, which had been there more than thirty hours, might have the privilege of landing first. But it was found impossible to start her, with their own vessel so heavily laden, and they were compelled to land their men first. Then they drew the Maryland from her long anchorage, and both of the regiments found rest and refreshment in the pleasant quarters of the Academy.

Annapolis was my first acquaintance with a slaveholding city, and of persons held in slavery. The place looked as if cursed by the crime it hugged to its breast. With admirable opportunities for growth, with a harbor and shores that would be filled with enterprise and taste were it not for this crime, the capital of this freest of the Slave States, is as shabby, mean, and crowded as the dirtiest quarters of the North End. I had quite a long conversation with some of the citizens. They had evidently experienced a new sensation. They had learned well the lesson of submission to slavocrats, and as one, who was with me, a Unionist from Kentucky, boasted of the number of slaves that he owned, they seemed to revere him as a superior being. But General Butler had given them a new idol to fear and to worship. And they responded as meekly and readily to my Massachusetts talk as they did to that of the Kentucky slaveholder. They listened almost reverently as I spoke of those terrible bugbears, Wendell Phillips and Lloyd Garrison. Do not imagine that there was any especial courage in me. I had on a sub-military rig, and they knew that five to seven thousand men were less than a mile off, eager to avenge so much as the mere nose-pulling of a Northern soldier. They had learned that there was a North, and that she had strength enough to do as she pleased, even under the eaves of the Maryland Capitol.

As the troops marched out to Washington, the different effect of their presence on the inhabitants was noticeable. The whites looked mad or scared, according to their social position, chiefly scared, and the blacks looked glad out of the eyes, though their lips were discreetly sealed. As we left the city, they began to be more free in the expression of their feelings. About two miles out, a colored family on a lonely plantation waved their handkerchiefs and cheered vociferously. The soldiers in response cheered lustily for the Union, and even kissed their hands to them in their enthusiasm. One old colored woman was in the Senate Chamber a day or two ago selling cakes and pies. One of the officers of the famous Sixth Regiment asked her what she thought of these times. "Why," she said, "you seem to us just like our Lord Jesus. He came down of His own accord to suffer and die to save us. And you also come to suffer and to die to deliver us." The piety of the old sister was not very much shocked by the analogy; I doubt if yours will be. Tears stood in the eyes of the officer as he told me her remark. He thought of those who had already died for this cause in Baltimore.

Camp in the Capitol.

What kind of a place do you imagine a camp to be? Something rural and rustic, I doubt not. Shady trees, running streams, green, waving fields, with tents nestling together, and soldiers with their environments, adding the life of humanity to that of nature. You can hardly take into account the march of improvement in making up such an opinion. You forget how we have improved our ecclesiastical camps from three or four stakes, and a sheet stretched over them, to the luxurious tents and dwellings of the Vineyard and Hamilton. Even so have military encampments caught the spirit of the age. And so we tabernacle to-day not as Aaron in the wilderness, but as his successors in the days of Solomon. Our camp is in the most sumptuous edifice on the continent, one of the most magnificent in the world. Our soldiers sleep under the splendid paintings and bas-reliefs of the Rotunda, or between the gray marble pillars of the old Representative Hall. The echoes of the voices of the heroic past, from Washington to John Quincy Adams, fill their souls with high inspirations. The officers lie on beautiful pavements of many colors, none the softer though for their velvety patterns, and lounge on crimson chairs and sofas, reveling before the battle in the rewards which usually follow only daring and danger. The fragrance of blossoming trees, and the music of bands of birds, salute the senses, not always unmingled with what Charles Lamb calls "the only manly scent," that of tobacco, and what boys think the only manly music, that of other two-legged and gay-appareled bands.

The glitter of muskets, the blare of drums, and

"Sonorous metal blowing martial sounds,"

the gay or sober uniforms, the even step of marching thousands, that revivifies the celebrated Virgilian line (changing "quadrupedante" to "bipedante"), as it shakes the dusty earth with its pulsing foot; these are certainly unwonted experiences for an American city. The "*putrem campum*" of that verse is exceedingly appropriate here. A more disintegratable soil, that professed to be a soil, I never saw. I can understand now how this city is able to almost constantly kick up such a dust as fills the eyes, ears, and mouths of the whole land. The winds here are all simooms, and the political storms are adapted to the climactic ones — of the earth, earthy.

There are probably more soldiers to-day in Washington than were ever gathered before in the same area in this country. And yet it is but a handful to the Parisian armies, and to what may be collected here or elsewhere ere this great rebellion and its greater cause are crushed forever. They are constantly coming. A thousand entered at nine o'clock last evening; another thousand at two o'clock this morning, their spirit-stirring music stirring spirits, and bodies, too, in a manner more stimulating than agreeable.

Notwithstanding the numbers of troops here, probably not less than twenty thousand, including the active militia of the District, the great buildings, where many of them quarter, are not overcrowded. Three thousand troops occupy the Capitol, and yet it looks as empty as a New York church of a Sunday afternoon. Many times that number could easily be packed into its immense halls, passages, and lobbies.

This building, where the nation's hopes and fears so anxiously and so justly center, is held by soldiers from New York, Pennsylvania, and Massachusetts. These three States stand together in the Capitol to maintain our liberty to-day, as they stood fourscore years ago to inaugurate it. It is more than a happy coincidence that the magnificent structure, which embodies the sovereignty and glory of our nation, should be intrusted to the watch-care of these ancient and constant allies. The most dangerous, and hence most honorable, post in it is occupied by the Massachusetts Sixth, who so nobly won the prize in their brave and rapid march to its defense.

I escaped to the elegant Congressional Library, hoping to avoid the din of arms, and throats, and drums that pervades every other part of the Capitol. Vain hope! The tremendous rattle of innumerable drums, as it seems to the drums of my ears, follows me here. From the lovely and usually quiet grounds in front of the Capitol, it arises like the rattling of hammers on the rivets of half a dozen engine boilers. If you want to know how military sounds sound when concentrated into an army, and void of fife and bugle, visit the "Novelty Works," or any other locomotive factory, and listen to the melody aforesaid. The poor birds, who were getting up a fine concert of their own, succumb, and hide their ears behind their wings. If my composition partakes of this intense rattling and ringing, consider it all the more military, and hence the more popular.

Camp at the Relay.

Camp Essex, May 16, 1861.

We have reached it at last.

"My high blown pride
At length breaks under me."

A greater than Jefferson the Little, even the bowed and aching octogenarian of Washington has issued his edict, and here we are. No more lounging on velvet chairs, no more looking through plate-glass, between bronze window frames and marble pillars, across the placid Potomac to Alexandria, and, with the mind's eye, to Richmond. We are on a retreat. We have left for the North.

Our change from our Capitol quarters was most willingly made. Like most persons in such places, we found ourselves sorely afflicted with the rich man's disease — nothing to do. So, when the order came yesterday to march, the soldiers gladly fled to arms and knapsacks. And well they might; for the real camp, which we have reached, is as much before the vain pomp and glory of the one we have left as dear, divine nature is ahead of hard and heartless art. If all pride has such a fall as this, it should not feel hurt at the operation.

Leaving our marble quarters, marching down the superb staircase, whose panels Leutze, or his successors, will hardly be able to fill with a more glorious picture than that then passing before them, we took the cars, and were dropped on the side of the hill, about half a mile from the Relay House.

The next morning the brow of the hill was appropriated to our use; and here, in the soft May air of Maryland, the white canvas town of Camp Essex "rose like an exhalation." The camp is not arranged precisely according to "regulation," yet nearly enough to give an idea of the ideal law, which in the army, as elsewhere, is fully realized but rarely. Close to the trees is a row of tents — the depots of the commissary and quartermaster, and the hospital quarters. The next row is that of the colonel and his staff; next, the tidy quarters of the major; then those of the surgeon and his assistants. The yellow flag of the surgeon is followed by the white one of the chaplain, with whom tents the paymaster. Arms, gold, and the gospel seldom come into such close conjunction as they do in this tent. At night the chaplain sleeps between a box of rifles and a box of money. The third and last of the official rows is that of the captains. At right angles to these are the streets of the privates, more closely built, and more densely populated, than those of the officers. Yet crowded into these tents are many who in wealth, culture, and position are fully the equals of their military superiors. The son of an ex-senator of the United States, and the son of a "Bell-Everett" electoral candidate — himself a Boston lawyer — do duty with the musket, each enjoying his undivided fifteenth part of the canvas ten-footer with as worthy fishermen and shoemakers, carpenters and sailors, for comrades.

Our flank companies are representatives of the flanks of the State — Pittsfield on the left, and Salem on the right. Next to the brilliant Salem Zouaves come the Marblehead fishermen. Captain Knott's Marbleheaders deserve special mention, as the first in all the land to respond to the call of the President. The very next morning after the summons left Washington, his company marched from home through a storm of driving sleet, and Faneuil Hall welcomed them first of all to the service of patriotism, with which it is identified. As they entered its honored walls, bound on a grander mission than any to which their fathers had responded, the "stone must have cried out of the wall, and the beam out of the timber have answered it," in honor of the perpetual valor of this most patriotic of towns. In no less than three of the historic pictures which cover the walls of the rotunda are representatives of Marblehead. The new pictures which shall reproduce this holier war will not be without her heroic presence. Beverly and Gloucester — wonderfully given to fun, frolic, and letter-writing — occupy the next street. Loquacious Lynn and conservative Newburyport share the last two streets. It would never have done to place all the argumentative shoemakers together: there would be no knowing how, with rifles and revolvers in their hands, they might have concluded to carry on their discussions. So Conservatism and Progress are hitched together; and the staid bearers of the name of Cushing, and the lively followers of the senatorial Crispin, balanced each other. Outside of the last street is Pittsfield, looking north and west, protecting the camp on its most assailable side. So seven hundred men are housed within four and twenty hours after leaving the Capitol.

15

The view from our camp is charming. At our feet lies a narrow valley, through which creeps the slumberous Patapsco, covering its face with willows. It has been hard at work miles above driving mills and factories, and now enjoys its release from labor: only temporary, however, is this recess, for it is soon caught again, driven into sluice-ways, and broken upon wheels, only finding lasting peace when it melts into the bosom of the placid Chesapeake. Just beneath us nestles the little village of Elk Ridge Landing — once a port of entry and a haven for ships. But the washings from the hills have choked up the channel, and choked off the trade. Now it seems devoted to the imbibition of whisky, of which, judging from the number of shops, enough is sold to reopen navigation, were it judiciously applied to that purpose. From the hill-top the village has a pleasant aspect, with its two churches, one embowered in trees, and the other standing in a field of blossoming clover, the white tombstones casting a moonlight luster on the green mounds beneath. But these are almost the only adornments of the village. The main street is a collection of wood and brick houses, with no sidewalks, and but few gardens and trees.

The walks around the camp are as delightful as its outlook. Deep ravines, heavily shaded, cover the northern and western sides. Through each of these trickles a tiny brook dancing down to the river. Threading the way through these glens, one enters the upland, which opens into varied vistas. Above the viaduct the Patapsco runs through a deep gorge, scattered along which are mills and the dwellings of the workmen. The summits are crowned with the dwellings of the landholders and their tenants. Looking from these eminences the landscape spreads out in those softly undulating lines which rich soils only can exhibit. A hard, thin soil requires mines of imported wealth, and generations of culture, to give it character. But this rich earth enriches everything. It thickens and deepens the foliage of the trees, softens the hard edges of the hills, and gives to the whole landscape a royal sweep and fullness.

Smoke Before the Fire.

The flames begin to shoot forth along the whole border — at Harper's Ferry, Western Virginia, Cairo, and St. Louis. This great seam in our Ship of State, that has been stuffed and stuffed with tow and pitch by ecclesiastical and political calkers for a couple of generations, is on fire. The flames, long pent within the vessel, have reached the surface, and, naturally enough, break out in its most inflammable part. Soon, perchance, they will lick the stars in their mad fury. "The strong shall be as tow, and the maker of it as a spark, and they shall both burn together, and none shall quench them." There is no blaze here yet — only intense and suffocating smoke, in which all things are hidden. We dwell where Dame Rumor has her seat; but this lady has always proved her close relationship to the father of lies, and never more indisputably than in the present smoke, preliminary, perhaps, to that of battle. One hour she positively declares that twenty-five thousand secessionists are within a day's march of the capital, and intend to storm it before the next nightfall. The next, she declares the troops at Alexandria are verifying Scripture, and fleeing when no man pursueth; that others are also hasting away from Harper's Ferry. So she flies up and down these streets, choking our ears as the dust does our mouths, and with equally unserviceable stuff. The fact is, we shall never know anything certain about the rebellious section until we march an army of observation, as well as of occupation, into its midst. The seceders love darkness rather than light because their deeds are evil. They keep up all kinds of contrary stories to delude the government, and especially the North. They wisely adapt their compound to the exciting of our fears and the allaying of our vigilance. So they say four hundred thousand men will, before midsummer, pour on Washington; or within a week the Confederate flag will float on the Capitol, if they condescend to allow it to stand. Then, having played the bugaboo enough, they pretend it is all practical joking. They have hardly any troops anywhere; only thirty thousand or so in all the Confederacy. Richmond is unprotected, and "only a miracle" can save that city from the government troops. I fear the Greeks bringing these telegraphic gifts. They must be watched and guarded from nearer heights than those of Arlington. We must arise and go down into the South country, and see for ourselves, and, if need be, feel in ourselves their hostile preparations.

The letter-writers and telegraph operators are in a dubious state as it respects matters in the Cabinet, as they are in respect to those in the South. Paul very happily describes the whole class in that keen sketch of the bustling know-nothing wise men of his day, of all skeptical days: "Ever striving and never able to come to the knowledge of the truth." The Vailed Prophet never kept his face more closely concealed than President Lincoln, General Scott, and Secretary Cameron do the face of military affairs. It is a fine time for our spiritualist friends to bring forth their mediums. Enormous prices would be paid by public journals for reliable facts that are undoubtedly transpiring in Virginia and the southernmost States — for more important facts that are as certainly settled and partially embodied in act in the brains of the antagonist leaders — rebels and patriots. How "stale, flat, and unprofitable" that folly looks beside these opportunities and urgencies for its existence! How fortunate it is that these silly women laden with lusts, and sillier men more heavily laden that lead them captive, have no such insight! It is the glory of God to conceal a thing; and this divine glory is partially shared by those who, in the exigencies of State, share also in his sovereignty.

LETTERS FROM CAMP.

II. SLAVERY DYING.

The Look of the Land.

Camp Essex, May 16.

AM sitting on the ground, in the door of my tent, like Abraham; like him, too, on a hill country, from which a large and lovely prospect opens. Like him, yet again, as our brethren in this vicinity would undoubtedly suggest if they sat beside me, I am surrounded by the patriarchal institution, to whose preservation they are ready to sacrifice liberty, civilization, Christianity, every good and perfect gift of God. Not very near is this institution, much less is it armed, as in his day, for the rescue of its master or his kindred from these invaders from the north country. The peaceful scenes over which his eye moved in Oriental quietude are before me, though not in the foreground. The peaceful sounds that crept into his ears are far from filling mine. The drums rattle around me. The loud orders of the officers, drilling their companies, break clear and shrill over the drum-beats, while the hurrahs of other troops welcoming their marching comrades, and the sharp sound of the musketry, or the reverberating roar of the cannon, of yet others who are practicing themselves

and their guns, mingle with the more peaceful chattering of the Gibeonites of the camp in their bustling service for the wants of the body, and are all often encompassed in the scream of the locomotive, and the roar of his train — a welcome proof and prophecy that the victories of peace are not only greater, but more lasting, than those of war. These shall perish, but those shall endure. We can add without irreverence, "Yea, these" signs and weeds of war "shall all wax old as doth a garment; as a vesture shalt thou" O Prince of Peace, "change them, and they shall be changed;" but the years and the triumphs of peace shall have no end. I trust they will be made more melodious in expression. Why cannot the movements of machinery be made as silent as those of nature? Why may they not sing as delightfully to our dull ear as the stars did to the keener sense of Messieurs Shakspeare and Addison? This hurly-burly of peace and war has suddenly ceased for a moment, and blessed Nature, the beloved disciple of her Creator, puts her arms of love and beauty around the distracted soul.

As I look out over the glittering white roofs and stacked bayonets of the camp, my eyes roam over as delightful a bit of scenery as ever enticed them from the drudgery of the pen. A valley lies beneath them, covering some two or three square miles, if its grateful irregularity could be Quakerized into such rectangular abominations as a square. Through it lazily strolls the river, gladly indulging its Southern indisposition to work, after the involuntary servitude into which some avaricious Yankees had forced it, just above the viaduct, for the sake of running their dirty and noisy nail factories.

Our Southern brethren do not believe in compelling anything to work except the negro. With great flourishes about the advantages to him of compulsory labor, and the dire effects of emancipation in letting loose upon their community a mass of idle men and women, they join a most hearty indifference to the idleness of all other creatures, human, animal, and vegetable.

An amusing instance of the unconscious power of this feeling occurred yesterday. A friend residing here, whose pleasant acquaintance I have made, speaking of a piece of meadow which was being devoted to the raising of osier, or basket willow, said the owner was getting twenty-five dollars an acre per annum for the meadow, and "didn't have to work it at all." That last consideration would have never occurred to a Northern man. This is one of the most important railroad centers in the country — trains passing and stopping almost every hour of the day and night; and yet I have not seen half a dozen teams in its streets, except those in the service of the troops, during my three days' residence. Here are three thousand men hungry for delicacies, and willing to pay for them, and not a farmer's cart has entered the camp. A half dozen black and white loafers with little baskets of cakes and pies, a wagon or two larger capitalists, with beer and oranges, are the whole trading force extemporized by our necessities. The exhibition day of a country academy in a Northern State develops tenfold more business activity than these multitudinous trains and troops can bring to life here. Great masses of the fat earth slumber in the sun. Many fine acres of grain and grass gladden my sight, or would gladden it, did I not think that the eye of the Holy Spirit was fixed on these same fields and their owners and tillers. How plainly His solemn tones sounded in my ear as He speaks to these transgressors, "Go to now, ye rich men; weep and howl for your miseries that shall come upon you. Behold, the hire of the laborers who have reaped down your fields, *which is of you kept back by fraud,* crieth; and the cries of them which have reaped are entered into the ears of the Lord of Sabaoth." That Lord of Sabaoth, the Lord of hosts, is marshaling His hosts for battle. May He not be compelled to employ them in the punishment of these defrauders, but may they speedily give unto their servants that which is just and equal. "Behold, the Judge standeth at the door."

I must acknowledge the fields look very lovely, whatever the mode by which they are cultivated, and are satisfactory because they are expressive of industry, even if unpaid. On some of their knolls, hidden in the already deep foliage, stand the cosy farm-houses, with their slave quarters, like the corn-barns and smoke-houses of Northern farmers, cuddling round the back door, near enough to bring in the corn-cakes without their getting cold by the way, and far enough off to keep up the idea that they are a kind of distinct order of beings — a notion which the white man in this region so sedulously and so foolishly cultivates. The slaves are housed, in location and in the style of their dwelling, about half way between their master and his other cattle. They have about the same position in the fancies with which he feeds his brain — a sort of half-way house between a white man and a fine horse.

Around this lazy yet lovely valley rise hills like the one where I am writing, though usually unoccupied, and either covered with wild woods or scarred with brown barren patches that have evidently been scratched by the slave's plow till they have refused to respond to such forced entreaties, and were then abandoned by their idle owners to an unnatural desolation. But the gay sunlight makes them pleasant to look upon at this distance, and they agreeably diversify the deep green of the rolling meadow and more rolling forest, among which they lie.

If I rise up, and walk or ride through the land, I can but see what Lot saw when he lifted up his eyes, that it is "well watered everywhere, even as the garden of the Lord, like the land of Egypt as thou comest unto Zoar." Is it not in other respects like the land Lot saw? Does not God see the weary bands that have often moved, handcuffed and chained together, along these roads, marching to the hotter fires of a more Southern hell? Does He not hear the voice of lustful command, of ferocious rage, of the blasphemous auctioneering of sacred woman, and lovely children, and Christian men, made in His image and regenerated with His grace? Does not His ever-listening ear hear these brutal sounds of tyrannic passion as they go up through this soft and palpitating air? A Maryland gentleman, once a slaveholder, told me that he heard the high sheriff of one of her counties, after one of these human auctions, say, "Lloyd Garrison never talked half bad enough about us. I am surprised that the earth does not open and swallow us up." Has not the Creator said of this and more Southern, and probably even more sinful soil, "Because the cry of Sodom and Gomorrah is great, and because their sin is very grievous, I will go down now and see whether they have done altogether according to the cry of it which is come unto me; and if not, I will know." He is making inquisition for blood. Who shall be able to stand?

I rejoice to see tokens of the departure of this cloud of darkness and death from this fair land. The rays of universal liberty are shooting through Maryland. They gladden with their novel radiance the mountains and valleys of Virginia. See the vote for the Union just cast here — the Union with an anti-slavery North, and under an anti-slavery government. See the new governor of Virginia, his associates, and the whole animus of his government. Kansas, too, stands tiptoe on those misty mountain-tops. Missouri has dethroned Satan from his usurped seat there. Here, too, is the light descending. The active complicity, or, at the best, supine indifference of the wealthy, the fear and feebleness of the working classes, the cowardice of the Church, and the cruelty of the State, are rapidly coming to a perpetual end. One can hardly conceive the change which has been already wrought here since the possession of its territories by the armies of an anti-slavery government. Its citizens begin to breathe freely, and even talk freely. Soon will healthful agitation breezes blow, and the work of regeneration be begun, never to stop till the blessing of perfect love to God and every man shall universally prevail.

"Behold how brightly breaks the morning."

How Slaves Talk.

It is quiet and peaceful here now, and I will avail myself of the brief interregnum to post the book of my experience and observation on the great matter which has kindled this great fire — the merchandise of the bodies and souls of men.

I am like one who should discourse wisely on all the currents, storms, and other grand phenomena of the ocean, when he had only stood on the rocks at Nahant, had seen the waves roll in on a pleasant day, and had thrown his eyes over the modest sheet that lies at his feet. I have only touched the edge of the great gulf of slavery, that sweeps for thousands of miles beyond me, with its terrific storms of lust and ferocity, its immeasurable depths of despair and dread, its awful, unutterable blackness of darkness. I walk along the beach, gather a few of its pebbles, listen to the solemn dash of its cold and cruel waves, and look out with wearied eyes on the gloomy expanse, as it spreads itself, southward and westward, myriads of miles, in a horror of great darkness.

The first person that I ever saw in slavery was at Annapolis. She was a pleasant, modest girl of ten or twelve summers. Her name was Mary. I thought how appropriate that the name of the mother of my Lord should be given to this poor, despised girl, whom somebody pretended to own; whom they could sell in the market-place, and subject to all unutterable horrors that overhang the future of these innocent maidens. Had slavery existed in Judea, the mother of Christ would have been a *slave*. For He must stand at the bottom of humanity that He might embrace it. In fact, he is asserted to have occupied this place. If the pro-slavery divines are right, in pressing out of measure the word "servant" in the letters of Paul, and if δοῦλος refers in all cases to slaves, then Christ was a slave; for Paul says, "He made Himself of no reputation, and took upon Him the form of a slave." I trust the poor slaves find comfort in that text, when they are drenched through and through with the pratings of preachers as to the duties of servants.

I suppose, if I had visited Havana, I should have heard my black brother called Jesus. I wish these man-servants, had this name. He who took their place would be glad to comfort them with His human title. The nearest we can come to it is Mary, and so I am glad they have the sense of kinship with Him which that name confers. But yesterday I dined with a slaveholder, a member of our church, who owned his cook, — and a very fine cook she was, too, judging from the dinner, — who was also blessed with this sacred name.

The name of John Brown, which so many good men of New England have not yet reverenced as they will, and the cause in which he is yet to be copied by this nation, and for which he laid down his life, find respectful hearers in the midst of this people, that have sat so long in darkness. But the other night, after a pleasant prayer meeting in the village church, quite a number of the members stood at the cross roads, and discoursed on this subject and on this hero. They knew him here. They said he traveled through this section quite extensively the summer before his death. One of them, a blacksmith, said that his horse was shod at his shop. He called himself a Baptist preacher, and had trusses for sale. As hernia, I have been told, is a very common disease with the slaves, this business gave him fine opportunities for making their acquaintance. He spoke freely against slavery, and was very ready with the Scripture in his discussions with the people. These last characteristics were marks of the man, no less than the former, by which he sought to relieve them in their physical weakness, and, at the same time, to fill their ears with the glad tidings that the year of jubilee had come. He died without the sight, yet he saw it by faith, and was glad.

The whites, as a body, ignore the blacks altogether. A good brother from Virginia told me, in Washington, he could not look upon them as the same order of beings with himself. He was perfectly honest, and, I am afraid, spoke frankly what yet abides powerfully in many breasts in New England. They carry this sentiment a little further here than in New England, though they only carry it to its logical issue. They say, if of a different species of humanity, radically, perpetually, then of a lower, as is apparent by their history and condition. If of a lower, then they are the servants of the higher. If divinely appointed for servitude, where's the harm in slavery, *per se?* Now, we cannot cure this brother's idea as to slavery, until we pluck the tap-root of caste and prejudice from ourselves. We must first cast the beam out of our own eye, and then we can see clearly to cast the mote out of our brother's eye.

This is the common feeling here. Hence they talk flippantly about the blacks not being able to take care of themselves — not desiring freedom — not being as well off when free as when enslaved — and much other white trash, which goes for good common sense in this section of the country. I thought I would go to the fountain head, and see if the waters tasted the same there. I would apply a little of Baconianism to the problem. So I asked the slaves and their free kindred themselves what they thought in these matters? How easy it is for a child to confound a philosopher, if the child has common sense and the wise man has not! I do not suppose all the gentlemen I have talked with on this subject—and they have not been a few—have conversed with as many of their colored neighbors, and in some cases, as I have been told by themselves, blood relations, on these vital questions, in all their lives, as I have talked with in the last forty days. They are regular Aristotelians on this subject of inquiry. They shut themselves up in their own exclusive Caucasian conceit, and theorize as to the state of feeling in their neighbors, with whom they never honestly converse.

Two interesting proofs of this occurred here but this week. I was visiting at one of the elegant seats surrounding our camp. The subject of slavery came up. The lady of the house was in great fear of insurrections in the Cotton States — the gentleman laughed at her fears. "Slaves wouldn't take their liberty if it was offered them," he said. He "tried it once." "Who will take care of the pickaninnies when they are sick?" says Juno. "Who will give me a dollar and a horse to ride to town if I am free," says Jupiter. So the king of gods and men, and his ox-eyed queen, *"soror uxorque Jovis,"* have their ears bored through, and well hung with brass pendants, and become bond servants forever to a lank, brown, strutting, tobacco-chewing lot of humans. (The gentleman aforesaid is not of this class. He is a Unionist and a non-slaveholder, having manumitted the "gods of Greece" in spite of their protestations.) How changed from those divinities who shook the world with their nod, and who sat in calm authority over the great Trojans and greater Greeks and Romans, in their long, eventful history! I thought I would hunt up some of these gods and goddesses, and if I did not worship at their feet, I would at least inquire reverently as to their feelings on the matter of freedom and slavery.

The next day I sat in the woods reading, when Jupiter came along disguised as an old black man, with a basket on his arm and a staff in his hand. Having been taught in Grecian mythology, I detected the deity in spite of the disguise. I addressed him respectfully. He was complacent and conversible. I asked him his name. He had assumed for the present that of John Diggs.

"Are you a slave?"

"No, sir."

"Have you ever been?"

"Yes, sir — till I was thirty odd years old."

"How did you get your freedom?"

"My mistress gave it to me at her death."

"How long have you been free?"

"Some fifteen or twenty years."

"Well, I understand you free blacks are not half as well off as the slaves. That is true, isn't it?"

"No, sir; I live better than I ever did when a slave."

"But they say you won't work — you are all lazy."

"They won't give us a chance, sir. They don't like to encourage the free negro, and so they hire slaves or the Irish, and let us starve. We would work as heartily as anybody if they would hire us."

"But weren't you happier when a slave? You had enough to eat and drink then, and wherewithal to be clothed."

"I didn't have any more than I do now; and, then, now when I sit down to my dinner and supper, I don't have somebody come blustering and swearing round the door, swinging his whip and flogging me away to any kind of hard work, though ever so tired. Ah, sir, I'm a great deal happier eating my poor supper nowadays, with my wife and chil'n, than I ever was when a slave."

"Have you any relations in slavery?"

"All my brothers and sisters."

"Where?"

"In Prince George's County, sir."

"They don't wish to be free, do they?"

"Yes, sir, every slave does."

"You must be mistaken. A good many gentlemen have told me that they don't want to be free."

"I would like to have them offer the slaves their liberty."

"But what makes you want to be free?"

"Why, sir, you know, when a boy's about thirteen years old, he feels as he'd like to be his own master, and the feeling don't grow any less as he grows older."

So ended my catechism and his replies. The twinkle of his eyes, as he told of his happiness over the scanty supper table, and the passion of boys for freedom, spoke far more than his lips. I asked him if he went to meeting.

"O, yes, I've been a Methodist for most forty years."

"Why don't you go to the church in the village?"

"O, sir, 'pears as the white folks don't like to have us worship with them, and so we have to have a house of our own."

"Well, religion is a good thing, isn't it?"

"Yes, sir, sweeter than honey, sweeter than sugar, better than coffee, sir."

I could appreciate that climax after forty days' drinking of camp coffee. I was glad to find that Jupiter had experienced religion, and become a humble and happy Christian. This war shows that Mars has met with a change also. I have talked with not a few blacks, and find but one sentiment. One old man, with but one leg, said he thought the war was for liberty.

"Liberty for whom?" I asked.

"For all of us, white and black."

I asked him if he would fight in the war.

"Yes," he answered, "as much as he could with his one leg."

At Washington I asked a waiter similar questions. He was free, had been born a slave, bought himself for six hundred dollars; his wife and children were yet slaves, and were sold from him to Tennessee.

I asked why he was so foolish as to work hard and raise money to buy himself. Everybody here said the slaves were better off than the free blacks.

"O, sir," said he, "I wanted to lie down massa and get up massa!"

"Out of the mouths of babes and sucklings," as these supercilious whites esteem their colored brethren, "has God ordained strength, that He may still the enemy and the avenger."

The Carrollton Manor.

As we leave Ellicot's Mills we enter the broad, handsome turnpike from Baltimore to Frederick. This is the finest road I have seen in this country; it is the only fine one in this vicinity. None handsomer, no one as handsome, goes out of Boston. It is a hundred feet broad, running directly west from Baltimore for nine miles, with undeviating steadfastness, turning neither to the right hand nor to the left. Nine miles out it winds round to the river to accommodate Ellicot's Mills, and then, going up to the high rolling lands it had abandoned for a moment, it proceeds on, as wide, hard, and straight as before. We entered upon this part of our journey with some misgivings. We had left pretty much all the Unionism of the section behind us. The turnpike gate seemed to have over it the inscription over Dante's Inferno: "All hope abandon, ye who enter here." Nevertheless Dante did not abandon his hope, nor did success abandon him. So I entered the infernal region, where scenes even more horrible than those that met his eye, often meet the eye of Him who rules over this, as well as the nether hell, for here is crime, not punishment alone, and crime against the innocent and holy children of God.

I heard some deeds worse than any which he records, but

I dare not put them in print. What they must be, you may imagine, when I say that his medieval frankness, not to say coarseness of speech, and his wonderful imagination have not conceived of scenes of barbarism, which men coolly spoke of as having been attempted by the present occupant of the grandest of these estates—the grandson of the signer of the Declaration. Nothing very marked or different from other places attracts you as you enter this Inferno.

The land lies very pleasant to the eyes — great fields stretch out before you. The trees gather often into clusters, and expand at times in grand forests; the corn, grass, clover, and cattle, and the human crop that raise or tend these, meet your eyes. A slumbering stillness is in the air. Only here and there a house is seen; not half a dozen in half a dozen miles. The houses of the proprietors are generally situated a mile or two from the road, in the center of their farms, and reached by a wagon path across the fields. The quarters of the negroes are alike hidden. The fields look as if of capacity for extraordinary culture, but are poorly tilled. One or two places are evidently well cared for. The one that seems the most like a Northern place is Mr. Hammond's, an ex-member of Congress, and a strong Union man, almost the only one, as far as I could learn, in the region.

The Carroll estate comprises twelve thousand acres. The turnpike runs for miles across it. One piece of woods is three miles wide. This will give some idea of a plantation, though it is but a quarter section beside some of those further South. It also suggests one reason why the Southron has so long ruled this country. There is nothing like land to implant in others and in its owner the sense of power. The possession of the treasures in the vaults of Boston banks would not give its owner or his poor neighbor such a realizing sense of his consequence as the calling of this farm his own. Our riches have been stored in factories and banks, in city houses and country seats, costly but small.

Theirs have been spread out over the earth: they can ride for miles on their own land; they own to the skies and the central fires. These last seem now to be breaking through the crust. What is a Fifth Avenue palace or millions of stocks to such possessions? England's nobility have maintained their preëminence by maintaining the proprietorship of the soil. These gentry would not sell a foot of their land; they buy, but never sell; they will not sell a white man a small farm any sooner than they would a black one himself. Now, add to this the owning of the men who till it, and of their wives and children, and you have an aristocracy as much prouder than England's, as their property is higher. These landed slaveholders rule this State; but sixteen thousand of them in a half million of white inhabitants, probably less than ten thousand of this class, and owning less than eighty thousand slaves; yet they sit supremely and quietly on the necks of their white as well as black neighbors, drain the State of enterprise, and keep its poorer classes in contemptuous degradation.

The manor-house is situated near the eastern edge of the lot, and near the turnpike. Turn from the road, and go south through a pleasant shaded roadway for about a third of a mile, and you come to the mansion. Near the road on the right is a heap of slave huts. The overseer's residence, a good-sized but shabby-looking brick building, stands among them. Barns and sheds are close at hand; on the right, through a long vista of trees, an eighth of a mile from the road, stands the revolutionary house. It is a low, spacious, wooden, yellow mansion, enlarged evidently at different times, one of its latter additions being a Catholic chapel. It has none of the costly elegance of the new houses of New York and New England, but looks much like the largest of the old mansions, made a good deal larger by plain additions. It had the comely, comfortable look of a grandee in his lean and slippered pantaloon.

I turned from the house to the quarters of its colored people, as they euphemistically call slaves here; they shrink from that word. I rode a little way beyond the house, having no invitation to stop; had I stopped, I should probably have found it rather difficult to get away, as the sympathies of this descendant of that patriot are all with the secessionists.

As I rode away, I met a slave woman dragging herself along to her work. As I had not the entrée to the master, I thought I would do the next best thing—cultivate the acquaintance of his most precious property. I asked her how many colored people there were on the estate. She said there was better than a hundred in these quarters, and there were other quarters above.

"Have you a good time?"

"Yes, Sundays. We have to work hard all the week, but we get together Sundays and enjoys ourselves."

"Where are you going?"

"To the field where the rest of the gang is — I have been to nurse my baby."

"How old is it?"

"Four months."

Fearing if I talked longer I should get her into trouble, and myself too, I threw her a quarter and bid her good by. She seemed amazed at the sight of the bit of money. I fancy her millionnaire owner had never given her as much, except at Christmas, in all his life.

The houses where these cattle are stabled are about as comely and cleanly as a pig-sty. I found it hard to believe that so rich and so lordly a man should put his choicest creatures in such huts. I contrasted them with the handsome cottages with which the great land-owners of the Hudson delight to adorn their estates, and in which they require their tenants to live in a neat and sometimes elegant style. But then these are compelled to treat them thus, or they will have to give them more than they wish to bestow. A neat stone dairy, just behind these huts, showed that the proprietor knew how to set off his estate with pretty buildings, if he only dared to do so.

Should he put his slaves in such houses, they must be taught to respect themselves; they must have beds and tables, and carpets and pictures, and all the little and big adornings of a real home. Could he compel the mother to work behind the plow, and walk back and forth two or three miles to nurse her babe, if she was living in this style? Could he drive the young, pretty girls, some of whom I saw, like field oxen, from such cosy homes, with their flower gardens, and inward comforts and elegances? His cultivated taste would revolt at that, and so he treats them worse than he does his horses; he has scores of these, handsome blooded animals, and their stables, close by the negro huts, far surpass them in respectability and comfort.

I drove out on the turnpike, and left the great manor of Charles Carroll of Carrollton with profounder detestation than ever before of the demon which possessed it, and which transformed its servants into slaves and its masters into tyrants.

A Slave Pen.

We leave the Marshall House at Alexandria, with its fresh and perpetual memories of Ellsworth's daring and death, follow the street west for half a mile or more, and reach a good-looking brick house, with a high fence on the east side, inclosing a yard, and some lower brick and wooden buildings that join the main building and run back from the street. Over the windows are printed, in large black and white letters, like the institution it advertises, the names of the enterprising proprietors of the establishment, with "Dealers in Slaves" under their "Christian" names.

Here is one of the depots of which so much has been written. We enter the rear quarters. Whitewashed and painted, they have no very offensive look. No Pharisaic tomb ever looked lovelier to a Jewish eye than this to a Virginian's. The difference between them was in favor of the latter. For the "inward parts" of this glittering tomb were sweet and attractive to his corrupted sense. No vampire ever delighted in the contents of a grave as much as he in the living creatures that had tenanted this spot.

The inner court was about one hundred feet square, paved with brick, with walls not less than twenty feet high, and a rude shed projecting from one side, as a shelter from the sun or rain. Here the "cattle" were permitted to run at large, and probably were sorted according to age or condition. Here the purchasers could make their selections; and hence the happy property passed away, like the pilgrims from the land of Beulah, to that perfect paradise, the plantation of the South.

My friend with me said he had often heard them singing as he had passed by. That shows how happy they were, and how cruel it was of the fanatical North to seek to prevent the spreading of this more than scriptural, even Southern, holiness and blessedness over all these lands.

I thought of Paul and Silas in prison — how they prayed and sang praises unto God. Now, as then, not only here, but over the whole region, through the vast prison of slavery, there is a great earthquake, so that its foundations are shaken, and many of its doors are being opened, and the prisoners' bands are loosed. I would that I could add, the jailers are penitent and converted. That will come in due time.

In this court were spread tables for some of the soldiers — a great change in one short month. I went into the dungeon. A trap-door, opening in the floor of the court, let me down into the cell underground, moderately spacious and immoderately dirty. As I stood there and thought of the free men who had been thrust in there, and of their sufferings and sorrows, my heart bled very fast. I remembered that though light had broken out here, there were such courts and cells at Baltimore still occupied by slaves. They were yet all over one half of our land, and I could but pray that this great conflict might not cease till each of them, like this, was occupied by the armies of the Republic, and their former occupants were standing in the fullness of their long-sought liberty.*

A Rational Beast and His Possibilities.

A grove of handsome trees, tall grass, and a stirring breeze are the accompaniments of this talk. I hope the reader will find some traces of their presence lingering in it, refreshing him with a vivacity not its own.

> "As sunbeams stream through liberal space,
> And nothing jostle or displace,
> So waves the pine tree through my thought,
> And fans the dreams it never brought."

Slaves are working just by me, and will give the letter the flavor of the palmetto rather than the pine. One of these "beasts" (they are as hard to name as the "ζῶα" the Revelator saw, and which our translators did into that wretched English) draws near me in his work. I bring my thoughts back instantly from their wanderings, and concentrate them on this central object to-day of all the civilized world.

"You like slavery, don't you?"

"No, sir; who ever liked to be a slave?"

"I've heard many say that you who were slaves preferred it to freedom."

* See Note IX.

"It isn't so; I should like to be free. Everybody wants to be."

"What do you want to be free for?"

"What a queer question that is! What does anybody want to be free for?"

"But you can't take care of yourself, if free, they tell me."

"Why not, sir? We take care of ourselves now, and make money for our masters. If we didn't, they would wish us dead right quick."

Verily hath a "beast" discourse of reason. I was as much amazed as Jacques, when, like me, he "met a fool in the forest," and found before he got through with him that he was himself the greater fool.

I am afraid I committed great treason by such conversation.

I, however, thus settled a very knotty question in natural history that has long troubled the savans, namely, if the lower orders of creation are endowed with the faculty of reason. Not only was that problem solved, but a very important discovery was made, that they could talk readily, and in as good English as the human, that is, the white, race can, among whom they live. Some of them, no doubt, may be taught to read and write, and acquire the more recondite sciences, and even may learn to cultivate the domestic feelings, filial, fraternal, parental, and conjugal, and possibly, in rare cases, can be taught to pray and preach, and make quite respectable Christian brutes.

I congratulate my Southern brethren on the wonderful *discovery they have made; that such an order of beings is* found among those creatures over whom God has given man dominion. They have been a little too modest about publishing to the world their treasure. They are getting bravely over this, however. Under the sacred inspirations of such teachers as Dr. Smith, Professor Bledsoe, and as many other prophets as gathered together once on a time at Mount Carmel, they have become convinced that they should not only tell to the listening and astonished earth the wondrous tale, but should fight with fire and sword every one who will not accept their opinion for truth.

I am constrained to confirm this statement of theirs, that they have a species of rational, feeling, Christian creatures, *which* (I cannot say *whom*—that pronoun belongs only to the human race) they can and do treat precisely as they do their horses and pigs, only the former do not have quite so easy a time or quite so luxurious living as the latter. I am sorry to add that they have not yet perceived the capacity for development which these creatures possess, nor the great variety of important uses to which they may be applied. They ought to take a few lessons in Goodyear, and see how he has worked his patent rubber into innumerable forms, and so work up their patent Negro to something near his capacity.

Even my untutored eye discerns that it is susceptible of immense improvement, and of employment in a myriad of ways that will pay. Excuse that Yankee thought. I find it is not totally unknown or disliked in this superior clime. This "strange beast," that can think, and feel, and talk, just like a human being, should not be confined to works that a steam-plow and reaper, a mere ox or horse, can do as well as he. He could be trained, I am positive, to the very highest of those labors by which we have to earn our daily bread. Only apply the right kind of culture, and give him the right sort of feed, and he will relieve the divine Caucasian of much of the drudgery which he has to undergo, and which is so hard in this hot country, and so degrading to that dignified head of creation.

I have no doubt that a doctor could train this animal so that he could diagnose as well as himself, and might be sent on those long midnight journeys, and could be compelled to go through those painful watchings by perilous couches, which exhaust the good white physician. Sleeping comfortably in his bed, lounging comfortably on his farm, he could send this creature, after being Rareyfied in colleges literary and medical, on these laborious missions. So the merchant might do his buying and selling, "shave" and be "shaved" through his chattel personal, he meanwhile "loafing" sumptuously every day. So the lawyer could get up and get off his pleas; the judge make up and pronounce his decisions; the sheriff execute his writs; the general drill his troops, and the troops themselves be drilled, —all by this admirable proxy. The editor could write those splendid editorials on State-rights, and the superiority of Southern statesmanship, society, religion, and civilization generally, and never himself write a line or think a thought on the inspiring themes. The legislator could decree and the governor execute by the same medium. Even the ministers, the hardest worked of all male people, could be relieved by using the gifts the gods provide. Wouldn't it be nice to feel no nervousness creeping over you as Saturday comes and finds you with no beaten oil of the sanctuary wherewith to fill the pulpit lamps on the morrow? Wouldn't it be pleasant to have the hot Sunday's sun rise upon you with no premonitory sweat oozing out of your pores at the thought of the work before you? All you have to do is to select one of the purest blood of this breed, send him to Randolph Macon, or Emory and Henry, where they know how to treat and train them, and then at every conference the itinerant rides away to his appointment with or on his factotum (they ride *on* them in Dahomey), sets him to studying, writing, preaching, visiting (the religious sort), all for his board and clothes, —just what it costs to keep his horse, —feed and harness.

If they wish for a specimen of the extraordinary development this creature can reach, who is a full proof of the feasibility of my plan, I can bring to Maryland one of this "kind," that was born and trained on her soil, and under the blessed influence of this benign institution, which not one of her ministers dares say is sinful, and many say is right. This Maryland animal has been trained partly under less favorable influences of freedom and equality, and hence is not as advanced as he would have been had he staid in the holy ordinance of slavery. Yet, despite this defect, he can as far surpass the greatest of the human orators of this State in art, pathos, reason, dramatic power, and all the other qualities that sweep an audience, as the white man by nature surpasses the black something. They should get this fine specimen of the capacities of their slave creature, and show it off in the Maryland Institute. The name of this excellent proof of the possibilities of slavery and Africa, is Frederic Douglass.

But I am getting enthusiastic. "The swelling theme" makes the style swollen. I can only say with Hosea Biglow on a like occasion, —

> "Forgive me, my friends, if I seem to be het;
> But a subject like this must with vigor be met."

I reluctantly abandon the enticing topic, only requesting that if, like Archimedes, Pliny, Ledyard, and many such, I perish through my too great desire to enlarge the bounds of human knowledge, I shall be held for a brief season in moderately grateful remembrance by my friends in this region for these discoveries and suggestions.

I have talked in the "Hercles vein," not because it is the only vein that bleeds to-day. Below the titillation of the surface flow swift and strong the deep currents of sympathy for those in this bounteous land who are bereft of all bounties. How plainly do I hear in this quiet wood, far from the noise of camp and street, —

> "The still, sad music of humanity,
> Not harsh nor grating, but of amplest power
> To chasten and subdue."

Arlington when first Captured.

From the gateway of General Lee's grounds the road soon enters a magnificent grove, as wild and massy as a White Mountain forest; though, unlike that, the ground is clear of underbrush, so that one can take in at a glance large spaces of the grand scenery. How cool and delightful is the change from the hot and dusty street to this charming forest!

The soldiers of the New York Eighth — dapper, small, and smart as are New York City soldiers — are scattered here and there along the road, lying on logs or stretched beside their tents. They give a novel and yet already familiar aspect to the scene. Winding up through this landscape and woodscape for a mile or so, we reached the broad summit where the house stands. Trees filled the large and level space close up to the house. In among the trees stands the main body of the tents of the regiment. The house is a spacious brick mansion, old-fashioned, gloomy, and decidedly seedy. Great pillars, large enough for a building thrice its size, support a portico. Before this the lawn rolls down over a score or so of acres to the woods that engirt it. Beyond lies the placid Potomac, and beyond that the more placid Capitol, glittering in the western sun as brightly as though no traitor's eye had ever looked on it from this spot enviously and murderously. Entering the house you find the old-fashioned look of the outside intensified. It seems to have none of the modern conveniences which the humblest cottages of the North enjoy. Fitted out elegantly two or three generations ago, it looks as much out of place as the perfect "one-horse shay" among the fancy turn-outs of Central Park. "'Tis sixty years since," seems written over everything. High-back chairs, high-post bedsteads, antique and very ordinary pictures, stag antlers, and many other venerable institutions, show that it is an heir-loom, and not of the living present. Northern houses of this sort do not disdain the modern comforts and conveniences. Gas and water can flow between old timbers as well as new. Modern chairs mix in with the ancient as children with old folks. But the pride of the real, Simon-pure, no-mistake Tom Thumbs, who style themselves F. F. V.'s, is to have everything old. Even the children here are probably born a hundred years old. Either pride or poverty, perhaps both, keeps the house in such a moldy state. Going to the rear, you notice the inevitable negro quarters, detached wings running from each end of the house, and, as I have noticed in Maryland, half way between the mansion and the stables. These buildings are large enough to accommodate, cattle fashion, quite a number of head. General Lee not being at home, I leave my card with his servants.

An old gray-headed negro, dressed in a neat black suit, sat on one of the door-sills. I looked in, and found a cellar some six feet deep, into which some broken steps descended. I asked him if those were his quarters. He replied in the affirmative.

"Had you no floor?"

"Yes, I had one, but the rats troubled me so I took it up."

"How long have you lived here?"

"Several years."

"Alone?"

"Since my wife died."

"Do you find it comfortable down there?"

"O, yes, pretty comfortable."

I looked down. There was an excuse for a bed in one corner, an old broken bit of a stove, a little table with a dish or two, candle-ends, etc., on it, a broken chair, an ax, a billet or two of wood, and the common earthen floor of a cellar; high up out of reach was a dirty window. Here was another proof of the old-fashioned notions that rule this region. An old man of nearly if not more than four-score years, modest, neat, courteous, living in a cellar, and in as much worse condition as any pauper I ever saw as a pauper's is worse than a prince's. My ears have been stuffed since I came here with the superior condition of the slaves to the free blacks. I have visited two of the grandest estates of this region, the Carrollton Manor and Arlington Heights. I have entered more than one of the free blacks' humble cottages, and I must say my eyes saw only filth and misery in the one, in the other neatness, self-respect, poverty, but pride also; yes, good reader, pride! Why shouldn't these scions of a mighty race have some of their haughty fathers' feelings? I entered one of the humblest of these huts near the Relay. The floor was as white as a Dutch dame's the morning after washing-day. Near the door stood an old trunk, the gift, probably, of some primeval mistress, — perhaps Noah's wife's to Canaan's, her granddaughter-in-law, and the first female slave. (*Vide* Dr. Smith and other very learned pro-slavery commentators, *passim.*) I never saw a cleaner house than that humble Christian's. The yard was swept as nice as the floor. Yet her husband had been a slave, and was then of that poor, despised company of free blacks whom so many here are ready to lift up their heel against. I have seen no slaves' quarters to compare with these bits of free soil.

I left the old man so tenderly cared for by those whom he has served so long, after commending him to Him who was as despised and rejected of men, and who had not even a damp cellar wherein to lay His head. Crossing to the opposite buildings, I saw a comely quadroon or octoroon washing. The floor was on her room, and half a dozen lively chattels on the floor. The breed is rather interesting in its adolescent state. Young lambs, and pigs, and dogs, and kittens have long been favorites of the farm. I don't think any of them superior to the younglings of this species of property. I found myself enjoying the gambols of these brown lambkins. It is really a fine-looking creature. Curly locks, quite too long for a lamb's or a negro's; large, laughing eyes; brown but well-cut features, much more closely resembling a Caucasian's than the ape's or gorilla's, to which they are said to be allied; fine-turned legs, and neat little feet, whose hollow did not make a very great hole in the ground, as they went capering about the house and the yard, — these are some of the characteristics of this king of beasts.

I asked the mother (dam perhaps I ought to say; ma-dam somebody will some time say), "Who do you belong to?"

"Mrs. Lee."

"Are you a member of the Church?"

"Yes, the Baptist."

"How many children have you?" (Pardon me for using the word children. She talked and acted so much like a Christian mother I didn't like to say "young ones.")

"Seven."

"Do you expect to be free?"

"Yes, sir; in about a year our time is up."

'Do you want to be free?"

"Yes, sir, I do."

"What for?"

"Because I do."

Didn't that reason show the woman as much as the baboonness? Not being acquainted with the latter's method of reasoning, I cannot be sure, but it struck me as a very familiar and conclusive answer. I bade her good by, a thing I never did a Northern animal, and threw some parting smiles at the jolly little contrabands who are to be transformed in a year or so from creatures that are appointed as meat for man (Genesis ix. 3) into beings made in the likeness of God.

A very tender Conscience.

A gentleman in our neighborhood supplied some of the officers' tables with milk. When Sunday came no milk came. Upon inquiry it was found that he had conscientious scruples about sending them milk that day. As they had no ice, and hence must be left destitute of this agreeable addition to the liquid distillment which the cooks called coffee, he finally relented and sent the milk, but would take no pay for it, — at least on that day. Yet this gentleman was a secessionist, a slaveholder, and had secured a valuable and beautiful estate, I understood, chiefly through the sale of human flesh. On one occasion it was said, that having received some thirty-four "head" (the very word I have heard used in speaking of slaves) of this stock as a marriage dowry, — what a gift to crown those sweet and sacred bonds! — he sold thirty of them. Were the King of Dahomey's funeral sacrifices much more horrible in the sight of God than the agonies which graced this Christian wedding festival?

Having coined their blood to drachmas, he moved hither with his fair bride and her remaining body-guard, and invested the drachmas, the price of innocent blood, in a beautiful farm. Is not this the Potter's Field which these many times thirty pieces of silver purchased?

As an offset to this slave-trading, I ought to set another fact in his history of late occurrence, in which he refused to sell a slave. Some of our brethren hereabout, and yonabout, too, for the matter of that, lay much stress on the fact that our slaveholding brethren never sell their slaves. Let me show how this virtue is illustrated in the life of my hero. A short time since, a free colored man from the South, I think from South Carolina, whose wife and children were the "property" of this gentleman, came here to see him. Whether invited, or whether a fugitive from Secessia, I know not. He is said to be a man of property, and was anxious to invest this property in his family. The wife being old, and lame, and fleshy, and otherwise of no great pecuniary advantage to her "owner," was graciously and freely given to her liege lord; though I understand no free papers were given her, so as to make the deed of gift of any real value. But her daughter, the only child left, a good-looking girl of sweet sixteen, he would not sell to her own father. The father offered thirteen hundred dollars for his daughter, but was refused.

Will not that do for a modern illustration of the ancient gnat and camel text? A man who would not sell milk on Sundays, and would not sell a father his own daughter, would sell a score or two of his brothers and sisters into hopeless bondage, and with their blood and bones live in elegance and abundance! Did he not strain at a gnat and swallow a whole herd of camels? What if I should cap the climax of this narrative by telling you that this conscientious soul-trader and soul-holder is a minister of our Lord and Savior Jesus Christ? It is even so. He is the elected guide and guardian of the morals and piety of a very influential portion of this community; and what is most astonishing is, that not the least objection is even thought of because of this conduct. I heard of some ladies who refused to attend on his worship because he was a secessionist. I heard others complain that he was too convivial in his habits; but I heard nobody find any fault with him for holding, selling, or refusing to sell, these children of a common Father, brothers and sisters of a common Savior.

I looked often at his tasty chapel, but could not make up my mind to desecrate the Sabbath by attending upon his ministrations. But happening to be at a quarterly conference of our own spotless and wrinkleless Church, where two slaveholders were nominated by the preacher in charge for stewards, and elected unanimously, without so much as an "affectionate admonition" from the excellent presiding elder, I thought I was myself getting into the gnat-straining condition by over-scrupulousness. So I concluded, being with the Romans, to do as they did, and see how near this worthy rector and I came to worshiping the same God.

Do you want to know how he looked and spoke? Descriptions of such persons will be curiosities of literature eagerly perused by future generations. This was a true successor of the apostles. No broken chain of descent was his, joined together by martyrial hands, and, perchance, by those of laymen even, often completely sundered, or united only by that unseen, and hence, for ecclesiastical purposes, useless Spirit of God, that carried the Church into the wilderness and supported her there. No; the bright links, clear and defined, and often of the finest gold, as, for instance, Alexander Borgia, Joan, Leo X., Laud, and a host of others, of whom not this world nor any other was worthy, glittered in the chain that bound this servant to his Master.

You expect a hard-featured, hard-voiced, hard-mannered man, with tones like the snapping of a slave-whip, and the manners of Haley and Legree combined. You don't understand human nature. So many paint Nero, who was really the most elegant gentleman of his age. We must remember that only in the other world does the inner nature body forth itself in the outer form. Here the reverse is apt to be true. The finest natures are hidden in the least expressible forms, and the vilest are not unfrequently, like Burr, and Goethe's Mephistophiles, witty, wise, and polished, handsome, gay, and sober, a perfect man in the worldly sense of perfection.

The preacher aforesaid is a middle-aged, gray, and bald-headed gentleman, of pleasant address, with a quiet, gentle, soft, pathetic tone and manner. I never heard the service read so beautifully. It had a melting cadence that glided into your secret heart. There was none of the hard and formal style of the mere reader, none of the airs of the rhetorician; but a subdued grace, yet full of life, that was very fascinating. With the constant undertone of my whole moral being conflicting with the sounds that met my ear, I could not but feel, as he read it, a newer and richer quality in that admirable service. Yet how some of the sentences he read startled me! I could but think of the medieval legend of the wonderful preacher, who, arrayed in black vestments, swept his audience with most pathetic and powerful appeals, and after he had left them they found it was the archfiend himself that had been thus lifting them to heaven. These were some of the solemn phrases that thrilled me so strangely, while he plaintively uttered them and I fervently followed him: "We sinners do beseech thee to hear us, O Lord God; and that it may please thee to show thy pity upon all prisoners and captives; that it may please thee to defend and provide for the fatherless children and widows, and all that are desolate and oppressed. O God, merciful Father, that despisest not the sighing of a contrite heart, nor the desire of such as are sorrowful, mercifully assist our prayers that we make before thee, in all our troubles and adversities, whensoever they oppress us, and graciously hear us, that those evils which the craft and subtilty of the devil or man worketh against us may be brought to naught; that thy servants, being hurt by no persecutions, may evermore give thanks unto thee in thy holy Church, through Jesus Christ our Lord." The psalms for the day were cxliv., cxlv., cxlvi. In them he read these words: "Save me and deliver me from the hand of strange children, whose mouth talketh vanity, and their right hand is a right hand of iniquity. . . . That there be no leading into captivity, and no complaining in our streets. . . . The Lord looseth men out of prison. The Lord helpeth them that are fallen. As for the way of the ungodly, he turneth it upside down."

His sermon was a practical discourse on a Christian's trials, and the comforts which, through the Spirit, he could extract from them. But I was preaching a good many sermons during this part of the service. I was asking, "Does he bring his bond-servants around him for daily prayer and religious instruction? Why are they not here at church with him? Does he ever go to the poor little chapel to which the wicked pride of the community exiles them and their kindred, and there comfort them with such readings and such discourses as these?" Especially I was anxious to preach a short sermon to him on the text that was printed around the stained window in the chancel: "Repent ye! for the kingdom of heaven is at hand." I presume I should have shocked the audience more than the rude Baptist did his hearers if I had read that third chapter of Matthew, and given its needed and divine application. I could not keep my eyes off that text. I thought it is not possible for this congregation to worship here and be unmindful of its meaning. Yet I was probably the only person that ever saw it that read it in this true and solemn light. Thank God, the kingdom of heaven is at hand. These troops, as those that gathered round John, are unconsciously, and many of them unwillingly, assisting in ushering it in.

The march of events in the political, the religious, the social world, all show that He is soon to appear who will unloose these heavy burdens, and let the oppressed go free, and break every yoke. His fan is in his hand, and He will thoroughly purge His floor. How glorious He appears in this apparel, traveling in the greatness of His strength! As the Liberator of His enslaved children He shines forth upon foes and formalists of this land of promise. His shoe-latchet, not only His most earnest advocates and forerunners, but much more these proud transgressors, are unworthy to stoop down and unloose. Blessed is He that cometh in the name of the Lord. Hosanna in the highest!

That tenderness of conscience which I have not spoken of as wrong in itself, but only strange in contrast with the hardness of the same conscience in other and infinitely more important matters, that evident apprehension of the spiritual significance of the word of God and of prayer, I can but think, show that in him yet live the germs of a divine life. May these germs burst the rocky soil of the hideous sin which now encases them, and blossom into beautiful and fruitful life. May he soon say to that congregation, but a very few of whom are partakers of that sin by actual slaveholding, and some of whom I know shrink from it as imperiling their own salvation,—may he say to them, "I have repented; I have brought forth works meet for repentance. I have laid the ax at the root of the tree. I give my slaves their liberty. I give them education, respectability, and, so far as I can by precept and example, I give them the grace which my Savior has given to me." What rejoicing will be in that Church, in that neighborhood, in this State, when he, or one like him, shall thus stand up for Jesus, and shall proclaim by act, as well as word, that the great and acceptable day of the Lord has here come.

LETTERS FROM CAMP.

III. PROFIT AND LOSS AFTER BULL RUN.

BALTIMORE, Wednesday, July 24.

ON a straw pallet, spread on a few rough, wet boards, lying loosely over the grassy ground, under leaky canvas, in the generally damp and sticky atmosphere of a tent in a shower, I am writing my last letter from the seat of war. A bit of candle, dimly burning, stuck in a tin cup, standing on the end of a valise, acts as a gas-burner. One of the private soldiers lies stretched in his blanket near me asleep, dreaming of the home he is hoping so soon to see. Round about are the odds and ends of a camp-tent, such as everybody ought to see, for at least one week in a year. But a sword hanging on the rear pole, and a musket or two on the floor, with haversacks, knapsacks, fatigue-caps, huge gray blankets, and sundry other military knickknacks, give the spot a little more of the Church militant air than it has in those heavenly seats.

Stereoscopic pictures are popular; and a true stereoscope delights in the little homely every-day nothings that make up our every-day life. So this last look of your correspondent may not be out of place, as he sits *à la* Turk, with his paper on his knee, in the only silent hours of a camp day, those that are close on to midnight, bringing to an end his long discourses, to which some readers may have given, he trusts, an attent ear.

The Monday when the tidings of our reverses came in was dark and rainy, but the news was far darker than the day. The copperheads seemed to think that the sky was wonderfully clear and warm, and were sunning themselves in great crowds at the corners where the secession papers, the Sun, Exchange, and South, are published. The poison of asps was under and upon their lips. Their mouths were full of cursing and bitterness, and their feet would have been swift to shed blood, had it not been for the military power, which measurably awed them.

How changeable are the affairs of this world! Sunday was the happiest day Washington has ever known; Monday the saddest. Light was on every Union countenance here. The forces of the nation were moving swiftly to the desired goal. The enemy fled before them. Many prophets were crying, "Within forty days and secession shall be overthrown." Suddenly the cry comes, "We are retreating; we are defeated; we are annihilated." Beauregard will be in Washington by midnight. So swift treads sorrow on the heels of joy. Everybody gave up everything as lost. The secessionists declared, and the Unionists half believed, that Lincoln would make another secret flight through Baltimore. Extra guards were set around the camps, and a thoroughly stormy and gloomy night set down on the homes and hearts of all this region.

But the morning cometh, if also the night, and the gray light of a new dawn began to glimmer around the great disaster. We began to hear courageous words from soldiers and civilians. One Baltimore man said he could march up to a masked battery; another, that he must certainly shoulder his musket; another was entreating General Banks to supply the Union men with arms. They boldly withstood the secessionists around their own newspaper batteries, — no longer masked, — and defended the cause of the nation in her hour of peril. The soldiers were equally cheerful. Their homesickness disappeared in a moment. They were ready to march to Virginia. I saw some of the Wisconsin troops on Tuesday morning. "Where are you going?" I asked. "To Richmond or to death," was the reply. This rallying and strengthening of spirits was one of the gleams of light.

A great disaster has befallen the national cause. What is it, and what are its consequences? Has it left us worse or better than we were when this correspondence began? Have we made any positive advance in the past three months? Shall we succeed? If not, what then? Much had been done. When the national troops began to pour through this city and State, three months ago, the capital was in the greatest peril. No fortifications, no troops, no preparations for defense. The enemy were at Harper's Ferry, Alexandria, and in Baltimore. Insolent, and flushed with Sumter victories, they boasted that the Capitol should be desecrated with their flag before the first of May. Maryland was in the hands of the mob. The bridges were burned, and the secession legislature was called together. The West was as weak and undefended as the East.

Now we have strong, well-armed, and occupied forts on the heights of Arlington and Alexandria. We have driven the enemy from Missouri and Western Virginia. We have put down insurrection in Baltimore, and banished all armed opposition from the borders of the State. We have the capital safe. We have expelled the foe from Harper's Ferry. We have raised and equipped an immense army, won many victories, and for a time filled the rebels with fear and despair. We have developed a military spirit of the grandest and deepest fervor, and, not least, have completely swept from the land that silly ostrich of a non-coercionist. Why,

I was up in Harford County yesterday, and heard some goodish country farmers say they were not secessionists and not coercionists. I looked on them as I would on pre-Adamite fossils; they seemed almost as historic and venerable as the bits of bricks which mark the pleasant site of Cokesbury College. When I heard that same ancient doctrine earnestly advocated by a gentleman of that rural district, whose clever discourse has a nipping and an eager air, I could not but think of Scott's Antiquary, and such Dryasdust Old Mortalities, so long has that once powerful humbug been gathered to its fathers. Yet, three months ago, no April ephemeron buzzed more conceitedly and authoritatively.

We have to grow by degrees in any knowledge, pleasant or painful. The threats of disunion it was never supposed would be carried out. Our duty to God and liberty compelled us to put those threats to the test. The secession of South Carolina dissipated our dreams as to the fanciful character of the long-threatened dissolution. It became a political reality. "It will not be general," said we. Virginia proved that an error. "It will not really assume a military and aggressive form." Sumter settled that question. "But a great uprising, a great military armament, a great expression of the determination of the government to maintain itself will scatter the armed and ferocious mob." Missouri and Western Virginia seemed to prove this theory true. But Bull Run has made it thin air. We see that the police service is no longer to be the legitimate business of the government. It will have to fight, to fight desperately, perchance for its very existence. We have risen to the obligations of previous hours. Shall we to those that are now being laid upon us? The people will. The government, civil and military, must. The deadly struggle is coming upon us. It will slay as many reputations as men. If the officers of the State and the army are not equal to the crisis, they must give way to those who are.

Be assured the people will not give over this effort to deliver themselves from an infamous thralldom without a struggle infinitely surpassing that of the last century. And be assured, too, that in this struggle the primal cause and curse will be throttled to death. A feud of nearly two hundred and fifty years' standing is being settled to-day. If the war holds on for a twelvemonth it will have only one phase. Everything else will be swept away, and one feeling fill every heart. Shall the slave power on this continent be supreme, or be utterly blotted out? Two hundred and forty years ago the seed was sown. At Jamestown a load of negro slaves was landed, at Plymouth a band of Christian pilgrims. Within a few years of that date, when the business had become brisk in Virginia, the Dutch slave-traders thought they would test the cupidity of the Puritans, and a cargo entered Boston Harbor. It was refused a landing and driven from the province. Then was the seed sown out of which this bloody harvest is being reaped.

The slave power has always ruled the continent. It ruled the colonies, it ruled the British cabinets as long as we were colonies; it was no small element in causing the Revolution, as Jefferson said in his Declaration. The Revolution was fought in the interests of freedom, and against the real slave power, which was intensely Tory. Hence all the Revolutionary patriots were abolitionists. But, the battle won, slavery again asserted its supremacy, and soon won it. The Constitution recognized it. Washington signed a fugitive slave bill, and Jefferson annexed Louisiana in its interest. It caused the war of 1812, the war with Mexico, and the present war. It is met to-day on its own merits. Our statesmen do not yet avow it, but they feel it. We may have to fight for political existence, for personal liberty even. Any treaty of peace now made would leave us colonies, despised more than their lowest slaves. We may have to hear our Patrick Henrys, Otises, Adamses, and Warrens, summoning us to the last fight for our liberties. If so, no quarter will be shown to slavery. That or we must die. As to the result there can be no doubt. If our fathers, weak and few, and scattered over an immense territory, drove out the proudest and strongest nation in the world, because of mere political disfranchisement, we shall trample under our feet the accursed system that would rob us of honor, liberty, and life itself. We are face to face with savages, with devils. The first-born of Satan is at our throats. Shapes hot from hell rush upon our armies. "We take no prisoners" is their motto. A soldier, I was told, in the late battle dragged some half dozen wounded comrades to a ravine and fountain, where he was tending them. While thus engaged a company of rebels came up and he escaped. But every wounded soldier was bayoneted.

Be not astonished at these things. The system they are defending surpasses in iniquity any on the face of the earth. What can it breed but hell-hounds? And yet but yesterday, on the blessed Sabbath, I could not make a good old Baltimore conference brother confess that slavery was sinful. Nay, he expressly and emphatically denied it.

> "O wisdom, thou art fled to brutish beasts,
> And men have lost their reason."

This event will preëminently teach us our dependence on God. We had begun to have too much confidence in ourselves. We thought the enemy was flying so steadily and universally, that the affair was to close without any especial humiliation before God; but we are brought to our senses. We shall have to call upon Him from whom alone cometh salvation. Unless He goes forth with us, we march in vain. Let the Church cry unto God, cry mightily, cry earnestly. Thus, and thus alone, shall the nation conquer.

Again, this repulse was needed to bring about the only object to which this war must tend, in which it must be consummated, if it be really successful. Had we marched easily and triumphantly to Richmond, we should have had an armistice and terms of re-union, which would have left Slavery in full power; slightly shorn of his locks, yet soon to have them grow again. Repulses and defeats strengthen a good, ruin a bad, cause. The object of God is to liberate these children of His, who have cried day and night unto Him for these many generations. Every defeat brings out this purpose the more clearly. The action of Congress today was bolder than it has ever been. It will grow in courage as disaster grows upon us. The defeat at Bunker's Hill paved the way to the Declaration. The defeat next year at Long Island only invigorated the spirits and nerved the arm of the people.

So will it be now. The ferocity, the inhumanity, the fiendishness of our foes, will only make us say that the cause that changes them to devils shall be extirpated. We shall advance to Senator Trumbull's position, and declare slavery abolished in the revolting States. I heard a Maryland gentleman say but yesterday, that he wished the government would issue that decree immediately. It will be issued if the war is prolonged. Let it go forward. What is your poverty, what, indeed, is the agony now rending a great multitude of Rachels, North and South, compared with the poverty and distress of the hundreds of thousands, of the millions upon millions, of God's dear children, in this fair land, for these centuries of bondage! The cup is being commended to our own lips of which they have drank so constantly and so deeply. They were despised and rejected of men,—men of sorrows, and acquainted with griefs. We hid, as it were, our faces from them. They were despised, and we esteemed them not. In my intercourse here I have heard frequent and bitter denunciations of their brethren and sisters, from the lips of elegant and excellent Christian ladies. I have heard some such inhuman utterances by

Massachusetts and New York ladies, but they had nothing of the ferocious intensity of contempt and hatred which marked these speakers. I could easily see how the secession feeling rages the hottest with the female part of the community, from Baltimore to New Orleans, when I heard the modest lips of godly matrons so full of ungodly speeches concerning their colored neighbors. All the Baltimore ladies are not like those above mentioned. Some of the most tender-hearted that I have ever known are here, showing their religion by their treatment of the degraded class among whom their lot is cast.

Let the fact teach us that He who made us of one blood is leading this nation, stuffed with pride and insolence, into the fires that shall humiliate and purify. These thoughtless, cruel-hearted mothers, and wives, and sisters shall bleed and cry, and come down from their seats of pride, and, like the desolated Egyptian haughtinesses of old, shall sit down in the dust beside their despised bondwomen, and seek for comfort from these long-suffering, and hence deep-experienced, souls.

This is some of the sweet juice the bruised reed of pride and hope yields to your taste. Is it unpalatable? Wait till the sorrow is yet sharper, and you may find your taste purged to apprehend its chaste and spiritual refreshment.

THE DAY DAWNS.*

"THE YEAR OF MY REDEEMED IS COME." — *Isaiah* lxiii. 4.

GREAT events are sometimes ushered into being with thunders and earthquakings; sometimes with the still small voice unheard of men. It is true that the kingdom of God cometh not with observation; yet in some of the chief movements of that kingdom to its ultimate and universal sovereignty, there is the utmost observation, and its final consummation will be accompanied with inconceivable pomp and glory. Both of these modes of manifestation have been connected with the coming of the kingdom of God in the work of emancipation in America.

The message which but yesterday flew through all the land, and is already leaping over all seas, is one of the great epochs of that divine movement. The rising waves of liberty lap the throne of national sovereignty. He who but a year ago, in most careful terms, promised the protection of the national arm to the Satanic institution, now declares that it must gather up its feet to die.

We may well exult over such a proclamation. It will cause rejoicings in the hut of the slave, in the palaces of

* A sermon preached in the Clinton Street Methodist Episcopal Church, Newark, N. J., Sunday, March 9, 1862. See Note X.

the princes, in the courts of heaven. If one could rescue a brute creature from the pit on the Sabbath day, and rejoice over its deliverance, much more can we over the fast speeding salvation of these children of our common Father, brothers and sisters of our common Savior, the Lord Jesus Christ.

I. Let us notice the prominent steps in the eventful history of this great reformation.

It started without observation.

Thirty years ago the whole nation lay dead and buried in the grave of slavery. The long struggle of the fathers had not prevailed against the evil. Jefferson had written against it; Washington had labored to abolish it; Franklin, the President of the first Abolition Society in America, and in the world, and the first petitioner to Congress, the first to any legislative body for the abolition of slavery, had died an abolitionist, but with his desire unaccomplished. The Presbyterian Church, after passing strong resolutions against the sin, had gone to sleep in its arms. The Methodist Church, after having labored, through such great foes of slavery as Wesley, and Coke, and Asbury, to extirpate it from her fold and from the land, after having emancipated forty thousand bondmen in Maryland had given over the effort, and was in the complete control of the slaveholding, slave-trading ministers and members of the Gulf States. Statesmen, having vainly struggled to keep the hydra-headed Barbarism from crossing the Mississippi, had yielded Arkansas and Missouri to its sway, and retired, weary and disheartened, from the great conflict, and were busy in the little and forgotten rivalries of the hour. Massachusetts, Pennsylvania, Connecticut, New York, New Jersey, New Hampshire, Vermont, and Rhode Island had abolished it in their limits, not by selling its victims South, as some of their own children ignorantly or irreverently affirm, but by liberating them on the spot, and from motives of conscience alone. But the great movement had paused in its march. An imaginary line was the nominal barrier; the mighty power of the Iniquity was the real barrier. The broad waves of freedom that had rolled to Mason and Dixon's line had been stayed, and a reflex tide of paralysis, of compromise, of complicity, set back upon us from that sea of death. All parties, all seats, all persons were submerged in its waves. The Samson of Liberty lay bound and shorn, and sleeping in the lap of the Delilah of Slavery. Then came there forth from an unknown quarter, in the city of Boston, a solitary beam of light, kindled from the embers of the abolitionism of the fathers, deep covered though they were with the cold ashes of silence and servility.

"It smote the dark with uncongenial ray."

A few souls saw the light and followed it, as the wise men did the star, unseen of the worldly and the wicked. It led them to a small upper room, where, among his scanty types, sat a young Quaker, who had lately been driven out of Baltimore, and who was weekly proclaiming through his little sheet the duty of immediate and unconditional emancipation — the very duty which Asbury and Garretson, and the Methodists of Baltimore, had proclaimed in that city forty years before. The darkness soon felt the light, and rose and raged around him. Ere many days, the men of wealth and standing of that city broke into a female prayer meeting, seized this brave and truth-telling young man, dragged him by a rope through the streets, with a mob howling for his life. He was rescued from destruction only by the strong arm of municipal authority, and the strong walls of a dungeon. From that hour to this, now in obscurity, now in the sight of all men, this Kingdom of God has been advancing. It brought men one by one into its service. Then single churches came, and from solitary altars the pure flame of the Shekinah of God's universal, impartial, life-giving and liberty-giving love shone forth. Then it organized itself into associations and parties, had internal conflicts, as Peter and Paul had, and separations, as Paul and Barnabas had, and errors crept into portions of it, as into the Church at Corinth and Galatia. But it sloughed off the errors, and rose in increasing beauty and majesty. Then it gained the mastery over States, and finally has placed itself substantially in the supreme seat of authority.

Meantime the counter elements were none the less active. They made the rulers submit to them. The organized forces, religious and secular, had taken no side, directly, with the oppressed, and so were swept into the grasp of the oppressor. They declared, through a President, that the mails, over more than half of our territory, should bear no message favorable to human freedom. They declared, through a Secretary of State, that Slavery was the Corner-Stone of our Republic, as Mr. Stephens says it is of the horrible fiction of a government, which that system, expelled from national power, has sought to extemporize. They seized upon the territory of a weak neighbor, with whom we were at peace, to give new outlets to their accursed merchandise in the bodies and souls of men. They passed laws, requiring, with threats of heavy fines and imprisonments, every person in the nation, man or woman, to aid in stealing their brethren, and in reducing them to bondage. A minister of the Gospel now lies in prison in Northern Ohio, one of the freest sections of the land, for refusing to commit that crime. They abrogated the solemn ordinance of our fathers whereby this fearful sin was forbidden to march northward of a parallel of latitude, and strove by every means, presidential, congressional, judicial, military, and mobocratic, to push the Car of Juggernaut into the Free Territories, and thence into the Free States. Only by heroic sacrifices, sufferings, and death, was their scheme made to fail. Our future history will contain no more honorable names than the martyrs of Kansas.

Those who are expected to hold the scales of justice evenly, and who are especially required, by the instincts of man and the Word of God, to defraud not the poor, nor take money against the innocent, the very fountain and origin of national justice, our Supreme Court, and its supreme head, had the blasphemous audacity to declare that no person of African descent could sue in our courts, or had any rights which white men were bound to respect. Though but one out of a million of the drops of blood in his heart traced its origin to Africa, and so to our common fathers, Noah and Adam, and all the rest were of purest Caucasian, he was prevented from appealing to the human representatives of divine justice, against any act of injustice, no matter how flagrant. The seat of Righteousness thus became the seat of Sin. How did the Divine voice ring in their ears, "What mean ye that ye beat my people to pieces, and grind the faces of the poor? saith the Lord."

The river of death staid not here. There remained one thing more for it to do. It must nationalize itself in the legislation of the land. All seaports must be open to its cargoes, all roads to its coffles, all houses to its victims. So a slave code for the Territories and slave-trade in all the States, were demanded, and, had it not been for the activity of the counter and Christian element, they would have been enacted; and over your railroads, and along your splendid streets, would have been lashed, to-day, the miserable droves of human flesh, in and out of our great commercial metropolis.

Minor, but not unimportant, events attend this career of national subjugation. Free speech and a free press were suppressed in the South. No party can stand there on the basis of Washington, Jefferson, and George Mason. All sects, organizations, journals, and tongues were compelled to adore the image the haughty dealers in human flesh set up, and whosoever fell not down and worshiped, that same hour was cast into the midst of a burning fiery furnace. All prostrated themselves admiringly before this worse than Babylonish idol. A little company of men, of the faith and courage of the Hebrew children, not only refused to bow down, but sought to snatch from the bloody jaws of the Moloch the poor victims he was daily devouring; and those who tenderly nursed the living idol with human flesh, caught the brave successors of those brave Hebrews, and hanged them on a tree.

Athens for centuries remembered, with annual festivities and ceaseless gratitude, the courage of Theseus, son of her king. To her children and her children's children, for many generations, she told the tale, how the Cretan pirates, having ravaged her coasts, would grant her existence only on condition that she annually sent fourteen of her choicest youth, seven of her finest young men, seven of her fairest maidens, who should be offered to the Minotaur, a man-bull, that was begotten in horrid lust, and kept alive by the more horrid sustenance of human blood. And they loved to tell, how once, as the vessel bearing this dreadful burden sailed out of the harbor, as many vessels have since sailed from Norfolk, Charleston, Savannah, and Mobile, with black sails, and full of lamentations and weeping, while parents, companions, or children stood on the shore overwhelmed with terrible distress, Theseus went with them, and with brave hands slew the boy-eating and girl-eating monster, and brought his kindred home. A greater than Theseus was Captain Brown; and though he fell in his effort to extricate his brethren and sisters from the cruel jaws of this worse than the Minotaur, begotten, as that, in lust, and kept alive, as that was, by the living agonies of myriads of human souls, still his soul is marching on. Two years have not yet elapsed since the last two of his friends mounted the honorable scaffold, whose remains this consecrated soil of New Jersey tenderly and joyfully embraces; and before that short time had passed, scores of thousands of men, singing praises for his courage and conduct, march by the spot where he was captured, along the road up which he was taken, mangled and faint, for a Pilate trial, by the jail where they chained him, the court-house where they mocked him, and the hill where they slew him. To-day citizens of Massachusetts occupy the hall where he was found guilty of insurrection, and treason, and murder; and the lawyer who acted for the State, the judge who represented its injustice, the governor, who, so far from washing his hands of his blood, washed them in it, even the State itself, whose wicked impulses these wicked men but feebly expressed, are in a condition of avowed insurrection, treason, and murder. She is being tried, condemned, and executed by the mighty armies of freedom moving over her soil, under the inspiration of the people who have sent them forth, and led by the Lord of Hosts, who mustereth his hosts to battle. Surely, never was a false accusation so swiftly hurled back upon those that uttered it. Never did He who says "Vengeance is mine, I will repay," so vividly and so rapidly commend to the lips of His enemies the cup they had forced down the throat of His servants. Insurrection, murder, and treason are written with the blazing finger of His justice on all, from the lowest servant to the State itself, who has dared to slay those who only sought peacefully to execute righteousness; who only remembered those in bonds as bound with them.

The slave power has thus, in every minor, major, and maximum form of iniquity, sought to throttle Democracy, Liberty, and Religion, in our land; and, finally, infuriated by the human blood it had drank, as such draughts are said to enrage those who physically drain them, it sprang at the government itself, and expected to have sat long ere this on the throne of national and undisputed sovereignty. Then comes a winter of discontent, a time of darkness, of helplessness, of despair; then the open revolt of States, and of officials of every grade; then the seizure of forts and munitions of war; then the assault on a helpless and starving garrison; then the marshaling of arms, and battle's magnificently stern array. Defeats rapidly multiply, and an hour of thick gloom rests down upon the people, and the war seems long, dubious, and almost hopeless; when, lo! one Sunday morning, Mill Springs is wet with the sacred blood of martyrs in this holy cause of nationality and liberty; but the blood of traitors flows more profusely, and the tide of defeat is turned. Fort Henry falls; Fort Donelson, the Western Thermopylæ, yields to the advancing forces of no Asiatic tyrant, but of democratic equality and liberty, and Bowling Green, Columbus, and Nashville are bloodlessly ours. The West seemed to be securing all the glories of the conflict, when a word from the banks of the Potomac, written by the commander-in-chief of our armies, the appointed head of the people, announces to the world a greater victory than any won on fields of blood, fraught with grander consequences, and sure of a higher renown.

We have thus led you through this very brief *résumé* of events, from the first blast of the trumpet of Freedom from the lips of a then obscure young Quaker printer, thirty years ago, to the last, which has just been sounded out from the Presidential mansion, foretelling the death of the monster, against which the youthful David then went out to battle. William Lloyd Garrison and Abraham Lincoln will stand together in our history. They are the ministers of God — the one the forerunner of the Divine Liberator, and the other the Chief of the Apostles, who establishes the liberty for which his predecessor had prepared the way.

II. Let us consider some of the fruits of this Message, which has been well declared to be the most important word spoken in this land since the Declaration of Independence.

First, it will give clearness and tone to the national mind as to the character of slavery. That mind has been exceedingly beclouded and debased by the presence and power of this sin. This debasement has not been confined to the region where it especially dwells. Even in the Free States are still found those who have thought any words hostile to the institution harsh and fanatical. Though such words have only embodied the sentiment of the Church in all ages, from Moses to Wesley, though they are spoken in a community whose fathers, from conscientious and religious motives, abolished slavery, still, so fearfully have we been poisoned with this malaria, that any strong and bracing word of truth seemed deadly and dangerous.

Hawthorne tells a story of an Italian physician who trained himself so that he could live a sickly life in a garden full of poisonous plants, whose effluence was fatal to all others. If another approached the inclosure, he dropped dead. But the former breathed freely in its poisonous air. Mithridates, to avoid death by poison, by constant habit was enabled to eat harmlessly all manner of deadly and forbidden fruit. As a nation, we have walked in a garden of death; we have lived on the fruit of the tree of death. In our insane lust of wealth and power, in our more insane fear of the slave-master and abhorrence of the slave, we have cried, —

"Give me agates for my meat;
Give me cantharides to eat;
From all natures, sharp and slimy,
Salt and basalt, wild and tame;
Tree of lichen, ape, sea-lion,
Bird and reptile, be my game;
Ivy for my fillet-band,
Blinding dog-wood in my hand.
Hemlock for my sherbet cull me,
And the prussic juice to lull me.
Swing me in the Upas boughs,
Vampire-fanned, when I carouse."

No wonder that other nations looked on with amazement. No wonder that coming here they were stifled in the fatal air. No wonder that the nation, at last, dropped, faint and dying, amid the miasma. Last winter, who believed, here or abroad, that we *were* a nation? This Presidential voice will clear the air. Slavery may a little longer

> "from her horrid hair
> Shake pestilence and war,"

but only against our earnest efforts for its extinction. The "rights of mankind," which our fathers died to secure, which are the proudest words on the memorial stone of Lexington, the proudest words in our Declaration,—these fundamental rights shall no longer be bartered away for aristocratic and tyrannic distinctions, based on the accidents of color and descent. Our fathers broke the chain that bound the poor white laboring man to his master; we shall break the heavier chain that hangs upon the neck of the poor laborer whose skin is sometimes a little more discolored than our own. We shall fall back on first principles. We shall say with Burns,—

> "That man to man shall brother be
> The whole world o'er."

We shall feel as Jefferson did when he wrote, "ALL MEN are created equal." We shall confess with Paul that God has made of one blood all nations of men for to dwell on the face of the earth. We shall say as Christ taught us and all mankind, "OUR Father who art in heaven," and feel as He taught us to feel—that our neighbor is he whom we most unrighteously loathe and despise; and only by treating him as our equal and our brother, can we be the children of our Father, or the brethren of our Savior.

The word of authority was needed; a word from a high, from the highest place. Such a word is this. When heavy and pestilential airs cover the low places of the earth, only the winds that sweep from mountain summits can displace them. So does this word dispel the heavy fog that filled many a heart with unnatural, with unchristian fear and hate. I stood one August morning on the summit of Mount Washington. All the valleys below were pressed down with clouds of vapor a mile thick. One could not see a score of feet beneath the peak. The winds raged, and great mountains of watery air, as huge, and seemingly as solid, as the hills they covered, moved over the face of the motionless ocean as icebergs over a waveless sea. But the instant that the sun arose, and fixed his eye on this mighty deep, the thick, oppressive air cleft asunder, the lowliest vales, with their trees and shrubs, and almost their very grass blades, stood forth to our view, defined and beautiful in the lustrous light. Upon those beneath, the sun undoubtedly shot down with equal suddenness and glory. So this declaration in favor of the abolishment of slavery pierces the mighty clouds of pride, and prejudice, and fear, that have hung heavily over the nation, and every eye sees clearly the great evil of slavery, and the necessity of its extirpation.

Hitherto many had failed to see. The convictions, the instincts, in their nature in favor of universal freedom, the authentic tales of cruelty which the system produces, repeated in thousands of instances, the political and infidel, though professedly religious, pretensions and progress of the slave power, its revolt and assault upon the government, even civil war, distress, and death, in all their horrors, found them stifled under the blinding vapor. This voice opens every eye, uplifts and regulates every conscience. No man here, no man elsewhere in our land, can again say, without not only knowing, but confessing, that the "truth is not in him," Slavery is right, is divine, is for the best good of the African, though he be an American of ten generations, and nine tenths of him be Caucasian. No one will wrest the Scriptures to its defense, or wrest democracy to its defense. That mean and miserable work this single word has destroyed forever.

Second. It will hasten the downfall of the rebellion. It will do this in three ways. 1. It will make other nations our allies, and compel their governments to cease to flatter the slavocrats with the hope of foreign support. They have lived on this hope. Mr. Yancey pleaded with the ministers of the British government that our government was as pro-slavery as theirs. The English journals in their interest have made like charges. This message, followed by correspondent action on the part of Congress, stops that argument, and, with it, all possible hope of success from abroad. For all Christian Europe hates slavery; God in Christ has wrought that work there perfectly. Though defective in the great democratic truth of equal rights, yet from emperor to serf they abhor human bondage, and no government, how much soever it may desire the disruption of this Union, is strong enough to interfere in the struggle in the phase it is now assuming. The people even of Spain and Austria, much more of France and England, would hurl from their thrones a monarch who should presume to fight for slavery.

2. Again: the word robs them of support at home by conciliating all classes, who, through desire or through fear, seek to support the government. The loyal slaveholder sees in his partial remuneration an advantage to him. For this so-called property is utterly valueless now, and never can be marketable again. I was told, when in Maryland, of a man for whom two thousand four hundred dollars was paid, not eighteen months before. He is worth to-day less than a Confederate note of a hundred dollars. The disloyal slaveholder may even hope for compensation under a proclamation of amnesty, or by the acts of his legislature, which the message does not propose to override. The various classes of the North will also agree. The extreme abolitionist, because he clearly sees at this new turn in the road, the depot which he has so long toiled to reach; the anti-abolitionist, if any such still exist, because it advises compensation, and

suggests the possibility of delay in the full execution of the work, and respects the verbal distinctions they cleave to, though they no longer really exist. The men of peace will approve it, because it makes for peace; the men of war, because they desire war only to break down the rebellion, and that step is soonest reached by such a measure. The great support, therefore, which the rebel cause has received from these varied and conflicting sources will cease, and with it much of their hold on power.

3. But a third and not unimportant reason why this will hasten the overthrow of the rebellion is, because of its effect on the slaves. Hitherto they could only see by faith that the war would work out their liberation. Now sight confirms faith. The tidings of this message will go by the underground telegraph to every slave cabin. Thousands this day have lifted up their heads in joy, for they see that their redemption draws nigh. They are not ignorant of the movements about them. When I entered Annapolis, with the first regiments that hastened to the rescue of the capital last April, I found the slave already aware of the real cause of our coming. They alone of all the people came out of their cabins on the road, and saluted the soldiers. At Washington I asked an old colored man if he knew what all this meant. "O, yes," said he, "it is for liberty." "Liberty for whom?" "To the white and the black," he replied. At a slaveholder's mansion, near Annapolis Junction, where we stopped for supper, the slaves, who were gathered near the barns, received us with smiles and cordial welcomes, and when we shouted for Union and Liberty, they responded with enthusiastic applause. While at the Relay, I heard a soldier of this regiment say to a colored man of Baltimore, "You also attacked us." "It is false!" he instantly answered, forgetting all about his skin, and his "natural inferiority;" "not a colored man in Baltimore touched you. We knew what you were coming for. Five thousand of

us would have defended you had we had arms." Like testimonies abound. This message will confirm their hopes. They see their prayers are being answered.

The year of God's redeemed is come. They could not rise, if they would, while every white man is especially armed and watchful. They will not now, as Freedom dawns peacefully upon them. But the power of their tyrants will be broken by these new hopes implanted in their victims, and they will hasten to make their peace with the government, and with those whom they have so brutally treated and despised. Thus will this word bring to a speedier close the already waning power of the rebellion.

4. But another great blessing which it foretells is the unification of the Republic. We have never been, in reality, one people. Blood has not separated us; for the French of Indiana and Illinois have coalesced with the English of Massachusetts; the Dutch of New York with the Irish of New Hampshire. Later immigrations flow into the ancient ones, and into each other, easily, spontaneously. Natural boundaries have not separated us. New Jersey is separated from Pennsylvania by more natural boundaries than Pennsylvania is from Maryland. Iowa and Maine are closer together than Ohio and Kentucky. There has been only one distinction, and that was slavery. Slavery, a peculiar institution, makes its supporters a peculiar people, though not the people of God.

"The Baltimore Christian Advocate," but a year ago, dwelt on the identity of the Southerners and their dispartation from the North in thought, life, and religion. They were excluded from the civilized world for their leprosy, and sought to make their infamy an honor. This was so at the beginning. John Adams calls them, in his day, the "Barons of the South." South Carolina and Georgia assumed the airs of aristocracy even thus early. The patents of this nobility have been vastly increased since that time, and their pride proportionally. We can never be one people, truly and perfectly, till slavery is abolished. Some of our citizens, of little money and less brains, foolishly suppose the Middle States more like the South than they are like New England; and others, more foolish, rejoice over this fancied resemblance. The truth is, that all the Free States are substantially identical. For they are alike in the great fundamental idea of free labor, of the dignity of labor, of the rights of labor. They are distinguished among themselves by grades of development of intellect, enterprise, and morality; yet they are fundamentally one. Hence, you can elect a mechanic to represent you in Congress, a mechanic to represent your State in the Senate, a mechanic for your mayor.* Hence you see the strong arm of a laborer, carved in stone, on the front of one of your costliest buildings, and the sign of a banking institution, too, that represents primarily capital, and not labor. These sights are not seen south of Mason and Dixon's line. All the Slave States are alike in despising labor. There, the holder, breeder, seller, of *human beings*, — he is the great man; the mechanic is the slave. Bishop Polk *owns* his farmers, blacksmiths, carpenters, masons, tailors, milliners, dress-makers, and cooks. What he does not want of these laborers he sells, as we do our cattle and horses, if we have more than are necessary for carrying on our farms.

I talked with a slave at Annapolis Junction, who said he carried on two farms for his owner, and never had a dollar for his sagacious and constant oversight. The tea and sugar on his cabin table, his wife, a free woman, bought with her labor. Is there a man capable of carrying on two farms for a Northern gentleman, thus paid? Is not such a superintendent always a respectable, often a leading, and even a comparatively wealthy member of the community? Such

* Such was the case at that time in Newark and New Jersey. Every one of these offices was filled by a mechanic.

is the universal state of affairs there. This must be changed. The great word of the Sixth of March initiates the reform. Free institutions and free labor will move southward. Man will be treated as man, woman as woman. A fair day's wages for a fair day's work, will be the motto there as here. Politics will conform to it. Said a friend of mine, a paymaster in the army, to a Maryland machinist, "Why don't you get up a workingman's candidate for Congress, instead of taking one of these slaveholding aristocrats?" The idea struck him as preposterous. Such an attempt would be laughed to scorn. But when slavery is suppressed, this universal custom of the North will obtain there.

So will the religion of the North move southward. They have a religion of their own. In it no stranger can meddle. An Episcopalian may be high church or low church here and in England. In the South a new Article, not written in the Book of Common Prayer, is introduced, which outvalues all that are inscribed there. You must say, "I believe in Slavery," or all the Apostles' Creed goes for nothing. If you say *that*, you are still Orthodox, although a heretic as to all the rest of the creed. So is it with Presbyterianism. You can go from Geneva, through Scotland, to Philadelphia, and be an accepted Presbyterian. Cross the unseen line and all your theology is changed to one dogma, and that a doctrine of devils. So the Methodists drop Wesley and Asbury, and follow diabolic fables that have not the merit of being even cunningly devised. Anti-slavery, inherited from their fathers, still lives in a part of the border. But it is like the shoal edge of the ocean, barren sand, always wet, often under water, and never harvestable, while it rapidly slopes down into the unfathomable gulf beyond, of abominable doctrines, and hardly more abominable practices.

This region must be regenerated. The waves of liberty, a Nile of wealth, must fertilize this American Sahara. Churches, schools, workshops and farms, must be filled with free worshipers, students, toilers. A vast country remains to be subdued — the richest and most beautiful in America. It is trodden under foot of the Gentiles. The voice of those who are defrauded of their wages cries to God, and He has come down to see if it be according to their cry. He finds they told the truth. Therefore will He destroy those husbandmen, and give that vineyard to others? Their enslaved neighbors shall till their own fields in freedom and happiness. Their poor white neighbors, now more despised than their slaves, will rise in intelligence, virtue, competence, and power. The great emigration of Europe and the North will pour over the wilderness, and it shall blossom as the rose. It shall blossom abundantly, and rejoice even with joy and singing. The glory of Lebanon shall be given unto it, the excellency of Carmel and Sharon. The victims of this terrific cruelty will at last be free, prosperous, and happy. The husband and wife, the babes and their mother, will dwell in peaceful and blessed communion. No more scourging lash, no more lordly lust, no more riven hearts, no more ignorance, idleness, or misery. No more such sights will be seen as would have made the Savior weep more bitterly than he did over Jerusalem. A colored man in Baltimore, now free, told me that he once received three hundred lashes for unintentional delay in attending to a tobacco field on Sunday. A member of the Baltimore Conference, a Virginian by birth, and an ardent abolitionist, told me that he knew a Baptist deacon, in the Shenandoah Valley, who carried the scalp of a slave at his saddle-bow, and a Presbyterian elder, who had taken off the skin of a slave, tanned it, covered his saddle with it, and rode upon it. Nat Turner's skin was cut up into relics, which ladies proudly carried; and John Brown's son stands in the Medical College of Winchester, a proof of the worse than Indian brutality of Southern gentlemen, nay, rather of Southern fiends. For they are not even men that can commit such barbarities.

These barbarities shall come to a perpetual end with the *monstrum horrendum* out of whose loins they have sprung. Some, in the last resort of unbelief, have asked wildly, "What are you going to do with these freedmen?" We answer, "Let them alone."

They will work; they will sell the produce of their farms; they are the most intelligent, they are almost the only intelligent, farmers of the South. They will be no burden to the government. Let their friends do as they are now doing. Let teachers and guides go forth as that ship-load went last week.* That was an event not second to this message. A new civilization went to South Carolina with them, and its results will speedily prove their fitness for freedom, to the overwhelming of our mean and wicked prejudice, with shame and everlasting contempt. It may even be shown that the superior race is the enslaved race; that as it was in Egypt, in Babylon, in Rome, so is it in the South. As from this class came, anciently, generals, scholars, poets, emperors, and statesmen, so may they yet, from this despised and down-trodden people. We may loathe this word, and him that declares it, as the Jews did Paul, when he asserted the equality of the Gentiles with themselves; but we cannot gainsay or deny it. They are of our blood, of the blood of Adam, of Noah, of Christ. They will prove

* The first vessel that carried out men and women for the establishment of schools and churches, and the organization of labor in the South, was the steamer Atlantic. She left New York, March 3, 1862, for Port Royal, South Carolina, with about sixty persons, under the superintendence of Edward L. Pierce, of Boston, and Rev. Mansfield French, of New York. Among them were fourteen ladies. She carried farming utensils, seeds, sewing machines, books, clothing, etc. All who joined the company took an oath of allegiance to the Constitution, and against all its enemies. This was the beginning of that emigration which has gone on so greatly since, and will proceed yet more rapidly under the peaceful protection of the future government. This "Atlantic" was the Mayflower that assured a New South after the Puritan and perfect pattern.

their honorable right to it in God's good time and way. A slaveholder's son in Maryland confessed to me that he had first cousins who were slaves, and who were equally talented with their cousins who were free. The best of Caucasian blood flows in their veins. They will yet show that it has not degenerated by commingling with the equally excellent, if more torrid blood of Africa.

But in the great uplifting of the Southern territory, this portion of the population will soon be lost sight of. Four millions, to the score of millions that will pour over that immense and beautiful country, will be less than the few thousands of them in New York to its myriad population. They will be merged in the great tides of life that will flow, freely and grandly, over all the continent.

5. There are other and not valueless fruits of this prophetic word. If carried out, or replaced, as it will be, by more thorough measures,* it will restore the Republic to its position among the nations of the earth. It will prevent the absolutizing of America by putting offshoots of the effete and discrowned families of Europe upon thrones propped on foreign spears. It will give us full and mighty power against the monarchical systems of Europe. It will abase the high heads that maintain, among men and Christians, factitious distinctions based on blood, not brains, on lineage, not character, on rank, not worth. All these will go down before the simple, majestic effulgence of a perfectly free and equal people. Therefore let us laud and magnify the name of our God. He has made us, who were less than a century ago no people, the people of God. He brought a vine out of Egypt, a vassalized, rank-ridden, priest-ridden Europe, and planted it in this goodly land. The wild boar of slavery has trodden it down and mastered it, and now is seeking

* The more thorough measure by which it was replaced was the Proclamation, six months after, of universal and unconditional emancipation.

to tear it up by the roots. Our God will not suffer it to be. He may chastise us, but He will not destroy. The signs of the times are propitious. The armies of the aliens are put to flight; distress has seized hold upon them. They are suffering the just judgment of God. "They have called evil good, and good evil; they have put darkness for light, and light for darkness, bitter for sweet. and sweet for bitter. They have justified the wicked for a reward, and taken away the righteousness of the righteous from him." Alas, how many innocent victims of their passions lay this last sin to their charge! "Therefore," says God, "as the fire devoureth the stubble, and as the flame consumeth the chaff, so their root shall be as rottenness, and their blossom shall go up as dust; because they have cast away the law of the Lord of Hosts, and despised the word of the Holy One of Israel, therefore is the anger of the Lord kindled against His people; He hath stretched forth His hand against them and hath smitten them, and their carcasses were torn in the midst of the streets. And in this day He roars against them like the roaring of the sea; and if we look unto their land, behold, darkness and sorrow, and the light is darkened in the heavens thereof."

It may be long ere this Presidential word shall be brought to perfection. It may be refused by the Pharaoh hardness of border slaveholders, in order that His strong arm may give the more speedy and more complete liberation which he threatens. The struggle with the hoary and haughty sin may be long, and fierce, and bloody. Seven years of suffering and death passed before the Declaration became the Deliverance. We have been partaker of their sins, and the measure of the judgment we have meted out to our enslaved brethren shall be measured to us again. We must suffer in our basket and store; we must suffer in our hearts, in our anxiety for those who go out from us to keep the foe from ravaging our firesides, in the dreadful griefs of wife, and mother, and child, over those who shall return no more. But yet we may rejoice that not all the desolations of war, nor even its chief miseries, are permitted by our loving and just God to come upon us. We may especially rejoice that His chastisements are leading us to repentance, that we are not only fasting before Him, but doing as He requires; preparing to "break every yoke, and let the oppressed go free." Then, after due infliction, after the godly sorrow has wrought its perfect work, after Congress and the legislatures of the guilty States shall coöperate in this divine work, or the President shall himself decree liberty, and shall with his own hand break the shackles from every limb, then, as He has promised, He will surely perform; "*then* shall thy light break forth as the morning, and thine health shall spring forth speedily. For thy righteousness shall go before thee, and the glory of the Lord shall be thy rereward, and I will cause thee to ride upon the high places of the earth; for the mouth of the Lord hath spoken it." Soon will the great Proclamation be answered by resounding praises from over the sea; sooner, by more grateful and more ringing hallelujahs from our Southern shores; and our nation, delivered from its enemies, delivered of the sin which has brought her to the verge of destruction, shall resume her place, shall ascend to a far higher place, among the nations of the earth. Her enemies at home, her rivals abroad, shall bend down to the soles of her feet, and all the other powers of earth shall

"perforce
Sway to her from their orbits as they move,
And girdle her with music."

Standing on the cheery hight to which the great words of our leader have lifted us, I have striven to speak, as Paul did in the storm, words of truth and of encouragement. The Ship of State, the Ship Union and Liberty, shall not go down. There shall be a loss, a blessed and eternal loss, of the accursed lading, but the ship shall be saved. We are flinging overboard that which caused the storm; we shall soon be able to sing, with our finest lyrist: —

"The good Ship Union's voyage is o'er;
At anchor safe she swings,
And loud and clear, with cheer on cheer,
Her joyous welcome rings.
Hurrah! hurrah! it shakes the wave,
It thunders on the shore;
One flag, one land, one heart, one hand,
One nation evermore."

LETTER TO THE LONDON WATCHMAN.*

ENGLAND AND AMERICA.

To the Editors of The Watchman: —

HAVING been lately permitted to make a brief visit to the land of my ancestors, and to behold for myself the spots made memorable by past deeds, as well as the great centers of present life and duty, I unexpectedly found all eyes turned away from their own things, historic or living, and fixed intently on those of America.

I could not ask a peasant the way, or follow a verger in his tour of curiosities, or "take mine ease at mine inn," but that, if they learned that I was an American, they instantly plied me with questions as to our present and prospective condition. The fullness with which our news is detailed, the frequency, elaborateness, and intensity of the leaders in your journals, the articles in every magazine and review,

* Letter to the London Watchman, written from Paris, July 4, 1862. See Note XI.

the excitement attending parliamentary debates on our mutual relations,—all show the depth and fervor of this feeling.

The Times attempts to ridicule us, by saying that we suffer all the extremes of intermittent fever, as conflicting reports rapidly succeed each other. It is properly so; for we feel that we are hanging over the sick bed of an intensely loved nationality—sick almost unto death; and every symptom, favorable or otherwise, naturally excites us. We are giving of the fruit of our body for the saving of our nation, and personal feelings are thus mingled profoundly in the struggle. But I see that here, without any such causes, almost as great excitement follows every important event; and British nerves respond as keenly as American to the varying telegrams that sweep over them.

I have found, with this deep and wide-spread interest, two other facts, painful to a lover of both England and America—to a lover of liberty and humanity. They are a want of sympathy with the United States, and an apparently intentional blindness as to the cause of the rebellion, and the course the government is pursuing against not only the revolt, but its primal and only cause. With few and most honorable exceptions, the tone of inquiry lacked that of sympathy. It was curiosity, not love, that prompted the querist. Especially was the ignorance of intelligent men of the connection of slavery with the rebellion, and of the movements of the nation against that sin, most evident and most deplorable. This last, I consider, arises from the first; for hostility or indifference of feeling will breed ignorance. And yet the latter affects, if it does not create, the former.

Will you permit me to attempt to remove this ignorance from any of your readers who may be thus affected? I am certain that, if removed, the fountains of sympathy will break forth. Will you allow me, therefore, to state in your columns the American cause as it appears to Americans. It may possibly clear away from some minds the clouds that darken them, so that they may see light in the light which the providence of God so powerfully casts upon the American people.

I do not seek to defend America at the English bar. I solicit no favors for her at its hands. She needs no defense. She seeks no favors. She asks for neither material aid nor moral support. She had a right to expect both. She would have received them gratefully, had they been, as they ought to have been, instantly and spontaneously offered; but she has never coveted them. Not that she despises the judgment of others; but when that judgment conflicts with the decrees of divine duty, that seem to her to be almost audibly uttered from heaven, so clearly, so powerfully do they address her, she can say, with a feeling akin to the Apostle, "It is a small thing to be judged of man's judgment," whether single, or associated and nationalized: "He that judgeth me is the Lord." A great nation is not to be tried and condemned by many or few hostile or friendly contemporaries. "God is judge; He putteth down one and setteth up another." To Him we appeal.

It is because she is so unfairly, so criminally, placed before the great reading, the still greater hearing, public of England, by almost all your influential journals and statesmen, that I ask the privilege of a hearing. It is because, rather, of the great interests of humanity, present and future, that are involved in this struggle. The position of your journal—more appreciative, and hence more sympathetic, than most of your neighbors—leads me to hope that my words will be given to your readers. They shall be written in all fairness and kindness of feeling, whatever plainness and honesty of speech they may be constrained to exhibit.

One question, more than all others, is asked by all kindly or hostile Englishmen. It is, "What is the war for?" They are in as great a state of perplexity as was Southey's child over Marlborough's famous victory. I can appreciate the laureate's difficulty in attempting to clear up the mind of his child. And, in the fact that the second, if not the greatest, of England's generals, and the one to whom she gave her most splendid testimonials, can give no reasons for his fighting, that the next generation shall be able to understand, I see the folly of endeavoring to establish the righteousness of the American cause on any other than enduring foundations. The rebellion began, and has been waged, solely in the interests of Slavery. There is no need of any argument in America to sustain this. There is no man nor woman, North or South, bond or free, white or black, that does not know it. And yet the rebels, and their allies of the press, and of Parliament, — allies, I am sorry to say, some of whom are world-famous abolitionists, — have had the effrontery to say that Slavery was not involved in the struggle ; that other interests caused the revolt — the tariff, or natural alienation of the people, or oppression of minorities. This is all chaff. We are one people, far more than England and Scotland, by marriage, emigration, language, interest, and feeling. Slavery, and slavery alone, has attempted our disruption. I beg you to consider these few facts as illustrative of this truth.

The slaveholders demanded, and secured, recognition in the Constitution. But slavery being given up, from conscientious motives, in the States of one half of the Union, and being impoverishing in its nature, it was expected that it would soon cease everywhere ; especially as the foreign slave trade was forbidden. But England, through her inventions, becoming the great cotton manufacturing nation, and the slaveholding States becoming the great cotton raising region, slaves rapidly rose in value, and with this increase of wealth came an increased importance to this interest. England's factories alone made this system mighty.

With this prosperity came also another power, working

on the conscience of the people, demanding the suppression of the iniquity. To this cry, we are happy to say, England contributed. Had she done so by refusing slave-labor cotton, we should have long since, and peaceably, extirpated the evil. The slave power demanded privileges not granted them in the Constitution. The free sentiment resisted, and in many ways, and with varying success, for twenty-five years the conflict has been waged. At last, and for ten years, not a single point of prominent and vital politics has divided the nation, except as connected with slavery. In 1860 the slaveholders refused to take Mr. Douglas as their candidate, because they knew that his doctrine of popular sovereignty, backed by the growing sentiment of the North, would be, ultimately, as fatal to slavery as the positions of the Republicans. They spurned him, though with him they could, undoubtedly, have retained their power, as his popular vote was over one million three hundred thousand, and was second only to Mr. Lincoln's. With Mr. Breckinridge's vote he would have had a quarter of a million more than any other candidate. Thus they revolted from the Democratic party, and set up as their platform a slave code in the Territories, and slave trade in all the States — that is, the right of free transit of slaves through all the States, and protection to that property, as to all other property, in the Territories. Defeated, as they expected to be, they revolted from the government, as they had intended and prepared to do. Drunk with long-continued success and dominion, they despised the North ; despised the party and principles that had legitimately and constitutionally risen to power ; and fancied that, affrighted by their warlike threats and preparations, and weakened by internal dissensions, we should speedily submit, and they could return to their seats of supremacy, or erect themselves into an independent nation, without opposition, almost with the whining solicitation of their foes. They never thought of tariff, of free trade, of majorities trampling on the rights of minorities, of the natural desire for different peoples to be independent of each other. These are cries got up afterward, and for a foreign market. At home it was Slavery, and only Slavery.

It seems unnecessary to quote the words of their so-called "Vice-President," declaring this to be the corner-stone of the new nation; to refer to the striking fact, that this class, and this class only, with their adherents and subjects, revolted at the election of a representative of the opposite sentiment, whose only vital article was the prevention of the further growth of the system. Their instinct is a sufficient proof of the truth of this position. They knew that if they recognized an anti-slavery government, their dominion was at an end. They revolted before it was established. They revolted only because it was to be established. They acted wisely, in the light of the wisdom of this world. Their supremacy was gone the moment they bowed to the sovereignty of the anti-slavery sentiment; and an evil principle, in man or state, cannot long exist except as supreme. They said, "We are strong enough to set up for ourselves. We will never submit to a party led by Messrs. Seward, and Chase, and Sumner." So they flung to the breeze the black flag of human bondage, and arrayed their legions under its accursed folds.

A simple illustration may set this more clearly before you, if it should need additional light. Suppose a great conflict had been raging in England for thirty years, between the principles of democracy and aristocracy; suppose that after many fluctuations in Parliament, and before the people, the democratic party should peacefully and constitutionally secure the passage of a Bill forbidding the increase of the peerage, and that, thereupon, the opposite party should revolt from the government and the sovereign head that made the Bill a law: could anybody doubt why they had rebelled? Could anybody doubt that democracy had achieved a great victory — a victory that extinguished the power of its rivals, and was certain, in a few years, to abolish their whole system? Would any pretense of difference of blood, and desire for separate national existence, give their rebellion character with a democratic people? What would you say if America should be deluded by such appeals, should recognize these aristocratic rebels as belligerents, and give them protection under guise of neutrality; while leading New York democrats should send them guns and ammunition, to defend themselves against their legitimate and democratic rulers? What must America say, when an abolition government and nation recognize these supporters of slavery as legitimately rebellious, and permits her vessels full of arms to leave her ports for their aid; and when, even, great Christian, and — alas! that I must say it — great Wesleyan, abolitionists are making fortunes through such atrocious coöperation? No blood-money wrung from the enforced toil of slaves is as bad as that.

Slavery, then, is the cause — the only cause — of the rebellion. To traffic in the bodies and souls of their brethren, to hold them as beasts, to use them for purposes infinitely worse than they use their vilest beasts, — for this they broke from the mildest and most liberal government that existed in the earth; for this they are seeking its destruction. There is no difference in blood; Davis, Stephens, Slidell, and a host of others, are of Northern origin. All are of one European, one American blood. There is one, sole, terrible difference, — it is Slavery.

But it is often said here, If slavery be the cause of the war, why does not the national government show it to be so, by striking directly at that system? I answer, The assailant and thing assailed are two different things, and it is the first duty of the government to defend, and, if possible, preserve that which is assailed. Slavery is the enemy. That which is attacked is the Union — that is, the government, the nationality of the United States. What she must first do is to defend that Union, and to preserve it from destruction. Though slavery is the *causa causans,* yet what she *does* is something very different from what she *is.* The gold the thief steals is a different thing from the thievish disposition. The loser seeks his money before he aims to abolish the propensity that robbed him. Slavery stole our arms, forts, ammunition; cast off the judicial, the executive, the entire national authority; organized armies, and assumed the prerogatives of sovereignty. What the government must do is, not first to abolish slavery, but to re-possess itself of its property, re-assume its authority, and destroy the insurrectionary armies.

Mr. Seward, the winter before the war began, well said that we must see what our enemies assail, if we would know what we should defend. They had ceased to oppose the anti-slavery policy in the Union, — they opposed the Union itself. The instincts of the people taught them that this was the point to defend. Hence their wonderful unanimity and enthusiasm for the Union; hence innumerable flags blazed along every thoroughfare, reddened every house-top, hung over every door, window, and mantel; children carried them in all their sports; ladies' bonnets, gentlemen's neck-ties, children's dresses, all assumed the national colors — the symbol of the nation's life. They even replaced the more solemn drapery of the pulpit with their glowing colors, and above the steeple's electric finger, or the heavenly cross, they waved, instinct with spiritual, with divine life. In the sacred voluntaries of the sanctuary the "Star-spangled Banner" was played; at every gathering its song was sung. This was not because of the especial beauty of its words or music; but it was the song of the flag, and so of the Union. Such a fever, so unanimous, so instinctive, so mighty, was never before seen in history. The people knew what was attacked, and what to defend; and they sprang to its defense with a zeal immeasurable, with a wisdom from above. It would seem as if this mighty feeling had been *providentially hidden in secret*, so that it should not be weakened by preliminary conflicts ; that when it should appear, the Southern sympathizer, who had prepared himself against the demands of freedom, and the timid conservative, who trembled at them, should both be swept into the current, and the one be filled with shame and silence, the other with unwonted zeal and heroism. So came this new descent of the Spirit of God on a praying and awaiting, but otherwise powerless, people, with the sound as of a mighty rushing wind, and it filled the whole place, the whole nation, with new, with divine life.

This defense, of itself, without primarily attacking the animus of its assailants, has been the course of every wise nation and ruler, when like exigencies came upon them. The good sense of America is simply the common sense of the world. England has suffered many insurrections. She never yet violently suppressed, or instantly attacked, the moving cause of any one of them. Ireland revolted under the lead of Romanism. Her rebellion was subdued, her Papacy pampered. The Sepoys revolted under the inspirations of Mohammedanism. Parliament makes no laws, generals strike no blows, at that superstition. William of Orange overthrows the legitimate king in the interests of Protestantism. He makes no edicts against the religion whose representative he had driven into exile, and whom he had dethroned, solely because of his adherence to that faith. So always did Rome, wise in the wisdom of government above all ancient nations. So, with equally consummate wisdom, acts America.

But while this is her idea, — simple, easily, universally comprehended, — yet let it be considered, that, in the working out of it, slavery inevitably, perhaps speedily, dies. Romanism did not long live a vigorous life in England, if

William of Orange abstained from assailing it. Mohammedanism cannot long live in India, if its power is completely broken. Ireland would have long since been Protestant, had she been treated as an equal, and not as a conquered, people. So Slavery, girdled, humbled, powerless to restrain the liberty of speech and of the press, will speedily vanish. It may linger for a generation in a feeble, dying state. It may, and probably will, flee as in a night. It is crushed, it must die. Nothing can save it but the success of the rebellion, and that cannot save it! The government is actually, earnestly, entirely on the side of freedom. It has abolished slavery in the District of Columbia; it has liberated thousands in the march of its armies; it has given them freedom, work, and wages, and opened schools for their instruction in Virginia, Tennessee, North Carolina, and South Carolina. It has declared that Slavery shall never exist in its Territories, in language such as no other government on earth uses. This is the preamble of her decree: "To the end that FREEDOM may be, and remain forever, the fundamental law in all places whatsoever, so far as it lies within the power, or depends upon the action, of the government of the United States to make it so." Such is the action of the government. It will go further, it will go to the uttermost, if the rebellion is not speedily overthrown. The struggle will never be ended by the success of the rebels till this last remedy is tried. God may require this at our hands; if so, it shall not be refused. The people are too determined to make any terms but those of submission; and slaves will be freed, armed, and arrayed side by side with their white brethren, if in no other way the government can be preserved.

This is the cause of this gigantic rebellion, as seen in the action both of rebel and loyal. The government steadily approaches that great magazine which they revolted to preserve. It may be compelled to put the torch to it. The explosion may be terrible, will be glorious. Four millions of men and women may enter into liberty with a Red Sea deliverance, with a Red Sea destruction of their oppressors. When God speaks to our Moses, "Say unto the people that they go forward," He will give the command, and they will march; and if the cruel oppressors still retain their hard and impenitent hearts, they will sink like lead in the mighty waters.

For this, be assured, is with the people of America a struggle for the highest national life. It is not a mere struggle for ordinary national being. They prize their Constitution and Union not because they *are*, but because of what they embody and guarantee. They are the seat, the center, in their judgment, we may say in the judgment of the world, of the highest civil life. They are based on one maxim: the majority of the people shall govern, if they govern according to the letter of a just Constitution. If they violate that, the minority have a right to rebel. If the Constitution fails in any part, or transgresses the divine law, out of which all human law ought to flow, it provides for its peaceful amendment, so that its letter may ever conform to the growing intelligence of the ages. Such a Constitution the world never saw before. If it be destroyed through the weakness of its friends and violence of its enemies, the cause of equal civil liberty fails in the world. This is the profound conviction of the American people; it may be the offspring of vanity, but for it they are willing to spend the last drop of their blood and the last farthing of their treasure. Their reasoning is simple, it is sublime. It is this: Only two modes of government can exist among men, one based on the decision of the majority of the people, the other on a class, elect and separate. The first is our system. We believe it to be the right, and the only right one. It is assailed; the minority refuse to abide by the decisions of the majority; they take no peaceable ways of securing their rights professedly assailed, but scornfully, violently, and murderously throw off allegiance to the government. To permit this is to confess that we have ceased to be a nation. It is to substitute the other system of government for the one we have adopted. It is to say the minority rules, for it has its way, not we ours. That is only the old world system over again. The slaveholders are our nobles, we their serfs. Out of their number, after long conflict among themselves, may come a William of Normandy, a Charlemagne, or a Napoleon, who will seize and transmit the regal power; and democratic equality, representative and constitutional liberty, fade away from the earth. So they said, so felt. And, feeling thus, as one man they declared this first rebellion against their fundamental axiom shall be overthrown. If the majority use their power wrongfully, revolution is just. But when used for liberty, for justice, for the best interests of the world, it shall not be trampled under foot by a despotism "built in the eclipse and rigged with curses dark." God helping us, this devil of an aristocracy shall not dethrone the angel of democracy. He will help us, and Michael shall prevail over the dragon.

It is not possible, it seems to me, for any European people thoroughly to apprehend the feelings of the American people in this great crisis of its history. They are on a lower plane of civil life. They are ruled over. We are the rulers. They reverence a class; we the whole. They have no part, or the least possible, in the administration of affairs. We are the sources of administrative power, and our King and his Ministers are required every few years to submit themselves as our representatives to our judgment. We feel, therefore, precisely as a king feels when his crown is assailed. Himself and his family are chiefly in his mind. It was not the interests of the people that troubled Charles I., or James II., or Napoleon, or the King of Naples, or any dethroned or attacked monarch, but family interests.

His crown is his fortune. To dethrone him is to rob him. Hence he fights for it. Hence he is careful to transmit it, if possible, to his children. So does every American feel. He is a sovereign. His sovereignty is assailed. He must defend it, even to the death, or he is a worm and no man. He must transmit this great inheritance to his children and his children's children. It is worth more than any crown or any kingly seat. Queen Victoria has no such gift for Albert Edward as the poorest man in America has for all his children. She can transmit authority over millions of subjects; he, authority, with millions of equals, over his rulers. They are all of royal blood, all equal heirs to kingly honors. This may, and probably will, seem vain and childish to many of your readers; so does a Christian's experience to many a proud listener. But it is true, nevertheless, and, like that, is in harmony with the profoundest reason. It is consistent, as we have seen, with the universal instinct. We have no class. We had one. It has tried to do as they all have done elsewhere — assume rights above its fellows. We have risen upon it; we shall grind it to powder. Its name shall rot. As William the Conqueror blotted out the great house of Alfred, and with it the royal dominion of the Anglo-Saxon blood, exterminating it so utterly that only French mottoes blaze on England's banners, and French phrases make its legislative wishes a law,* so shall this uprising of an aristocracy — of a cacocracy rather — be blotted out in America. Not by a selfish and cruel man, for his own selfish and cruel interests, but by a great people, for themselves, their children, and the world. For it is another peculiarity of American feeling,— in the opinion of others, perhaps also a vanity; in their own, an inspiration, — that they are fighting the battle of the world.

* The Queen, or her Minister, acknowledges the enactments of Parliament by a French phrase — *La Reine le veut.*

Great Britain, in her conflicts, is inspired by the cry of Nelson, "*England* expects every man to do his duty;" France appeals to the glory of France; America feels that she is struggling for the rights of mankind. It is no new feeling with her. You will find it on the monument to her heroes that fell at Lexington, "Sacred to Liberty and the Rights of Mankind." You will find it in her Declaration of Independence. That great paper is the statement of the rights of all men. You will find it rooted and grounded in her earliest history. It inspired the Pilgrims of Plymouth, the settlers of Rhode Island, of Pennsylvania, of Maryland, of Georgia. It is on its greatest and probably final trial to-day. The war of the Revolution made her a nation. To become and be a nation, a people must first secure their liberty, then defend it from without and from within. America had secured hers after seven years of terrible suffering. She had maintained it, so that all the caste powers of the earth feared, if they did not respect her. In her unmailed arm they saw her sleeping thunders. With but the skeleton of a navy, with not a score of thousands in her army, she protected her citizens, native or adopted, in every sea and under every flag. Now comes the assault from within. If she yields, if she is humbled, equal liberty disappears from the earth. "The bubble of democracy is broken," as Nesselrode said, and kings and rulers may revel, unaffrighted by Belshazzar visions of dissolving kingdoms and vanishing scepters.

She sees the eyes of the *peoples* of Europe fastened upon her, no less than those of their rulers. She knows that if any people are yet blind through ignorance and degradation, their children will come to her light. She knows God has lifted her up, for the world's benefit and blessing; and, so knowing, a grander inspiration possesses her. She may be ridiculed for this. Yet she is not alone in her pride. One cannot read a British journal, or hear a British speech, or hardly open one of her books, where her greatness is not set forth in full if not fulsome phrase. France is as little afflicted with modesty. Both are partly right; both have honorable qualities, and, in many things, an honorable fame. Yet the achievements and the liberties of America are far greater than theirs. France owes whatever of liberty or equality she possesses to America. America owes their germs to England, but their growth and greatness are her own. It is the seed of the age of Cromwell, first betrayed by him, and then trodden under foot by succeeding dynasties, which has found a good soil there, and is bringing forth fruit a hundredfold. It will be transplanted to Europe, and all nations shall sit under its blessed branches.

For these armed and separated kingdoms must become peaceful, United, States. Destroy distinctions in society; make the ruler subject to a written Constitution; choose him out of the people, to return in a brief time to the people; in a word, make the people sovereign, and armies and armaments will cease. Terror of each other, wasteful expenditures to defend themselves against each other, yet heavier ones to maintain a costly and useless pomp of government, will also cease. England, like New York, will be simply a great State, with its governor and local administration of affairs. And New York is to-day as wisely and liberally governed as England; far more liberally in the matter of education. Scotland, in like manner, will enjoy the blessings of a real and not, as now, a *quasi* independence and union. Ireland will have its governor elected by its people; France, Austria, Italy, Spain, each theirs. Each is no larger, no better, than the States of the American Union. Each, I may proudly say, with all its great history, has no equal history; for in none of them is the most vital of all social and civil duties — the education, the elevation, the liberty of all — so thoroughly carried out. These shall yet be one Republic, a European Union; copying the American, forerunning the World Republic. Call not this a fantasy. It is the democratic prophecy of England's laureate, drawn from our living example. It shall be fulfilled in the earth when —

"The war drums beat no longer, and the battle flag is furled
In the Parliament of Man — the federation of the World!
Then the common sense of Most will keep a fretful realm in awe,
And the holy earth will slumber, lapped in universal law."

It is essential to this era of accomplished bliss that the American Republic be preserved; for it is, what "Blackwood" has long jeeringly called it, "the Model Republic." Not that it is developed to the fullness of its own principles. This very conflict has been thrust upon it by Divine Providence because it had become unfaithful to those principles. It had ceased to regard all men as equal. Through social, financial, and political interests it had been tempted to disregard the cry of the slave; it had allowed his masters to rivet the chains which previous generations had cast upon them. God rose upon us in judgment. He made us feel that our boasted strength was perfect weakness; that we should disappear as speedily as we had arisen, unless we gave full scope and play to those principles which He had breathed into us, which were our breath of life, and by which alone we had become a living, national soul. Everybody saw it in the flashing of an eye; and hence the unanimous cry, "The Union shall be preserved; let Slavery die." This takes a much stronger form in most, but its lowest expression is this.

We have yet a great work to do in this matter — a work which no European can comprehend, which almost every American yet shrinks from, but whose preliminary steps, to our honor it shall be said, we are willing to take, letting Providence direct the issue. It is this — the African race is in among us, in slavery or akin to it. It is unlike every other race, who are welcomed, whose lineage is speedily forgotten, and whose blood mingles freely each with each.

The distinctions and pride of European races have totally disappeared there. I know eminent families in whose blood a half dozen of these races are represented. We therefore cease to talk of English, Irish, German, French, Celtic, Teutonic, or any such clannish blood. We call ourselves the Caucasian — the white race. Yet this is clannish. And as these narrow feelings dwell in European nationalities, so this like narrow, if larger, sentiment works in us. Now the problem is thrust upon us by Providence, of the relation of the Caucasian to the African race — the white to the black. Our fundamental and most vital theories require that we make no distinction; that we be as unmindful of the accident of color as that of birth or tongue. But our feelings are powerfully averse to the conclusions to which we are thus driven. We cannot deny our foundation principles; we cannot instantly overcome the repugnance of generations.

It will not do for Europeans to say, *We* have overcome it; there is no distinction of color here. This is not quite true. I saw but three colored men in England, and they were all engaged in menial occupations, and one was dragging his heavy mistress round the streets — a service to which no Southern slave was ever humiliated. I have seen like few in France, and in no case have I seen gentlemen and ladies freely associating with them. They seem to be alone. At the Madaleine an elegantly dressed lady of color sat alone, and though in a most eligible seat and a crowded assembly, the chairs near her were left vacant.

But if received, they are only admitted to the lower grades. Let us see them in your House of Commons, in your House of Lords, generals in your army, riding in state and authority above the people. Let your prince follow the greater of Hebrew princes, and make a daughter of the dark race the sharer of his throne, and you would see whether England was as free from prejudice as she boasts.

If every sixth person in Great Britain was more or less African; if, in some counties, two out of every three were of this color; if you, that were white, had imported them or their ancestors as property, and still regarded them as such; or if, becoming weaned, by Providential dispensation, from that conviction, you were instantly required to look upon them as equals, to grant them all rights and privileges, social and civil; yea, more, if you were required to place them in your ruling class, to make them your nobles and kings, you would have some idea of the work of America.

She can have no lower class. She cannot, by virtue of her very nature, persist in distinguishing between men on account of complexion. She knows no Europe, no Asia, no America, before the law; she must know no Africa. Yet this non-recognition brings in its shadowy train many a yet abhorrent recognition. If all avenues are thrown open, who knows whither they will mount? Hence her principles and her feelings are engaged in a terrific struggle. Nothing but the danger of losing her own liberties could have made her grant the African his. Nothing but the sacrifice of his own equality would make a white citizen admit the black as a sharer. The slaveholders had an immense leverage in the depth and universality of this sentiment. They believed the people would prefer them as rulers to the admission of Africans as equals. The people have rejected them, in view of the possibility, the probability, of the latter alternative. This is far from being settled; but the first steps are taken. Many seek to expatriate the negro; but he will not go, and they dare not drive him out. Hence they wait the movements of Providence. It may be that higher than all their thoughts, far beyond all their desires, we are working out another problem that must be solved before the Millennium comes. It may be that the unity, as well as the equality, of the human race is to be first reëstablished in America. The dispersion of Babel, continued for thousands of years, yet potent in all the earth, may cease there first. To her may the gathering of *all* the nations be. The extreme races of mankind are forced together in a land whose greatest, all-engrossing idea, is the perfect equality of all men. They are being welded in the fiery furnace of war, and weakness, and sorrow. They may become one and indivisible. If so, and if, being so, the central idea of her nationality is unweakened, if all men, of whatever shade or origin, move freely in the great currents of social and civil life, then has she indeed a high, the highest possible honor. Then will she be the guide and example of the world. At present it must be honestly said, she desires no such honor. It is a greatness, of the kind which Bacon says is thrust upon man. But she is determined to be faithful to her principles in view of even such a possibility. The time will come when she will hail it as a privilege. Europeans of the higher and middle classes, even, shrink to-day from such relations with their own blood in the lower classes with unutterable abhorrence. They can throw no stones at Americans. What fearful processes our Creator may employ to break up all these prejudices, everywhere prevailing, He only knows. They must be abolished; for He Himself makes no such distinction among the children of Adam. They must be like Him in this regard in respect to each other.

It is not necessary for me to say that we do not condemn the course of all the citizens of Britain because we must that of their government. We gratefully recognize the sympathy of not a few of her eminent and private men. We gladly commend the foresight, wisdom, as well as constant abolitionism of George Thompson; the bold and true democratic utterances of John Bright; the faithful and able services of the Star and the News, and of a few other sheets in the minor cities of the kingdom. We rejoice that Dr. Jobson, and William Arthur, and Robinson Scott have not failed us in this hour, but have steadily approved our course, and confidently awaited our success.

Let it also be remembered that America does not refuse to recognize any excellences in England, though her leading journals and statesmen find it very difficult to see any good in America. She acknowledges her indebtedness to the men who wrested the Magna Charta from an unwilling despot; to the greater men of later date, Hampden, Vane, Russell, Sydney, Granville Sharpe, Erskine, Fox, Wilberforce, and many others, who, by their labors, dangers, and in not a few cases by their martyrdom, advanced the cause of human rights not only in Britain, but throughout the world. She rejoices that the encroachments of aristocracy and monarchy on the liberties of the people have thus been resisted and beaten back, and that these powers have been at least girdled and limited. These are proud names, which she delights to honor. They have labored, and she enters into their labors, not to revel idly in the fruit of their toil, but to carry forward the work they so perilously, so gloriously begun. A saying of Algernon Sydney is the motto of Massachusetts — the spirit of Sydney is the spirit of America. There these great Britons find a more congenial home than in their own yet half-liberated land. There it is that Milton's spirit, as well as language, is the mother tongue. Every heart beats in unison with his principles; every institution conforms to their high behests. What is discordant must disappear, what concordant must go on to perfection.

Neither does America quarrel with the crowned heads of Europe because they are crowned. She has had imbecility, if not treachery, in some whom she had appointed to maintain her authority. She knows that with the most irresponsible powers an Antonine ruled wisely. She acknowledges the good sense and admirable virtues of Victoria, and rejoices that she feels the gratitude, as a mother and a sovereign, which her government, as subjects, have forgotten. She recognizes the consummate tact of Napoleon, the wisdom of Victor Emanuel, and the larger, because more liberal, nature of Alexander of Russia, — more worthy than the first of that name to be called Alexander the Great. Yet these exceptional cases cannot blind her eyes to the wrongfulness of the system on which, though not of which, they flourish. As excellent have been not a few slaveholders. Does England therefore approve of that institution ? So she feels that the structure of society on this basis is wrong, and that, as great and virtuous, far more so, as a whole, would their rulers be, if from and with the people.

It only needs a Washington and Jefferson to prove this. They will appear when the people shall call for them ; and when that call is made, you, too, may feel the throes of civil convulsions. They have always attended the birth of new liberties. England, France, Italy, have organized in the State the new demands of human nature only with fierce civil wars. It seems to be a necessity laid upon man that every triumph of Freedom must be through blood. Would that the powers now leagued against her here would take warning from the fate of their natural allies in America, and yield without resistance to her divine demands. But it is not probable that they will thus learn wisdom. Wrong power never has. It has always to be overthrown by armed right. Sydney's and Massachusetts' motto is painfully true: *Ense petit placidam sub libertate quietem* — She seeks *with the sword* serene repose under liberty. Hence it is more than probable that England's now peaceful and lovely fields will again reëcho with the ragings of civil war. Almost every rood of her soil has been made fat with fraternal blood ; and the warfare is not yet accomplished. It is but just begun. Her masses with but little culture, comfort, civil rights, or social equality. A few persons cover all her lands with their seal, while, as Tennyson declares, and declares too truly, —

> "Her poor are huddled and hustled together, each sex like swine;"

the right of primogeniture separating between children, and impoverishing all but one, that he may be unnaturally honored; a ruling class, based on birth, not worth; a church claiming exclusive privilege, protection, and power; a chief ruler born to his seat, and, as history has proved, almost as frequently a curse as a blessing to his subjects, — these radical and profound evils, as they appear to Americans, as they are appearing to all men, must be abolished. Before their abolition, they must be boldly assailed. Said I not truly the warfare has hardly begun? It will begin. The August day of wealth and quiet which she is now enjoying is no greater than that which America enjoyed two years ago. We had to arise and attack a gigantic foe or surrender our liberties. So must Britain arise. Somebody must sound the democratic trumpet here, and call the people to contend for their rights, peacefully, sternly, unto the triumphant end. He who calls for this glorious warfare may find that the traitor's gate of the Tower can still be opened, and that the headman's ax is yet sharp, if rusty.

More than one has had to lay down his life in America before the conflict came to its armed and final issue. Lovejoy died at the hands of a mob, defending liberty of speech. Torrey expired in a Maryland dungeon for seeking to deliver the captives. Others have been offered on the altar of this faith, until the traitor's gibbet was honored with the heroic martyrdom of John Brown and his devoted band. For some yet unknown heroes in your land the hemlock and the laurel are perhaps now growing. I hope and pray that this work may require no such sacrifices, but that, by peaceful agitation, this divine purpose may be accomplished. But it must be begun, and on their heads be the guilt who seek thus to suppress it. When accomplished, — whether, as we hope, peacefully, or, as may possibly happen, by such a conflict as America is now passing through, — there will be a new England, far lovelier than the past or present; an England not only of charming ruins, and fields, and roads, and sheep, and kine, of castles and villas, where a sumptuous nobility or the comfortable middle class, dwell in delightful seclusion, but an England where the multitudinous masses are upraised in intelligence, comfort, and dignity; where all have equal rights, and legislators and governors, elected by the people, feel that they are one with the people. The kindness which now beautifies many in these high stations will not then be, as now, one of condescension, but of the promptings of equality and fraternity. Then, and not till then, shall the saying of the Great Alfred (one of our founders as well as of yours, for both peoples were in his loins) be fulfilled, that "England wishes every man to be as free as his own thoughts."

It is no child's play that is laid upon the Englishmen of to-day. It is no chaffering between two pampered and purposeless parties, whose quarrels are almost as powerless for the good of the State as were those of the Court of Louis XV. They may be swept away, as those were, by the strong wind of a political revolution. May the men of Britain see and seize this arduous, glorious calling. May they gird their loins to the great work. Then will disinthralled America forget the conduct of the present ruling caste, and with the Commonwealth of England hold firm and eternal concord; for they will be one in feeling, work, and victory.

But I may be intruding upon your courtesy by such utterances, though they have legitimate connection with the whole argument; for, to the American mind, democracy is in debate on her fields, and anti-democracy alone is the baleful animus of English silence and practical complicity. But these words, to be effectual in England, must be proclaimed by Englishmen. My excuse for the liberty I have indulged, if any is needed, is that, though writing in France, I am writing to England. Here a government professedly based on seven and a half millions of free votes dare not allow a single obscure word in an obscure journal to question its pretended popular sovereignty; but Britain has long rejoiced in perfect liberty of speech and press. We trust it is no vain boasting. It must be perfect, or it is no liberty; if it cannot discuss the system as well as the policy of its government — the constitution as well as the administration — it is as much paralyzed as though stricken with utter dumbness. I remember, too, that one of your own poets has said, —

> "Let us ponder boldly; 'tis a base
> Abandonment of reason to resign
> Our right of thought."

But freedom of thought is not freedom unless that of speech accompany it.

As the utmost license of honest utterance exists in respect to every other subject, so it must in respect to this also. Our Creator subjects His nature, government, and movements to the scrutiny of all His intelligent creatures. If He thus casts His works and Word, His Gospel, and Himself in His Incarnation, in His Trinity, in all His nature and workings into the crucible of honest discussion, certainly this far lesser idea of civil government cannot claim exemption. If kings are kings, as they say they are, *Dei gratia,* then they must be content with the condition He has imposed on His own royalty. "It is enough for the servant that he be as his Master." But it has no exemption in reality. Their own government is discussed privately by Europeans, in every parlor, kitchen, and workshop, as much as the American is in America. It must be publicly here as it is there. Let not the advocates of any system fear for the result. As was said of an infinitely greater cause, involved in an infinitely more vital controversy, so may it be of these conflicting ideas of government: "If they be of man, they will come to naught; but if of God, we cannot overthrow them, lest haply we be found fighting against God." Napoleon said Europe in half a century would be Republican or Cossack. The Crimean War prevented the triumph of the latter; the rule of the slave power in America has thus far prevented the former. If that be overthrown, it is not too late in the remaining decade of time he suggested, to have his prophecy fulfilled. He saw at least that the world was too small for such hostile systems to long hold equal sovereignty. It is getting smaller every day. All men must soon decide whether they will rule themselves, or be ruled by a self-elected few. Four *réunions* of the world's industry within ten years show us how compact, how interwoven, is the family of man. In like manner the world's politics should be calmly, carefully, and courageously considered by the world's representatives. It will be considered, but whether in this or a more violent form, God knows.

But, finally, it is perhaps only a proper expression of gratitude for an American to speak thus freely to Great Britain of her great defect and duty. You sent one of your most eloquent orators to America to show us our sin, and to summon us to the work of its extirpation. You have faithfully and constantly set before us this duty in your journals, in the resolutions of religious and philanthropic associations, and even in the documents of State. A humble son of America may show the gratitude which he and many of his people truly feel for this faithfulness on your part, by a reciprocal service. As Mr. Garrison said of some of his warm English sympathizers, "Each nation, as each individual, has its own cross to bear. Your duty is not ours. It is ours to abolish slavery. It is yours to abolish aristocracy, from the knight to the throne." Both will then arrive, though by different paths, at the same high and glorious table-land of universal liberty, equality, and fraternity May our motto be an improvement of that of England, and instead of the selfish Norman's proud French, "God and my right," may it be the better, the best watchword, "God and the Right." And may He give us grace and strength as nations, as well as individuals, to see and to do our whole duty.

With great respect,

I remain, truly yours,

G. HAVEN.

PARIS, July 4, 1862.

THE STATE A CHRISTIAN BROTHERHOOD.*

"LET US KEEP THE FEAST, NOT WITH OLD LEAVEN, NEITHER WITH THE LEAVEN OF MALICE AND WICKEDNESS, BUT WITH THE UNLEAVENED BREAD OF SINCERITY AND TRUTH." — 1 *Cor.* v. 8.

"ARISE; SHINE." — *Isa.* lx. 1.

"ALL NATIONS SHALL CALL YOU BLESSED; FOR YE SHALL BE A DELIGHTSOME LAND, SAITH THE LORD OF HOSTS." — *Mal.* iii. 12.

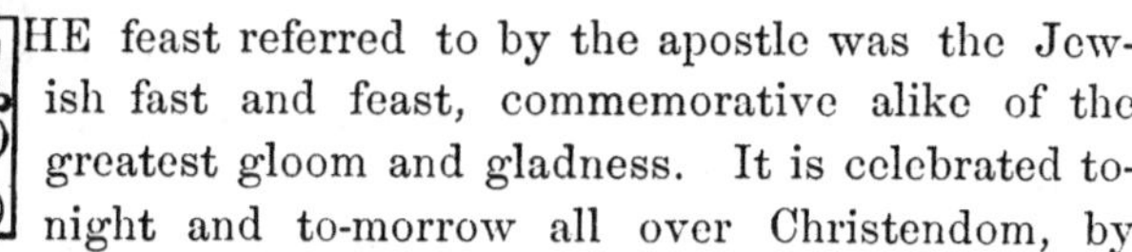

THE feast referred to by the apostle was the Jewish fast and feast, commemorative alike of the greatest gloom and gladness. It is celebrated to-night and to-morrow all over Christendom, by both Jews and Christians, — the solemn sacrifice, typical and memorial, of the blessed Lord. With Paul, we see the sacred supper, and the more sacred garden that eternally sanctify this day. With him we behold the consummations of the morrow, — from the midnight betrayal to the midnight burial, — the scorn and scourging, the mob, from publican to priest, seething with ferocious rage, the cross of agony, the torn and bloody hands, and feet, and head, the blackened heavens and rent earth! How they overwhelm

* A discourse delivered before the New England Conference of the Methodist Episcopal Church, at the High Street Church, Charlestown, Mass., on the occasion of the annual State Fast, April 2, 1863.

us, as we stand on this distant point of earth and time, and look upon that Form, high and lifted up! The preliminary services of many generations also rise before us; even back to that Thursday night, when there was wrought out the earthly salvation of a nation, type of the earthly and eternal salvation of the world. We see the poor slaves, aroused by the screams of their hitherto haughty neighbors, hastily cooking their unraised cakes, and, in great terror, as well as great joy, fleeing from the house of bondage. The light of four thousand years shines solemnly upon us. We feel our unity with the emancipated founders of the memorial sacrifice — with Him in whom, in "the form of a slave," it was divinely consummated.

But our responsibilities lie not with the past. We gather from it incentives to duty; but the Duties themselves are here and now. The apostle introduces these words in an earnest expostulation with his brethren for a local, Corinthian sin. So we, if we would rightly eat the unleavened bread and bitter herbs of a true fast, must do it by purging ourselves of the old leaven of malice and wickedness within ourselves, and by eating the unleavened bread of sincerity and truth, in respect to present and personal obligations. The cause of this gathering is not to keep the passover, not even to dwell on the great event, which, more than all others, should be held by the Church in perpetual remembrance. It is by invitation of this Commonwealth, through its elect head, to deplore our national sins, and implore national forgiveness and salvation. We may with especial propriety, therefore, consider those questions of morality and religion that connect themselves with our civil and social institutions.

In what respect must we, as citizens, must our nation, as a nation, purge itself of the old leaven of malice and wickedness? What are the new works, sincere and truthful, demanded of us by the God and Savior of nations and of men? May God help us to speak and hear in the enjoined spirit of sincerity, the εἰλικρίνεια, or translucent clearness of spiritual vision, by which, and by which alone, we detect the perfect proportions and exquisite beauty of absolute truth. If the green scum of pride cover the soul's vision, if the muddy elements of prejudice float in it, if the violent winds of passion toss it, if, as is often the case, all these combine, a dead surface, muddy center, and vehement commotion, then we shall not discern the truth. We may fancy that we have found it, but it will be a lusterless, crystalless thing, the worthless compound of our own gross natures. We shall rage on those who do discover it, and set it before us. Not in Christ's day, alone, did swine trample pearls under their feet, and turn and rend those who set before them these gifts that were then esteemed more precious than diamonds. The human heart, here and everywhere, in you and me, tempts to this same act. It is a swinish heart, full of swinish conceit and appetite, that the grace of God alone can purge and purify, and uplift to the style and manners of the sky. Let us implore for ourselves the presence of His Holy Spirit, which alone can give us the eye serene and the transparent medium by which we may see the very thought of God in all its perfection of beauty. May we be lifted up by His side, in a revelator's vision, and behold our land and ourselves, as His eye now beholds them. Then shall we gather from the thoughts of the hour both increasing purity and increasing knowledge. The truth that thus shines out to our humble-lidded eye will itself dissipate any remaining darkness in the medium of vision. We shall see the more clearly from seeing it the more clearly.

It is a favorite conceit with all famous peoples that they have a mission. "For some especial purpose God has raised them up," they say, forgetting that this purpose may be, in their case, as it was in Pharaoh's, to show forth His power and His wrath. They forget that it is the simple, universal, every-day mission of doing justly, loving mercy, and walking humbly before God, and that it is the national, as well as private, observance of those probationary tests that shall fit us for, and insure us admission to, the citizenship of the heavenly nation. But worldly people dream that they have some great earthly thing to do, and cry out with Pharisaic agony of conceit, How are we straitened till it be accomplished! So has it always been. Egypt, undoubtedly, fancied that she had a mission, and, looking on her pyramids, obelisks, sphinxes, and temples, dreamed that the problems of the universe were to find solution only in her. So, evidently, felt Nebuchadnezzar and the powers of Nineveh and Babylon. So did Athens, and Turkey, and Venice, and mediæval Italy. So did Spain and France. So, to-day, do England and America.

It will be noticed that only as a people rise to wealth and power do they begin to assume these airs, and when that wealth and power leave them, much, if not all, the sense of their peculiar mission departs also. Another fact is also noticeable. The institutions under which they have happened to flourish receive all the glory of their success and the ardor of their propagation. Athens thought her style of a slave democracy the world's panacea. Sparta was certain that her fashion of a slave oligarchy was the only remedy. Rome would Romanize everything. So is it now. The British fancy that their Constitution is the sole cause of their prosperity, and that, could it be applied to all the weak bodies politic of Europe, it would effect an instant cure; while the truth is, her Constitution, for five hundred years, never made her great. Protestantism and the discovery of the Cape of Good Hope are the causes of her wealth, and her wealth the cause of her arrogant self-esteem.

We are treading in the same path. Is it a divine one, or

is it but the fantasy of a heated vanity? One is constrained to feel that much of it is the laudation with which success crowns her votaries. She delights to wreathe the laurels of virtue with those of victory. Yet there is a basis for this universal sentiment. It is this. All nations, at their beginning, or at the hour of their especial development, measurably recognize the equal rights of all. The Arab and Turk, flying with the crescent, symbol of their bloody cimeter, across three continents, offered equal privileges to every soldier. The meanest serf was one with the haughtiest bashaw before God and His prophet. A like sense of equality won Marathon and Salamis, and founded the Grecian power. Rome's greatest victories were when she was a republic. Gibbon begins her decline with her Cæsars. Venice, Holland, and republican France, all felt this inspiration sweeping them on to power. Yet these have perished. They are broken in pieces as a potter's vessel. They departed from God and God from them. It would seem as if nations would be taught by their fate. But nations, like individuals, are but slightly impressed with another's experience. England is traveling the same path. In the day of her wealth and power she is doing precisely what Venice, Greece, and Rome did in theirs. She tramples on the rights of her despised people, from whom alone is her real life. Unless she is converted, she will follow her proud predecessors to their eternal grave.

What is our mission? It is of precisely the same character as theirs, and as all men's—to fear God and keep His commandments. Being the latest birth of time, the principles on which and of which we must live are so clearly recognized, that they have found expression in our organic law. They are twofold.

First. Universal toleration of religion, with the acknowledged supremacy of Christianity.

Second. The universal equality and fraternity of man.

I. We may properly consider, as preliminary to the first topic, the marked difference between this idea and those which have been followed by previous nations. Religion has always been recognized as the supreme idea of the State. In Israel orthodoxy and obedience were identical; so were heterodoxy and treason. When Christianity became potent in the Romam empire, it ascended the throne as the supreme object of reverence. It supplanted heathenism, which, for four centuries, had attacked it with instinctive and increasing ferocity. Not without earthly wisdom did Herod search for his rival to the throne of David among the babes of Bethlehem. Not without the bloody instincts of self-preservation did he slay the whole, that he might the One. He knew that the scepter of earthly sovereignty was grasped by the appointed Heir of all things. He saw that his central and sacred throne would be the first that He would ascend. Every pagan emperor acted with like worldly wisdom. The refusal to worship their dead predecessor was a refusal to acknowledge their own legitimacy. If unhindered by their clemency or carelessness, it must result in the overthrow of their dynasty. Could Napoleon allow citizens of France, or Victoria those of England, to openly acknowledge a Bourbon or a Stuart as their sovereign? Then they could a president, and where are they and theirs? The same instinct of self-preservation worked alike in rulers as sanguinary as Nero, as gross as Caligula, as statesman-like as Trajan, as clement as Marcus Aurelius, as devotional as Pius Antoninus. They all, with one accord, sought to uproot the pestiferous treason—treason against the gods, and, therefore, against the State. In the triumph of Christianity the same law obtained. It was Christianity, not Constantine, that overthrew Paganism at the Pons Milvius. Under its inspiration, he slays the gods in the person of his rival Maxentius. Not without significance, too, may we not say, not without Providence, did this heathen bring into the conflict the holy vessels of the Hebrew service — three hundred years before, with their nation, brought captive to Rome. As Jew and pagan united in killing Christ because He assumed to be their king, so they again, and for the last time, appear together to prevent His elevation to the throne of earthly dominion. The apostate Church and apostate world are confederate against the Lord's Anointed. It is in vain. The ark that once embodied the rejecting and rejected Church, and the golden candlestick that suggested its vanished light, follow the idolatrous Cæsar, the incarnation of pagan supremacy, to the bed of the Tiber, while the Cross, waving in the skies, leads the triumphing eagles of the Christian Cæsar to the throne of the world.

From that hour till the organization of the American government, Christianity had allowed no real toleration to hostile or indifferent faiths. However Christless it was, it yet assumed an undivided sovereignty. Whatever civil wars it had in itself, those wars never questioned its supremacy in the affairs of state. Latin Occidentalism fought for centuries with Greek Orientalism for the control of the empire. Protestantism, in many preliminary skirmishes, and for generations after the Reformation dawned, contended mightily with Romanism; but none of these forms of faith ever dreamed that they were contending for toleration. They were striving for the mastery. Their success involved the utter overthrow of their rival. Such were the wars of Germany and England for two hundred years. As soon as any especial type of faith prevailed, it demanded the complete obedience of its foes. Presbyterianism was as zealous for the rack and thumb-screw against Episcopacy, as both against Papacy. Janet's stool, hurled against the robed and prayer-reading Churchman in John Knox's kirk, was but a symbol of the national feeling. Cromwell was as severe against the liturgists as Charles II. against non-conformity. The reason why the true faith outlived these persecutions was, because it was the true faith. Had it been false utterly, as were the pagan systems, it would have died and made no sign. Constantine was as rigid in requiring subjection to his religion as Diocletian, just before him, had been. But Diocletian struggled to slay the divine truth, and hence rightfully goes down to history as a persecutor; Constantine, to extirpate a false, though famous, faith, and its advocates either yielded an outward conformity, because it gave them no inward support in their extremity, or else, resisting and perishing, have been accounted, by their victors and their posterity to this day, as worthy of death and infamy.

It is well to notice here the charge that is often laid against our Puritan, not Pilgrim, fathers, for the Plymouth Pilgrims learned toleration in their exile, and were the first to practice it in the world. But the Puritans of Massachusetts Bay had suffered less and learned less. They simply conformed to this, till then, universal principle. They revolted from the ritualistic forms of worship, and for almost a hundred years had striven with it for the mastery of England. They had been defeated. They must conform or fly. Had they succeeded, their rivals must have done likewise. They did so obey or fly in the reign of Cromwell. Defeated they retreated to America. No wiser than their generation, than all previous generations, they made their creed the supreme law of the land. Any shade of difference was, so far forth, treason — any avowal thereof must be punished as rigidly as theft or murder; more rigidly, for these concerned but the estates or bodily lives of their people — that, if allowed, imperiled their eternal salvation. The idea of toleration found occasional expression, but it was rather the dream of a fanciful thinker than the resolute opinion of a sturdy believer. Lord Bacon held to it, but Lord Bacon was hardly thought to be a wise master-builder in ecclesiastical matters.

The first man who introduced it formally into the constitution of human government, grew to the height of his *great argument in the prolific soil of Puritan politics.* Roger Williams "saw the light and hailed it in his joy," when, seeking deliverance from the trammels of a human creed, he found himself restrained by the bolts and bars of human laws. It was the conflict of conscience with conscience that struck out the spark of the inviolable sanctity of conscience, which has become the peculiar light and glory of America. It is not unlikely that had he been allowed a measure of liberty in prophesying, he would have been contented with his chains. He certainly shows the inconsistency which every strong nature somewhere reveals, in that, while contending for the utmost liberty of conscience in the State, he should exclude from the Church all who refused compliance with a mere form. Had his colony been as great and prosperous as its neighbors, it might have returned to their system. To expel unimmersed Christians from the Church is as much greater violation of human rights than to expel non-conformists and non-professors from the State, as the Church itself is greater than the State.

Less catholic was the Catholicism of Maryland. Like that of Rhode Island, it was constrained by events. Unlike that, it was not developed from principle. James would establish a colony. He wished that it should be Papal. His power was not equal to his desires. A Prostestant Parliament was hostile. He secured his ends only by making league with the most ultra of his opponents; and on the basis of perfect toleration the most extreme of Papists and Protestants outwardly, not inwardly, united. Maryland was the fruit of the strange marriage; — an unnatural child, she reveals the unmingling contraries of her origin, even to this day.

The American idea, therefore, of the equality of all Churches and Christians before the law is of the latest origin. It is also to-day as purely an American institution as the civil equality of the people. There are but few religious bodies and no Christian governments elsewhere that yet desire such a boon. They are as much afraid of spiritual, as of social and civil democracy.

The Protestants of France accept subsidies from the State, and submit to the restraints with which it pays for its aid. M. Monod, one of the most able of the Evangelical preachers of Paris, told me, with especial and unconscious pride, of their success in building up congregations to the standard required before they could draw on the government for the support of a pastor, and of the various increments according to which that aid was graded. He did not seem to feel the ignominy of receiving his bread from such a hand as Louis Napoleon's — a professed Papist — a real Infidel. He did not feel the further degradation, as it would seem to an Englishman even, for they have grown to that stature, of being forbidden by his patron from saying anything controversially against the Papists. Napoleon keeps up the show of impartiality by requiring like pledges of the Papal priests. It is one of the shrewd dodges of that arch hypocrite, by which he apparently serves the cause of liberty, and really that of slavery. With Paris, thoroughly, openly, universally Catholic, there is as little need of the priests declaiming against Protestantism as in the days of Louis XIV.; while the possibility of Protestants converting those whose errors of doctrine they are not allowed to oppose, would be as hopeful as the like silence imposed by the Sanhedrim on Peter and John, had they submitted to that decree of the State, would have been in the conversion of the Jews. To carry out his crafty trickery, he puts a policeman in every church to see that it does not violate this law, and all — whether native or foreign, Wesleyan or American — are thus preserved from the errors of free speech, and bold denunciation of dominant apostasy. What Monod and his friends ought to do, would be to cast the gold of the emperor at his feet, saying, "Thy money perish with thee," and, departing from his presence, proclaim the whole truth as it is in Jesus. He would undoubtedly make a vigorous attempt to suppress their liberty, but they would grow with persecutions. The days of St. Bartholomew are passed. He would be constrained to concede what they piously and persistently demanded. But they content themselves with faithfully laboring in the imperial fetters, hoping for some movement of Providence that shall set them at liberty.

Like, though less servile, are the dissenters of Britain. The universal tax to support the Establishment is quietly submitted to by millions of anti-Churchmen. If there were but a uniform refusal to pay it, it would soon be swept away. A single item illustrates the power of this tithe. In the Epworth Church, where Samuel Wesley was rector, a son of a Lord, Rev. and Hon. Charles Dundas, is the present incumbent. His congregation, on a beautiful June Sabbath, was not over fifty; less than twenty staid to the sacrament. In the village around the church are, at least, three churches or chapels of Wesleyans, Independents, and others. Yet the income of the rector is over eleven hundred pounds, or nearly six thousand dollars. Four fifths of this is drawn from the poor neighbors who never attend his preaching. This is a poor country parish, and bears no comparison to the enormous wealth of some of the clerical estates. Walking on the uplands near Shakspeare's cliff at Dover, I asked a peasant who owned the land about me. "The Archbishop of Canterbury," he replied. Yet this was twenty-five miles from Canterbury, and a hundred from his real residence, which is in London.

Such a system, of course, prevents real toleration. Liberty of conscience is never perfect where one is compelled to pay for the support of a religion he does not approve. Nor is the liberty of the National Church itself more than a name, when politicians, like Palmerston, appoint their bishops and station their preachers. But the non-conforming mind, as a whole, is not ripe for a perfect independency. The Free Church of Scotland, though it spurns the aid of a patronizing State, would willingly receive it, if the State would not interfere with its operations. Were that Church strong enough to bring Scotland over to its view, it would dictate terms, under threat of dissolving the British Union; would become the State Church, and take the moneys of the government for the support of its preachers, while it maintained its superiority over the State, and did not — as the National Kirk meekly does — place the sovereign or her lordly representative in a royal gallery, far above the moderator, the real head of the Church.

Like ideas and usages prevail in Protestant Germany. In fine, everywhere but here, is there more or less of a subjection of the Church to the State, whereby the Church receives its stipends and surrenders her sovereignty. The Roman States are the only exception. There the Church is the State, as it was in the original Jewish nation. When one sees in Rome officials, judge, policeman, custom-house officer, all, receiving their salaries from a clergyman, whose council of state are also clergymen, he has a lively conception of Palestine under Samuel, and the high priests of a later period. Even their kings were but the collectors and disbursers of the Church tariffs — never the supreme head of the Church, as in England.

The Church and the State have thus experienced all the evils of alternate authority. Now the Church rules the State, and now the State the Church. Here, for the first time, they agree to dissolve partnership. They who have been united for good or evil, for better or worse, in life and in death, in all previous ages and races, who have never conceived a dissolution possible, have agreed to make the experiment. The collisions of conscience have compelled this — not the advance of political science. Had the Conscience been a unit, the State would have remained its servant. Dissensions in the Church made statesmen of indifferent conscience—as Jefferson and Franklin—see that the independence of each high contracting party was better for both.* Others, more conscientious, adopted their views, and thus was launched the great national idea. It is new in history, and new in two important respects to ourselves.

1. It has not been universal with us till the previous generation. But two or three colonies were without an established Church at the beginning of our national existence.

2. A more important consideration is, that this toleration had never been extended among the most extremely liberal commonwealths, so as to place all faiths and non-faiths on the same basis as Christianity. The colony of Roger Williams was a Baptist colony, with all its toleration: so was Penn's a Quaker. Both were Christian. The deposition of Christianity from the supreme seat is an act almost of our day. It is not yet everywhere formally accomplished, though the force of the current sweeps thither.

This idea seems to us eminently practical. It is not so necessarily. It has its most grave and perplexing problems. Like all things human, it is defective and mortal. It will have its day, and cease to be. But we live in the hour of its supremacy. We are required to make full proof of the ministry we have received of the Lord Jesus during its dominion. We ought carefully to consider, then, what are the dangerous tendencies of such a system, and what are the duties of the ministry in view of these tendencies.

The greatest peril of such a disunion is, that the State ceases to recognize Christ as its Head. We may be so tolerant as to be intolerant of Christianity. We may allow such liberty as to reject the authority of the Author of all our liberties. We are attempting to build up and make mighty in the earth a nation that is Christian in reality,

* Mill on Liberty, p. 20.

and not in name. How difficult, if not impossible, such a work is, can only be seen by comparing it with every other great nation in history. The four kingdoms that Daniel described to Nebuchadnezzar were pagan powers, crushed by the stone cut from the eternal mountain. The governments since the days of Constantine have been imperfect portions of that kingdom that is to fill the whole earth. This divine kingdom is going on to its completion, and every power to whom God giveth prominence must consider itself as one of its component parts.

The successive rise of these Christian empires has been because of their partial allegiance to Christ — their successive fall, because of their subsequent revolt from Him. The present hour beholds four great powers influencing the world — England, France, Russia, and the United States. Each of the others is the representative of a grand division of the Christian Church. We profess not to represent the Christian Church in any of these great divisions. Further than this, we profess not to represent Christianity itself. The first position is right. The second is wrong. It is proper for us to say we are not a Papist or Protestant nation. It is proper to amply protect Jew, Mussulman, Pagan, and Infidel, in his worship or non-worship; but it is not proper to refuse to recognize Christ as our national Head. It is not right to carefully abstain, in every presidential message and proclamation of fasting or thanksgiving, from mentioning the name of the Savior of the world. Such liberality is licentiousness. Such fastidiousness is fatal. We aspire to the leadership of the world. But it must be only as the lieutenant of Christ. If we hope to thrust ourselves into the front rank of the race, at this period of the world's history, and so near the millennial reign, without any especial cognizance of Him by whom are all things, and for whom are all things, we shall find that we have made a dreadful mistake. We shall surely and most suddenly be ground to powder under the steady and rapid advance of that divine Stone. We shall be as though we had never been. God would make small account of us, no matter how large we made of ourselves, did we thus trifle with His decree, made before the world was, and confirmed often since man began his career: "Ask of Me and I will give Thee the heathen for Thine inheritance, and the uttermost parts of the earth for Thy possession." Christ has asked, has earned the gift. It shall be given. Who art thou, Goliath of America, that dares to talk about establishing a kingdom with no Christ in it, or with Christ put on a level with Mahomet or Buddh, Paine or Parker? "The nation and kingdom that will not serve Thee shall perish. Yea, those nations shall be utterly wasted." It is as true now as in the days of pagan Nero; as true here as in Mohammedan Turkey. You may say we *are* Christian. So we might be if the majority governed; but this is a case where the minority govern; and no President dares acknowledge Christianity to be the religion of this nation. It may offend some unchristian conscience. The call to prayer and fasting that appears in to-day's papers confirms the statement. There is no Christ in it. It is contrary to our cardinal principle. If this is to be the doctrine of America, she will never live out half her days. The attempt now being made to introduce into the Constitution the confession of national faith in God and Christ ought to be pressed forward. The blessing of God will attend its success.

Already two great sores have broken out upon us in consequence of this latitudinarianism — one, the irreligious character of many of our public men, and of the masses of the people; the other, false notions as to the minister's relation to politics or the affairs of State.

1. It is a rare thing to see a man in the presidential seat who is a professed Christian. I am not aware that such an one has ever been elected to that chair. It is prob-

able that not one of them was a member of an Evangelical Church. This evil is not cured yet. We have had moral men, and those who were far otherwise. But a man that was willing to avow himself a Christian, that was connected with a Christian church, and received its sacraments, is yet a most rare novelty there. The same is true of the majority of our high officials. Whatever the party in power, that fact remains unaltered. The representatives of the cause of liberty are as unwilling to personally profess Christ as are those of the cause of slavery. This is strikingly contrary to the managers of nations abroad. Whatever defects they have, — and they are many, — however bitterly they oppose the rights of the people, they recognize the rights of Christ. They are professors of faith in Him, and trust to Him alone for salvation. The prominence that they thus give to personal Christian faith is not without marked benefits. It recognizes the necessity of that faith. It rebukes infidelity. It popularizes religion. We may complain of the feeble fruit of such a divine seed, as we see their adhesion to hoary errors and violent perverting of justice ; but we forget that we, as a people, have been, and, in a degree, are even now, guilty of like devotion to hideous sins. Their corrupt sentiments and unchristian conduct are not Christianity, and multitudes who are affected by the fashion of the great men more than by their sins, may thus be led to a simple and saving knowledge of Christ. Certainly the prevalence of a lack of Christian faith, on the part of our representative men, reproduces this irreligion in a fearfully increasing ratio as we move through the masses of society. The great majority of Americans have no religion. They are worse than the worst heathen, for these do revere and worship something higher than themselves. Even in New England, the majority, probably, of most towns have no personal faith in Jesus Christ as their Savior. So fearfully does this irreligion in high places reveal itself in the low.

In Europe the poorest classes are very generally religious. However low the tone of their piety, — however ignorant all, and immoral many may be, — there is in the masses a knowledge of Jesus as the only Redeemer, the consciousness of the need of His blood for their salvation, a willingness to confess such a need, and, perhaps, according to the light they have, through the half-teachings of their spiritual guides, as strict a conformity to the demands of their faith as with us. All this is directly contrary to our experience. How few attend our Sunday services! When there, how impious their bearing — sitting and staring through the prayers as coolly as at a play — coming to Sunday evening meetings in large numbers, but with no thought of worship — with no idea that they are expected to feel a sentiment of godly fear, or sorrow, or faith, — while myriads never darken the doors of a church, and spend the Sabbath as thoughtlessly as they do a holiday! These are solemn, they are dreadful truths.

They may well make us pause in our rejoicings over the perfect equality of all religions. They show us that we may have gone further than the scriptural warrant, than the liberty that is in Christ Jesus. I do not read that the heavenly worlds put atheism, diabolism, and every other foe of God, on a footing with God Himself. If they did, hell and paradise would be identical, and Satan be as much protected in his idea of worship as Michael in his. Nay, more. The synagogue of Satan would be on a perfect level with that of Christ, and the impartial and tolerant Governor of the universe would represent the two parties by being Himself without any religion whatever, as are our public schools — the neutral point where the two contraries become a zero. This idea of God, which Emerson sets forth in some of his most nervous infidelity, is but the fitting expression of our popular religious principle: —

"There unlike things are like;
There good and ill,
And joy and moan,
Melt into one."

2. But this is not its only defect. It is not negative exclusively. No error is. It is eminently active, and one of its activities is, that religion and the State being divorced, ministers, the teachers and representatives of true religion, must not meddle with politics or the affairs of State. "They don't belong to your parish," say the self-elected leaders of civil affairs. "Let us alone. What have we to do with thee, thou minister of Jesus, the Son of David? Hast thou come to torment us before our time?" And they do not cry out thus, cowering and trembling as did most of their kindred of old, but with the effrontery of the same kindred when they baffled the ministers of Christ at the foot of the mount of transfiguration.

"You attend to the Church, and we will attend to the State." It is much as if one should shut you up in a spacious house, which he had no desire to enter, and say, "Stay thou there while I roam at will through all the adjacent fields, and streets, and homes. I have all out of doors to myself, and all in doors but that one habitation." In due time such a haughty doorkeeper to the house of God goes a little further. He not only forbids your leaving your palace, which he thus makes a prison, but he forbids your speaking, when there, on matters and things outside of your walls. If he deigns to visit you, you must not dare to give him advice as to how he shall have his conversation in this world. You must not presume to discourse upon the principles involved in his profession and career. You are debasing your profession, if you do. You are intruding on domains forbidden to clerical feet. You are dragging your robes in the mire of political strife. "Preach Christ," he impudently says. Poor creature! A full Christianity is the last thing he wishes to have preached. A Christ who is Lord of lords — to whom belong the kingdoms of this world — who demands that they and all their subjects conform in all things to the kingdom of heaven — He is what such transgressors especially dislike and dread.

Even church members, — and I am surprised and grieved to say it, but it is true — even the very ministers of Christ themselves, have measurably yielded to this pressure of antichrist. And in our land, alone of all lands since Adam, has the doctrine been avowed by the Church and its minister, that they have nothing to do with the movements of the State. Far from it. They have everything to do with it. They always have had, they always must.

What does God keep mankind on the earth for? Only that He may build them into a holy temple in the Lord. But is one part of the temple open to the feet of His servants, and not another? Laymen could not enter the holy of holies; but priests could go everywhere, from the court of the Gentiles to the altar and ark. So is this great temple of humanity open to the inspection, under the surveillance, of the ministry and the Church.

Thus has it always been. More than once did the Hebrew kings seek to break away from the intermeddling clergy; but God smote the politician, not the prophet. "Art thou he that troubleth Israel?" cries the secessionist Ahaz to the political preacher Elijah. Thus his traitorous descendants in America yet confront the descendants of that prophet. Saul meddled with Samuel's duties, and God took his kingdom from him. But Samuel never was censured for his frequent intermeddling with the affairs of Saul. David had to submit to the authority of more than one priest. No priest was ever compelled to silence before him. Isaiah, Ezekiel, Jeremiah, Hosea, Amos, all the preachers of righteousness, dwelt on social and civil sins. They dwelt on hardly anything else. So the beginner of the new dispensation laid down his head because of a bit of political intermeddling with the affairs of the government, and Christ was bolder than all His followers in denouncing the conduct of the real rulers of the people.

The whole history of the Church since has been a history of its conflict with the world and the rulers of the world. The first Christians were executed for treason. The officers of the empire required them to take the prescribed oath of allegiance — the recognition of the divinity of the emperor. They refused, and were cast to the lions. It was as legitimate treason as that of John Brown's, and their death was for the same folly.

It has continued thus ever since. The wars of Charles Martel and Charlemagne against the Mohammedan and heathen irruptors from Northern and Southern Asia, were inspired by the clergy ; and the great Charles was crowned by the Pope solely because of his zeal for the Church. They show you the field where Zwingle fell, in a religious civil war in Switzerland, at the head of the Protestant cantons — struck through with a lance because he would not pray to the Virgin.

Cromwell's rebellion was inaugurated and sustained by the clergy in the interests of the Church. James' conflict was solely on matters of religion, and the famous trial of the Seven Bishops, for meddling with the decrees of the State, was the real cause of his expulsion. The prisoner of Chillon, made memorable in Byron's verse, but more memorable by his six years' confinement to a subterranean pillar by a chain not ten feet in length, was a minister who, from his pulpit, dared to defy the government of the Duke of Savoy. And God, to release him, stirred up a civil war in all that region, and brought the men of Geneva and Berne to reduce that fortress. The conversion of Geneva, which was Roman Catholic when he was cast into that dungeon, to the reformed faith, of which it has been for three hundred years so eminent a defender, was due to the faithful political preaching of Bonivard, the prior of St. Victor.*

The necessity of defending such a thesis as this shows the peril of the nation. As a law against an especial offense proves the prevalence of that crime, so the many words that have had to be spoken in America by clergymen within the last few years in defense of the right to speak, show how far we have departed from the custom of the world elsewhere, and of America herself, till this generation.

England, who keeps nearly a score of prelates in her highest house, whose first nobleman is a minister, the successor of Augustine, never dreams that the clergy degrade themselves by mingling in the civil strifes of the day. The religious journals discuss political questions as freely as religious, and the opening editorial of the London Watchman, the Wesleyan organ, is almost always a political article. So was it here. What is this anniversary, of more than two hundred years' standing, but a recognition by the State of the duty of the minister to enlighten the community on national sins and duties? What is thanksgiving but a like recognition by the State of its obligations to the God and Savior of nations and men?

Let me not be understood as undervaluing the central duty of the Church and ministry, when I declare that our chief peril, as a nation, is in refusing to avow ourselves Christian, and in excluding the appointed embassadors for Christ from the questions that agitate society. Their chief mission is to preach the Gospel; but the Gospel is not con-

* "The range of the history of the Church is as wide as the range of the world which it was designed to permeate. The Christian Church is but another name for Christendom, and Christendom merely another name for the most civilized, the most powerful, the most important nations of the modern habitable world."— Stanley's Lecture on the Province of Ecclesiastical History, in the introduction to his History of the Eastern Church, p. 33, *et seq.* See other admirable remarks on the Identity of Church and State, *in loc.*

fined to a repentance and faith that have no connection with social or civil duties. The Evangel of Christ is an all-embracing theme. It is the vital force of everything in earth and in heaven. What the ancients dreamed respecting the relation of the earth to the worlds around it is true in a spiritual sense. The Cross is the centre of the spiritual, and therefore of the material, universe.

If so, then must all things, human and temporal, acknowledge its supremacy. Literature, science, politics, business, the status of society, all charities, all reforms, — there is nothing that you can conceive that has not an intimate relation, friendly or hostile, to the Cross of Christ. The God-appointed bearers of that Cross have no right to omit the consideration of these topics. They are traitors to their Commander-in-chief if they do. Every knee and every thing shall bow to Christ, and it is our duty to bring all these matters to that divine test. It is thus alone that the kingdom of Christ can be universally established. It is thus alone that it can be preserved in any measure of purity and vitality.

You can easily see what would be the result of yielding this point through cowardly complicity. The politician says, "You must not preach politics;" and then goes on establishing the State on injustice, and framing iniquity by a law, while you set before him, with great assiduity, the savorless salt of an exhausted and tasteless Gospel. He opens his thousands of grog-shops in defiance of you, as he has in Boston for years. He expels the Bible from the public schools. He seeks to abolish the death penalty, giving free scope to murderous passion. He abolishes, as they almost did last week in our Legislature, the chief penalty for adultery, undermining the corner-stone of human society. Thus he cunningly thrusts Christ from His temple, and puts His enemy on His throne.

The evil stops not here. It invades His inner sanctuary.

The crafty Philistines have entrapped the clergy in this diabolic doctrine of State rights — the parent of its better known, but not baser kindred. They are shorn of their strength. The pulpit must not preach against usury, the besetting sin of business communities, — that is not Christ Crucified. Some rich brother, who has waxed fat on these ill-gotten gains, will denounce you as an intermeddler, while his conduct uncensured, and himself undisciplined, keeps scores from the Church. You must not talk against the opera or theater, for that is a social matter, and "Christ Crucified" does not touch the pleasures of life. "It is not forbidden," they say, "in the Bible, though it was then the most popular amusement." In this respect it is on the same level as slavery, according to its apologists. What an age has passed since their base pleas defiled the nation!

We cannot denounce the insane passion for fiction, even when it is running wild over the Church itself, and so infecting all the tiny vines of the nursery, that when we shall hereafter look that they bring forth grapes, they will bring forth wild grapes. Is there any connection between what we shall read and "Christ and Him crucified"? Thus the enemy constrains us to throw down the hedge around the Church itself, and invite the boar out of the wood to waste it, and the wild beast of the field to devour it.

Do you say, "Such possibilities are the foolish fancies of a mere theorist? Why not tell things as they are?" In this I am no dreamer of dreams. The results of this divorce have been seen in this country in a more shameful prostitution of the ministry and the Church than in any country in modern history — almost than in any country in any history. We need not go outside of our own history as a Church for the painful proof. We have seen in its brief life a large portion of its clergy in the presence of an enormous sin, refusing to confront it, declaring that to say aught against it was to preach politics, and for this cause they were not sent. Though they knew that the political face of the many-headed dog of hell was the last and least, though they saw the infinite immorality it engendered, the blasphemy against Christ and His Church, the social, private, universal corruption that broke out everywhere in the regions it occupied, — still they said, to preach against it is to preach politics, and our business is to proclaim Christ Crucified.

So they broke away from their brethren who protested not against their silence, not even against their clerical communion with the monster. The episcopal contact was all they shuddered at. They felt that his anointed hands, fresh from the scourging of slaves, could hardly impart ordaining grace. His friends resented such a reflection on them. They revolted, and set up for themselves as a Church of Jesus Christ — a pretense as profane as the claim of the most corrupt of Popes, that he is Christ's vicegerent.

They entered into an alliance with this crime. The sons of God married themselves to this daughter of Satan,

> "Seems woman to the waist, and fair,
> But endeth foul in many a scaly fold,
> Voluminous and vast — a serpent armed
> With mortal sting. About her middle round
> A cry of hell-hounds, never ceasing, bark
> With wide Cerberian mouths full loud, and ring
> A hideous peal."

The Church and the State were made one flesh, and horrid flesh it was too; and to-day the deluge of fire is pouring down upon the doomed region, and that haughty Methodist Episcopal Church South, where is it? With the antediluvian cathedrals and congregations of Cain. They pretended to be opposed to meddling with political and social sins. They became their slave. "And God has wiped them as a man wipeth a dish, wiping it and turning it upside down." So He dealt with His beloved Ephraim. So with the more beloved Judah. So He will deal with every Church that deals thus with Him. Only by repentance and a turning with their whole heart to Him can this Church be saved. May such repentance and salvation yet be theirs.

He appoints His ministers to watch over souls as those that must give account. It is His duty, therefore, to make every thing contribute to their salvation. Will a wicked system of government imperil the spiritual welfare of its subjects? He must resist it unto the death. Will social vices tend to their corruption? They must be attacked and overthrown. Will false doctrines delude souls to destruction? They must be rebuked. Would not a holy society, a correct system of government, correctly administered, a pure and lofty literature, — in fine, a virtuous civil and social organization, — tend to the salvation of more souls than corrupted morals, despotic government, and debasing literature? Christ Crucified, preached to a community under the pressure of all manner of inward and outward lust, would be proclaimed almost as vainly as in Pandemonium itself. He is most successfully lifted up when all the surroundings approximate to the divinity of this central truth.

Only thus does He keep the field at all. To keep the standard flying we must take care of the wings of the army. We must prevent flank movements, and all manner of subtle assaults. What matters it that you gather round the flag, if you desert the outposts. Great Britain fought for herself by trying with Nelson's fleet to confine Bonaparte in Egypt, as much as by setting a guard in the English Channel. Wellington was defending London when campaigning in the Peninsula.

So is it with the Gospel of the Cross. Christ Crucified is the grand banner of the Church, in its conflict with the world. It is the only Name whereby the world can be saved. It must be always and everywhere proclaimed. It must be always and everywhere defended. But to come and hug that flag-staff with apparent fondness, while the enemy is plowing the outer lines with his diabolic artillery, is not affection, — it is cowardice; and the officer who thus comports himself receives contempt, not commendation, from his Master. Take your flag with you, and rush thither. Smite down the enemy in this remotest assault, and you preserve your army from more central peril.

The indifference of God's ministers to this great social duty has undoubtedly bred infidelity. The very Cross of Christ, the ark of God, has it not been taken, in our pretense that we must be so busy in defending it, that we cannot speak on a political sin? The politicians we patronized despised us. The men of conscience and moral vision, who were blind to the full truth of the Gospel, also despised us for truckling to popular and powerful sin, and both became skeptics as to the very truth which we professed to be so anxious to keep from harm.

Bear with me, my brethren, if my words seem overmuch. They spring from the profoundest convictions of my moral being. They seem to me eminently, preëminently appropriate to us, to the occasion, and to the land in which we are required to make full proof of our ministry. The greatest problem that we are working out here is not the equality and fraternity of all the children of man, unspeakably great as that is, but the power to preserve the utmost liberty of worship and the utmost liberty of no worship, with a pure society and a predominant Christianity. It is an attempt to trust the human race with the offers of salvation, without endeavoring, in the least degree, to compel their acquiescence. It is the last possible combination of the divine and human in man's history. It is not unlike, one may fancy, the probation of the angels who keep, and those who kept not, their first estate. It is the very opposite of the position of the Father of the Church. Abraham served God with the whole world, to a man, against him. A State or a national Christianity could not, therefore, then be possible. David lived under a system in which every statute and ceremony, civil and religious, was of divine appointment. European Christians have these outward constraints abounding. We have no constraint at all.

Yet so much the more must the Church rule everywhere. It is a calcium light, shining out over the whole field. It is commander-in-chief, riding and ruling everywhere. It must bring every thought into obedience to Christ. Whatever subject or practice affects the morals, and so the basis of religion, it is not only legitimate for the ministry to bring to the Gospel light, that it may be seen what manner of spirit it is of, it is absolutely commanded them so to do. And he who refuses — no matter what excuse he may put forth — is verily guilty of treachery to the cause of his Master. He may not so purpose in his heart, but that is the fatal end.

Therefore, my beloved brethren, be ye steadfast and immovable in this great duty. Let the churches rejoice to co-operate with their leaders in this work. Hold up aloft a full Gospel, that shall illumine every custom, thought, and feeling of the society, every path of human activity; that shall make all daily pursuits, mercantile, manufacturing or otherwise, holy and unblamable before God; — how far they are from it let usury, adulteration, fraud, all the tricks of trade, answer; — that shall rectify and exalt civil government as the confessed servant of Christ; so that while granting the utmost liberty of conscience, it shall be none the less bold to declare that it is a Christian government — a State of the great world-federation whereof our Lord is to be the unseen, yet always seen, Sovereign.

II. The other topic connected with our theme and occasion deserves ampler attention than we are now at liberty to give. We have said that the mission of America seems to be twofold. First, to prove that the utmost liberty of conscience can co-exist with a ruling Christianity; and, second, that the utmost liberty and equality of all men can co-exist with a stable and prosperous government. The last is as unsolved a problem as the first. It is being tested to-day. Only the power of true Christianity can secure its success. Many of you will say, "There is no question as to its success. Have we not welcomed all Europe to our shores? Are we not proud to acknowledge Ireland and England, Germany and Italy, Hungary and Poland — every exile from a murdered or a murdering nation, as our friend and brother?" What does that prove? Do we call the Prince of Wales a democrat because he says, "I am willing to marry any one of a certain rank?" We look on these peoples as first cousins. They are near of kin. Of course it is no disgrace for us to recognize their equality.

But there is another people among us — another portion of our Father's family as much beloved of Him as any European. How do we look on them? How do we feel towards them? What merchant here will put behind his counter an intelligent, accomplished, virtuous, gentlemanly youth, whose blood is known to have come in ever so slight a degree from the oldest continent and the oldest child of Noah?

By the rights of primogeniture, Ham had precedence of all his brethren. He should have been the father of the Son of God. But sin in him, as in Cain, Esau, and Reuben, deprived him of his birthright. And, lo! his youngest brother's sons, not those who took his place — for the children of Shem, the brothers and sisters of our Lord, have no aversion to those of Ham — not those of Japhet even, as a whole — but a little clique of this youngest brother's children put on airs of immeasurable superiority, and talk of colonizing their elder cousins by themselves, and of the impossibility of treating them as their equals and brothers, their color is so *very* abhorrent, though many a darker European than multitudes of them, have, in the same eyes, the most aristocratic of complexions.

But we must welcome them as brothers or die. There is no alternative. God, our Creator and theirs, has brought us to this shore, foreign to both of us, that He may here develop the fullness of that Gospel scheme He is seeking to establish in the earth.

The division of languages and of man was because of sin. It was the first punishment after the flood. In carrying forward His enterprise of subduing the world to Himself, He found that He must first separate the human race by long-enduring boundaries. He must make them so substantially independent creations, that some of their half wise men should declare they had many original centers of dispersion. They had but one, — in the plains of Shinar, at the tower of Babel.

As the world is approaching its ultimate paradisiacal estate, it must approach the conditions of the primitive abode. There must be one language and one family. The language which seems to be in advance of all others as a world-subduing tongue, is the English. Though, when one has spent months among millions of people who have never heard of this tongue, he is constrained to doubt its speedy universality, still, it occupies to-day more diffused and more numerous centers than any other tongue, and seems to be engirdling the earth. America will, undoubtedly, contribute largely to this end; not a little by the enormous emigration which she will yet draw from every nation of Europe.

She will also contribute, in no small degree, to the accomplishment of the other equally dubious and seemingly remote but most certain event — the solidarity of the human race. As in Adam all were separated, so in Christ shall all be united. In that oneness there shall be neither Greek nor Jew, barbarian nor Scythian, bond nor free. This was the apostle's bold declaration to the proud Greeks of Colosse. He did not add "white or black," because there are no whites, as we call them, in that dusky clime. He touched the marrow of their sensitive prejudice in putting Scythian and barbarian on a level with themselves. His equally bold declaration to the most fastidious Athenians, that God made of one blood all the nations of men, must yet be verified in the earth. America seems to be the spot where this divine purpose is to be first accomplished.

Other countries are in advance of us in some of the elements of that perfect society. But in no one are all of them in such rapid process of solution and recrystallization as here. The three essentials of that state are well expressed in the French democrat's saying, yet burning on the triumphal arches of Louis the Great in spite of all the obscuring efforts of their present tyrant — "Liberty — Equality — Fraternity." The equality and fraternity of the African and Asiatic are perfectly carried out in Egypt. A like equality and fraternity of the African and European exist in Mexico, the West Indies, and the Southern States. One of the first scientific scholars of the country,* long a resident in Alabama and Georgia, informed me that seven eighths of the colored people of the South are partly white.

But in neither of these eastern or western experiments is there a corresponding liberty, culture, and Christianity. These are needed to make the other three of any value. All these may, and if we are true to our national mission will, exist in this country. Here we have, as our foundation-stone, the European democrat's triad. We have it elevated and consecrated by universal education and the fullest expression of Christianity.

There we stop. To apply these to ALL our people — "aye, there's the rub." It is dreadful to many undeveloped natures that God, upon opening for us this fountain of living waters, should have invited our brethren of other climes to come and drink also. He has built an ark for humanity, and, lo! as we very clean beasts are pompously marching in, these strange and most unclean creatures also enter.

* Alexander Winchell, LL. D., Professor of Natural Science in Michigan University.

We wanted the gifts all to ourselves. Like Peter, amid the glories of the transfiguration, have we been in the transfiguration of His truth in our land. We have been perfectly willing to abide in it ourselves, and have been utterly thoughtless of these our brethren: nay, not utterly thoughtless, cruelly thoughtful in our aversion to their sharing with us this excellent glory. Had Peter seen a Gentile coming up the hill that moment, he would undoubtedly, in his hot, self-confident, American fashion, have insisted on Christ interrupting his conversation with the resplendent spirits while he expelled the loathsome intruder. "Dost thou dare," he would exclaim, "to intrude upon our dear, delightful, Judean banquet! Don't you see that it is Moses and Elias that are talking with our Lord? Only the chosen people can come up hither. Begone to your outer darkness!"

Peter afterwards had a bitter trial of what he called conscience and Christianity, but which was only a satanic prejudice, when, on that tanner's housetop he was invited to the unseemly feast. Go to your dinner to-day, and see toads, and snakes, and snails upon the table, and you would find it easy to comply with the request of the Governor. But if, in addition to our so-called natural abhorrence, we found in the Discipline, by special inspiration of God, through the lips of our founder, an express command to abstain from them as unclean, we should shake off the dust of our feet against the profane host, and betake ourselves to more Methodistical and more decent quarters. Yet God, who had interdicted them through Moses, now says to this zealous disciple of Moses, "What I have cleansed, that call thou not common," — says it to you and me to-day, no less than to Peter at Joppa: as hard bound in carnal prejudice as he, and, unlike him, without any shadow of Scripture authority to support our contempt.

The vision is precisely adapted to us. We, like Peter, call a portion of our neighbors and kindred common and unclean — unlike him, in this respect, too, that he seemed to have divine command so to call them, for they were separated from him by decrees of His appointment. We loathe our brothers of the same Gentile family. We look on them as of another race. We talk about colonizing them, giving up to them the Gulf States, or the torrid sections of America, —

"Anywhere, anywhere, out of the world," —

so that we can rid ourselves of their abhorred presence. We are theoretically, vociferously, valiantly in favor of equal rights. We pour out our money and our lives for the great cause. We fill the heavens with our jubilant reverberations on the national birthday. But when it comes to the little practical matter of letting our darkly-hued neighbor sit at our table, work at our bench, tend behind our counter, enter into business partnerships with us, be our teacher, doctor, or stationed preacher, ah, how the Petrine nature swells indignantly within us, and we exclaim, "Not so, Lord." Yea, we are ready to cry in the ears of God, my brother, though we fancy it is only in those of man, "Away with the fellow that talks such abominations from the earth. It is not worthy that he should live."

Yet hither is God's providence drawing us. A profane Bostonian lately said, "I never did, and do not now, care anything for the negro. But I have about concluded that God does." The tide sweeps with increasing force and volume against these deep and ancient prejudices. They will be overwhelmed. And when buried, we shall be borne forward by the rolling waves of superior truth to the headlands of superior vision. Did not that faithful Jew feel a strange enlargement of soul when he saw the centurion and his house receiving the word of the Lord? When he touched his holy Jewish hands, wet with the sacred water of baptism, on that till then accursed brow, the preacher received a greater baptism of the Holy Ghost than the candidate. There fell from his eyes as if it had been scales. He saw the Gospel limited to no inconsiderable race and spot, but, like the sun, shining with equal glory on every land and on every man.

So we, emancipated from the base-born feeling of caste, which now rules us with its rod of iron as tyrannically as it does the Brahmins of India or the nobility of England, will feel something of the length and breadth, the depth and hight of His purposes and feelings toward our race. To call every man brother, unmindful of all outward aspects; to feel that he is YOUR brother, absolutely, entirely; to treat him as such, unconscious of any distinction between you, — how will the heart, thus freed, grow in the likeness and after the stature of its Creator and Redeemer! It will have climbed the last of the mountains interposed that have made enemies of nations and of men. The whole landscape of man's futurity lies before him; the land of Beulah, whither the race, with many weary pilgrim steps, is slowly tending, —

"A land of corn, and wine, and oil,
Favored with God's peculiar smile,
With every blessing blest;
There dwells the Lord our righteousness,
And keeps His own in perfect peace,
And everlasting rest."

We shall see all the sons of Adam at peace with themselves and with their God. They speak one language. They feel the pulsations of a common brotherhood. While they have all the distinctions of a family, in taste and action — one a scholar, one an orator, one a merchant, one a mechanic; while each nation may have its special character after this sort, — as Italy is the home of art, Germany of thought, France of taste, and England of business, — yet like brothers of varied tastes and pursuits, they will rejoice in this diversity of gifts, but the same spirit. The varieties of complexion will be as agreeable as is now the variety of beautiful countenances. They will feel, not only no estrangement, but a vehement rush of blood to blood.

> "Thither the warm affections move,
> Nor shall we call them thence."

The whole earth will not seem too large to that Christian family — girded by steam, bound together by that electric cord which transmits the feelings and thoughts of the whole world as instantaneously as the brain communicates with the heart, they,

> "Like kindred drops, will mingle into one." *

In the glory of that fast coming prospect, how the petty contractedness of our unseemly prejudice drops from us as fetters from the emancipated slave, as a strait-jacket from a cured maniac, as the weight of imbecility from the enlightened idiot! This effluence of spiritual illumination will strike us more powerfully than it will our dark-complexioned brother. It will be a novel outgleaming to us, not to him. He has long felt the truth of the unity of Man. He has long known that he is your brother. It is strange, inconceivably strange to him, that you have not known that you are his. You so intelligent, so superior to him in your advantages, not to know this simplest and most fundamental of truths. The words of Christ are his sole refuge in his perplexity. "I thank Thee, O Father, Maker of heaven and earth, that Thou hast hidden these things from the wise and prudent, and revealed them unto babes. Even so, Father, for so it seems good in Thy sight."

How great the strides made in America in the last two years to this glorious consummation! A friend of mine, a New York lawyer, had a fine Afric-European superintending his farm. The morning after the call for the first seventy-five thousand volunteers, the young man informed him that

* See Note XII.

he could not work for him any longer. "Why not?" "I am going to war." "But you can't go." "Why not?" He was ashamed to answer the glowing patriot, but he had to: "Because you are black!" The poor fellow stood paralyzed, as if a bullet had pierced his heart. He had forgotten all about his brown complexion. His heart was red with the hottest of patriot blood. The call made no reference to white men. How was he excluded? He shrunk back to his enforced shame, and we went about the task of saving the country without the aid of, with violent hostility towards, such as him, full one sixth of our people.

God has taught us that we cannot be saved unless they are saved also. We are beginning to accept His terms. That young man can now be enrolled as a soldier. He may soon take rank as an officer. He, or such as he, may yet outrank and command their proud and half-hearted despisers, whose blood is of the same complexion as their skins. They are the true Copperheads that will save the Republic. They will go into this war, as Frederick Douglass says, not as hewers of wood and drawers of water, but as men. They will come out of it our recognized equals and associates. We shall be blood relations then, as never before. A common baptism of sorrow and death will make us, at last, one people, and thus prepare the way for a universal family.

The last thought, though distasteful to some of our brethren elsewhere, cannot be offensive to us. For last year, by a unanimous vote, we adopted a resolution denouncing the sin of caste. You remember the pregnant words:—

"Resolved, That we deprecate the unchristian spirit of caste so prevalent throughout the North, and even among many professed anti-slavery men with respect to people of color, and we can never regard our reformatory work accomplished till they enjoy equal rights and privileges with other classes."

It is a high honor for this Conference to thus lead the Church, and for once to lead the reformatory section of the nation in the great movement. As our fathers, some of whom are still present, though most have fallen asleep, in advance of all other bodies of ministers, twenty-eight years ago proclaimed the duty of immediate and unconditional emancipation, elected delegates to the General Conference on that issue, and began the agitation which, with all its imperfections, has purged the Church, if not the Discipline, of arrogant slaveholders in the ministry and membership, and is fast purging the land, if it cannot the Constitution, of the like mass of proud and putrid flesh; so this resolution is the first utterance by the Church of what will yet be a truth, universally and proudly recognized.

Let our words and works agree. To do this will require the discharge of many duties yet in violent conflict with our pride and prejudice. May I mention a few of them?

1. We must expunge the word "colored" from our Minutes. It ought never to have found a place there. How abominable that epithet must appear in the eyes of the Savior, by whom these His brethren were cleansed with the same blood, and, perchance, at the same moment and the same altar! He does not write it in the Lamb's book of life—the heavenly Minutes of His church. Born into His divine family, we are nearer of kin to them than brothers of a human household. And yet we shamefully degrade them. How unchristian and inhuman such conduct is, may be seen from a single example. Suppose an unfortunate dwarf should join this church, and the pastor should return three hundred full grown adults and one dwarf; or if a dozen mutes, or blind, should become members, and we should make the like distinction, how quickly should we revolt from the revelation in ourselves of the old leaven of malice and wickedness! What a torrent of indignation would be poured on our Missionary Board if they should publish in their East

Indian returns their Brahmin and Pariah members in separate columns!

But the worst feature in this iniquity is, that it casts reproach on those who, by the pressure of an ungodly world, are already oppressed. The Gospel is especially tender towards the lowly and despised. We are especially cruel. It also inevitably breeds in us hardness of heart—the extreme opposite of the new heart, whose law is to esteem others better than ourselves.

I was struck with this years ago, in a revival that occurred in a country town in the State of New York. The preacher, a godly brother, though not educated in this truth above the community in which he lived, was inviting sinners to the altar. Seeing some of his congregation urging the few of this class present to go forward, the thought dimly struck him that they were included in "all the world" whom they were singing about as being invited by Christ. So he said at the close of his invitation, "If there are any colored persons present *who have souls*, let them come forward also." To such a request no colored person who had a soul would be apt to respond. The same brother, in summing up the fruits of the revival, announced to the church that so many "had been converted, and John, Jane, and Dinah, colored persons." He was unconsciously but correctly conforming to the practice of our church.

This distinction is the *primum mobile* of all our weakness. Had we boldly taken the ground of Paul at the beginning, refused to know white or black, bond or free, in the Church, made emancipated slaves our preachers and bishops, as he did Onesimus, mingled the whole in one pure and holy brotherhood, we should never have met with the difficulties we have. We should have grown less yet more. Our pro-slavery foes would not have been as they have been, and still are, those of our own household. Our strength would have increased uniformly, steadily, mightily. As it is, it has been as it has. Let us go back to first principles. Let us cling to the corner-stone of Jesus Christ, the Brother alike of all men, the Brother especially of the poor, the oppressed, and the despised.

2. This resolution involves home duties also. Some of our churches yet permit invidious distinctions to be made between His brethren in the house and at the table of the Lord. They compel a portion of His family to sit together in an ignoble place, and to come together to His feast after they have concluded their banquet. Perhaps they think these servants of men are also servants of the Lord, and are therefore properly placed at the last table. I am afraid they, much more than their fellow-servants, are indeed the servants of the Lord. How do James the Just's searching words try our reins and our heart in the light of such conduct. "My brethren, hold not the grace of our Lord Jesus Christ with respect of persons; for if ye say unto the" white member or visitor, "Sit thou here in a good place, and say unto" your colored brother, "Stand thou there, or sit here under my footstool, are ye not then partial in yourselves, and become approvers of evil thoughts? Hearken, my beloved brethren, hath not God chosen the poor of this world, rich in faith, and heirs of the kingdom which He hath promised to them that love Him? But ye have despised the poor!" And that too, because of a complexion God gave them, and as handsome in His eyes as yours in yours. We should cease to allow this evil to be done. It should be instantly abolished from every church in this Conference.

3. We should also abolish every colored church. All should melt into each other. All ye are brethren.

4. These flourish for another and yet worse reason, which springs from the same false root. God is pleased to call some men to preach His gospel that are much nearer than we are to the complexion and lineage of Christ and His apostles. He pours grace upon their lips, so that all the

world runs after them. But we call them negroes, or the more classic and more contemptuous word by which we designate this class, even if the Lord's anointed. They cannot minister to white people. They cannot associate with their not always whiter clerical brethren. We have no humility by which we love to kneel down and wash their feet, though that very deed was done by Christ, on this very night, to teach us this very lesson. It is not learned yet.

We compromise with conscience by setting off others of our brethren to whom they shall minister. Thus America presents a spectacle seen nowhere else in Christendom, — seen never before in Christendom, — of a body of poor believers, compelled by their brethren to worship by themselves under the ban of public infamy, and a body of God's ministers, in like manner, compelled to make full proof of their ministry under like disgrace. I say it is not seen nor known anywhere else in the world, past or to-day. James thought he had touched the bottom of sinful distinctions when he dwelt on the partialities displayed in the same church. What would he have thought had the Holy Ghost required him to give warning to Christians against pushing a portion of their brethren, and of their ministry also, into separate churches — separated for no fault of their own, for no leprosy or disease that whitened skins, but because of a heaven-daring pride on the part of their kindred.

This must be changed if we hope for the blessing of God. The ministry must lead in the change. The proudest churches in Europe are open to every body. You will find the beggar and the noble worshiping side by side at Westminster, the Madaleine, St. Peter's, everywhere. A minister is a minister there, no matter of what blood or color. They are not without their prejudices, even against color. But they do not carry it to our extreme. On the contrary, they sometimes bravely overcome it. See Rev. Mr. Martin, of Boston, invited to two churches in London. The most eloquent preacher of his denomination, and probably of any denomination in our city, able to fill the Tremont Temple every Sunday, he was stuck in a poor little house in the Pariah quarter, and the Temple remained empty. Now he is the welcomed pastor of a church of Englishmen — the proudest blood in Europe to-day. Should a brother of like graces approach our doors, what would we do with our resolution? Stand by it, should we not? Admit him as our perfect equal, and cast the weight of our influence in favor of his receiving such a station as his talents merit.

That this is the question of the age, a multitude of signs show. We cannot pass over one. From it learn all. You are aware of the great impression produced on the millions of people from all parts of the world, at the Great Exhibition, by Story's statue of the African prophetess — the Lybica Sybilla, as he called it. It took its place as the greatest contribution of genius; and critics, in London reviews, discussed with much learning its relations to Greek and Egyptian art; when, lo! it appears from Mrs. Stowe's article in the Atlantic, that it is but the statue of a New York slave, seventy years of age. She is known to many here — an old John Street Methodist, who cannot read, but who can do what is far better, she can talk. Sojourner Truth is the rude, ungainly name of a rude, ungainly African of the purest negro blood, who is the model of a statue surpassing the Moses of Michael Angelo; for that is but a marvel of genius; this is the gospel for this generation — a new sermon of Christ's in stone. Europeans of every rank, with their yet haughtier American fellows, like Joseph's brethren, bow down to her whom they had sold into bondage — to all her race in her.

But I have long since wearied you. I shall be happy if I have inflicted no heavier burden. I could not say less and fulfil the injunctions of the text. I feel that America is the center of the history of the world to-day. For good or evil, in wrath or mercy, God has lifted her up before all men — He has endowed her with preëminent privileges and opportunities; an estate of wondrous breadth and beauty; fundamental ideas of civil and social life, that have been only the dreams of good and wise men in all other ages and places — a people knowing good and evil, full of enterprise, of resources, of capacity, individual and concrete, such as all nations else have never seen; an intelligence diffused like the light; a quickness of conscience that is like fire shut up in the bones. Over such a nation, with such a heritage, in such an exaltation, what infinite responsibilities hang! To be its guides and molders, as God has made His Church and ministry, is a duty from which they may well shrink — of which they may justly be proud.

Our liberties must be preserved and extended only through the Church. And the Church must be kept in its first estate and advanced to its complete perfection chiefly through its ministry. Upon you, then, as its divinely appointed officers, comes the responsibility. The ministry, the servants of the Church, are its authorized and responsible officers. God, not man, made the Church. He, not man, officers it. And He holds us accountable to Him, not to our fellow-Christians, much less to our fellow-men, for the manner in which we discharge that high office. If we bow down to them, and serve them; if, like Aaron, at command of the people, we make golden calves for their idolatry, their blood will He require at our hands. "See, *I*," not the Church, nor the Conference, nor the bishops, "*I* have set thee a watchman on the walls of Zion," on the towers of time.

It is but for a moment that we stand here. Death soon shoots us down. A more insatiate archer may first slay us, if we are not vigilant and courageous. It is but a little step from our post to the headquarters of our Commander. Hither we must ceaselessly go for orders. We must proclaim them at the head of our several regiments, and see that the subordinate officers and soldiers observe them. We must proclaim them to the hosts of rebellion, without fear, without bitterness, without favor, without weariness.

Our encouragements may come partly from the Church, but preëminently from God. It is a good and blessed reward for one to have his praise in all the churches. It is far better to have the approval of God.

There are times when every Church needs to be lifted up out of itself. The Seven Churches required such treatment. They were settling down into worldliness. They must be stirred up, or they sleep the sleep that knows no waking. He is seldom popular who is set for this work. Paul had to say to his Corinthian brethren, with almost an air of hauteur, "With me it is a *very* small thing that I should be judged of *you* or of man's judgment." Edwards was driven forth into the wilderness, and among savages, by his aristocratic church of Northampton, after it had been blessed, under his labors, with the greatest revival it had ever enjoyed, simply because he scourged a popular sin. They show you the narrow, low door beside the chancel of the Epworth Church out of which John Wesley was thrust, as Christ out of Nazareth, by his fellow-townsmen, led by his father's successor and his father's vestrymen. St. Mary's, the university Church of Oxford, yet testifies, in its Christless vibration between Romanistic formalism and Broad Church rationalism, to the crimes of those who, a century and a quarter ago, expelled from her pulpit the same great advocate, because he proclaimed that central truth of Luther's preaching, and of a vital Christianity, Justification by Faith.

Yet these men were not alone; nor will you be, if ordered to like duty. The Captain of the Hosts of the Lord is with you. His still, small voice ever strengthens you.

Finally. To save this land to universal liberty and universal brotherhood, supported by universal law and sanctified by universal piety, is to save all lands. It may take all our sons, all our treasure, all our generation to destroy the enemy that is seeking to prevent this consummation. It may take a longer time and greater struggles to destroy the enemy within us, that with profounder and more powerful force works for the same diabolical end. But if we are faithful to our principles and our God, we shall triumph over both. We shall subdue the rebellious host without and the rebellious spirit within.

Then shall other nations behold the image of the transfigured Christ shining in our uplifted face, that will glow, like that of Moses, with the radiance of His divine countenance. European caste and tyranny, tottering everywhere to its downfall, will speedily disappear, and the same Christian union and liberty, "like a sea of glory, will spread from pole to pole."

"Half of Europe will come to America if you break up this rebellion," was the last word almost that was spoken to me as I was leaving the city of Liverpool. All of America, in its influence, will go to Europe, will go over the earth, not in the boastful spirit of national pride, but in the humble spirit of Christian love. We have nothing we have not received. We shall then only be a member of an equal, universal, happy family, the family of Christ.

However dim and distant that glorious hour may seem to our weary-watching eyes, we are required to labor for it, in private and public, in ourselves, the Church, the nation, the world. May we to that end, to-day, purge out the old leaven of malice and wickedness, that we may be a new lump, sanctified and set apart for the Master's use. Then shall this beautiful parable of the poet be to us henceforth and forever a blessed realization:—

"A Brahmin on a lotus pod
Once wrote the holy name of God.

Then, planting it, he asked in prayer,
For some new fruit unknown and fair.

A slave near by, who bore a load,
Fell fainting on the dusty road.

The Brahmin pitying, straightway ran,
And lifted up the fallen man.

The deed scarce done, he stood aghast,
At touching one beneath his caste.

'Behold,' he cried, 'I am unclean,
My hands have clasped the vile and mean.'

God saw the shadow on his face,
And wrought a miracle of grace.

The buried seed arose from death,
And bloomed and fruited at his breath.

The stalk bore up a leaf of green,
Whereon these mystic words were seen:

FIRST, COUNT MEN ALL OF EQUAL CASTE,
THEN COUNT THYSELF THE LEAST AND LAST.

The Brahmin, with bewildered brain,
Beheld the will of God writ plain.

Transfigured then, in sudden light,
The slave stood sacred in his sight.

Thereafter, in the Brahmin's breast,
Abode God's peace, and he was blest."

THE CHURCH AND THE NEGRO.*

THE Church Anti-Slavery Society: — is not that tautological? A repetition that ought to be, if it is not, vain? The first includes the last. If it is truly the Church, it is also by necessity the Anti-Slavery Society; for the greater ever includes the less.

Thus it was when its creed and sacraments were first given. The Hebrews had two articles of faith — anti-idolatry and anti-slavery. The first had been taught them by the divine miracles, the last by their own suffering and salvation. Bunsen says that "History was born on the night of Exodus." So was Abolitionism and the Church as a congregation of believers. These twain were twins.

Never before had human slavery been abolished by divine decree; never since, by a single act, on so grand a scale, save by the decree of last January. But the difference between the two was the simple, yet all-important difference, between a proclamation and an execution. God *abolished* Hebrew slavery. He set *His* millions free. He made their enemies to sink like lead in the mighty waters. We only

* An address delivered in Tremont Temple, before the Church Anti-Slavery Society, June 10, 1863.

say ours are free, and still but half protect the freedmen, even if in our armies, from worse than Pharaoh's assaults.

The Old Testament cannot, therefore, indorse human bondage. It was based on human freedom. Its original people were, by creation and necessity, abolitionists. While as yet no glimmering of the hideousness of slavery had dawned upon the moral sense of the world, God revealed its character by emancipating a race.

These freedmen He organized into a nation. For the corner-stone of their constitution He placed Abolitionism. On the top of Sinai, before He enunciated a moral or a civil institute, — the higher and the lower law, — He proclaims His abolitionism. "I am the Lord thy God, which brought thee out of the land of Egypt, OUT OF THE HOUSE OF BONDAGE."

His edicts not only abolish slavery, they abolish caste. The laws of Moses are the essence of democracy. In all eastern and all old countries there are families that have served for generations, as there are those that have ruled. To prevent this tendency, God proclaims every seven years, and at the outside, every fifty years, a complete abolishment of such relations. No father shall entail his servitude, however slight, on his children. All persons are equal. Had these laws been faithfully executed — which they never were — they would have preserved Israel from a monarchy, and so from ruin. This perpetuation of the inferior status of a family, from generation to generation, is the distinguished peculiarity of England. It is the stronghold of its aristocracy and its throne. It is against the pattern of civil society given in the Mount, which was a democracy of equal freemen.

It may be said that they were permitted to enslave the heathen. Not so. Their time and labor were bought for a season, as was that of the poorer of our ancestors in the early emigrations to this continent; but they could not make a contract that held over seven years, except in most rare cases, when the heathen were permitted to bind themselves, not their masters to bind them, for a lifetime. The Jews could not then sell these self-bound servants, nor had they power over their children ; nor could they hold them a moment after they acknowledged the true faith.

How long would slavery have existed in the South if these three conditions had been imposed upon it ? How long, if the last only had been adhered to ? It was so once in Maryland. The baptized slave became a free man ; now he is sold for a higher price. By the law of Moses, as rendered by these critics, the masters should be slaves of their slaves, for they are by far the worse heathen.

How profane, in the light of these facts, have been the ceaseless utterances of the Southern pulpits, and the too general utterance of the Northern, that the Israelites established slavery. Their laws were against it, their animus against it, their origin against it, their God against it.

The New Testament is equally anti-slavery. It is more spoken against than theatric exhibitions or gladiatorial shows. These are never specifically condemned, though they were universal. They are frequently employed to illustrate the Christian life. The apostle refers to an experience of the latter class among the beasts of Ephesus, with no hint that it was immoral. So is it almost speechless against the sin of war, then universal, and inspired solely by lust of robbery or power, and unspeakably cruel against the innocent. Yet see how John seems to revel in it ! Had he spoken thus of slavery, what a perversion would its monomaniacs have made of his illustrations ! Slavery is condemned more frequently and more severely than them all.

The New Testament Gentile Church was comprised almost as exclusively of slaves as was the Mosaic Church, — as has been the real Church of Christ in the South. The lowest class chiefly embraced it. The Abyssinian eunuch was an Ethiopian slave. They of Cæsar's household were largely Cæsar's slaves. Why should the apostles preach to them of the evils of slavery? They knew it by a fearful experience. We have prated loudly about the divine right of slavery, but there was one class of the population to whom we never addressed such remarks — the slaves themselves. How superbly foolish would have been such preaching. Equally foolish would have been like preaching on the part of Paul and his associates. Paul rejoiced in his freedom. The Centurion declares how much it cost him. It was a subject that was evidently one of intense interest to both parties. The very fact of Paul's being free, and proudly availing himself of its privileges in avoiding punishments to which his brethren were often subjected, speaks volumes as to the opinion of the early Church on this question.

More than this, the New Testament especially enjoins upon the master to give his slave liberty, and upon the slave to run away if he has a fair chance of thus securing his freedom.

If a sympathizer with slavery happened to be a preacher to slaves, as too many have been, and he should scatter among his parishioners this sentence of Paul's, "If ye may be free, use it rather," how would they understand it? How would their masters, if they should hear of it, treat such a circulator of the Scriptures without note or comment? The frequency of like remarks by the apostles gives tone and character to all the New Testament. It is in marked contrast with all cotemporary literature.

Slavery was abolished in Europe by the Church. She sold the sacred vessels from her altar to redeem her brethren. She bought your yellow-haired fathers, chained captives in the market-place of Rome, from their dark-skinned "owners," who, undoubtedly, entertained very strong prejudices against their red locks and white faces.

She would have abolished aristocracy and monarchy had she not been betrayed into an oligarchy herself, and so became the natural ally and servile tool of kindred castes in the State.

"The Church Anti-Slavery Society" is, therefore, a verbal repetition. If we appeal to its origin and early history, it is a real repetition. Alas! that it is not in its latest and American history. It is too late now to repent. The mission of abolishing slavery was offered to the Church of America, as it was to that of Europe. Theirs was faithful to their trust, ours not. And so God has been compelled to take the work into His own hands. He has poured out upon us the plague of war and its abounding miseries, because His Church would not testify and toil for the salvation of their brethren; because it arrayed itself by indifference or by open violence against its brethren. He had not forgotten the preamble of His Sinai declaration of Hebrew independence. He had not forgotten His like proclamation at the beginning of His ministry in Nazareth. He had not forgotten our declarations both as a nation and as churches. We had.

I do not say that all the Church was silent and sinful. Many testified, as local bodies, as individual preachers, striving according to His working, which worked in them mightily to save the Church from apostasy and silence, their brethren from slavery, and their nation from war and destruction. But no great ecclesiastical body, as such, engaged in this work. They almost unanimously strove against it. They resisted those who sought to bring them into active and determined hostility to the sin. They wilfully extracted the vigor from resolutions they could not table, and carefully abstained from the execution of the tame decrees they were compelled to declare by pressure of outward fear, and not of inward inspiration.

This is a painful but most patent truth. What is written is written. We cannot recall the past. Our record of the past generation, as the American Church, is laid up in the archives of history. It will be collated and kept, with the records of other eras, places, and branches of the Church. It is laid up on high. Where is the bishop who, like Gregory of Rome, has used the treasures of the Church for the emancipation of our enslaved brethren? Where is the synod, assembly, or conference of a whole Church that has expelled the "owners" of their own members from their communion, proclaimed themselves, exultingly and ceaselessly, abolitionists, and uttered the decree of God without wavering, and with divine boldness, in the ears of a slumbering and sinning nation?

We ought not to have spent a dollar for missionary work abroad. It ought all to have gone for the manumission of slaves at home. Such testimony, backed by such liberality, would have cleansed the land of its curse, placed the Church, where she is not, far above all rivalries of anti-church reformers, and given her a position and influence that to-day would have covered this land with the fullness of millennial glory. How painful the contrast. See it in that perfect daguerreotype of ourselves — the Church of Thyatira. "These things, saith the Son of God, who hath eyes like a flame of fire. . . . I know thy works, and charity, and service, and faith, and thy patience, and thy works, and the last to be more than the first. Notwithstanding, I have a few things against thee, because thou sufferest that woman Jezebel, which calleth herself a prophetess" (that is, a Christian minister), "to teach and seduce my servants to commit fornication. . . . And I gave her space to repent of her fornication, and she repented not. Behold I will cast her into a bed, and them that commit adultery with her into great tribulation, except they repent of their deeds. And I will kill her children with death, and all the churches shall know that I am He which searcheth the reins and the hearts."

The churches and the world have known it. The Southern Church, the chief transgressor with this Jezebel, has suffered the most with her. We have partially repented, and so have partially escaped.

It is useless to dwell constantly on the past. It is right to repent, to see what might have been, and to lament what is. Yet it is wrong to pause there. The future is yet before us. The sincerity of our repentance must be shown by the manner in which we fill that future.

The Church, as an Anti-Slavery Society, has but little work left for it to do. The red right arm of God is achieving the redemption which He would fain have wrought through his Church. Yet there is a mission before us as great as that we have neglected. It is possible for us to cover the shame we cannot obliterate with valor and vigor in a service that peculiarly belongs to the Church of Christ.

"What," you exclaim, "are we to have no rest from this agitation? Shall we not be permitted to devote ourselves exclusively to personal and ecclesiastical edification, without further intrusion of this offensive theme?" Nay, the Church has no pause in her mission, any more than her Maker has in His. "My Father worketh hitherto, and I work," — she, as well as her Master, must ever say, —

> "Beneath the solemn arch
> Naught resteth nor is still."

To purge herself and the world of sin, to build up human society after the model of the heavenly society, demand unceasing effort. The real cause of all this woe is far from cured by universal emancipation.

The slave is gone, the negro remains. Many abolitionists, and all mere unionists and partisans, have fancied their sole work was to liberate the slaves. It is their least work. We are to be made one family. There are feelings and usages contrary to this, almost as abhorrent, yea, every whit as abhorrent in the sight of God, as the ownership of man, which lie in our hearts and in the customs of society a hideous lump, "heavy as lead, and deep almost as life."

The basis of slavery is caste. That feeling of caste yet prevails exceedingly over all the land. The blackness covers our hearts deeper than it does the faces of our brethren. It must be removed. Nowhere in the world except with us does it have powerful dominion. In Asia, Mexico, West Indies, the Southern States, it is practically unknown. It has no real existence in us. Black coverings are preferred for the top of the head, as the abundance of advertisements of hair dyes testify. How much worse is the hair than the face? The black-gloved, and so black-skinned hand, is esteemed comely; so is the black-clothed, and therefore practically, black-skinned body. A strip of white linen around the neck and on the breast, and a bit of white flesh between the forehead and the black-bearded mouth, are the only specks of Caucasianism in an American gentleman in full dress. From hat to boots, Paris declares, and Broadway confesses, an "inky suit of customary black" is the requisite of a gentleman. And yet we pretend that we have a natural antipathy to color. How foolish! A black man in a white vest is more of a white man than we in our fashionable costume.

The Southern States will soon settle this problem when peace and liberty prevail there. A Baltimore gentleman, of the highest social standing, said to me, "that he had long advocated the admission of half negroes to social equality with their white kindred." That event will come, and with it the inevitable recognition of the other half of their blood, and so of the whole of the attainted color. And when Southern gentlemen lounge through our Saratogas and Newports with their elegant quadroon wives on their arms, we, who follow fashion more than principle, will be as profusely eulogistic and servilely imitative as we have been in commending and copying their diabolic contempt.

It is unchristian: they are our brethren and sisters; they should be treated as such. Dare you insult your own sister for any real or seeming deformity? Dare you expel her from the family circle? Would you allow another to taunt her with her sinless misfortune? How dare the Church to allow others to treat thus her sisters and brethren; nay, how dare she to treat them herself as she has, and yet hope for the blessing of God? "I thank Thee that I am not as this negro," has been our daily prayer in the temple of God. Have we gone down to our houses justified of God? Our first duty is to make ourselves one with these, as Christ's first duty was to make Himself one with us. He became like unto His brethren; so must we. Will the Church seize the opportunity, trample out this prejudice, and thus deliver herself from destruction? I cannot say yes; can you? I am afraid she will not.

Both army and people will give the highest military and political honors to the black man before the Church concedes him equal rights with his brethren. The regiment that is to inaugurate the era of real democracy in our land will march through our streets to-morrow.* We have not yet dared to make its officers of the same blood as its privates; but we shall. We could to-day without awakening any feelings of animosity. I asked Mr. Douglass, when at the camp the other day, why he had not command of the regiment? "Don't insult me," he replied. "I have had hundreds of applications from white gentlemen to use my influence to get them commissions, but they tell me the times are not yet ripe for commissions to our people." They soon will be. They have had straps long enough upon their backs; it is time they had them on their shoulders.

* See Note XIII.

And yet that day, I fear, will find the Church fast bound in these chains of Satan. Frederick Douglass may be Major General, may be Senator Douglass, representing the Empire State in Congress, and, as I heard a New Yorker say, "the only Senator Douglass that will be known in history," before any one of his clerical brethren will be settled over such a congregation as this. They are already in the bar of this city, in the medical fraternity of this State, the acknowledged equals, often the associates of our first lawyers and doctors. Into what conference, association, or synod are they admitted as co-workers and brethren?

God will chastise the Church if she persists in the hardness and impenitence of heart, by not only taking, as Christ threatens, the vineyard from her, but by giving it to these with whom she refuses to fraternize. See one token of this: The regimental banner of the Fifty-Fourth is a cross of gold, with *In hoc signo vinces* inscribed beneath. This is the first Christian banner that has gone into the war. It is the first Christian flag ever unfurled in the American nation. It is the oldest flag of Christianity. Is it not significant? God has thus made this despised class the leaders of the nation. "He has put down the mighty from their seats, and exalted them of low degree." The last shall be first. They are the true Christ-bearers. They have borne His Cross in unspeakable misery, oppression, agony, and degradation; they are now bearing it in honor, we believe unto great glory. At one step they take precedence of the million of their white forerunners. No regiment in the United States has had grace enough to put that upon its standard. This has: they shall not lose their reward. They stand up for Jesus; He will for them.

Let us, my friends, gird up our loins for the great duties of the future.

> "Never had Christians such high call before;
> Never can Christians hope for higher one;

And if they are but faithful to their trust,
Earth will remember them with love and joy;
And O, far better, God will not forget!"

Let the Church take up this class, in the infancy of its freedom, in her arms and bless them. God delivered Israel in a night; it took forty years to make them a people — so may it now. It is a work that will bless us more than them. He would have done that work in two years had that people been willing to coöperate with Him. So will He hasten to bring this people into their promised land. They are ready to obey Him. Will we lend an accordant hand? Will you be co-workers together with God? Will you cease to harbor this most unchristian pride and bitterness? Or will you act the Moabite and Edomite to these your kinsfolk, wearily approaching your borders, and seek to drive them back into their bondage, or to keep them from their purchased, and promised, and most fairly earned possessions? If you do thus treat them, be assured that God will punish you as He did those disdainful relatives of His chosen children. "God will smite thee, thou whited wall," shall be said to every white-skinned scorner and repeller of his browner, and, in this feeling, better brother.

As our Master gained a Name that is above every name by humbling Himself to us outcasts of the universe, so will the Church be uplifted by descending to these her brethren. Uproot and expel the iniquitous prejudice from your souls. Say with the fairest and finest of Shakspeare's heroines, —

"I see Othello's visage in his mind,
And to his honors and his valiant parts
Do I my soul and fortunes consecrate."

The hour is propitious. The great deeps of social pride are breaking up. The Church can take the lead in these divine movements if she will. She can drive this spirit of caste from the Temple of Christ — a spirit more mean and sinful than that which He scourged from His Father's house. Let us cast it out of our stores, our shops, our families, our pews, and our pulpits, yea, and first of all, out of our own hearts. Then shall it flee the land, and the Church, redeemed by her valor and faithfulness from her shame and sin, shall be without spot or wrinkle, the Lamb's wife, winning and transforming the whole world to her own loveliness, blessedness, and peace.

THE WAR AND THE MILLENNIUM.*

"THEY SHALL MAKE WAR WITH THE LAMB, AND THE LAMB SHALL OVERCOME THEM." — *Revelation* xvii. 14.

HE relation of the present conflict to the Millennium? "A very distant relation," you may say. Can war and the thousand years of warlessness be kindred? Can the bloody feet of battle be shod with the preparation of the gospel of peace? Such is the doctrine of the Word and Providence of God. War is the forerunner of the Gospel, the one who cries, "Prepare ye the way of the Lord!" and what he cries, he does. The Bible describes the advent of that hour as full of the tumults and deaths of strife. They may have a Biblical, a divine conjunction. Is ours one of that class? Is God appointing and directing it to the consummation of His desires, or is it simply a bloody feud without meaning or end?

To see this more fully, consider,

I. What is the Millennium?

II. What are the principles involved in this struggle?

III. How are these related in affinity and time?

* A sermon preached in Boston, on Thanksgiving Day, November 26, 1863. The battle of Lookout Mountain was fought on the 24th of November, and that of Missionary Ridge on the 25th.

I. What is the Millennium? We need not plunge into the morass of speculation as to the time or circumstances of the Millennial year. Some fancy that it precedes the final resurrection, some that it follows it. Some believe the present race and earth will be destroyed, or rejuvenated by miraculous intervention in the present order of things; others believe that the present race of man, under its present circumstances, will occupy the present earth, changed in naught save sin. Whatever be our theories as to the mode of its coming and existence, all who believe in it agree as to its character. It is simply the triumph of Christ over Satan in the hearts and lives, the laws and institutions, of man. What that war is between Christ and anti-Christ, all hearts that know themselves, too painfully understand. It is spiritual, vital, all penetrating, all embracing. It is a struggle as to whether man shall be saved from sin, or kept in sin. It is an attempt to make the earth a heaven or a hell.

This war begins in our moral nature, and in the sovereign head of that nature, the free will. It extends through every emotion, sensibility, intellect, appetite, habit, custom, law, or institution, whether of the individual or society. It extends its vast, imperceptible influences to the lowest orders of creation, and even the lifeless elements of earth and air. At the first revolt of the reigning will in man from its super-reigning Creator, —

> "Earth felt the wound, and Nature from her seat
> Sighing through all her works, gave signs of woe
> That all was lost."

The ground was cursed because of his sin. It rolls in waves, it cleaves in fire, it is frozen in winter, it is parched in summer, for thy sake, O man. Not the ground alone is affected, the whole creation groaneth and travaileth in pain together until now. The whole creation is to be restored only by the restoration of man. His new creation can alone renew the face of the earth. As is the fall, so must the rising be. As the struggle, so the triumph. The plunge was through Satan unto sin, the deliverance must be through Christ unto holiness.

The perfected deliverance is the Millennium. It is God again at the helm of the soul, voluntarily restored there as He was voluntarily expelled; God moving thence through every thought, impulse, volition, bringing all into subjection to Him; God thus sanctifying every part of every soul, and making them communities of holiness, centers of sacred life, sweeping away by their personal and united grace the curse and the crime of civil and social life, working in healing influences in the animate creation and in the earth itself, until "the statelier Eden comes again" to a long-degraded and ruined world. This is the essence of the Christian, the Bible Millennium. This was promised to the first transgressor on his first repentance. It gladdened far off his penitent eyes, —

> "Fair as a star when only one
> Is shining in the sky."

It grew nearer and clearer to the faith of Abraham. The solitary star had become a cluster, a hemisphere sprinkled with beaming hopes. The Lord Jehovah Jesus, in the solemn midnight, centuries ago, visited him in his little black, goat-skin tent, under the rocky range of Hebron, and brought him forth from its lowly, flapping door into the hollow of the darkened hills. Far up the clear depths within depths he beheld —

> "The abyss where the everlasting stars abide."

"Look now toward heaven," said his divine guide, "and tell the stars, if thou be able to number them. So shall thy seed be. And in thy seed shall all the nations of the earth be blessed."

And yet he was then the only representative of that

multitude and blessedness in all the earth. The mighty idolatries of Egypt, among which he had dwelt, were in the hight of their seemingly eternal solidity of strength and glory. Their temples, stout as the pillars of earth, were then going up. Their pyramids, defying the shocks of the reeling globe or the bolts of shattering lightning, were then exquisitely cutting the crystal sky with their perfect lines. The Assyrian kingdom, within whose boundaries he was born, and whose Euphratean metropolis he not unlikely had visited in his youth, was then exultant in the unlimited pomp and sway of a Satanic faith. The deluge of spiritual death rose higher than the highest mountains of society, filled the whole earth, every dell, and cleft, and crevice of every heart of every people. His soul alone floated on the desolate, rainy seas, a spiritual ark, built and guided of God, in whose holy recesses the faith of his wife and son, and to a less degree his nephews, were also carried.

Jacob's dying eyes beheld the like vision under a slight increase of the on-marching light. A few score of his own blood, separated from the rest of the world as unclean, are all that profess the true and saving faith ; and these are worldly, violent, corrupt, differing from their heathen neighbors in but little more than their creed, and often inferior to them in dignity and excellency of character. Levi, the father of the priestly line, was shamed by the mildness and manliness of Shechem, the pagan. Judah, from whom Christ came, stamped himself and his tribe with indelible infamy. Reuben had gone still further in sin, and done deeds that even in that darkened age struck the public conscience with abhorrence, and called down upon him the dying maledictions of his father.

Yet with these men standing about his couch, the aged patriarch sees the coming Shiloh, the Messiah of God, and declares that to Him shall the gathering of the peoples be. The blessing that Abraham saw conferred in Christ upon all the world, Jacob sees is responded to by all the world: The nations shall gather about the Sent of God. Though not a nation then acknowledged Him; though only a few wild, wandering men, sons of a thrifty, itinerant shepherd accepted this announcement without perception of its meaning or desire for its consummation; though judging from his commandments concerning his bones, Joseph was the only one present that really possessed his father's faith in his father's clearness and confidence, still the word is spoken. The world shall come to the feet of Him who comes from God through the line of Judah.

How this ray is multiplied in the widening light of Scripture history! How proud stand David and Isaiah on the misty mountain tops of this dawning glory! How clear, and round, and shining it cuts the horizon at Bethlehem and Nazareth, so simple, so lustrous, so pure, so grand, the very brightness of the glory of God in the face of Jesus Christ! How this light increases in the pages that follow that advent and conclude the oracles of God! The confinement of the truth to a single man, a single family, a single tribe, a single nation, the necessity for all who would receive it to become members of this household, is suddenly changed. As in the night we can overcome the darkness only by seeking the light, while in the day the light seeks us, so in the ages before Shiloh came the world must ally itself to Judah, if it would enjoy heavenly vision; but after His advent the divine light goeth out into all the world. The deeds of the apostles show that this power is moving out for the subjugation and ingathering of the world, East, West, North, and South. Down to Ethiopia, over to Syria, up in Asia Minor, far over to the forest depths of Illyricum, out to the gates of Gibraltar, to Damascus, most ancient of cities, Antioch, most wealthy, Athens, most cultivated, Corinth, most luxurious, Rome, most imperial, everywhere mightily grew the word of God and prevailed. This omnipotent assault of the Spirit of God on the spirit of evil abounds and superabounds in the closing chapters of the Book. Then all the trumpets of heaven, with one acclaim, are ringing out the conquests of Christ over Satan in all the earth. The slow, dubious, often utterly imperceptible movements of the pre-advent age are changed to the most intense and increasing energy. Vials ever pouring, horsemen, as on battle-fields, fiercely riding, war rapidly following war, the Captain of the Hosts of the Lord pressing home His victories, giving His baffled enemy no chance to rest and repair his loss, driving him from his central throne, within twelve generations after His crucifixion, and thus expelling Him from the sovereignty of what is called in the New Testament, "the inhabitable world," and in the Roman writers, the "òrbis terrarum," the globe of the earth.

Driven to his savage devotees, Antichrist rallies these vilest of his slaves and hurls them at the Christian empire. The empire, backslidden, is seemingly destroyed, when, lo, the savages, under the genial penetration of Christian grace, become the saviors of civilization. They are as fresh soil to worn-out lands. Christianity converts them, not they it. Thus Christ advances, till to-day only three organized and prominent powers in all the earth deny the divinity and redemption of our Lord Jesus Christ,—the Chinese, the Turkish, the Japanese. The first two have yielded practically their independence, and live only by the sufferance or mutual jealousies of their Christian neighbors, while at the gates of the last the guns of three powers are now thundering, the unconscious servants of Christ, battering down, not Japan, but its idols and false worship.

The rebellion of man under the inspiration of Satan grows weaker year by year. The Revelator's far-off vision from the sharp, bare cliffs of Patmos, is our careless, every-day, mid-noon brightness. The power of Antichrist was then supreme. Across the smooth, black waves the hills of

Ephesus could be easily seen. On their farther sides, perhaps visible through the opening which gave her a harbor, Diana's wonderful temple glitters in the golden light of that gorgeous clime. Across the opposite and wider sea—

> "The earth then wore the Parthenon
> The brightest gem upon her zone."

No decay then blackened its shining pillars, no rifts marred its matchless symmetry. Its goddess, sixty feet tall, of ivory and gold, towered as the representative of that worldly wisdom which is to-day the most pretentious of all the enemies of Christ. Just below, Corinth was ablaze with a magnificence that was all devoted to the most open and shameful lust. Below Ephesus the horrid foulnesses of Phenician abominations flourished in opulent Antioch. In sight lay the birth-place of Homer, who had clothed the false offspring of false gods in the regalest robes of melody and imagination; and close beside him was the home of Pythagoras, who had sought to give them the dignity and authority of reason. Everywhere about him was Rome, in closest amity with the enemy of God and man. Zealously she followed his commands and shook her sceptre, full of fear and death, over the trembling, scattered sheep of Christ. Yet he saw through and beyond, above and around all this dominion of darkness the bright, divine future, and was glad.

Such is the Millennium in prophecy and history, in progress and perfection.

II. What connection has our war with this consummation? The progress of the promised grace has subdued its first enemy, idolatry. This destroyed man's allegiance to God. It must subdue the second enemy, which is man's hostility to man. This hostility assumes civil and social forms. It is monarchic, slavic, disuniting. Against these, march democracy, unity, fraternity, every man the equal and the brother of every man. To gain this victory we are now contending.

1. The separation of man by artificial social barriers is one of the earliest and deepest expressions of our rebellious nature. Ambition, if the last infirmity of noble minds, is the first of ignoble. Success gratifies it, power solidifies it. When solidified, immediately the priest consecrates it, and to deny its divinity is sacrilege. That is the way the monarchic and aristocratic systems have always grown. England's social structure, the proudest, and richest, and wickedest of any that controls civilized society, has grown exclusively from this seed. A robber chief, with a few hundred retainers, lands on her coast, throws his sword into the balance of a civil war, reduces both foes and allies to slavery, parcels out the lands, confers titles, appoints bishops and cardinals to sanctify his crime, and thus establishes the present government of England. The crimes, in which Kinglake so forcibly shows that the present Napoleon laid his power, were few and trifling beside these out of which Victoria's throne has been built. But few and small as they were, they were of like character, and show that the eight centuries that separate their commission have not modified their nature.

All governments based on the few, by the few, and for the few, are hostile to the government of Christ, and must be abolished before His glory fully comes. They were conceived in sin and shapen in iniquity. They breed pride, licentiousness, violence in the ruler, — poverty, cowardice, sycophancy, ignorance, lawlessness in the ruled. The Papal Church, and its eldest daughter, the Church of England, are oligarchies. They uphold civil by religious tyranny. Not so the first and future Church. That is Democracy. Her people are equal each to each, and their pastor's superiority is not one of authority but of service. The governments of man and of the Church must correspond. Both must be a brotherhood of equals.

2. Then comes the unification of Man. Unless he is one, Church nor State can ever be one. Christ cannot be the Head of our household. Whatever opposes this consummation, — blood, language, color, caste, — must give way, that Christ may be all and in all.

These vital principles are involved in our struggle. The first we saw at the first. So the whole world, kings and peoples, instinctively saw that the struggle was over that idea, over both ideas. The nation hailed the first with unbounded fervor — Union for the sake of Union. But thoughtful men hailed the grander idea that rose behind and above it, —

> "Another sun risen on mid noon,"—

the Equality and Fraternity of Man. Union, not for ourselves alone, but for all men, was our strongest, our most general feeling. It carried us safely over the disastrous days of our first defeats, through that first winter of fearful idleness, when the riotous rebels built their camp-fires and boiled the bones of our slain heroes in sight of our capital. It carried us through the still more terrible calamities of the Peninsula defeats, and the yet severer defeat of our confidence in the commander of that campaign.

But the people clung with increasing devotion to their idea, and its embodiment in American nationality. Three hundred thousand men hastened to cast themselves into the gulf, that Union and democracy might be preserved.

The second, and even darker winter, came upon us; a winter of woful discontent. Treason triumphed in many of the States of the North. The Proclamation of Emancipation,—a glad and glorious vision to holy hearts,—was surrounded by clouds and darkness, even like Him from whose chambers it had truly proceeded. The Mississippi was still fettered by stronger bands in its Southern windings than the icy ones nature had imposed on its upper currents.

McClellan removed, Burnside defeated, Hooker defeated, Fremont cashiered, how thick the darkness, how faint the national heart !

Still her purpose failed not. Why ? It was the salvation of popular government. The Union must be preserved, not alone because it was essential to our own welfare, but because through its preservation would the divine doctrine of popular government live among men. If America is lost, the world is lost.

Under this chastisement the people accept that other truth — the Identity of Man. God compels them to take this truth, just as very sick persons take very disagreeable draughts, not that they like the medicine, but that they may get well. Only this medicine of God is truly His best of food ; the choicest of His gifts to men as men. The Union is the American passion — a passion which no European appreciates. England sneers at it, and, if friendly, looks blank and ignorant at such enthusiasm. "Why this fury for the Union ?" "We have had one for two hundred and fifty years, and nobody on either side feels for it an impulse of enthusiasm or patriotic affection." "Why this talk about 'our country'?" Country, to an Englishman, is simply the region not occupied by large cities. "The Times" acknowledges that it does not understand Mr. Beecher when he talks so much about "our country." An incident current in their drawing-rooms illustrates this remark. An American lady, who sought to conceal her American origin, as if ashamed of it, was charged in company with being an American. She reddened with shame and surprise. "Why do you make such an accusation?" she asked. "Because you said 'our country.' No Englishman ever uses that expression."

But our passion for our country is also and chiefly a passion for liberty. We fight for empire, because empire means democracy. We shall wage this war fifty years, if need be, because everybody, with more or less clearness, sees that its success is essential to the preservation of those ideas. It was not so at the first. Abolitionists, though sound on the rights of man, were, as a whole, unsound on the necessity of the Union to attain and maintain their rights. Different classes of the people were the depositary of different ideas. The one cried "Union at any cost. Down with the abolitionists who are disturbing it. Union is liberty. Union is democracy. Let it alone, even if it becomes the patron of slavery. Some way and some time it will emancipate the State from that iniquity." The other party, with equal and superior fervor, cried, "The Rights of every man at any cost. Down with the Union, if it stands in the way of liberty.".

As in the material world, the orbit pursued is the resultant of the forces employed upon the orb itself, so here. The centrifugal lovers of Liberty, and the centripetal lovers of Union, whose representatives were Phillips and Everett, were each at heart lovers of the democratic and federative ideas. Both sought their preservation. Both contended together, because each felt his own principle was in danger of destruction through the purpose of his antagonist's idea. The shock of arms united them. The one saw that Union now meant universal liberty. The other that abolitionism meant Union, and only under its banner could the nation be preserved. Equal rights were seen to mean every man's rights. Democracy was identical with abolitionism. Hence no men were more ardent to strike down the slave power than the life-long democrats, — democrats who were honest believers in the corner-stone of their creed — the equality of man. Dickinson of New York was such a democrat; Butler of Massachusetts, another. They said instantly, "free the slave; make him a soldier; cut out the cancer over the heart of the republic."

3. But a greater truth than all the rest was born of the

exigencies of this hour. We found we as yet had known nothing, as it were, of the scope and fullness of that word Democracy. It was with us, at the worst, equality of white people, and the slavery of all other complexions; at the best, equality of the whites, and the liberty, but not fraternity, of the blacks. Not the oneness of man as man, — never, never. We fell into spasms at the thought of that divine truth, as a mushroom lord of England might at his equality with his servant.

But the wisdom of God is wiser than men. You did not create the doctrine of human fraternity. You may have fancied that you did; that it was your patent, and could be limited and controlled at your pleasure. So did the Athenian democrats. Where are they? So have the Southern slavemongers. Where are they? God, my friends, not you, made man, of one father, that all might be brethren, that each should in honor prefer one another, esteeming others better than themselves. He is pushing us forward to His, not our, Millennium. He is using and blessing us if we choose to work with Him. If not, He is none the less using us, while also chastising, for the advancement of mankind to the same goal. He maketh our wrath or righteousness alike to praise and prosper Him. Whether gradually, and by the operation of laws that have been molding and transforming man for ages, or suddenly, and by the breaking up of the present order and institution of a new earth and new man, as some devout students of the Bible believe, whichever be the way, the end is sure and the same. The Millennium is a world of men, equal, brotherly, united, and holy. Every approach to that state now renders its violent introduction less necessary. If it can be effected by natural causes there will be no need of the supernatural. It is being effected. The divine doctrine of democracy has become choked with weeds and stones. We said "It is true and grand, but it is only for white folks.

Do you dare to say that that negro and I are of one blood, and should be one in social and civil life? that it is as much his duty to ignore my complexion as it is mine to ignore his? Horrible!" And so we stone the prophets who simply preach to us our own doctrine of democracy, rationally and divinely developed.

But God is taking vengeance on us for destroying His servants, and is compelling us to rise to the hights of our own principles at the threat of losing all its lower developments, which we see to be our essential life. We listen, refuse, yield, and most reluctantly obey.

Now comes another word of God. Arm him as a soldier? We refuse; we scream in fear and hatred at that word. When Charles Sumner said, at the Massachusetts Republican Convention,* that such was the course of Marius to save Rome, and such must be ours to save the country, the journals of our capital denied the correctness of his quotations, and scouted with horror his proposals. To such a pitch of fear did they reach, that on carrying a defense of his scholarship — as if it could need defense — to the most learned of our journals, which had been severest in denunciation of his scholarship, I was told, after the article had spent a night in their editorial rooms, that if they should dare to publish that simple statement of the language of Plutarch, their building would be torn down before night. Another journal, "The Traveller," to its honor be it said, admitted the article, and what was better, stood by the principle, without loss of building or character.

Such opposition only new punishment could cure. So God sent our enemies again upon us. They ate up our boys as the ox eateth up grass. He develops demand for work at home to subdue the recruiting fever. He makes the draft unpopular and difficult. He wastes our armies, and shows that they cannot be replenished from their pre-

* September, 1861.

vious sources. At length, crushed with calamity and nigh the gates of the grave, we whiningly and meanly, yet honestly say, "Come, you nigger, and fight for us." He comes. Disregarding our hearts, mindful only of our danger, he comes and fights like well tried warriors; fights so grandly that an officer at Port Hudson urged the appointment of white officers over them, because if led by their own men they would have certainly stormed those hights, and every man been slain. Whoever heard before that it was the business of an officer in battle to restrain the daring of his men.

We are being led gradually to higher hights. Providence is using this degradation for the furtherance of His ends. What means the cry that has just made every heart bleed afresh. Our sons are starving in Richmond prisons! Why not exchange them? We cannot. Why not? Because the rebels refuse to recognize the white officers of colored regiments as prisoners of war, and are putting our colored soldiers, whom they have taken captive, into slave-pens and worse than slave miseries. If we call these men to fight for us, we must, at least, protect them if captured, equally with their fellow-soldiers. There, at least, white and black are alike. The people are sad, but, thank God, are firm. They might not have been, had the rebels used those white officers as they do our other officers. They might have said, "Let the blacks be enslaved, but release my white sons by exchange for yours." God has made this trick of the devil a clasp of his own to bind us to our despised brethren.

We must yet give these officers position. We must let them serve in what regiments they choose. We must let them rise in that regiment, if they are worthy, to the chief command. We must make them generals, not of black men, but of armies. This war, if greatly prolonged, will not close till this progress is wrought. It is not as great as has been achieved. It must be done to make our ways straight for the coming of the Lord. God will not rest until, either through this war, or by subsequent conflicts, which He shall create and control, He has abolished this iniquity from every institution and every heart.

The last word of commendation which Mr. Beecher received in England was from the students of the non-conforming colleges, the heirs of the blood, principles, and sovereignty of Cromwell and his associates. In that address they urge him to labor for the abolition of all distinctions in society based on color. It will be done, and we shall yet see in Baltimore, as in Boston, people of African descent moving freely in the best society. Africa is as good a country as Asia, whence we are supposed to have come, and its children will be held in as high an honor.

Thus shall the millennial day break upon the world. It may be in a day. Events are hastening it forward. Every step in Europe is to emancipation, equalization, unification. There is no possibility of peace there on any other basis. Nor is there here.

Christendom thus unified, heathendom and Islamdom will soon be regenerated. Social vices will abate their violence. Liberty and unity will prevent wars and armaments, royal houses, and luxurious absorption by a few families of the people's wealth. Legitimate industry will pay the old debts of kings and crimes, and easily supply the slight demands of a popular and peaceful government. Intemperance, Sabbath-breaking, infidelity, all the fruits of crowned and Catholic Europe, will be replaced with the graces of Christianity. The Lord Jesus will be the real and recognized, if not visible, sovereign of the world. "Unto Him shall all flesh come, and every knee bow." By Him shall rulers reign, and judges decree justice. In Him shall all the world, consciously, happily, completely, live, and move, and have its being.

"Yea, truth and justice then,
Will down return to men,

Orbed in a rainbow; and, like glories wearing,
Mercy will sit between,
Throned in celestial sheen,
With radiant feet the tissued clouds down steering,
And heaven, as at some festival,
Will open wide the gates of her high palace hall."

Say not this is all a golden dream. It is scriptural, rational, inevitable. It is hardly now a prophetic vision, so much of it has been accomplished. The blindest-eyed can see, through the vista before him, the glad consummation. Compared with the dreary ages that are past, how brief, how pleasant the remnant hours! Gigantic sins can be brought low as in a moment. Three years ago, and the most hopeful souls in America could see no immediate end to its most awful sin. Here and there was one who said the election of Mr. Lincoln begins the end. But this gave it nearly or over a score of years in which to die. The multitude saw not even those misty mountain tops. They looked over the immense territories ruled by the masters of these sins, and no glare of sunshine greeted their eyes. Wickedness stalked crowned, haughty, through all that land.

"The free were only they
Whom power made free to execute all ills
Their hearts imagine; they alone were great
Whose passions nursed them from their cradle up
To luxury and lewdness — whom to see
Was to despise — whose aspect put to scorn
Their station's eminence. The wise, they only
Obscurely waiting till the bolts of heaven
Should break upon the land, and give them light
Whereby to walk! The innocent, alas!
Poor Innocency lay where four roads meet,
A stone upon her head, a stake driven through her.
Who that was innocent did care to live,
The hand of power did press the very life
Of Innocency out."

That horrid shape, most said, can never die. For centuries, certainly, will it flourish. It arose in arms. How the whole land trembled at the neighing of its strong ones! How we quailed and whitened at its imperial front! Never before was a nation so despised by its rebels. No epithets could body forth their scorn. Egypt did not so disdain her Hebrew slaves, nor the Philistines, with Goliath at their head, the unarmed refugees of the cliffs of Judean wildernesses. They had bounds to their contempt. Not so our Southern masters. "Mudsills," "greasy mechanics," whom "we can drive into the ocean with a lady's riding-whip,"— these were the A B C of their scorn. They looked abroad, and every aristocrat was nodding and winking approval, chief of whom in this crime against God and humanity was the aristocracy of Great Britain.

Our hopes were in our principles, our people, and our God. They have not failed us. And the hideous iniquity which we dared not touch, which we went round and round to get at those who, sheltered behind its Gorgon-headed shield, laughed us to scorn; that Gorgon-hissing shield we at last struck at and struck through, and the monster lies prone for many a league, prone over half the land, prone forever.

Coifi, a priest of British paganism, at the time of that island's conversion, and before its present backsliding, at the risk of death from the insulted gods, rode full tilt against their temples, before a ghastly crowd, who believed instant death would be visited upon a priest who should dare, armed, to approach these shrines, and were expecting that such would be his sudden fate. But, as the poet tells us,—

"He crashed
Through the inclosures, ever sacred held,
And gained the central space unharmed, and rode
Thrice round and round, and in his stirrup stood,
And with a high defiance on his lip,
Smote with a clang an Idol, monster faced;
E'en as he smote, the foul thing, reeling, fell,
And then from every heart the icy hand
Of fear was lifted.

Within the crowd a sacred fury wrought;
The deities were tumbled on the grass,
The pales and the inclosures were torn down,
And one a torch applied, and towers
Of flame rushed up, then licked the air and died,
While white-robed priests, together standing, sung:
'Down falls the wicked idol on his face —
So let all wicked gods and idols fall.' "

Thus have the fears of our monster idol been dispelled, and the demon that has burned to death screaming myriads in his arms of fire, has been smitten of God and tumbled into the lake of eternal burning, while we have stood amazed and glad beyond all power of praise. Its priestly devotees and lordly defenders are howling in sorrow and shame, defeat and destruction.

Let us not despair of further victories of the Lamb. This demon slain, there is no such other hydra cursing the earth. European tyrannies will fast follow it to its dishonored grave. Asiatic abominations and African savagery will feel the warm rays of the Sun of Righteousness, long held in disastrous eclipse by this horrific sin. They will wilt down at His presence, as when the melting fire burneth, the fire causeth the waters to boil.

Our own social sins, intemperance, Sabbath-breaking, infidelity, immorality, will be more easily restrained and extirpated after this Satan among the lesser fiends is cast into the bottomless pit and chained there forever. Our prejudices, born and fostered of him, will likewise disappear, and brotherly love and unity possess all hearts.

The glad tidings of yesterday assure the speedy overthrow of Pharaoh and his hosts. This great and growing soldier, with a rare fitness, joins his victories to our national holidays. They are thus twice blessed, in what they give to these rejoiceful days, in what of higher quality they take from their ancient worthiness, and add to their own high meed of fame. Vicksburg crowns the nation's birthday with an undying glory, and Chattanooga, relieved of its long-exultant enemies, fills the most ancient of our festal days with the tides of exultant life. See that band creeping round the shaggy breast of yon sharp peak; amid the blasted pines, the prostrate firs, the loose stones, their perilous path they keep, up and up, till a cloud receives them out of our sight. Not a cloud of heaven, but of earth, a cloud soon to flash with unwonted brightness, to rumble with thunder-claps of death. The battle opens, rages, grows closer, hotter, deadlier. Pressing ever on and up swing the gallant troops around the last smooth precipitous wall, that sits a crown of smooth, high rock upon the mountain's brow. The rebels break and flee; along the wild edge, headlong plunges the host. The fiery Hooker is fleeter of foot. Upon the plains beneath he breaks, like torrents into which the mountain cloud seems to have burst, torrents sweeping all things in their wild and fatal flight.

Across the plains, on a low ridge, hangs a heavier cloud of war. It stretches for miles along its summit. In the valley below, with Chattanooga at its back, but a mile or two distant, on a little knob, stands a little man reconnoitering the scene. The plains are filled with mustering squadrons. Advances are made along the line up this bristling hill. Here Sherman holds his enemy by the throat, each bleeding, each firm. Then Thomas pushes forward his columns, and below Hooker sweeps up the less precipitous but more perilous sides, with his untamed daring. Day and day writhes the mighty anaconda of the plains, and the hills are wreathed in agony of strife. That point is reached at last which every great general knows, and only great generals, when, each side exhausted, that which summons all its strength crushes its foe. The word is given. The army summon up the spirits; the hill is stormed, is swept, is ours. The rebels, who but now had thought themselves invulnerable, leap from their rifle-pits and intrenchments, and fly in panic irrepressible.

This is the thanksgiving feast that the calm general sends to a nation drunken with delight. This crushes the dragon in all the region above the Gulf States, except that spot where he raises his head sparkling defiance from his green and deadly eyes. The West is free from slave or rebel, and shall be free forever.

This victory assures the end. Slavery is doomed by the fiat of the nation and the arm of Grant. They have fought with the Lamb, and the Lamb has overcome them. No State, we fondly hope and believe, can ever resume its place in the Union with this crime on its hands. Other blessings shall speedily follow — all blessings. The glory of the Lord shall cover the earth as the waters cover the sea. Already its beams cover thick the morning sky.

> "Come forth, O Light, from out the breaking East,
> And with thy splendor pierce the heathen dark,
> And morning make a continent and isle,
> That Thou mayst reap the harvest of Thy tears,
> O Holy One, who hung upon the tree."

WHY GRANT WILL SUCCEED.*

"AND THE LORD SAID UNTO JOSHUA, FEAR NOT, NEITHER BE THOU DISMAYED; TAKE ALL THE PEOPLE OF WAR WITH THEE, AND ARISE, GO UP TO AI: SEE, I HAVE GIVEN INTO THY HAND THE KING OF AI, AND HIS PEOPLE, AND HIS CITY, AND HIS LAND." — *Joshua* viii. 1.

HE land trembles with the conflict that has been raging for more than a week in the seat of the rebellion. The smoke of the great agony curls up in the central heavens, and almost casts its lurid darkness over our visible skies. Under its sulphurous canopy our sons and brothers have been wrestling in a death struggle with those who should be our sons and brothers, for principles and privileges that are dearer than life. We gather in this quiet house of prayer, far from the scene of the contest; yet we hear but little save the rapid pelting of the musketry or the fearful boom of the artillery. Our ears are filled with the hurrahs of our boys as they fly up the steep sides of rebel earthworks, or the Indian yells of our foes, as they leap in mighty masses upon our serried columns. The piled dead lie before our vision, ghastly,

* A sermon preached in Boston, Sunday, May 15, 1864, on the occasion of the advance of General Grant on Richmond. See Note XIV.

torn, trampled, their eyes glazed, or "staring in muddy impurity." The wounded, sinking, fainting, groaning, bleeding, fill our souls with inexpressible anguish. We see not each other's faces, we hear not each other's voices. These sights and sounds fill sense and soul to a staggering fullness.

> "The fires of death,
> The bale fires, flash on high; from rock to rock,
> Each volley tells that thousands cease to breathe;
> Death rides upon the sulphury siroc;
> Red Battle stamps his foot, and nations feel the shock."

Amid such powerful presences it is difficult for congregations to gather in churches to-day. Telegrams, not texts, are our spiritual food. The battle, not the Bible, draws our attention. The lives of myriads, nay, the life of the nation, hangs on the dreadful die.

We do not condemn this feeling. Were one of your family to-day struggling with disease, and life or death hung trembling in the balance, you would not be a listener here. You would be busy in the chamber, nursing and praying. The quiet worship of God's house is sometimes more profane than the active worship of out-door philanthropy. Should you, on coming hither, see a horse cast in the street, and say, "It is Sunday; I cannot miss my seat and sermon to relieve this poor beast," you would find no spiritual nourishment in the service. God would scorn your advances. How much more, then, when your country is struggling for existence, when the principles of civil and Christian society are cast into the wavering scales of war, when the welfare of the living generation and unborn generations is subjected to the risks of battle; then, if ever, in every church and congregation, should prayers, meditations, and eloquence, all conspire for one end. Do you suppose, had Joshua's battle been on the Sabbath, that Eliezer and the Levites would have forbidden the non-combatants to think about their contending kindred on that day? Or that

Phinehas would have told the worshipers at Shiloh, "Your brethren are having a terrible civil war down at Gibeah to-day, but you must think only of your sacrifices and ceremonial service." Nay; he would have said, "Leave here thy gift before the altar, and let us hasten up to yonder hill, where perchance we may see the fearful strife. Let us earnestly pray for their success; let us fly to the dreadful scene, and administer our aid and comfort to the wounded and dying." So now we may, we ought, to pray and talk on the all-absorbing theme.

We are led hither, also, by the request of our Chief Magistrate, who desires us to acknowledge the goodness of God in crowning our onward movement with victory. Especially should we consider this subject, that we may lift it above the bloody phases it presents to the natural eye, or the mere shifts and windings of politics that it exhibits to some minds, into the grand hights of divine workings. God moves with our moving army; God fights with our fighting soldiers; not for the welfare of America, as an especial and peculiar nation; that is a heathen's idea of God, who thought Jove or Zeus was his god only; and not the god of his enemy. He contends for us, because He has certain ends to be consummated on the earth, that can only be effected through the overthrow of the doctrines and usages of the rebellious confederacy.

We may not see Him. Perhaps Joshua did not when he stole up the high wall of the Jordan valley, and through its passes wound his way to the long and lofty hill upon which Ai frowned contemptuously upon him. He knew that that city must be taken or the hill country of Palestine could not be occupied by his people. He knew that the narrow gorge of the Jordan would soon cease to contain them, if they failed to gain a foothold upon the hights. It was a military necessity. It was an absolute necessity. He saw not that his success involved even the redemption of man.

He did not fully know that out of it would come salvation for the world. Even though this inspiring vision did lift itself before his eyes, yet he felt none the less that his work was to deliver a nation of fugitives from destruction, and establish them upon immovable foundations. As in all greatest duties, there was the vision of future perfection, and the present obligation, hard, painful, bloody.

> "God has conceded two sights to a man —
> One of men's whole work, time's completed plan,
> The other of the minute's work, man's first
> Step to the plan's completeness."

So Joshua might have seen the infinite necessities that compelled the capture of the hostile town ; but the strong, hard duty of the hour was its capture. We, too, looking over the bloody and blackened field of wasting strife, looking at the yet unsettled, and perhaps most desperate future, may rightfully inspire our hearts, as was that of Joshua, with visions of the plans of God that necessitate our victory.

This last and greatest ground for our assurance of success covers the final issue. Others, like those that pressed immediately upon the mind of the Hebrew captain, press upon us. The future of revelation may be near or distant — dim or clear. In it America may appear shining with a celestial glory, or may be blotted out as completely and indifferently as are Egypt, Assyria, and Rome, or may shine in as baleful light as Judea, whose central principles and Person, like that nation, it may have scornfully rejected.

Whatever be that ultimate summing up of God concerning this nation, depends upon the manner in which we respond to His calls at the present moment.

It is often said that we are settling the question for the rights of man in America and in the world. We are not doing exactly this. For the question of the success of the rights of man does not depend upon America, but upon God. If we follow His orders we may be His favorites —

the ministers of this divine purpose. If we fail to follow them, we shall be cast aside as unceremoniously as we have cast aside disobedient or incompetent generals, and He will make others His officers, servants, and friends. So, then, we are led, in considering our grounds for hoping to succeed, solely to the consideration of the manner in which we have responded to the demands of God. We have no political or merely military problems to discuss. We trace our defeats and victories to no incompetent or competent generalship. A higher law regulates these matters. Not that we despise generalship. Not that we believe victory usually follows virtuous imbecility and defeat vicious ability. Success requires sagacity, even in the way of righteousness. Folly is not God's favorite. Moses was as naturally as he was supernaturally gifted. David was of extraordinary powers independent of their extraordinary subjugation to the divine will. Paul was the acknowledged leader of the Jewish leaders before he became the head of the Christian Church. Luther, Calvin, Wesley, were men of the amplest parts, independent of the lofty purpose in which they employed their genius.

And yet the wisest of minds set against the will of God is weaker than the weakest working with that will. The mightiest steamer tugs in vain against Niagara's current, the tiniest feather flies resistlessly upon its rushing floods. So, in estimating the reasons for our success, we shall ever bear in mind that though great generals are a great necessity, great ideas are a greater. Joshua was a great general. No superior appears in Hebrew, if in any other history. Yet at the very beginning of his campaign he meets with an ignominious repulse. He is chased down the mountains of Bethel a ruinous rout. Why? He had ceased to ally himself with God. He was but a lieutenant of the Divine Captain. He was not in unison with his commander-in-chief. He flies as miserably as the weakest of his soldiers before the impetuous mountaineers — the avowed rebels of the cause which he was tamely supporting. So the eleven tribes — for the clerical tribe coöperated largely in the patriotic and holy enterprise — fled twice in utter disgrace and confusion before their corrupt and abominable brethren of Benjamin and Gibeah. They had as good leaders, doubtless. But they were not in earnest against the sin of their brethren. They took up the quarrel compulsorily, and not seriously — fearing for their Constitution more than for their God, and He drove them down the rocky slope and across the broad meadows at its base in unspeakable panic, until they had begun to fast, and repent, and search their souls, and seek for God's way before they expected any victory.

In the light of this high principle we see why we did not succeed at the first. We had become almost as deeply implicated in the sin of the nation as our revolting brethren. We refused to let the cry of the slave rouse us from our torpidity; even after the shot at a national vessel and the capture of a national fort had stung us into a war for national self-preservation, we still vociferated at the top of our lungs, "War for union, not for liberty — for white men, not for man — for the Constitution, not for the right." So we rushed to Washington — bravely, no doubt, as did Joshua's men up the sides of Ai; yet vain-gloriously, godlessly, profanely — stuffed with hate, and prejudice, and all uncleanness. Then came Big Bethel, Bull Run, Ball's Bluff, with their chastening experiences. But they did not chasten us. The leaven began to work, yet wrought slowly, slowly. A young Napoleon came down from the Alleghanies, and was going to conquer without God; nay, against God. His army lies around him, superb in equipment, gay in caparison, matchless on parade, encumbered with material which a lavish nation squandered upon them. He wanted to conquer. Everybody does. He wanted to substantiate the fame which danced before him. But he said, "I must be the victor of a people united on the old basis—slavery must go out gradually—not by my right arm." He did not like it, did not approve it. He wished its death. But he would not touch it. It was the sacred Hyena before which we bowed in adoration — which at least we would keep carefully pastured and folded — not caged exactly — for though inclosed in bars, he had wide ranging-ground and ample privilege to eat men, women, and children by the million.

One event, like Achan's little wedge, showed the rottenness of that army, and the certainty of its fate. God sent two or three sweet singers into the winter's camp, to beguile a lonely hour of the soldiers with their melodies. They were honest singers. Not such as black their faces, and travesty all sincere and truthful things to beguile bewitched ears of their money and their time, but men that feared God, and would sing, as did Miriam, and Deborah, and David, the songs He taught them. They essayed to sing the grandest hymn of the war; solemn and stately as the oracles of heaven. You know its deep pathos.

"We wait beneath the furnace blast
The pangs of transformation;
Not painlessly doth God recast
And mould anew the nation;
Hot burns the fire
Where wrongs expire,
Nor spares the hand,
That from the land
Uproots the ancient evil.

"What gives the wheat-fields blades of steel?
What points the rebel cannon?
What sets the roaring rabble's heel
On the old star-spangled pennon?
What breaks the oath
Of the men o' the South?
What whets the knife
For the Union's life?
Hark to the answer — Slavery!

"Then waste no blows on lesser foes,
In strife, unworthy freemen;
God lifts to-day the vail, and shows
The features of the demon!
O, North and South,
Its victims both,
Can ye not cry,
Let Slavery die,
And Union find in Freedom?"

That hymn the soldiers were forbidden to hear. From that hour dated the disasters of the Peninsula, and the disgrace of to-day; while the general who was the mouthpiece of his commander in that crowd has lately crowned his practical treason at Manassas with complete defeat at Shreveport. Then God left us to the pride that goeth before destruction, and the haughty spirit that precedes the fall. He went not with us into that campaign. Miserable destruction overwhelmed us.

And yet, as if to show how clear was His line of action, there was going forward at that very time another movement on His basis. A general who had started out determined to conquer—but hoping to do it without touching the great iniquity, who had offered to protect the slaveholders of Maryland against the fugacious losses of their human property — had been whelmed in disgrace and defeat at Big Bethel. Unlike every other defeated man, he instantly saw that if he would win he must be true to truth. And he was as instantly and as thoroughly converted. He goes to New Orleans in the power of that conversion. Its forts fall before him, as did Jericho before Joshua. He ruled that great city in justice. He decreed liberty; gave the freedman a uniform, long before Massachusetts wrung from a defeated government the privilege to organize her now famous "Fifty-Fourth." He did what the government has not yet done — put men of color in command of the regiments he raised. Success throngs to him; he rises before the nation, before his foes, before the world,—the man who has done more than all others to really save the country. He alone of the generals who were first appointed to lead the assault upon the rebel Capitol is to-day in the field, and under the gates of the city. And he to-day stands so strong in the judgment and conscience of his countrymen, that should he be defeated by superior forces, or superior military scholarship, he would suffer no real loss in their hearts. They know that he means to be right. He may not know all about war. He knows that which is of more worth. He may have been a blasphemer, a persecutor. So was Paul. But in this matter, if in no other, he is true.

We did not succeed, notwithstanding the light that shone at the mouth of the Mississippi; the government refused to speak the word of Liberty, and destruction came. That word appeared, and light broke dimly over the black and maddening waves. The waves still roared, and were troubled. The mountains shook with the swelling thereof. But a new creating spirit was brooding upon its turbulent depths. The influences of regeneration moved through the seething mass. The enemy arose and defeated the idea at the polls. It raged again in mobs and massacre; it was savage, unrelenting. The kings of the earth took counsel together against us. All that passed by wagged their heads, exclaiming,—

"She has gone down, our evil-boding star,
Beneath a hideous cloud of civil war,
Strife such as heathen slaughterers abhorred,
The lawless band who would call no man lord,
In the fierce splendor of her insolent morn,
She has gone down — the world's eternal scorn."

It was too late — that hate and scorning. She had begun to live. But not yet was she deserving success. The slave is freed by compulsion, not by love. Not honestly, but meanly, did we

"Do good by stealth, and blush to find it fame:"

blushed with a real sense of shame. We disliked our colored fellow-men. We hated to call them truly brethren. They must not enter our armies, they must not stay in our borders. We will free them, and expatriate them. Therefore successes come slowly. The waters dash against the light, and almost obliterate it. Burnside moves out only to be miserably defeated. Hooker takes up the gage of battle, and with a larger army than the one that is now sweeping down to Richmond, is completely destroyed in the Wilderness. Flushed with success, and welcomed by bloody insurrections and secret machinations, the foe moves down upon us out from its fastnesses. Wasting and destruction are in all our borders. He is barely repulsed. We sit down before him, unable to take Ai or Gibeah, unable to get anear it.

Meantime in the West is another general, who believes in ideas no less than arms; who sees and accepts the call of God. As little and unknown as David among his flocks, he would have remained unknown but for that God saw his heart was simple, right, and true. Being thus, he clothed him with power, and the West stood disinthralled from the fetters of the rebellion. God's gift for our partial service was the freely flowing Mississippi. His punishment for our yet Egyptian longings and rebellions of spirit was Fredericksburg, Chancellorsville, and the invasion of Pennsylvania.

But we grow in righteousness. The spirit of the people is becoming penitent and sincere. We see that not only is slavery wrong, — caste is wrong. It is abominable in the sight of God for man to look with loathing upon his fellow-man. He made us all alike — all of one blood, all brothers and sisters, as close as those born of the same father and mother. We are not yet cured of that iniquity, though we are advancing thitherward. We put them into our ranks. In one or two instances we conferred on them commissions. Still we held them in the servants' place and at servants' wages. That brings disaster, Fort Pillow, Plymouth, Shreveport. The campaign opens most dismally. The government pompously refuses to raise their wages, and shoots one who asserts, and justly, that he was enlisted under false pretences on the part of the government, and that it has no claim upon his services. Mutiny mutters through all the army.

Had Grant moved upon Richmond with that iniquity unremoved, he would be to-day a disgraced and ruined man. We call him a great general, and so he is; but his generalship could not have saved him. God would have given him into the hands of his enemies, as He has given another at New Orleans, whose reputation has been hardly less than his; but who defrauded the freedman of his right to negotiate his own terms for labor; who compelled him to receive the pittance that secession land-owners proposed to give, and forbade his being paid but half of that before the close of the year; who shut him up on the plantations, and forbade his crossing the boundaries without a pass — the hideous reminder of his old condition; who stripped the epaulets from the shoulders of wealthy gentlemen, that had won them by their valor, simply because they were slightly tinged with a browner complexion than his own; who disfranchised two thirds of the Union men of the State, and compelled the election of a rebel in heart over an honest lover of union, liberty, and the rights of man. And then, having inaugurated with a monster concert from one who had desecrated Puritan Massachusetts with his Sabbath amusements, his new, false, and unjust government, he moves out to subdue his foes, and is dashed back upon his capital, like a weed torn up by the sea, and hurled on the rocks. As a Presidential candidate,

"He falls like Lucifer
Never to hope again."

And this man was one of the ablest minds in the land; the pet of his commonwealth; the hope and pride of the nation. What has killed him? God. He set himself against the Almighty. He scorned the doctrine that there was sentiment in politics; that soul should appear in government. He is dashed to pieces. All is gone. Honor, fame, hopes, and more than all, a good conscience. Never was there a fall in this nation so sudden and so irremediable. And why? Not because he lacked generalship. Other generals have failed. He lacked principle. His fate is a warning—a painful, dreadful warning to every man. Sooner or later, in such hours as this, everything short of truth and justice is burned up, and every one who makes these idols his trust is burned with them. "The strong shall be as tow, and the maker of it as a spark, and they shall both burn together, and none shall quench them."

So, too, would our chief army have perished, but for timely repentance and its meet works. The President declares for ten months that he has no power to treat colored soldiers as soldiers. All at once, fearful lest Congress will not give him, in time for the advance, the power that he has said he did not have, his attorney general informs him that the original bill granted him this power. Could he not have found that out before ten months of disastrous trial had opened his eyes?

Then marches the new army to battle, with colored soldiers as soldiers; with colored cavalry sweeping up to the gates of the rebel capital. And then and therefore comes the victory. That is why we shall succeed. Our men are converted to the truth. They treat their associates in arms as their equals, their friends. They march together, fight together, bleed together, shout together, die together, triumph together, — brothers in blood and brothers forever.

How must the trembling sinners of Richmond look aghast as they see the dark faces of their slaves riding insolently up to their walls. Nemesis, shod not now in wool, but with fire, is marching upon them. She brings the death of

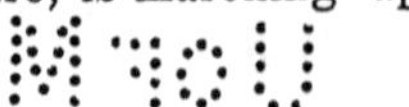

their pride, their power, their all. Their end is coming. "Go up," says God; "for I have given them into thy hand."

But this success will avail us nothing unless we purge ourselves of the least and last remains of this iniquity. We must put away from us the unclean thing. Not those we call unclean, but our prejudices, far more unclean and abominable in the sight of God. Your soul, not your neighbor's color, your God hateth. We must abolish colored regiments, colored conferences, colored churches, colored pews, and colored distinctions in everything. Our full salvation depends on our faithfulness to this duty.

For, my friends, be assured God cares but very little for you unless you will aid Him in carrying out His designs on the earth. To that design if America is willing to contribute, well for her; if not, she is broken in pieces as a potter's vessel. That design is the brotherhood of man in Christ. If we coöperate with Him, He will make us His vanguard. If we refuse, He will do with us as He did with His more chosen and more beloved people—cast us off, and raise up another people who shall follow His guidance.

The world looks to us to obey His commands; to expel from our hearts the accursed thing; to lock foot and heart with these our brethren, for a courageous march across the world. Europe hangs on the destiny of this hour. If we come out of this struggle clear and glorious, if a man irreproachably just and fearless shall lead this nation out of its slime and sin, then the hundredth anniversary of our Independence will not see a throne in Europe, so ripe is that continent for liberty.

May God help us so to go on to perfection, that with the certain fall of the stronghold and strong arms of the rebellion before our Joshua, there shall be a more perfect downfall and destruction of the stronger holds of false and fatal pride, that have so long ruled and ruined our souls.

Then, fearful as are our calamities, distressful as is the

fate of many wounded heroes, and riven and bleeding hearts, we shall feel that their tears and blood are not shed in vain. As the blood of brave Hebrews won the citadels of the hills from heathen foes, and made them the fair and chosen seats of the Lord for a thousand years, so will these sacred gifts secure for us generations of peace and joy.

> "God's hand within the shadow lays
> The stones whereon His gates of praise
> Shall rise at last."

And in those ages to come, when that temple shall stand complete, no honors too great can be paid to our memory. The world's feet will pass by the tomb of the great Washington, to pause at the mounds where his children, with superior heroism, poured forth their blood to preserve and to perfect the blessings he partially secured. Throughout all nations shall strong men weep for gratitude over their unspeakable valor, and all the world, Asian, European, African, American, with one united and unceasing impulse, in a regenerated and fraternal brotherhood of man, shall rise up and call us blessed.

> "Triumph not, fools, and weep not, ye faint-hearted.
> Have ye believed that the divine decree
> Of Heaven had given this people o'er to perish?
> Have ye believed that God would cease to cherish
> This great new world of Christian liberty?
> And that our light forever had departed?
> Nay, by the precious blood shed to redeem
> The nation from its selfishness and sin,
> By each true heart that burst in holy strife,
> Leaving its kindred hearts to break through life;
> By all the tears that will not cease to stream
> Forever, every desolate home within,
> We will return to our appointed place,
> First in the vanguard of the human race."

THREE SUMMERS OF WAR.*

THE REVOLUTION AND THE REBELLION.

"WHOSE ARE THE FATHERS." — *Romans* ix. 5.

E have just slowly waded through the third summer of blood. The waves still roar and are troubled. The mountains shake with the swelling thereof. It is well in such an hour to strengthen our souls with the experience of our fathers. The third year of our revolutionary struggle may be properly placed beside the third year of our war. They were waged for the same ends, by the same people, against the same pretensions. Our foe, like that of our fathers, speak our language ; like that, seek our annihilation as a nation in the interests of slavery and despotism. Our fortunes merit and will reward comparison. The analogy naturally resolves itself into the military, the moral, and the financial.

1. In a military view, if we take our stand at Philadelphia, July 4, 1776, and look over the country which had just been declared free and independent, we see not an armed enemy in all its borders. Four months before they had been ex-

* A sermon preached in Boston, July 4, 1864.

pelled from Boston. The nation was seemingly master of the whole land. Yet they were far from being its undisputed possessors. Though Britain was ousted, she was rapidly entering. On that very day the white sails of her army-laden navy, moving down from Halifax, were off Staten Island. The troops soon occupied its shores, and New York was a beleageured town. On the 27th of August their Bull Run occurred at Brooklyn. Two weeks later there was a second panic at Harlem, when Washington vainly attempted to keep his men in front of the enemy, and exclaimed in dismay, "Are these the men with whom I am to defend America?"

So great was the depression of the public mind by that disastrous defeat, that Washington, in a letter to the president of Congress, dated the 2d of September, writes in almost a state of despair. "The check," he says, "that our detachment sustained on the 27th ult. has dispirited too great a proportion of our troops, and filled their minds with apprehension and despair. The militia, instead of calling forth their utmost efforts to a brave and manly opposition in order to repair our losses, are dismayed, intractable, and impatient to return. Great numbers of them have gone off; in some instances almost by whole regiments." The British were as jubilant and hopeful as the rebels at Manassas; while, to complete the analogy, General McClellan appears on the stage in the person of General Lee (ominous conjunction) as the dreamed-of deliverer, while the defeated Washington is despised, if not rejected. An American officer in the camp writes to a friend, "General Lee is hourly expected, as if from heaven." He had had some minor successes at the South, like our then favorite, and was looked upon for more than two years by many patriots as our only savior.

We were soon driven from New York, and the American cause would have perished that year but for the brilliant raids of Washington at Trenton and Princeton. The next spring he was driven from Philadelphia, after the two fatal fields of Brandywine and Germantown. The campaign was redeemed only by the capture of Burgoyne, in which Washington gained nothing, and Gates everything.

The terrible winter of Valley Forge settles down as a shroud over the handful of bleeding and starving soldiery. The French alliance alone relieves the dismal prospect. The arrival of a French fleet the next spring at the mouth of the Delaware compels the British evacuation of Philadelphia. Washington pursues and fights the drawn battle of Monmouth. In fact, no decisive victory in open combat ever crowned his arms. The triumphs of Greene and Gates were added to his other troubles.

Thus stood affairs in the summer of 1778. Burgoyne defeated, the French alliance effected; only these. The following year was one of unvarying disaster. We attempted to take Newport, in conjunction with the French fleet, and failed. New Bedford was burned, and the adjacent country laid waste. The coast of New Jersey was similarly ravaged, and a body of infantry, under Pulaski, was surprised and bayoneted, after the fashion faithfully followed at Fort Pillow. The winter saw Savannah and Charleston, with the whole country south of Virginia, fall into the hands of the enemy. Norfolk and Portsmouth were burned, and property to the amount of two millions of dollars destroyed. New Haven and the Connecticut coast were sacked. Washington with a little force was cooped up in the Highlands, incapable of relieving the ravaged sea-coast, or of descending upon New York, and avenging the insults on the head of the enemy. Thus stood the military situation at the end of three years. A ragged, mutinous corps was all that were between the country and its subjugation. They were powerless to assail or to defend. The capture of Stony Point, ten days afterward, was almost instantly followed by its abandonment, so difficult did Washington find it, before Wordsworth, —

> "To keep
> *Heights* which his soul was competent to gain."

Compare this condition of affairs with ours in the same space of time.

Every post south of the Potomac and the Ohio, at the beginning, was in the hands of the rebels; the whole of Kentucky, of Missouri outside of St. Louis, of Virginia, West and East, of the Mississippi below Cairo. The Relay House was our advance post. Three years have passed, and where are we? Swept back in terror from our first field, we have steadily gained ground. Western Virginia is ours, and the most of Eastern; Missouri, Kentucky, Tennessee, Arkansas, most of Mississippi, portions of Louisiana, including the metropolis of the Gulf, Northern Alabama, and Georgia, the edge of Florida and South Carolina. The lines of the rebellion are pressed back in their center from the Ohio almost to the Gulf.

The Mississippi has been stripped of its batteries. No frowning forts prevent commerce. Its capital receives Massachusetts principle from a Massachusetts governor. Their second city, Nashville, second to none in its pride of place, is ruled by the candidate of the friends of union and liberty for the second office in the gift of the nation. The foe is penned up in Charleston, Richmond, Atlanta, and Mobile, except the few that ravage the plains of Texas. All of these are under investment. Charleston is half consumed, and Richmond threatened by the national cannon.

We are not compelled, as was Washington, simply to repel assaults on our intrenchments. Our troops celebrated their last 4th of July, not as they did the one before, in victories won on Northern soil, but in the very center of the rebellion, with their hand at its throat and their foot on its heart. Richmond and Atlanta, the two *foci* of the blazing comet that

> "From his horrid hair
> Shakes pestilence and war,"

are within the guns and the grasp of our armies. How superior are our successes to those our fathers had won in the same space of time!

2. The moral victories are not less striking, nor is the comparison of the two wars in the progress of their ideas less valuable. The Declaration was thought premature by many friends of the cause, as has been its twin brother, the Proclamation. At the first ballot in Congress, June 8, only seven States out of the thirteen voted in its favor. Introduced by Richard Henry Lee of Virginia, and seconded by John Adams of Massachusetts, it was opposed by Dickinson and Wilson of Pennsylvania, Robert R. Livingston of New York, and Edward Rutledge of South Carolina, not because it was wrong, but premature. July 1, it was opposed by four States, and was finally carried, with New York silent, but hostile. There was a like division of sentiment outside of Congress.

Mr. Lincoln's Proclamation has provoked far less bitterness among the friends of the Union than did the Declaration; yet we find that two years later, when British commissioners appeared in New York, and sought to beguile us from our steadfastness, they were unanimously, and even contemptuously, repulsed. It was then that the offer of ten thousand pounds and a high office to Dr. Rush drew from him the famous reply, "I am not worth purchasing, but such as I am, the king of England is not rich enough to buy me." They declare that Great Britain has granted all the colonists originally demanded, appeal to the colonial government against Congress, seek to stir up Protestant and Puritan prejudices by calling the French allies Papists, entreat the lovers of peace not to let the ambition of a few members of Congress ruin their whole people, and threaten increased chastisement if their offers are rejected.

All their efforts were vain. Congress coolly publishes their appeal in the public journals, and treats them with confident disdain. So great had grown the public sentiment in these two years of most moderate success.

In other respects the public conscience had not grown. Though the war was waged professedly for the rights of man, they still failed to see the iniquity of slavery. In no instance did a state decree emancipation, and summon its slaves to its banners. These were treated usually as they are by the rebels to-day — made useful in the camp, sometimes in the field, but with no idea of granting them their rights as equals. In the third summer of the war, 1779, a body of soldiers, having captured some slaves with a British outpost on Lake Erie, sold them for five hundred pounds, and divided the money as booty. To-day, our soldiers, making such a capture, would put arms in their hands, and welcome them to their side as brethren.

But as they progressed rapidly in their main idea of independence, so have we in ours of liberty and union. It is doubtful if, in the winter of 1860–61, one man in a thousand believed in a free and united nation. The South was defiant, the North indifferent. If the Union stood, it seemed evident that it would be only as the tool of the slave power. Now, the men who believe in its dissolution are as few or as powerless as those who then believed in its salvation; while through the South, in a multitude of places, are its numerous, fearless, and tireless friends that then were gagged by the mailed hand of secession.

So also — and herein we augur the best of results — the public conscience has grown more rapidly than the public resolution. When the war broke out, how deep was our detestation of the negro! how feeble our hatred of slavery! Probably three fourths of the three months' soldiers were far better haters of the cause of freedom than slavery. They went not chiefly as volunteers, but because they were members of already organized regiments. The first regiments of volunteers were of a far different composition, though even these grew slowly in the faith. Yet they grew. Negro soldiers, but a year ago, marching through the streets of Boston, amazed the whole land; now they are as unnoticed as their white brethren in Baltimore, and even march, though fortunately for their foes, as prisoners and without arms through the streets of Richmond, exciting unspeakable terror even in this unsubstantial military form in their Macbeth murderers. They have won their way to the front; they will yet to commissions and commands. All honors await patient and steadfast souls.

Meanwhile elsewhere the renewal of the land goes forward. Congress has abolished all its fugitive slave law iniquities, including that which George Washington signed and Josiah Quincy resisted. It has also abolished distinctions of color in the cars of the capital, opens the courts to their testimony and their rights as appellants — compelling Judge Taney, we trust, ere he shall vacate his seat, to respect many a right where he declared none existed. It prohibits slavery in the Territories, and almost secured universal suffrage there, and the abolishment of slavery in all the land. Maryland accepts the ordinance of 1787 at the same time that Congress abolishes that of 1793.

Thus in our ideas we have advanced as rapidly as our fathers did in theirs. They waxed strong in independence amid the storms of disaster and death. So have we in our equally great idea of union, and far greater one of liberty.

3. The financial question is of far less importance than that of ideas or arms. We could afford to sacrifice all our business and all our wealth so that we should preserve unweakened our national boundaries and political principles. Yet in this field we have great ground for gratulation.

Many are affrighted at the value of gold and the depreciation of the currency. They may find encouragement in the history of their fathers.

The issues of paper began with the issue of the Declaration. In eighteen months it amounted to twenty millions of dollars of Continental currency, besides large colonial issues. Thus far there had been no depreciation. In this they were our superiors as financiers, for our gold remained at par a year only after the war began. Their decline, however, was much more rapid. Loans, lotteries, and other devices were tried, but without success. New bills of credit must be issued; they were refused by the people. Congress declared that they "ought to pass current, and be deemed equal to the same nominal sums in Spanish dollars," and that "all who refused to take them should be considered enemies of the United States." But still their best friends declined to receive their currency as equivalent to silver. The States were called upon to make this refusal penal, but declined. They were urged to tax their people, but also refused. Again appear the Continental greenbacks. Sixty-three and one half millions were issued in 1778, making the total to that date over a hundred millions of dollars. By the 4th of July, 1779, they had reached one hundred and sixty millions of dollars. The dollar went down to five cents. The loans and foreign debt were only thirty-seven millions and a half. A riot broke out in Philadelphia while Congress was in session in consequence of this disastrous condition of affairs. At the end of the year the issue had reached two hundred millions, and the value, three cents.*

Thus stood, or rather thus fell, at the end of three years, the finances of the Revolution. There was a deep beyond this lowest deep, whither they plunged before the paper Declaration of 1776 became a living reality. How do our three years of conflict compare with these? Our loans are nogotiated readily, our interest paid in gold steadily. Our

* See Note XV.

currency has reached six hundred millions, or, with the local issues, eight hundred millions; not thrice the amount of theirs. Two dollars and a half, not thirty dollars, can buy a Spanish dollar. Our real estate and other property, which was estimated at more than sixteen thousand millions in 1860, has not decreased in value. In this most tremulous of all the nerves of society there is unspeakably less agitation than in the days when Jay brooded, like Chase and Fessenden, over this question of finance, and Congress wore anxious brows in their painful and ineffectual deliberations.

The results of this state of the finances were not unlike what prevail to-day. The extravagance and seeming abundance of these times obtained then. "If I were called upon to draw a picture of the times and the men," says Washington, in a letter to Colonel Harrison, the father of the future president, dated December 30, 1778, "from what I have heard and seen, and in part know, I should in one word say that idleness, dissipation, and extravagance seem to have laid fast hold of most of them; that speculation, peculation, and an insatiable thirst for riches seem to have got the better of every other consideration, and almost of every order of men; that party disputes and personal quarrels are the great business of the day, while the momentous concerns of an empire, a great and accumulating debt, ruined finances, depreciated money, and want of credit, which in its consequences is want of everything, are but secondary considerations." At Philadelphia he saw and lamented the folly and extravagance of the people, "spending three and four hundred pounds for an assembly, a concert, a dinner, a supper, while the great part of the officers of the army, from absolute necessity, were quitting the service, and the more virtuous few, rather than do this, were sinking by sure degrees to beggary and want." "Meantime," says Irving, "it was hard to recruit the armies. There was abundance of employment, wages were high, the value of money low, consequently there was but little temptation to enlist." How aptly do these times mirror forth the same image! Washington, too, found contractors his bane. He calls them "the murderers of our cause," and exclaims, "I would to God some one of the more atrocious in each State, was hung in gibbets upon a gallows five times as high as the one prepared for Haman. No punishment, in my opinion, is too severe for the man who can build his greatness on his country's ruin." He would have deemed Forts Warren and Lafayette slight repayal for our modern plunderers. The rise of "shoddy" was more marked, and its sway more perfect, than in this day. Says Hildreth, "In place of the old mercantile interest, almost annihilated by the Revolution, a new money interest had sprung into existence since the war, and as the resources of Congress and the States diminished with the rapid decline of public credit, began to exercise a constantly increasing influence over American affairs. Sudden fortunes had been acquired by privateering, by rise in the prices of foreign goods, by the sutlers who followed the camp, and by others who knew how to make money out of the great public expenditure. It was remarked that while the honest and patriotic were impoverished, rogues and Tories were fast growing rich."

They had no stocks in those days, and so put lotteries in their place — a fitting substitute.*

* In this matter of finance we are following precisely the experience of England in her attempts to ruin Napoleon. "For eighteen years she suspended specie payments in her desperate struggle with France. Bank of England notes were made, in effect, a 'legal tender,' by every person being protected from arrest who offered them in payment of a debt, and by the bank being guarded by law from any suit for non-payment of its notes. For eighteen years there was thus in Great Britain an inconvertible paper currency. From 1797 to 1815 the Bank of England *tripled* its circulation, and the country banks increased from two hundred, in the same time, to nine hundred and forty, or almost *five times*. The depreciation was, of course, enormous, not shown so much in the price of gold, which only reached forty-one in 1812–13, but especially in values: one

4. In other respects their condition was more deplorable.

(1.) Mutiny broke out in the camp. Whole regiments, with their officers, being ordered upon expeditions, refused. With great difficulty did Washington prevail upon them to abide faithful. Poverty at home and nakedness in the camp were destructive of patriotism.

(2.) Sectional jealousies embittered the army. The South loathed the North; the North was jealous of the South. New York despised New England; New England hated New York. The French assumed superior airs, which terribly inflamed the American mind. It was even thought dangerous for D'Estaing to moor his fleet in Boston harbor.

(3.) Added to this were the jealousies and feuds of the officers. Duels were not unusual. Gates, Lafayette, Mifflin, and others were involved in them. Stark threw up his commission in a pet at being slighted; Greene chafed at his post of quartermaster-general; Wilkinson, Conway, Gates,

pound in paper became worth but ten shillings in 1813, and, according to Doubleday, fell to seven or eight shillings, that is, a depreciation of nearly seventy-five per cent. The price of wheat rose from 53 s. 1 d. a quarter in 1797 to 125 s. 5 d. in 1812; oats from 16 s. 9 d. to 44 s.; wool from 3 s. 8 d. to 10 s. The rent of arable land increased from £88 6 s. 3¼ d. to the hundred acres, in 1790, to £161 12 s. 7¼ d. in 1812. But unlike America, no increase of prices arose in England from diminished labor; on the contrary, labor was supplied in abundance, and wages did not rise with other values; the final rise being only about twenty per centum in many parishes. In this depreciated currency, worth forty or fifty per cent. below what the foreign fund-holders had supposed themselves pledged to receive, did England pay her former creditors. Individuals, of course, complained, but it was manifest she could do nothing else, and this 'repudiation' has never, we believe, been thrown in her teeth. The enormous volume of paper money, amounting, according to the best authorities, to four hundred and fifty millions of dollars in 1815, naturally stimulated speculation and extravagance to the highest degree, and left its bad effects on the national habits. Still, despite all the inflation, and with a public debt in 1815 of some sixty-seven hundred millions of dollars, England resumed specie payments within four years after the termination of the war, and began a career of prosperity which has made her the richest nation in the world."

Schuyler, and many others were removed, or removed themselves. Above all, cabals flourished against the commander-in-chief. He was for a time less popular than Gates with Congress and the nation, and came near losing his command through the violent conflicts that raged around him.

In these minor yet not unimportant points we see how much more kindly Providence has dealt with us. No starvation has wrought mutiny in the camp; no jealousies and feuds among the officers have proceeded to blood; no cabals have materially weakened our cause; no sectional jealousies have separated the soldiers. The flags of every State have waved together in the smoke of battle, filling their followers with a common enthusiasm, which has only provoked them to love and good works. If we consider how frequent were personal encounters in the West and South before the war, and how intense were sectional jealousies and animosities, especially against New England, we have great reason to thank God and take courage at the marked harmony and cordiality of men and States during the fearful struggle.

"After the fathers shall be the children." In duty, in suffering, in reward we are the rightful descendants of these patient, persistent, triumphant heroes. Our cause is as holy, our success as sure. We may be called to emulate their virtues amid yet greater sacrifices. We may see our wealth melt away. National bankruptcy may be our experience also. Our credit may vanish from foreign markets and our own. Our tables may be thinly spread with the poorest fare; our garments may be of the coarsest fabric; our wharves, vessels may rot at them; and before our cities foreign armaments may hover. The dead may lie in every house, and mourning fill all the land. Still the great question is before us. Shall we prove our right to the blessings God has conferred upon us? Will we show ourselves heroic sons of heroic sires?

To that state our foe is reduced. What is their money

worth? Yet do they fight less strenuously? And for what? An empire of sin and hell — freedom to iniquity of every kind and of every degree of baseness; to overthrow the government and the institutions upon which hang the hopes of the world; to establish despotism here, to establish it everywhere; to put Maximilian safe upon his stolen seat; to abolish liberty in Chili and Peru; to extirpate democracy in Europe and America. If they succeed, we die. Crushed by enormous debts, distracted by standing armies, by burning animosities and divisions, we shall crumble into fragments, and the millennial glory that seemed breaking upon the earth will fade away, while the darkness of death will enshroud the people. Then let the minions of tyranny exult.

"Shout, through your dungeons and palaces, Freedom is o'er!"

What are our losses, actual or possible, to such a catastrophe? Shall Boston and New York be as Hamburg, mere commercial towns, with no influence beyond their suburbs? Shall rent and rending States tear each other in their mutual ferocity? Shall liberty become servitude, and the world be thrust back into the cave of despair, from which it is emerging? Then let us whine, and talk of ruin, because gamblers crowd gold toward three hundred per cent. Ruin? Well would it be if this insane thirst for wealth that is maddening the people were instantly ruined. Well would it be if trade should retire to the legitimate channels that it has so fearfully and destructively overflowed. Well would it be if our conceit and arrogance were ruined. But not our cause, nor our country. Of these we must say, "I am persuaded that neither poverty nor anguish, neither false friends nor fierce foes, neither treason nor death, shall separate me from the grand, eternal principles of our fathers, of our fathers' God."

Upon us the ends of the world have come. We are the depository of the civil principles of the millennium. There is nothing more theoretically perfect in the secrets of

Divine Wisdom for the construction of human society than has been given to us. If we shall abandon them through love of gain, or fear of poverty, we shall be accursed of God and all mankind, as were his chosen people for like treason. The American name, now the highest, will be the lowest in all the earth. The American flag will be the emblem of dishonor. Did England ask, How much will it cost to defeat Napoleon? Reverse after reverse for a score of years did not daunt her purpose. A Nelson slain, and the supremacy of the seas slain with him, an impoverished currency, distractions at home and disaster abroad, — these made her not waver. She persevered unto the end; and for what? To overthrow democracy in Europe, in England, in the world. Shall we be less faithful to the truth than she was to error? Shall we cringe, and crawl, and submit to disunion or a viler reunion because politicians plot for perfidious peace, and speculators press prices to fabulous hights? Not if they multiply their stratagems and their prices a thousand fold.

There may be worse years before us, as there were before our fathers at the close of the summer of 1779. Our loans may fail, our currency depreciate, distress and death may stalk through the land. What matters it? If faithful to God, He will give us the victory. The work will be done. Slavery shall die. Our foes shall be made our footstool. Our fathers shall not disdain their sons. Let us be of good courage, and take joyfully the spoiling of our goods, knowing that there is in store for us a more abundant recompense.

"O, well for him whose will is strong;
He suffers, but he will not suffer long;
He suffers, but he cannot suffer wrong.
For him nor moves the loud world's random mock,
Nor all calamity's hugest waves confound,
Who seems a promontory of rock,
That compassed round with turbulent sound,
In middle ocean meets the surging shock,
Tempest-buffeted, citadel crowned."

THE CRISIS HOUR.*

"TURN YE, TURN YE, FROM YOUR EVIL WAYS: FOR WHY WILL YE DIE, O HOUSE OF ISRAEL?" —*Ezekiel* xxxiii. 11.

THREE years of war! The three months which we were told at the beginning, by the most influential man in the nation, was to see its completion, have been painfully stretched into years. Again and again, and yet again, have our harvests of brave men been swept down by the reaper Death. Myriads of souls of heroes have descended untimely to Hades, and still the bloody sickle is thrust in, and still the dreadful harvest is gathered.

A nation that had almost ceased to believe in war, where peace societies flourished, and peace ideas were in authority, where a uniform was a bauble pleasing chiefly to the eye of children, where soldiering had become the synonym of folly and extravagance, where every one was fancying that the era of armed settlements of difficulties had passed, at least for this country, and that the Supreme Court and the ballot-box were its permanent substitutes — in such a land has raged for forty months the most terrific, the most bloody,

* A sermon preached in Boston on the occasion of the National Fast, August 4, 1864.

the most costly, the most violent war of the age, — we may truly say, with the great Napoleon's campaigns before us, — of the century and of civilization. For that great captain, in the same space of time, neither mustered nor mastered such mighty armies, neither swept over such breadth of territory nor slaughtered so many milliards of men. Not less than three millions, probably three millions and a half, of men have been engaged in active strife on this lately most peaceful soil. A number almost exactly equal to that of the victims whose cries to God caused the conflict, have thus been busily and too successfully striking at each other's hearts. Strange coincidence! Nay, a marvelous Providence, rather — a revelation of the righteous judgment of God. He saw His children writhing under the lash, and the lust of their oppressors, under the neglect, and scorn, and contumely of the whole nation. He has meted out a measure according to our sin. "There are four millions crowded into that black hole of America," He says — "four millions of My dear, despised children. Thirty millions walk proudly the upper deck, lift up haughty eyes to heaven, and present a daily prayer that My soul hateth. 'Lord, I thank Thee that I am not as this negro.' The four millions of their brethren also, daily, from the depths of their darkness and distress, cry to Me." And the Lord hearkened and heard. He descended from heaven. He set the battle in array. He made brother spring at the throat of brother, until, to the number of the enslaved, including even their wives and little ones, the mighty men are set against the mighty, while death and mourning fill all the land.

For the fourth time since this collision cast its bloody blackness athwart the heavens, have we been summoned by the National Executive to prostrate ourselves at the footstool of God in penitence and prayer for the salvation of the nation. Each time the wail has been deeper, as if the fear increased rather than diminished with each year; as if rather the true sense of our peril, and of the only source of our salvation, began to break more and more upon our blinded, hardened hearts. The wounds of the Great Surgeon and Physician probe deeper and deeper. Our cries break forth more and more sharply. The sense of our awful crimes and our just punishment grows and grows in our affrighted souls. We almost begin to confess our sins. We have not yet done it. This Proclamation comes the nearest to it. Yet this fails to mention it. We bow the head, but not yet the knee. We pour forth prayers, but no confessions, especially no tears. The nation has never yet broken forth in the penitential cries of David, when he had been guilty of a far less sin. We have been guilty of the enslavement and murder of multitudes of Uriahs. We have been guilty of the ruin of millions of Bathshebas. We have sold from them the children they have been compelled to bear, reducing both the innocent victims of our shame and their innocent offspring to more horrid bondage. Again and again did God send His Nathans to tell us our sins. Again and again, so far from listening to His prophets, and prostrating ourselves before Him, have we stoned those He sent unto us, and, sitting in our palaces of power and pride, have despised God and feared not man. We have never acknowledged the greatness of our sin. We have never cried, "Against *Thee*, THEE *only*, have we sinned, and done this evil in THY sight. Have mercy on us, according to Thy loving kindness: according to the multitude of Thy tender mercies blot out our transgressions. Deliver us from bloodguiltiness, O God."

Instead thereof, how carefully we have refrained from any confession of our sin! Not yet in a single Executive summons to penitence is there a direct reference to our national transgression. In the last it is glanced at only covertly and by indirection. The first cry burst from the lips of the retiring President, by whose connivance the crime of national destruction became organized and outbreaking. He dreamed not that God was to punish us because of our submission to the devil of slavery. He desired Union, but hated Abolitionism, and asked this people to entreat God to defeat the last and preserve the first, insulting Him by petitions against His most clear desire and purpose. Those that our later and better leader has issued, if less hostile to God, have not been more penitential or more honest in their confessions. Not one has mentioned the sin that has ruled us. Not one has asked this people to pray for its extirpation, nor for the uprooting of its baleful cause — our hatred of our brother for certain distinctions made by God Himself. The last comes nearest to the demands of God, and is, therefore, the most hopeful of all. It contains these lines, in the congressional resolution which the President has made the basis of his appeal : "To implore Him, as the Supreme Ruler of the nations, not to destroy us as a people, nor suffer us to be destroyed by the hostility or connivance of other nations, or by obstinate adhesion to our own counsels, which may be in conflict with His eternal purposes ; to implore Him to enlighten the mind of the nation to know and do His will ; humbly believing that it is in accordance with His will that our place should be maintained as a united people among the family of nations." Under such circumstances we come together. With a mighty war raging fiercely ; with wasting and destruction in all our borders ; with the heavens brass and the earth blood ; with the vultures and wild beasts of prey hastening from across the seas to devour the remains of the Great Republic ere it is dead ; with traitors on every side and in every haunt ; with a monstrous debt, rapidly accumulating ; with armies imperilled and almost exhausted in the long and doubtful conflict — surely never had a people greater cause to cry mightily unto God to come and save them.

Let us sorrowfully and prayerfully consider our duties

and perils in this dark hour. Dark as it is, God can make it light — God only. Let us implore His guidance, and, hardest of all, do His will, —

> "Hang on His arm alone
> With self-distrusting care,
> And deeply in the spirit groan
> The never-ceasing prayer."

The cause has a bright face, if we have the humility necessary to behold it.

Consider, 1. Our perils. 2. Our duties. 3. Our encouragements.

Our words may be familiar, even to the breeding of disgust. But that should not prevent their solemn consideration. Novelties are unseemly in the house of mourning. And such is this house to-day. Novelties are not needed in the front of the army. Earnest, courageous, steadfast discharge of most familiar duties alone deserves the victory. So with us. It is not flights of fancy that you need, if you crave them; not subtilties of casuistry, not windings of metaphysics, not poetry, nor rhetoric, nor oratory; these are as much out of place as they would be in a fire engineer seeking the extinction of a furious conflagration; as they would be in a captain striving to get his ship, freighted with a precious cargo of humanity, from the rocks against which she is dashing. How hollow and heartless would seem fine phrases and postures from such a man in such an hour! Much more now should we feel that our sole business is to hear and do the will of God. Hear with trembling, do with zeal; hear with contrition, do with hope.

Gather about His oracle. Stand upon His tripod. Let His afflatus breathe its divine breath into our weak and earthly natures, and lift them up to the stature and the manners of the sky.

I. First, then. What are our perils, or why may we fail? "Fail!" you say: "impossible:" the very word is treasonable. Nay, that depends on the spirit with which it is uttered. Isaiah was no traitor because he warned Israel that unless they repented they should perish. Nor Jeremiah, nor Amos, nor John the Baptist, nor Jesus Christ. The traitor is he who wishes or seeks the ruin of his land in the interests of iniquity. Not so the patriot. He warns that he may save. So, by divine direction, scattered through His word, by the authority to me committed, I must declare to this people the possibility of failure. Our efforts so marvelous and so mighty, our expenses so great, our sacrifice of life so costly, our zeal so fiery, may avail naught. The Ship of State may go down among the breakers, among which she has so long been rolling. Why? Why may we be blotted out of the family of nations? Because of our unfaithfulness to the divine idea upon which this nation alone can live. Our perils are not from our foes, but from our God. Is there evil in the city, and the Lord hath not done it? Did He not tell His chosen people in the solemn threatening of Moses that, if they kept not His commandments, He would blot them out of the earth? And has He not long since fulfilled that threat against five sixths of the nation, including the very tribe to which Moses belonged? It was He that brought the armies of the heathen to their gates. It was He that drove them into captivity, and made them servants of their enemies. It was He that abolished Israel from among the nations of men. Thus does He now "speak unto us in His wrath, and vex us in His sore displeasure." Our perils are not from Lee and Davis, nor from Napoleon and England, not even from Vallandigham and "the Courier," but from God. These are but the instruments wherewith He executes His punishments.

We may fail, for two reasons. 1. Because we are so false to Christ as a people. 2. Because we are so false to the lower professions we boastingly avow. When one stops to consider how glaring, how intense, how universal is the impiety of this nation, he may well tremble for its existence. In this city of the Puritans, hardly a thousand young men avow themselves the servants of the Most High God. Hardly ten thousand, young and old, are active members of Christian churches. Where you meet one God-fearing, God-praying youth, you will meet ten who drink and swear, and are lovers of themselves and of sinful pleasures rather than of God. The same proportion exists throughout the country. Not four millions of the twenty-four in the Free States profess religion — not one million of its twelve millions of males — not one quarter of a million of its four millions of young men between sixteen and thirty. Not one in ten, the whole land through, are voluntary servants of the Most High, — hardly one in twenty. With the female portion of society the ratio is less horrible, yet it is sufficiently fearful. The vast majority of them, who in other lands are almost entirely devoted to the Church, are utterly indifferent, and usually hostile to the claims of the Gospel. We are a prayerless nation. We lament the wickedness of Europe, the desecration of her Sabbaths. But we forget that their worst Sabbath-breakers attend service at least once in the day — that the church is crowded, if also the theater. We, with a more baleful consistency, seeing that the two are incompatible, abandon the Church entirely, and throng the haunts of pleasure and of sin.

Should we not tremble for our country when we think of this sin? Why should God strive to preserve a nation of idolaters, idolaters of the vilest kind, worshipers of self and sin? What reason has He for covering this continent with a deluge of Sabbath-breaking, worldliness, infidelity, and crime? The righteous few He can save, or transfer to heaven. Let the Christless many perish in their sins.

2. But this peril is increased, if we consider how false we are even to the pretensions we make. As a people we avow our independence of Christ. We never take His

name upon our official lips. We never recognize Him as our Sovereign, nor His Gospel as our law of life. But we make great professions, nevertheless. No people were ever more boastful; not the English, not the French, not the German, all very boastful nations, ever bragging of their prowess, their talents, their taste. Yet none of these proclaim their principles as their glory. None of them say, "I am the believer in the equal rights of every man." An almost obliterated inscription upon the arch of St. Martin, in the Boulevards of Paris, has the faded words, "Liberté, Egalité, Fraternité;" but they do not blaze, by decrees of her emperor, from her present Arcs de Triomphe, her halls, her flags, her journals. They are not on the lips of her rulers. No word has been more upon our lips these last three years than Democracy, — not the false, but the true. We are the representatives of its claims among men. We are its armed defenders. In our victory it lives; in our failure it dies. We have stirred our assemblies with harangues upon its nationalities. We have fired our soldiers with appeals for its preservation. We have filled our press, our pulpit, our people, with its inspirations. Yet we still hideously disregard its most plain and palpable injunctions. We compel one fifth of our people to live by themselves, to fight by themselves, to marry among themselves, and even to worship by themselves. They are more apart than the lepers of Jerusalem. Here and there we grant them the ballot-box; here and there the privileges of schools. But never do we ignore the color of their face or the crinkle of their hair. Never do we say, "Away with the most violent foe to our organic idea! All are one in Christ Jesus." As a nation, we burn with contempt. We call them to our armies, but it is to hold inferior places. We give them no commissions, nor commands. We separate them into regiments by themselves. We give them posts of honor and of danger, but still by themselves. Why should we put them thus apart from their brethren? Why cling to our prejudice more violently than an Englishman to his? A murder is committed there in a first-class carriage. The public is affrighted. How shall its repetition be prevented? A dozen devices are suggested, but the simplest device of them all — the introduction of the American rail-car — nobody dares to propose. Why? This compels too great familiarity. "We must be by ourselves," says wealth and blood, "even if murderers buy seats in our carriage and kill us, because of this excess of gentility. So we say to our African blooded people, "Keep by yourselves, even if such separation causes our national destruction."

What an answer to our loud-mouthed professions of equality and fraternity! What a mockery of our lives against our lips! It would be ludicrous were it not for its awful results. The Jews, who proclaimed themselves the depositary of God's will, and then slew His own Son, were not greater hypocrites than is America to-day; nay, they were not so great, for their light and knowledge was far less than ours. They did not know that He was truly the Son of God; we do know that these are truly our brethren. Our Declaration is read every Fourth of July, and broken every other day of the year, and that also. Our friends and neighbors, who have dwelt in this land as long as we, nine tenths of whom have English blood in their veins, and one half of whom have more of that blood than of their original African, all of whom, if entirely and directly from the lowest tribe of Africa, are included in our national creed,—these fellow-citizens and fellow-men, born of our blood and on our soil, are shut out of the legitimate workings of that creed. They are disfranchised in thirty States of this Union. They are despised in them all. Why should we talk of victory? Why dream of it? What claim have we to it? Is the Church erect and godlike in this matter? Is any Church? Is ours? We had many jubilations in our quadrennial council, because we concluded no longer to harbor a certain class of sinners, when there were no more of these sinners to be harbored. But when the question was asked whether there was any objection to admitting a colored brother to our Conferences, it was answered gravely by the committee to whom it was referred, and their report accepted by the Conference, that "there was no *legal* objection"—as if there were moral; thus elevating their prejudices into the dignity of divine law. Then they proceed to organize colored Conferences, but give them no right of representation in the General Conference. Church and society join hand in hand in this sin, and God is not letting them go unpunished. Society stamps upon them, crushes God's image and Christ's brethren, and their own, into contemptuous dust. What Church would imitate the example of the first Gentile Church — that of Antioch? Simeon, called Niger, put his ordaining hands on Barnabas and Paul. Where is the Church composed chiefly of white members, where a black man is one of its officers, and ordains its ministers? even such ministers as an apostle, and such an apostle as Paul.

The like treatment the nation, as a whole, gives to its children, its poor, its unfortunates. Its orphans cannot have the same asylum as those of its white neighbors, though both may come from one house, nor can its children attend the same school. Everywhere, save in a few of the New England States, does this curse reign. Is it any wonder that we are in peril? We are wrestling with the Almighty, not for a blessing, but a cursing. We annul His laws, despise His children; and can we hope for prosperity?

II. But perils nerve true men to their duty. An enemy at our gates makes the coward pale, makes a hero cool and calm. God, who sends the dangers because of our sins, sends salvation, if we repent and forsake those sins. We may see our duty in the dreary horror of our danger. As the brave commander sees his when his vessel shivers in the roaring breakers, as the competent officer discerns and discharges his in the surprise and shock of battle, so should we. We who profess to be Christians, let us seek and follow the way of escape. "Gird up thy loins as a man," is God's reply to us, when we faint, and whine, and beg, as we are rebuked of Him. When Joshua lay on his face, and asked God if He was going to destroy the nation which He had redeemed with such great wonders, the Lord answers with appropriate scorn, "Get thee up. Why liest thou thus upon thy face? Israel hath sinned, and they have also transgressed My covenant which I commanded them, for they have even taken of the accursed thing, and have also stolen and dissembled also." How have we dissembled! "Therefore they could not stand before their enemies, but turned their backs before their enemies, because they were accursed; neither will I be with you any more, except ye destroy the accursed from among you." Joshua instantly leaps up, and sturdily follows the will of God; and lo, ere the week is out, so far from being driven down into the valley of the Jordan, back upon his camps and his families, he is chasing his enemies down the opposite hill-side, across the plains of the Mediterranean, and halting sun and moon in the heavens till he completes the work of subjugation. Had this nation been as earnest in its fastings and prayers, had its President and Cabinet, Generals and Congress, been as sincere in their humiliations, they would years ago have chased their enemies into the Gulf, and peace and liberty have long possessed the land. But they are not sincere. We are not honest before God. Our honest President here fails in honesty. He was honest in seeking the expatriation of this portion of his people, he is not in seeking their elevation. He still refuses to pay two Massachusetts regiments the same as the rest are paid. He refuses lieutenancies to those who, were they white and foreigners, would have been made major generals for their skill and valor.

What must we do?

1. Pray for the conversion of this people. The Holy Spirit must renew us after the image and power of God, or we perish. This nation must be holy or unholy, Christian or infidel. It must be converted. The Church should rest not, day nor night, praying and laboring for its salvation.

2. The nation must conform to its lower but hardly less vital principle of democracy. There is no alternative betwixt a perfect democracy and a monarchy. Europe has proved this again and again. She attempted a mixed democracy in the Italian cities, in Venice, Florence, and Ferrara. They became soon dukedoms, and then appendages of a kingdom. She tried it in Holland, but the Princes of Orange despoiled their people of liberty in conferring upon them nationality. She tried it in Flanders, but Ghent and Bruges gave allegiance to a ruling class, and lost their rights and liberties by their error. France tried it, but developing a military leader to preserve her liberties against leagued tyrants, that leader robbed those he assumed to protect. So will it be here, if we persist in declaring our rights are based on color. If we, who are of the aristocratic blood, declare that any tinge of Africa expels its possessor from the heritage of equality, we shall assuredly resolve ourselves into a monarchy. We shall become as Greece, Rome, Venice, and Holland. We shall lose all our rights as equals. The dominant class will be reclassed, as in all aristocratic countries, and the stratifications of our society will be solidified and permanent. As the Irish, who hate the Negro, are almost as completely excluded as their next lower neighbor from the superior rank of Americans, so shall we find others above us, and on the top of all some selected families, with ducal, royal, or imperial pride and power.

If we would escape this calamity, we must abolish our prejudices. We must be true to our principles. Will we be? God waits for our answer. To-day, if ye will hear

His voice, harden not your hearts. Our fathers hardened theirs, and He swore in His wrath that we should not enter the desired rest. Will we persist in our sin? If we scoff at His commands, if we nickname His principles, as His people and His work have always been nicknamed by a mocking world, when they started upon their mission, then He will laugh at our calamity and mock when our fear cometh, when our fear cometh as desolation, and our destruction cometh as a whirlwind, when distress and anguish cometh upon us. Calamity and fear, distress and anguish, are all upon us. Beware lest you hear the scorning voice of a scorned God sounding through terrified souls, "Where now is thy confidence, thy strength, thy glory? Woe to rebellious children, who seek counsel, but not of Me. The Lord doth have them in derision." Let us hasten to expel this kind that go not forth without prayer and fasting.

3. A third duty, not less imperative, is to cordially support, while encouraging, the Church and the nation. We are not of that class who abandon those they seek to convert. We do not hate the Church because we condemn her short-comings. We do not traitorously oppose the government we hope to save. With all its faults the American Church and the American nation are, to-day, the advance guard of the human race. They may be chastised, they may be slain, because of their sins. That work belongs not to their children, but to their Creator. He can create and He destroy. It is ours to correct, to instruct, to aid by our prayers, our utterances, our sacrifices. For this work we may be required to lay down our lives. The period of volunteering for this service is past, that of drafting is coming. We may in honorable ways maintain our government without the surrender of our lives. We may loan the government our moneys; we may restrict our expenses; we may give liberally for the relief of our sick and wounded soldiers, and for the desolated families of the fallen heroes; we may thus,

in many ways, illustrate our patriotism. But we may be required to go yet further in our zeal and our service. The call of the nation may summon us to its service. Substitutes may not be secured, and if secured will not always answer the summons to duty. The cause of liberty and humanity may demand our life. Let us not refuse the gift. It was right and proper for the persecuted Christian to try to escape from his persecutors; but if caught, if summoned to trial, then he must manfully face his fate. Paul could not say, "I stand by my vows, but I will hire a trained gladiator to fight the lions in my place." These were duties that could not be transferred. So now it may come to us. Let us meet it as the sons of our fathers, as the brothers of those who are now in battle array, or who have fallen for our salvation. You, too, may yet be called to give the parting kiss and start for the perilous field. Humanity hangs in the hazardous balance. Let its principles not fail for lack of your support. Pray, speak, fight for Christ and your fellow-man.

III. What are our encouragements? Many say, "To what purpose is this waste of life and treasure?" We have seen it is for purposes of punishment; we shall also see that it is for purposes of mercy. God has chastened us very sore, yet far less than our desert. He has compelled North and South, alike guilty, if not equally, to scourge each other with bloody rods. He has arrayed millions against millions, and made the whole land rock with His thunders. In the midst of our sufferings, He has wrought salvation for His sufferers.

1. Slavery is practically dead. Whichever way this war terminates, this iniquity ceases. If the South maintain their independence, without foreign aid they can keep no slaves in their borders. The nations that desire their success will scorn their alliance with that barbarism alive. They will, undoubtedly, adopt an oligarchic system of government, in which white and black will hold inferior, servile perhaps, but not slavish positions. Those awful sights, so

frequent and familiar in this land but four years since, are gone forever. The auction-block, the separated families, the plied lash, the illimitable concubinage, the enforced ignorance and bestiality, the chained coffles traversing the States, the prison-house, the whipping-post, the hell upon hell of torture, shame, and sorrow, the land of darkness and the shadow of death, we can never see again. Many talk pertly of this, and say, "Five dollars expended in cowhides will restore the old system." Others as pertly say, "An amendment of the Constitution alone will save us from the returning flood. Hasten to erect this sea-wall while the tide is out." My friends, the Constitution did not kill and cannot kill slavery. It died BY THE VISITATION OF GOD. It can never come to life again. As easy is it to revive gladiatorial shows in Rome, or Druidic burnings of children in England, or the wanton worship of Venus at Corinth, or cannibalism at Otaheite. The slaveholder himself is cured of slavery. Jefferson Davis declares they are not fighting for slavery, but for independence. Their only cry for thirty years, increasing in the culmination of the outbreak, was, "We fight for slavery, not independence." They know they cannot restore that system. With no fugitive slave law, with a North intensely hostile to slavery, with the world hating it, they must abandon their darling demon. It has gone down, down to its wicked hell, down beyond all resurrection. Enough has been accomplished for all the dreadful cost. With a great, but not too great a price, have we won this freedom. An institution many believed would endure for ages, lies prone for many a league. Millions of its victims, escaped from its devouring jaws, are exulting to-day in irreversible freedom. State after State is wheeling into the line of liberty. Praise God from Whom these blessings, so great, so marvelous, have flowed.

2. Hardly second has been the great uplift of the despised race. Much yet remains to be done, but much has been

achieved. They walk our streets with erecter mien than ever they wore before. The scornful white begins to discern comeliness in their countenances, and grace in their steps. The lighter shades, Mrs. Kemble Butler can assert, are improvements on the mere white and red of our complexions, and many respond, "Amen." The lovely children of slavery are smothered in the ardent embraces of fastidious and lately loathing dames and damsels. They are warmly welcomed to our pulpits. They are made the advance guard in our most desperate assaults. They will mount the ramparts of Richmond, and aid in dictating terms of peace to their once arrogant masters.

That the work is not accomplished should not make us repine. If Grant fails to take Richmond, and Sherman Atlanta, the campaign has not failed. We have marched to the heart of the Confederacy. We have kept their armies pent up in their capitals, with but brief and temporary escapades therefrom. We have possessed ourselves of two thirds of their territory east of the Mississippi, and one half of that beyond. We have not yet drained our first quota of fighting men, between twenty years and forty-five. The large class below and above those ages are still unsummoned. If Grant is delayed before Richmond, it is not for our destruction, but purification. The new draft of five hundred thousand men must embrace two hundred thousand blacks. Ere another year, if the war lasts that long, they will be Colonels and Brigadier Generals in the United States army. The favorite nickname of the negro and the nation, "Sambo" and "Samuel," is of the same origin. Is not this prophetic of their future identity? Our victories are encouraging; so are our defeats. We have moved forward as fast as we deserved to move. There is much to be done before the war for democracy can be closed by complete victory of democracy. Desdemona loved Othello because he had saved her country from destruction; so must we his American kindred.

When Jules Girard, the lion-killer of Africa, had slain one of these devourers of the people, he says, "Even the women crowded around the man with thanks and praises, who a month before would have fled from him as from a noxious beast, whose very appearance is repulsive. Now they talked, and wondered, and chatted, with a mixture of familiarity and respect that they would not have shown even to one of their own countrymen." So, when this rebellion, the awful master of our land and lives, shall have been slain by the very hands which it was started to enslave, we shall fall upon our knees in gratitude to our deliverer. And as deliverers are always beautiful to those they save, so will these who were to us before like the French soldier to the Arab women, "a noxious beast, whose very appearance is repulsive," like him become objects of respect and admiration, of regard and love. We shall see in them the features of a common parent. Adam and Eve will beam from their countenances. We shall welcome them as brothers and sisters, and the long nightmare of our fears and hates will break up, while the flood of bliss in us, and the sunshine of peace streaming upon the land, will make us glad with exceeding great joy.

3. The last encouragement we should do wrong to omit is that which comes to us from foreign lands. Not the decrees of monarchs, not the scowls of titled leaders and their toady flunkies, but the honest, earnest, unanimous, passionate regard of the people. There was more joy in Manchester than in Boston when the Kearsarge sunk the Alabama; as much delight in Paris as in New York. The people are with us. It is their war. All people are here fighting their masters. The "mudsill" is contending with the Corinthian capital; "the greasy mechanic" with the scented lordling. The revolutions of the last century paved the way for the progress of this. If we win, Europe is theirs. The United States of Europe will wheel into line with us, perchance ere the century shall close, and kings, nobles, and

standing armies, palaces, pride, and aggrandizement of lands and houses, will be scattered like Charlemagne's bones, so that none shall gather them. The movements in England against primogeniture and for manhood suffrage * will triumph soon after we shall subdue the rebellion, and then the family of the Conqueror will bid a long farewell to all its greatness.

There is no other possible solution for that ever-recurring problem, if we win. And we shall win.

> "This fine old world of ours is but a child
> Yet in the go-cart. Patience! Give it time
> To learn its limbs; there is a Hand that guides."

Great as is our impiety, our insolent scorn of God and His children, our infidelity, our worldliness, our crime, yet He will spare us. He will redeem us. The world's future shall not be blotted out with our destruction. As He spared His rebellious people in the wilderness, not for their sake, but for the sake of the world, so will He now spare us. As He punished that generation with destruction for their unbelief, so He may this; but our children, growing up without our prejudice, with more than our patriotism, shall preserve this land for liberty, for fraternity, for God and His Christ. They shall dwell together, unmindful of color and of origin. They shall be one in love, and in life. As in heaven, so in earth, this region of all nations, kindreds, tribes, and tongues shall dwell together in unity — Asiatic, Afric, European, American; Chinese, Negro, Indian, and all; one people, the people of God, with one law, one liberty, one destiny; the founders of the New World, wherein dwelleth righteousness. "For a small moment have I forsaken thee, but with great mercies will I gather thee. In a little wrath I hid My face from thee for a moment, but with everlasting kindness will I have mercy on thee, saith the Lord thy Redeemer."

* Her victory for suffrage was won in three years after our war ceased, that of freedom of lands will soon follow.

THE WORLD WAR.*

"BEHOLD, THIS ONE IS SET FOR THE FALL AND THE RISING AGAIN OF MANY." — *Luke* ii. 34.

AMERICA proclaimed war against the thrones of Europe when she declared her Declaration. The irrepressible conflict began at that moment. It has continued ever since. It is increasing to-day. It may come to blows to-morrow. The babe Christ, as Simeon told Mary, was set for the fall and the rising again of many in Israel, that the thoughts of many hearts should be revealed. Herod's palace and Hell's palace felt His presence. Great disputes, greater wrath raged in both. The events were noised abroad in hill, country, and valley; from shepherds to Eastern magi and kings. Not only were the events a subject of discourse; issues sharp, violent, deadly, instantly arose from them. The massacre of the babes and the flight into Egypt were but the beginnings of a warfare that has gone on, unceasing and without truce, even to this day. How many empires have fallen; how

* A sermon preached on the occasion of the Annual State Fast, in Boston, April 4, 1864.

many have risen since that hour! Not always were His allies flying or Himself in flight. The Babe was triumphant, even in seeming disaster. Gods, devils, and sinners were alike controlled by Him.

> "They feel from Judah's land
> The dreaded Infant's hand;
> The rays of Bethlehem blind their dusky e'en;
> Our Babe, to show his Godhead true,
> Can in His swaddling bands control the damnéd crew."

So was it with the American nation in its infancy. When born it amazed tyrants. When but a child it confounded the doctors of monarchical political philosophy, and now, when tyrants, doctors, and the ruthless mob of sycophantic priests and press cry "Let it be crucified!" they cry in vain. Christ only once yielded His life to His murderers. Death hath no more dominion over Him. No more hath it over His. In His Church and in His State, — the body whereof the Church is the soul, — shall He go forward conquering and to conquer.

The words which announce my theme should not affright you. Many people are very fearful of a war with Europe. "Don't proclaim the possibility of a war with England. Have not we enough on our hands to-day?" My friends, we *are* at war with England. We have been at war with her for almost a hundred years. We must continue it till one or the other is subjugated. It is a war of ideas, a war of principles. Whether or not it shall clothe itself in armor and flow in blood, God knows. He ordained the conflict, He will conduct it to its divine, triumphant issue. Let us on this day of national humiliation and prayer consider these most vital, national questions.

Man cannot escape his responsibilities. Gifts and duties are born together, by the creation of God. We are required to-day to view those gifts, not in their own blessed light, but in the shadow and more serious glooms of their attendant duties. The Christian, when he first feels the pulses of the divine life rising in his soul, fancies his life is to be a Gaudama paradise of the perpetual contemplation of his delight. He soon finds that not only must he fight if he would reign, but he must fight if he would live. So we long fancied that we were to enjoy the blessings of our wonderful system of Union and Liberty without disturbance from within or without. We were aroused from our luxurious trance by internal enemies rushing fiercely upon us, disarmed and enervated in body and soul. We leaped to our feet, and looked hither and thither for aid; and, lo, the very faces that smiled so blandly upon us an hour ago, how cold, how scowling now! What hauteur, what undisguised contempt, what sensitiveness to the remotest and most unintentional interference on our part with their pretended rights and dignities! What hastening to cast loving side-glances at our foes!

Did we say, "France is our old ally. Surely she will sympathize with us?" We were compelled to read, as a response, the imperial letter, declaring our dissolution essential to the safety of Europe. Did we say, "England, our mother, our commercial ally, who boasts in her liberty, and boasts in her abolitionism, she will earnestly espouse their cause who represent this liberty and abolitionism in the fiercest struggle to which they ever have or can be subjected?" We were surprised to behold her, in advance of all others, proclaiming not merely the desirableness, but the *fact* of our dissolution, conceding our rebels belligerent rights, and aiding them with vessels, armaments, men, means of subsistence, and far from least, unceasing words of compliment and encouragement, through Parliament, the platform, and the press?

They were consistent, we not. They were wise in worldly wisdom, we fools. But we have acquired wisdom in the painful school of experience — the only school in which it can be learned. They saw that an earth so small as to have five World Conventions of its industry in ten years, whose ocean channels, bridged with multitudinous ships, would practically disappear when the telegraphic wire should make both hemispheres throb with one pulse; whose industrial wares and devices were simultaneously sold in India, Europe, America, and Australia: such a pent up Utica could not endure two radically and bitterly hostile systems of government in equal supremacy. The American Idea appeared among these throned powers and pretensions, as the Nazarene among the gods of Greece and Rome. It could allow their existence neither as equals nor inferiors. No niche in the Pantheon satisfies its claims. One or all must die.

Their wisdom will be the more clearly seen, if we notice how vital are the differences between the two systems of society. What is this man-child of America, against which, from its infancy, the kings of the earth have instinctively set themselves, and the rulers taken counsel together?

I. Three ideas were born into organized society in the birth of the American nation.

1. A successful revolution in favor of human rights. Other revolutions have transpired in the world's history, not a few. This was the first that appealed to the world in behalf of the world. "A decent respect for the opinions" of mankind is in the inaugural sentence of the Declaration. It is fittingly completed in the enunciation of certain "inalienable rights" — not of themselves merely or chiefly — but of "all men." Rev. Jonas Clark, who heralded the Revolution by brave words, that were half battles, spoken often in the church on Lexington green, by which his flock was strengthened to begin the armed strife, by brave deeds there, was permitted at the close of the

century to write the inscription for their monument. His youthful political sermons glow in its first line: "Sacred to Liberty and the Rights of Mankind."*

What previous people ever proclaimed such a doctrine, ever felt its inspiration? Their revolutions were local reactions from local oppressions. The Cromwellian revolt was against the absolutism of Church and State. It did not affect the world, because it did not feel its oneness with the oppressed of the world. Its religious character was thus expansive, not its political. Hence every religious, but no civil Protestant, saw and sought the Protector's protection. The Protestant Waldensians felt his uplifting, the Papal Irish his descending arm.

The Dutch uprising was a brave resisting of a foreign foe. They regarded themselves alone, their deprivations, their duties. Hence they never flashed their energies into like suffering and seeking peoples. They had so died out of the memory of men that their eloquent historiographer has enjoyed the privileges of the novelist as well as historian in his narrative of their exploits. Earlier revolts were usually the struggles of slaves against the cord; if successful, slaves still, revelling, like triumphing usurpers, more bloodily than their dethroned masters, in the spoils of victory.

This was the first that stood upon principles as broad and deep as human nature. Hence the inspiration it has breathed into the human race. Hence, too, the ceaseless, Herodian virulence against it of all the monarchic and aristocratic tyrants of man.

It would be a curious and valuable study to know how and whence these vital ideas became the soul of our Revolu-

* This striking American usage has been revived in our present struggle; President Lincoln's immortal Proclamation closing in the Revolutionary style, with an appeal to "the considerate judgment of *mankind*."

tion and our national being. How did the cry of taxation and representation—the whole preliminary struggle become lifted up into the hight of a contest of a people for the rights of man? Was Puritanism or Rousseauism its father? Or did both of these seemingly most hostile elements unite in their common basis of personal liberty, and so build up the great idea of social, civil, and universal liberty? Was it not rather that the fullness of times had come, and God sent forth this new truth to renovate and unite the earth?

2. A second element of our national idea is the organizing of the disrupted mass into planetary States, wherein the central idea of liberty should have fullest scope under righteous law. It is an easy matter to destroy; the difficulty is to build up. The Israelites could be delivered in a few days. It took forty years to make them a nation. More miracles of Omnipotence, and the greatest of all miracles, the infinitude of the divine patience, alone changed the enfranchised mob into a mighty people. Cromwell could behead Charles. To rehead the State, "there was the rub." France found like difficulty. So have the Central and South American republics. Their triumphs were failures because of this weakness.

A far greater feat, therefore, than the accomplishment of our Revolution was the organization of the revolted colonies into self-poised, prosperous commonwealths. This work demanded the highest qualities—self-respect, obedience, industry, education, temperance, religion. They exhibited them in the highest degree. The sobriety with which they drank the cup of liberty amazed the world. Expelling from the continent the only power that could affect them, Europe looked to see here as elsewhere liberty speedily becoming licentiousness. But they failed to see the sight as logically as heartily desired. We were the lesson and the pattern of the world in our organific more than in our revolutionary life.

We built up our political temple in perfect liberty and in perfect solidity. Its pillars were of the hardest marble, though their finish was as velvet, and they touched the earth with the ease and grace of

> "The herald Mercury,
> New lighted on a heaven-kissing hill."

The State became the home and garden of liberty, sheltered by the walls of law. It brought forth fruit after its kind, of many kinds, and of unspeakable sweetness and refreshment, while the leaves of its tree were for the healing of nations. Thus, before the Union was formed these independent communities had attained civil manhood. They were separately free and prosperous, though as yet disunited, and therefore weak and chaotic in their relations to each other and the powers of Europe.

3. There must be a force added that shall make them one, and so change chaos to cosmos, worlds to a universe. This is our greatest apparent characteristic. By this we become the *American* nation. Had it not been formed, no such nationality would have been known, for no State could have been recognized as the representative of this continent. Virginia, New York, Massachusetts, or the united New England might have had boasting sons. Not one of them could have spoken the proudest word man as man has ever uttered,—"I am an American." To say, "I am a Roman," was but to proclaim one's self connected with a city. To say, "I am an Englishman," is but to boast of connection with a bit of an island. To say, "I am a Frenchman," "German," or "Italian," is proclaiming a nationality narrowed to a strip of a continent. "I am an American," asserts an heirship to a hemisphere. It is next to saying, "I am a man."

This step was necessary to create a nation. The segregated sovereignties must become a congregated sovereign.

How shall it be done? Can it be done at all? It is an experiment that has never succeeded. Palestine tried it and failed. Greece tried it and failed. Rome, Venice, Holland, and others, have called themselves republics, but they never made their provinces their equals, much less made the whole a unit, of which they were but the same fraction as their fellows. Nothing in history was encouraging. Yet necessity was laid upon them. They saw that their freedom, personal, social, civil, would avail them nothing if contending States were to dismember the continent. The Union must be, and it was.

This made us a people. Europe took small note of our quarrel with Britain, only as the separation humbled a haughty neighbor. France helped us more out of revenge for losing the Canadas than from any hope or fear that we should become a powerful nation. Our disorganized state, for several years after peace, was after the former pattern. "There is no escape," shrewd politicians of Europe say, "but in the old way — a monarchy gradually developed out of weak and warring tribes." There was but one way of escape, and of that they dreamed not. It was by framing a Union, in which some of the most vital rights of sovereignty, such as the making of war and peace, regulating commerce and currency, and representation at foreign courts, were forever relinquished; while others equally vital, as the tenure of property, and punishment of death, were retained.

The Union closed up our pupilage. We entered on our majority. It lifted us out of the obscurity of barbarous and fighting clans into a compact, vigorous, free nationality, and made the world behold the dawning of a new day for humanity.

It may be asked, "Was not the trail of the serpent over all this?" Yes, but Eden was Eden if the devil had crept in there. The theory of our fathers was right. It was faithfully applied to all our people, save one fraction. It was conferred in form, though not in feeling and in fact, upon them in some of the States. Our present struggle to preserve the last of these blessings, is because we had become false to the principle that gave life to the first, and so to all. We are wrestling with principalities and powers without and within, to the intent that our Union and Constitution may conform to our primal and preëminently vital doctrine—the liberty, fraternity, and unity of mankind. This is the threefold cord of individual, State, and nation, which binds America together. The least right of the least citizen is preserved intact by the State in its sphere, and the Union in its, while the volitions of all flow in a mighty and steady volume through the whole realm, and move it, as with one impulse, to universal influence, perchance universal dominion.

II. Such are the principles first introduced into civil society, on a grand scale, by the organization of the United States of America. Can we fail to see that they are in most direct and violent conflict with the civil institutions of Europe? The supporters of those institutions see it if we do not. It is written in the history of Europe ever since that day. The very year that saw the inauguration of Washington saw the fires of democracy burst forth from beneath the throne of France. Within four years from that date they had consumed that throne and him that sat upon it. The oldest and haughtiest house in Europe had set in blood, while the titled blood of its supporters had daily flowed, a dark and dreadful stream, past the Tuileries into the reddened waters of the Seine.

The kings of Europe banded themselves together against it, determined to put out the direful conflagration, or at least to keep it within its original bounds. Vain hope. Their very effort spread the flames. Democracy defied, marched forth in defiance. The flames leaped over the whole continent. Armed liberty swept away every throne in middle Europe, and cleansed the churches of their trophies of idolatrous obsequiousness. Crowns were trampled as mire in the streets. Imperial dust sleeping haughtily at St. Denis, Aix la Chapelle, and Spires, was driven into eternal exile. It swept on, a vast prairie fire, through France, Germany, and Italy. Everywhere the traces of the great conflagration are yet visible. All monarchic and aristocratic elements melted in the fervent heat. It changed at once, and in spite of momentary reaction, changed forever the face and the soul of the civilized world.

III. The question naturally occurs at this point, Why were not these successes successful? Why did a reaction set in that has maintained its supremacy, in spite of all attempts to the contrary, to the present hour? The answer usually is, that the people of Europe were not fit to enjoy the liberties they had secured. John Adams began this charge as early as 1790, when, in the interests of aristocracy and England, he called the French people "a nation of thirty millions of atheists." Others fastened upon them other equally false imputations, such as their ignorance, violence, lawlessness, brutality. They are the staple excuses with which the tyrant ever defends his tyranny. The people of France, even in the bloody outbreak of the September massacres, as a body, were peaceful and placable. That fatal month but feebly repaid the contempt and cruelty of centuries. They would have maintained their liberties, and developed them in solidest and comeliest perfection, but for three reasons, for none of which are they directly responsible — the hostility of the priesthood, the league of frightened royalties, and, sad conjunction, the neutrality of America. The first caused infidelity, the second, war, the third, defeat and re-subjugation.

The Papal Church clove to its natural ally, the throne. Of one aristocratic nature, they share one destiny. The sense of right in the breasts of their devotees they strove to trample out with the hoof of ecclesiastical authority. The people saw their rights; they saw no form of Christianity asserting and defending them, and they renounced the truth for a season, because it was made the servant of a lie. Yet never substantially out of Paris, never in the masses there, was Christ rejected. They staggered blindly, without the appointed guides, but they groped not in utter darkness. The same experience has partially transpired here. Men of active conscience and profound sense of the right saw the Church speechless before the horrid demon of Slavery; nay, in many of its organizations prostrate before it; and they have been tempted to reject, not only the sinning Church, but the divine truths which have thus been held in unrighteousness. Yet as here so there, the people would have rallied from the shock their infidelity gave to their conscience; the Church would have been rent as here, and its ministers largely allied themselves to the cause of man as well as of God, and faith and worship would have crowned and sanctified a triumphing democracy. This consummation was prevented by the war into which they were drawn by the league of all the thrones against them, and the refusal of this nation to aid them in their struggle to maintain their liberties. This neutrality created immense excitement at the time of its adoption, sundered Cabinets and Congress, threw Washington, though President, into the minority, and organized the party which is now breathing its last, and which is dying solely because it abandoned the only principle on which it began to be, earnest devotion to the rights of man everywhere.

This doctrine has been a chief source of evil to ourselves and to our cause at home and abroad. It was a departure from principle under the guise of selfish policy. It was the first temptation and the first fall of the American nation, and the prolific parent of all our woes. The sword has been found two-edged; and the stout British arm has made it cut as deep into our vitals, as our youthful arm did into that of the more youthful French republic. The chastisement it has inflicted has revived the once potent views as to its character, and the restraints, unjust, unbrotherly, ungrateful, and unwise, which it imposes on our proper duty in the affairs of nations.*

Slavery, the parent of our aristocracy, and parent of disunion and war, sprung into new life on Washington's proclamation of neutrality. The first Fugitive Slave Law was signed in the same year and by the same hand that had signed that proclamation. So soon did this fatal germ shoot up from the error-planted soil. That tree has grown with steady rapidity. We sat weak, sick, and dying beneath its pestilent shade. By a clear working of Providence, the bitterest and extremest foe to our national ideas grew out of their very root, because we sought to selfishly confine them to ourselves. The essence and perfection of anti-liberty and anti-Union flourished in the soil of a selfish liberty and Union. Had we vigorously aided in the establishment of the former ideas abroad, the latter would have never flourished at home. Our spirit would have informed our action, and the earnest defense of liberty there would have speedily delivered us from the power and the presence of slavery here. Had we aided our friends then we should have had no enemies now. That neutrality destroyed our friends and multiplied our enemies. No less than six republics, the fruit of our loins, have we sacrificed to this mistaken policy. We refused to hear France when she cried to us, as she saw the armies of Europe gathering under the lead of our greatest foe. "Let the galled jade wince," we wickedly cried; "our withers are unstrung." Lafayette had exerted no small influence in giving Washington a free nation. Washington refuses to aid Lafayette in maintaining the freedom to which they had attained. The Poles appealed to

* See Note XVI.

our arms, but appealed in vain. Ireland twice sought to deliver itself from the clutch of its oppressor: we blandly witnessed its failure. The Central South American republics asked for coöperation: we gave them a resolution. To Greece we sent brave words but no sword. We have calmly seen Napoleon trample out in Rome the sparks that our hands had scattered. Garibaldi and Mazzini looked to us for aid, and looked in vain. Finally, Kossuth was sent to us, to save us, if possible, from ruin, by bringing us into active coöperation with our European brethren. He passed through the land, the most fêted and most lauded of orators. But he effected nothing. We were stupefied with the enchantments of neutrality and slavery. "What's Hecuba to me, or I to Hecuba?" we selfishly proclaimed. "Let us eat and drink, for to-morrow we die." Too true was our unconscious prophecy. We were then struck with death. "Material aid for Hungary? Hungary, torn by the talons and beaks of the double-headed eagles of Austria and Russia? Ah, no! Hungary has our sympathy, you our ears, — no more." We had eaten the lotus. It was not for us to go a Quixoting over the world rescuing imaginary Dulcineas from imaginary robbers. "Liberty and Democracy for Europe," did you say? Our grandfathers heard that cry, and stopped their ears. Why should we unstop ours. We were born deaf.

"Our voice was thin, as voices from the grave,
And deep asleep we seemed, yet all awake,
And music in our ears our beating hearts did make."

And with one voice the nation cried, —

"Let us alone. What pleasure can we have
To war with evil. Is there any peace
In ever climbing up the climbing wave?
All things have rest, and ripen toward the grave
In silence: ripen, fall, and cease;
Give us long rest or death, dark death or dreamful ease."

We refused to listen to his cry. He turned sadly from us, and lo, we were waked with the knife of our brother at our throat, while we cried wildly for help and no help came. How we staggered in blindness, and fell, weak with loss of spirit, of confidence, of friends, of the blood of our sons. Had not God lifted us, and animated us with principle, the higher and only life, we should have been as when He overthrew Sodom and Gomorrah.

Thus have His laws had their revenge. We have experienced the only possible result. The disease our fathers hated and feared, and hoped would depart, by the very inactivity they imposed upon us grew to an awful magnitude. The farewell address says, "Let us keep what treaties we have made, but make no more." Live in the swaddling bands of selfishness. Be the Japan of Christendom, and lo, our bandages, like a Chinese lady's shoe, compel weakness and corruption, not strength, sweetness and beauty. Our evils and perils, not repressed and eliminated by a vigorous out-door exercise, but nursed by an in-door luxury of indolence, make us faint even unto death. We have lived solely by the miraculous goodness of God.*

IV. But if we refused to accompany our principles with our prowess in their march through the earth, the principles themselves went forth conquering and to conquer. They could not be hidden under a bushel though we hid ourselves there. Our relations were, in reality, in spite of our adjurations and mercenary spirit, far more political than commercial. Our doctrines affected the theories of publicists; they soon affected the practice of the people. "Every continental writer on civil government, with a very few exceptions," says J. Stuart Mill, "for two generations, has been an ardent democrat." He traces this as directly to America as the tides in the harbor are traced to the outer sea. "A democratic republic," he says, "came to occupy a large

* See Note XVII.

portion of the earth's surface, and to make itself felt as one of the most powerful members of the community of nations." Had it been free in fact and free to act, it would have long since republicanized Christendom.

Every country felt that earthquake. Enceladus stirred, the volcano muttered, and kings trembled. Thrones rocked on the sea of a restless democracy. They would have been buried in its waves but for the rise of one man, who, like the inheritor of his name and seat to-day, sought to destroy the very principles through which alone he became the arbiter of Europe, its kings and its peoples. Still his course was ever felt to be against thrones and kings. On the walls of a hotel in Coblenz I saw a little picture of a company of European kings, to whom a messenger is announcing the escape of Napoleon from Elba.

"My God," cry they, with white lips, "is he come again?" Such a picture in that town, full of soldiers, and strengthened with the finest fortifications of Europe, is as significant of the popular sentiments as would have been a portrait of John Brown in the cabin of a Charleston slave. For though he betrayed the cause of democracy, he was ever and instinctively the enemy of the feudal aristocracy. Marrying into them, he was still like Samson with his Philistine bride, none the less the foe of her brethren.

Great Britain preserved herself from the eruption of these ideas in two ways. Having waged a long war with us in attempting to suppress these doctrines, her people, as is usually the case in belligerent nations, became largely hostile to the principles of those with whom they were contending.

But this cause was slight to that created by the fears and the vigor of her nobility and gentry. For forty years they struggled to suppress the growth and extirpate the root of the tree of liberty. In America, in Europe, on every sea and shore, they waged ceaseless war. Burke became their defender, and sold his birthright for a mess of royal pottage, doing for the cause of man, that had nursed him to greatness, precisely what his great successor, Brougham, has done in our day — turning on the principles and people that had elevated him, and fawning at the feet of a despising royalty. He had impeached king and nobles when he dared to confront Hastings, and king and nobles knew it, and never condemned that faithful ally. Not many years elapse before he whines, in eloquent terms, for the king and nobles of local oppressions as deep and damning as any committed in India. He leaves the people out of his category of British rulers. He was so sensible of his treason that he chose to be buried in a wooden coffin, that dissolution might be the more speedy, and his body escape the profanations with which the anticipated triumph of democracy in England would, he feared, assuredly visit it.

But the ruling class was not content with the service of pamphleteers, however able ; they imprisoned those who assumed, with any earnestness of purpose, the popular side — poets like Montgomery and Leigh Hunt, editors like Cobbett, lecturers, almost voiceless thinkers, every one who dared avow their sympathy for the cause of man. They have suppressed substantial freedom of speech to this day.*

* Speaking of the difference between English and continental publicists on theories of government, Mr. Mill significantly says, p. 11, "A similar [that is a democratic] tone of sentiment might by this time have been prevalent in our country if circumstances, which for a time encouraged it, had continued unchanged." He elsewhere declares (p. 33) that "the law of England on the subject of the press is as servile to-day as it was in the time of the Tudors ; " and while declaring in the text that there is no danger of its being enforced, has to confess in the notes that it was enforced as late as 1858. These laws were rigidly carried out by Castlereagh and Ellenborough, and caused a worse reign of terror in England than prevailed in France. Here a few tyrants lost their heads, and executions raged for a single month. There for two generations every lover of equal human rights has been prevented from declaring his sentiments. To do so now would insure the utterer a speedy acquaintance with the cell and axe of the Tower.

They stirred up a war with France, and compelled the Continental monarchs to make their territory the battle-ground against humanity. They developed the power of Napoleon, and thus attained their end, his triumphs establishing the despotism that they loved, and overthrowing the republicanism which they feared.

V. The present state of this conflict is not less important.

The degradation of our people before the slave power, and the almost total extinction of our liberties, the utter extinction of our sympathy as a nation with the peoples of Europe, had made their oppressors less fearful. Our name was yet a spell, perhaps, to evoke the spirit of democracy withal, but they saw that when we boldly supported and sought to extend the most anti-democratic institution in the world, that our name might call this spirit from the vasty deep, but they did not fear that it would answer us. They could safely send hither the heir apparent of their throne to receive our adulations, and to witness, with pitying contempt, an enslaved and dying democracy.

But the uprisal of a great people in the cause of its fathers, its fame, and its God, quickened all these ancient fears. They had visions of corresponding insurrections at home. Their martyrs for liberty, from Vane to Orsini, arose to avenge their cause by creating the free and equal state for which they had died.

Hence they instantly arrange themselves on the side of our foes. They leap to embrace the hideous monster of Slavery. Its bloody hand is at the throat of democracy. They trust it will stifle its divine life here and everywhere forever and forever.

1. The British government lead off in this degrading alliance. It brought forth fruit after its kind. The recital of the acts in which the feelings of the British aristocracy found expression would be longer than that in which our first Congress indicted its king. Before a battle had been fought,

even before an army on either side had been gathered, it took every possible step to insult, weaken, embarrass, and destroy our government, except that of active hostilities, and this was withheld only from fear of civil war at home. It sheltered piratical steamers in its harbors; and when our vessels of war lay in wait for them in the Channel, it put its men of war under their bows, with directions to blow them out of the water if they presumed to obey the orders of their government. And this too, not in British waters, but upon the high seas. It forbade our national vessels from staying in its ports over twenty-four hours, or coaling there oftener than once in three months, while its own vessels rode at anchor in our harbors. It recognized the rebels as belligerents before they had fought a single battle; when they had only mastered a single fort and a starving garrison. To do this was to recognize them as a nation; for nations only have a belligerent, that is, a war-making power. This it did not grant to Italy till all her battles had been fought and won. This it never gave to Hungary, though she was for months successful, and was only overthrown by foreign intervention. This it did not give to Poland, though she maintained for over a year a provisional government by arms as ably as the Confederates did theirs, and that too against a power it hates and dreads almost as much as it does the United States. The all-important difference is, that the rising of Poland is against it own institutions, our insurrection is in its favor. Russia is dangerous to its empire, America to itself. Russia may rob it of India, our ideas will rob it of England.

The whole scope of its proclamation was to confer nationality upon the rebels. So they understood it. So did we. So did England herself. It would have been followed by its legitimate acts but for the grand uprising of our people, and a fear of the future at home.

Her course subsequently was consistent. In her feelings

as well as policy that were exhibited in the Trent imbroglio, in allowing armed privateers to sail from her ports, in refusing to amend her laws while acknowledging their inefficiency, so as to control these pirates, she acted according to the theory she wished and purposed should prove true. Lord Palmerston was called in Paliament "our Confederate Premier" amid the applause of the house. He declared in his seat that "the difference between him and Mr. Cobden consists in the fact that Mr. Cobden considered that but one government exists within the original boundaries of the Union, while the administration have, *from the beginning*, ACTED as if there were two." That is, they gave the rebels a practical, but not formal recognition.

All this has been done by instinct. "Instinct is a great matter." It made them detect and worship monarchy in the disguise of the robber Slavery, as it made Falstaff discern and respect his master in the garb of a highwayman. It has been as natural and universal with the ruling classes, as has been our enthusiasm here for the Union. "Five sixths," Mr. Cobden declared, "of the upper classes were in favor of our disruption." As here a few adhered to slavery and secession, the apparent, against freedom, the real national idea, so there a few have stood forth for the theories and boastings of the nation against its root and ruling principle. These few were most rarely in governmental positions, much less of titled and gentle blood. Almost every lord, however mushroom, was meanly unanimous. Abolitionists like Brougham and Shaftesbury, liberals like Morpeth and Russell, men of tact without principles like Palmerston and D'Israeli, all took counsel together against us. The Duke of Argyle was almost the only titled exception to this universal law.

The gentry, who are the wall-flowers of the nobility, — outside wall-flowers, ever trying to creep over into the sacred inclosure, even if of such blood as Buxton and Wilberforce, turned up their noses at the dead democracy of America. "An ounce of civet, good apothecary," they cried, "these west winds smell dreadfully."

The lackeys of the Church, press, of the counting-house and factory, fell into like spasms. They all wore livery. They worshiped the upper, and trampled on the lower classes. They joined the upper in their detestation of America.

The Times declared that not a gentleman, member of Parliament, nobleman, nor representative Londoner sat on Mr. Beecher's platform at Exeter Hall. It carried its sycophancy to such a pitch that it asserted that "the two essentials of a government to-day are monarchy and money." Thus stood ruling England till success crowned our arms; thus in feeling stands she still.

It is in no spirit of invective that we make this record, but simply as students of natural laws, which work as clearly and inevitably in the realm of politics as in that of science and religion. They are the creatures of the idea that controls them — an idea irrepressibly hostile to that which has been in debate on our fields and seas, and which has come forth the unquestioned conqueror. They will yet rejoice in its overthrow, and in their absorption into the grander name than Queen, Lords, and Commons — even that of the People of England. That people we profoundly esteem. They have acted as nobly in their chains, as our slaves did in theirs. We doubt not their future sovereignty, and an increasing glory to the national name when that hour dawns.

2. But our conflict with continental crowns is none the less positive though less marked. It is less marked because those crowns have had all that they could do to keep their places on their masters' heads, — so intelligent and determined are their peoples. Blondin has too much to do in keeping his balance over the deadly-flying glassiness of

Niagara's stream to attend to the difficulties of rival gymnasts. The Pope, Francis of Austria, William of Prussia, Victor Emanuel, the King of the Danes, all are tossed on the wildest seas, and may in a moment be dashed upon the fatal rocks of Democracy.

Napoleon was the only one that could look abroad, and he more because he *is* a Blondin, the prince of tight-rope dancers, than because his vigilance is less or his peril less. From him learn all. He made our traditional friendship with France a deceitful brook. Why? Because his France is not France. She is garroted. He speaks for himself, not for his people. They are intensely democratic. Their elections show the vitality of their democracy. He knows that our salvation is his destruction, our destruction his preservation. Therefore has he steadily sought our ruin. With the complicity of England, Spain, and Austria he seized Mexico as the basis of operations against us. His success there drew forth the public congratulation of every crowned head on the Continent. They trusted that this triumph assured our overthrow.

The European Church, in its highest officials, has been their close ally. The guns of St. Angelo exulted over the fall of Mexico. The Pope went still further in revealing his fears of democracy, when he called Jefferson Davis "Illustrious President." The Protestant State Churches have been equally unfriendly. They see that the bands of Church and State will be the first to dissolve when the state and the people are one. John Bright, the future Premier of England, has already more than hinted at such a separation.*

VI. Such is the past and present conflict of America with Europe. It has a future. We can read it in their light.

* This step is already taken in the election of a Parliament pledged to disestablishing of the Irish Church. The elder must follow her daughter, and State and Church cease to be one.

It is simply this, *Europe must become a Union of Democratic States,* in league, if not one with America. The instinctive cry of the people of France and America just threescore years and ten ago must be answered, — "We are One."

Great truths are always simple. When first announced they are apt to appear visionary. Yet when once embraced they become as familiar and pleasant as light and life. The truth of the absolute unity of Man, how simple, how sublime! And yet when we see in a brightness above the brightness of the sun, whither it is leading us, how many start back appalled, —

"And each particular hair doth stand on end,
Like quills upon a fretful porcupine."

So this self-evident, imperative, fast-hastening event, how few believe, how few delightedly embrace! How many say, "Why, they are not fit to govern themselves." So we said, till within three years, "The slaves are not fit to be freed at once. They must be trained to liberty." Nobody but a little clique of so-called fanatics dared to cry, for thirty years, "Immediate and Unconditional Emancipation!" and they did not dare, had they desired, to add, "By the red arm of War." If they had, they would have perished, or ere their truth was born. But God has answered their cry, though in a way of which they dreamed not. The slaves were liberated in an instant, thrust out in a night, as were Pharaoh's, through our fear for ourselves, not regard for them. New Year's eve will ever be the American-Afric's Passover. And lo! at the sight every one exults. They declare it to be marvelously natural and proper. In fact, it is the only possible way.

So shall we see concerning this truth. It started from Independence Hall. It will not cease to march till it has subdued the world. Its line has gone out through all the earth, and its words unto the end of the world.*

* See Note XVIII.

Not a state, except the free state of Switzerland, and the wealthy state of England, but that has been rent with this new cloth sewed into its moth-eaten purple. The new wine is ever bursting the rotten bottles of hereditary privilege, from which they are trying vainly to exclude it. They are ever busy repairing their ragged robes of royalty, which the people are ever rending, but the Sartor Resartus has to do his patching with new cloth — popular suffrage, constitutional government, or some fresh-woven bit from the American looms.

The conflict is springing up in England. Her political managers are the shrewdest in the world. They have steered, with remarkable skill, their Ship of State. Through the war they held high carnival. They were warm supporters of the murderer of Liberty in France: they talked about Poland, but declared they would do nothing to save her. They allowed the people to compliment Garibaldi, while they rejoiced that Victor Emanuel had shot him. I heard Mr. Disraeli thus sharply and truly retort on Lord Palmerston, when he declared that the cause of the unity of Italy required the countenance of his government.

"The noble lord observed that not any generous word of sympathy, no word of approbation, ever came from me in favor of the Italians. That cannot be said of the noble lord. Words enough he has given the Italians; but what more he has given, the Italians know best. I can only say, that if all the encouragement they have received, and all the assistance they have had in their hard fortunes, were furnished by the noble lord, I doubt very much whether they would occupy the position which they now do."

Even these "windy inspirations of forced breath" were not given until a year after their liberties had been achieved. And these same rulers of a Protestant nation have since allowed Napoleon to suppress liberal institutions and freedom of religion in Mexico, and to seek to establish monarchy and papacy in that land, solely that their class might not be absorbed by the natural growth of democracy here and at home.

But that democracy is growing. Every ardent advocate of America is a latent or patent, a nascent or adult democrat. John Bright, their Quaker leader, — like our Quaker leaders, he who started the great reform, and he who for a quarter of a century has written the battle-songs of freedom, — is a bold and earnest fighter in its ranks. His head may yet grace the block in behalf of the cause of man. He has had the courage to say that a President elected by the suffrage of a free and equal people, is in a far loftier seat than one inheriting a throne. He talks of a world-republic after the model of America. His coadjutors, just returned to Parliament, will replace the fallen Cobden in their zeal for the people. Hughes boasted that the men of toil gave him his seat, and Stuart Mills was yet more pronounced in his adhesion to the principles which will necessitate democracy. Gladstone appeals from the most conservative to the most radical of constituencies. He must regard the people who trust him.

Poland, in its brief insurrection, revealed the same tendency. The proclamation of the national committee was based on that of President Lincoln's. The serfs were promised freedom and the possession of the soil they till, — in this respect in advance of our proclamation and action, — while loyal masters were to be reimbursed from the national treasury. Such decree, if carried out, would change the face of Europe. Lest it should be carried out by the success of the people, the three powers of England, Austria, and France hastened to inform Russia that she must make some concession, or they would take the matter into their own hands. Not by recognizing this decree and establishing the republic of Poland — a thousand times, no! but by the erection of some sort of a kingdom, whose movements should not jar too harshly the Prince Rupert's drop in which each of them dwells. The success of Russia in suppressing the uprising made them rescind their demands. It was not to humble her, but to save themselves, that they were so active. That success will yet result in failure: the principles of that uprising must prevail if their nationality fails.

Italy is thus breaking the bonds of centuries. Michael Angelo's gigantic, heavy slumbering Night is changed into the more gigantic, arousing Day. What life, what strength, in its Samsonian limbs! It will speedily awake, arise, and go forth as a bridegroom out of his chamber. He who has once trodden its soil, and seen the enthusiasm of its people for Garibaldi, whose bust and picture are everywhere, knows that its present government is but the brittlest of cords that holds for a moment the upsoaring eagle. France alone can stay the unification and republicanizing of that land.

Greece cast off the incubus of ages in an hour, and proceeded, in calmest style, to elect her ruler. I saw that election in Athens. It was exactly like one in America—the same talking in the streets and at the cafés, the same running of carriages with voters for rival candidates, the same counting of the ballots at the polls, in fine, a purely American idea, as is universal suffrage carried out in purely American style, in that most ancient and most famous of democracies. The ostracizing and approving shells and pebbles, carried round the Pnyx, were replaced by poll booths, inspectors of elections, ballots, and all the other paraphernalia of her sister more than twenty hundred years younger. Had not England restrained her, she would have declared herself of the political faith of her fathers. In conjunction with Napoleon, that power compelled them to continue their throne. They called a pale lad from the Rhode Island of European kingdoms to rule a nation of democrats, whose constitution, like ours, forbids any citizen from wearing a title. More than one Athenian said to me, at that time, that England would not allow them to establish a republic. She appoints their head as indifferently to their wishes or to the popular suffrage, over which they were so jubilant, as an Arab is to his daughter's choice of a husband, or a slaveholder's to his slave's choice of anything. A great time they had with their universal suffrage. The king they get had not a single vote. The prince they almost unanimously ask for, as well as the nation that invites him, are quietly snubbed by the Great Powers, so called, that adjust the affairs to suit their own convenience; and yet when there is an outbreak there, people say they are unfit for liberty. They had no outbreak till their rights as a people were trampled in the dust. King George affects the citizen king, going about in plain costume and unattended. If he is equal to this rôle he may reign a few years, because he recognizes the people; and he may not. Whether he reigns long or short, the inevitable future of Greece is freedom and democracy.

So is it everywhere, and everywhere it is taking more and more the threefold American form.

A revolution in favor of the equal rights of all. This is accomplished in Switzerland, Greece, Italy. No titles are allowed in the first two to any citizen, but few in the last. It is substantially so in France, and becoming rapidly so in Poland, Russia, and Germany.

The organization of these people into States, electing their rulers, and enjoying local independence and liberty.

Their union into one nation.

The pronounced sympathies show how rapidly this union of feeling, antecedent to a union of fact, is pervading Europe. Huge Garibaldi meetings were held in England, suppressed by the government professedly out of fear of the Irish, but really out of fear of the Ideas. Like meetings assembled in behalf of Poland, in London and Paris. The leaders of the same idea, in different states, are beginning to see eye to eye. Kossuth works for Garibaldi ; Garibaldi sends a proclamation to Hungary as he starts for Rome. Victor Hugo and Garibaldi issue proclamations to the Poles. Failure only binds them closer together, and nerves their souls for future victory. As Washington in Virginia, Adams in New England, Hamilton in New York, Franklin in Pennsylvania, and Pinckney in South Carolina, saw the absolute necessity of union for success, so these wise men are working together for one end. As the kings conspire against their peoples, so do these leaders of the people breathe one breath against their oppressors, — Union of all, Liberty for all.

Before this goal is reached, civil war will doubtless break out over the whole Continent. From Belfast to Moscow, from Scotland to Greece, the uprising may be bloody, desperate, universal. England, the slowest of all European states, is rapidly developing three parties — the radical democrats, radical monarchists, and timid go-betweens, whose sympathies incline them to the former, and fears compel them to the latter. In a late number of the London Watchman, the organ of the Wesleyan Church, the whole subject is summed up in an article against John Bright. It says, "That democracy may rule forever, from ocean to ocean, is a project so precarious, though so vast, that no wonder Mr. Bright's eyes can be so dazzled by it as not to perceive the Red Sea of blood which is now weltering between. We hope that the honorable gentleman, in the lack of other topics, is not about to preach up republicanism in England."

The people of Great Britain will follow Bright, or any other leader, through that Red Sea to the Canaan of equal rights that lies beyond. The very lull in English politics which that article notices, is precisely like that which occurred here as we were approaching the dread crisis. The questions of bank, tariff, foreign population, and papal influence, that had organized great armies under their banners, died out of the public mind, and one sole absorbing theme took their place.* Whether Mr. Bright has the qualities for the leadership in this struggle remains to be seen. He may be too old and too peacefully educated for the full demands of the hour. He may be the John Quincy Adams, seeing and saying what others will achieve. Some younger man, whom his sentiments shall inspire, may take up the standard when he pauses, and advance to death and victory. When begun, whosoever first falls will be followed by his destroyer. This lull can only be changed by the coming conflict between aristocracy and democracy — first with voice, then, we fear, with arms. The late election portends this future. The voice of the people was low, but it was clear; never so clear before. Their leaders must come to this issue, or give way to those that will.

On the Continent is witnessed a like uprising. The king and representatives of Prussia have been in a permanent feud for more than three years. They are getting into closer conflict. He is suppressing liberty of speech, as he has the liberty of the budget. But one issue can come ultimately of the struggle.† Napoleon and Paris are in open opposition. Denmark's late king threatened to transform his kingdom into a republic on certain contingencies. Though he failed to keep his promise, his people may not fail to remember it. They may say, "We thank thee, king, for teaching us that word," and proceed to do for them-

* The excitement that has sprung up since, and the center around which it revolved, confirm these views. The ballot has been extended, and a long stride made toward a democratic republic of Great Britain.

† The vast changes in Prussia are really the triumph of the people. A united Germany insures a German republic. Bismarck discerns this future, and is preparing the way for it.

selves what he shrank from doing for them. The tongues of fire leaping out of every crevice of the tottering statecraft of Europe, betoken an inextinguishable conflagration. Into this war we may be drawn.

VII. The many attempts at liberation that have been made for almost a century, have failed, for three reasons: the leaders of the people had no concert of action, while their masters were in close league; they had no sympathy nor guidance from the Church, and, especially, they had no nation to help them, while many nations were banded against them.

1. The first, as we have seen, is being changed. European democrats feel that as their arms and interests are one, so must their efforts be. But one barrier separates them — language; and that is ceasing to be a barrier. Switzerland, their model in its government, is their representative in its condition. Italian, French, and German almost equally divide their territory. Among the mottoes for a national celebration at Neuchatel, was this: "Our enemies say we speak so many languages they cannot understand us. Let them attack us, and they will find that we have but one tongue — the cannon." So will it be with the people of Europe, They will yet speak one word — Liberty — with one mouth, the cannon, against one foe — their masters, for one object — a European republic.

2. The second cause of their prolonged failure lay in the want of sympathy of the Church with their movement. The position of the Church in our Revolution was most valuable. "The opening ball of the Revolution," John Adams pronounced young Mayhew's sermon on the Higher Law, that he preached in the West Church, Boston, in 1750, on the anniversary of the execution of Charles I.; which the Puritans were compelled to recognize, but which he turned into an opportunity of defending the deed, and of inaugurat-

ing our liberties. It took a generation then, as it has in our present revolution, to develop the truths that must, ere they be perfected, bear

"The blood-red blossom of war, with a heart of fire."

With him, and after him everywhere, the clergy came to the defense of the great principles of Liberty and Independence.

Not alike fortunate was European democracy in its earliest conflicts. The Church was its chief adversary. It was constrained to oppose her in its attempts to obtain its rights. This wrought the scoffing infidelity of Voltaire and Rousseau. This, too, wrought her destruction. An atheistic democracy was more dangerous to the people than a corrupt and slavish priesthood. But to-day this powerful class are joining and leading the people. The dissenting clergy of England are becoming more and more identified with the political, as they have always been with the religious principles of their ancestors, the Puritan ministers of the Commonwealth. The Protestant clergy of France, by their unanimous letter to us of sympathy and encouragement, show themselves fit to guide their great nation in its escape from the Giant Despair castle, where treachery and violence have so long chained and beat it. The archbishops of Greece, first of all in the public ballot signing their names for a Protestant prince, while the constitution forbids any one not of the Orthodox or National Church, to ascend the throne, proved that they are willing to lead their people toward liberty at the expense of a wrongful edict of their constitution. Eleven thousand Italian priests petitioning the Pope to abrogate his temporal sovereignty, proves that Garibaldi has high and numerous helpers in this most, we might almost say only, influential body in that land. The Catholic and Protestant clergy of Hungary are largely identified with the people.

They refused greater privileges offered by the Austrian government than they hoped to obtain in their own independent action. Thus is the Church coming up out of the wilderness, the leader and benefactor of the people. Her conversion will go forward, and insure to the future European republic a stable and Christian triumph.

3. The last defect we may have to remedy. To save ourselves we may be compelled to save others. We shall then be the inspiring and molding nation that they have long needed. As England molded and inspired all Europe for a quarter of a century to resist and overthrow republicanism in Europe that she might preserve her own aristocratic institutions intact, so America, her grander daughter, may have to guide those peoples in a conflict for republicanism, however long, however costly, however bloody. We are the only great nation that represents the sovereignty of the people. We may be compelled to maintain that sovereignty everywhere with the sword. They turned our neutrality between themselves and their people into a like neutrality between us and our slave-mongering rebels. They set at naught a compromise *we* made, not they, by which, without their solicitation, we abandoned Europe, and declared this continent should be ours. We must abandon a vow, that we should have never made, to confine ourselves to this hemisphere. England is nearer than Mexico, France than South America. We may have to carry freedom there, in return for their attempt to bring slavery here. Mr. Sumner in his speech on our foreign relations, more than suggests this issue. He describes the armed intervention of Cromwell in favor of the Walensians, in words that glow with a kindred enthusiasm for the like oppressed, and struggling, and despoiled Hungarians, Venetians, and Romans of to-day. He says, —

"A mightier pen than that of any plodding secretary was enlisted in this pious intervention. It was John Milton, glowing with that indignation which his sonnet on the massacre in Piemart has made immortal in the heart of man, who wrote the magnificent despatches in which the English nation of that day, after declaring itself 'linked together with its distant brethren, not only by the same type of humanity, but by joint communion of the same religion,' naturally and gloriously insisted that whatever had been decreed to their disturbance on account of the reformed religion should be abrogated, and that an end be put to their oppressions."

He shows that Cromwell was not content with mere pronunciamentos, but sought to enlist the Protestant powers in their favor, and proceeds, before such a league can be effected, to intervene with arms. This martial display wrought the desired end. Had it not, the flag of St. George and the Cross would have waved in the mountains of Savoy, beside the banners of persecuted Protestantism, for the cause of Liberty of the Soul. Of this event, Mr. Sumner makes the following pregnant application. In his concluding passages, after describing our relation as a Republic to the European monarchies, he adds, —

"Born in this latter day, and the child of its own struggles, without ancestral claims, but heir of all the ages, it will stand forth to assert the dignity of man, and wherever any member of the human family is to be succored, there its voice will reach, *as the voice of Cromwell reached across France, even to the persecuted mountaineers of the Alps.* Such will be this Republic — upstart among the nations. Ay, as the steam-engine, the telegraph, and chloroform are upstart. Comforter and helper like these, *it can know no bounds to its empire over a willing world.*"

Even if this third element be kept from the seething caldron of European politics, so far as armed intervention is concerned, the other components will unceasingly disturb and ultimately dissolve their thrones. If we refuse to hear the cries of those who are "linked together with us by the same type of humanity and by joint communion of the same" political faith, our institutions and success will fight for them.

The two ideas are abroad in the earth; they are wrestling for the crown of the world. Democracy has clothed itself with continental thunders, is regnant in a mighty state. The world is too small for two such hostile systems to hold equal sovereignty. All peoples are fast becoming one people. They can have but one system of government. It must be that of themselves. We are its divinely appointed representatives and defenders. We may be its divinely armed and appointed propagandists.

Such is the clear, unanswerable logic of principles, the necessary precursor of the more evident but not more certain logic of events. Our propositions are stronger than Euclid's. They are the mathematics of humanity, of morals, of the Spirit of God.

Thus stand the relations, past, present, and future, of America to Europe, its kings and its peoples. The first century of our nationality is rapidly concluding. It is a century of greater progress in political thought and life than any, in some respects, than all its predecessors. In all this activity America is foremost. She is a sign that is spoken against. Yea, a sword has pierced through her own soul also, that the thoughts of many hearts, at home and abroad, may be revealed. Many states have already risen, and fallen, and risen again under her involuntary influence. That influence is but just begun. If she casts off the grevious sin that has beset her, if she humbles herself before her God and Savior, if she carries out faithfully her own principles of equality and fraternity through all her social and civil life, ignoring distinctions of color as she does those of language and birthplace, she will stand forth, under Christ, the redeemer and mistress of the world. The enslaved of Europe will hail her midday glory with greater acclamations than they have her dawning beauty. They will struggle the more fiercely in their chains. They will snap them asunder. We are set for the fall of tyrants and the rising of the nations. Our influence will not be confined to this continent, but will renew and unite the world. The nations that have so long sat in darkness, and have now seen the great light, will come to that light, and kings to the brightness of its rising. Thus and then will wars cease to the end of the earth, the millennial glory rest upon the world-republic, and universal liberty, equality, and brotherhood bring universal peace.

THE END NEAR.*

"THE MORNING COMETH." — *Isaiah* xxi. 12.
"THROUGH THE TENDER MERCY OF OUR GOD, WHEREBY THE DAY-SPRING FROM ON HIGH HATH VISITED US." — *Luke* i. 78.

FTER a long, long night of clouds, and darkness, and storm, thunderings, and lightnings, and tempests of blood, with faint gleamings of the muffled stars at times, to show us that the heavens still abide, yet with no grayness even betokening the actual dawn, suddenly we see the "King of Day rejoicing in the East." The shadows flee, the golden glory covers the horizon, and shoots its radiance across the whole heavens. Even the blindest bats of night, that beat their leathery wings and eyeless heads against the walls of the national temple, confess that something bright and beautiful is stealing over their feeble senses. They know not what it means or is. For they have torn out their eyes with their own claws. They feel a warmth, a sunniness, pervading their spirits, that compels their unwilling recognition of the coming day. But these poor, darkened creatures apart, the people see

* A sermon preached in Boston on the day of National Thanksgiving for General Sherman's capture of Atlanta, September 11, 1864.

the light, and rejoice in it, and hasten to the brightness of its rising. Most true in this case was the familiar saying verified — the darkest hour is just before day. Last July and August were probably the gloomiest months since the night of war closed us in. Our armies lay in their trenches while marauding bands vexed their rear. Our mines exploded only to our loss and not the enemy's. The North was invaded, and triumphantly trampled by robbing feet. For the first time since the war the enemy cut off our communications with the capital, and defiantly approached its very gates. Our villages were sacked and burned to the ground. Gold leaped up to three hundred. Provisions and wares followed at a yet swifter pace. The earth burned like an oven. Nature, too, lay sick with a fever, and seemed to be dying with the dying nation. And, as a fitting crown of all the calamities, thousands upon thousands of traitors, a generation of vipers, "a coil voluminous and vast," assembled in one of our greatest cities, the especial symbol and proof of the magnificent workings of our free institutions, on the birthday of our first great traitor, Benedict Arnold, great, but far less than these his children, and there under the guidance of men who had been openly consulting with our open foes for months before, with jubilant and hopeful hearts, plotted the dismemberment, the reënslavement of the nation — nay, not plotted, boldly exulted in her ruin.* Through the words of one who had once been placed by the nation in its highest seat, they defied the government to prevent traitors from seizing and controlling the polls, declared the only rebellion in the land to be that of the rulers against the people, spoke no word of reprobation against those who for more than three years have struck terrific blows at the national life, and but for God's right arm would have long since cast it as dead among the nations as Egypt or Rome. Such was the dreadful record of those

* The Chicago Democratic Presidential Convention.

burning months; drouth in the heavens and on the earth, the war hanging dubious, weakness in the hearts of the people, and treason stalking boldly through all the land.

> "The red-ribbed ledges dripped with a silent horror of blood;
> Echo, whatever was asked her, answered, 'Death.'"

Yet, lo! almost in the twinkling of an eye, the scene changes. The heavy clouds not only seemed to shut out the day, but to proclaim an everlasting night — the night of death and national destruction. Beasts of prey roamed everywhere through our land. Their hideous howls affrighted our ears. Across the continent rolled their cannon. The grave yawned, and multitudes of ghosts of cowards and traitors went gibbering through the streets.

And now we cry, the morning cometh! — the blessed morning of peace and liberty! It is really breaking. These are no cold, deceitful, auroral beams betokening a deepening winter. They are the true dayspring. The Dayspring from on high is visiting us. The present Thanksgiving Proclamation of the President has a more confident and cheerful tone than any of its predecessors. He penetrates the dread entangled forest. This valley of the shadow of death, with its fiery, flying serpents hissing and stinging, with its darkness, and storms, and desolation, its groans and death, — how dark, how woful, how deadly; he can almost see through it. Dangers yet stand as thick around him as serried soldiers, but a glimmering comes through the strait and narrow way that he is steadfastly pursuing, which bespeaks a blue sky, peaceful fields, and the light of heaven.

With these encouragements we are invited to assemble in our respective places of worship, and offer thanksgiving to God for His mercy in preserving our national existence against the insurgent rebels, who have been waging a civil war against the government of the United States for its overthrow. And surely no locality is more worthy of our assemblage than this. We are within a few rods of the spot where John Adams declared that the opening gun of the Revolution was fired. Where a young minister, in a city subject to a foreign power, and with all its wealth, office, and influence supporting that power, dared to preach a sermon on the Higher Law, defying that power in the name of his God, and first starting in the mind of this city the doctrine of Independence. To the same mind was due the other focus of our orbit, — the body of which Independence was the soul, — Union. Both came from one brain, and his a minister's. For while meditating upon the disconnected, and hence useless efforts, of the patriots of Massachusetts and Virginia, New York and South Carolina, as he was preparing to go to an association of ministers, he thought, Why not have such an association of patriots? why not of provinces? He instantly wrote his thought to John Adams, and the Union then first began to be. With such auspices hanging over us, we cannot be untimely in considering the great duties of the hour as Christians, as men.

But what proof have you, some half-hearted, perhaps some over-cautious soul may say, that the night is far spent? Are not the rebels yet firm and undaunted? Are they not armed, and organized, and active? Have they not possession of their original capital? Do they not yet rule in Charleston? What are your signs of promise? Let us put them into one bird's-eye view.

Suppose Jefferson Davis had been able to carry out his boasted threat at Montgomery before the opening of the war — that if war should come from secession, it was the North and not the South should be its theatre; we "should smell Southern powder and feel Southern steel." Suppose that in carrying out this threat New York had been taken by his armies within a year after that time, and had been kept in their grasp firmly to this hour, while two South Carolina generals had been its actual governors; suppose the Mississippi had been opened to its fountain, and St. Louis, and all the cities were in their hands; suppose an army had penetrated into New England, and secured Springfield, the center of our railroads, and the chief depot of our military stores, and had annihilated, by the same act, the last but one of our great armies; suppose that every one of our seaports was captured or invested, leaving only New London as a place where we could smuggle in a few of the necessary supplies for our army and our people; suppose that Boston was half burned,—Fort Warren a chaotic mass of brick and stone, — the lower half of this city, including its shipping, warehouses, and stores, up even to Tremont Street, all in ashes and abandoned, and that daily in our more retired portions the deadly shell should drop from the enemy's vessels which filled the outer harbor; suppose that gold had long since ceased to be an article of trade, and that our greenbacks had become so worthless that it took eight hundred dollars of them to buy a barrel of flour; suppose that Washington had been held in close siege for four months; that Lee had carried out his contemplated invasion of the North last spring; that on May last he had drawn Grant back from Fredericksburg, from Culpepper, from Manassas, and had thrown his troops around the south, and east, and north of the city, leaving only the west open; suppose that he had clung to this position ever since the middle of May, now throwing himself on one side of the Potomac and now the other, and, at last, by a sudden movement, had got possession of the Baltimore Railroad, from which assaults after assaults on our part were unable to dislodge him; suppose that provisions had risen in that city to famine prices, and even then our people, and our soldiers too, had scarcely nothing to eat: should we not think our end was near? Should we not prepare to accept any terms our victors might demand? This is an exact picture of the rebellion to-day. Its state is even worse than this. Three of their States are supporting the administration through military governments — Tennessee, Arkansas, and Louisiana. Only Eastern Virginia and the Carolinas are able to retain any efficient hold upon their peoples.

If every north-west State was thus ruled by military governors of the confederacy; if Pennsylvania and half of New York were theirs; if only Massachusetts, eastern New York, and the State between were ours, the parallel would be complete. Study your map, and your faith and patriotism will have free course and be glorified.

But if the night be so far spent, what is our duty?

1. Not to desert our posts. The morning is coming, but is not come. Should the watchmen engaged in protecting your houses and stores desert their posts at the first gray glimpse of dawn, your city would instantly swarm with thieves and murderers. They would rush out from their dens and coverts, whither they had been driven by your protectors, and lay waste and destroy. So if we slacken our arm, if we withdraw our troops, if, as some traitorously advise, we throw open our doors to their murderous feet, instantly they would swarm from every hole in the South where they are now shut up. They would rush to the Potomac. They would slay every Union man, white and black, in that whole region. They would open their ports to foreign emissaries and associates. They would assume their old defiant attitude with yet greater defiance, while we, craven of spirit, would hide ourselves from them, as we should from armed rioters, if they had possession of this city.

No, the only duty is to fight it out on this line, if it takes the whole century. There is no release in this war except by the death of its cause. There should be no relaxing of our efforts to compel their complete subjugation. The army should overflow with soldiers. The exhausted fighters, through this long, long night, should be encouraged by the faces of their friends thronging to their support. The young men, untrammeled by family cares and duties, should fly to the field. When Burgoyne seemed almost in the net which Schuyler, and afterwards Gates, had prepared for him, he was intrapped only by the multitudes that flocked to their banners. So when their last great army is penned up in its first stronghold, everybody that can leave his home and handle a musket should swell the heroic ranks, and see this huge, amorphous sin die its eternal death.

2. But our duty is also to support the government with our voice and vote at home. Every presidential election is important, but none has been so important as this. It was vastly important that the gigantic slave power should be opposed by the people ; that the great national uprising should be indeed an uprising, not a mere rolling over in sinful and slavish slumber. Therefore all the preliminary contests for liberty for twenty years were vital. It was vital that Birney should be nominated and voted for in 1840. Unless the child was born, it could never become the strong man. Unless the sentiment against slavery had condensed itself into political form then, it might not have conquered yet. For four presidential canvasses it was the subject of insult, of scorn, of neglect, and in the minds of few wise enemies, of fear. Said John C. Calhoun, "While abolitionism contents itself with talking, we are in no danger ; when it begins to vote, we are dead." Yet not till 1856, till arrogance after arrogance had been successfully exhibited by the slave power, till the right of petition in Congress, freedom of the mails, rights of citizens in Southern ports, rights of pleadings of State against State in the Supreme Courts, the freedom of territory north of 36° 30′ beyond the Mississippi, the right of fugitives from slavery

to their liberty, the rights of any man of any portion of African descent in the courts of the nation, had been all stricken down, a foreign state invaded and dismembered in the interests of slavery, members of Congress smitten for declaiming against the monster, a war waged with all the powers of the government for the subjugation of liberty in Kansas; not until these assaults on the national ideas and life had been committed could the people be sufficiently aroused to see their sin and their danger, and to declare their purpose to return to the old paths. Even then they failed to see it. Many honest men hoped for other ways of escape than by confronting in battle of leagued and banded States.

Another four years in the wilderness and Canaan was reached, the Jordan crossed, and the tribes of God in possession of His inheritance. Then came the long and bloody struggle, as with them after the passage of the Jordan. Four years of war and we appear again in our tribes to choose our ruler. Some say, "Enough of war! Let us make peace with the rebels. Any peace that will insure Union, or that will not." Joshua and his lieutenants are objects of unspeakable abuse. What shall the people do? Shall they elect a chieftain who will make terms with the idolatrous Canaanites, whereby one half of the territory wrested from them shall be restored to their control? Shall we give up Jericho, so miraculously conferred upon us, or Ai, for which we so bloodily contended, or Bethoron, down whose steeps we pursued the hostile chiefs in rout and ruin, while God held the light for us in the heavens to enable us to complete the work? Shall we restore the Gibeonites, to whom we have made solemn pledges, into the hands of their enemies, who will reduce them to bondage, and waste them with furious slaughter? "O, yes. Depose Joshua, and elect some one of those who cowardly advised against taking possession of the land. Depose him, and appoint one who shall secure for us a dishonorable peace and an everlasting war."

In such a crisis every lover of God and his country has but one duty to do. He must stand by Joshua. Treason in the camp is as fatal as the foe on the field. He must bear aloft the banner of liberty and righteousness, unfurled twenty-four years ago, and never to be laid up till the victory is entirely won.

Some object to the political canvass at such an hour. Yet it has its advantages. It allows the country to say whether it has confidence in its own principles and purposes. Had the vote been taken in this nation in 1779, at the darkest moment in our history, after three years of almost unsuccessful war, whether George Washington should still head the armies of the republic, and John Adams its Congress, it would have encouraged them more than a score of victories, and paralyzed the arm of their oppressors more than a hundred defeats, to have had the people, by an immense majority, declare their purpose to support their heroic leaders unto the end. So will it inspire our soldiers with fresh courage, stagger our enemies more than the loss of ten Atlantas, and cause the whole world to settle down into the conviction of the intense earnestness of the American people, if we reëlect our leader to the seat he has so ably filled.

The Church should unite as one man in this exigency. Prayers should go up daily for success in this election. Her salvation depends upon her faithfulness. She has had much to do with this revival of pure and undefiled religion. From the beginning her children have been found fighting for the cause of liberty and of man. She did more to develop the sentiment that was crowned in the elections of 1860 than all other influences combined. The great revival was a fitting and necessary prelude to that great election. Let her continue faithful and the work is done. Let her once more march to the ballot-box, an army of Christ, with the banners of the Cross, and deposit, as she can, a million of votes for her true representative, and she will give the last blow to the reeling fiend; she will keep, where she belongs, in the fore front of the nation in civil and social righteousness; she will be stronger to assail the fortress of religious error, and to effect the renewal of the land in holiness.

If she refuses this duty, if she listens to the siren voice of a seductive but fatal peace, if she is beguiled from her steadfastness by those who hate her with an unblushing and ferocious hatred, who in every bar-room and gambling hole throughout the land to-day are heaping upon her all manner of curses and revilings because she is true to the cause of God and man — if she shall league with these, her fate is sealed. She goes down, with Jerusalem of old, into dust and desolation. Her enemies mock at her, crucify her, kill her, and God will grant her no resurrection. The Church must do her duty in this hour, and that duty is, by every righteous means in her power to secure the reëlection of Abraham Lincoln.

3. But a third duty of the hour is, to maintain the whole truth as to the questions at issue in this conflict. The morning cometh, but a higher morning is also breaking upon the land. When the women were hastening to Christ's sepulcher on the morning of His resurrection there was a rosy flush upon the Mount of Olives. How gay and glad danced the flames upon the distant hills of Moab! How bright the face of Nature! Trees were rustling in their new spring robes, flowers were pouring forth their fragrance on the balmy air, birds were filling the sky with their matin music. They, perhaps, felt that the outward glory did not well conform with the inner darkness. The sun should still be darkened. It should rise every day in the garments of

mourning which it assumed in those dread hours of the previous Friday. But when they come to the sepulcher and find the stone rolled away, and the Savior arisen, they see with their souls' eyes why the sun seems to dance in the heavens, and the birds emulate the angelic chorus, and trees drop balm, while

> "Flowers laugh before them in their beds
> And fragrance in their footing treads."

Another morn had broke upon the world, a divine, eternal morn, of which this earthly and perishable one was but a feeble emblem.

So if we will lift up our eyes we shall behold another morning breaking on the land. The Dayspring from *on high* is visiting us. Peace comes with healing on her wings. There might have been a peace full of infamy, full of calamity, a peace that came from cowardice, that created disunion, that was sure to be the fruitful parent of unceasing war. Not such shall we see if faithful to the new sun that is now arising. This day began to dawn more than two years ago. When the President, in March, 1862, issued a proclamation to the Border States, urging them to abolish slavery with national compensation, and informed them that in case they did not, its abolishment might come from another quarter, then the day began to break; that was the first gray ray which pierced the involving dark. When six months later he announced emancipation in all the rebellious region, if, after three months' warning, they did not return to their allegiance, the grayness became golden. The east was ruddy with the rushing dawn. And when, on January 1, 1863, he proclaimed their liberty in all the land, and required the army to welcome them as such, the first segment of the solid globe of fire appeared above the horizon. The enrolling and arming of the slave, the abolishment of invidious distinctions of color in courts and cars, are further evidences that a true and glorious day is breaking; a day that no night shall follow, and in which peace shall be one with brotherhood; in which true democracy, the rights and fraternity of all men, shall be universally recognized and practiced. When there shall be no school to prepare white men to rule colored regiments, but such regiments shall be abolished, and men, without distinction of color, rule and serve in all the armies of the republic; when there shall be no white nor colored churches, but all in Christ shall be one in Christ.

This morning is dawning. Thanks be to God. This is more than the victory of Farragut and Sherman. Far greater is he that conquereth his own spirit than he that taketh a city. If the nation shall conquer its own proud, rebellious, unbrotherly spirit, it will do a far greater work for God and man than if it should annihilate every hostile power in the world. We know that work is the most difficult. Let us address ourselves to it, therefore, the most diligently.

While we do the first and second works, supporting the army and the government, let us not leave this undone.

Let us labor and pray that the only divine morning may indeed come. Our fathers had a rosy peace, but it was only for an earthly day. We found twilight fast gathering over it when this generation appeared on the stage of action. That disastrous twilight deepened into night — a night of storm and darkness; a night like that in Egypt, in which every household has sent forth exceeding great and bitter cries, for in every house has been one dead. We are emerging again into day. Shall it be like the other, a day of earth, stormy and brief? or shall it be a day of heaven, calm and eternal? That depends entirely on our faithfulness to the principles of God and His Gospel. Mr. Seward declares that if peace comes, slavery, as well as all other questions, must adjust themselves to that basis. If by this he means that this nation is not to uproot slavery, and caste, its tap-root, then will our peace be brief and worthless. If by it he means that these duties must go forward under the new conditions, it is well, but go forward they must, or we go backward. Our fathers made much more rapid progress in the storms of the Revolution than in the peace that followed. We must beware that our morning is not darker than our night. Fearful as that has been, the eye of God has shone upon us, as it did upon the Israelites in the tempest's gloom and destruction of the Red Sea. We have

"Touched God's right hand in the darkness,
And been lifted up and strengthened."

Go forward in that strength. Cleanse yourselves, and prepare for the duties of the coming day. The light is not given as a luxury, not for idle saunterings, but for labor. Man goeth forth to his work when the sun comes out of his chambers. We have a great and glorious work to do. We have our land to cleanse from its sins, to deliver from its enemies, to make the glory of all lands. We must educate this people so that all nations may seek after the same likeness and image. We must take the foreigners, who are rushing by thousands, and will by tens of thousands, to our shores, and inspire them with the gospel of truth and brotherhood.

The war draws near its end. In forty days, we might almost say, and Richmond shall be overthrown. With her vanishes the last rebellious army from the field, and the last hope from their breast. As Lord North, when tidings were brought to him of the capture of Cornwallis, threw up his arms as though a bullet had pierced his breast, and pacing up and down his apartments, exclaimed wildly, "O God, it is all over!" thus will the grand instigator of this unlawful war cry out as he flees from his proud citadel to hide his dishonored head when the conquering armies of Union and Liberty shall enter Richmond.

See to it that the third word is added, — Fraternity, — or, as sure as there is a God in heaven, there will be another war in America; a war more fierce, more bloody, more fatal than this — a war of races and of extermination. Justice and brotherly kindness can alone prevent this sun from going down. They can. Let us so live and labor that the peace and the nation shall be perpetual, universal, celestial.

It may seem improper to prognosticate evil when the good is breaking upon us, but truth is truth. Our fathers would have cried out at him who, on the day of Thanksgiving for the capture of Yorktown, had declared that unless they abolished slavery there would come upon their children a fiercer war than the one from whose red waves they saw themselves emerging. And yet he would have told them the truth. Liberty for all has had to be purchased at a great price, because they would not then bestow it freely upon all. So our war has established universal liberty. I have not the least doubt that slavery, under no subterfuge of compromise and complicity, can long live. Should the rebels succeed, should Mr. Lincoln be defeated, slavery must die. But Fraternity, the oneness of man, is yet an unsolved problem in this land. Our hearts still hate our brothers — still we thrust them from our arms. We have not half completed this work of regeneration. We have hardly begun it.

It must be begun, it must be completed, or a future war grows out of the seeds of an imperfect peace. We must conquer our prejudices, or God will again cast us into weakness and agony. Be assured that this word is of God. It is written on every page of His Bible, on every page of history, on every promise of the future. Man can exist on the earth happily, righteously, divinely, only as one. Five millions of our brethren held insoluble amid thirty or one hundred millions, can only disturb, and, unless cured, will destroy the body politic. They must be treated without special consideration or contempt; without special exclusion or inclusion. The sons of the first parent differed: the older despised the younger, and hence death and disunion to this hour. We must go back to Eden. We must say, and show it as a natural trait, —

> "That every person who shall lift again
> His tongue against his brother, on his forehead
> Shall wear forevermore the curse of Cain."

Gird on, then, the armor for God and your Country — for Liberty, and Union, and Fraternity. The day breaks, the shadows flee. Ere long the last grand note of triumph will fly through the land, over the seas. The dragon is broken in the midst of the waters. Slavery is gone down forever. The power that four years ago defied the whole world — that said to America, "Submit, or we will destroy you;" that said to Europe, "Acknowledge us or your people shall starve in their huts, your factories be silent, your ships rot at you wharves;" that said to itself, "We have climbed to the top of human sovereignty — the South, the East, the West, the North are ours." Where is it now? "Perished from the earth it has so long so grievously cursed." Hallelujah! the Lord God omnipotent reigneth!

One more blow on his accursed brow by our soldiers, one more by every patriot arm at the ballot-box, and he lies dead forever. He enters history, cruel as the burning Moloch, vile as the wanton Baal, proud as the imperious Satan, the demon of America cast out forever from the earth, thrust down forever to the lowest hell.

"Up then, in Freedom's manly part,
  From gray-beard eld to fiery youth,
And on the nation's naked heart
  Scatter the burning coals of Truth.
Now break the chain — the yoke remove,
  And smite to earth oppression's rod,
With those mild arms of Truth and Love,
  Made mighty through the living God."

THE WONDERFUL YEAR.*

"THE YEAR OF THE RIGHT HAND OF THE MOST HIGH." — *Ps.* lxxiii. 10.

THE year 1666 was long known in British annals as *Annus Mirabilis*, The Wonderful Year. Dryden celebrated its marvels in one of his ablest poems. Yet its wonders consisted solely in a few forgotten victories over the Dutch and the great fire of London. Much more will the year 1864 stand forth in our annals as wonderful.

The year naturally divides itself in two parts — our progress in arms, our greater progress in principles. Let us first consider the least, though the seeming greatest.

I. Our military progress is a cause of the highest national exultation. One year ago our situation was far inferior to what it is to-day. We held, under menace, Chattanooga and the Rapidan. We were beleaguered in Knoxville; a proud and confident foe ranged through the valleys of East Tennessee. We were holding foolish revelry in New Orleans, while the enemy, growling and hungry, were prowling through the whole interior, and often upon the banks

* A sermon preached in Boston, January 1, 1865.

of the Mississippi, looked in contemptuously upon our silly junketings. Great activity prevailed through the hostile region in the recruiting of their armies and the replenishing of their military stores. Never were their ranks so full; never their cannon so numerous; never their muskets so many and so good; never their spirits or their stock so high. They were sure that this year would conclude the war in their favor. Their friends, here and abroad, were not the less sanguine. Six times had we sought, under as many different commanders, to break the line of their Richmond approaches, and each time had been bloodily repulsed.

The opening of the year was disastrous. Our gay and festive army at New Orleans abandoned its gayety and festivity for a season, and sailed pompously out, down the coast of Texas, only to sail back again, shorn of their pomp, but not their vanity. Again they essay a land attack; and, like Braddock in the equipage of a muster field, with trains of cotton speculators in their ranks or rear, they march into the deadly ambuscades of Shreveport. The scattered fragments pick their perilous way back to the hilarious city, and the conquered hero comes North to receive an ovation from his exultant fellow-citizens. At Chattanooga the results were equally disastrous. We had sought to move out southward, only to be surprised and nearly annihilated at the bloody streamlet of Chickamauga. One wing and one chieftain alone preserved us from complete destruction — the same chief that has just crowned himself with fresh and unfading glory in his utter annihilation at Nashville of the same army that there so nearly routed ours.

Driven back into Chattanooga, the enemy had followed, and the hills about the city were covered with the insulting foe. The railroads were under their control; means of subsistence had failed; their shot and shell dropped daily into a defenceless camp, and the extinction of the army of the Cumberland was daily expected — would soon have been consummated. From this calamity General Grant had saved us; and under his bold generals had stormed the hights of Missionary Ridge and Lookout Mountain, and forced the foe back from the bloody fords of Chickamauga. Here he had paused; and here only did a gleam of sunshine glitter upon our bayonets till more than a third of the year had passed. Nay, so thick was the darkness, that as late as May our fortified posts on the North Carolina coast were attacked, and all but Newbern captured. Forrest made sacred forever the waters of the Mississippi with the blood of our massacred soldiers — blood that, flowing from dusky veins, gave the stream the holy redness of our flag of national freedom and fraternity the holier redness of the heart of Christ. With insolent ferocity he raged through Kentucky, and made good his boast that he would water his horses in the Ohio. Of our three armies, one was annihilated, one barely holding its own in the heart of the rebellion, and the last, long considered the first, held at bay in the same spot, beyond which it had essayed for three years in vain to march.

Now witness the contrast. In these eight months we have thrown our army upon Richmond, and held it there. Steadily have we pushed our lines around the fated city, and the line once formed has never been broken. In a series of battles that have had no equal on this continent, and no superior on any, have we won our way to its gates. Its chief line of communication is sundered. Its army, cooped up within its walls, is constrained to helplessly behold the overthrow of its coördinate armies in other sections of the field. Its general, by far the greatest, almost the only great one in its service, looks painfully on the desolations that are made in the very heart of his territory, but with no power to stay the march of the desolator. He awaits in sullen silence his own steadily approaching doom. The troops that lay in Chattanooga, helpless under the fiery shower from the surrounding summits, now look upon the blue sea, in possession of the second commercial seat of the rebellion, after a fierce and deadly march of over two hundred miles, to the seat of the armaments and military factories of the rebellion, and with a subsequent march of three hundred miles, most agreeable, most peaceful, most triumphant.

The deluded foe seeks to take vengeance by recapturing one of its own cities, that it now with a prophetic instinct calls ours, only to meet with complete and everlasting destruction. Thus rests the field to-day. One repulse alone shades the picture — that of Wilmington; offset, however, by the victory of Farragut at Mobile, who shows that on the sea, as with England in the days of Nelson, we have one captain that always conquers. To him the two remaining posts of the rebellion may bow, as the two greatest have, unless Sherman captures them by land as he has Savannah.

In this military review we should not fail to see the different status of affairs between this winter and last, in the langour that invades the spirits and the purposes of the rebellious leaders. A year ago they were alive with activity. The conscription was everywhere gathering in its strong grasp their idle or cowardly subjects. They were a unit in purpose and in action. To-day distractions rule their counsels, inactivity pervades their movements; no new levies, except those of slaves; no new armies springing out the earth to cope with our victorious legions; the faintness, the chill, the tremor, the horror of death invade this huge, tyrannic frame. The Giant Despair rages in blind passion, and staggers to his eternal doom.

How dark was the prospect last May. How impenetrable the gloom of last August — the darkest month of the whole war. How wonderful the brightness of this new year's morning. Surely must we exclaim, with most humble, most grateful hearts, Thy right arm, O Lord, hath gotten us the victory!

II. But other and greater victories await our attention. The triumphs of principles surpass those of arms.

One of the most important battles ever fought among men was waged in the late Presidential contest. Over myriads of leagues the combatants contended. Three thousand miles, from ocean to ocean, the line of battle stretched. Three millions of soldiers were in the field. The gage of battle was equally grand. Not only the life of a nation, but the life of humanity, hung trembling in the balance of the hour. Milton's imagination is of the sublimest order; yet his description of the war in heaven excels not the plain statements of the actual events that have transpired in America to-day. Were he living at this hour, and in this land, in his moments of repose from the duties to which his patriot soul would devote itself, his pen would revel in the grandeur of the scenes that have moved forward under our half-apprehensive eyes. It will assume its place in history as one of the last turning points, may we hope, in that divine highway which is being cast up among men, and which ends in the

"Shining table-lands,
To which our God himself is moon and sun."

1. Its importance will be the more clearly recognized by contrasting it with its predecessor — the election of eighteen hundred and sixty. In every respect will it be found superior.

(1.) It is superior in the circumstances under which they were fought. Then the land was in apparent peace. Quiet possessed its borders. No tramp of armed men resounded through our streets. No cannon shook the skies. No groans of wounded multitudes made the heavens mourn.

No maimed thousands limped about our doors. No weeds of hopeless sorrow shadowed the souls of mothers, wives, and children, "grieving over the unreturning brave." No dreams of war, horrid war, affrighted men's hearts. Here and there a fevered vision might fancy it discerned it. Here and there, possibly, a clearer eye did behold it. But none imagined that it would assume such a fearful magnitude. The wildest dreamer did not so fill the land with blood. Among peaceful fields, from the Rio Grande to the St. John's, the discussion went forward, and the decision was made. Shotless cannon announced the victory, and tearless eyes overflowed with joy.

This battle was fought in the midst of gloom and anguish. Blood, and fire, and vapor of cannon smoke filled all the air. Hundreds of thousands of our bravest and best had entered untimely graves. Hundreds of thousands breathed painful breath, eating the bread of affliction in Southern prisons, lying torn and shattered on the nation's couches, or wandering among us, with riven frames and pallid faces, fragments of their then vigorous and manly selves. Crape covered many a heart that then was bright with bridal bloom. Children cried for fathers, whose bones unburied looked up to the pitying and avenging eyes of God. Mothers by scores of thousands had become Naomis and Rachels. Wives by tens of thousands were going down in sorrow to the grave. What a land! lamentation and mourning, the screaming ball and the wailing household joining in doleful miserere. Starvation over hundreds of miles that then flourished in plenty; and worse than all, brothers aiming the rifle at each other's hearts that then were dwelling together in unity.

Can we say that an election proceeding under such circumstances is superior to its peaceful predecessor? Yes, even in these very elements is it superior. Look beneath the calm exterior of the former campaign. Over all that vast domain, where now war rolls its bloody surges, rested the gloom of hell. Millions of delicate women wrought daily in the field without reward except the lash of the master, and were nightly scourged to most horrible service. Millions of men were subject to like unmitigated toil, and to hardly less agony unutterable as they were compelled helplessly to behold their dearest selves the dreadful victims of their oppressors' lust. Everywhere the auction-block was mounted by Christians, while demons in human guise discussed their points, as they would those of beasts, but with a ferocity of passion such as no legitimate and lower merchandise awakens. The husband and wife, whom God had joined together, man rent asunder. The babe was torn from its mother's breast. The saintly maiden was cast into the lecherous clutch of a fiendish buyer; and all this was sanctioned by the professed Church of Jesus Christ. Deacons, vestrymen, and class-leaders, ministers, and bishops, vied with the rumseller, the gambler, and the avowed libertine, in this traffic of hell. Not of the Father's house, but of the Father's sons and daughters, did they make merchandise. All churches ran together to see which should soonest reach this goal of Satan. They all alike threw off the impediments of Northern conscience and communion, that they might the more easily surpass their rivals in their diabolic race. Bishop Polk and Bishop Pierce, Dr. Palmer and Dr. Manly, led their several hosts down the steep places of sin into this gulf of perdition. They yet retained the form and likeness of sacramental hosts of God's elect, though with no divine presence within them, and only divine justice overhanging them. As we saw their seemingly sacred forms, Abdiel's exclamation at Satan's yet undimmed glory leaped from our lips.

> "O Heaven! that such resemblance of the highest
> Should yet remain, where faith and fealty

> Remain not! Wherefore should not strength and might
> There fail where virtue fails, or weakest prove
> Where boldest, though to sight unconquerable?"

They have thus proved. Their brightness, their strength, their good name is gone. Those then puissant congregations and commanders have sunk into as complete infamy, and will into as complete destruction, as the less apostate churches of Ephraim and Jerusalem.

Is not this election preferable? The auction-block has rarely exhibited its atrocities since the fires of heaven fell upon this hideous Sodom, whose very Lots had become partakers of its vilest sins. Rare have been the forced separations, then so frequent; rare the lash, then so constant; rare the unspeakable shames, then so universal and so awful. God has suspended these atrocities, even where he has not yet led them into liberty. Their Pharaohs have paused in their career of abominations where they have not yet let them go. Baleful as were the attendant miseries of the last election, they were blessed as the smile of heaven in comparison with the agonies that then rolled up from half the land in a wail that made the angels weep.

(2.) In another respect it may be said this last election is inferior to its predecessor. "That was held freely over the whole country, this only over a fraction." But this statement is not true. This was a freer and fuller expression of the people's sentiments than was that.

In one half of the land four years ago, no man could have deposited a ballot for Mr. Lincoln without the sacrifice of his life. Freedom of the ballot was as much precluded from the States below the Ohio as freedom of men. There was immeasurably greater liberty of voting at this election in Kentucky, Tennessee, Virginia, and Maryland, than was ever known there before. A friend in Baltimore told me that it was at the risk of his life that he gave his vote for Mr. Lincoln in 1860. Now that city rolls up a heavier vote for him than even Boston. The alarm cry of our regiments at the Relay, fearing midnight assault, was "Baltimore;" the midnoon shout of joy to-day is "Baltimore;" so swift tread time and truth.

(3.) The late campaign is superior to the former in its relation to the great evil against which they fought. Both are but parts of one stupendous whole. Both are steps of God in His march through the earth. Each involves more than it formally asserts. Their declarations of policy and purpose show how great has been our progress in this brief hour of time.

Four years ago, the highest we could reach was the non-extension of slavery. To touch it where it ruled, was declared impossible. To lift the fetters from a single neck, to even express sympathy for those who wore them, was forbidden. Our unpeopled territories should be free. So said only a minority of the people, and they not its representatives of fashion, wealth, or influence. To-day, by a great majority, the people say, "No more slavery. If the Constitution does not forbid it, amend the Constitution. Not territories alone but States, not wilds but cities, shall be cleansed of this plague. The nation shall be pure." How vast that stride! Then defensive, almost in a posture of entreaty, now aggressive and defiant, liberty wraps her starry robe about her, and marches forth to the sovereignty of the continent.

We saw the gradual approach of the sun of Liberty. We knew that it was the first blow slavery had received from the arm of the people, and that from it she could not recover. Though it might fight long and die hard, die it must; yet we could not believe it would die so soon.

The first word spoken against it doomed it. Though Church and nation subsided into silence and submission, still that word lived. It broke forth with new power through the pen of Mr. Garrison. And for the first time since he leaped into this conflict with all the power and populace of the land, could the great revivalist of this reform approve the nomination and aid in the election of a chief magistrate. He ought to have been on the electoral ticket of Massachusetts with Edward Everett. The dullest eye would then have seen the mighty change. The two antagonists of Mr. Lincoln, each from an opposite side, the one the conservative candidate for the vice-presidency, the other the most radical denouncer of any presidency upon such a Constitution, the extreme lover of the Union and the extreme lover of liberty unite together, to uphold both of these great pillars of our national temple.

(4.) This conflict is greater than its predecessor in its effect upon foreign nations. The former election was local and unknown. It was not seen across the Atlantic save by a few discerning eyes. The masses, whether titled or without a surname, whether in robes or rags, saw nothing. To-day they see nothing else. The quarrels of Europe were unseen. Their international politics, once so grand to their unwidened vision, appear as the battles or diplomacies of pigmies. What matters it if Denmark is disparted, or Italy united, or Poland subjugated? They are baubles of an hour, tiny eddies of the great current whose gulf stream sweeps across America. Even the pregnant movements of this continent, the imperializing of Mexico, and nationalizing of British America, are unlike unnoticed. Europe pays no regard to them. "What is that rent and bleeding Democracy going to do?" cry these pallid kings. "Will she assert her purpose to fight it out on that line, if it takes a century, or will she succumb to her foes and her wounds, and, sinking amid the waves her blood has reddened, leave the ocean of the future free to our monarchic sails?"

"Will she," cry their half-despairing subjects, "will she abandon the struggle for our rights no less than for her own? Will she be slain in her own home by her own children, the most horrible matricide in history? And shall we weep in unutterable sorrow the death of her who might have been the mother of free empires wide as the earth, enduring as time?" How they gathered to their shores! How they fastened greedy eyes upon our great controversy! How they prayed for our salvation! How they leaped for joy at the glorious result! We were exultant, but with no such happiness as beat in every peasant breast of Europe.

As the first election awoke the greatest exultation in the cabins of Southern slaves, so has this in the hardly less degraded cabins of England, and Scotland, and France, and Germany. It carries dismay and death to kings and their minions, life and light to their down-trodden brethren. Never before did such a message cut the skies.

2. But the greatness of this election is better seen by a more direct contemplation of its actual results. Not alone in the questionable superiority of war over slavery, or publicity over privacy, does it deserve its title of great, but by the principles which, through it, have become the unalterable masters of the nation, the certain masters of the world.

Three ideas essential to the consummation of the divine desire in Christ with respect to man have been established by this decree of America.

(1.) The first is that of Union. The debate on that topic is closed. Till this year it has always been questionable whether the Union would endure. It was effected with great difficulty. It was imperiled at the start by the wrongful demands of some of the States, by the wrongful pride of others.

When effected by the partial, and, as we have too painfully learned, by the fatal surrender of principle, it was still expected to survive but for a season. In 1798, within ten years after its organization, the Virginia Democrats set State sovereignty above the Union. The resolutions of Kentucky, which were written by Thomas Jefferson, became the serpent that the Satan of slavery entered and seduced the new-born nation from her rectitude. To what depths of weakness and disgrace it brought her, the closing hours of Mr. Buchanan's administration have written with the point of a diamond. Under their formulary the nation saw her forts and armaments seized, her power triumphantly defied in her own domain, and herself the scorn and derision of every petty princedom.

Not only did resolutions thus early foreshadow this struggle; the purpose to sever the Union was itself avowed in the same century that witnessed its birth. It assumed many forms, and was never formally passed upon by the people, unless the reëlection of Andrew Jackson, by a great majority, after his suppression of South Carolina nullification, was an expression of their hostility to it. If so, the determination still lived. It flourished more and more. The re-awakening of the national conscience to the great evil of slavery, gave its supporters the pretext they desired. For thirty years they waged the ceaseless strife. At last, when the people had mildly said to this iniquity, "Thus far shalt thou go, but no further," they sprang to arms. "The United States," cries Keitt, of South Carolina, in a jubilant voice to his rebellious associates, "are scattered unto a thousand fragments." "Disunion forever!" reëcho the leagued traitors, as they hold by the throat eleven States, more than a third of her commonwealths, more than a half of her domain.

To this shout of disruption, the nation with a universal voice, responded, "Not yet!"

"Not yet the hour is nigh, when they
Who deep in Eld's dim twilight sit,
Earth's valiant kings, shall rise and say,
'Proud country, welcome to the pit!
So soon art thou, like us, brought low?'
No, sullen group of shadows, No!

"For now, behold, the arm that gave
The victory in our fathers' day,
Strong, as of old, to guard and save, —
That mighty arm, which none can stay, —
On clouds above and fields below,
Writes, in men's sight, the answer, No!

"O country, marvel of the earth!
O realm, to sudden greatness grown!
The age that gloried in thy birth,
Shall it behold thee overthrown?
Shall traitors lay that greatness low?
No, land of hope and beauty, No!"

The first cry for the Union was an inspiration. It sprang unconsciously from every lip. They said "a picnic excursion to the Potomac will settle the business. Seventy-five thousand men, in holiday costume, lounging in Baltimore and Washington hotels, and easily moving down upon Richmond, will re-cement the Union in its old and immaculate perfection." They knew not with how great a price this treasure was to be bought. One army after another must perish. The pleasure excursion must become funereal. "Death must come up into all our windows, and enter into our palaces, to cut off the young men from the streets." After three years and over, of such a price paid for the Union, the people reaffirmed their solemn vow, not as at first in thoughtless exultation and enthusiasm, but in a tearful, a humble, yet most resolute purpose to carry out that divine inspiration, at whatever expense of money or of life.

So intense was this feeling, that no one presumed to ask our suffrages who would not publicly consecrate himself to the Union. But some held out the olive branch to the rebellion; complained of the war and the sacrifices of purse, of life, of liberty that were essential to secure its perpetuation; and the people decided, with an agreement that has since been made unanimous by the willing coöperation of all, "the Union shall be preserved; at whatever cost, at whatever hazard, at whatever suffering, we will be still one people." From the Calais of our continent to its Golden Gate, a space larger than that which Europe spans between her Calais and her Golden Horn, with a depth, a solemnity, an enthusiasm that was unutterable, the heart, the voice, the vote said, "We are, we will be one." That debate has closed; 1864, it will be said by the future historian, settled the question of America's nationality. No longer will State-rights resolutions vex and frighten the people. No longer will we foolishly say, "Our system is an experiment." It has ceased to occupy that place in human affairs. Once the press was an experiment; so was the railroad, so the steamship, so ocean steam-navigation, so the telegraph, so Protestantism, so Christianity. But they have ceased to hold such positions. The American Union has likewise; it stands forth before the world the most tried, the most triumphant form of government that exists among men.

(2.) The election settled the greater and more doubtful question of liberty. The President had proclaimed emancipation; but would the nation proclaim it? It was his act before, his alone. Congress had not confirmed it. The Supreme Court had not constitutionalized it. The people, "the masters," as the President happily says, "of Congress and the courts," sat in judgment upon it. They heard the appeals of the contending attorneys. They carefully deliberated. They enthusiastically affirmed it. Henceforth it stands as enduring and sublime as the Declaration and the Constitution.

Already has it brought forth perfect fruit. Congress, the servant of the people, has uttered its decree, and the nation is redeemed forever from the yoke of bondage. Four years ago we only dared to stay the progress of this deluge of death. We promised to preserve it inviolate where it was. We would have passed an amendment to the Constitution, pledging ourselves to secure it national protection in the States where it existed, if that would have appeased our enraged masters. Charles Francis Adams offered such an amendment, and only the hopelessness of its acceptance by the slaveholders prevented its passage; and now another amendment has passed, not to preserve it intact, but to sweep it from the land. Then the President, under his inaugural oath, promised it the support of his official arm; now the same President, before the campaign opens, and when policy requires those declarations that are the least offensive and the most popular, announces his purpose to labor for its universal extirpation.

No equal reform was ever so speedily effected. Never before has a great nation so suddenly swept away an iniquity which was so inwoven into its whole fabric of social as well as civil life as to have received the familiar title of "the *domestic* institution." Till within four years it governed the land. It had elected our presidents, appointed our judges, sent abroad our ambassadors, chosen our Congresses, enacted our laws, controlled our commerce, dictated our fashions, tyrannized over society; had been the only constant, the supreme power in the land.

Thus stood the system then. The people after years of exhortation gained courage to look the monster in the face; they dared to say to it in its onward march, Halt! It raged on them with supercilious scorn. "If war comes," says its arch-leader, "it shall be on Northern soil. They shall smell Southern powder and feel Southern steel." Little did its myrmidons fancy its future. They were assured of unquestioned dominion.

How are the mighty fallen! Three fifths of their territory is wrested from them. One half of their slaves are national freemen. One half of their States have broken from their allegiance, and have adopted constitutions forbidding slavery. And now we are on the verge of universal emancipation. Ere this year shall close, liberty will be proclaimed by the agreement of the ratifying States throughout all the land to all the inhabitants thereof. Hallelujah! the Lord God omnipotent reigneth! His right arm hath gotten Him the victory!

Wise men, even when believing in Abolitionism, counted those foolish who said when the former election occurred, that under peaceable movements slavery would cease before 1876, but if war came it would not last five years. War came, and where is it? You may diligently consider its place, but it is not. As the antediluvian world in forty days was washed out of the earth, with all its wealth and pride, with its solid temples and palaces, so that the keenest antiquarian can find no trace of its existence, so has this system, wicked as any the antediluvian sinners imagined, much less did, been buried under the deluge of God's indignation through the myriad arms and votes of His obedient people.

(3.) This election was the victory of Democracy. Union might have been maintained and true democracy destroyed. So was it well nigh in the "save-the-Union" victories of 1852 and 1856. So is it utterly in the strong league of the slaveholders to-day. But our victory was the triumph of the equal rights of all men, without distinction of color or origin. "I vote the white man's ticket," said one on depositing his ballot for the unsuccessful candidate. "I vote all men's ticket," might have been the just response to his anti-democratic democracy. This question, deeper far than that of Union, deeper even than that of liberty, was also in the thickest of the great conflict. It was the unspoken word, louder than any that was uttered. It was the undertow, stronger than any which agitated the surface, that moved the Ship of State on its God-appointed course.

This victory has already achieved great results. Its greatest we have mentioned. It alone produced the amendment and purged the land of its ancestral curse. Another result, hardly inferior, deserves a record. It caused the elevation of Mr. Chase to the Chief-Justiceship. Had his principles not triumphed in that campaign, he would not sit, to-day, on the throne of national justice, their most permanent, and, with one exception, most exalted embodiment.

For a generation the people had been made to err in judgment. One who occupied that bench had begun his career as an abolitionist, but abandoned it under the temptations of ambition. That seat became the fountain of injustice. The whole bench became corrupt. Every judge became a partaker of the sins of his chief. If one died who kept his ermine spotless amid the great defilement, his place was supplied with one fouler than the rest, until at the last the whole was a unit of sin and shame. The circuit judges, and even the commissioners, were infected with the same poison, so that no human being pleading for his liberty found favor in the eyes of these unjust judges. The fact that they sought it was made the ground of its refusal. The more they wearied them the less they obtained justice. In Boston as well as in Charleston did this iniquity sit in the throne of judgment.

At last their Chief spoke, and, like his master in Eden, gave the lie to all the principles in which we were created. America, the child of equal rights, gives no rights to one sixth of her population. Free or slave, they are all without the pale of law. They cannot plead at her bar for property, liberty, or life. They cannot testify for themselves or others. They cannot defend themselves, their wives, or their children. They have no rights which this nation is bound to respect.

God heard that hiss of hell, and He too entered this Eden and walked among a fallen people, who sought to hide themselves from Him by impudently denying His authority and His law. He said, "If My children have no rights, you shall have no peace. If they cannot hold their property, I will take yours away. If they are deprived of their liberty, your sons shall pine in a more loathsome prison-house, beside which the hut and the fare of My negro child are princely. If their lives are not protected, yours shall be wasted." How fearfully has He avenged His own elect who cried day and night unto Him! We have heard and heeded, and through this election brought forth a great work, meet for our great repentance. For that God-vacated office the national voice nominated their candidate. It was God's appointment, not theirs. He had identified himself with the oppressed from the beginning. He had been a consistent, humble, faithful lover of God and his fellow-man. He had plead their rights unheard at the very bar where now he sits supreme. Greatest of all our victories is this. More than the triumphs of Grant, and Sherman, and Farragut; more than the reëlection of Mr. Lincoln and the assertion of our unity and abolitionism, is the elevation of Salmon P. Chase to the Chief-Justiceship of America. Those were wrested from our foes, this from ourselves. Those were the expressions of pride, this of principle. Those sought to save the national life, this the national soul. Those insured our existence, this our glory.

His was more than the appointment of Jay or Marshall. Upright as they were, they were not selected especially in view of the relation of their uprightness to existing wrong. Justice Chase was. He will uproot with his judicial ax not slavery alone, but its worse roots, caste and prejudice, and all the undemocratic and unjust treatment of our fellow-citizens and fellow-men, and complete the work that is so gloriously begun.*

* In the light of this position of Mr. Chase, his private words, written to Theodore Parker, are worthy of our attention. They are found in the Appendix to Mr. Parker's Life, p. 520. Thus he writes: "I don't pretend to be a very wise or expert statesman, or anything of that sort;

3. The consequences of this decision are twofold: those that concern foreign states, those that will affect our own.

(1.) This election will be an important step in the liberation of Europe. As the "bubble democracy" has not "burst," that of aristocracy must. The two systems are wrestling for the mastery of the world. Three millions of bayonets support a half dozen thrones on the necks of a hundred millions of men. Those hundred millions have heard this great decision; their half a score of masters have heard it also. Victoria sees in it the hand of America, her nation's first born, writing the doom of her family on the walls of her palace. Napoleon beholds in it his dream dissolving, of Mexican domination and California acquisition. The breakwater he had hoped to have set across our Southern line to the deluge of democracy is swept away, and the refluent waves will not only drown his American pretensions but his central throne.

Already "The Times" confesses its influence on the rising demands of the disfranchised masses of Britain. Already the Secretary of her Treasury declares that manhood is the only right basis for suffrage. Already the peasants and patriots of the continent are uniting together for the common weal.

The suddenness and completeness of our emancipation is but a type of that which will yet renew the face of the earth. In a day has this nation been born. In one shall those of England, France, Germany, Italy, Greece, and Russia; not in their present disintegrated and hostile condition, but like ours, a unity of life, of liberty, of name; one nation, free, fraternal, Christian.

(2.) But more important duties invite our service. We

but a roughly-trained practical man, who wishes to *do* something for truth, justice, and human progress, and who would prefer that what little he does or says should be so spoken of, that nothing in his example of word or deed shall even seem to contribute to the upholding of wrong."

too have a future as well as a present and a past; and it would ill become us in our rejoicings over what we have attained to be unmindful of what yet remains to be accomplished.

This battle has settled two great questions that have been in fierce debate and in perilous position throughout our history. It has shown that the nation is rooted and grounded in the doctrine of Union and the doctrine of liberty. These pillars of its common weal it will stand by so long as its nationality endures. There is yet one step it must take,—Fraternity. The French democrats wisely put this as the climax of their creed. It is there and everywhere the highest grace, and the last attained. We have decided for democracy. We must carry out the principles of democracy. That principle is no distinction of man from man by any accidents of color or clime. "All ye are brethren" is its sole creed. We have yet failed to embrace this truth. The Cleveland Platform declared the right of all men to suffrage. Congress in its territorial constitutions, Maryland and Missouri in their new free constitutions, limit that right to white men. They are not yet wholly free. Only by consistently obeying this call of God can we preserve that whereto we have attained. Cromwell and Napoleon both failed in the great revolutions they achieved; and why? Because they were false to the fundamental principle of those revolutions. The Pilgrims of Plymouth gave Cromwell the model of a free commonwealth. Equality and fraternity were the *foci* of its orbit. He created himself lord, and the Lord of lords cast him down headlong, and his work fell with him into a grave, where it has lain for more than two centuries. Napoleon was the child of democracy. He denied the mother that bore him, and was cast out and trodden under foot of his enemies. This grace he could not retain. The peasant Frenchman the Emperor's equal? Never. Do not we feel like him? Would we not welcome to our tables to-day a rebellious slaveholder sooner than his loyal slave, even if the latter was as well-mannered as the former? Would we place one of this class in our stores or shops, however capable? Would we accept the brightest scholar in the land, if of this race, as a professor in our schools, or the most eloquent preacher, whose lips God has anointed with grace, as our pastor and guide?

This prejudice exists only in this fraction of our continent. It must be overcome here. The conductor on the cars from Cairo to Alexandria was as black as ebony, while nearly all the passengers were either Europeans or Arabs; and the African was the easy master of the turbulent Asiatics and the haughty Caucasians.

To the removal of this prejudice every lover of Christ and his country should devote himself. If we pause now, we fall back into a deeper pit than that out of which God has most mercifully and most miraculously delivered us.

That such is our peril, the history of the great party whose career is just closing clearly shows. No party ever had a more glorious beginning. It sprang into life as the friend of man.

It won the power, and war arose. In the hight of the war the Federalists assailed it and were annihilated. An era of good feeling sprang up. The Democrats rejected the doctrine of the equal rights of all men, the headstone of their corner, and it has become the headstone of their grave. Jefferson favored slavery, of which he had declared God had no attribute that did not make war upon it. He urged its extension beyond the Mississippi. The democracy passed the Missouri Compromise, and in that day, dying it died. Never since has it breathed its natal air. Never since has it been the defender of the rights of man.

4. But if the year has been thus wonderful in its deeds, the duties it imposes are not less vital. What is the service to which the Master calls us? This, and this only: —

To abolish from the national action and the national heart all distinctions arising from color or origin.

(1.) In the discharge of this duty we must seek to abolish the unrighteous distinctions which are made in the composition and control of our armies. Had it been announced to our foreign-born population, "You can only serve in regiments of your own nationality; you are forbidden to march in the same company with American troops," how would they have scorned the summons of such a government! How justly would they have said, "Let Americans save America, if they persist in oppressing us with such invidious distinctions!" Equally just would it have been for colored Americans to have said, "You compel us to keep in regiments by ourselves; we will march in no regiments at all. You brand us with prejudicial infamy; we will not voluntarily accept the insult. If your government shall draft us and compel us to fight, we are powerless to resist; but not of ourselves will we rally to the flag; that is not fraternal."

This distinction must be abolished. A citizen, if he volunteers, should join what regiment he chooses; if he is drafted, those that most need his musket. We shall then cease to read of the valor of white or colored troops as separate bodies, but of men and patriots, whose complexion may be various, but whose blood and bravery are one.

We should abolish also the refusal to grant them commissions and commands. This glaring injustice will be patent to every eye, if we consider what would be the feelings and conduct of other privates should such a law degrade them. Were it announced to the army that only West Point graduates could hold commissions; that their valor, their skill, their experience can only elevate them to a sergeant's bands, how long would they serve such a land? Yet there are a hundred thousand of our soldiers who fight under this insulting opprobrium. However valorous, however endowed with military genius, however prodigal of life, they are not only compelled to serve in the ranks, but to see less competent white men set over them, and that solely on the ground of their complexion. This great injustice, this democratic lie, must be abandoned. It is part and parcel of the system of aristocracy that we have formally decreed shall vanish away. The work has been initiated by the conferring of a lieutenant's commission on one of these soldiers. It should be hastened forward. Congress should abolish the unjust distinction, and the man, whatever his complexion or origin, who wins his shoulder straps, should wear them studded, if he deserves it, with the three stars of a lieutenant-general.

(2.) We must grant them civil equality and fraternity.

The question of negro suffrage is assuming an importance, not only to the true Democrat and Christian, but to the most feeble or most false professor of democracy and Christianity. It will be found that here as in the army we must call on those we yet despise to come and save us. Professor Lieber shows that by abolishing slavery we have increased the basis of representation in the Southern States by the two fifths of the slaves who were before constitutionally excluded. If these are forbidden to vote, it increases the power of the white man in those States against his fellow of the North, by that large addition to a census-counted but non-voting population. If the rebels should be allowed to return with any powers and privileges, such as would have been accorded them in the late peace conferences, they would avail themselves of this iniquity to reëstablish themselves in more than their former power. Our only and sure cure for this peril, is for Congress to decree the right of suffrage for national officers to be without respect of color.

Again, the loyal white men of the South must call on their equally loyal brothers, often of more white than colored descent, to come and save them from the voting of their secession neighbors. These once active rebels, when these States resume their forms of civil life, will outnumber their loyal neighbors, and snatch again the scepter after having thrown down the sword with which they had sought the murder of the very government they will then represent. The loyal whites will be cast back into the pit out of which the national arm has dragged them, unless they will lift their like loyal colored fellow-citizens to equal honor.

But not as a measure of necessity should this be urged. It is one of duty. In many States of the Union this cruel disability exists. With proud, rebellious hearts we say, "The foreigner may vote, the native shall not. The brutalized victim of Papacy, whom priests and pope make hostile to our ideas and institutions, may oppose the government that protects him with ballot, almost with bullet, and yet lose no right of suffrage; while the most Protestant of our Protestants, the most godly of the godly, the most faithful of the faithful, shall not utter his voice at the ballot-box against these foreign foes." We should instantly annihilate every such barrier, and make suffrage and manhood identical. What Gladstone demands for England, Congress ought to bestow upon America.

"But," cries one of timid soul, "if this right is conferred so freely in States where the blacks have a majority, they will become its governors and representatives, and a black man may sit as a senator in our national Capitol!" And why not? Ought not the larger fraction of the population of South Carolina, who are among the most loyal in the land, to have the administration of the affairs of that Commonwealth? And if the most conservative citizens have for years contemplated with approval, and aided with their liberality, the rising glory of Liberia, can they object to a more truly named Liberia growing into majestic life on the ruins of Charleston, so long the seat of the beast? Will not Captain Robert Small be as good a governor of South Carolina as Michael Hahn, far less loyal, is of Louisiana? Is not his first office prophetic of his future, and is not the master of "The Planter" yet to be the master of the planters?

But not alone in the States where they are numerically superior will they justly claim the position their merits shall secure for them. In every State the same privileges must be accorded. No more and no less in Carolina than New York should they rise higher than they merit. Here as there, whoever deserves the highest seats, should sit there. Frederick Douglass, one of the first orators and clearest headed statesmen of America, should be the representative in Congress from his district. He has no equal in the national estimation within its boundaries. He would soon show that he was worthy to follow his great Auburn neighbor into the Senate chamber and the Cabinet. He might win what the other has lost, because to his ability is joined more popularity if not more principle — the highest honor the nation can bestow. "*Palmam ferat qui meruit*" is the only motto for a democratic people. If he deserves the palm he should carry it, by the votes and with the applause of all the nation.

(3.) This work should be carried forward in the Church. Sad is the fact, but most true, that those who call themselves the disciples and representatives of Jesus Christ are in their body, the most tenacious of this iniquity. Whatever the name of the Church, her spirit and act is the same. No professed Church of Jesus Christ here has reached the hights of fraternity which every other profession has allowed. The medical and the legal bodies have admitted them as equals ; not so the clerical. They visit around the same couch, they act as attorneys for the same client as their whiter fellows ; they cannot belong to the same conference with us, travel the same circuit, or be settled over the same congregation. And yet the Church professes to represent, and should represent, the highest ideas that man can receive or entertain. It is the depository, the vehicle of God. His best truths he commits to her as a distributing reservoir to all the world. Her ministers He deigns to call

His servants and embassadors ; her members, His sons and daughters ; and yet when His Son, the brightness of His glory, and the express image of His person, calls himself especially the Son of man — not of men, much less of a class of men, and that white men, but the Son of MAN ; when His Spirit orders His servant to declare to the Churches that in Christ Jesus the middle wall of partition is broken down ; that in Him there is neither Greek nor Jew, Barbarian nor Scythian, bond nor free, male nor female ; when He forbids the setting off one portion of the Church by itself for any outward distinctions ; against the words of Christ, the teachings of the apostles, the lessons of history, the testimony of every conscience in the sight of God, the Church in America gives herself earnestly to the support of this heaven-hated sin. She compels these her brethren and sisters to form Churches of their own. She separates God's ministers, if the least tinged with this complexion into conferences by themselves. If any of these Christians come into her Brahmin assemblies, she hastens to commit the very sin that James rebukes, and has "the faith of the Lord Jesus Christ, the Lord of glory, with respect of persons," saying unto his brother, often of the very complexion of James and the Lord Jesus Christ, "Stand thou there, or sit here under my footstool." How those holy words rebuke our haughty sin ! "If ye fulfill the royal law according to the Scripture, Thou shalt love thy neighbor as thyself, ye do well. But if ye have respect of persons, ye commit sin, and are convinced of the law as transgressors." Then comes that dreadful imprecation, so awfully fulfilled upon the apostate Churches of the South, so fearfully experienced in our own griefs and calamities : "For he shall have judgment without mercy that hath showed no mercy."

O, that the Church would arise and wash herself of this abomination ! She should instantly invite her despised brethren to sit in her exalted seats. She should abolish the iniquity known only to Protestant America, the colored Church. She should invite all those whom God has called to serve at her altars, which are not hers, but His. She should throw her mighty influence against this cruel and false prejudice, and drive it from the land. She should proclaim the great doctrine of the Bible, the central doctrine of the Cross, the unity, the fraternity of man, and should declare that what God hath put together man shall not put asunder. Then, and then only, will God's smile and benediction rest upon her. Then shall she go forth, not as now, to feeble victories and frequent defeats, but to constant, glorious, and increasing triumphs. Scriptural holiness will spread rapidly over all the land, and the coming of Christ speedily redden the divine horizon.

To this high and heavenly work the great election calls us. This grand future opens its celestial vistas to our waiting eyes. Union, emancipation, democracy, the triad of triumphant principles, will insure the unification, the liberation, the fraternization of America. Her sons, of whatever hue, shall wear her honors of whatever hight. Sella Martin will be the popular pastor of a popular Church, having no taint in its composition of the present bitterness of Christians against their better brethren, but composed indiscriminately of those who, though of many complexions, are of one Lord, one faith, one baptism. John S. Rock will sit as judge where now not one of his race can sit as a juror even when those of their own color are on trial for their life; and the perfection of justice will be consummated, and God the Judge of all, be satisfied then, and then only, when one of this blood whom our late Chief-Justice declared had no rights, shall occupy his seat as the administrator of equal rights to all the land. Such a one is the Queen's highest judicial representative in Jamaica to-day. Such will be America's in Washington to-morrow.

Such are some of the results and obligations which spring

from that national decree. The work is not yet accomplished. Our brothers yet pine in prison-houses, and suffer unto death on the bloody field. The foe is yet stiff-necked and rebellious. It may be long ere the high lands of perpetual peace are reached. We may see days as dark as any which have covered us. Yet the end is sure. The grand uprising assures its coming. Does it also that higher, that diviner end to which the whole creation moves? Will the nation, will the Church, will every Christian, every minister, every man gird himself for this greater task? If so, that higher glory will speedily dawn. The sun will rise that knows no setting. The kingdom of Christ will be established. The whole earth, one family, will dwell in Him, knit together in love, in labor, in faith, in joy; while over it all will bend the cloud of witnesses, with celestial faces, the martyred and sainted dead of every age and clime, not the least in honor and happiness those of our own age and clime, reliving happiest lives in their more saintly children, the inheritors of their sacrifices, their grace, their renown.

> "For all they thought, and loved, and did,
> And hoped, and suffered, is but seed
> Of what in these is flower and fruit."

THE VIAL POURED OUT ON THE SEAT OF THE BEAST.*

"AND THE FIFTH ANGEL POURED OUT HIS VIAL UPON THE SEAT OF THE BEAST; AND HIS KINGDOM WAS FULL OF DARKNESS; AND THEY GNAWED THEIR TONGUES FOR PAIN, AND BLASPHEMED THE GOD OF HEAVEN BECAUSE OF THEIR PAINS AND THEIR SORES, AND REPENTED NOT OF THEIR DEEDS." — *Revelation* xvi. 10, 11.

WE have often been summoned to the sanctuary, in the progress of the great controversy so near its end, at times to exult, but chiefly to mourn. We have been constrained to set forth the national sin and the national danger; to point to the cloud charged with God's thunderbolts, that hung black and fiery over a vain and careless land, and to urge upon the Church and the nation the tears, the words, the deeds of repentance. We have seen that cloud gather blackness as the nation and the Church went plunging from sin to sin, until at last it broke forth in such a storm as has not fallen upon any land since the fiery shower fell upon Sodom. Under that cloud, through that sea, we have waded forward, slowly and tremblingly,

* A sermon preached in Boston on the occasion of the Fall of Charleston, March 5, 1865.

stumbling often in the mire of our own corruptions, refusing often to listen to the command of God, which ordered us onward, trusting in arms of flesh, in compromises, in pride, in self, in sin. But as these fancied helps broke under the weight with which our weakness compelled us to burden them, we found ourselves sinking, with a faintness almost unto death, upon the only Arm that could save. The unwelcomed duty sounded dreary as a funeral knell in our frightened ears, and only to preserve ourselves from destruction did we heed its hated summons. A merciful God granted us salvation even under such undeserving circumstances. Though with great and sore chastisements, with misery and death multiplied manifold, He saved us from utter extermination. He is bringing us out into a wealthy place.

We are, we hope, on the verge of complete victory. The last steps to this divine consummation are being taken. One more, and the goal is reached. That step must, ere long, follow, and the arch-rebel flees for life through the regions where for years he has ruled in power and great glory, and where he fancied his glory was to be perpetual. In the progress of these achievements we have reached one event that ought not to pass unnoticed. The fall of Charleston will be more memorable to the future student of this war than that of any other city. Its capture will surpass in interest that of all its rivals in iniquity, from New Orleans to Richmond. In the ruin that has overwhelmed it, God has written out in the eyes of all the world His just displeasure, His inevitable vengeance against sinners. In dwelling upon this theme we are raised to the hights of the divinest truth, where the dread vision of a sovereign God, exercising His power in justly punishing willful, persistent, and awful transgressors, stands forth before our awe-struck eyes. The angels of His vengeance are flying in the midst of heaven. The vials of His wrath are poured upon the air. We see the fearful devastations; we see the Lord, strong and mighty, sad, and solemn, and serene, quietly casting His enemies into destruction.

Let us draw near this mount that burneth with fire, that is enshrouded with blackness, that trembles, and rocks beneath the footsteps of a descending God. Standing afar off we behold the fearful spectacle. As the shells drop bursting upon the doomed town, it seems as if they were lightnings darting from the very heavens. That cannon's roar is but the muttering of the voice of God in angry thunder. As Abraham, from the distant hills of Hebron, beheld the smoke of Sodom go up as the smoke of a furnace, so may we behold the smoking ruins of the haughtiest and wickedest town that has existed in this generation on the face of the whole earth. Nowhere has there been such sin, nowhere such just and terrible punishment.

In considering this subject, let us study more closely the sin and punishment of this city, and draw from this divine act such lessons of national and individual duty as it is intended to teach.

I. Its sin. The Seat of the Beast. No place in modern history has achieved so infamous distinction as the city of Charleston. Rome is supposed by many to be in the eye of the revelator when he wrote this vision. That city has truly been drunk with the blood of the saints. It has been full of pride, and malice, and murder. Its inquisition stands beside its cathedral. Tortures fill its walls with stifled cries. Dungeons and death bury the victims of liberty and truth alive in their ponderous and marble jaws. It has sent its emissaries and influence throughout the world, and repeated its pride and cruelty in every clime and age. Yet Rome has never equalled Charleston in crime. Paris is a worldly, sensual, wicked town. It fosters vanity and vice. It is the seat of a ruler who is subtle, comprehensive, active, bold. He marches forth his armies into Italy and Mexico to subdue liberty in the name of Liberty. It is the seat of the most powerful foe of European rights that Europe contains. Yet Paris is Paradise compared with Charleston.

London is a mighty mass of swollen wealth and pride, poverty and corruption. She keeps millions of her natives poor, ignorant and disfranchised, downtrodden and despised, that bloated thousands may strut the lordlier. The crime of London, as the centre of the ruling forces of England, is written with the point of a diamond. It will, unless it repents, assuredly feel the awful judgments of God. Yet London is heaven by the side of Charleston.

The metropolitan city of America is far from being perfect before God. It is given into the hands of wicked men — plundered by its officials, abandoned to pleasure, to avarice, to crime. And yet New York is spotless before the little city by the sluggish streams and amid the sultry marshes of Carolina. She is preëminently the Seat of the Beast.

What is the pride of London or of Rome to hers? They boast, the one of its commercial, the other of its spiritual supremacy. They despise others. Their population is largely paupers or beggars. Their political prisons yet immure or threaten the lovers of liberty with their hated walls. But they do not forbid the lowly citizens from acquiring the rudiments of knowledge. They do not compel them to work without any wages. Their leading merchants do not take these rewardless toilers to their centers of trade, causing them to mount the auction-block, and, sitting haughtily around, despite the strong crying and tears of their victims, knock them down to the highest bidder.

The Jews' quarter at Rome is nightly shut with iron gates; but its occupants are not rung to their dens by the bells of St. Peter's, nor is one of them who is found without seized and cast into prison, horribly scourged, and more horribly sold into bondage. They are not subject to unutterable crime, boastingly wreaked upon them by their disdainful lords and owners. They are not shipped in chains, or driven across the land to distant hovels, torn from loving hearts, and cast into a fiery furnace, whose flames burn with intolerable fierceness, though the Son of God walks with them in its midst. These horrors of horrors were reserved for Protestant America, for more Protestant Charleston. One third of her population have been subjected to these direful cruelties. They walked by stately school-houses which they could never enter. They were driven forth to daily tasks for which they received no wages. They were compelled to hasten to their huts and rags at the stroke of the evening bell on pain of punishment and the lash. They were the victims of immeasurable crimes, which God and hell can only punish. They were marched through the central street in the heart of the city, into a building with "Mart" rightly stamped upon its front. It needed no prefix, as it was the chief, in fact, the only trade of the city, all others centering in this traffic in slaves and the souls of men. Here they were driven up and down a platform, sixty feet in length, to show off their points to their critical buyers. Here, in smaller rooms, they were blushingly exposed to the unblushing eyes of their own fathers and brothers. Hence they tottered, trembling with anguish and despair, to their new fields of toil, and terror, and most welcome death.

What city has such a record? Where has the Seat of the Beast been so clearly established? We look abroad for this fulfillment of the Book of Revelation. We find it at our own door. The Bible is not a prophecy of Babylon or Rome alone, but of America, of the United States; not of yesterday, but of to-day. Here and now is the vial poured forth on the Seat of the Beast.

But though in distinction from European and even heathen capitals, this city is by merit raised to her bad eminence, it may be asked, How is she the superior of her sisters in sin? Is not Savannah, or Mobile, or New Orleans, all flourishing depots of cotton and humanity, her equal? Is not Richmond, above all other places, the breeder and the seller of human flesh and soul, from whose wharves and depots hundreds went weekly to their living graves,—is she not deeper than Charleston in the gulf of transgression, and will she not be in that of perdition? Nay, these associates were subordinates, not equals.

She was the chief in sin, because she threw around the iniquity the threefold robe of civil, and social, and religious character. She made slavery her idea. To it her ablest minds devoted their ablest powers. By the pen, in the forum, on the bench, from the pulpit, they justified, they glorified, they deified Slavery. From the beginning they exhibited this tendency. They erased from the Declaration the words Virginia inserted that reflected upon the slave trade. They inserted in the Constitution the words that Virginia sought to erase, which gave Slavery the protection of the national flag, and raised it from a local and limited, and therefore dying crime, to a national and dominant institution. They avowed their purpose, despite these concessions, to destroy the Union that protected their demon, because it did not promise to propagate it. They sought to break its bands more than fifty years ago; and more than thirty, lifted the standard of revolt, professedly in the interest of the tariff, actually then, as now, in that of slavery. Failing in this, the State set about the nationalizing of the accursed thing. She made her chosen son Secretary of State, and through him declared, with the approval of the government, that Slavery was the corner-stone of the American Republic. In its interests her representatives wrought untiringly, and wove the web they meant for her coronation, but which has become her shroud.

She first saw the man-child of Abolitionism, and sought its destruction in its cradle. She drove the gray-haired representative of human rights violently from her doors.

She gagged those who raised a voice in its defence in the halls of the Union. She struck down with the bludgeon its senatorial defenders. She challenged its representatives to mortal combat. Her clergy rent every Church in twain, that would not bow the knee to her Baal. She first leaped up in revolt when the people had decreed that her infamous reign should cease. She avowed her purpose to reopen the slave trade, and to make the ocean a Styx, swarming with worse than Charon's boats—even those that conveyed none to Elysium, all to Tartarus.

Well may she be called the Seat of the Beast. Well may she stand forth in history beside, nay, before, Egypt, Babylon, Rome, whoever enslaved the people of God and exulted in their hideous deeds. They sinned against little light; she against much. They were the children of darkness; she of the light. They fell from earth; she from heaven. They entered the grave; she hell.

But, if great is her sin, great also is her punishment. The Vial is *poured out* on the Seat of the Beast. Such destruction has visited no other center of the rebellion. Her servile vassal, the capital of the State she controlled, has fallen justly into a like burning grave. But she alone of the rebellious cities has seen, or is likely to see, destruction. New Orleans lost nothing but her chains. Savannah, Nashville, Natchez are unharmed. Richmond may share her fate, but will probably remain entire, a monument of the persistence of arms, not of ideas. Virginia, the seat of the traffic in slaves, and Charleston, the seat of the influence of slavery, have felt the heaviest the hand of God. Her wharves are empty. Her palaces deserted, dismantled, and torn from top to bottom with the plunging shell. Her own sons, in the rage of their despair, turned their shotted guns upon her, cast the torch amid her inflammable cotton and more inflammable gunpowder, and by one stroke destroyed both of the props on which she trusted for success in arms.

Her citizens cared nothing for the miserable poor that still sought shelter there ; nothing for her ancestral name, nothing for her still existing wealth. Like the progeny of Sin and Death, whose kindred they are, they " gnaw her bowels for repast." They even rejoice in her ruin. How their hearts must have sunk within them as they fled trembling and astonished, by night and by day, leaving the seat of their pomp and pride to the foot of the conqueror. Surely the bitterness of death cannot surpass, hardly can equal, the agony of shame, remorse, and rage, every passion but penitence that blazed in their yet haughty and hating souls. " Their kingdom was full of darkness. They gnawed their tongues for pain, and blasphemed the God of heaven, because of their pains and their sores, and most truly '*repented not of their deeds.*' "

How faithfully doth the seer depict her doom : "Her sins have reached unto heaven and God hath remembered her iniquities. In the cup which she hath filled, He hath filled to her double." The potion she has so long poured down her innocent children she is compelled to drink, even to the dregs thereof. " How much she hath glorified herself and lived deliciously, so much are torment and sorrow given her. For she said in her heart, I sit a queen ; I am no widow, and shall see no sorrow. Therefore have her plagues come in one day. Death, and mourning, and famine, and she is utterly burned with fire, for strong is the Lord God who judgeth her. Rejoice over her, thou heaven, and ye holy apostles and prophets, for God hath avenged you on her."

No such destruction has overwhelmed a sinful power since the French nobility, gorged with the blood of their people, went down in the night of terror. Nay, they fell less, for they had sinned less. They have sunk like the angel's millstone into the sea, and they shall be found no more at all. Their mighty names have become titles of weakness and dishonor. Their Barnwells, and Rhetts, and Hamptons, and Haynes, and Prestons, pipe and whistle in the ghostly sound. Poor and fugitive, they apprehend the feelings of those of their slaves who have fled in like fear and trembling from their enraged pursuit. "With what measure ye mete it shall be measured to you again," must sound sadly in their painful ears. It is no bloodhound's cry they hear, but the tramp of armed men, the roar of hostile cannon, the crackling of burning roof-trees, the shouts of liberated slaves. These make doleful music to their exiled steps. They go a way they shall not return. They shall continue powerless names. As the Tory rulers of Massachusetts, the Olivers and Hutchinsons, fell into utter nothingness with the fall of their State, so shall these be in South Carolina as though they had never been. They shall wander, seeking bread from the slave they have sold. They shall sink to the bottom of the society they have ruled. Their glory has vanished away. Thus has God poured out His vial on the Seat of the Beast. Thus has its sin found it out, and its fate overtaken it.

But this punishment had not been complete without the instrument by which it was perfected were considered. They were not captured by the Western troops marching a hundred miles behind them, nor by white troops galloping up to the town. Their own slaves were left to receive the keys of the city, and to walk her streets as conquerors. Through them alone can her mayor find access to the provost marshal. They alone preserve its safety by night and its quiet by day. The slave is the ruler of the land. A few whites are associated with him, but he is the substantial master. From his hands the impoverished tyrants must sue for daily bread. How wonderfully is the Word of God fulfilled! His truth, His ways, His word, are the same yesterday, to-day, and forever. "The sons of them that afflicted Thee," yea, they themselves, "shall come bending unto thee; and all they that despised thee shall bow themselves down at the soles of thy feet."

We pause, oppressed by the sacred lesson. What are its teachings ?

1. It teaches us that no greatness is aught against God. How these men once boasted ! How they defied the nation that made them great ! With what insolent self-confidence they paraded the streets of their slave metropolis ! Not the patrician of Venice who stood beneath the corridors of the Doge's palace, where no plebeian was allowed to walk, was so contemptuous as the patricians of Charleston to their white and black slaves. But as Austrian soldiers freely tread those desolated pavements, so do the slaves of Charleston march where late their masters rode.

Great and mighty are thy judgments, O Lord God of Hosts. Thou bringest man to destruction, and sayest, Return, ye children of men. His pride, as his years, are as nothing before Thee. At Thy rebuke he flees. At the breath of Thy nostrils he vanishes away.

2. It teaches us the regeneration of the earth. Charleston is not to be destroyed. It is to be rebuilt in righteousness. The church of St. Michael, so long perverted to hideous uses of pride and sin, will become the ministrant of truth and love. That name is not inapt. Michael, the archangel, triumphed over the dragon. It was the favorite picture of ancient and enslaved Christendom. It betokened their deliverance from the grasp of their tyrants. So does it those who have heard for generations its bells with horror. To them Michael may mean their deliverer, the slayer of the dragon of Slavery. He has fought with the devil for the souls and bodies of these children of the Father, and has won their salvation.

These freedmen shall renew that beautiful region in righteousness. They shall not build and another inhabit. They shall not plant and another eat, as they have for these hundreds of years, but they themselves shall long enjoy the work of their hands. Those excellent school-houses their *children shall enter. In those spacious churches they shall* worship a God who shall be well pleased with their humble, happy offerings. Those marts shall flourish in legitimate traffic. They shall be rulers where they have been slaves. Happy, happy, happy day! Already it breaks upon them. They look on their deliverers as the Messiah himself. And they are. Jesus is yet walking the earth incarnate in this Republic, breaking these heavy chains, opening these prison doors, and bringing to these, His children, the great and acceptable year of the Lord.

3. Take warning from this awful punishment. If God spares not these, no more will He spare you, though He bear long with you. With these He has borne for two hundred years. Their iniquity is full. The day of vengeance is come. And yet they are unrepentant. No sorrow fills those sinners' souls for their dreadful guilt. Those ministers, — Methodist, Presbyterian, Episcopalian, Baptist, Papal, — are as bitter in their hatred of the first law of the Gospel as when they flourished in power and authority at the head of the community. We have seen no penitent bishop of that apostate Church. We have heard no churches moaning for their sins. They faithfully follow the words of our text: "They gnaw their tongues for pain, and blaspheme the God of heaven, because of their pains and their sores, and *repent not* of their deeds." Beware lest you fall under like shocks, with like anguish and like impenitence. We may sin as fearfully against God here as they there. In your bodies, in your souls, in pride, in passion, in unbelief, in carnal-mindedness, in pursuit of the world. You may reject Christ, and be rejected of Him. As a church member, you may fall into the lowest hell. Many of them were such. So were the Israelites of the wilderness. So were Caiphas and Judas. So may you be. Watch, pray, strive, agonize, or you will plunge into sin, into everlasting destruction. Behold, the Judge standeth at the door!

4. Remember that this great work is not accomplished. The saddest, most solemn, most religious message ever delivered by an American President, was spoken at his inauguration by the great and good man, who, for the second term, has begun his arduous duties. Let me read to you some of those weighty words.

"Fondly do we hope, fervently do we pray, that this mighty scourge of war may speedily pass away. Yet if God wills that it continue until all the wealth piled by the bondman's two hundred and fifty years of unrequited toil shall be sunk, and until every drop of blood drawn with the lash shall be paid by another drawn with the sword, as was said three thousand years ago, so still it must be said, The judgments of the Lord are true and righteous altogether."

How they infold the past, the present, the future. How they point to our only success — God and duty. Our armies in the field, our legislation in Congress, our principles at home, our God in all of these, through them all, above them all — these are our salvation. Only by adhering to the right shall we triumph — the whole right. We must uproot from our hearts that most unchristian and inhuman sentiment which makes us distinguish between man and man, between Christian brethren, on account of certain outward traits. These must be swept away, or the wrath of God will again rest upon us. The Seat of the Beast may be transferred from Charleston to Boston. We may feel this outpouring of divine displeasure. May this fate be averted by our earnest embracing of the whole truth as it is in Jesus. May our victories speedily be consummated, the greater victory of right be equally accomplished, and the Holy Spirit renew every heart, and all the land, in the purity, and peace, and brotherhood of heaven.

JEFFERSON DAVIS AND PHARAOH.*

"AND THE LORD SAID UNTO MOSES, RISE UP EARLY IN THE MORNING, AND STAND BEFORE PHARAOH, AND SAY UNTO HIM, THUS SAITH THE LORD GOD OF THE HEBREWS, LET MY PEOPLE GO, THAT THEY MAY SERVE ME. FOR I WILL AT THIS TIME SEND ALL MY PLAGUES UPON THY HEART, AND UPON THY SERVANTS, AND UPON THY PEOPLE; THAT THOU MAYEST KNOW THAT THERE IS NONE LIKE ME IN ALL THE EARTH. FOR NOW I WILL STRETCH OUT MY HAND, THAT I MAY SMITE THEE AND THY PEOPLE WITH PESTILENCE; AND THOU SHALT BE CUT OFF FROM THE EARTH. AND IN VERY DEED FOR THIS CAUSE HAVE I RAISED THEE UP, FOR TO SHOW IN THEE MY POWER; AND THAT MY NAME MAY BE DECLARED THROUGHOUT ALL THE EARTH." — *Ex.* ix. 13-16.

ISTORY sometimes reproduces herself with photographic accuracy. Past and present then are one. The very man who molded that dusty past after his image and likeness, seems to be stirring in the disturbed elements of the present, and fashioning them after the same form. Plutarch sought for such a parallel between the chief men of Greece and Rome. The present Napoleon has set up his great ancestor and the first Cæsar as of like lineaments, labors, and, he might have added, fate. Yet none so strikingly in their rise, rule, and fall resemble each other as Pharaoh and Jefferson Davis.

* A sermon preached in Boston on the occasion of the State Fast, Thursday, April 12, 1865.

Living thousands of years apart, under different skies, institutions, and religions, they have had a history and will have a fame well nigh identical. Their resemblances and contrasts will be the theme for our consideration.

We may properly engage in such contemplations, because the hosts of our Pharaoh are cast into the sea. On the triumphant shore stand victorious our Aaron and Moses, — Lincoln and Grant; with their hardly less grand associates, Sherman and Sheridan, the Caleb and Joshua of the hour; while a rescued country, and the liberated millions for whose especial deliverance God hath raised up both Pharaoh and Moses, lift up glad hands in exultant hallelujahs to Him whose right arm hath gotten Him the victory.

With overpowering emotions of thankfulness and praise we crowd His courts to-day. Our fasting is turned into feasting. The bridegroom is with us — how can we fast? The bands of wickedness are broken — why should we fast?

> "Let the hills clap their hands, let the mountains rejoice,
> Let all the glad earth raise a jubilant voice."

With our eyes fixed upon the ingulfing waves, that have drowned forever the great rebellion and its greater cause; fixed yet more steadily and gratefully upon Him at whose command the waters disparted to let His people go over dry shod, and then closed eternally over their mighty oppressors, let us dwell upon the analogies our subject suggests. We shall find in them fresh cause to adore the wisdom, power, and goodness of Him who worketh all things after the counsel of His own will; who, never interfering the least in the freedom of His creature, still holdeth the reins of sovereignty, and guideth the affairs of the universe.

The proper way to contemplate the great struggle, which seems so near its end, is to take our stand by the side of God, and look upon it from His point of observation. We have, as a nation, chiefly observed it from the side of Union.

To us it has been a struggle for sovereignty, for empire, for integrity of the national domain. The Flag has been the chief symbol of our sentiments and resolves. Nationality the inspiring energy of our souls. Not so with God. Our nationality is of small account with Him beside righteousness. He has inaugurated and conducted the war chiefly, we might almost say solely, in the interests of Liberty. He allowed, He encouraged our passion for the Union, because thus He could best work out His plan for emancipation.

Then, too, we have dwelt almost constantly upon the rebellious leaders and their hosts. Their policy, their progress, their prospects, have absorbed our minds. It is as if we studied the Mosaic deliverance from the movements of Pharaoh, his ministers and his people. That we never do. We look at it from its Mosaic, its divine, its slave side. We study the movements toward emancipation. We see Pharaoh not aggressive, but resisting the desires and decrees of God. The slave Moses, not his master, is the center around which those events are organized. So should it be here. Not the slaveholder but the slave, not the rebelling armies, but the organizing troops of Freedom; not the stately pronunciamentos of Jefferson Davis, but the prayers and prophecies of the captive, should be now, will be the future nucleus around which this Thirty Years' War will inevitably revolve. The movements of abolitionism, political, social, religious, military, from the rise of Garrison to the consummation of Lincoln's election and proclamation, of Sherman's marches and Grant's victories, as well as the hostile forces in the Senate, society, the pulpit, and the field, all gather around that Christian bondman. They are the chosen people of God who for three centuries have groaned in their prison-houses, and whose liberation and exaltation, not our Union nor our liberties, are the great, almost the sole cause, of the outstretching of His arm, and the more than Mosaic miracles that pass before our half-observant eyes.

Taking our position, therefore, by His side, and looking on the war with His eyes, we see it to be, as all Europe sees it, a war of God for emancipation.

Three difficulties stood in His way: the words and construction of the Constitution; the aversion of the North to abolitionism, and the purpose of the South to prevent it. Each of these seemed strong. All must yield, or be crushed to powder beneath His omnipotent march. How can they be removed or reduced? Only by strengthening the last.

The dread of touching the Constitution had become a disease. The people feared it, as our fathers did their idols—the work of their own hands. They said, The Constitution forbids us to touch slavery where it is. We cannot, we will not, violate that instrument. The slaveholders' will alone compelled them to forget their idol and fear God. They or it must die.

Behind and beneath this lay a horror of touching the slave. "Emancipation! haven't we opposed it from the beginning? The black man will become our equal, our master. He is a brute, an ape; does not want freedom, will not work, will not fight." Mr. Ten Eyck, senator of of New Jersey, declared in the Senate, after the war had begun, that if slavery was abolished in the District of Columbia, the slaves would be pouring down upon the North, and his State would not take care of them. He has just lost his rëelection because he would not give them their rights in his own State. This aversion was profound, was universal. How could it be overcome? Only by the firmness of the Southern purpose. The lesser evil can only be overcome by strengthening the greater, and God gives it that power. For this purpose He raised up their strong leader, and endowed him with extraordinary nature, in order that against His will these fears and prejudices of the nation might be dashed to pieces, and our glorious end be sublimely accomplished.

The study of His character is, therefore, the study of all this gigantic movement. It was said, a year ago, "The rebellion is Jefferson Davis. His will is its sole support and life." It was so from the beginning. It has been more and more so to its ignominious end.

Consider then, —

I. The resemblances between our Pharaoh and the one who was the needful point of resistance in God's first war for emancipation.

II. The end God had in view in raising him up.

The parallel is seen in their freedom, their character, their work, and their fate.

1. They were alike in freedom of action. For this purpose God raised them up, that He might show forth His power in them. Yet they themselves freely elected the course they pursued. Many theories concerning the condition of Pharaoh's will have been propounded by students of his history. Some have argued that his freedom of will was supernaturally suspended, so that he was a mere machine worked by Almighty power for its own ends. Others have thought that he expressed the ordinary relation of every man's will to that of God, though under extraordinary circumstances of expansion. The last are right in this position, though they err in saying that this relation is the actual absorption of his volition into the volition of God.

The truth may be clearly seen in the parallel which is before us. Jefferson Davis has freely resisted the most pressing and repeated appeals of God. Never has he felt that the mission he was set to do was one forced upon a reluctant will, or one that constrained that will to any course other than it freely and enthusiastically accepted as its highest, strongest, only choice. In him, as in the great Egyptian, the divine intent was directly the contrary of his own. Their purpose was to aggrandize themselves, each by retaining a mighty mass of slaves, the one to preserve and increase the glory of his kingdom, the other to found an empire that should absorb the continent, and be, as was that of Pharaoh's then, the leading power of the world. God's plan was to liberate His enslaved children, and to employ them in the extension of His kingdom throughout the earth. Their wills, then, are and were precisely like yours and mine — like the humblest of their retainers, the most degraded of their slaves.

God gave them this freedom of action, but gave it, as He gives everything, subject to the laws of its constitution. One of those laws is, that exercise, in whatever direction, strengthens the faculty in that direction. Had they yielded honestly but a little, they would soon have yielded all. Their resistance intensified resistance, so that by the laws of their nature, that is, by God the Creator and Sustainer of all law, they both hardened their hearts, and yet God hardened them also. He allowed those natural laws to work their perfect work in them, because that thus the more fully could His own ends be accomplished.

To go further than this, is to make God the Author of their deeds, and so of their sins. It is to annihilate their responsibility and their humanity. It is to make them vessels of wrath fitted for destruction, with no more sin or punishment in them than in the fire which has devoured the palaces of Charleston and Richmond. Such is not the teaching of Scripture. Such is not the feeling of every heart. They are responsible, they have sinned, they are punished. They are men of like passions with ourselves, who have rejected the counsel of God against themselves. With their own hands they bound themselves, they kept themselves bound to the potter's wheel. Of themselves have they allowed God to make them vessels of wrath fitted for destruction. As they have sown, thus do they also reap.

2. Their characters are alike.

This work is to be accomplished by human agents, acting

among men, and according to the nature of man. It was as easy for God to have taken up the children of Israel, their wives and their little ones, in their beds, and to have transported them bodily into the land of Canaan, as it was to work the wonders that He did for their liberation. He could have slain Pharaoh at the beginning as easily as at the end of the conflict. He could have so inspired the Egyptians with terror, or whelmed them in destruction, that they would thrust out their slaves as readily at the first as at the last. But He never violates human nature while working with or against it. He respects most carefully the freedom of His creatures, whether He saves or slays them. He had two ends to accomplish — the development of manhood in His people, so that they might become fit for the sovereignty which He designed for them, and the destruction of Egyptian pride and purpose, so that they should voluntarily let His people go. To achieve these ends, the progress of events must be gradual. They would not yield freely at first, neither would the slaves assume their rights and duties and burdens at first freely. Moses found this fact preventing his success, when "he supposed his brethren would have understood how that God by His hand would deliver them; but they understood not." How precisely similar was our conduct to our Moses. There must, therefore, be one man whose nature is so firm, whose mind is so clear, that he sees the possible and intended end of every movement in the opposite direction, and who is set like the eternal hills to resist their progress. Upon that rock shall the purposes of the people be broken. Upon it shall those of God be established.

The characters of these men are alike in three respects. (1.) Their clear perception of the end from their beginning. (2.) Their steadiness of purpose. (3.) Their power to develop such strength and steadiness in others.

(1.) Pharaoh, like Jefferson Davis, saw that the first step

toward emancipation, if not resisted, would inevitably lead thither. When Moses asks for a three days' camp-meeting around the base of Sinai, an old and familiar usage of the Egyptians, the quick-sighted king detects the whole scope of the petition. He instantly answers, "Who is the Lord, that I should obey His voice to let Israel go? I know not the Lord, neither will I let Israel go." And when they humbly renew their request, declaring "The God of the Hebrews hath met with us: let us go, we pray thee, three days' journey into the desert, and sacrifice unto our God, lest He fall upon us with pestilence or with the sword;" he savagely retorts, "Wherefore do ye, Moses and Aaron, let the people from their works. Get you unto your burdens." And he instantly bound their burdens the heavier, ordering their overseers to take away the straw, but not to diminish the tale of bricks.

So, when the public conscience had grown in this land that it began loudly to demand of the slaveholders the abolition of slavery, Jefferson Davis stood forth chief in audacity, coolness, and firmness to resist its demands, and by the aid of supple tools, among whom, alas! was our own great statesman, he bound upon the already heavily-burdened slave the additional atrocity of the Fugitive Slave Bill. There was a feeble ray of relief before. If they reached our borders they were substantially free. Now the human blood-hounds scented them through the streets of every Northern city, and in the lanes and fields of our most rural communities. A gray-haired minister of Jesus Christ, stationed close beside us, was compelled to flee for his life, as were the African bishops Cyril and Athanasius from Alexandria, and Paul from Damascus. The cry rose yet more bitterly to heaven. Gates hundreds of miles thick suddenly shut in upon them, grating harsh thunder in their affrighted ears.

Each thus early apprehended the full significance of the movement, and sought to stifle it in its birth. This perception of the intent of the Hebrews was stimulated to greater ferocity with every miracle. So, since the nation put its authoritative word in the mouth of its Executive, has the heart of our Pharaoh become the more hardened against the liberation of his slaves. He saw its end when Mr. Lincoln was elected, and avowed his purpose to resist it. He seceded when as yet no overt act had been committed, and in spite of our protestations of faithfulness to imaginary constitutional demands, that were like the beggings of Moses before the Lord, unlike, in this respect, that our President made his before Pharaoh; a degradation Moses never reached. He saw that allowing the Territories to be free, was abolishing slavery. The little favor the Republican party was constrained to beg, the occupancy of the wilderness by Liberty, notwithstanding its profuse promises that it would not harm the gigantic sin where it ruled and reveled; that the fugitive slave bill should be yet more firmly supported; that the four millions of captives should have no hope of release, but should be given over to the extremest cruelty of their oppressors; that the coastwise slave-trade should still go forward, and the slave-masters yet rule the nation; in spite of the promise to amend our Constitution so as to prevent the Northern conscience from ever disturbing the iniquity, the Pharaoh of the South saw the end. He knew that wilderness inheritance insured the ultimate possession of the whole land. He knew the recognition of their political inferiority must end in their political annihilation. He knew that acknowledging the black anywhere as equal, as would be the case in the recognition of Liberia and Hayti, would result in his universal equality. Therefrom he instantly and resolutely ordered secession. He visited Richmond and Charleston, and the other chief centers of this sin, and organized revolt. He gave the diabolic enthusiasm the needful energies of his potent will.

(2.) In strength and steadiness of will they are alike.

Pharaoh never actually yielded to their petitions. Several times, when great reverses came upon him, he felt like relenting a little. Once he got so far as to agree to let them go, providing they went without their families and their flocks; but even that he repented of, and they left, at last, without any direct orders from him.

So has it been with our Pharaoh. In some of the great reverses that have befallen his arms, he has half inclined to substitute a temporary system of serfdom for his pet horror of slavery. To win the recognition of England and France, to secure needful help to his armies, he has almost said, "I will give these slaves a partial liberty;" knowing that after the crisis had passed he could easily resubjugate them to slavery. And once, when the thick darkness of disaster covered his whole land, save the cabins of the slaves, where the light that shone upon Goshen was again shining, when the Mississippi was lost and Georgia cleft in twain, and the enemy lay around his capital, and darkness that could be felt, that was fearfully felt, pressed down upon every rebellious heart, then he partially relented. Then he said, "Let us arm the slaves, and free those we arm." Not free their wives and children, but themselves. Let them go free for a little season till this calamity be overpast. God repelled the insulting proposal, and prevented the attempt. His heart became hardened against even this compliance, and he awaited in sullenness the blow that annihilated him. He knew, military man as he is, that Richmond must soon fall. He knew that the last stroke would soon be dealt. He had seen these movements of the Delivering God become more and more severe. Savannah had fallen, South Carolina had been traversed, Charleston and Columbia were in ashes, the enemy was gathering on every side of the doomed capital; still he stood firm. He received his death-blow in the church of his idolatry, at the altars of a false god, whom he had set up in the place of the true God and our Savior

Jesus Christ, and calling him by that holy name, was fervently adoring the hideous idol. At these altars of a foul and bloody Moloch did he fall. Here did the true and eternal God of liberty and love smite our Pharaoh. Fitting was the hour and spot of his destruction. As Cæsar fell under the statue of the rival he had slain, as Napoleon fell on the fields most consecrated of all in Europe to the liberty he had betrayed, as Judas fell in the very spot which the price of his treason was to purchase, so fell Jefferson Davis in the very church that for generations had set up a false god as the true, and that had steadily and rapidly increased the foulness and ferociousness of its idolatry; on the Sabbath, too, which had been so horribly profaned by him and his with pretended worship of a Savior whose precepts they had most fearfully despised and rejected. "Just and true are Thy ways, thou King of Saints."

Yet here, as in his prototype, he remained unshaken. No cry escaped those thin, pallid lips; no quivering of that firm-set mouth; he leaves the church as calmly as he had entered it. He leaves the city of his pride and hope with as little outward tremor as when he rode in, triumphant, four years before. He offers no freedom to his slaves. They take it. Just as the Israelites took their actual liberty, without the order of Pharaoh, who would have granted the three days' journey, but not emancipation, so do ours theirs. Their unbending tyrant gives no sign of submission. He falls, like Satan, upon his eternal ruin, unsubdued, unterrified.

(3.) Like Pharaoh, he possessed the power of infusing his strength into others. That monarch often felt the will of his subordinates failing him. Once and again they entreat him to yield to the demands of Moses. "How long," they say, "shall this man be a snare unto us? Let the men go, that they may serve the Lord their God; knowest thou not yet that Egypt is destroyed?" But Pharaoh's heart did not relent. He still refused to hear the voice of God. He strengthened his subjects to endure the vials of wrath which Omnipotence was pouring constantly upon them.

Even so has our Pharaoh been entreated again and again by his people to make terms with the enemy, even at the sacrifice of slavery. Governor Brown of Georgia, Senator Hunter, Vice-President Stephens, and not a few of her generals, have been advocates for peace and Union. But he stood firm. One word he writes as his sole orders to the embassy that met our President at Fortress Monroe but two months ago — "Independence." * And he inspires that embassy with his resolution. Every one of them saw the impossibility of carrying out that purpose. They were ready to yield. Not so he. He compelled them to his service ; he made Johnson, and has just made Lee fight his battles, after they had acknowledged that even victory could not save them. That sally upon Fort Steadman, that three days' battle behind Petersburg, were all compelled by Jefferson Davis. Like Pharaoh, he rallied his hosts for the last encounter. Perhaps like him he will still make another desperate assault upon God and Liberty. Perhaps the Red Sea, where his hosts and his power shall perish, has not yet been reached. The midnight cry in Richmond, and flight from its mighty walls, may not be the last of this tyrant. We shall see. But we shall see that if he gathers his legions for a new resistance, and is again overthrown, he will still die haughty, stern, defiant. His allies may cower. He never. No such correspondence will pass from him to President Lincoln as General Lee wrote to General Grant. He dies as he has lived, with firm and steadfast mind, fully set to do evil. These three qualities of far-sightedness, steadiness, and power to inspire others with strength, are striking counterparts of his great original.

* See Note XIX.

3. But their work is as analogous as their characters. For what purpose did God raise them up? To show forth His power, and that His name might be declared throughout all the earth. How remarkably do their histories compare. The first has been famous throughout the earth and throughout all generations. Other Pharaohs have ruled in Egypt. Some built pyramids, some temples, some ran through Syria and the East with their all-conquering armies. Some erected gigantic statues, which still remain for the astonishment of modern eyes. Yet all are forgotten beside this otherwise unknown king. Some suppose he was the great Ramesis, the Napoleon of his dynasty. But no proof of this is extant. And if it is so, not for his deeds of war, or government, or architecture, or piety is he famous. In these he is utterly unknown. Only as the one whom God raised up, by whom to free His people, is he ever heard of among men.

Thus is Jefferson Davis to be known; thus only. Men knew him before as an astute politician, as a brave and accomplished soldier, as a gentleman in culture and bearing, as the easy master of his party and its administration of the government. They have known him since his usurpation as one who is perfect master of himself; who can express the most abhorrent ideas in the calmest, strongest, and most elegant language; who can organize armies in every part of the vast region that recognizes his sway; who can make every State legislature and his Congress, in spite of malice, and envy, and failure even, embody his will; who can so influence the courts of Europe that they covertly recognize his embassadors, and one of their first statesmen can say, in an extorted admiration, "He has created a nation." It is not too much to say that the accomplished, courtly, sagacious Davis has appeared before the world to vastly greater advantage than our rude, stammering Moses, who only utters a finished sentence by mistake, and stumblingly presents the demands for which alone he too has been raised up.

Yet with all his abilities and his fame, Jefferson Davis will be known in history only as the one through whose needful resistance God wrought the liberty of His people. For this purpose God hath raised him up.

How necessary it was that Pharaoh's heart should be strong. Had he yielded early, the Israelites would have made their journey and returned; and so His purposes and promises would have been defeated. He must refuse the first pleas in order that the divine end shall be accomplished. His people were not ready to go. The great and terrible wilderness made them naturally affrighted. They still loved the flesh-pots of Egypt. They feared the enemy behind and before; they had but little if any confidence in the leader, and he as little in himself. The Egyptians would not have aided their departure with the needful gifts. The work must grow. It must grow around a point of resistance as well as a center of resolve. Moses and Pharaoh both developed gigantically in the long conflict — a conflict certainly of months, probably of years. So have Lincoln and Davis. Had the usurper yielded, as most expected that he would at the beginning of the war, the great purpose of God would have been unaccomplished. That purpose, be it ever kept in mind, was Emancipation. Nothing short of this would satisfy His will. To bring us up to the willingness to proclaim it, He must make that strong will stronger in resisting every attempt at any other settlement. He does not alter the will, he does not deprive it of its essential freedom. It chooses sin. He nerves it so that it persists in sin. It would still prefer it. There would be no inward conversion in him, as there is not to-day in the subjugated aristocracy of Richmond, in Lee and Ewell, and the imprisoned leaders of their armies. He allows its free choice to continue; but gives its strength strictly according to its law by which it abides firm in its free election.

Note how often this appeal has been made and resisted, because God's ends would not have been attained in its acceptance.

First came the Peace Congress, before the first inauguration of Mr. Lincoln, that offered to make the Crittenden resolutions the basis of settlement — extending slavery to the Pacific, and confirming it in the States where it existed, by constitutional amendment. Four fifths of the South would have accepted that. Davis said, "No : — Independence." Charles Francis Adams next offered like amendments in Congress, with the coöperation of Mr. Seward and Mr. Lincoln. The firm refusal of Davis alone prevented the miserable humiliation of their passage.

Mr. Lincoln next makes every concession and promise in his inaugural ; still he is defiant.

We seek to relieve a starving garrison, taking bread, not balls, to their help. He orders his men to fire upon the merchant ship, and fire at the same time the Southern heart.

The President issues the riot act, and calls upon them to lay down their arms, promising universal pardon. They and their leader laugh him to scorn.

Bull Run follows, and they exult the more. A long winter of pride and luxury succeeds, during which they rest assured of victory. The spring opens with the fall of Fort Donelson and the capture and government of New Orleans, in which events appear almost simultaneously before the public eye, the three representatives of our naval, military, and moral victories, — equals in honor and in fame, — Farragut, Grant, and Butler.

Still Davis is unyielding. McClellan's defeats confirm his confidence. Then we are forced to issue the Proclamation. With how much hesitation that word of God was uttered ; with how great hostility on the part of the nation, history will painfully record. The President declares, just before he makes it, that it is like the Pope's bull against the comet. He holds it back for a year, and would have held it back till to-day, but for the bloody scourges of an angry God. Even then it gave the rebels time to come to their allegiance. Strong in his faith and purpose, their Pharaoh ridiculed the offer and the threat.

Again the spring opens dark with disasters to our cause, that he might be confirmed in his resistance and we in our duty. Drafts are called for. Riots break out. The enemy get the reins of government in their hands in New York and elsewhere. Gold goes up. Business goes down. What next? "Arm your colored men!" "Impossible!" "Arm!" says God. "I will not!" say you. "Treat these niggers as men, as fellow-soldiers. 'Is thy servant a dog, that he should do this thing?'" "Arm!" sounds solemnly from the voice of God. And we most reluctantly obeyed. Still we said we will arm them as servants, not as soldiers. Ten dollars a month shall they have, and none shall hold rank above the sergeant. They enlist, they fight, they die, they compel our unwilling admiration. Still they are not paid as soldiers. Congress refuses to pay them. The President opposes it. In answer to our partial faithfulness God gives us partial success. Vicksburg falls, and Gettysburg repels the invader. But Chattanooga is besieged, Louisiana is overrun, Fredericksburg is defiant. The spring opens with Chattanooga ours. But Banks is repelled with great slaughter, and the coast of North Carolina largely retaken. Grant prepares to move out on his campaign, now so triumphantly concluding. Before he goes he demands of Congress equal pay for his soldiers. Some of you will remember that I preached on the occasion of his departure, on "Why he would succeed," and laid that down as the corner-stone—the making of all his men equal in their pay.* More than his genius is that justice. Still

* See p. 393.

Davis hardens his heart; and last summer, when his emissaries plotted for peace at Niagara Falls, our President had grown to the stature of the divine will. Never before. Peace on the basis not of Union alone, this had always been his previous error; but also on that of Emancipation. Then came success after success,—at Atlanta, at the polls, at Savannah.

Still the chief was defiant. Till but two months ago it seemed as if this divine demand might be sacrificed. Had he said to his commissioners with Mr. Lincoln, "Peace and Union," the country might have compelled the President to submit to the ignomy. Leading abolitionists, like The Tribune, were more clamorous for peace than for liberty. But God hardened Pharaoh's heart, and he said, "No Union." Hence no peace. Even when Sherman had reached North Carolina, and Grant was about to move on the enemy's works, Davis proposes to talk of peace, but with no offers of Union. Independence is still his cry; to it he clings, to the bitter end. Then comes his overthrow as in a night, and with him is buried, in an eternal grave, not only disunion but slavery. "For this purpose I have raised thee up, that I might show forth My power through thee."

My children shall go free. Despite their timidity, despite the unwillingness of the people of the North, despite the hellish purpose of their masters, they shall go free. The tyrant's firmness shall breed strength in the heart of his enemy, until the word *peace*, in its mildest form, when proposed by their chief general as the basis of his submission, is carefully excluded by his conqueror. No terms, but military; not peace, but surrender.

Thus has Jefferson Davis been lifted up before all the world. Thus has every eye in Europe, peasant's or prince's, seen the strong-willed enemy of God steadfastly resisting His divine decrees, and manifesting the very power of God, because He thus constrains the further and full expression of that power, to its glorious accomplishment in the complete deliverance of His long enslaved people.

4. Their fates are similar.

Whether Pharaoh perished in the Red Sea or not, he perished from history at that hour of his overthrow; so whether Davis is caught and hung, or escapes and dies in exile, or at home, his career as a leader and a man of influence is closed. No longer will kings and emperors accept his ministers as their guests and friends. No longer will Earl Russell answer respectfully and officially their formal notes. No longer will the Pope send him letters, and the emperors of Africa — congenial tyrants — their best blooded steeds. No longer will his name make the theaters of Oxford and Cambridge reëcho with applause. No longer will parliamentarians argue for his recognition, and all aristocratic Europe envy him his dignities. No longer will commissions signed with his name protect pirates upon the seas, and robbers upon our borders.

Jefferson Davis is no more. The President of the Confederate States, head of a million soldiers, the pet and pride of eight millions of supporters, is a panting fugitive, glad to hide his diminished head in the depths of the forest, in the huts of the slave. His name is cast out and trodden under foot of men. Let him live. Napoleon at St. Helena was a far bitterer pill to his European worshipers, than if he had been guillotined on the Place de la Concorde. So will Davis be in the obscurity of London or Paris. His end is reached. The Red Sea of blood has drowned his hosts, his power, his fame. Let him rot in a living grave.

Thus has God shown that He is the perpetual Master of the world. Whether on the banks of the Nile or the Mississippi, whether thousands of years ago or to-day, whoever of His oppressed people calls upon Him, He will hear, He will answer. He is the same God, visiting the iniquities of the fathers upon the children to the third and fourth generations of them that hate Him, and showing mercy unto thousands of them that love Him and that keep His commandments.

Consider, in conclusion,

II. What are the ends God had in view in this display of His power.

1. The first, of course, was to release millions of His beloved children from the awful bondage under which they had groaned. Of this we have no need of further words. Whoever believes in God believes in His hatred of oppression — and such oppression — not the mere subjugation, but the sale of His children; not the sale only, but their separation also; not their separation merely, but their subjection to unlicensed lust. The only wonder is that He withheld His arm so long; that He could listen for generations to their dreadful cries, and not appear on the clouds of heaven taking vengeance on their oppressors. He has thus appeared. Fire has fallen from heaven, in the curvetting shell of General Gilmore, upon the Sodom of the iniquity. Fire has consumed its kindred Gomorrah with its destruction. He has avenged His own elect, who have cried day and night unto Him.

2. But God's purposes in this redemption is to confer great honor on this people. Many sneeringly ask, Is not a white man as good as a black man? I am afraid we shall be compelled to answer, "No." Were the Egyptians as good as the Israelites? They thought themselves much the better, and treated with ineffable scorn, and shunned, with what they thought, instinctive horror, their neighbor, the Hebrew. Yet who were highest in the thought, and love, and purpose of God? Who in the history of man? Where are the Egyptians? Where not the Hebrews? So with us. Which of our peoples has exhibited most of the elements of goodness? Which has the most faith, the most patience, the most long-suffering, the most charity?

Which obey most strikingly those commands of the Gospel, "When ye are reviled revile not again; Bless them that curse you, and pray for them that despitefully use you; Love your enemies?" I have talked with many a fugitive and freedman, and never heard one breathe a word of harshness against his oppressors. When telling the story of their sufferings, horrible as they were, no railing accusation was raised, none was felt against those worse than murderers. What does all this betoken? It shows us where the sweetest fountains of grace are in this land. It shows us who are most like the apostles and martyrs of the primitive ages. These did not surpass our martyrs in faith and love, as they could not in suffering. They shall be exalted into equal honor. God intends to make that the choice blood of America. Not our proud Anglo-Saxon, not the Celtic, or German, or any other of the representative races, shall climb to the top of American society, but the African. He has the most of Christ. He is the nearest God. If he maintain his piety in prosperity that he has in adversity, if he grows in grace as he grows in culture, then shall he be the leaven of our too hard and impious mass. He shall season our worldliness, selfishness, and irreligion with his heavenly salt. In humility shall he be raised to sovereignty.

As the Israelites were delivered, not merely because of God's hatred of slavery, and sympathy with its victims, but because they were His chosen people, out of whom He intended to make for Himself a name in all the earth; so has He delivered these from their house of bondage, that He might set them among princes; that He might make for Himself a people humble, holy, faithful; the best expression on earth of His divinest nature.

3. He has emancipated them in order that He may thus reunite all mankind in one blessed brotherhood of blood and love. A descendant of this same Pharaoh gladly accepted

the hand and the throne of a descendant of these same slaves, and lives in history only because of this alliance. So shall it be in America. The daughters of these haughty Southerners, who have shrunk from their touch as leprous, shall yet gratefully accept the offers of the sons of their father's slaves, and their parents and themselves shall feel their house exalted by the alliance. That day is near at hand. Not ten years may pass ere such marriages will be frequent. So completely will society be reversed, and the true relations of humanity appear in that clime.

In fact, their independence could have hardly delayed this result, so ripe was that region for that change. It will be precipitated with a rapidity that will astonish all scoffers and infidels when once peace resumes her sway, under the banner of Union and Abolitionism. Gentlemen and ladies, as well as the poorer classes, will delight in such legal, happy, God-appointed relations. And the despised blood will become the honored and even enviable blood of all that region. Thus will He who has delivered them crown them with abundant honor.

Let us fear and praise the God of these Hebrews. Let us be of those Egyptians who joined themselves to them. Let us behold the clear revelation of His will and purpose in the rapidly unfolding events of the hour. Those who four years ago were slaves, are now free; who were forbidden in Massachusetts to bear arms, now hold Savannah, Charleston, and Richmond under their guns; who then were shut out from the alphabet, are now the hungriest and most progressive students in the land; who then were not accounted men, are now demanding their equal rights as citizens, and will soon enjoy all the prerogatives of manhood.

Be valiant in this cause. Let not the mistaken policy of our President, as revealed in his speech of this week,*

* The last address Mr. Lincoln made only advocated partial and very limited negro suffrage. It was the indorsement of Governor Banks's policy in New Orleans instead of General Butler's.

become the law of the land. May he who will be always known as the Liberator, be also known as the Regenerator. Let not those rebellious States be reorganized without conferring the right of suffrage on every loyal man. Twelve thousand half loyal whites of Louisiana refuse the petition of six thousand thoroughly loyal colored men to give them equal suffrage. Shame on this nation if, after having been led so far in the way of duty, when the moment of success dawns, it shall cast itself back into the mire of its own sins. Shame on it, if having won its triumphs by the valor of men of color, it shall refuse those men that franchise which it bestows on any Northern traitor who has done his uttermost to oppose the government, and even upon the Southern rebel, on his taking the oath of allegiance — an act of easy and frequent perjury.*

Shame, too, on the Church that seeks to separate these best children of God from their prouder but less pious brethren. South and North, in Boston and Charleston, there should be no such thing known as a white or a colored Church. All should be knit together in love. All must be, all will be.

Let us then, my friends, hail the future. Our Pharaoh is perished. He steals, a homeless wanderer, through the regions he so lately ruled. He is of the past. We are of the future. The redeemed Israelites remain — the redeemed nation. May we not, because of our unbelief and unwillingness to obey God's most clear commands, be compelled to wander forty years in the wilderness, as we have for the seventy years that are past; but may we instantly recognize and obey His will, so that our Canaan shall be speedily gained, and our rest shall be glorious.

* This was the policy so persistently and fatally followed out by Lincoln's successor.

THE UNITER AND LIBERATOR OF AMERICA.*

"THY GENTLENESS HATH MADE ME GREAT." — *Ps.* xviii. 35.
"HE SAVED OTHERS, HIMSELF HE CANNOT SAVE." — *Matt.* xxvii. 42.
"ALL NATIONS SHALL CALL HIM BLESSED." — *Ps.* lxxii. 17.

THE appalling deed of the last Good Friday begins to put on the fixed lineaments of the past. As that face and form, then so full of life, are frozen in death, so he who animated them is fast becoming solidified and shapen in the unchanging marble of history.

Still standing in the horrible shadow, how can we carve the features of the immortal dead? The chisel shakes in our trembling hand. The rain of sorrow blinds our eyes. In the ghastly darkness, we but faintly discern the spiritual form that has so suddenly and forever vanished from the eyes of man. He, who but yesterday was the center of all human observation; whose every word, as he himself declared but three nights before his death, was in no unimportant sense a national decree; from whom were the issues

* A Memorial Discourse on the Character and Career of Abraham Lincoln: delivered in the North Russell Street M. E. Church, Boston, on the Occasion of his Assassination, Sunday, April 23, 1865.

of life and death to the imperious leaders of the rebellion and their too willing subjects; upon whose course foreign potentates fastened watchful eyes, and foreign peoples were yet more intent; the foremost man in all the world, — now lies he low in his shroud of blood. A nation weeps around his bier. The world bemoans his fate.

Never before did so wide and bitter a cry pierce the skies. Never before were the heads of so many millions waters, and their eyes fountains of tears, weeping day and night for the slain of the daughter of their people. The great day of the Church has become yet more solemn in the annals of America. Let not the 15th of April be considered the day of his death, but let Good Friday be its anniversary. For then the fatal blow was struck. He died to the conscious world ere the day had died. We should make it a movable fast, and ever keep it beside the cross and the grave of our blessed Lord, in whose service and for whose gospel he became a victim and a martyr.

That crime I cannot dwell upon in such an hour. The criminal is not the object of my revenge. Justice will demand his death, to whom no less would it be a mercy; for it would shut him from the sight of the race he had dishonored and the earth he had polluted. Not the awful transgressor nor his crime, not even the gigantic abomination of which this deed was the natural and inevitable fruit, shall becloud the hour. Let us look the rather upon him whose earthly work is done; not upon his form, laid out in "long-stretching death," that is slowly moving amid tearful myriads, through mighty cities, by the side of inland seas, across yet vaster seas of billowy or level green, to its beloved home in the heart of the land, fit resting-place for him who shall ever live in the heart of the nation; but upon the features of his life, that we may learn why he grew to such a hight, and how we may, in our humbler sphere, attain an equal perfection.

The character and career of Abraham Lincoln will therefore be the appropriate subject of our mournful meditations. These are harmoniously united. His career was but the flowering of his character, — his character the seed and germ of his career. Extraordinary circumstances gave that nature a fulness of opportunity for its development such as has most rarely, probably never before, fallen to the lot of man; but they did not make the man. The most fruitful ground does not create the character of the seed it multiplies. It imparts a possibility of richness and fulness that inferior earths cannot afford. Still their own nature abides, and the oak is an oak, the ivy an ivy, in the richest as well as in the poorest soils.

His character was as complete when wrapped in the vesicles of his early privacy as in the grand uplifts of its wonderful consummations. As a child, a youth, an industrious, studious, obscure workman, a lawyer and politician of Illinois, he displayed the peculiar qualities which in his higher sphere bore such abundant fruit. His first speech was as brief, as witty, as compact, as simple-minded, and as good-natured as his last.*

For these traits he is not to be praised. He was created in the frame of soul that he ever exhibited. For their culture he alone merits eulogy.

God needs various workmen for his varied work. And as a wise master-builder uses a great variety of material for his manifold edifice, and works this material into a yet greater variety of forms, that the whole may be a unit of perfection, so does the Divine Master-builder in His infinitely grander structures of soul, erected on earth for time and for eternity.

The stately cathedral has its massy stone, lying in huge boulders under its visible foundations, rising in shapen blocks to its roof and pinnacles, carved in daintiest delicacy

* See Note XX.

around its pillars, doors, and altar. This solid earth it lightens with graceful forms of wood, as though the heart of oak blossomed like the gentlest flower into fragrant beauty. These are yet more relieved by tints that flush the cold face of stone with life, and this vitality puts on its highest expression in the scenes, sacred and divine, into which the walls change under the touch of the great masters, as the shapely face of death becomes radiant with life and love under the inspiration of its Creator.

Thus does God build up the nation and the world. Thus does He use every style of character, every quality of spirit in His sublime cathedral of man, which He is patiently and persistently erecting, in truth and love, out of a redeemed and regenerated humanity, on the earth and in the heavens.

I. What, then, were the traits of soul which this eminent agent in the plan divine received from God, and faithfully, usefully, and rewardfully developed?

1. We should only respond to the sentiment of every heart, hostile or friendly, when we place at the foundation of his character, honesty. This was his familiar appellation in obscurity. It has been none the less so in the greatness of his exaltation. Yet it fails to express the whole idea which it strives to embody. It is the rude, ungainly trunk, which, despite its rough exterior, is both the upholder and the nourisher of all the attractions that rejoice above it. It branches out in graceful boughs, with their rustling robes of green. It turns under the smiles of spring into an orb of odorous flower. It hangs in an autumn ripeness of golden fruit.

Honesty in him was not the calculating wisdom of the world as shown in its favorite and unworthy employment of that word. It was not from selfish policy that he was honest. Such honesty is really most dishonorable. It meant in him its true and original signification. It was sincerity, simplicity, impartiality, honor; in fine, the scriptural conception of this nature, guilelessness. Look down as deep as you may into his profound nature, you will see that it is clear as a moteless fountain. It may seem to be shallow, it is so pure; and yet a second sight convinces you that though your eyes are sounding deeply, they touch not the bottom. As you look skywards on a clear day, you first fancy that you sweep the whole depth of the dome with your glance; a second and more penetrating gaze shows you that you have only caught its lowest outlines. As it rises hights above hights, you exclaim, —

> "The *chasm* of sky above my head
> Is Heaven's profoundest azure,
> . . . . an *abyss*
> In which the everlasting stars abide."

Thus do you gaze into this pellucid nature. It is as simple and open as a child's, yet you cannot penetrate it; not because it interposes barriers to your gaze, but because your vision fails. It is none the less clear because it is so deep. Could you look farther, you would find the same nature, honest, unselfish, child-like; "an Israelite indeed, in whom is no guile."

The soul of this characteristic is absence of selfishness. That is the root of guile. Though not without the temptations common to all men, he was remarkably free from this propensity. This freedom from self-seeking is the more noticeable in contrast with the characters of most great men. Milton declares ambition "the last infirmity of noble minds." This passion implies a subtle love of self, and frequently mars the most exalted natures. Only one President before him seemed almost utterly free from it. Jefferson talked indifference, but was a ceaseless schemer and mover of political wires while professedly absorbed in his laboratory, study, and farm. Adams, Franklin, Jackson, Clay, were men of great parts, but a sense of their necessity to the movements of the nation gave to their strength the weakness of men. Their personality was to them an *essential* element in the events of their age. Not so with Washington and Lincoln. They were the priests placed over the abyss divine. The breath of God bore them onward in the accomplishment of His purposes. They were His willing servants, but servants only. They were not necessary to His success. Each looked forward to the hour when he should repose peacefully in the quiet of their homes. Each felt that others had greater wisdom than they. Each bent his ear kindly to hear what their more creative minds should say. Each sincerely sought the truth. Other men of might feel that they possess the truth. They do not seek it. It comes to them. It is an inspiration. They must declare it or die. "Woe is me," cry Phillips and Everett, cry Sumner and Beecher, "if I speak not that which I feel stirring within me." The President had no such call. He waited to hear their words. In sincerity of heart he deliberated, decided, acted.

This trait gave him that slowness of action, which was not unlike the stammering of Moses. He must hear the voice thrice ere he obeyed it. He must consider, as he cannot create; deliberate, as he does not divine.

2. But this guilelessness of heart and impartiality of judgment were joined to great faithfulness in adhering to the truths he had espoused. His step was as firm as it was careful. Having done all, he stood. Hampden's motto might properly have been his — *Nulla vestigia retrorsum*. No step did he ever take backward. Men of ideas often fail when those ideas are born into actual life, and the Herods rise up for their destruction. They are bold in the closet and the forum, but timid in the field. Demosthenes was not only the greatest orator of Athens, he was her greatest democrat; none of her men of might equalled him in courageous defence of her central doctrine. And yet when she must sustain her idea at Chæronea, he fled before the legions

of monarchy, and denied in shame the faith for which he had so valiantly contended. Cicero was equally courageous in words and cowardly in deeds, — a Roman in the forum, but not at the front. .

So have been many idealists and reformers. Their shields have been thrown away when the enemy assailed them. Such are not the most renowned. They have the strength of soul both to create and to sustain. Socrates, Huss, Luther, Paul could fight as well as speak, — die as heroically as they lived. Still this faithfulness is more sure to be revealed in those who accept the truth in full view of the perils it involves. Who takes the oath of allegiance before the enemy's guns will be apt to abide by it in the succeeding charge. Lincoln believed in these truths from the beginning. But he did not embrace them as objects of duty till he saw the whites of the enemy's eyes, as they were rushing upon him to his evident destruction. Then seizing them as if they were, as they were, loaded cannon, he henceforth used them steadily and valiantly in repelling and discomfiting his foe.

This trait was the more necessary in the tremendous fluctuation of popular feeling and current events. When the waves roared and were troubled, when the mountains shook with the swelling thereof, it was well for the nation that one held the helm who steered carefully, but calmly and steadily; who, if he did not hasten, did not go back ; if he did not so soon as we prayed make the desired haven, never ran his vessel back upon the breakers we had passed. His faithfulness was one of his most admirable and most necessary traits.

3. We should be unjust to his character if we shrank from noticing his playfulness. In common with many superior minds, he was as sportful as a lamb. He liked a good story better than a great honor. No one ever more enjoyed

"Jests and youthful jollity,
Quips and cranks and wanton wiles,
Nods and becks and wreathéd smiles,
Sport that wrinkled care derides,
And laughter holding both his sides."

A merry twinkle ever sat in his eyes. Ever when saddest with sorrow, a ray of this sunlight played on their salt drops. Napoleon, Luther, Socrates, Cicero, Cæsar, Wesley, Franklin, Webster, many great men, were of this nature. A jest-book attributed to Cicero was current in Rome long after his death. Cæsar was ever pointing his speech with these glittering specialties. Napoleon was full of mirth and jokes, even on the night before Waterloo. Their bon-mots were as brilliant as their battles. Lincoln, next to Franklin, if next, was the most famous jester of America. Each of these ever used a witty story to point an argument; and many was the laughable word uttered by the great diplomat of the Revolution, that did the people of that sad hour good like a medicine.

This playfulness was not unmanliness. It was the relief of an intensely overstrained nature, — the dimples of childhood dancing on the cheek of age, — the reminiscence of the past and prophecy of the future, that kept his heart green and juicy amid the furnace of fire, heated seven times hotter than ever before, where he was called of God to walk. It was an important element in his career. Without it, neither he nor the people could have walked erect. Those mirthful, melancholic stories creeping out on the top of great disasters, like light playing upon graves, relieved the people in their terrific gloom. Not that he did not weep. No President ever wept so much. Not that he did not soberly gird himself to his fearful responsibilities. None ever wrought so patiently and persistenly. But by a pleasantry he lightened his and our bursting hearts, that would otherwise have sunk like lead in the mighty waters.

4. His integrity was remarkable. In fact, all the traits we have mentioned, save perhaps the last, may be summed up in the one word — Integrity. Here is his honesty, his simplicity, his impartiality, his steadfastness. He was an integer — a unit. His soul was one. There was no disunion there — no conflict there. Its surface might be tossed, not its depths. He had doubts as to what policy to pursue, and often changed it with the changing moment; but never did he doubt his country, his cause, himself. It was the spinal column, that supported not him alone but the whole land. To it, as to a mighty tower, the people fled, and felt that they were safe. Thousands of millions passed through his hand; no itching palm caught the most soiled fragment of the tiniest currency. He assumed the errors, even the asserted peculations of his subordinates, as his own. The country smiled, but laid not the assumed sin to his charge. Its faith in his rectitude was unbounded. The most envenomed shafts were never aimed at that mark. Here, at least, his bitterest foes confessed that he was invulnerable.

5. But even this was not the seat of his strength. That lay in his love. His gentleness made him great. Sincere, honorable, faithful, true, he might have been, and yet not beloved. Franklin was as mirthful, Washington as incorruptible, Adams as just, yet for none of them did the people shed such floods of tears. Children and graybeards, man and woman, slave and freeman, beggar and prince, all poured forth their tributary tides of woe. "Behold, how they loved him!" will all Europe say, as they hear this exceeding bitter wailing. It was because he loved them. The condition of the highest love is essential here. We loved him because he first loved us. He was the first President of the United States who seemed to carry in his warmest heart the heart of all the people. The pertinacious, cold-blooded leech of an office-seeker did not feel that he was answered in the

selfish spirit which inspired his zeal. There was a fatherly affection even in the refusal. The bitter secessionist, even the relentless rebel, found only gentleness and love in his eye, and voice, and grasp. They were constrained to feel that they had become prodigals from, nay enemies to, a most tender and still affectionate father.

If these selfish or hostile men found such a welcome, how much more did the loyal. The degraded slave felt the warm clasp of that paternal hand as a benediction. The most garrulous griefs were poured into a sympathetic ear. His patient heart allowed every head to lie upon its broad, soft pillow. The people felt the throbbings of that heart warmly beating for them, and, like a tired child on its mother's bosom, sank trustfully to rest.

Far more than his sagacious judgment, incorruptible integrity, and playful humor, did his deep affection for the nation support and carry us through the darkest night of our history. It is not his mother's knowledge of what is best for him, not her lightsome nature, not her unceasing faithfulness, that makes the sick child commit himself so confidently to her arms. It is her love that makes him trustful. Her judgment may err, strength may yield, joy may flee, but love never faileth. Many waters cannot quench it nor floods drown it. His greatest weakness only increases its strength. His dying makes it live forever.

So has the nation rested in his loving arms. She knew that his judgment was often at fault, however carefully he exercised it; that sometimes even his strength of purpose almost trembled under the fearful pressure to which it was subjected; that his pleasant smile became sadness, and the sunny wrinkles were channels for many tears. He had never spoken confidently of success. The mighty struggle he feared might result disastrously; the sick nation might die; but dying or living, she felt that he loved her. That quality of his soul was undiminished. Nay, it was the soul's self, and grew the stronger when all else grew weaker.

Never did a great people so universally recognize and repay such love in its ruler. Never did a ruler so love his people. Cromwell loved religion first; Wellington, duty; England was the second in their heart; her people, last. Napoleon loved himself, not France; Cæsar, power, not Rome; Washington, the country more than its people. All the great leaders of the Revolution, all the great living leaders, reformatory, civil, and military, are devoted to the idea that controls them: this to liberty, that to union; this, America's glory, that, her destiny; this, philanthropy, that, piety; this, justice, that, honor; this, empire, that, prosperity. Not one of them can in a peculiar, profound, and personal sense be said to love the American people. That grace they want. Not that they do not love the nation; far from it. All have, all do; but it is a general, not a special regard; an affection that reveals itself in other forms than mere love. Not so with our great President. He held every one in his heart of hearts; he felt a deep and individual regard for each and all; he wept over the nation's dead boys at Gettysburg as heartily as over his own dead boy at Washington. Their death, more than his own child's, was the means of bringing him into an experimental acquaintance with Christ. That sorrow wrought in him a godly sorrow, which has become a joy forever.

Here then may we properly conclude his portraiture. It arises, like that of Him in whose image he and all of us are made, into the hights of love. Without profanity we may say Abraham Lincoln is love. By that nature will the future hail him. A John among the disciples, he, of all our public men, the most truly possessed and expressed the nature of his Lord and Master. Without revenge, without malice, without hardness or bitterness of heart, he held loyal and disloyal, slave and master, black and white, rebel soldier and rebel leader, in his equal love. Had his dying lips been allowed to utter one sentence, we think it would have been the dying words of Christ; and for his assassin he would have prayed, "Father, forgive him, for he knows not what he does."

It is for this trait that such mourning bows the land; for this are the streets of his funereal journey lined thick with weeds of sorrow, thicker with mourning multitudes; for this do the subdued eyes of millions of strong, cool men,

> "Albeit unused to the melting mood,
> Drop tears as fast as the Arabian trees
> Their medicinal gum."

It is for this, preëminently, that the despised race, free or slave, pour forth their most piteous lamentations. Their tears of joy but yesterday are almost tears of blood to-day. He was the first President that took one of them kindly by the hand; the first that acknowledged their equal right with every other citizen to his official recognition. He was not merely their military liberator, breaking their bonds only because he could thus deliver himself from his enemies; but he was their friend and their father, carrying them in the same paternal arms in which he bore the rest of his children. Well may they cry out, as they see him thus suddenly leap into a chariot of fire and ascend to his reward, "My father! my father!" Well may they bewail because of him!

For this do ten thousand steeples knell their pathetic minor, while all listening hearts, as never before, beat responsive, —

> "Keeping time, time, time,
> In a sort of Runic rhyme,
> To the throbbing of the bells,
> Of the bells, bells, bells,
> To the sobbing of the bells;
> Keeping time, time, time
> To the rolling of the bells,
> Of the bells, bells, bells,
> To the tolling of the bells,
> Of the bells, bells, bells, bells,
> Bells, bells, bells,
> To the moaning and the groaning of the bells."

Thus stands forth the character of this great man : of unblanched and unbending soul ; without selfishness, yet full of feeling ; without pride, yet ever regardful of the dignities of his position ; without ambition, yet ascending to the topmost hights of sovereignty, and absorbing into himself more than dictatorial, far more than imperial and kingly powers ; without the least malice, yet waging the bloodiest of wars ; without boastful bitterness, yet making myriads of his enemies lick the dust ; whose most loving heart ever irrigated, yet never drowned his wise brain, making that, which is often in others a verdureless summit, in him a well-watered garden full of choicest life.

> " A laborer with moral virtues girt,
> With spiritual graces, like a glory, crowned."

Such was the nature of him to whom the heart of the people has gone out as never before to any ruler. They revered Washington, they respected Adams, they believed Jefferson, they admired Jackson, they loved Lincoln. God's gentleness had made him great.

II. How this character revealed itself in his career, there is no need that I should relate unto you. The details of that life will be the theme for many a historian. Irvings will yet arise who will devote their graceful pen to the portraiture of this second Washington. Carlyles will make the splendor of their genius glow around the head of this greater than Frederick, or Cromwell. Napoleons will make him a more faithful study and model than Cæsar. With every luxury of art and wealth shall the grand career of the cabin-boy of Kentucky, the Uniter and Liberator of America, stand in the libraries of kings and statesmen, in humbler shape and larger love, on the shelves of all their people whose future that life both illustrated and assured.

1. Two dangers threatened the land when he assumed the reins of government — disunion and slavery. The Scylla

and Charybdis were on either side of the tossed and leaky vessel when he took the helm. Fierce broke the waves on the rocky Scylla of disunion ; more fiercely did the Charybdian sands of slavery threaten to suck the ship in their shifting and ceaseless maelstrom. Both, in influence, invaded the whole land. A great party in the North supported disunion under the specious phrases of State sovereignty and no coercion ; while all the land alike hated the slave and his kindred, and refused to touch, in the least, the iniquity or its victims. The President shared the feelings of the last, if not the sentiments of the first. His predecessor yet occupying the seat of government, if government it might be called which had ceased to govern, was calling on the people to fast and pray, that the wayward sisters might return. Great men carried monstrous petitions wrapped in the powerless American flag and laid them before Congress, entreating that body to consent to the nationalizing of slavery by giving it the best half of our territory and all our Constitution. The most widely circulated paper in the land declared for the Montgomery constitution, and had its rebel rag all ready to fling to the breeze when Fort Sumter should be attacked, the nation utterly cowed, the government overthrown, and Jefferson Davis made President of the twenty-seven Confederate States of America — New England alone being excluded from the general league. She might be permitted, if she chose, to retain the belittled title of the United States, with its plucked eagle and lowered flag, — the Switzerland of America, — safe only in the contempt of her tyrannous neighbors, wide ruling the continent.

Beneath all this turbulence was the crowded dungeon of slavery. Its imprisoned millions toiled and suffered, sighed and prayed, saw visions and dreamed dreams such as the despised Galileans saw in Jerusalem when prelate and Pilate, ignorant and scornful, were seeking, by reconciliation and compromises, the union of the God of the Hebrews with the idols of Rome. What cared we for these? "Touch slavery where it is?" "Never!" "Free the slaves?" "Hang him who dreams that dream." "Up with John Brown and his crazy gang, who fancied himself the Moses of this abominable Israel." How that first martyr but now welcomed the last to the rest and reward of the faithful! Brothers in this service, they shall be brothers in heavenly fruition and eternal renown. "Abolish slavery instantly and forever?" "Impossible. The slaves will cut their masters' throats; will invade the North, and expel our laboring population; will become the vagabonds of the continent."

Thus warred the elements.

> "Who shall calm the angry storm?
> Who the mighty task perform,
> And bid the raging tumult cease?"

We pay no unwarranted eulogy to President Lincoln when we declare that the peculiar qualities of his nature adapted him to this especial work. We well understand that God was beneath and above all this chaos, breaking the grievous yoke of His children, and moving this unwilling nation into higher spheres of life and duty. But He works ever through instruments, and as we properly study the relation of the human nature of Moses, of David, of Paul, to the work He laid upon them, so may we that of our leader to what he was set to do.

(1.) We see how admirably that nature was fitted for its first and most important work — the uniting of the North. Whatever other duties should arise ere the gigantic task was completed, the first duty evidently was to make the loyal States one. They were weakened by the severing of Southern ties. The whole structure rocked to its base. North-western, Pacific, Central, and North-eastern confederacies were projected. Even cities threatened to assume their independence. The Mayor of New York publicly declared that no troops should pass through her streets, no cannon leave her wharves for the coercion of the rebellious States. Unless we could be united the whole was lost. There was otherwise no means of staying the movement of disunion; no fulcrum upon which to plant the lever of emancipation; while to secure the Union was to destroy slavery, as every rebel knew. Therefore this must be done.

His conciliatory character, joined with his perfect simplicity and integrity, was the centre around which the Union sentiment rallied. The people felt that they could trust him with their liberties, for he would not abuse the trust. The hostile party found it hard to complain of so paternal a despot. They might rave at his acts but not at him. They saw that the salvation of the country was his first and last concern; that he had no private, no party ends to serve, but only those of God, his country's, and truth's. He addressed them kindly and generously, as in his letter to the Democrats of New York, — being, we presume, the first great ruler in this or any land who wrote letters to his people as frankly as to his family. He thus brought many of their leaders to his side, so that in his army and in his cabinet, as well as in less prominent but hardly less important fields, many of these earnest foes of his party became his warmest supporters. General Butler and General Dix, Senator Dickinson and Edward Everett, Secretary Stanton and Senator Douglas, with thousands of others, gave him their earnest and cordial support.

His conciliatory nature is strikingly seen in the composition of his first cabinet. It contained all of his rivals for the nomination, with one exception, that of General Banks, and he would undoubtedly have had the bureau for New England, had he not taken up his residence in the West. Such a combination of independent and leading minds, rivals of each other and their head, has never been seen in this land since the first cabinet of Washington, which embraced in it three rivals of each other, if not of him, — three favorites of the nation for his chair; two of whom sat in it, and the Constitution was modified solely that the third could also, — an event which might have happened but for his assassination by Aaron Burr.

This course had the desired effect. The country rallied round so gentle a leader, and the union of the yet undismembered fragments was secured. The feeling of the land found expression in its chief, and the various orders and mighty number of traitors yet with us were compelled by popular sentiment, and sometimes by popular violence, to conform to the general will.

(2.) Then came the second step, — the conciliation of the border. Each side essayed this work. Their sympathies and their sins inclined them to the rebels, their instincts and obligations to the nation. The presence of our army constrained its eastern edge to our side; the influence of ideas, its western. The line swayed low in the center, and Kentucky became the battle-ground of this sentiment. Slowly and surely the truth prevailed there. Against their prejudices, their education, their habits, their institutions, they ranged themselves under the flag.

The openly rebellious region must be reduced only with arms. How these fluctuated, and how they triumphed only when fortified with the other and greater idea of the war, history will faithfully show. Here his nature had no chance to exert its influence. Generalship, not statesmanship, was what that work demanded. It was, however, beginning to do so when his career closed. He had other material than a discontented North or a divided border to operate upon, and might have failed as completely there as he had succeeded wonderfully before. Through his armies there, through himself here, he had closed up the hideous rent secession had made, and beheld North and South, East and West, again and forever, one. He was the uniter of America.

2. But a still greater danger, duty, and glory were before him. We were an enslaved as well as a sundered people. The sighing of the captive had upheaved the nation from its foundations. The closing quotation of Mr. Sumner's first speech against our national sin was being awfully fulfilled: "Beware of the groans of the wounded souls; oppress not to the utmost a single heart; for a solitary sigh has power to overset a whole world." We disregarded those sighs, not solitary, but multitudinous and perpetual as the heavings of the sea, and we were fast reeling to our downfall. To be set aright, this dungeon must be opened. Its millions of innocent captives must go free This people must be our people, their God our God. How terrible this task! It is ever easier to conquer our judgment than our prejudice. We surrender our reason sooner than our heart. The nation hated, despised, detested, the black man. It preferred slavery, with all its horrors, to immediate and unconditional emancipation. So did Mr. Lincoln. But God is greater than man, and to our martyred leader's eternal honor shall it ever be said, God found him willing in the day of His power. How slowly these steps were taken, how reluctantly, how unbelievingly even, we all know. Yet taken they were. Like Jacob, having so many feeble ones to carry, he must needs travel slowly; yet he moved forward. Every day found him further than before.

Conciliation was his favorite feeling and policy. But that cannot be adjusted to this most embittering duty. It must stand aside for a season, and deeper traits must be brought into service. His sense of right, the backbone of his nature, which alone made him strong in the fearful strife, saw that there was no other path than this. His training and his feelings shrank from the negro: his desire to shun distracting elements made him shrink from him yet the more; but duty said, "Go forward! Pronounce the decree of emancipation! Let my people go! Take them by your official hand, and recognize them as yours!" And he obeyed.

There was another great conciliator by his side, the head of his armies, the worshiped of the land. He heard the like voice, but refused to listen. Reconciliation and emancipation he declared were impossible. He had the ear and the heart of the President. He warned, he threatened, he besought. Kentucky begged him to desist. He would mar all her prospects of Union if he pursued that course. The influential half of Missouri petitioned. Many wise friends from the North entreated. He hesitated till disaster overwhelmed the chief adviser of this delay, till the volunteer inspiration had gone out in blood, and the suggestion of a draft was met with scowls and threats of defiance from every quarter. The ship was lying on her beam-ends. All God's waves and billows were going over her. The rocks of anarchy were thrusting their sharp fangs into her. Only the throwing overboard of this demon can save her. He clung to the idol yet a little, and made one more prayer to its worshipers to come into the ship and save their god. They heard and jeered. They had a better craft, built for the sole worship of their deity. They entered no amalgamating vessel of freedom and slavery. He kept his word. Slavery was tumbled into the bottomless gulf. The waves roared and hissed the fiercer. Secession broke its bands among us, and raged in the streets of Northern cities. But all in vain. The Ship of State began to right itself. The voice of Christ calmed the sea. The rocks of disunion were submerged, and the quicksands of slavery disappeared forever from the view. The slave became a man, a warrior,—will soon be a citizen, and, merged in the currents of society, be lost in the indistinguishable throng that, from all nations and lands, rejoice in the common blood and name of American.

Thus will he stand forth in all coming time. To him was decreed the greatest honor history has conferred on man. His sole peer is the father of our country; and he is not his superior. Alike in many traits of character, alike in many points of career, they will share together the reverent gratitude of succeeding generations. Their statues will rise in every city, before every eye. The one delivered the nation from the yoke of vassalage to a once paternal, but then tyrannical power; the other released her from the deadlier grasp of a once fraternal, but then far more tyrannical dominion. The one organized her embryotic communities into States and a Nation. The other reorganized these belligerent republics into a solid and perpetual Union. The one liberated three millions of his own hue from foreign despotism; the other liberated four millions of another color than his own, from a despotism infinitely more horrible. The influence of both shall go forth for the redemption and regeneration of all lands. The whole world shall sit rejoicingly at the feet of Washington and Lincoln. Happy, proud America! that from her soil sprang, over her soil reigned, in her soil sleep the creator and the redeemer, under God, of her land and of the world.

We will not dwell upon the defects in this character; for the service it was set to do, it was fully competent; from other service God has mercifully relieved it. As his prototype failed to see and to carry out the full workings of the principle he inaugurated, — as another Virginian was to be the perfecter of the doctrine of democracy which God intended should here have complete expression, and the great leader was removed so that his influence might not embarrass this movement of Providence, — even so may this second Washington have been summoned to his reward, in order that the perfection of that democracy may the more speedily hasten forward. It could not, perhaps, have been done before. The country had been so reduced by previous theories of State rights, and of long submission to an oligarchy of human flesh, that it could not instantly know, much less discharge its whole duty. The web of the new era might have been rent, had it been then subjected to severer strain. But this crime has made its lace iron, — the Northern iron and the steel, — and we shall henceforth be strong enough, we hope just enough, to confer equal citizenship upon all the nation. We must not only nor chiefly punish the rebellious leaders. This may be our primary, though not our principal duty. The loyal freedman must have his full rights as a man. For this is the new President raised up; not, as most say, to be the juster judge, but to be the truer democrat. The last involves the first. The conditions of the rebel and his former slave, excepting slavery, may be reversed. No citizenship for the rebel leader; perfect citizenship for his slave. No land for the chiefs of the rebellion, homesteads for his loyal bondmen. Expatriation, which was urged upon the negro, not three years ago, may be enforced upon his master. The African had no rights these would respect. These may have none the nation will respect. Outlawed, homeless, exiled, — these once mighty rulers of the land may thus expiate their crime of treason, while their victims take their homes and their crowns. The first shall be last, and the last first.

Whatever be the fate of the rebel, the enfranchisement of the negro alone can renew that land. We have found that our salvation could not be effected without the aid of their bullet. We shall yet find that it cannot be preserved without the aid of their ballot. It is impossible to hang, banish, or disfranchise the half a million former aristocrats of the South. Neither confiscation of their lands nor emancipation of their slaves can annihilate their power. They cannot thus be prevented from vaulting into authority again. The white serfs who have so faithfully fought their battles will assuredly honor their military commanders with civic power. What can make and keep them powerless? Negro suffrage. Nothing less is needed. Set the four millions of the freedmen over against the six millions of white peasantry, and let them grapple. We shall soon see who are the real *men* of that region. These loyal masses will see to it that the disloyal tyrants do not trouble the nation further. They will be the owners of the soil, and the masters of their masters. They shall rule over their oppressors, and preserve thus the liberty, the unity, the peace of America.

To this consistent and complete democracy the new Jefferson is summoned. If true to his principles, and triumphant over the base prejudices of birth and breeding, he will shine by the side of his forerunner, equal in service, gratitude, and fame. We trust that he will be thus faithful, and that we shall grow as steadily after the divine pattern in the healthful sunshine of a hastening peace, as in the fearful midnight of the most bloody of wars.

Let us not be blinded from higher duties by our just vengeance against the assassin. His sin will quickly find him out. That sin no death can adequately punish. Yet Booth is but a babe in iniquity compared with Lee. The assassin never reigns in history by the side of the rebellious chief. He has secured a horrible notoriety. With Clytemnestra the assassinator of Agamemnon, king of men; with Ravaillac, who slew the best king that France ever knew, he shall hang forever on the gibbet of infamy.

Yet he is but the dagger's point; Lee is its polished handle; Slavery the force that drove it home. Shall we wreak our vengeance on the bullet, and let him that fired it go free? The miserable felon assassinated our leader. The yet unharmed general attempted to assassinate the nation. We have been wrestling in his murderous clutch for four years, and received innumerable stabs in our attempts to prevent our destruction. Is the nation less than one of its citizens? Shall we fawn upon her would-be murderer, and tear his, in our rage, into a thousand atoms? Nay, he too is a murderer. Not alone of the hundreds of thousands whom he has slain in battle, but of the multitudes that he has starved to death in his prisons.* He has ridden daily under the walls of these charnel-houses, where they were perishing for a crust of bread, and never relented for an instant at the piteous moanings that almost made the walls to groan. When the bony arm of one of our boys is thrust between the bars, he not daring to put his face there, knowing that the sentinel's bullet would strike him dead, and a poor slave-woman thrusts a bit of bread into his hand, that sentinel's bullet instantly spatters her brains upon the sidewalk. And that guard was a soldier of Robert E. Lee, a traitor colonel of the army of the United States, who, despite his barbarities to our men in the field, our captured soldiers, and these lowly creatures, whom we are, by the command of God, especially required to protect, dwells among us unharmed, almost in honor. What was the miserable actor's crime to his? We should do solemn justice to the greatest traitors in our hand, as we shall to him if Providence shall place him in our power.

But whether we are firm or feeble, God will make both to praise Him. How marvellous are His ways! Out of unspeakable crimes He has revealed His glory. Out of the violence of the slave-master has come liberty to all he held in bondage; out of the attempted murderers of the nation, a more perfect nationality; out of the successful murder of its head, a more thorough and speedy regeneration. Thus has it been most strangely verified before all nations, in the experience of these transgressors, that

> "Power to the Oppressors of the world is given,
> A might of which they dream not. O, the curse,
> To be the awakener of divinest thoughts,

> Father and Founder of exalted deeds,
> And to whole nations, bound in servile straits,
> The liberal Donor of capacities
> More than heroic! This to be, nor yet
> Have sense of one connatural wish, nor yet
> Deserve the least return of human thanks;
> Winning no recompense but deadly hate
> With pity mixed, astonishment with scorn."

Such is the fate of Davis, Lee, and Booth. They have the painful consciousness of having been the unwilling instruments of the very ends they strove to frustrate. They have united, liberated, fraternized America, and yet are and ever shall be linked with Pharaoh and Judas, Caiaphas and Pilate, the execrated of men.

Thus have all things worked together for our good, so far as we have loved God. From the beginning has He held us in His hand. He has ever prevented our sins from destroying us. Good and evil were in our earliest history, as in our latest. Raleigh and the slave-trade gave their contrary impress to Virginia; the Pilgrims and persecution to Massachusetts; Huguenots and slavery to South Carolina; the Dutch greed of gain and love of liberty to New York. The wheat and the tares have grown together until now. Yet always has He been guarding the wheat from utter spoliation. He has eliminated the evil, and educed the good. He has made our sins and our sufferings go hand in hand, our penitence and our progress. He has changed New England intolerance into firmness for the right, New York covetousness into rivers of beneficence. He will change the Virginia slave-trade into righteous traffic, and South Carolina slavery into the grandest liberty of this continent. The conscientious contraries shall also become a harmonious whole. The Huguenot of Carolina and the Puritan of New England, the Roman Catholic of Maryland and Episcopalian of Virginia, the Quaker of Pennsylvania and Dutch Protestant of New York, the Baptist of Rhode Island and Methodist of the prairies, shall yet form, not the broad, but the true Church of our Lord and Savior Jesus Christ, on whose divine foundation the nation shall stand in perpetual unity, holiness, and love. Thus may we learn to more perfectly confide in His guidance and grace who has so wonderfully revealed His constant presence in our planting and our growth, and who has shown here, as elsewhere in His kingdom,

> "That many things, having full reference
> To one consent, may work contrariously;
> As many arrows, loosèd several ways,
> Come to one mark; as many ways meet in one town,
> As many fresh streams meet in one salt sea,
> As many lines close in the dial's center,
> So may a thousand actions, once afoot,
> End in one purpose."

Let us, then, show our grief for our loss by greater faithfulness to the cause for which he died. The grandeur of this cause, in its past, present, and future, was remarkably revealed in his most memorable word and most memorable deed, with which his career was properly crowned. The last inaugural is that word, — the entry into Richmond, the deed. That word is the most truthful, humble, and Christian, that a ruler ever addressed to his people. It contains the clearest recognition of the divine will, the humblest prostration before His offended goodness, the amplest confession of the righteousness of His punishments, the largest beneficence to his own most deadly foes.

How sadly it prophesies his own fate! His, too, must be of the blood which God requires from the sword to repay that drawn by the lash, for two hundred years, from the shrinking flesh of His innocent children.

His dying speech from the national throne will be read with wet eyes by our children's children. If the farewell address of Washington will ever be cherished by the nation, much more will this more profound and pathetic confession of our sins, more resolute expression of our duty and purpose to eradicate them, be admiringly read by remotest generations. It lacks no element of perfection. So short that he that runs may read it; so simple that the most childish can understand it; so statesmanlike in its principles that the rulers of the world can profitably study it; so religious that the most pious can find in it the holiest nutriment; so philanthropic that largest souls can grow larger in its air; so clement that the hardest heart cannot but melt in its perusal, — it is the consummate flower of executive orations. Jeremiah could not wish it more penitential, Ezekiel more resolute, John more affectionate.*

It was a worthy requiem. He sung his swan song, sad, sacred, solemn, sweet. The voice of the ages, from David to Christ, went wailing through the strain. It will yet be, as it should be, the most popular and powerful word of America.

But if the last inaugural was his litany, the advent into Richmond was his jubilate. No picture of the war will be so frequently painted. It was in extraordinary agreement with his whole life and character, in extraordinary disagreement with that of every other eminent ruler. Here was a more than emperor, who for four years had waged severest war with a portion of his own people, that had made this their capital. Under many generals had he essayed its capture. Blood had flowed around it like water. Still had it

* The "London Spectator" truly says of him and it, "He has persevered through all obstacles, without ever giving way to anger, or despondency, or exultation, or popular annoyance, or sectarian fanaticism, or caste prejudice, visibly growing in force of character, in self-possession, and in magnanimity, till in his last short message of the Fourth of March we can detect no longer the rude and illiterate mold of a village lawyer's thought, but find it replaced by a grasp of principle, a dignity of manner, and a solemnity of purpose, which would have been unworthy neither of Hampden nor of Cromwell, while his gentleness and generosity of feeling toward his foes are almost greater than we should expect of either of them."

proudly resisted the whole strength of his armies. At length, after bloodiest encounters and almost a year of siege, it had fallen into his hands. How should he take possession of his prize? How have all conquerors exulted over such a conquest? When Charles the Bold captured Liege, he compelled its citizens to batter down a new entrance in their walls, through which he marched in triumphant pomp and scorn. When Louis the Great's, and David's generals reduced a rebellious city, they sent for their royal masters to take stately possession. Our grand monarch is near by when his great general, as great as their greatest, has won for him the long-coveted prize, and all the country is aflame with joy. Does he enter it in royal state? He sends a grand deputation to take formal possession of rescued Sumter. He himself walks up the streets of the capital of the rebellion attended by twelve marines and half a dozen officers and friends, without music or banners, or military or civic pomp. Thousand of unshackled slaves dance around him in an uncontrollable ecstasy of delight. They look upon the face of their deliverer. To them it shines like that of Moses as he descended from the mount. Like the lame man unchained of his life-long fetters of infirmity, they precede and follow this to them chief of Christ's apostles, walking and leaping and praising God. They too have been unchained of life-long fetters, that have made them sit at the Beautiful gate of the temple of knowledge and liberty, powerless to move, hopeless of salvation.

Their sneering master and mistress (such, thank God, no longer!) scowl from their windows upon him and the tumultuous crowd of beggared blacks that throng him, as Saul's daughter did upon the rejoicing David, despising him in their hearts. They do not mar his calm content nor the delight of the noisy escort who guide the ruler both of themselves and of their former masters to the residence of the fled usurper. He is indifferent to their contempt, and only regards the wonderful salvation of which he has been the chosen instrument, but which Jesus of Nazareth has alone effected.

As Christ entered into Jerusalem, the city that above all others hated, rejected, and should soon slay Him, attended by those, but now lame and blind and deaf and leprous, whom He had cured, so did this, His servant, enter the city that above all others hated and rejected him, and would soon be the real if not intentional cause of his death, attended by thousands who had been saved from worse maladies than those bodily diseases, out of whom, in a moment, legions of devils that had long possessed them had been instantly and forever expelled by the same Divine Redeemer, through His appointed word. "Behold thy king cometh, meek," is most beautifully true here and now. The haughty tyrant is gone, the loving father is come. Well may their glad hearts dance for joy. Well may the air ring with their jubilant hallelujahs. Well may the paternal President feel the comfort and strength of the hour. The blessings of those that were ready to perish came upon him. His work draws near its close. The nation is united, the rebel subdued, the slave set free. His cup is full. He can well exclaim, "Now, Lord, lettest thou thy servant depart in peace, for mine eyes have seen Thy salvation, and the glory of Thy people Israel."

How near that departure was! This was his Palm Sunday. Ten days elapse, his Good Friday comes, and he follows his Divine Master, through like bloody hands, to his Savior's glorious eternity.

Thus did our king enter his strong city. Thus did he triumph over his Philistia. The story will be wrought in song and canvas, over the world and adown the ages, as a most beautiful and most rare expression of a Christian triumph. It will live with the last act of John Brown, — his kiss upon the slave-child's cheek, — each the perfect flowering of his earthly life. With such a word as the inaugural, and such a deed as this, we may truly feel that his life was rounded to a perfect close. He could properly hear the voice of the Master saying, "It is enough; come up higher! Thou hast been faithful over a few things, I will make thee ruler over many things. Enter thou into the joy of thy Lord."

His work is done. Ours is yet unfinished. His place in history, and, we trust, in heaven, is sure. Ours is yet to win. We shall show our admiration for him more by completing his work, than by standing too long gazing steadfastly into the heavens whither he has ascended.

As he constantly moved forward with the advancing hour, so must we. To pause where he stopped is to go backward. Let us keep step with God in every path of Christian and patriotic duty, enlarging the bounds and upbuilding the walls of the kingdom of Christ by our faith, our zeal, our love. Then shall we best express our sorrow over him who fell so untimely, yet so timely, and become, if not, like him, a martyr, at least a witness for and a worker with our God. Then shall we be a sharer of his labor and his reward. What a reward it is to him whose most peaceful nature was compelled to most stormy and repulsive service! How ineffably sweet must be the quiet and repose of the banks of the river of life, after this dark and bloody night of earth and time! There he rests from his labors, and his works — how many and how mighty! — do follow him, and shall forever follow. There he worships the Chief of the martyrs, — whose form like his was pierced by the murderous stroke, whose soul like his was bowed with sorrows not His own, whose life like his was given for the redemption of others than Himself. Before that Savior does he, thoughtless of self, bow in bliss and gratitude unknown to earthly hearts. Through His infinitely greater service and sacrifice has he, a poor slave of sin and hell, found everlasting redemption and equal citizenship with the unfallen angels of God. Let us, like him, though with eyes dimmed by tears and time, gaze, in faith, on the illustrious Martyr of the universe, our Savior, our Redeemer, our God. Let us consecrate ourselves, soul, body, and spirit, to that divinest purpose, for whose establishment He poured out His soul unto death, and to whose completion He has allowed so many of His disciples to feebly but gratefully follow Him afar off, in like sacrifice of themselves upon the altar of their faith, — assured that, under His supervision, despite the seeming triumphs of men and devils, that cause is steadily advancing to its earthly and eternal consummation.

PEACE: HER GIFTS AND DEMANDS.*

"THEY ARE DEAD THAT SOUGHT THE YOUNG CHILD'S LIFE."— *Matthew* ii. 20.

"THE LORD GAVE THEM REST ROUND ABOUT, ACCORDING TO ALL THAT HE SWARE UNTO THEIR FATHERS; AND THERE STOOD NOT A MAN OF ALL THEIR ENEMIES BEFORE THEM; THE LORD DELIVERED ALL THEIR ENEMIES INTO THEIR HAND. THERE FAILED NOT AUGHT OF ANY GOOD THING WHICH THE LORD HAD SPOKEN UNTO THE HOUSE OF ISRAEL; ALL CAME TO PASS." — *Joshua* xxi. 43–45.

UT one Fourth of July has ever occurred that equals the one which has just been celebrated with tumult and joy unspeakable. That was the first that came after peace was made, and our independence was acknowledged by the parent government. After eight years of wasting war; after thousands of their youth and men of years had fallen in death; after their prosperity had given way to long and fearful poverty, and the national sovereigns, crowns, shillings, and even pennies, that had been the stable and general reward of industry and basis of wealth, had given place for years to a miserable

* A sermon preached in Boston, Sunday, July 9, 1865.

paper, many dollars of which could not buy a British shilling, and whose fluctuations, even on its almost worthless base, paralyzed trade and defrauded labor of its due ; after anarchy and hatred of brother against brother, such as only our Southern section has lately reproduced, had raged through all the land, as violently in Boston as in South Carolina, then came the gray flush of the approaching day. Exhausted England rested long and longer between her attacks, until at Yorktown, hemmed in by allianced France and America, she surrendered her hold and hopes, and acknowledged our independence. The following Fourth of July was a day of widest and wildest delight.

Such has been the past anniversary. We have heard the joy and praise that with bell, and martial march, and music, and roar of multitudinous cannon, have shaken the skies ; that with the voice of praise, and prayer, and discourse of reason, and passion of oratory, have lifted the souls of the people to Him whose right hand and whose mighty arm hath gotten Him the victory. We, too, have just emerged from a wide and wasting war. Our finances have plunged into an abyss, which, but for the unexampled confidence and strength of the people, would have proved as fatal to our wealth as was the continental currency to that of our fathers. Our foes have been they of our own household. Brother has wrestled with brother in dying agonies. Half a million of our sons sleep in their own blood. The cloud of sorrow has wrapped millions of hearts in the pall of the grave. For four years has the terrific struggle gone on, until at last the sulphurous cloud moves off, and the light of returning day gladdens every eye.

It is well to come together in the house of God, and lift humble and grateful hearts to Him. It is well in the awakening day, to consider the blessings and the duties with which He is now crowning us. Let us then turn our eyes inward and heavenward, discerning the will of God and the willingness of man.

I. The first great blessing which peace brings us is Peace. She herself is a treasure worthy our warmest love. War is ever horrible. Whatever grand disguises it puts on, in pomp of dress, array, and melody; in the excitement of the strife, when men put on the action, and put within them the heart of the tiger; in the bloody feast of telegrams and pictures of the battle, on which the public appetite feeds with a greediness of delight that reveals our kindred to our cannibal ancestors, and shows that we are one with those who yet find their most exhilarating beverage to be the blood of their victims, and his flesh to be their sweetest viand. Notwithstanding all these terrific uplifts of soul which it creates, it is still a volcano of death and horror. You may admire the armless, legless heroes that feebly move through your streets. You would hardly wish to exchange your soundness of body for their wounds and weakness. You may seek to cheer the weeping father, mother, wife, and child with your cheap phrases of duty, patriotism, and glory. But you would not exchange your embodied love for theirs, disembodied and unapparent. You would not empty your house of its head or its heart, in order that you might fill your desolate soul with memories of goodness or greatness. Human hearts crave visible, embraceable beings, on which to lavish their love. Heaven to the heartsore is desirable, because it will disclose the evanished faces of the loved, and restore to our arms their long-lost forms.

Those who, therefore, prate flippantly of the glories of martyrdom for the right, are not those who bleed inwardly and constantly in consuming sorrow. You never hear the parents, whose son will brighten their aged eyes no more, parade this theme in wordy eulogy. You never hear the widow, cast into an outer and inner mourning, that only death can cure, by the dreadful disasters of battle, who is ever crying out in the darkness of her home and heart, —

"O that it were possible,
After long years of pain,
To feel the arms of my true love
Round me once again!"

You never hear such wounded souls discoursing on the beauties and grandeur of war. That is well enough for orators, and editors, and parlor knights, and dames; it is not the speech of these who humbly say, with firm-set lips, and tumultuous, agonized heart, "I was dumb, and opened not my mouth, because Thou didst it." "Thy will, not mine, be done."

Nay, war is a horror of horrors. Thank God it has finished its direful course. Thank God that the marches of our mighty legions have ceased; that we no more sup on such horrors as were served up to us on the dreadful night of Bull Run, and by Ball's Bluff, and Chickamauga, and Murfreesboro', and Fredericksburg, and the Wilderness, and Spottsylvania, and Fort Pillow, and a hundred other like fearful names. These telegrams, dripping, nay, deluged in blood, are not served up as our daily food. And those more horrible accompaniments of the bloody feast, — Libby and Belle Isle, Andersonville and Salisbury, — they too are gone, and gone forever.

Talk not of the glories of war. As well talk of the glowing pageant of the Judgment, when the great day of God's wrath is come, and who shall be able to stand. Some may fancy that they will gaze with artistic eye on that terrific spectacle. They have so dwelt upon it in earthly imagination; they have set their highest genius to depict the scene. Rubens, Cornelius, Fra Angelico, and greatest of all, Michael Angelo, have set forth its fearful splendors with sublimest pencil. Yet what are they by the side of the unspeakable reality? — the blazing earth, the dissolving heavens, the arising dead, the assembled multitudes, the great white throne, from whose presence earth, and heaven flee away, and there is no place found for them; the Judge severe, the wonderful Son of God, the enraptured saints, the shuddering, flying, falling sinners. Ah, why fancy that a Michael Angelo, by covering a narrow wall of a little chapel with pigment, can body forth that spectacle of spectacles!

So dream not that your talk of war, or pictures of war, embodies its realities. No tongue, no heart can. Its riven frames, its ghastly dead, its unutterable groanings, its shock of demons leaping at each other, — all this is over, may it be, forever. That blessing peace bestows.

But peace also gives us the blessing of ordinary law. War not only destroys the happiness, it weakens the stability of society. We have lived for four years in fear of losing our liberties as well as our lives. Those liberties have been suspended. The ancient and essential landmarks of human progress and protection have been submerged in the deluge of blood. Our prime minister not only said that he could, by touching a little bell, consign any one to prison: he did it. Had he so chosen, he might have consigned them to death also. Hundreds were thus, without warrant or accusation, cast into jail; others were banished from the land, and all held their liberties at the tenure of the government. The Constitution as well as the laws was suspended, and military despotism swayed the land. The government professed to maintain some of its forms, yet it claimed the power to disregard them all, and did often disregard most. The President appointed generals, who held commissions as members of Congress, contrary to its direct letter. He refused to execute laws which

Congress enacted; refused to remove those whom it ordered to be cashiered; and though carefully regarding their will, when he could consistently with his own duties, he as carefully disregarded it when he decided that such disregard was best. This lawlessness and super-Constitutionalism have come to an end. The forms of law resume their authority. The President becomes again the servant of the Constitution. The little bell of his secretary can no more be a knell, summoning its hearer to heaven or to hell. It has lost its power over the liberty or life of man. The courts resume their benign .and calm control; Congress can legislate, supreme in its sphere. The people enjoy the serene repose of liberty under law. Great, unspeakably great, is this gift of peace.

II. But while peace in itself is thus blessed and blessing, this peace witnesses, though it did not not confer, yet greater blessings than deliverance from war and despotism. It ushers in the morning of Liberty. What a contrast does this national birthday exhibit in comparison with its late predecessors. Five years ago this anniversary was celebrated with quaking hearts. For thirty years the great iniquity had grown by the national principles, and policy, and power upon which it had fed, until it domineered over most, and threatened all the land. The nation rocked under the Presidential conflict. Bitterest hate burned in multitudinous breasts. The Union should perish if the candidate of freedom was elected. Many hearts fainted with fear. Others, and enough, were courageous despite their fears. That Fourth of July was black and lowering. The next was far darker. Our men lay in their intrenchments beyond the Potomac. Bloody skirmishes in Baltimore, and at Alexandria where Ellsworth had fallen, betokened the coming storm. Washington was surrounded with fortifications; the country was filled with armed men.

> "The steed,
> The mustering squadron, and the clattering car,
> Went pouring forward with impetuous speed,
> And swiftly forming in the ranks of war."

Three hundred thousand soldiers were summoned to arms. The white villages of Northern invaders dotted many a Southern knoll, and the blue-breasted hosts trod defiantly their hostile fields. Anxiously, tearfully awaiting the rising of the curtain, and the opening of the great tragedy, the people gathered to their birthday festival. What solemn appeals marked that hour! what stern resolves! what earnest declarations of duty! what searching of ourselves. Yea, what indignation; yea, what fear; yea, what vehement desire; yea, what zeal; yea, what revenge. In all things we were approving ourselves to be clear in the great matter with which God was testing the sincerity of our repentance. But the cloud lay along the sky black and muttering, and shooting forth occasional shafts of death. The storm broke soon in all its fury. Not twenty days from that, Bull Run was lost, and panic and seeming national dissolution swept the land.

The next anniversary was more doleful. We had gathered up courage, plucked a young commander from the Western mountains, glorified him with the title of the Young Napoleon, put him at the head of two hundred thousand men, and sent him down to sweep away the enemy. Meantime a hardly regarded officer had opened the gates into Tennessee, and another had fought his way down the Mississippi, while a third had seized the harbors of North and South Carolina, and still a fourth had taken possession of New Orleans. But all eyes were turned from these lesser lights of Burnside, and Dupont, and Butler, and Farragut, and Foote, and Grant, and gazed intently on the commander of the Potomac. That Fourth of July saw him defeated, and after untold slaughter, driven from the eaves of the rebel Capitol in irretrievable disgrace and ruin.

Again the nation was on its face, and sorrow and dismay tore its soul. That Fourth of July covered a year of blood and anguish. What multitudes had bit the dust! Since less than three weeks after the previous anniversary, when Bull Run opened the sluiceways of blood, what channels of gore had poured over the land! And all seemingly in vain. Their heart was yet unsubdued; their resources mighty; their territory scarcely entered.

Another year rolls round: the great word of Liberty had been spoken, but the more greatly longed-for word of Peace had not been heard. So far from it, those three days previous the most terrible battle of the whole war had been raging, and multitudes were lying unburied on the field of Gettysburg. And though the Mississippi was opened, its tidings did not intensify the morning pæans. War still raged; the conflict was yet uncertain. The foreign powers looked scorningly on; the breaking waves dashed high over the laboring vessel. That Fourth of July was as sad as any of its forerunners. The smile was enforced; the cheer hollow; hope deferred was breaking the heart. Still the nation stood firm to its principles. It went steadily onward in its career of justice and righteousness. It grew higher and higher in the divine stature.

Our last birthday was in some respects our darkest. Each side had put forth all its strength for the final struggle. Each felt that it was the last time. If defeated, it did not seem possible that we could rally again. We had brought to the head the best military talent at our command, and had given them every soldier and weapon they could use. The two who had risen by steady success to the highest positions, were each held at bay by unsubdued armies. One had already sacrificed threescore thousand even in his march to Richmond, and was powerlessly battering its gates. The other was pushing slowly and painfully through the rocky ramparts of northern Georgia, far yet, and seemingly hopelessly far, from the walls of Atlanta. No gloomier hour has shut down upon us since the war began. The bells almost tolled, ring them merrily as they may, so dismal were our rejoicings. The whole head was sick, the whole heart faint. The resolution of the Lieutenant General hardly sustained the public faith. The mercury sank into the bulb. Traitors stalked boldly through the land, and held open conference with the armed rebels against the government. The Presidential contest was beginning to agitate the nation, and liberty and nationality were to be subjected to a test such as they never before suffered, much less endured — that of a popular vote on the very question of the national existence, in the hour when almost one half of her children were in arms against her.

Dark, how dark, total eclipse, was that hour! The sun was turned into blackness, and the moon into blood. The stars of heaven fell as when a fig-tree shaketh its untimely figs. We almost saw the sheeted dead walk gibbering through the streets. If we failed in the field and at the ballot-box, if we failed in either, all was lost. Liberty went out into returnless night. The rights of man disappeared from the face of the earth. Free institutions were at an end. Cæsarism was the law of this, as of all preceding ages. Democracy was a vanished bubble, man a slave, humanity a delusion, Christianity a lie.

No one will ever forget that dreadful day. The guns were almost minute guns, firing a funereal salute over the dead empire of man. The orations were earnest and courageous, but plaintive and dreary. Congress issues a most penitential confession and cry to fasting and prayer. The nation put on sackcloth, and lay upon its face before the Lord.

Thus similar in sadness, solemnity, and anxiety were our

last five anniversaries. How different this! Peace might have brought us another kind of a gift. It might have come with our armies overthrown, our land rent in twain, our liberties gone, defiant and triumphant hosts lining the farther bank of the Potomac and the Ohio, feuds raging in every Northern State and city, our debt, currency, business, and wealth alike worthless, while Slavery lifted her crested head, and hissed her triumphs in the ear of an amazed and ruined world. No blessing would such a peace have won us, but misery and death.

Far otherwise has been the gift and goodness of God. He bestows upon us a peace that is full of richest rewards; one in which the spirit of rebellion, rampant in the land for thirty years, raging like an unloosed menagerie for four years, has been disarmed, if not subdued; in which the fiercer demon of Slavery has been cast out of the nation at once and forever, and four millions of her long-suffering children are sitting at her feet, clothed and in their right mind; one in which the nations of the earth that despised us, and desired our destruction, are constrained to stand in awe of the majesty of our strength and the greater majesty of our continence, and behold their systems of restraint and misgovernment crumbling like banks of mist before our rising sun.

The salvation of other vital ideas is worthy of especial rejoicings. Peace has not only brought liberty, it has secured the perpetuity of a free, and equal, and united nation. They are dead that sought the young Child's life. The best civil expression of the Gospel of Him of Bethlehem was in extremest peril. It was the youngest of political forms, too often spoken of by ourselves as an experiment; always thus regarded across the seas. Against this central necessity of a truly Christian state, against the only possible system of permanent and righteous government, arose the mighty rebellion. It not only planted itself on human bondage, it allied itself with thrones. Mr. Mason claimed the sympathy of the British aristocracy, because the idea and purpose of his government were one with their forms and principles. He won it because of this unity. The young child of a democratic Union was thus fearfully assailed. It has survived its assailants. So far as possessing any power of renewing their attack, they are dead that sought the young child's life. The Gospel of the Son of God can now grow in its civil and national expression, unalarmed by the foes of its own household. They have become its footstool. They will yet be its faithful servants and supporters. All the imperial powers that joined in heart and lip in the murderous endeavor, will acknowledge its triumph, and conform their institutions to its ordinances divine.

Such are some of the gracious favors with which God has been pleased to crown this hour and people. It is the grand Sabbatic jubilee of the nation. She rests from her painful labors. Her work of creation has greatly progressed, if it has not attained completion. She can justly rejoice in the propitious hour.

"Grim visaged War has smoothed his wrinkled front."

The bells have rung merrily their sacred summons to the altar of thanksgiving. Again, and as never before, can we join in the psalm of peace and praise.

"Joy to the pleasant land we love,
The land our fathers trod;
Joy to the land for which they won
Freedom to worship God;
For peace on all its sunny hills,
On every mountain broods,
And sleeps by all its gushing rills,
And all its mighty floods.

"The wife sits meekly by the hearth,
Her infant child beside;
The father, on his noble boy,
Looks with a fearless pride.
The gray old man, beneath the tree,
Tales of his childhood tells;
And sweetly in the hush of morn
Peal out the Sabbath bells."

Especially can we add the last verse of these lines, and feel that the joy and peace are now truly attained. Then the poet was constrained to add.

"And we are free — but is there not
One blot upon our name?
Is our proud record written fair
Upon the scroll of fame?
Our banner floateth by the shore,
Our flag upon the sea;
But when the fettered slave is loosed
We shall be truly free."

That fetter has fallen, that liberty secured, and calm is complete.

III. But the Sabbath, though a day of rest, is still more a day of work. Never do duties press more steadily upon us than on these days of God. Never has the Creator been more active than since He ceased from six days of creation, and entered upon the present Sabbath of earth and time. The grosser work is ended of forming sun, and moon, and stars, and earth; of bringing into being trees and plants, fish, and bird, and beast; even the highest of this material handiwork, the fashioning of man; but the spiritualizing of that man, his preservation in purity, his growth into families, communities, nations of holy ones, his restoration if he falls, and by a long and painful path, which God Himself must build and traverse in sorrow unto death, his attainment of the beatific state of universal brotherhood, a developed, happy, holy world — all this is the work of the seventh day, the Sabbath of God and of the world.

So we have accomplished the grosser work of physical subjugation, and are called to enter the spiritual service of regeneration. The armies are scattered, the forts possessed, the cannon mounted by trusty soldiers, the flag respected and obeyed, the whole land freed from open rebellion. This work of creation is completed.

But a greater yet remains. The inward work is yet to be done — a work in us no less than in the region this sin has so long made a hell, and God's judgments have made an Aceldama.

That work is one in idea, though manifold in form. It is this, and this only, and this entirely — to erase from our statutes, our tongues, our hearts, every recognition of color as a badge of distinction or separation between man and man. The outer work of this regeneration is accomplished, the inner is yet unachieved; the material, or six days' work, is done, the spiritual or Sabbath duty is begun. The outer work was to break the chains of the slave, and put a musket in his hands, to fight for himself and his country. These two acts accomplished, proved him at the least, and at the most, but a physical man. The harness of slavery had made him a brute. He was like the ox and the mule by whose side he toiled. I have seen one driving his team afield, with a vivid sense of the slaveholding feeling that they were substantially one. Both had been bought or raised on the farm; both had a market value; both had been or could be sold; both were as much objects of property as the plough which united them. The purchaser of stock put them together in his bill, the assessor in his schedule, the sheriff in his sale. The people spoke of so many head of slaves as they did of so many head of cattle.

Until this yoke was removed no inward regeneration could be effected. God might shine in upon him and sanctify him. He might warm his heart with the breath of earthly love, make him a devoted son, husband, and father, make him an humble, joyful Christian; but man could not recognize these inner and spiritual gifts, as they were not marketable commodities. They must not interfere with their marketable qualities. Suppose a steam engine should fall in love, and awaken in his mate reciprocal emotion; suppose they should feel that they must go and keep together, irrespective of any rights of corporations or individuals, what would the business men say at such an intrusion upon their domain? They would declare this thing must be stopped, or all our property vanishes. If the internal heat of locomotives takes this amorous and self-dependent form, what may happen to our stores, and houses, and fields, and cattle, even stocks and gold? These coldest of creatures will feel the general warmth with which Lucretius tells us all nature reciprocates the affection of its Creator.

Two elephants, the papers said, last winter, hybernating together at Pittsburg, fell in love. Their tender attachment was the theme of much gossip and amusement on the part of probably their more callous keepers. Spring came, and their different owners said they must be separated. Grief and rage extreme tore the hearts of the noble beasts at the enforced decree. Alas, multitudes of men and women, tender, deep, and true, whose hearts and lives God had made one, have been torn apart by far more cruel hands over half our land for hundreds of years. The wants and wishes of their proprietors came between the feelings of these legal beasts, and husband and wife, mother and babe, have been as carelessly parted as dam and foal, or cow and calf, a span of horses, or a yoke of oxen.

I had before me as I was writing this discourse the auction bills of Charleston, in which are described the creatures to be sold, with their names and ages. I read such names, ages, and descriptions as these: "Cicero, 55, driver; Hester, 20, field-hand, prime, one eye lost by an accident." The accident that happened to this young lady and "prime field-hand" may be easily imagined. It was probably not unlike that accident which happened to Isabella Joyce, that terminated her life in awful tragedy. "Maud, 16, field-hand, prime." A pretty name, a Maud Muller, only with an infinitely worse fate. "Infant, 6 mos." The creature had not yet attained to the dignity of a name, save that name which makes every parental heart throb in love — a babe upon the block, and no mother specified. One among the lot may have been its agonized mother, and may not. "March, 35;" who is described as "a field-hand, and A 1 cook." "Joe, 18, prime field-hand, two years at carpenter's trade," is yoked, we trust lovingly and righteously, with "Julia, 16 years of age." This young carpenter and his youthful companion, knocked down to the highest bidder, like a pair of horses at auction, give you some faint idea of the horrors of that hell of hells. Listen still further: "Flora, seamstress, 24," with "Jemmy, 30, and James and Charles, 5 and 1," probably their children, James being the dignified title with which she honors her husband in his boy. "Abram, 2 years old," and "Binah, 2 mos.," are on the list. "Lucy, a cripple, 60," "Lucy, a nurse, 58;" another carpenter, also named "Joe, aged 25." Perhaps this name was given to these artisans because the father of the Lord Jesus Christ was of that name and trade. It was an appropriate title and calling. No doubt their Lord and Master often toiled with them at their task. This Joe had a little family, "Amey, 27, Louisa, 8, and Joe, Jr., 3." They all brought seven hundred and fifty dollars, as a clerkly pencil writes on the paper. Kate, a babe of a year, goes into the iron mill; William, of the same age: Molly, standing alone, a maiden of 22 summers, brings the handsome figure of thirteen hundred and fifty dollars. "May, 9 mos., Aaron, 6 mos., Lizzy, 1 year, Emma, 3," pretty names are these; pretty faces we doubt not; pretty souls, certainly, as they look weeping and agonized up to the face of their like weeping and agonized Lord. More than a hundred such names are on these three bills of sale at The Mart, as this haunt of hell was by distinction called. How they point to the myriads whose fate they shared!

See you not, my friends, that slavery must be destroyed ere the first step in manhood is taken. These sons and daughters of the Lord God Almighty must be taken from the list of merchantable things and made into men and women.

Before this, not human feelings alone were disregarded, the Divine Spirit was despised. He might renew them in holiness. He might say to them, "Ye are no longer your own; ye are bought with a price; ye are the servants of the Lord your Redeemer." But these men step in, Christians professedly, and say, "We hold them still as ours. What care we for the Holy Ghost? He may renew their heart. He may make them free men in Christ Jesus, He cannot make them free from us. Should a revival of religion break out among our mules, would that spoil them for our fields or markets." So they mocked the God of heaven, and he has rained upon them fire and brimstone, and a horrible tempest, and this has been the portion of their cup. Beholding such dreadful deeds committed by lordly merchants, supported by eminent jurists and statesmen, sanctified by consecrated divines, carried on for generations, against every pulse of humanity, every call of conscience, even entreaty of God, how could we expect any other doom? It is only amazing that God has borne with it as long as He has. His long suffering is greater than when "He waited in the days of

Noah while the ark was a preparing." His ark now has been long preparing. The North has been ripening in conscience under the preaching of many Noahs until the nation was ready to become the ark of shelter for these suffering children. Then came the flood. Death has leaped into their houses, while their slaves walk out in freedom. Their sons perish by myriads, their prophets flee, their pride falls: what pride and what a fall! Their ruin is complete, while those that they had stolen, and sold, and scourged, and ravished, and treated with unutterable inhumanity, dwell harmless amid their conquerors' desolation. Never was there such a contrast in the same land at the same time. The slave lost nothing for they had naught to lose. The hatred and fear of the master prevented his employment of them in battle, and so they have escaped the death which has invaded every other class in all the land. They were valueless as merchandise, and therefore their sale and separation ceased. They were eased in toil and free from the lash, for they found favor in the eyes of their masters when it was seen that the families of those who fought for their bondage must be intrusted to their keeping.

Thus has light been in captive Goshen, while darkness was on Pharaoh's palaces; thus have no death-wails broken from their riven hearts, while in almost every other household has there been lamentation and bitter mourning.

As we see this divine punishment and protection, we can but exclaim, Just and true are thy ways, Lord God Almighty. Thou hast cast down the mighty from their seats, and exalted them of low degree. It has come to pass in this day that the Lord has given them rest from their sorrow, and from their fear, and from their hard bondage; while those who held them captive are themselves captured, and all their pomp and power have become a burning and a desolation forever.

"The blood that they have shed could hide no longer
In the blood-slaken soil, but cried to Heaven.
Their cruelties and wrongs against the poor
Have quickened into swarms of venomous snakes,
And hissed through all the earth, till o'er the earth,
That ceases now from hissings and from groans,
Rises the song, — How are the mighty fallen!
And by the peasant's hand. Low lie the proud,
And smitten with the weapons of the poor, —
The blacksmith's hammer, and the woodman's ax.
Their tale is told; and for that they were rich,
And robbed the poor; and for that they were strong,
And scourged the weak; and for that they made laws,
Which turned the sweat of labor's brow to blood, —
For these, their sins, the nations cast them out;
The dunghills are their death-beds, and the stench
From their uncovered carrion, steaming wide,
Turns in the nostrils of enfranchised man
To a sweet savor. These things come to pass
From small beginnings, because God is just."

1. These chains broken, the next step is to recognize the slave as a man outwardly. This was done by putting the rifle in his grasp. True, a soldier is largely a machine, but he is a human machine. We use horses for riders, not for fighters. The ancients employed elephants, moderns confine themselves to men. Their valor, obedience, and skill have tested this quality of their manhood.

The outer line is carried. The inner is yet to be won. The country has been compelled to recognize the physical manhood and brotherhood; it must now their spiritual.

In this duty, as in the first, much is to be done here. It was almost as great a deed to organize a colored regiment in Boston as it was in Richmond. Governor Banks vetoed the whole Revised Statutes, a volume of a thousand pages, because it struck the word "white" from the militia law. Had he been her Governor, Massachusetts had not led the column in this onward movement. Governor Andrew faced a frowning and a sneering city when he called his neighbors to arms. The President did not dare to march them through New York. They would have met a worse fate than did the Sixth in Baltimore. We hated and despised them as much as we did Davis and his myrmidons. We have partially, and but partially, overcome that feeling.

This chain must be dissolved from their necks and from ours. On its various links I shall not enlarge. They are evident to every man's consciousness. The right of suffrage may be won at the South only at great expense of time and toil, and possibly of blood. Were there more blacks than whites in this State, and you whites held the whole power in your hands, would you admit them to its privileges without a struggle? No party holding such power ever yet abandoned it gratuitously. There are more blacks than whites in Mississippi and South Carolina, if not in the other States. The present Governor of Louisiana declares that to give him the ballot gives him the country. But yesterday's paper reports him as saying to his white hearers, "If after having taken this country from the red man, and holding it for more than a century you have become so charitable as to give it to the black man, I can only submit and bow to the will of the people." The *people* he understands to be not the majority of its citizens, but its former voters, four fifths of whom were and are rank rebels. They must deprive their loyal fellow-citizens of equal rights, or the State goes into the hands of the man of color. It is something of an advance for him to call him *man;* something to say the people may, if they will, give the State into his hands. The white people will not grant this, but God will. They may shrink from such a complete overturn in their society, but it is inevitable. The South must admit the black, not to the supremacy, but to equality. Their blood must mingle as freely in the channels of social unity as it has on the fields of carnage. They are at antagonism to-day. Some event may arise, will arise, that will force them into an indissoluble unity.

2. This future in the State is none the less the future of the Church, and the duty of peace is to insure this future. It is all comprised in one text. There is neither Greek nor Jew, male nor female, barbarian, Scythian, bond nor free, but Christ is all and in all. Its workings everybody feels, but few are willing to acknowledge, fewer are willing to obey. That a church can stand permanently on any other foundation is as impossible as it is for God to lie. That brethren in Christ are to be set apart because of their color from other brethren ; that the ministers of Jesus Christ are to be forbidden from serving in pulpits, to which their talents summon them, because of their complexion; not even because of this, but because they happen to have a small portion of descent from one of God's continents and peoples, is a scandal and offence, a stench in the nostrils of the Almighty. Not their skin, but our pride, is rank, and smells to heaven. Nay, more, "it hath the primeval, eldest curse upon it, a brother's murder." For he that hateth his brother is a murderer ; and we all hate our brethren of this blood when we seek thus their segregation and degradation. The church of the South, the church of the North, must be reconstructed on this basis. We talk of reconstruction in the State, and negro suffrage. There must be equal reconstruction in the Church.

To this work dedicate yourself. Ten years only are wanting to complete the first century of our national history. What a century has it been. How grand in promises. How far grander in fulfillment. Dr. Styles, of Yale College, in a Thanksgiving sermon, preached before the Legislature of Connecticut, May 8, 1783, with the title, "The United States raised to Glory and Honor," is lavish of his prophecies on the future of America. Any but an American reading his words would have called them the ravings of fanaticism. But they are more than fulfilled. His grandest dreams are trivial by the side of the realities of history. Our last incubus is cast off, cut away from us by the sharp knife of the Divine Surgeon, with great loss of blood, and almost with loss of national life. Yet we survive, and ere this century of our Lord concludes its course such a progress is to be witnessed materially and spiritually as we never yet imagined.

Europe, Asia, and probably Africa, will pour forth their millions over the fat earth of the West and South; the mines will cast their inexhaustable treasures into the national lap. The negro will rise to posts of honor and authority in all the land, will sit in Congress, will rule as governor where till yesterday he toiled as a slave, will be settled as pastors in the highest pulpits, will be partners in our largest houses, guests in our most aristocratic parlors, residents in our richest palaces, and men shall smile at the idea of distinction of color, as they now do at the divinity of slavery. The grace of our Lord Jesus Christ shall renew the land in holiness and love. The Churches will melt into harmonious oneness, each esteeming the others better than itself. Law will everywhere forbid the sale of intoxicating drinks as a beverage, will give universal education and universal protection.

Thus shall the regeneration of all the lands be perfected. The Church shall rise to her true hights of divine brotherhood, the State and society shall conform to her in all their lower but powerful activities. The inward holiness shall be wrought into outward virtue. The Sabbath work shall crown with its ineffable glory the humbler labors of preceding generations. The earth shall rest in gladness and laugh in harvests. The industry of man shall find full rewards. The unity and married calm of States shall be perfect and perpetual. The people of God shall be one people, none biting and devouring each other, but all moving like a mighty army of many battalions and many commanders, under the Captain of our salvation, to the bloodless victory of the human race and the consummation of a perfect eternity.

> "Then comes the statelier Eden back to man;
> Then reign the world's great bridals, chaste and calm;
> Then springs the crowning race of humankind, —
> May these things be."

AMERICA'S PAST AND FUTURE.*

"TO-MORROW SHALL BE AS THIS DAY, AND MUCH MORE ABUNDANT." — *Isaiah* lvi. 12.

OW many weary years contribute to the triumph of this hour. Standing on this summit, beholding the glory that is breaking forth upon all our land, feeling the joy that pervades every breast, we can hardly fail to look back upon the steps that slowly led, through indifference, hostility, storms of war, and streams of blood, to these Delectable Mountains. One who hung delighted over the peaceful Paradise, where Adam and Eve in their fresh-created perfection walked in a garden of calm and fragrance, could not refrain from vivifying the scene by contrasting it with the previous elemental war, the darkness and confusion of chaos, creatures fierce and gross of nature, that filled the mighty carboniferous forests with their roar, the whole abhorent, unelevating scene: —

* A sermon preached at Medford, Massachusetts, on Thanksgiving Day, November 26, 1868, on the election of Ulysses S. Grant to the Presidency of the United States.

"Wrapt in impervious mists, which ever steamed
Up from its boiling oceans, without form
And void, it rolled around the sun, which cast
Strange lurid lights on the revolving mass,
But pierced not to the solid globe beneath:
Such vast eruption of internal fires
Had mingled sea and land.

* * * * * *

Earth to its center shook; and what were seas
Unsounded, were of half their waters drained;
And what were wildernesses, ocean-beds;
And mountain ranges, from beneath upheaved,
Clave with their granite peaks primeval plains,
And rose sublime above the water floods;
Floods overflowed themselves with seas of mist,
Which swathed in darkness all terrestrial things,—
A world unfurnished, empty, void, and vast."

Out of this wreck of matter came the perfection of Eden, and the blessedness of the holy parents of our race. As the angels beheld the darkness and destruction, how could they anticipate the coming light and life? Only the consciousness of an indwelling and overruling God of infinite right, and love, and power, gave them the desired assurance. Resting calmly in that knowledge, they beheld the prevailing darkness, the baleful government of the Prince of the Power of the Air, the mighty conflict, the ever increasing signs of the progress of the kingdom of God, the subjugation of one foe after another, of fire and fog, of savagest beast, huge, amorphous, with many a scaly fold, voluminous and vast, whose presence, whether as lizard, mammoth, or winged and web-footed monsters, would have made the earth uninhabitable to man. They saw the conflict increase in fierceness as it began to consummate itself in the final victory; the death-ocean of ice from pole to pole being the last, and, to other eyes than those of faith, the complete annihilation of all life positive and possible. But in faith they still looked and labored. Conspiring with their Creator, they aided in the resurrection of the earth from this sepulcher of being, and again beheld it glowing in more beautiful and more abundant life on the Paradisaic morn of the human creation and their Edenic home .

I. So we can note the mighty war of spiritual, and even of material elements, that has attended this new creation of our land and people in the truth and love of God. We can look back over centuries, and behold the beginnings of that iniquity whose overthrow this victory completes. Nay, centuries measure not its horrid life. From the first sin, this principle has possessed the hearts of men ; from the first sinner, it has found foothold in human society. "Thou shalt rule over her," was the estate into which one half of the race was plunged by the first transgressor. "Thou shalt rule over him," the first declaration made to Cain concerning Abel, cast a large portion of the other half into the same chains. The husband held his wife as property, and beat, petted, or sold her, as his passions prompted. The father owned his children, the eldest son his brothers. In fact, the law of sin was a law of bondage. Slavery was the first-born of Satan and the fallen pair ; slavery of mind, and heart, and body. It is the favorite term of Scripture to express the relation of the lost soul to its lost master.

This iniquity developed rapidly, and prevailed like the flood over all the earth. Whole nations were made slaves in an hour ; one mighty overthrow of its protecting army by an invading host reduced every person in the realm to property. Cities were thus changed from liberty to slavery in a moment ; states were transformed in a day. All Israel went into captivity after one battle. All Egypt was reduced to vassalage by one conquering hour of Persian, Grecian, or Roman arms. India's multitudinous millions fell thus beneath the victorious stroke of a foreign general. All Northern Europe became the slaves of Cæsar.

"He hath brought many captives home to Rome,"

is the praise for him that Shakspeare naturally puts in the lips of Antony.

Whatever mitigation this law might receive through the clemency of its executors, or the difficulty in its execution, it was still the law of society, and, as a whole, faithfully adhered to through vast ages of degraded humanity. Athens, in the hight of its power, had twenty slaves to one freeman in its population—slaves of the same blood, speech, and nationality as their masters. Rome had an equal proportion in her own walls, and far greater in her Italian domain. The whole world was one vast plantation, where slaves toiled and suffered without recompense or hope. Only Judea, in the time of Christ, had become a free state. It stood alone among kingdoms, recognizing in its laws no property in man.

It is an answer alike to all professed religious progressives, and to all contemners of Jewish Christianity, that this State stood solitary in its doctrine of the liberty of all men. Why had not Grecian culture and philosophy, of which we so loudly prate, effected a like amelioration for that beautiful clime? Pericles had ruled, Phidias carved, Plato written, Demosthenes spoken, Socrates talked, Homer sung, and the men of Marathon and Thermopylæ had fought; yet Greece was still a state of slaves. India, too, the favorite haunt of modern skepticism, where it is fancied the first rising of modern thought and faith can be clearly seen; whose Buddha and Brahma it is pretended are the sources of all religious truth—where was India in its humanitarian development when Christian Judea acknowledged every man free and equal, and was practicing that "declaration of independence" which we have yet failed to fully receive? India was the greatest slaveholding state in the world. A few of a higher caste held hundreds of millions of their kindred in chains—hold them to this day in more than adamantine fetters; for these can be broken; no power can yet dissolve, only One can ever dissolve, these bonds of caste — and that is the power of Christ Crucified; to the formalist and unprogressive Jew a stumbling-block; to the haughty-minded Greek, foolishness; but to them that believe, both Jews and Greeks, Christ the Power of God and the Wisdom of God.

This liberty the chosen nation lost by rejecting its sole Author, and on its captivity, the human race was plunged again into universal slavery. Out of this deluge that overwhelmed mankind in a worse than material destruction, society slowly emerged through the diffusion and energy of Christianity. The Church broke these bonds. She abolished slavery in Italy and the Orient. She tamed down its horrors in Northern Europe, and swept it away in gradual centuries from every European Christian country. Had she been more faithful, her victories would have been earlier and greater; and long since she would have redeemed the world to Christ and Liberty.

As it is, her work has been great and her progress steady. Rome broke the chains from the body if she bound them on the soul. Athens became Christian and free. Egypt, under her bishops and other clergy, emerged from her idolatry and her serfdom. England broke the yoke from our Saxon fathers, and stopped the slave trade between Ireland and England, that flourished even after the invasion of William and the erection of Victoria's throne. Kingsley, in his Hereward, or the "Last of the English," describes this traffic in language not unsuited to the Charleston and Richmond of our own generation.*

This emancipation was not completed till our own day; and the present Emperor of the Russias has the honor of closing the list of European sovereigns who have released from bondage European peoples. None of that branch of mankind are now held in servitude, save such as Turkey binds, or as on our own continent, in Brazil and Cuba, have

* See Note XXI.

their blood tinted with the hues of a fraternal race, soon to disappear from these dominions.

II. But while slavery was thus dying at the bidding of Christianity, — and at her bidding only, — it still existed in regions unvisited by her rays, and intruded its baleful presence into lands that had been settled exclusively in her interests. Driven from Europe, it took refuge in Africa. Denied sovereignty of men of white complexion, it infamously suggested to the carnal heart that abolitionism depended on color, not on humanity: that it was wrong — of course it was, now that it could no longer be sustained — to enslave white people, Caucasians, the ruling race, the divinely appointed head of creation; but that fact not only permits, it *requires*, the enslavement of the antipodal race. The white skin is emancipated because it is white. That logic necessitates the enslavement of the black skin. So the devil feeds our too susceptible hearts with the Satanism of caste, and sweeps the whole Christian Church — at least in America — into bondage to this opinion. He makes us look on our brother with loathing. He makes us separate him from ourselves as an abhorred thing. He makes us exclude him from our table, our pulpit, our pew, our shop, our store, our homes, our hearts. He diffuses such a murky mist of prejudice over society, that we inhale its miasm as our constant atmosphere, and under its cloud work out his plans for the perpetuation of his power over us and our victims as long as he can keep us under his sinful influence. Expelled from the white class, this iniquity begs permission to invade the black and ruin it. And so a legion of evil spirits rush upon the hapless victim, and drive him headlong into the abyss of shame and agony. For three hundred and fifty years has this abomination flourished. From the first modern African slave-maker, stealer, and trader, Prince Henry of Portugal, the first navigator of Western Africa, and the sea-father of Vasco de Gama and Columbus, even until now, has the Afric shore echoed with the screams of these victims, the ocean been incarnadined with their blood. Before America was discovered, from six to eight hundred Africans were annually imported into Portugal. The Moors were the chief traders, and their horses their chief coin. They bought ten to eighteen men for a Barbary steed.

Columbus deserved his end for his treatment of the Indians, who received him as a god, and to whom he became a demon. He stole them by the thousand, and sold them in Spanish ports. He offered to supply four thousand annually to Ferdinand and Isabella, and estimated the revenue to the crown, from their sale, at fifty thousand dollars per annum. He was the father of all the Indian barbarities that yet curse our government, and make our line of advance to the Pacific Sea a red line of the red man's blood. But Columbus did not introduce the negro to save the Indian; nor did Las Casas, the emancipator of the Indian, as is too frequently charged. He accepted him to his subsequent regret, but he did not first import him. The African was brought over by the earliest traders as an item of commerce, when as yet Indian slavery was flourishing, and bishops, priests, kings, governors, and colonists alike flourished upon it. He was a captive here as soon as his American brother. He has outlived him as a slave, he may also as a freeman.

From that hour to this you see the strides of this giant iniquity. How it overrun all the India Islands, the neighboring shores north and south, crept down to Brazil and up to Mexico, crossed over to the Pacific, and swept the coast from its southern to its northern belt of ice and so-called civilization; how it struck at the Christian colonies of France and England, and whatever their diversities and hostilities of creed, compelled them alike into bondage to this crime. The Puritans, Churchmen, Papists, and Quakers, the sons of the martyrs of Holland and France, Huguenots and Synodists of Dort, the followers of Cromwell and of Charles, all creeds, classes, tongues and tribes, plunged into this cruelty and crime. And to this day, those who bear this mixed religion and national blood in their veins are the bitterest foes in the world of the negro and of emancipation. They despise him in all the North, they hate his liberation in all the South. Of one blood are we and our rebellious brethren, in our near origin, and in our feelings toward our long-enslaved kindred, the oldest of our race from the oldest of our continents.

III. The controversy God has waged with us because of this sin we all know by heart, especially its last and bloodiest chapters. We know how our Constitution admitted seemingly, and in the intent of its founders, this iniquity, though it also enunciated principles that made it actually unconstitutional. We all know how Washington violated these fundamental principles in signing the first fugitive slave bill; how Monroe and Congress again violated them in approving of the extension of slavery into free territory beyond the Mississippi; how the Church and the State descended together to the pit of destruction, and sank so low that the Church refused to listen to the testimony of one of its sisters if she had been ravished of her virtue by her owner, provided he was also a member of the same church; while separate States inflicted upon these victims every conceivable and inconceivable barbarity, and the nation forbid any one from harboring those who might escape from this den of lions, and even prohibited his refusing to assist in their recapture under penalty of heavy fines and imprisonment.

Thus Church and State were married by and to the Devil. Thus an offspring burst forth in all the land and in every household of bitter contempt and malice toward God's children and our own brethren; an offspring of pride, and passion, and avarice; an offspring that made the minister of

Christ the minister of Satan; that erected the auction-block for human souls under the shadow of Christian churches; that made our flag protect cargoes of chained citizens on the long ocean pathway from the Chesapeake to the Rio Grande; that filled thousands of pulpits with prayers and preachings, to which God responded, "My soul hateth;" that changed our hearts to stone before the beseeching cries of our own brothers and sisters; that wrought evil after evil by the arm of the State and the sinful blessing of the Church, until the line forbidding slavery in millions of miles of territory was blotted out; the rights of the man of color, whatever the dimness of his tint, declared invalid before any national court; the right to prevent his introduction as a slave into any free State taken away; and slavery had become, in the language of its most eminent advocate, "the corner-stone of the Constitution."

Against this prevalence of iniquity God raised up enemies, in the Church and out of it, in the nation and abroad; in the principle with which he fired our hearts, and the scourges with which he compelled our sins to chastise us; everywhere the forces of the Almighty were aroused and organized to confront this gigantic sin. How His flag sunk and rose in the varying conflict. How the hearts of His followers failed them for fear, and inflamed them with hope, as alternate failure and success attended their efforts and their prayers. Especially did fear possess them as they saw the end of all their preliminary battles; as clear and more clear the determination of the slaveholder "to fight it out on this line" became evident, and confidence in the willingness of his foe to meet him on the bloody field failed to be developed with equal certainty. Many were the attempts made, not by the slavocrat, but by his antagonists, to avoid this issue. We offered to extend the Missouri line to the Pacific coast. We offered to introduce an amendment into the Constitution forbidding the National Government from ever emancipating a slave. We kissed their hands and feet in fear of the threat of disunion which they constantly flourished over us. Many went yet further, and advocated the dismissal of the slave-holding section. Even some of our wisest leaders fell into this snare. Phillips and Garrison, Chase and Greeley, advised this course. They did not believe the people would endure the test to which the Union would compel them. They feared slavery would subdue the North, rather than the North abolish slavery. They dreamed that, cut off from the North, the slave would soon compel his master to emancipation. But the wisdom of God is wiser than men. He allowed His enemies to most daringly defy our national principles, organization, and even existence. He strengthened His friends to meet defiance with defiance, treason with faithfulness, hatred of the country and its principles with increasing flame of devotion to every vital national idea. They sought to extirpate its love of liberty. He excited it by innumerable harangues. They denounced the Union. He fed the sacred flame of devotion to this outward and essential body of the national soul. So, when the night of staggering weakness and seeming dissolution came; when men's hearts were everywhere failing themselves with fear, and with a looking for the things that were about to come upon the earth; when the head of the nation threw up his imbecile hands in confessed powerlessness, and allowed his chiefs of State to rob his treasury and arsenals, to scatter his petty navy and pettier army, while he, like a sick girl, cried "No coercion," "I shall be the last President of the United States," as he certainly will be the least; when the President elect had to steal into his capital in disguise, and foreign observers were writing home, "The Constitution of the United States can be bought on Broadway for three cents, and that is a higher price than the people set upon it" — even then the slowly-growing opposition was solidifying itself for the coming struggle, and at the first word of command from the authoritative source, sprang up in arms as cheerfully, as enthusiastically, as multitudinously as the angels leaped to the call of their Lord for the overthrow of the rebellious host, and the unity and liberty of the Heavenly Kingdom.

> "The mighty quadrate, joined
> Of union irresistible, moved on
> In silence, the bright legions to the sound
> Of instrumental harmony, that breathed
> Heroic ardor, to adventurous deeds
> Under their godlike leaders, in the cause
> Of God and his Messiah."

IV. That struggle gave birth to our coming President. He was one of those who saw and felt the full force of the conflict, at least in its material form. He measured the greatness of the war before a soldier had been summoned to arms, or a blow had been struck by the enemy. In that doleful winter of our weakness he, the humble merchant of a country town, was carefully studying the forces of the rebellion. His minister spent an evening with him at that time, and saw him as he rose up in the enthusiasm of his discourse, and stood with form dilated, filled with the vastness of his theme. When he left, he said to his wife, "Did you notice how much Mr. Grant resembled Napoleon?" Little did his guests think how complete that resemblance was, and how all the world, before three years elapsed, would recognize him as the successor to this soldier in the military annals of the century.

His wife had a clearer vision. To this same gentleman, expressing on the morning of his departure hopes that her husband would return in safety, she replied, "I hope he will return major general, or something of that sort." She was probably the only person in the country that saw this capacity or entertained these expectations. His father to this day seems to have no apprehension of him. He still says, "Ulysses accomplishes all he does through hard work," having no perception of that genius which alone makes that hard work create victory out of defeat, and a world of renown out of a chaos of ruin.

1. Six years ago no man was more unknown. To-day his deeds are written broadest of all our soldiers' on the pages of our history. No general before him has an equal record. He has made the fields of Trenton, Yorktown, Bunker Hill, Buena Vista, and Cherubusco sink into insignificance beside the names of Shiloh, Vicksburg, Chattanooga, and Richmond. His military power is sure.

But greater than his prowess is the cause he served. He saved the best of nations; he slew the worst of crimes. Through his gift alone was the Republic of America preserved unbroken, preserved at all. No other general appeared that seemed equal to the necessity. Sherman's gifts were not such as could put squadrons in the field, nor conduct tedious and perplexing sieges. Sheridan could hurl his forces like storm-driven waves upon the line of his foe, scattering them like spray in the swiftness and mightiness of his blows. Thomas alone revealed powers that might have won for him the chieftainship. But even he failed to reveal the combination of organizing, steadfast, far-seeing, daring, and impetuous qualities that tower in the character of Grant.

He has kept intact our vast boundaries, and insured their vaster expansion. He has changed the contempt of all nations into respect, and implanted a dread of our prowess and our ideas that is a sure precursor of a fast-hastening change in all their states conformable to our triumphant principles. He has insured the essential extension of America over the world. Already the United States of Europe are openly advocated in congresses from all her peoples; and that more distant and dubious title, the United States of Asia, looms up mistily from the far horizon. Even the United States of Africa will be born in due time into the family of republics; while the United States of America shall encompass the whole continent in her oceanic lines. Thus from this victory over the rebellion will arise a fraternity of nations, few in number, divided by no alienation of language, government, or faith; ultimately to become one with each other, with Christ, with God.

To this consummation the man just elected to the headship of the Republic has chiefly contributed. Joshua's arm alone could batter down the walls of Ai, and Gath, and Askelon. Moses, the Lincoln Liberator, must give way to the conquering warrior. David's military genius alone enabled Israel to complete its appointed boundaries, and send its banners and its laws from the Euphrates to the Nile. So the mighty foes of this nation — mightier than ever before arose from the heart of any State for its overthrow, and failed in their undertaking — could never have been suppressed by any genius save one that instinctively grasped the whole field of deadly debate, and as instinctively discerned the path to the mastery.

This ability may have included more than it had opportunity for exhibition. Had France succeeded in Mexico, and proceeded thence to assail the Union, his acquaintance with that territory might have been called into requisition to smite this new foe in the farther South. Had England followed out the instincts of all her ruling classes, and engaged in the support of the rebellion, even to the refastening the fetters on the neck of the slave, his military genius would have reënacted the victory of Scott on the field of Lundy's Lane, and the triumph of Wolfe on the Plains of Abraham. The controversy of Nova Scotia would have been settled by its absorption into our nationality, and the ambition of Canada been more than gratified by becoming an integer in the Continental Republic.

His administration may witness this Northern and Southern extension of our boundaries by the arts of peace, which, had France and England dared to enter our field of civil debate, might have been speedily accomplished by deeds of war.

2. But while we thus linger around the services which our General and President have rendered to our nation and to all nations, and behold the pleasant visions of coming consequences of his great victories, we should be forgetful of his chief victory and its chief duty if we failed to dwell upon the grandest results of his arms. Unlike all other great generals, his military fame is indissolubly united with the emancipation of millions of slaves. Alexander drove back the Eastern powers, and put Europe for the first time where England and Russia keep her to-day, on the neck of Asia. But he gave no people their liberty. His triumphs were military alone, or at the best political. Cæsar, undoubtedly the first of warriors in the ante-Christian ages, reduced free nations to slavery, and added vast multitudes of bondmen to the already glutted man-market of Italy. To no race nor man did his powers bring liberty. He even put the dagger to the Roman Republic, and was the acknowledged founder of an imperial dynasty whose name is yet boastfully assumed as their own by a ruling house of Europe, while his spirit animates the most despotic of emperors.

Of every later captain the same sad fact is true. Napoleon reduced liberated France to bondage. Wellington tied the English and European nations to aristocratic and despotic institutions. Only Washington and Cromwell made their arms deliver their peoples; and they did not break such yokes or bestow such liberty as it was given to our General to achieve. His genius was employed not to enslave, but to emancipate; not to beat back aggressive tyrannies, but to uproot them; not to release from civil bondage, but from human; not to save states, but men.

This puts his name as far above his rivals as the deeds of humanity surpass those of mere ability. The inventor of a needle-gun may show as great genius as the inventor of the needle in the sewing-machine. But the latter has made his talent relieve the toil and enrich the gains of millions of the poor, while the former only increases the number of the slain in the field of battle. The mere military genius, as such, is often the least valuable gift of God to man. The poet is of more worth ; the preacher a far better blessing ; the inventor, and discoverer, and educator are his superior. He is but a boxer on a bigger scale. He fights with others' fists, as John Morrissey gambles with others' hands, as every master works through his subordinates. He masses force, and hurls it upon opposing force. If his force crushes its contrary, it is but the gift of a thunderbolt, an earthquake, a trip-hammer. For what is his genius exerted? That alone decides its value. Byron writes as good poetry as Cowper; perhaps better. But which serves God and his generation with his heaven-given gifts? Davis had as great fitness for statesmanship as Lincoln. Whose talents are put to divine using? It is the end they serve that makes their real value.

So Grant's genius was fortunately devoted to the highest ends. His military skill, like Stephenson's inventive talent, like Wesley's poetic, was employed by God for the best possible service. He struck down not only an army, but an institution. He won not victory merely, but liberty. He rescued not imperiled troops, but an imprisoned race. What God might have done through others had he not arisen cannot be told ; what He did do through him can never be told. Every father then in chains who walks to-day a freeman ; who meets his joyful family around his own thanksgiving table ; every such mother who clasps her babe the closer to her breast, as she feels that no power can snatch it from her arms except He who gave it, and He always leaves it on her heart, whether He holds it here or in heaven ; every child of these parents playing in the unconscious gladness of childhood, not knowing what wonderful brightness lights up his path that never illumined their childhood — these millions owe their innumerable millions of blessings under God to his military ability. Surely, never was a gift divine more divinely honored.

V. What means this election?

The past is past. The future is before us. No man, no nation can go back. We must advance. The London policeman's word in a thronged thoroughfare is the order of the Creator to mankind — "Move on!" What is the path on which he orders us to march? What are the principles which this election is designed by him to settle?

1. It ordains order. The primal element of all progress is peace. Crystals can only be formed in still media. Even the fiery uprushings of the volcano make no gems until they sink in repose. Grant's election assures that condition. He has met the enemy on its last organized field. He has put to rout the assassins as he did the soldiers. The ghosts of rebel fighters, as the Ku Klux profess to be, revisiting the glimpses of the moon with revolvers in their skeleton hands, and murder in their fleshless hearts, will subside again into their unquiet graves. Rest, perturbed spirit of slavery and murder, rest. The man who subdued you living, will subdue your dead. Those that have dared to assume these grave clothes for the indulgence of their own diabolical malice, must cease their bloodthirstiness or join their dead comrades. Through all the South shall there be as complete peace and liberty as throughout the North. "Charley," said our President elect to one of his friends, "Charley, if I am President, every man everywhere shall be protected in the liberty of uttering his opinions."

That vow will be kept. Every rebel knows that it will. He has seen the man who says it at Fort Donelson and Shiloh, at Vicksburg and Chattanooga, in the Wilderness and at Richmond; and he knows that he always keeps his word. In Kentucky, he made peace by driving out the rebel soldier; he will again, by driving out the rebel assassin. In Tennessee, and Mississippi, and Virginia he made peace, sending "the great river unvexed to the sea," sweeping away all armed hostility from Nashville around to its capital, driving the enemy's cannon from the Rapidan to Richmond, and from Richmond into our own victorious lines. They fear his arm. They will crouch, and tremble, and obey. As the devil and his angels fled and fell before the mighty Michael, Prince of God, so will this new revelation of the same evil spirit submit to this new revelation of the decree of the Almighty.

It is a glad dawn for our loyal brethren.

The fugitive loyalist, black and white, has feared the glance of a passer-by, as if it were, as it has too often been, the glare of a murderer. He has trembled when the night closed around his dwelling, lest the ghostly knock should call him from his slumbers to the sleep of death. Never were the lamentations of Jerusalem's prophet over the afflictions of his land more painfully fitted to any people. "We got our bread," must they say, "with the peril of our lives." "They hunt our steps, that we cannot go into our streets." "Our persecutors are swifter than the eagles of the heavens; they pursued us upon the mountains, they laid wait for us in the wilderness." Most sadly identical, also, is the cause of all the misery of Zion and the South. "For the sins of her prophets and the iniquities of her priests that have shed the blood of the just in the midst of her, they have wandered as blind men in the streets, they have polluted themselves with blood, so that men could not touch their garments. The Lord hath accomplished his fury; he hath poured his fierce anger, and it hath kindled a fire in Zion, and it hath devoured the foundations thereof." In this awful condition of promiscuous massacre, the helpless ones have turned despairing eyes to a hostile President and a powerless

Congress. They have made every Christian heart exclaim with the Christian poet, over like horrible barbarities inflicted by the Papal fiends on their Protestant brethren of Vaudois : —

> "Avenge, O, Lord! thy slaughtered saints, whose bones
> Lie scattered on the Alpine mountains cold."

On this darkness peace breaks. The cabin shall be sacred as the castle, the laborer shall toil and travel unharmed. Complexion shall not imperil life, but shall be a bond of mutual affection. The impartial President shall fold all in his protecting arms, and the South shall at last accept in practice the motto of Massachusetts, as she has already adopted her principles. Under liberty shall she enjoy calm quiet through the sword.

2. But if order is heaven's first law, it is only the first. Something must be done. "Quiet, to quick bosoms, is a hell." Quiet is only a condition for life to work in. What is the life that is to work in this condition ?

It has revealed its earliest stages. The universality of suffrage and the equality of legal and civil rights. These steps have been taken in the South in form ; but they are not yet everywhere successful in spirit. They have not been yet taken in all the North in form, though they are largely successful here in spirit. In both regions form and spirit must unite. The South must everywhere cease to forbid the legitimate voter his suffrage ; the North must everywhere cease to forbid its citizens from becoming legal voters. Georgia and Connecticut to-day are practically united. Both exclude law-abiding and patriotic citizens from the ballot. One does it with Colt's revolvers, the other with Colt's workmen. Ohio is as wicked as Louisiana. She has sunken from a hundred thousand majority for liberty to fifteen thousand, because she refused to do this God-demanded duty. She will go into bondage to the enemy, unless she is delivered from this crime. Universal suffrage must be enacted and enforced by the National Government. If we make the South allow her black voters their rights, we must also, through a constitutional amendment, or by congressional enactment, make the North do equal justice. It can only be done by one of these causes. The intensity of prejudice would to-day make almost every State that voted for Grant, where this suffrage does not exist, vote against its bestowal. Missouri cast her ballot for Grant and Slavery. She voted down the rights of man, and voted up the representative of these rights. She struck at her citizens while she struck for the nation. All her sisters would do likewise. Iowa and Minnesota would have no followers in this right action to-day.

It must be done at Washington. The Constitution demands it. The President should urge it — Congress ordain it. Only thus can the blot which stains this jubilee-hour be wiped away. General Grant has not received all the votes that legitimately belong to him in this election. Thousands of brown hands would have gladly put his name into the ballot-box, had not this wicked prejudice forbade. They felt the insult and the ignominy all the more keenly as those same hands have pulled the trigger in the hottest of the fight, under the same great General, for the salvation of the country. To-day they are refused the privilege of serving in the bloodless battle, while it is now years since they were allowed, or gladly hastened, or were in not a few cases even compelled, to stand upon the fiercest ridge of war.

How long shall this evil continue? Every one must labor and pray that the root of slavery shall be extirpated, and that our President at his reëlection may receive the vote of every man who shall desire to express his gratitude for the liberty which he has secured to them from this cruel fetter of ingratitude and injustice.

3. But equality at the polls is not the only work laid upon the coming government. There must be such a disposition of its patronage, such a steadfast expression of its conviction, such an employment of its influence, as will tend to the abolition of the whole mass of prejudice that still defiles the national heart. I am aware that this evil cannot be utterly abolished by any enactments. The leprosy lies deep within. It dwells in our churches, in our souls, in our education, in society. It still makes us look on many a human face with repulsion which is of the complexion of the mother of our Lord — nay, of the Lord himself.* It still leads us to erect barriers between us and our kindred, and to make us and them talk of "our race" as if they and we had a different parentage, Savior, and eternity. It must come to an end. It is coming to an end. This election is a great advance toward that end. If the Administration as faithfully adhere to its ruling idea, and put men into office everywhere without regard to color and with regard only to capacity, it will greatly prosper this great reform. Let him make Frederick Douglass a member of his cabinet, and the nation will commend and imitate his courage.

But under it, as well as through it, will the work go forward. Senators and representatives will enter Congress of the condemned hue. They have already become mayors, secretaries of state, lieutenant governors; they hold no small influence and office in the uplifted South; they must yet more. Mississippi, with her half a million; South Carolina, with her majority of this tint; Tennessee, where they stand between the loyal whites and annihilation; Louisiana, where they have wealth, culture, and talents in their ranks—these must cast down all bars and gates, and let the tides of human, civil, social, and Christian life flow freely among all the people. To this complexion shall we come at last.

4. Yet more: our feelings of aversion will change to feelings of regard. The complexion at which we now profess

* See Note XXII.

to revolt we shall look upon with pleasure. Vice is not the only thing that is at first hated and afterward embraced. Virtue is more frequently subject to this experience. It is very rare that a real gift of God is fallen in love with at first sight. How few behold in religion all the charms with which she is divinely invested. How many turn with disgust from her pleading, pleasing countenance. How few are instinctively drawn to temperance, to study, to work. The world beholds in vice everything charming, in virtue everything repulsive. But acquaintance changes this experience, and we cling to the good we at first disdained. Nay, we usually are the more fond in proportion as we were hostile. It is the law of our nature that we choose that which we say we will never have. If you hear a person declaring that he will never be a Methodist, be sure that he will yet be of the most earnest type of that religion. If he says, "I will be anything sooner than a Congregationalist," you may mark him as fore-ordained to be a sober deacon of that orthodox church. When the young lady says, "I'll marry anybody but Mr. Simperton," she will soon be found casting her most languishing meshes around that just despised youth. When pompous young Jones says, "I hate the very looks and even name of Miss Marigold," be you certain he will ere long say to her, "Your face is angelic, you name is sweeter than the lutes of paradise. I can only live in the light of your affection." So shall we treat our brethren and sisters of color. We shall "see Helen's beauty in the brow of Egypt." We shall say, "What a rich complexion is that brown skin." "It is Italian, Greek, Oriental, perfect. How far it excels our chalky hue." We already paint our houses after their color. Our girls crinkle their hair after the natural curliness of their sisters' locks. This is one of God's modes of curing us of color-blindness. We shall see, as Mrs. Kemble says, that there are qualities in the human skin superior to a pink and white tint, and that in velvety softness, in fineness of fiber, in richness of tone, this despised flesh surpasses our own.*

We shall be attracted to this hue because it is one of God's creatures, and a beautiful one too; because it is a favorite hue of the human race; because, chiefly, we have most wickedly loathed and scorned it. He will have revenge, and will yet compel us to discern the loveliness of this most abhorred virtue, and to become enamored of it. The Song of Songs will have a more literal fulfillment than it has ever confessedly had in America; and the long-existing, divinely-implanted admiration of Caucasians for black but comely maidens, be the proudly acknowledged and honorably gratified life of Northern and Southern gentlemen.

But this law rests on no mere quip of the fancy, nor is it a rebound of a vehement passion, as wrongfully right as it had been wrongfully wrong. It is the grand undertone of all marriage. It is the Creator's mode of compelling the race to overleap the narrow boundaries of families and tribes, into which blood, so called, invariably degenerates.

"Not like with like, but like with difference,"

is the law of marriage. The light complexioned turns to the dark, and the dark to the light, as day to night and night to

* These are her exact words: "Their skins are all (I mean of blacks generally) *infinitely* finer and softer than the skins of white people. Perhaps you are not aware that among the white race the *finest grained* skins generally belong to persons of dark complexion.

"While I am speaking of negro countenances, there is another beauty which is not at all unfrequent among those I see here. A finely-shaped oval face — and those who know (as all painters and sculptors, all who understand beauty do) how much expression there is in the outline of the head, and how very rare it is to see a well-formed face, will be apt to consider this a higher matter than any coloring, of which, indeed, the red and white one so often admired is by no means the most rich, picturesque, or expressive." — *Journal of a Residence on a Georgia Plantation in* 1838–9, *by Frances Ann Kemble.* Pages 41, 42. Harper & Brothers.

day. The tall seek the short, and the short the tall; the small the large, and the large the small. Opposite temperaments also thus incline to each other. Bishop Morris says that he can select husbands and their wives in a large company by this law of like and difference. Contrast whets appetite. Dr. Holmes's ten lovers dangling in the silken noose on the fatal trap of Cupid, being asked the color of the eyes that caused their ruin, —

> "Ten shadowy lips said 'heavenly blue,'
> And ten accused 'the darker hue.'"

The last five of these victims were undoubtedly blue-eyed swains, and the first of brown complexion.

By this law only will yellow-haired Germany and dark-skinned France become one. Only thus will the mediæval feud between light-eyed England and dark-eyed Ireland come to an end. Let their youths follow their instincts, and the differences that now seem barriers of eternity, will become magnets of eternity. Thus, too, will our dividings cease. The lightest and darkest of the children of Adam and Noah are divinely planted together in this land, that they may, by obeying this law of God, work out the perfect oneness of the race of man.

Already, too, our romancers and poets, the imaginative fore-flyers of the slower-footed fact, are putting this future into their fascinating tales, and all the greedy crowd of novel readers are finding their freshest morsels flavored with this celestial truth. The stage makes an octoroon a heroine, and wins thousands to the admiration of a color on the boards, which they still falsely profess to detest in the parlor. Mrs. Child, in her "Romance of the Republic," gives a vivid portraiture of the wrongs and rights of this married life and love in conflict with the curse of caste. Anna Dickinson waxes yet bolder, and, in her "What Answer?" shows how inevitable, how beautiful is this true affection, despite, nay, including this difference of color. And the hour is not far off when the white-hued husband shall boast of the dusky beauty of his wife, and the Caucasian wife shall admire the sun-kissed countenance of her husband, as deeply, and as unconscious of the present ruling abhorrence as is his admiration of her lighter tint. Desdemona was as deeply fascinated by Othello's visage, as was he by Desdemona's. That hour is not coming — it already is. Not a few of these marriages which God has made, and whose legal validity man, in some instances, has reluctantly acknowledged, are already filling homes with happiness, and both prophesying and leading the way to the future unity and blessedness of America. Amalgamation is God's word, declaring the oneness of man, and ordaining its universal recognition. Who art thou that fightest against God?

5. But General Grant's peace opens the way for yet further victories, if any in your minds can be further. The suffrage of woman must follow that of the African. The proudest female must march behind the lowliest negro. She is a citizen already, frequently a tax-payer, always of equal intelligence, often of superior virtue to man. She is our mother; and who believes he knows more than his mother, or is better able to understand and exercise any duty? She is our wife; who that deserves a wife believes himself the superior of that wedded soul? She is our sister; and who does not know that when in school together she more frequently led him in scholarship than he her? She is of the Commonwealth, having equal rights with every other member. She is bone of our bone and flesh of our flesh. Surely, all enforced exclusion of her from her just claims is the greatest injustice. If we preëminently despise the man who strikes a woman, how should we feel toward the State who thus strikes down all its women, and robs them of all power of defense from its blows?

Above all, we need her help. Christ is seeking to establish His empire in the earth. It is an empire of peace, of unity, of righteousness, of love. It is to be established in good-willing men, in holy laws, in sacred institutions, in purified society. How can this be done except by the co-operation of the best and most numerous members of that society? Only by woman's vote can the kingdom of God be completely established. Only thus can we save the State from debauchery and utter demoralization.

That work will go forward. It is advancing everywhere; and when the next election comes may we see our sisters sitting by us, and transforming the dirty, smoky atmosphere of the voting-rooms into sweet and quiet parlors, full of pleasure and peace.

The temperance movement must go forward. It has been held back by the imperative demands of the cause of freedom. It met with a repulse from misjudging men, under wicked leaders; but it will rally and move on. It has a grand foundation laid in the convictions of every heart, the conclusions of every understanding, the decisions of courts, the statistics of jails and almshouses, the annals of crime, a generation of totally abstaining people, and the success of the experiment of prohibition. Every good and evil inure to its benefit. With the departure of the giant crime of Slavery to its own hell, the movement against its hardly inferior associate will be recommenced. We have exchanged the slaveholder's ring for the whisky ring. The one elected Presidents; the other has preserved one of them in his undeserved seat. We have abolished the one; we must the other. To this reform every youth should consecrate himself. In every State it should be agitated. Congress should be implored to establish it in the Territories and the District of Columbia. The new South must adopt it to save her new citizens from utter demoralization. Great will be the happiness of the nation when no village shall be cursed with a grogshop, when every city shall be as pure from this vice as the rivers of Eden, when our youth shall be untainted with this appetite, and our men shall not err through strong drink. May that hour soon break upon the waiting realm, and National Prohibition of all that can intoxicate deliver our land from its last and heaviest burden.

Not a few other blessings wait on the coming hours. As clouds of angel faces surround the heads of victor saints, misty yet distinct in beauty, so do clouds of reforms, the faces of the true angels, messengers of God to man, encompass the victor President.

Black were the clouds about the head of Lincoln when first he became the head of the nation. A winter storm of darkness and death beat upon his head. How dark, how dreadful that hour! The flush of morning joy at his success was instantly extinguished in the sulphurous folds, shooting lightnings, rumbling thunders, portending ruin. How sadly, wearisomely, patiently did he wade through the sea of troubles, and by opposing, end them. A slightly brighter cloud encompassed the last election. Still it was a dreary mixture of light and darkness. Grant was still held at bay before Richmond. Sherman yet lay in the heart of the enemy's country, and the march to the sea was but a crazy dream of those two generals, as it seemed to loyal and rebel minds. Thomas had scarcely relieved Nashville of its beleaguered hosts. Gold still hung high above the hundreds. Europe still believed and hoped that Jefferson Davis had created a nation. Mexico was still a principality of France. Charleston was the same haughty hold of slavedom. Mobile snarled defiance from all her forts at all our fleets. Lee was still the bepraised general, far before Grant, in English and in rebel judgments. Slaves were still held by the millions in every State, from Kentucky, by way of Virginia and the sea-line, up to Arkansas. Our poor boys were still rotting to death by the thousands at Andersonville and in the Libby Prison. Much had been done; but all would be lost were not much more done. His reëlection was but a pledge, a sign of pluck, a charge on the enemy's lines, a determination never to submit or yield till the victory, how far soever distant, should be attained. To-day all this is past; and the new heavens open around us in abundant light. American ideas are breaking in pieces all nations. They have invaded England, and elected the first People's Parliament that ever sat in her realm; they have overrun Germany, and unified that long disparted nation; they have entered Spain, overturned the Inquisition, driven forth a ruler whose seat had been held by her family for three hundred years, and probably in some line of her blood for a far longer time, and are even now discussing the establishment of the Republic of Iberia. The British Provinces have organized a nationality which is a precursor of their admission into the greater nationality of America. Mexico has expelled Napoleon, and sustains her own independence, preparatory to her absorption into our domain.

In enterprise the world is also careering like a ship before the wind. The girdle of the nation will belt her zone before another year, and our President enter the Pacific cities — the longest journey ever made by the head of a nation through its territory. The South will be filled with peaceful, loving, laboring populations. Emigration will set in from Africa, Asia, Europe, and the islands of the sea; and the world make gigantic strides to the glory and calm of the millennial year.

To this work, and honor, and reward may all be devoted. Let Christ abolish sin from your souls, of whatever sort, by His indwelling grace. Let your heart become His peaceful realm, with its every passion, thought, and purpose subject to His sway. Labor by every word and work to make all other hearts equally perfect. Strive to bring the laws of society into subjection to His control. Root up the gnarled tusks of prejudice. Toil cheerfully, hopefully, faithfully, to bring in the Grand Sabbatic Year, the Jubilee of Heaven.

> "The visions seen far off, and sang of old
> By holy seers and prophets, grasped by faith,
> And longed for, though the half could ne'er be told
> In language, nor by hope itself conceived,
> Will have accomplishment, — a waking bliss, —
> The rest foreshadowed by the Church of God,
> The golden dawn of Everlasting Day."

NOTES.

I.

The Fugitive Slave Bill. — (Page 1.)

After a struggle of over seven months, the bill for the rendition of fugitives passed Congress, September 13, 1850. It was the first act of the national government in avowed support of the institution of slavery, after the great debate had sprung up. Its previous laws of this sort had been enacted in the state of darkness that had beclouded the popular mind concerning the duty. In the conflict that had been raging for nearly twenty years, the slave power had met with sympathy from the general government, in its refusal to receive petitions, in the attempt to purge the mails of what were called "incendiary publications," and in other minor expressions of hostility to abolitionism. But it had never done anything in direct support of slavery. This act was of that character.

It immediately caused intense excitement in all the Free States, and the question of the prerogatives of law was universally discussed. Pulpits defended not this act especially, but the duty of obeying every act of legislation, as the only foundation upon which society could exist. They also in all cases apologized for, and in most cases defended, the system of slavery. Among many others, two sermons, setting forth this view with much acuteness, were published in the "Journal of Commerce." The public mind was made timid by these warnings and pleadings, and the cause of humanity seemed in danger of destruction through fear of touching the sacred ark of law.

But God raised up many defenders of His imperilled cause. Pulpit contended with pulpit, press with press. Out of the conflict the public conscience grew to a clear perception of the principle, that that law only can be law, in its true sovereignty, which embodies the conscience of man and dwells in the bosom of God.

II.

The Assault on Charles Sumner. — (Page 57.)

The Nebraska Bill brought forth fruit after its kind. Conceived in iniquity, it bred civil war. The seat of this war was in the southern territory of Kansas, though the act that inaugurated it was known by the name of the upper territory of Nebraska. As the compromise repeal was not followed immediately by an enactment recognizing slavery as existent in these dependencies, it was evident that if the North should first settle the territory, she would have some chance to shape its character. Emigrant Aid Societies were, therefore, established, and every appliance put in force to stimulate immigration. Bold leaders guided bold followers to the first battle-field in America, where blood mingled freely with the ballot as an arbiter in the strife. Heroes sprang up almost autochthonous. Men never known before became known forever, of whom John Brown, the martyr of Virginia, was by far the chief. The slave power poured in their men; but, as in all the subsequent contests, so then, they could not equal the friends of freedom in numbers. The aid of the national government, and their savagery, made up for their lack of numbers. The administration constantly favored their cause, decided their minority constitution, which established slavery, alone authentic, and endeavored to force her admission into Congress on that basis. This was fiercely opposed, and by the vigor and daring of the anti-slavery leaders, was successfully resisted. May 19, 1856, Charles Sumner, Senator from Massachusetts, delivered a masterly oration upon the course of the government and the slave power. This freedom of speech, it was felt, was harming the cause of the slaveholders. He must be punished, and it suppressed. So with the knowledge and in the presence of their leader, Senator Douglas, who was then expecting the nomination to the Presidency, on May 22 an assault was made on Mr. Sumner, as he sat at his desk, writing, by Preston C. Brooks, a member of the House of Representatives from South Carolina. About fifteen very severe blows were inflicted on his head. He pulled up his seat in his endeavors to escape his would-be assassin. He was nearly killed, and for several years was unable to do any public service.

The country instinctively felt that this was a new step in the march of the iniquity. It had defrauded the Territories of their rights. It now sought to extinguish all State equality. For if freedom of debate in Congress was suppressed, all State rights were practically annihilated. Only as the slave power allowed would any State presume to act. The "United States" ceased to be, and an oligarchy became the sole sovereign of the country. The following resolution, adopted at Faneuil Hall, is an example of that sentiment: —

Resolved, That in this outrage we see new encroachments upon Freedom, new violations of State rights; that the attack is to be rebuked, not only as a cowardly assault upon a defenseless man, but as a crime against the right of Free Speech and the dignity of a Free State.

The Massachusetts legislature also declared, in its resolves, that it was "a ruthless attack upon the liberty of speech, and an indignity to the Commonwealth of Massachusetts." She also demanded for her Representatives in Congress freedom of speech, and announced her determination to sustain them "in the rights of American citizens."

Thus the blows upon Sumner were the natural precursor of the shot at Sumter. Both were against the Nation and Humanity. Both came from Disunion and Slavery.

The act made the presidential campaign, then beginning, yet more fierce, and greatly increased the anti-slavery vote.

The discourse on this subject was published in "The Westfield Newsletter," the newspaper of the town where it was preached, at the request of a number of leading citizens. It is with pleasure that their note of invitation is here reprinted, both as a memorial of old times and old friends, of whom the greater part continue to this present, but some are fallen asleep, and also as a proof that its words were only levelled up, if even that were possible, to the hight of the hour. These gentlemen of business, social and religious standing, by their indorsement, show how deep and wide the tide of feeling flowed.

WESTFIELD, June 11, 1856.

TO REV. MR. HAVEN.

We, the undersigned, having listened with the deepest interest to your discourse of last Sabbath afternoon, and feeling that such wholesome truths ought, at the present juncture, to have a widespread circulation, would respectfully request the same to be published.

In making this request, we feel we are but expressing the unanimous sentiment of the large audience convened on that occasion.

H. HARRISON,
SAMUEL DOW,
JOHN KNEIL,
GEORGE S. SAVAGE,
D. N. DAY.
B. R. LEWIS,
M. D. MOORE,
ELIJAH PORTER,
T. P. COLLINS,
RALPH LAY,
P. N. WESTON,
ALBERT A. RAY,
E. A. RAY,
A. P. RAND.

Messrs. HARRISON, DOW, KNEIL, and others.

Gentlemen: Agreeably to your request, I submit the remarks made last Sabbath afternoon to your disposal, hoping that they may aid, though slightly, to a right perception of the sin and peril of our beloved nation, and to the instant and earnest employment of all the means approved by our Creator for our present and perpetual salvation.

Very truly yours,

WESTFIELD, June 11, 1866.

G. HAVEN.

III.

SLAVERY'S LAST TRIUMPH.—(Page 87.)

The fiercest political battle that till then had been fought in America, had resulted in the defeat of John C. Fremont, the candidate of the anti-slavery forces, first known as the Republican party in this campaign, and the election of James Buchanan of Pennsylvania. It was a victory that ruined the victors. The strength of the friends of freedom was made known. Their party had grown from 157,123 in the last presidential election, to 1,340,514. They had elected a Congress, which was so largely impregnated with the free sentiments, that it restrained the Executive from his full and fell purposes. The discourse was therefore a declaration of the intent and scope of the triumphant party; a declaration that was substantially fulfilled in all the leading efforts of the administration in respect to Kansas, Cuba, the Dred Scott decision, which deprived every man of color of every constitutional protection, and the decision from the same court prepared, but not declared, that reopened the slave traffic in every free State. Lincoln's election alone prevented that declaration. During its existence, and with its connivance, the foreign or African slave trade was reopened, and invasions of Mexico and Central America were carried out; while its bequest of the most terrible civil war in history, far surpassed and more than answered all the statements of its intent and effort, and showed that had not our people been willing to die by the hundreds of thousands, this roll of lamentations, mourning, and woe would have been more than fulfilled.

IV.

"IT WILL BE DEMANDED OF US, DROP FOR DROP, BY THE GOD OF JUSTICE."—(Page 112.)

Eight years afterward, President Lincoln, in his last inaugural, thus spoke: —

Yet if God wills that the war continue until all the wealth piled by the bondman's two hundred and fifty years of unrequited toil shall be sunk, and until every drop of blood drawn with the lash shall be paid by another drawn with the sword, as was said three thousand years ago, so still it must be said, that the judgments of the Lord are true and righteous altogether.

V.

Canaan's curse nothing to do with the African and his Slavery. — (Page 124.)

The position was long held by abolitionists, that the curse upon Canaan was a prophecy of his political subjugation to the children of Israel, and that he was not the father of the African race, and his curse had given no authority for African slavery. This was opposed with intense vigor by the Southern pulpit and its Northern sympathizers. Even so late as 1869, a lecturer could make "cursed be Canaan" a title for a witty satire against slavery and caste. But how false it was, and how thoroughly exploded, may be seen from the following extract from "The Christian Advocate" of January, 1869, published at Nashville, the official organ of the Methodist Episcopal Church, South. Its learned editor, Rev. Dr. Summers, thus confesses the wrongfulness of that famous plea for American slavery: —

> The descendants of Ham's fourth son, Canaan, were exclusively involved in Noah's malediction; but they were not negroes, nor, so far as appears, any darker in their hue than the Jews, to whom, as Shemites, they were brought into servitude, as they were afterwards to the Greeks and Romans, the descendants of Japheth.
>
> We do not doubt that the black races of Africa, including all the negroes, descended from Cush and Phut, two of the sons of Ham, with perhaps a little intermingling from the descendants of Mizraim, another of his sons, who settled in Egypt.

VI.

"One half the family the property of the other."— (Page 132.)

A clergyman of the Methodist Episcopal Church, Rev. J. D. Long, when travelling a circuit in Maryland, stopped at the house of one of his congregation. After dinner they went to walk.

"Did you notice anything peculiar about my family?" said his host.

"Nothing especial," was the reply.

"Did you not see the girls that waited on the table?"

"I noticed that there were some."

"Those girls are my daughters, the children of my first wife, who was my slave. I lived happily with her, and as honorably as the State would allow. When she died, I married my present wife, a white lady, whose daughters sat at the table. The older sisters are the slaves of the younger."

"The elder shall serve the younger" was strangely fulfilled in this instance. It was one of a myriad of examples of the mixed condition of slaveholding families.

VII.

The Movement at Harper's Ferry. — (Page 153.)

The seizure of the arsenal at Harper's Ferry was made on the night of October 17th, 1859. It was arranged for the 24th; but Captain Brown suspected a traitor in his band, and struck earlier to escape his treachery. The consequence was, that many of his supporters, both from the North and among the slaves, were not ready, and his plans thus failed of connection and of success.

He intended to make his rendezvous in the hills, but delayed, fatally for himself, all the forenoon in the arsenal which he occupied. He had twenty-two associates, sixteen whites and six colored. When a workman asked the guard of the arsenal by what authority he had taken possession of public property, he replied, "By the authority of Almighty God."

The excitement of the nation was wonderful. No event of the war produced such a startling effect on the public mind. Every one saw that it betokened a new phase of the growing struggle. Only one of the daily press, however, had the courage to avow the justice of the act. "The Evening Post," on the day of its announcement, stood by the principles involved in his action. Most Republican journals denounced him. The country has not yet fully discerned the value of this courageous and Christian deed. A complete history of the event has not yet been written. It will be found to be far more wisely and skillfully arranged than is even now allowed. It was undoubtedly the needed deed. The words and acts of the reform required this step. They had done their work. A blow against it was the opening gun of the war. The soldiers soon detected its value, and the famous "John Brown song" became the most popular song of the army and the war. It was first sung within less than three months after the fall of Sumter, by the Massachusetts Twelfth, marching down State Street, under the command of Colonel Fletcher Webster, son of Daniel Webster. Captain Brown will undoubtedly stand forth as the John Huss of this reform, one the most exalted of its many martyrs in the love and honor of future generations.

VIII.

Bunker's Hill and Harper's Ferry. — (Page 195.)

The analogy between these two historic events has been suggested by several speakers and writers. It has not been as carefully elaborated as it deserves to be, and will be by future historians. It may not be amiss to state a few of the points of resemblance they will detect, both in respect to the enterprises themselves, and their real leaders.

They are not unlike in rashness, viewed in the light of cool, sagacious generalship. Consider the former. Fifteen hundred untrained soldiers, with only four rounds apiece of cartridge and ball, planted themselves behind a mere bank of turf and sticks, thrown up in less than twelve hours, within a few rods of a ship channel, where the enemy's men-of-war lay, and whence they could rake them on three sides, and cut off their retreat on the fourth. Consider, further, that a great city was less than a mile distant, full of ammunition and thoroughly trained soldiers, and its nearest eminence, in hight and distance, commanded their site as perfectly as though it had been perched over their heads but a rood off. Is there greater military wisdom in putting such a handful of raw militia into such a trap, than Captain Brown showed in his operations? Wellington nor Washington would have never undertaken the former any sooner than the latter.

If we look at each of them, as they appeared to the hopes or even the dreams of Warren and of Brown, we shall find them not dissimilar. No historian ever has clearly set forth the immediate practical good that the encampment on Bunker's Hill was intended or desired to effect: we doubt if they ever will. It could not have been dreamed for a moment, that their position could be retained for any length of time. Without shelter, without rocky ramparts, or means to erect them, without ammunition or cannon, or provision, shut off from all communication from the main army as completely as if in a besieged fortress, they could not have hoped for anything but a bloody battle, fruitless in its immediate results even if successful, or a final submission of the whole force by the slow, but, in this case, most certain process of siege. Had not the British been rash with rage and pride, they could have had the whole fifteen hundred in their hands in less than a week without the loss of a man, as easily as the Virginians could have starved Captain Brown into surrender. had they, too, had the grace of patience. It may be said the Americans made a blunder, and located themselves nearer Boston, and on a lower hill, than they intended. So the leader of the Harper's Ferry entèrprise said he made a blunder, and did not follow any of his plans in entering the arsenal. History will give them both the benefits of their claim, if she gives either. What then? The hill they intended to occupy is just as completely shut off from the camp as the one they fortified. It has only one advantage over the latter. This one is overtopped by Copp's Hill in Boston, that one, not. It is, however, within reach of its fire, as well as that of the fleet. The mountains on which Brown said he meant to establish himself, are not subject to like objection. The enterprise of Putnam, Prescott, and Warren has not any such claim to real necessity as must be allowed to the fight at Lexington and the fortification of Dorchester Hights. It was a *trial* battle. It would have always been branded as criminally foolish, but for the higher than strategetical, or so called practical reasons, which incited it, and especially but for the wonderful fruits it brought forth in the hearts of friends and foes. Will not the future historian of the great conflict of slavery and freedom find like analogies in the events of Harper's Ferry? In one respect we pray and believe they will totally differ. The former was the prelude of a long and cruel civil war. The latter, we hope, will prove to be the only bloody interruption to the peaceable progress of this cause. It will certainly have this relation, if the slave masters learn more wisdom from this event than our British masters did from Bunker's Hill.*

We cannot fail to notice the remarkable resemblance of the real leaders of these enterprises, both in respect to their own temperament, as well as in their relation to their associates in the general movement. Warren differed as much from the other great leaders in the cause of liberty then, as John Brown did from those of to-day. His voice was fierce for war long before the others considered the argument of peace exhausted. His deeds were like his words. On the Lexington day, he was fighting in the ranks, while Hancock and Samuel Adams, equally great patriots, and esteemed by the king far more dangerous rebels, felt it their duty to seek safety in flight. His rash courage almost sealed his fate that day. For at West Cambridge a ball passed so near his head as to carry away the pin that fastened his earlock. Had he been captured at Bunker's Hill, as he undoubtedly would have been but for the fortunate stab of a bayonet, he would most certainly have been hung within a month on Boston Common, by the Governor of Massachusetts, for "murder, treason, and inciting to insurrection."

There are only two points of difference between these transactions. The first, that those who fought were, in the one case, themselves the victims of the oppression, in the other, chiefly sympathizers with these victims. This is not quite true, though constantly asserted. For colored men, free and slave, were engaged at Harper's Ferry. Some were slain, some escaped, some were captured and hung. It was planned and perfected, theoretically, among the fugitives of Canada. Colonel Washington's favorite slave was among the slain, and no one knows, no one can know, till slavery is abolished, how great an army was pledged to meet at the rendezvous in the mountains.

The second point of difference is, that much legislative and military preparation preceded the former encounter, none the latter. It will be noticed, in connection with this fact, that the ruling government of Massachusetts had allowed, for many years, mass meetings, congresses, peti-

* This note is printed as it was published in December, 1860. The analogy has grown more complete with the events that have since occurred.

tions of its subjects, the collection of military stores, and, at last, permitted fourteen thousand of these rebels to be encamped under arms within three miles of its Capitol. Suppose Virginia had granted its subjects such privileges, would they not have developed civil and military leaders, and executed enterprises of great pith and moment, without the aid of a foreign arm? Let us reflect that history, which is the voice of humanity, never takes into account, in its ultimate and irreversible judgment, immediate success or failure. The *final cause* rules here as everywhere. Warren and Bunker's Hill are still, and ever will be, the most thrilling names of the Revolutionary struggle. Those to whose liberty they are dedicated, have compelled all nations to do them reverence, by their own unceasing, enthusiastic devotion. So the like, yet far greater admiration of the Afric-American race, when they shall have achieved their freedom, will compel all the world to revere the names of John Brown and Harper's Ferry. Their representative shall yet stand with the descendant of John Brown and the successor of Governor Wise, in mutual amity and grateful reverence before a commemorative monument at Harper's Ferry, as the descendants of George the Third * and Joseph Warren lately stood with the representative of emancipated Massachusetts, cordial and reverent, before the sacred memorials of Bunker's Hill.

IX.

"The open Slave Pen."—(Page 244.)

The following lines from the late poems of John J. Piatt, are a fitting memorial of a vanished horror: —

We start from sleep in morning's buoyant dawn,
  And find the horror which our sleep oppressed
A vanished darkness, in the daylight gone —
  The nightmare's burden leaves the stifled breast.

Yet still a presence moves about the brain,
  Some frightful shadow lost in hazy light;
And in the noonday highway comes again,
  The loathsome phantom of the breathless night.

So, while before these hateful doors I stand,
  I feel the bordering darkness which is past,

* The Prince of Wales and the President of the Bunker Hill Monument Association, Hon. George Washington Warren. What connection of names and men could be more significant? Governor Wise has since approved the abolition of slavery. The Bunker Hill Monument, at Charlestown, Virginia, will as surely crown that spot with its glorious memories.

Or passing surely from the awakened land;
  The nightmare clutches me and holds me fast.

Back from the years that seem so long ago,
  Return the dark processions which have been;
Lifting again lost manacles of woe,
  They enter here — they vanish, going in.

Hark to the smothered murmur of a race
  Within these walls, — its helpless wail and moan, —
Which, for the ancient shadow on its face,
  Called not the morning's new-born light its own!

Imprisoned here, what unforgotten cries
  Of hopeless torture, and what sights of woe,
From cotton field and rice plantation rise! —
  These walls have heard, and seen, and witness show.

The human drove, the human driver, see!
  Hark, the dread blood-hound in the swamp at bay!
The whipping-post reëchoes agony;
  The slave mart blackens all the shameful day.

The wife and husband, see, asunder thrust!
  The mother dragged from her far children's wail!
The maiden torn from love and given to lust —
  The Human Family in a bill of sale.

All sounds reëcho, all sights reappear;
  (O blindness, deafness! that ye cannot be!)
All sounds of woe that have been heard, I hear!
  All sights of shame that have been seen, I see!

O sounds, be still! O visions, leave the day!
  What thunder trembled on the sultry air?
What lightnings went upon their breathless way?
  Behold the stricken gates of old despair!

The writing on these barbarous walls was plain;
  The curse has fallen none would understand;
God's deluge ere another happier rain;
  His plow of fire before the reaper's land!

The awful nightmare slips into its night,
  With cannon-flash and noise of hurrying shell.
O prisons, open for returning light!
  The sun is in the world, and all is well.

X.

First Abolition Proclamation.—(Page 269.)

The first proclamation that declared for the abolition of slavery, was read in Congress, Friday, March 6, 1862. In it Mr. Lincoln proposed the following joint resolution:

Resolved, That the United States ought to coöperate with any State which may adopt a gradual abolishment of slavery, giving to such State pecuniary aid, to be used by such State in its discretion, to compensate for the inconvenience, public and private, produced by such a change of system.

He argued that this would "initiate emancipation," and prevent the border States from going with the Confederacy in case the government should be forced to acknowledge the independence of one part of the disaffected region.

Congress and the country recognized the importance of the step. The telegraph declared "the President's Message excited deep interest in the House to-day. It forms the theme of earnest conversation." "The Tribune," of March 8, said, "It is one of those few great scriptures that live in history, and mark an epoch in the lives of nations and races. The first era of the supremacy of the rights of man in this country dates from the Declaration of Independence; the second began on the 6th of March, 1862, with the Emancipation Message of President Lincoln." It was an unnoticed coincidence, that Webster's speech, surrendering himself, and so far as he could, his party and State and section, to slavery, was pronounced on the same day that this message was read, March 7th. Twelve years to a day had reversed completely that fatal descent of the North, and raised the nation to its true hight. Thenceforward to the next and bolder step, universal and unconditional emancipation, was easy and inevitable.

XI.

Letter to the London Watchman.—(Page 291.)

The circumstances attending the writing of this letter ought to accompany its publication in this form, as a defence for what might seem to some an inappropriate intrusion of American ideas into a British journal. Having a letter of introduction from Rev. Dr., now Bishop Thomson, to the late and lamented Rev. J. A. Riggs, then editor in chief of the Watchman, on calling upon him, a conversation ensued on American affairs. It was remarked that the British public seemed but little conversant with the questions involved in this controversy, and

41

the position of the American government. The editor requested a communication setting forth these points. It was suggested that a full statement would not be acceptable to his readers. The reply was, that free speech was always allowed. In Paris, a few weeks after, on the Fourth of July, the letter was written. The proofs were sent to Paris, with a note, asking if we wished it to publish treason, and if our American editors would allow articles against a Republican form of government to appear in their journals. It was replied that it "was asked to publish nothing. Free speech was declared to be the law of all British journalism. Any American editor would admit a defence of British ideas, monarchy included, in his journal. The editor had full liberty to accept or reject the article."

It was accepted, and one half published, [to the bottom of page 303]. That portion caused so much excitement that a committee was called of the managers, and the balance read, and forbidden to be published, although it was already in type. The letter, as thus prepared and printed, and half published, is here presented. Its only objection, as the editor himself declared in a conversation afterward, was its statement of the real cause of the anti-American sentiment in England. He agreed as to the coming of democracy there, and said that "if they had a king like George IV., they would be a republic in ten years." He has since died; a true Christian gentleman, whose heart was in sympathy with our ideas no less than with our struggle.

XII.

The Ultimate Oneness of Mankind. — (Page 350.)

The vision of saints and poets, the declarations of prophecy, and the necessary triumph of Christianity, in bringing all the world to one language and one heart, is well set forth in "Yesterday, To-day, and Forever," in the Millennial Year. The poet thus describes the unity of language: —

Babel's confusion was unlearned. And one
Melodious language, wherein every thought
Found utterance, overspread the circling globe,
A language worthy of the sons of God.

XIII.

The March of the Dark Brigade. — (Page 369.)

The following editorial, from "The Independent" of that date, illustrates the feelings which the event excited.

"It is not often 'that the hub of the universe' shakes on its axle.

But last Thursday it fell from its steadfastness. It was the Fifty-fourth Massachusetts regiment which cast the shadow of its coming on our last week's columns, that stormed and took the city.

"We gather from various sources the incidents of the march, and submit to our readers the raw materials for the future poets and historians. The cars from the neighboring cities came in crowded, as at the Prince of Wales' reception. Extremes meet. The heir of the proudest throne and the most despised of mankind created like *furore*. The streets were thronged. Nature smiled propitious. So did the citizens.

"About ten o'clock the cars landed the regiment, and the line of march was taken up through the principal streets. Gilmore's band led the column. A colored band that did not play, and a colored drum corps that did, and well, followed. Then came the strange spectacle — a thousand black forms and faces. Some expressions looked hard, and almost brutal, as if they had just emerged from their long prison-house, and had only two ideas — liberty and vengeance. Others, and most, were refined and thoughtful, and full of high inspiration.

"They sweep along from curbstone to curbstone, with even, steady tramp, their knapsacks and coats piled upon their shoulders, their guns erect against them. Nemesis is marching to South Carolina. Not shod with wool, as Horace talks about. The wool was on her head — and will be a sacred fillet when those who wear it shall be sacrificed upon the altar of their country's salvation. No doubt the slaveholders in Richmond and Charleston heard the solid tread.

"They came to the State House. The Governor, Senator Wilson, Adjutant-General Schouler, and other dignitaries, were received into the opened lines, and the march was continued down Beacon Street. The *crême de la crême* crowded the aristocratic windows. Handkerchiefs fluttered, and loud cheers rent the air. In one of the most aristocratic houses, the residence of the colonel, colored ladies and white stood in the parlor windows.

"How those soldiers must have felt at such an ovation! Did they remember their life-long degradation? Did they remember anything else? Many had just been slaves. Their backs were hardly healed of the scourge. What contrasts in their lives! No novelist has dreamed of such.

"The Common was crowded. The Governor and his staff marched around the straight line of battle. Never did his Excellency seem to feel and look so excellent.

"Then the troops defiled before him in company line, and with far better precision than most new regiments and many old ones exhibit. Thence they march out of the Common, down Tremont Street, down Court Street, by the Court-House, chained hardly a decade ago to save Slavery and the Union. Thence down State Street, trampling on the very pavements over which Sims and Burns marched to their fate, encompassed by soldiers of the United States.

"'Their sisters, sweethearts, and wives,' — a familiar quotation in the notices of previous departing regiments, but looking a little odd in this new place, — ran along beside 'the boys,' giving their parting benedictions of smiles and tears, telling them to be brave, and to show their blood! The crowds cheer even *The Courier* office — the soldiers sing the John Brown song — the boat is reached, and the sensation is solidified into history of the United States.

"All attempts to express the feelings of the crowd or the soldiers seem to read stale and flat. Yet, as Goldsmith said that the weakest jokes were received as wit by the circle of the happy Vicar, so these attempts were treated as successes by the happy crowd. One man said it was a verification of Shakespeare: —

> Know you not *Pompey*?
> You have climbed up to the walls and battlements,
> To see *Great Pompey* pass the streets of Rome.

"One fact should be chronicled. Their regimental banner, of superb white silk, had on one side the coat of arms of Massachusetts, and on the other a golden cross on a golden star, with IN HOC SIGNO VINCES beneath. *This is the first Christian banner that has gone into our war.* By a strange, and yet not strange providence, God has made this despised race the bearers of His standard. They are thus the real leaders of the nation."

XIV.

THE PAY OF COLORED SOLDIERS. — (Page 393.)

Senator Wilson, in his history of anti-slavery measures in Congress, narrates the long struggle to put the laws right upon this subject. It lasted from January 8 to June 11, 1864; and even then had to be left optional with the Attorney General to say whether soldiers from the Slave States should be reckoned as entitled to the same pay as white soldiers. The President could not wait for this slow action of Congress, and under the pressure of General Grant, who wished to get his army into the best fighting trim before he started from Washington, he reversed the previous decisions of his Attorney General, and pronounced all soldiers equal in their pay. Though this act of General Grant's was inspired by military judgment, it was none the less excellent in its nature and in its effects.

XV.

Depreciation of Continental Currency. — (Page 414.)

In the Annals of the American Pulpit, Vol. IX., p. 11, are two or three items from General Muhlenberg's correspondence, which shows how worthless the Continental currency had become.

On the 5th of January, 1780, he purchased a load of hay for £50 currency.

March 10, 1780, he bought a horse for a journey from Pennsylvania to Virginia, which cost him £1025, or over $5009. The previous gold value of the horse was £15 to £20, or less than $100. That journey of himself and family cost him £10,000, or $50,000. This was three years before the war closed.

XVI.

American Neutrality: its History and its Effects. — (Page 450.)

These facts will show how baneful has been the sway of this doctrine in our councils, both upon our foreign and domestic relations, and upon the liberty of the world.

The French Revolution began in 1789. The Republic was established in 1793. Every American, every European saw that both the Revolution and the Republic sprang from our loins. It was our first born among the nations — the beginning of our strength. It had consummated itself in the execution of the king; a deed as necessary for their salvation as it would have been for our fathers to have expelled the British sovereign from our soil, and to have hung him had he persisted in demanding his rights as separate from those of the people. Their execution of Louis XVI. is as justifiable as that of Charles I.

They established a government based on the broadest principles of democracy. The event was hailed with enthusiasm in every part of the country. In Boston, an ox roasted whole, was carried through the city and served up on State Street. Sixteen hundred loaves of bread were distributed, and the fear of the Maine Law being then, unfortunately, unknown — two hogsheads of punch. Each child of the public schools received a cake marked "Liberty and Equality." Balloons were sent up, bonfires blazed, the State House was illuminated, and a public dinner at Faneuil Hall was presided over by Lieutenant Governor Samuel Adams, the father of the Revolution. Governor Mifflin presided at a like jubilee in Philadelphia. Charleston was ablaze with the same enthusiasm. For once, and for the only time till now, Massachusetts and South Carolina struck hands in favor of universal liberty. They are coming together again!

Then came the practical test of their zeal. The Republic was instantly met with an offensive alliance of Great Britain, Austria, Prussia, Sardinia, and New Netherlands. They declared war against it. They mustered their forces for its subjugation. The terrific cloud of American independence and equality had moved across the seas, had broken over their heads in the deluge of France. If they should remain quiet, it would speedily drown their thrones in its mighty floods. They take arms against the sea of troubles. France sees her peril, and well she may. A mass of emancipated serfs, led by men who had been equally despised and but little more privileged than themselves, — what can they do against the European world? They look to America, their nearest friend, their only parent. Citizen Genet is sent as embassador by the Girondist government, as noble and pure a body of rulers as ever failed or triumphed in any land. Our first Congress that passed the Declaration, our last that has just confirmed it by its corresponding acts, were not more unselfish, broad-minded, sagacious, and honest than the government that executed Louis and established the French Republic.

Genet landed at Charleston, and was welcomed with great rejoicings. His entrance into Philadelphia was an ovation. His mission was publicly proclaimed and heartily indorsed. He said that his object was "to draw the United States, as far as possible, into making common cause with France." His government "desired to effect a true family compact on a liberal and fraternal basis, on which to raise up the commercial and political systems of two peoples, all whose interests were confounded." Thus did she look to us, her mother, in the hour of her first trial. She hastened to us, she begged, she entreated us to aid her in maintaining her liberties.

But while the people were willing, another spirit ruled the government. It hastened, with equal zeal and alacrity, to identify itself with the enemies both of the country and its principles. The doctrine of Neutrality was then born into the political world — a cup that has since been faithfully commended to our unwilling lips, by the power that then won the chiefest benefit from its creation. How perfectly the type and antitype agree. England's course toward us is exactly copied after that which we pursued against the French Republic. As soon as war was proclaimed Washington called his cabinet together. Hamilton, an aristocrat, and almost monarchist, proposed to them, in writing, certain questions, all favoring the doctrine of neutrality, none of fraternity. He sought to commit them to his side before they had assembled. Jefferson opposed it, or sought for such a moderate and transient expression of it as he hoped might be carried in the cabinet, and knew that the winds of popular feeling and the force of events would soon sweep away. Hamilton prevailed, and Washington issued his proclamation, April 22, 1793, in less than a fortnight after the news reached him of the declaration of war by the allies, and while the embassador of the new republic was known to be on his way to the capital. How strikingly does the Queen's proclamation, in less than a fortnight after the news of the fall of Sumter reaches England, and while our embassador is on his way thither, photograph our own conduct, and hoist us with our own petard.

Citizen Genet was coldly received by the President. In the pressure of his necessities, and relying on the enthusiasm of the people to protect him against the decree of their government, he presumed to issue commissions and make spoliations of British commerce in our waters. This brought him into conflict with our authorities and damaged his position, though not enough to lose him the moral and hearty support of the people. The country was alive with excitement. The word Democrat was imported from France, and adopted by its sympathizers. Jefferson allied himself so strongly with their cause that he was compelled to leave the cabinet. Madison was alike its earnest and active friend. Monroe had pledged his country to the Republic in Paris, and had been recalled by the government for his ardor for liberty, only to be hailed everywhere by the people. The next Congress, the first of the second administration, was carried against the administration and neutrality. Frederick Muhlenberg, of Pennsylvania, was elected speaker on this issue. Albert Gallatin was chosen senator from Pennsylvania on the same question. Bache, Franklin's grandson, and the inheritor of his principles, was its editorial champion. There never was a movement, in our political history, better officered, more popular, or more just, and yet it failed. Selfishness, timidity, greed of wealth, opportunities, which increased vastly with the prospective ruin of the English carrying trade, through French privateers — these moved us from the principles of brotherhood and liberty by which we had become a nation. We not only refused to do to others as we would that they should do to us; we refused to do as they had done to us. We had won our liberty solely though the help of France. Now she may groan and die, while we look out for ourselves.

The immaturity of our institutions, and their experimental character, were pleaded as an excuse for our course. But we find as the result, what we knew in our hearts at the beginning, that the only way for a nation, as for an individual, to maintain their rectitude, is to *work* righteousness. He who saves his life shall lose it. We lost ours at the very moment we sought thus sinfully and selfishly to save it. Most honorable as were the motives of Washington, his judgment failed him. The enthusiasm of youth yielded to the fears of age. He shrank from war, as well he should; but he also shrank from confidence in the cause he had so greatly assisted in establishing, and whose preservation might demand war. He distrusted the people. He revealed his real feelings when he told Jefferson that an American monarchy " was not what he was afraid of: his fears were from another quarter; that there was more danger of anarchy being introduced."* The only right way to repress both dangerous tendencies was to keep the Republic alive with its own spirit; to make it zealous for its radical ideas, and faithfully support them wherever they were in peril.

This fearful spirit possessed the whole of the second administration of Washington, and is the controlling animus of his most famous paper — the Farewell Address. In fact, the chief cause and topic of that document are not the perils of disunion at home, but of union abroad. Its strongest and most animated sentences are directed against this duty. Its sentences so cold, and unworthy of the great soul that penned them, are the very gospel of selfishness. How they contrast with the gospel of humanity which Jefferson wrote, and Congress proclaimed, not twenty years before, and of which Washington had been the military executor. A few extracts will confirm our position. Far below the highest statesmanship is this statement of the relation of great powers to each other.

"The great rule of conduct for us in regard to foreign nations is in extending our commercial relations, to have with them as little political connection as possible. So far as we have already formed engagements, let them be fulfilled with perfect good faith. Here let them stop."

For such an embargo on all intercourse but that of a mercenary character, he gives this reason: —

"Europe has a set of primary interests which to us have none or a very remote relation. Hence she must be engaged in frequent controversies, the causes of which are essentially foreign to our concerns. Hence, therefore, it must be unwise in us to implicate ourselves by artificial ties in the ordinary vicissitudes of her politics, or the ordinary combinations and collisions of her friendships or enmities."

And yet, not long before, Merlin de Douay, the president of the convention, which had overthrown Robespierre, and wiped out the blood stains of his administration, in welcoming Monroe as Washington's embassador, had used these words: —

"The French people have not forgotten that it is to the American people that they owe their initiation into the cause of liberty. It was in admiring the sublime insurrection of the American people against Britain, once haughty, now so humble, it was in themselves taking arms to second your courageous efforts, and in cementing your independence by the blood of our brave warriors, that the French people learned in their turn to break the scepter of tyranny, and to elevate the statue of liberty on the wreck of a throne supported during fourteen centuries only by crimes and corruption."

Does this sound as if "Europe had a set of primary interests, which to us have none or a very remote interest"? Were controversies raging on

* Irving's Washington, V. p. 113.

such a field foreign to our concerns? Alas, Great Master, thy noble heart forgot its inspirations in its fears. In truth, the *only* political activity in all Europe, making her quake and rend under its mighty tread, was the gathering and wrestling of armies, bearing on their several banners each but one sentence, learned in our school alone — "The Rights of Kings," "the Rights of Man." The first born child of America was struggling in its cradle with the crowned hydras of tyranny; yet its mother refuses to hear and to help her throttled babe — and that, under the plea that these "controversies are foreign to her concerns."

There is much more in like vein. The Atlantic is spoken of as separating us. It was forgotten that the Atlantic did not separate us from our enemy and our allies in the great fight of the Revolution; and that Franklin's diplomacy at Paris, as much if not more than the sword of Washington, had achieved our liberties. Yet with these clearest of facts before him, he says, —

"Our detached and distant situation invites and enables us to pursue a different course [than to intervene.]

"Why," he exclaims, "forgo the advantages of so peculiar a situation? Why quit our own to stand on foreign ground? Why by interweaving our destiny with that of any part of Europe, entangle our peace and prosperity in the toils of European ambition, rivalship, interest, humor, or caprice? It is our true policy to steer clear of all permanent alliances with any portion of the world."

Is not this the gospel of selfishness? Is this the true and eternal principle of nationality? Is this rightfully reading our own history? Had Holland, and Spain, and Russia, and France so treated us, he would long before have been hung as a rebel, or have been a fugitive and vagabond on the earth, while the people over whom he ruled would still have been "born colonists, born slaves."

The farther history of those times is not without its painfully appropriate lessons. Hamilton, sought in the spirit and intent of the neutrality act, as England has, in our late war, to abrogate the force of the treaties we had made with France, and on substantially the same basis: —

"Because she had changed her government she could not hold us to the responsibility to treaties made with a view to a totally different state of things, and which, if carried out, might impose obligations on us and expose us to dangers never dreamed of when the treaties were made." *

Again, the French Republic and the American began to quarrel on the same grounds that we have fallen apart from England. They seized our ships carrying contrabrand of war to their enemies. We claimed that

* Hildreth's History, IV. p. 414.

free ships made free goods. They acknowledged the principle, but plead necessity, as Mr. Seward said we might have done in the Trent affair. We glowered, talked big, and insultingly demanded, as England has of us, retraction under threat of war. It was precisely what John Bright calls England's course with us, "a cold neutrality." Cast off by us, who should have fraternized with her, she turned upon us in hate and scorn, just as we have upon England. She defied us, and trampling over her foes without our aid, despised us and proceeded to yet greater lengths of impudent contempt for our claims. Our neutrality was pushing us into a war with our only child, our best and only friend. Washington's declaration that "our detached and distant situation" saved us from all need of exercising the feelings of brotherhood and delivered us from the toils of European ambition, interest, and caprice, had hardly been uttered and he retired to his longed-for retreat, before he was summoned forth to lead our armies against our ally, who had been made our enemy by the principles and conduct that had animated that address. The European complications of France alone prevented the horrid sight of the only two republics in the world, neither of them ten years old, and separated by a vast and stormy ocean, springing at each others throats in mutual ferocity. How would the monarchies of Europe have rejoiced at that spectacle! Why did they not suspend their assaults upon France and allow Washington and Lafayette to thus throttle and destroy each other? Thank God, those powers by the swiftness of their own rancorous hatred prevented that catastrophe.

Meantime, Massachusetts had been bribed into silence by giving her son the Presidency, and Samuel Adams, closed the last of her truly democratic rulers, not to be begun again till more than half a century had rolled away. Governor Andrew was his first political son that reigned his stead. Hers was a wilderness wandering of more than forty years.

When the Democrats came into power, the French Republic had become far advanced towards a military despotism, constrained to it, by our refusal to aid her in preserving her liberties. The influences of the contrary doctrines of the late leaders, and especially our warlike threats and preparations, conspired with these tendencies to repress our enthusiasm. Still Jefferson sympathized with France, reversed the current that set so strongly towards England, and brought on a war with that power, though too late to preserve the liberties of Europe.

Munroe, his pupil, and warm friend of the French people, made his name immortal by declaring the doctrine that Republicanism should possess this continent: a step exactly opposite to that which Hamilton and Washington had taken, for it could be maintained only by permanent alliances with foreign powers and armed intervention in behalf of those foreign republics. It is a step too that may yet lead us, as we have lately seen, by the way of Mexico or some other invaded Republic, to the high table land from which they had descended — the ground that our affinities and duties are limited by no oceans, tongues, or creeds, but that where "Liberty dwells there is our country;" and where liberty is struggling against armed foes to maintain its hold, there should our eye melt in sympathy, our arm be revealed in salvation.

All the results of this doctrine are not yet innumerated. By the usual movements of Providence, the evils it was hoped that it must have suppressed have flourished the more for its enactment, while the good it had hoped to win, turned to ashes on its lips.

Democratic ideas troubled the aristocratic tastes of Hamilton, Adams, and Washington. Though not monarchists they were not Democrats. They distrusted the people. The French Republic was a perfect democracy. It struck at the vitals of their theories. They feared the rising waves. They sought to sweep out the Atlantic tide with their neutral broom. They were washed away by it. Hamilton and Adams lived to see their power utterly broken, and themselves and their ideas "in the deep bosom of the ocean buried." Washington, by a kind Providence, was relieved from the mournful spectacle. A dread of foreign war also troubled them. Our civil war with its streams of fraternal blood flowed from that unbrotherly timidity.

Their third motive was the most honorable and most powerful, and most dearly has it been paid for. The country must be unified. All distracting influences must be kept in abeyance. A new war with England in behalf of human rights will breed distractions at home. So thought these great and good men. Total mistake! It would have condensed the people as never before and never since. From the hour that neutrality was adopted disunion began. Charleston and Boston were enthusiastically united in the cause of Freedom and Republicanism in Europe. The young men who had been born and reared during the commotions that had preceded and accomplished their independence, were, as the young devotees of a triumphant principle usually are, more earnest in their defense and propagation than the men who had established them. The young men of South Carolina, of Pennsylvania, of Virginia, of New England vied with each other in their laudations of their brethren in France. Munroe, Madison, Bache, Gallatin, Muhlenberg, Randolph, the men who soon obtained and for twenty years retained the leadership of the nation, represented these ideas.

Had they been heard, the two great evils of disunion and slavery had never raised their snaky crests in the land, while the outside evil of dominant monarchism and hostility to our existence, would not have conspired with these inward foes to compass our ruin. He that saves his life shall lose it.

Our present war is thus legitimately traced to that unmanly shrinking from a just war. The most tyrannic and abominable of aristocracies ever known in the civilized or uncivilized world — an aristocracy based *exclusively* on the ownership of human flesh, sprung from this unjust fear and dislike of popular rights; and the very Union, to save which all these sacrifices of principle and humanity were made, has been rent by the hands of its children, and has only been cemented by rivers of fraternal blood.

XVII.

Difference between American and British Neutrality.

(Page 452.)

In this analogy we would not be understood as granting to the British and French governments the protection of our course for their own misconduct. It shows that our error bred mischief to ourselves, not that it approves their crime. They appropriated our invention to their own use, and in directions that we never approved. Our neutrality was exercised between actual powers, with whom we had treaties of alliance. We did not proclaim neutrality between the French throne and the Directory, — the throne was abolished, and a government unquestioned exercised sway throughout the whole territory, It was between this *de facto*, this recognized government, and foreign powers that we declined to interfere. This we had a perfectly legal right to do. We were under no obligation of international law to cast ourselves into the arena. Our complaint has been based wholly on moral grounds — the higher law of amity and justice, which demanded of us the help that we refused to give.

Not so with British neutrality. That was illegally as well as unnaturally exercised: that not merely refused to form compacts, it violated those already formed; that practically and intentionally interfered in favor of a rebellion in the interests of slavery against a power to which it was bound by solemn vows of treaty. Washington's proclamation did not invest the French Republic with nationality; it had that already; Victoria did the Confederate. Washington was scrupulous to regard British rights in our waters, to the extent of incurring the hostility of France and of his own people. Britain was as unscrupulous in its indifference to American rights in British waters, although those rights were supported by treaty obligations as well as the cause they represented. America proclaimed neutrality between recognized political powers; Britain between a nation and a rebellious faction. America shunned alliance in favor of liberty and the rights of man; Britain solicited one in favor of the vilest despotism and the most hideous bondage the world has ever known. America adopted this perfectly legal course, to preserve her infantile democracy from the risk of annihilation on

European fields. Britain, her perfectly illegal one, that she might destroy this matured democracy in its last national stronghold, and insure, through the universal prevalence of Monarchism, the perpetuation of her own political institutions.

While, therefore, we are justly blamable, morally speaking, for the course we pursued, and have suffered greatly for that selfish fear; while we have given our foes a word and an act that they needed, and have hastened to use against us, we are not responsible for their mode of using that word, which is, in every respect, novel, unjust, and in violation of solemn obligations and international law. Mr. Bemis, in his able pamphlet, as well as Mr. Sumner and M. Gasparin, prove this conclusively.

XVIII.

AMERICAN INFLUENCE ON THE WORLD. — (Page 460.)

Very forcibly is this put by M. Montalembert, in his "L'Eglise Libre dans L'Etat Libre." What confession can surpass this: "La Société nouvelle, la democratie pour l'appeler par son nom, existe; on peut même dire qu'elle existe seule, tant ce qui n'est pas a peu de force et de vie. Dans une moitié de l'Europe elle est déjà souveraine; elle le sera demain dans l'autre moitié."

A new society is in existence, called democratic. One can hardly say that it exists merely, since it has no small strength or vitality. In one half of Europe it is already sovereign. It will be in the other half to-morrow.

XIX.

JEFFERSON DAVIS AND INDEPENDENCE. — (Page 540.)

The persistency with which Mr. Davis clung to the idea of independence was most remarkable. In the summer of 1864 he said to Messrs. Jaques and Gilmore, an informal commission who visited Richmond, "We are not fighting for slavery, we are fighting for independence; and that or *extermination* we will have" After the meeting of his commissioners, Messrs. Stevens, Hunter and Campbell, in February, 1865, with Mr. Seward and Mr. Lincoln, at Fortress Monroe, he said, at a public meeting in Richmond, "Sooner than we should ever be united again, I would be willing to yield up everything I have on earth, and if it were possible, would sacrifice my life a thousand times." Even at Danville, after he had fled from Richmond, he issued a proclamation, in which he declared, "I will never consent to abandon to the enemy one foot of the soil of any of the States of the Confederacy.

No peace shall be made with the infamous invaders. If by stress of numbers we should be compelled to withdraw from her [Virginia's] limits, or those of any other border State, again and again will we return, until the baffled and exhausted enemy shall abandon in despair his endless and impossible task of making slaves of a people resolved to be free."

This was surely a strong will, surpassing even Pharaoh's. He yielded when his land was filled with his dead. Not so his antitype. Milton's imagination of another enemy of God and man is exactly fulfilled in the language of Jefferson Davis: —

> What though the field be lost;
> All is not lost; the unconquerable will,
> And study of revenge, immortal hate!
> And courage never to submit or yield,
> And what is else not to be overcome,
> That glory never shall His wrath or might
> Extort from me!

XX.

Lincoln's First Speech. — (Page 553.)

It is reported, on good authority, that when Mr. Lincoln was a candidate for the legislature, at twenty-three years of age, after returning a victorious captain from the Black Hawk war, he made the following speech: —

Fellow Citizens: — You all know me. I am humble Abraham Lincoln. My speech will be short and sweet like an old woman's dance. I am in favor of a protective tariff, internal improvement, and a uniform currency. If elected, I shall serve you as well as I can. If defeated, I shall try to feel not very bad about it.

He failed in the district, though he received all the votes of his precinct but nine. That speech prefigured his presidential career. Its three points were never so completely carried out by the national government as in his administration; the highest tariff, the greatest system of internal improvement, even to the taking possession and the running of many railroads, and a remarkably uniform currency, were its characteristics. The figure he uses is very humorous, and very like him.

XXI.

English and Irish Slave Trade. — (Page 607.)

In Charles Kingsley's "Hereward, or the Last of the English," one of his characters, Martin Lightfoot, servant of Hereford, thus describes his parentage. Its veri-similitude to Southern slavery is striking:

I was born in Ireland, Waterford town. My mother was an English slave, one of those that Earl Godwin's wife, — not this one that is now, Gyda, [the famous Godiva of Coventry,] but the old one, King Canute's sister, — used to sell out of England by the score, tied together with ropes, boys and girls from Bristol town. Her master, my father that was, [how perfectly Southern, this] got tired of her, and wanted to give her away to one of his kerns. She would not have that, so he hung her up, hand and foot, and beat her that she died.

XXII.

What was the Complexion of Christ? — (Page 622.)

"*It still makes us look on many a human face with repulsion which is of the very complexion of the mother of our Lord, nay, of the Lord himself.*"

It is impossible, of course, to declare certainly the complexion of our Savior. Our only guides are the people of the land where He lived. Some fancy He was a white man. But this could not be, except in violation of every law of race. The natives of Palestine, Jews and Arabs, except the few of the former, imported from Germany, are of a brown complexion, almost the color of the bright brown mulatto. The women of Nazareth, who still gather at the well of Annunciation, are of this dusky hue. The most beautiful lady we saw abroad, one of the loveliest we ever looked upon, was a brown Bethlehem Jewess, who passed us at the tomb of Rachel, on her donkey, with her brown, bearded, and turbaned lord and lover walking at her side, a perfect type of the Rachel and Jacob of four thousand years before. Just such complexions may one see to-day in those who were but lately Southern slaves. A very comely and attractive Bedouin, of a bright brown complexion, went up the pyramids with us and stood under the sphynx. When asked to come to America, he replied, "You will sell me." We had been selling multitudes of his complexion for generations. Dean Stanley describes Abraham as a Bedouin sheik. Except in the faith, he says, "In every aspect the likeness is complete between the Bedouin chief of the present day and the Bedouin chief who came from Chaldea nearly four thousand years ago." One of these "aspects" in complexion, and the Arab of Palestine and the Wilderness, is very like Frederic Douglass in this particular. Abraham and his wife were both of the present wandering race. Isaac's wife was of his parents' parents' Mesopotamian origin — and so was Jacob's. Joseph's was an Egyptian lady of color. Moses married an Ethiopian. Salmon married the Canaanite Rahab, Boaz the brown Moabitess beauty, Ruth. David's Bathsheba was a Hittite, a wild slip of the land, very comely, but as far from white as from black. Solomon had a swarthy daughter of Pharaoh to wife. The later marriages were no lighter; and undoubtedly Mary was of the likeness as well as lineage of David and Bathsheba and Ruth and Rahab and Rachel and Rebecca. Jesus Christ stood midway between the complexions of man, that He might lay His hand upon both and blend both together in Himself. The Asiatic is the solvent of the Caucasian and the Negro, and his color is almost exactly reproduced in the mulatto of America, the amalgam of the two opposite complexions. A light-haired, light-skinned Italian, or a dark-skinned German, is far more natural than a light-skinned native of that hot clime, and these are extremely rare. Every Arab, wild or tame, is of one color, and that is almost exactly the hue of the mixed blood of America, whom we so foolishly and falsely profess to naturally abhor. "They are of the very complexion of the mother of our Lord, nay, of our Lord himself."

www.ingramcontent.com/pod-product-compliance
Lightning Source LLC
LaVergne TN
LVHW021049110826
845150LV00001B/21

* 9 7 8 1 4 2 5 5 6 8 1 3 9 *